Northamptonshire
County of

SPIRES

AND

SQUIRES

Artwork and Text by Derek F Blunt

First published in the United Kingdom in 2012
by EddyLynNorthampton.

Text and Illustrations copyright 2012
by Derek F Blunt.
The moral right of the author has been asserted.

A catalogue record for this book is available from
the British Library. ISBN 978-1-909424-01-2

Printed by Lonsdale Print Solutions Ltd
of Wellingborough, Northamptonshire

As buildings and objects vary quite significantly
in size the drawings included in this publication
are not to the same scale.

Whilst every effort has been made to check the
accuracy of the information contained in this
book I accept that circumstances are continually
changing and errors can occur for which
I apologise and it would be appreciated if any
such errors can be made known to me so
as to be rectified in future editions.
(derekfblunt@sky.com)

DUST COVER PICTURES
'SPIRES'
Wilby/Kingsthorpe/Kettering/HighamFerrers/Geddington
'SQUIRES'
Front – Southwick Hall /Althorp House /Kirby Hall
Back – Boughton House

Other books by the author

LANDMARKS
Parish Churches in Northamptonshire
published 2011

ISBN 978-0-9568576-9-9

BIBLIOGRAPHY

ALLISON K J & others
The Deserted Villages of Northamptonshire
Leicester University Press 1966

BRIDGES John
History and Antiquities of Northamptonshire
ed P Whalley 1791 – 2 vols

DOMESDAY BOOK
21 NORTHAMPTONSHIRE
Phillimore.Chichester 1979

GREENHALL R L
A History of Northamptonshire
The Darwen County History Series
Phillimore and Co Ltd 2000

HOLMES Clive
Northamptonshire
A Portrait in Pen and Ink
The History Press 2010

JENKINS Simon
England's Thousand Best Churches
Penguin Press 1999

KINGSCOTT Geoffrey
Lost railways of Northamptonshire
Countryside Books Newbury 2008

NOBLE Tony
Exploring Parish Churches in Northamptonshire
Jema Publications 1999

NORTHAMPTONSHIRE WI
Northamptonshire Villages
Countryside Books Newbury 2002

PEVSNER Nikolaus
Buildings of England - Northamptonshire
Penguin Books 1973 (Revised)

POULTON-SMITH Anthony
Northamptonshire Place Names
Amberley Publishing 2010

RCHM inventory of Historical Monuments in
Northamptonshire Book I – VI 1975-81

WEBB Peter Gorham
Portrait of Northamptonshire
Robert Hale Ltd 1977

WILSON Ron
Churches in and Around Daventry
Troubadour Publishing 1999

NORTHAMPTONSHIRE
COUNTY OF
SPIRES AND SQUIRES

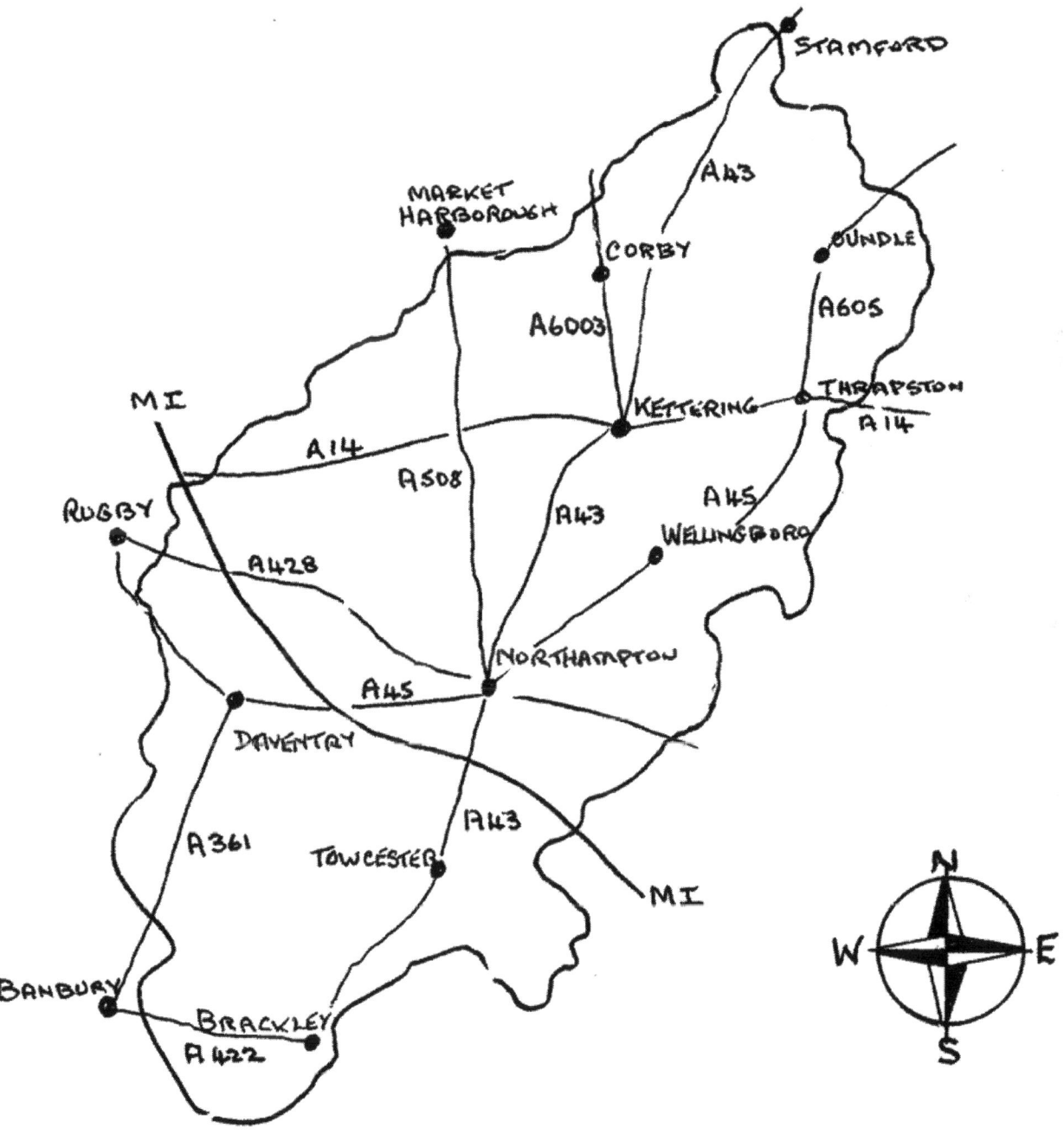

ACKNOWLEDGEMENTS

From my point of view writing this book has not only been very challenging but also very rewarding.
During my research I have travelled extensively within Northamptonshire visiting every hamlet, village and town
not to mention churches, stately homes and museums - in most instances on more than one occasion.
I have met a countless number of people from all walks of life from the 'little old lady' to the Lord of the Manor,
many of whom would have talked enthusiastically all day about their area or particular interest.
Some have just pointed me in the right direction, drawn my attention to specific items of interest, or simply
related anecdotes about their locality. To all these people I would say a **Big Thank you**.
If you read this book you may well come across something you said.
Thanks must also go to those who, in the past, have written leaflets, guides and histories of their church,
stately home, village or town which have been valuable sources of reference.

Last but not least I cannot overlook the work of two I have never met and am not likely to!
Both of their works have been used extensively in my research and are frequently quoted.
William the Conqueror was famous for the Domesday Book.
When learning about the Great Survey as a school boy I never imagined I would spend hours in later life poring
over this work, learning about Northamptonshire in the years surrounding the Conquest.
Almost 800 years later John Bridges of Barton Seagrave wrote 'The History of Antiquities of Northamptonshire'
which gives an interesting insight into the life and times of the early 18th century.
Without this imput both past and present it would have been impossible to compile this book which I hope the
reader will find interesting and informative and will encourage them to discover for themselves
just what treasures our **'County of Spires and Squires'** *has to offer.*

CONTENTS

INTRODUCTION

In many respects Northamptonshire is one of England's hidden counties – almost, it seems, unwilling to make itself known to the wider public. With a few exceptions you will not find Northamptonshire on any 'Tourist Trail'.

Although being a landlocked County with no mountains and few areas of outstanding natural beauty there are many attractive villages and superb buildings among which are numerous beautiful Parish Churches and a considerable number of Stately Homes.

All of the village churches and a few of the town churches are featured in my earlier book
'LANDMARKS' - Parish Churches in Northamptonshire   (ISBN 978 0-9568576-9-9)
www.derekfblunt.com
Of the almost three hundred churches included, almost a third has a spire
which feature prominently particularly along the Nene Valley.

Among the most majestic are those at Oundle, Rushden, Higham Ferrers,
Middleton Cheney and Kings Sutton, all of which rise high above the surrounding houses.
Some spires have been lost over the years mainly on account of neglect or lightning strikes.
Most notable losses are those at Rothwell, Moulton and Little Harrowden.
Although most churches are ancient, spires did not start to appear until the late 13th century.
Churches are free to visit and if they are not open a key holder can usually be found nearby.

With a few exceptions, Stately Homes in the County date from about the 16th century at a time when wealth was
being re-distributed following the Dissolution of the Monasteries and honours were bestowed
on prominent figures in the field of law, politics and royal favour.
In a number of instances such as Holdenby and Kirby, grand houses were built in the hope of hosting the monarch.
Others were rebuilt on the site of earlier buildings, whereas some were enlarged in accordance
with the newly acquired status of their owners.

Most villages had a Squire and a 'Big House' and although many of the Houses have been lost over the years particularly
following neglect during and after the Second World War the County still has a large number although many have been
converted into residential apartments and are therefore off limits to the general public.
A number are still family homes and others are maintained by a Charitable Trust.

The most important for the visitor are Boughton House (*Duke of Buccleuch*) Althorp House (*Lord Spencer*)
and Sulgrave Manor (*Washington*). Others open occasionally to the public include Deene (*Brudenell*),
Stanford on Avon (*Cave*), Cottesbrooke (*MacDonald Buchanan*) and Southwick (*Capron*).
Of the grand houses lost forever the most impressive must have been
Holdenby (forerunner of the present Hall) and Pytchley Hall.
Kirby Hall is a romantic and preserved ruin and together with Apethorpe Hall is now cared for by English Heritage.
Canons Ashby House is protected for posterity by the National Trust.
Overstone Hall on the other hand (damaged in a fire in 2001) is a sad and decaying sight.

Some Stately Homes are so secluded that the traveller rarely sees them, whereas a number open their doors to visitors at
certain times on payment of an admission charge to help cover maintenance costs.

As far as the villages themselves are concerned you are free to wander almost at will and the most attractive parts are often those off the beaten track. My visits to every town and village in the County have sometimes been quite exhausting but nevertheless very rewarding. Although I have lived and worked in the County all my life I have come across many attractive buildings and unusual sights I did not know existed.

I hope that you will enjoy my book and will be encouraged to discover more about Northamptonshire, its heritage and its

SPIRES AND SQUIRES

DUKES OF NORMANDY
(SIMPLIFIED)

Richard I – the Fearless d.996

Married 1) Emma of France   Married 2) **Gunnor**   d 1031

Emma d 1052   Robert d 1037   Mauger d 1033

Richard II – the Good d. 1026

married 1) Papia   married 2) **Judith** de Rennes d 1017

Richard III d 1027   William d 1025

Robert 1 – the Magnificent d. 1035

Mistress – **Herleve/Arlette** (who later married **Herluin** Viscount of Conteville)

Adeliza d 1083
Married three times
m2) Lambert of Lens

WILLIAM THE CONQUEROR
1028-1087
married Matilda of Flanders d.1083

Odo d. 1087
Bishop of Bayeax
English Earl

Robert d. 1090
Count of Mortain

Countess **Judith**

Robert II	**Richard**	**William II**	Cecilia	Adeliza	Matilda	Agatha*	Constance	**Adela**	**Henry I**
Curthose	d.1074	Rufus						married Stephen	Beauclerc
d.1134	aged c20	died 1100						11 children inc.	married
aged c80	while	while						King Stephen	1) Matilda
Duke of	hunting	hunting						of England	2) Adeliza
Normandy									12 children &
									at least 20
									acknowledged
									illegitimate
									children

* Existence uncertain

PART OF BAYEAUX TAPESTRY (Death of Harold)

WILLIAM THE CONQUEROR

William was the illegitimate son of *Duke Robert* the 1st of Normandy (known both as 'the Magnificent' and 'the Devil') and *Herleve* (also known as *Arlette*) daughter of a common, albeit prosperous, tanner in Falaise. His is probably one of the best known names in English history - the Norman Conquest and the Battle of Hastings in 1066 being among the earliest memories from our schooldays.

He was born in either 1027 or 1028 and his illegitimacy shaped his life. His mother *Herleve* was married off to one of *Duke Robert's* vassals and she went on to have two more sons - *Robert* who became *Count of Mortain*, a mighty Anglo Norman Baron and *Odo* who became *Bishop of Bayeaux*, an equally mighty power in the church. Both names appear frequently in the Domesday Book of 1086.

Duke Robert died suddenly while returning from a Pilgrimage to the Holy Land in 1035 leaving the 8/9 year old boy as *Duke of Normandy*. For a time the Norman Lords kept their word and recognised *William* as their lawful Duke but as time went on friction developed and many nobles perished in their attempt to gain the upper hand. Despite many attempts on his life the young lad survived with the help of friends and relatives and when he was 19/20 years of age he went to war against his cousin *Guy of Burgundy* to defend his inheritance and on winning forced the rebels to swear allegiance to him.

He went on to become ruthless, powerful, greatly feared and the undisputed Duke of Normandy.

He married *Matilda,* a daughter of *Count Baldwin* of Flanders and although they appeared an ill matched pair, he being over six feet tall and muscular (turning to fat in later years) whilst *Matilda* was slender and of small stature it appears to have been a remarkably good marriage particularly in the political sense.

The union produced nine or ten children, two of whom went on to become Kings of England - *William II (Rufus)* (1087-1100) and *Henry I* (1100-1135).

Edward the Confessor, King of England had a Norman mother and had lived in exile at the Norman court until 1042 establishing a close association between the two countries.

William claimed that in 1051 during a visit to his cousin *King Edward*, who had no heirs, he was promised that he would be his rightful successor. *Edward* died in 1066 and *Harold Godwinson, Earl of Wessex* and brother in law to the deceased King had himself crowned as *King Harold II* in 1066 with the consent of his peers although *William* declared that *Harold* had previously promised on oath to uphold *King Edward's* wishes.

Fearing an invasion from Normandy *Harold* gathered together his forces in order to oppose the enraged *William* but received news of an insurrection in the north orchestrated by his brother *Tostig*, the deposed the *Earl of Northumbria* and *King Hardrada* of Norway. Reluctantly *Harold* left the south coast unprotected and marched north to do Battle at Stamford Bridge on the 25th September 1066. The Viking invaders were routed and both *Tostig* and *Hardrada* lay dead.

In the meantime *William* raised an invasion force of some 600 ships and around 7000 men (including 2000 - 3000 cavalry) and sailed to England. He landed unopposed at Pevensey Bay in Sussex on the 28th September 1066 and within a few days raised fortifications in nearby Hastings. *Harold* and his men dashed south to meet this threat but his forces were exhausted with all the fighting and travelling and were no match for the Normans.

Battle took place between the opposing forces at Senlac Hill near Hastings on the 14th October, 1066 during which *Harold* was killed – hit by an arrow in the eye and then mowed down by the sword of a mounted Knight.

On Christmas Day of that year the *Conqueror* was crowned *William I* in Westminster Abbey which had been founded by *Edward the Confessor*. Three months later he was confident enough to return to Normandy leaving his half brother *Odo* as Regent to administer the kingdom but on both sides of the channel there was constant plotting and fighting.

Apart from the Battle of Hastings *William* is best known in England for his Great Survey which came to be known as the Domesday Book. It was completed in 1086 by which time the Conqueror was dead having fallen from his horse at the Siege of Mantes whilst fighting *Philip I* of France. *William* is buried in his Cathedral in Caen, Normandy.

DOMESDAY BOOK

One date most people will remember from their schooldays is 1066 when *William, Duke of Normandy* defeated the Anglo Saxon *King Harold* at the Battle of Hastings. *William* brought with him from Normandy a great army of nobles and knights and on being anointed *King of England* on Christmas Day of that year set out to reward his supporters by bestowing family, friends and nobles with grants of land or 'manors'.

He needed to raise money to meet his debts and to pay the mercenary army to defend his kingdom and to this end commissioned a Grand Survey of the land and resources under his control.

This led people to compare it with the Last Judgement or 'Domesday' as described in the Bible when all people would appear before God on the Day of Judgement and there would be no appeal.

Officially it was known as 'the Book of Winchester'. The name 'Domesday Book' appears to have been adopted to describe this Grand Survey in the late 12th century.

The survey provided extensive records of landowners, tenants, the amount of land they owned, how many people occupied the land (villagers, smallholders, servants, freeman) the amount of woodland or meadow, the number of ploughs and the value of any mill.

What was not included were castles, nuns or monks as they were outside of the normal source of income and revenue.

Needless to say *William* did not do the work himself - he engaged others for the task. In fact he appointed two groups of Commissioners to ensure that nothing had been overlooked and no-one gave false information.

The results were recorded by hand in Latin and consisted of two huge books completed in 1086 by which time *William the Conqueror* was dead. The final version of the Domesday Book ran to four hundred and thirteen pages and was written by one scribe and checked by another. It was written on sheepskin parchment using black and red ink only. The survey only recorded heads of households so it is impossible to give an accurate figure for the population - one writer estimated the total population as between one and a quarter and two million - quite a margin for error. The total value of land recorded in the Domesday Book was £73,000.

The basic unit of land was the manor (not to be confused with Manor House) and could be larger or smaller than just one village - some villages had more than one manor.

Some of today's villages were not mentioned either because they did not exist or were part of another manor.

It is notable in that it was the only census in England before 1801.

As far as Northamptonshire is concerned there are recorded about 580 estates distributed among sixty landowners. The King held vast estates in the County. Among the other main County landowners were the *Count of Mortain*, the half-brother of the King with ninety nine and *Countess Judith,* the King's niece with more than sixty estates. Peterborough Abbey held fifty one estates.

The County was divided into twenty nine Hundreds in which are mentioned 326 settlements some of which were split between Hundreds - e.g. Easton on the Hill was in both Upton and Willybrook Hundred.

Only about forty of our modern villages are not mentioned although more than eighty settlements which are recorded have now disappeared or are very much shrunken to only one or two properties.

The total number of households in Northamptonshire is recorded as 6882, of which there were 3452 villeins (villagers), 1808 bordars, 849 sokemen, 680 slaves and 93 other groups.

Based on a ratio of 4.5 persons per household the County population in 1086 has been calculated at approximately thirty thousand not much more than Daventry in 2012.

Sixty one priests are mentioned but only three churches at - Halse, Guilsborough and Pattishall.

NORMAN CURRENCY

After 1066 the Normans used their own French coins in Britain each impressed with a small star.

The Norman French for 'little star' was esterlin.

The pound sterling was a pound weight of esterlin – roughly 240 coins so 'esterlin' became anglicised to 'sterling' for the whole currency. Pennies are believed to be named after King Penda of Mercia.

A penny in 1086 would be worth about £30 today. The penny symbol 'd' is from denarius - a Roman coin.

Shillings came from the old English 'to divide' – the coins were often cut to make smaller denominations.

A shilling in 1086 would be worth about £360 pounds today.

NORTHAMPTONSHIRE AFTER 1066

In order to eradicate opposition from Saxon or English noblemen *William* decided to redistribute the land to those who were loyal to him and would render him service. Of the thousands of English landowners before 1066 virtually none remained by the time of *Williams's* death on the 9th September 1086 after being thrown from his horse. It was estimated that only 8% of the country was left in English hands.
Most of the previous landowners were either dead, impoverished or in exile overseas.

A feudal system was introduced in England such as was well established in Normandy and other parts of Europe. This was based on tenancy rather than ownership of land. The King was the overall owner and the favoured aristocracy, mainly new Norman Lords became 'tenants in chief' and held vast estates in return for military services. These Lords imposed similar conditions of service on their under tenants who imposed like conditions on their villeins.

Of the land distribution in Northamptonshire at the peak of the new feudal system the King possessed some fifty nine manors and estates. Other major land holders in the County included:-

Odo (12 manors) – *Bishop of Bayeaux* – also *Earl of Kent*. Half brother to *William I*.
Regent in his absence in Normandy and Commissioner of the famous Bayeaux tapestry.
He died in 1097 on the First Crusade.

Robert (almost 100 manors) – *Count of Mortain* – Younger brother of *Odo* and half brother to *William I*.
He was the largest landowner in the County after the King. He died in 1090.

Countess Judith born in Normandy in 1054/5 - (66 manors) - daughter of *William's* sister *Adeliza* by her second husband *Count Lambert de Lens* who was killed in the Battle of Lille in 1054.
She married a Saxon noble *Waltheof, Earl of Northumbria* in 1070 and is thought to have had three daughters.
Waltheof joined the revolt of the Earls against *William* but was betrayed by *Judith* and eventually beheaded on May 31, 1076 at St Giles Hill near Winchester. He was buried in Croyland Abbey in Lincolnshire which became a place of pilgrimage as a result of reports of miracles attributed to him.

Judith inherited all *Waltheof's* possessions including many manors in Northamptonshire.
One of *Judith's* daughters, *Maud*, was married to *Simon de Senlis* who with his son and grandson, have gone down in Northamptonshire history as builders of Northampton Castle, founder of the Priory of St Andrew and likely builder of the churches of the Holy Sepulchre and St Peter. Judith died about 1086.

William Peverel (26 manors) is thought to have been the illegitimate son of *William I* by his mistress and took the name *Peverel* from his stepfather following his mother's marriage.
He is said to have been a favourite of the *Conqueror* and he and a relative, *Renoir,* are both in the Falaise Roll as having fought at the Battle of Hastings. As a soldier *William,* who died in 1114, helped the *Conqueror* to subjugate the kingdom in the years after the invasion.

Geoffrey (36 manors) - *Bishop of Coutances* (also called *Bishop of Lo*) – *William's* trusted friend.
Rebelled against *William Rufus* and died in 1093.

Hugh de Grandmesnil (19 manors) – Constable of Leicester Castle - died there in 1094.

Peterborough Abbey and its Knights (51 manors).

Since the time of the Domesday Book Northamptonshire has experienced many major national events, four of which in particular have influenced the size, shape and wealth of the County. In chronological order they are:-

THE BLACK DEATH 1348-50 AND ITS AFTERMATH

Although the Bubonic Plague affected England more than once it had its greatest impact between the years 1348-1350.
It is estimated that in medieval England approximately 1.5 million people died out of a total population of 4 million.
The disease was carried by rats and death often occurred within three days.

Whole villages faced starvation as fields were left unploughed, harvests were lost and animals neglected.
Some villages disappeared completely or became grossly de-populated and in the list of lost or shrunken settlements in Northamptonshire (see page 467) are many which come under this category.
As populations dwindled landowners had fewer people to work the fields and so turned their attention to sheep farming which required less manpower.

Feudal law stated that peasants could only leave their village if they had the permission of the Lord of the Manor, but so many landowners were short of workers that they actively encouraged peasants
to move and work for them and the old feudal system was in danger of collapse.
In an attempt to curb mass movement of peasants from one land owner to another the Government introduced the Statute of Labour Act in 1357:-

' No peasants could be paid more than the wages paid in 1346.
No Lord should offer more wages than paid in 1346.
No peasant could leave the village they belonged to'

The labour shortage led landlords to give peasants on their Estates more freedom and paid them to work on the land in the hope of retaining their services although they had to work for free on church land for two days each week making it difficult for them to grow sufficient food for their families.

The imposition of the Poll Tax in 1381 on peasants already having difficulties in meeting their expenses led to their revolts which were quickly suppressed and their leader, **Wat Tyler** was murdered but the Lords of the Manor did not have it all their own way as owing to the shortage of labour, they had to pay up when peasants were needed for harvesting, etc.
The rallying cry of the peasants would become popular :-
" When Adam delved and Eve span - who was then the gentleman?"

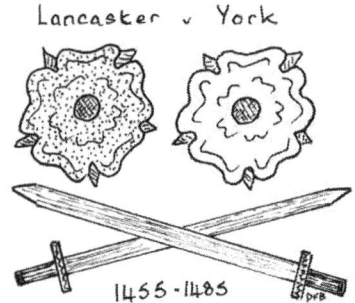

Lancaster v York

1455-1485

THE WAR OF THE ROSES 1455-1485

The War of the Roses is the name given to the struggle between two branches
of the Plantagenet family for the English throne.
The argument stemmed from both Yorkists and Lancastrians claiming their inheritance through
the complex lines of descent from *Edward III's* twelve children.

At the commencement of the hostilities the Lancastrian *Henry VI* was King but he became insane
and a distant cousin, *Richard, Duke of York* was appointed Protector.
War broke out after *Henry* recovered and the rival supporters
(Yorkists and Lancastrians) took up arms.

One of the earliest battles took place in the fields south of Delapre Abbey, Northampton
on the 10th July 1460 when the King was taken prisoner.

Richard was killed at the Battle of Wakefield in December 1460 and the new *Duke of York* (*Edward*)
claimed his inheritance. He won the Battle of Towton for the Yorkists on the
26th March, 1461 – probably the most bloody battle fought on British soil.
He was crowned *King Edward IV* and secretly married *Elizabeth Woodville* of Grafton Regis much
to the annoyance of his greatest supporter the *Earl of Warwick,* with the result that he took the
King prisoner and executed many of his close family and supporters.
When *Edward* died in 1483 his young son became *Edward V*.
With his brother, another *Richard* (born 1473) he was confined in the Tower of London.
After their mysterious 'disappearance' *Edward IV's* brother
was declared *Richard III* although he was extremely unpopular as many thought
he was responsible for the death of the two young Princes.

King Richard met his death at the Battle of Bosworth in 1485 against the forces of *Henry Tudor*
who became *Henry VII* and then married *Elizabeth* of York, daughter of
Edward IV and *Elizabeth Woodville* thus bringing about a union between the rival Houses
and an end to thirty years of hostilities.

Most of the population were not particularly affected by the war but nobles and knights
suffered badly if they were on the defeated side and many lost their great Estates and even their lives.

DISSOLUTION OF THE MONASTERIES 1534-1536

Prior to the beginning of the 16th century all churches were Catholic
and adhered to the authority of the Pope in Rome.

Abbeys held great swathes of land and had become rich and powerful.
All this changed when *Henry VIII* wanted to divorce his Spanish Catholic wife,
Catharine of Aragon and marry *Anne Boleyn*.
Unfortunately for him and many say for the country the Pope refused to give permission
for an annulment and the King took his anger out on the church.

Within a very short time *Henry* declared himself and not the Pope, Head of the Church of England
and ordered *Thomas Cromwell* to send commissioners out to establish the wealth and land ownership
of all the principal Monasteries, Nunneries and Friaries.
Although prominent people in each area carried out a similar survey and were generally against the
total destruction of the religious houses and the confiscation of their property they were overruled.

In the majority of instances the religious foundations had rendered
invaluable service to their communities particularly the sick and the poor.
Henry however, was adamant and refused to make any concessions.
As a result the establishments concerned were closed, the buildings made unserviceable and the land
and property confiscated.
The monks and nuns sought compensation and a few received generous pensions.
By 1553 the Catholic church had effectively been abolished in England.

Villages in Northamptonshire such as Canons Ashby, Pipewell and Catesby were changed forever
and Colleges attached to churches such as Fotheringhay, Irthlingborough, Cotterstock and Higham
Ferrers were dissolved although the churches were saved for the parishioners.

At the time of the Dissolution it is estimated that as much as a quarter of the total wealth
of the country changed hands.
In Northamptonshire alone up to two thirds of the wealth held by the church
found its way into the hands of local gentry.
It was the largest redistribution of wealth since the Norman Conquest some 500 years earlier.

St Marys Church - Canons Ashby

ENGLISH CIVIL WAR 1642-1645

Since the mid 16th century when *Henry VIII* declared himself Head of the English church and
began to drive out the Catholic religion there was conflict between the supporters not only
of these two groups but also from new groups or 'Dissidents' who wished to worship in their
own way without any compulsory form of worship, they became became known as Puritans.
Along with many other prominent men they opposed the King's divine right
to govern and objected to him raising taxes and imprisoning protesters.
As a result *Charles* decided to abolish Parliament in 1629 and tried to rule alone.
Problems arose when he wanted to raise taxes to crush a Scottish rebellion.

War broke out all over the country between supporters of the King (Royalists) and supporters of
Parliament who were to become known as 'Roundheads' (originally a term of abuse) following the
establishment of a New Model Army under *Sir Thomas Fairfax* in 1645.
Towcester became a Royalist stronghold although Northampton sided with the Parliamentarians.
The local landowners were divided in their loyalty resulting in family members
fighting on opposing sides
As in the War of the Roses some of the gentry lost their Estates and their lives.

There were a few minor skirmishes in the County during the Civil War but the best known
is the Battle of Naseby which was fought on the 14th June 1465.
Although it was not the last battle between the opposing forces it was the most decisive
and the Royalists never again gained supremacy.

The Parliamentarians were led by *Oliver Cromwell* who was born in Huntingdon, the son of a
small landowner. He entered Parliament and was very active in the events leading up
to the Civil War at the end of which he was a member of the special commission which tried
King Charles I and condemned him to death.
Charles was beheaded in Whitehall, London on the 30th June, 1649.

Cromwell went on to become Protector – a King in all but name -
and held that position until his death in 1658.
The restoration of the monarchy under *Charles II* followed shortly after but the monarchy
never again had the same power as before.
Cromwell is immortalised in a statue alongside the Houses of Parliament
and is known for his approval of the desecration of churches
and damage to monuments and statues and the abolition of Christmas
(many today wish that Christmas in its present form had stayed abolished!).

 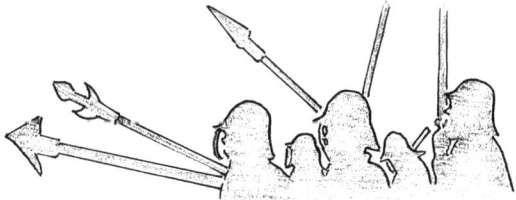

NORTHAMPTONSHIRE SPIRES

Northamptonshire, known as the

'County of Spires and Squires'

is blessed with a large number of beautiful and majestic church spires.

The compact Oxford Dictionary describes a spire as a *'tall pointed structure on the top of a building especially a church tower'* - the word comes from the Old English meaning tall plant stem.

Some writers use the alternative word 'steeple' whereas I have seen steeple referred to as the tower and spire combined.

The most noticeable feature of most parish churches is their tower or spire which makes the building stand out above everything around them and can often be seen for miles around.

Spires started to appear in the 13th century and quickly became the 'must have' of wealthy benefactors wishing to outdo their neighbours.

Even the Saxon churches at Brixworth and Brigstock did not get their spires until at least the 14th century.
Of nearly 300 parish churches in the County almost a third have a spire - many of these are congregated in the Nene Valley.

The design of spires altered over the years from a simple squat spire to a very tall and highly decorated feature.
The tallest spires in Northamptonshire are at
Oundle (210ft – 64 metres),
Kings Sutton (198ft – 61 metres) and
Raunds (186ft – 58 metres).

Spires can be made of stone or wood covered with lead, or as in the case of Silverstone, Evenley or Syresham shingles (wooden tiles) and come in a variety of shapes.

Almost from the outset of spire building it was decided that the octagonal form was most suitable leaving a gap in the corner where it met the square top of the tower. This was overcome by the installation of broaches (small triangular additions). One of the earliest examples in Northamptonshire can be found at Deene although the best broach spire locally is generally agreed as being the one at Aldwincle (St Peter). Later alterations in style included the provision of parapets at the base of the spire, decorative pinnacles, flying buttresses and crockets (small leaf like spurs) up the vertical angles.

Sadly many spires have suffered damage over the years particularly as a result of lightning strikes, fire or deterioration of materials.   Many were rebuilt but some including Rothwell, Little Harrowden and Moulton have been lost forever.

NORTHAMPTONSHIRE SQUIRES

In the *'Return of the Owners of Land'* in 1873 it is recorded that in Northamptonshire 57% of the land was owned by one hundred and two landlords with Estates of over 1000 acres and of these thirteen landlords owned Estates of 5000 - 20,000 acres.

It is not surprising that Northamptonshire became known as the *'County of Spires and Squires '* the Squire generally being associated with the 'Big House'.

Prior to the reign of *Henry VIII* there were many wealthy landowners partly as a result of their association with the great religious houses and colleges – some could trace their history back to ancestors who arrived from Normandy with *William the Conqueror* in 1066.

With the Dissolution of the Monasteries and other religious houses in the 1530's and the acquisition of their land and property *Henry VIII* was in the position to grant favours to those close to him or those who could be relied on, or bribed, to support him in the future.

It is estimated that up to two thirds of the wealth of the monasteries and religious colleges in Northamptonshire found its way into the hands of local men. Much land was sold off cheaply and the chief beneficiary locally was *William Parr.*

Others to benefit included *Sir Edward Griffin* who acquired the house and land of the Knights Hospitallers at Dingley, *Sir Thomas Tresham* received much of the land of Pipewell Abbey. *Sir Walter Mildmay* benefitted financially by virtue of his family's involvement in *'Receiving the Surrender'* of the Monasteries.

Not all acted honourably in order to enhance their wealth. Some acquired land in other counties.

Increased wealth and enhanced status resulted in a period of house building or re-building, in many instances recycling stonework or features from monastic type institutions.

Many of these grand houses were built in the hope of attracting a visit from the monarch and the Elizabethan style E-plan featured strongly.

Some of these noble families suffered disastrously owing to the Civil War in the 1640's either through death or loss of land and possessions.

The *Tresham* family of Rushton who were often in trouble because of their Catholic faith at the time of the Protestant Revival and their association with the plot to blow up Parliament became extinct on the death of *Sir William Tresham* in 1634.

The *Catesby* family at Ashby St Ledgers also suffered as a result of their involvement in the Gunpowder Plot.

Nevertheless in 1873 there were still thirteen landlords with estates of 5000 - 20,000 acres in the County as follows:-

Boughton – *Duke of Buccleuch and Queensbury* – 18,000 acres plus 460,000 acres elsewhere (branch of the *Montagu* family)

Althorp – *Earl Spencer* – 17,000 acres plus 24,000 acres elsewhere

Overstone – *Lord Overstone* – 15,000 acres plus 30,000 elsewhere

Castle Ashby – *Marquess of Northampton* – 9,600 acres plus 15,500 acres elsewhere

Cottesbrooke – *Sir J. Langham* – 9,200 acres

Wakefield – *Duke of Grafton* – 8,500 acres plus 30,000 elsewhere

Fawsley – *Sir Rainald Knightley* – 8,000 acres

Lilford – *Lord Lilford* – 7,800 acres

Deene – *Countess of Cardigan* – 7,200 acres

Oundle – *Jesse D. Russell* 6,300 acres

Dingley – *H. Hungerford* – 5,300 acres

Kirby – *Earl of Winchilsea* – 5,100 acres

Easton Neston – *Lord Hesketh* – 5,000 acres

Of these only Boughton, Althorp, Deene, Lilford, Oundle (Biggin) and Cottesbrooke are still family homes. A number of houses have been in the same family or its descendants for hundreds of years such as Deene *(Brudenell),* Althorp *(Spencer)*, and Boughton *(Montagu)*. Rockingham Castle is unique in the County as it was a Royal Castle for over 500 years before being turned into a family home *(Watson)* in the mid 16th century – over a 1000 years of history.

All are well worth a visit.

ABTHORPE

Three miles south west of Towcester
Population: 1801-393   2001 – 285
*Thorp, Thorpe or Torp are common elements in English place names deriving from the Scandinavian word for 'village' or 'farmstead'. The prefix comes from **Abba** a local tribal leader.*

Abthorpe is located in a rolling rural landscape in the valley of the River Tove.

It is fortunate that a minor road between Towcester and Helmdon skirts the village leaving the centre around the Green and the church relatively peaceful although parked cars can be a problem.

Around the church are some attractive buildings including a house dating back to 1682.

On the Green stands a village pump and some well placed seats to enjoy this idyllic English scene.

At the heart of this delightful village stands the church of **ST JOHN** the **BAPTIST**.

Internally the building is very reminiscent of a non-conformist chapel.

Abthorpe was originally a Chapelry of Towcester until 1736 when a new parish was formed with the addition of Charlock and Foscote.

Eventually permission was granted to rebuild on the site of the former Chapelry and this work was completed in 1871 making it one of the newest village churches in the County.

There was insufficient room at the west end to build the tower with its broach spire so it was built at the north west corner of the nave.

Disaster struck on the nights of the 7th and 8th of February 1984 when high winds caused severe damage to the spire which then fell through the nave roof. After repair the spire was damaged again two years later. Attending the Dedication was the ***Duke of Grafton*** who made a considerable contribution towards the rebuilding and used to own much of the land in the area.

Until the 1920's the Grafton Hunt would meet on the Green.

The population has declined over the years and now most people work outside the village.

In the past villagers worked in lace, silk stocking making, shoe making and agriculture.

One public house, The Stocking Frame has closed but the name continues on the house.

The public house near the church which is still open is called the New Inn and has an inglenook fireplace.

There is no longer a shop or a post office.

A Methodist chapel was built in Wappenham Road in 1925 but sadly owing to declining support finally closed in 1996.

The old school which was built in 1642 has this inscription:-

'Feare God, Honour Y King
Jane Leeson hath builded
this House for a free school for ever.'

The date is significant in that it marked the start of the Civil War at the end of which the King was executed.

Robert Porter appointed in 1690 was School Master for forty nine years and became first Vicar of Abthorpe in 1747. From this time, well into the 19th century, the classes were either taught by the Vicar who lived in Leeson House, which had become the Rectory, or more often the Assistant Curate who lived in the schoolroom.

Remarkable amongst these was the ***Rev. Pryce-Jones*** of Caersus in Montgomery (1793-1831) whose salary was withheld from 1819-1829 because he had taken to the bottle.

This Georgian scandal was commemorated in the ditty:-

'Abthorpe is a village of peculiar people
A drunken Parson and a wooden steeple'

Modern educational requirements result in children now having to travel out of the village for their schooling although the building which is now used as the village hall until recently echoed with voices from a playgroup.

The Old School -- Fibthorpe

The parish includes the lost/shrunken medieval settlements of Charlock and Foscote.
Neither appears by name in the Domesday Book presumably because they either did not exist
at that time or were taxed elsewhere.

CHARLOCK

I can find very little history of this settlement which is thought to have been situated
to the south of the parish around Charlock (Challock) Farm.

Alicia, daughter of *Jordan de Chaldelake,* by Deed gave her lands in Chaldelake (Charlock)
to the Priory and Convent of nearby Luffield during the reign of *Henry III.*

FOSCOTE

The name is self-explanatory. Here was a cottage alongside the Roman Fosse Way between Lincoln and Bath.
This settlement is thought to have been located north east of Abthorpe in the area around Foscote Hill Farm.
Records of 1405 show the sale of all the trees and underwood in the orchard and grove of Foscote manor
and this was followed by some depopulation about 1488.

I was interested to read that in 1530 *Edward Knightley* had a case against him before *Chancellor More*
for having bought Foscote Manor *'from an idiot to the detriment of the vendor's widowed mother.'*
Edward Knightley appears to have been an unscrupulous rogue and was regularly being sued or suing someone else.
He came from a wealthy family as his father held forty one manors in the Midlands
but this did not stop him from upsetting all and sundry.

There were originally two manors here. The owner of one manor, *John Assheby* enclosed his land and evicted
twelve tenants and the other manor was acquired by the *Fermor* family of Towcester.

DSTONE

Seven miles south of Daventry
Population: 1801 – 161   2001 - 84

DOMESDAY BOOK
ETENSTONE/ATENSTONE

There are two different spellings in the Domesday Book.
*The origin is thought likely to be from **Aettin's** tun - farmstead.*

In addition to two different spellings Adstone also gets three references in the Domesday Book and not surprisingly included in the list of land holders is the ***Count of Mortain***.

This is now a very small village whose population has halved in the past two hundred years and sits almost unnoticed on the old Banbury Lane. The whole of the village which has been a Conservation area since 1991 includes six listed buildings and a number of listed chestnut trees.

The small church of **ALL SAINTS** is hidden down a little lane just off the main road.
It dates from the 13th and 14th centuries but was totally restored in the 19th century when the chancel was added.
There is no tower but a simple bellcote sits at the west end of the nave.

In Catholic times the church was served by the Canons of nearby Ashby who owned most of the land in the area prior to the Dissolution.

It is said that visiting monks stayed at 10 School Lane (***Charlotte's*** Cottage).

Among the oldest buildings are the Grade II* listed ironstone Manor House on the north side of the Green which is thought to date back to the late 17th century but has undergone alteration and Manor House Farm overlooking meadows which was built in 1656 by an ancestor of ***George Washington***.

The 17th century Manor Farm provides a wide range of leisure activities including quad biking, clay pigeon shooting and archery.

In his *'History of Northamptonshire'* published in the late 18th century ***Bridges*** noted quarries in Adstone.
The Methodist chapel dates from 1849 in the Georgian tradition but is now unused and is in a sorry state.

There is no longer a shop or public house and the old school is now privately owned.

All Saints Church Adstone

LDERTON

Three miles east of Towcester
Population: 1801-183   2001 -248
(figure includes Grafton Regis)

DOMESDAY BOOK
ALDRITONE

*According to research the name appears to have nothing to do with alder trees but derives from the personal name of a local leader - **Ealdhere**.*

There is evidence of an ancient settlement here as artefacts from the Iron Age and Roman and Saxon periods have been found on **'The Mount'** an English Heritage Scheduled Ancient Monument which although privately owned is open to the public. It was the subject of an investigation for the TV programme
'Time Team' first broadcast in January 2001.

In 2009 archaeologists picked up where the 'Time Team' left off and uncovered what they believed were remains of the only medieval stone castle in the area.
Further excavations took place in 2010.

There are some medieval fish ponds to the south west of 'The Mount' and these now form part of the garden of Manor Court.

In 1086 the Domesday Book records the **Count of Mortain** as owning the manor although part was held freely by **Edwin** and **Eadmare**.

This is a delightful, peaceful little village just off the Stony Stratford to Northampton road and it is hard to imagine that such a small isolated place had a Market Charter in 1270.

The Manor House was located to the north west of the village and was acquired by **Henry VIII** who leased it to various local families including the **Haslerigs**.
During the royal progress in 1605 **Anne of Denmark** is said to have stayed in the Manor House although I also read that on this occasion her husband **King James I** lodged at Grafton Regis.

The Mount. Alderton

Tucked away is the 14th century church of **ST MARGARET** which was virtually rebuilt in 1848 but without a south aisle.
The Jacobean pulpit is dated 1633 and there are some box pews and a six hundred year old font.

On the floor in the chancel is a rare oak effigy of a cross legged Knight thought to be **Sir William Combemartyn**, once Lord of the Manor who died in 1318.

At one time the village also had a place of worship for Protestant Dissenters the funds for which were mostly donated by the **6th Duke of Grafton** on condition that they did not worship at the same time as the established church. The chapel was demolished after 1980 but there are still many old houses some of which are thatched.

The only public house, The Plough, closed in 1958 and there is no shop, post office or school although there is a plant nursery.

In 1935 the parish was merged with Grafton Regis but an independent Parish Council for the village was established on 1st April, 2004.
In 2009 Alderton was recorded as having 109 residents.

ALDWINCLE

Two miles north of Thrapston
Population: 1801-349   2001 -345

DOMESDAY BOOK
ST PETERS - ELDEWINCLE
ALL SAINTS - ALDEVINCLE
The Saxon word 'wincel' (sounds like a sea snail!) means at the place of a bend.
*The prefix may be from **Ealda**, an old name or alor, an alder tree,*

The name seems very appropriate because the River Nene has a great double bend on its way from Thorpe Waterville to Wadenhoe.

This delightful little village with some lovely thatched cottages is virtually surrounded by water, either lakes, resulting from sand and gravel extraction, or by the river.

In 1967 during gravel diggings about a mile south of the village, evidence was found that at the time of the Roman occupation the Via Devana between Leicester and the Ermine Street crossed the river here over a timber bridge and causeway.

The presence of so much water means that the area used to be flooded regularly and on the minor road between Aldwincle and Thorpe Waterville is a raised walkway as a reminder of those times.

The Nene Way - a seventy two mile long footpath running through the County follows the Nene alongside the village but the whole area is superb for walking and attracts not only walkers but many fishermen and birdwatchers
One of the bird hides is sponsored by Oundle school in memory of **Sir Peter Scott** the famous ornithologist who frequented the spot when a pupil at the school.

At the time of the Domesday Book there were two parishes here which were recorded separately for taxation purposes.

St Peters seems to have been a little neglected at that time as it was worth thirty shillings but:-

*'If it were well worked
it would be worth 100 shillings'.*

The manor of All Saints held by *Guy de Raimbeaucourt* included a mill rendering six shillings per annum and ten acres of meadow.

Both parishes had a church, a Manor House and a Rectory but they were amalgamated in 1885.

The two Rectories were associated with famous families – *John Dryden* the poet and playwright and Poet Laureate to *Charles II* between 1668-1685 was born in 1631 in All Saints Rectory (now Dryden House). He died in 1700 and his funeral procession to Westminster Abbey included one hundred carriages.

The other Rectory - *St Peters* - was demolished in 1790 but was, in 1608, the birthplace of *Thomas Fuller* best known for his book the *'Worthies of England'* which was published after his death in 1661.

The beautiful church of **ALL SAINTS** with its superb 15th century embattled Perpendicular style tower became redundant many years ago and is now under the care of the Churches Conservation Trust.
It is still consecrated and although devoid of church furniture is used occasionally for services, plays, concerts, etc. and it is here where you can see the *Dryden* memorials.

Still in use is the church of **ST PETER** dating from the late 12th century.
It has many interesting features including an elegant broach spire which is reputed to be one of the best in the County.
The west window dated 1900 is in memory of *Thomas Fuller* but it was the millennium window that caught my eye as it depicts the church's Saint (*Peter)* in vivid Pentecostal flames with the *Risen Christ* overhead.

The Baptist chapel was built in 1823 and is still in regular use and is beautifully kept.

Near the church is the attractive village hall with a variety of children's play equipment in the garden.
Young children have the advantage of a new Primary school - the old school dating from 1872 is now used as commercial premises.

There is still a shop and garage in the main street but no longer a public house although the Pear Tree Farmhouse has a popular tea room, bed and breakfast accommodation and an approved camping site at the rear.

Off the main street is a Pocket Park on land that was formerly a quarry and area of old woodland.

A former public house -The Castle Tavern (now the Tavern Cottage) in Lowick Lane has an interesting plaque on the wall.

It is said to have been transferred in 1954 from a row of cottages in nearby Titchmarsh and features castellated towers and masons tools with the date 1834 and the inscription in Latin translated:-

'Believers in Christ have Eternal Life'

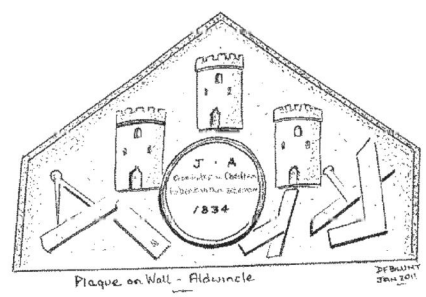

Plaque on Wall - Aldwincle

ALTHORP

Five miles north west of Northampton
Population: N/A

DOMESDAY BOOK
OLLETORP
*The name derivation seems to indicate that this was where **Olla** or **Ali** lived.*

Now classified as one of the County's lost villages it is thought to have been located on the south west side of the park immediately east of West Lodge. The correct pronunciation of the name is 'Oltrup'.

At the time of the Domesday Book there were ten households and in 1377 fifty people over fourteen years of age were assessed for the Poll Tax but the population then declined. The reason for the decline as in so many cases was land enclosure by the Lord of the Manor, in this instance the *Catesby* family in the 15th century.

Althorp now consists of little more than a Grade I listed mansion with its large park and Estate buildings.

Railway trains on the branch line between Northampton and Rugby still run through the Estate grounds but the imposing Althorp Park Station, (the station for Althorp House) closed in 1964. When members of the Royal family attended the interment of *Princess Diana* at **Althorp House** in 1998 they had to disembark at nearby Long Buckby station.

Headlines were made in 1892 when the headless body of *Annie Pritchard* was discovered near Althorp Station.
She had been brutally murdered by *Andrew George McRae* and is buried at East Haddon where she is said to haunt the churchyard.

There are many stories of ghostly happenings around Althorp including a groom carrying a lantern, a baby, a dead man attending a party and the wanderings of an old servant - I keep clear of the place after dark!

It is said that *Charles I* was playing bowls at Althorp when word came through that a party of horse under *Cornet Joyce* had arrived at nearby Holdenby to arrest him.
In 1984 Althorp was the setting of the film *'Another Country'* the story of one of the Cambridge spies.

CORNET JOYCE

According to some accounts *George Joyce,* was a tailor in London before joining the Parliamentary army. He served in *Cromwell's* Regiment of Ironsides and in *Fairfax's* Regiment of Horse where he held the rank of Cornet (the lowest commissioned rank).

At the end of May 1647 he led 500 horse to Oxford to secure the Army's train of artillery after Parliament had ordered its removal to London.
Claiming he had *Cromwell's* personal authority he then rode to **Holdenby House** where *King Charles I* was in semi captivity under the protection of Parliamentary Commissioners and removed the King to Newmarket. *Fairfax* wanted *Joyce* court martialled but no action was taken – he appears to have had the tacit approval of *Cromwell* and *Ireson.*

He fell from favour in 1653 and his arrest was ordered after the Restoration when the astrologer *William Lilly* claimed that *Joyce* was the masked executioner who beheaded *King Charles* but *Joyce* escaped to the Netherlands where he was last heard of in 1670.

Spencer

Althorp House

Althorp House and the Spencer family

*The **Spencer** fortunes were founded in sheep and wool and this enabled **John Spencer** who farmed at Wormleighton in Warwickshire to buy the Estate at Althorp in 1508 followed shortly afterwards by lands at Wicken and Nobottle.*

He set about building a house at Althorp in red brick surrounded by a wide moat and in 1512 obtained leave to create a park of 400 acres around the property. The area appears to have been cleared by a previous owner.

*When **Sir John** died in 1522 his successor, another **Sir John**, set about enlarging the House by adding an enclosed courtyard and two projecting wings on the south side.*

By 1577 the family had 14,000 sheep on their Estates at Althorp and Wormleighton.

*The wealthy **Robert** (1570 -1627) was a diplomat for **James I** and was created 1ˢᵗ **Baron Spencer** in 1603.*
*Robert's grandson (3ʳᵈ **Baron Spencer**) fought for the Royalists in the Civil War and was created*
***Earl of Sunderland** in 1643 just three months before he was fatally wounded at the Battle of Newbury.*
His widow had the courtyard roofed over and added an imposing staircase in 1660-2.
The very imposing ironstone stables with Tuscan portico were added about 1732.
*The House was further remodelled in 1787 for the 2ⁿᵈ **Earl Spencer** who amassed a great private library including many works by **Caxton**. In keeping with the family's rising status the red brick House was then clad with light grey mathematical tiles made to look like stone, together with Corinthian columns.*
*When the House was further altered between 1876-88 the family resided at nearby **Harlestone Hall**.*
*The 5ᵗʰ **Earl** (1835-1910) was known as the 'Red Earl' due to his distinctive long red beard which made him stand out in a crowd.*

Family members have held many high political offices including Secretary of State, Leader of the House of Commons, First Lord of the Admiralty and Chancellor of the Exchequer.
*Female members have also gone on to be famous including **Lady Georgiana**, daughter of the 1ˢᵗ **Earl Spencer** who became **Duchess of Devonshire** and more recently **Lady Diana** daughter of the 8ᵗʰ **Earl** who married **Prince Charles** on 29 July 1981. **Princess Diana** died in a car accident in Paris in 1998 prior to which most people had probably never heard of Althorp. Since then many thousands have visited her childhood home and seen her place of rest on an island in the Estate grounds, although many people believe, contrary to official reports that she was laid to rest together with her forebears in the family vault at nearby Great Brington church (pages 194/195).*

*The family represented by the 9ᵗʰ **Earl** still live in the grand House of Althorp with its wonderful collection of furnishings and works of art which is open to the public at certain times during the summer.*

APETHORPE

Five miles north of Oundle
Population: 1801 – 231   2001 – 133

DOMESDAY BOOK
PATORP

*It is thought that in the Domesday Book the name was recorded as Patorp rather than Aptorp owing to a clerical error. Whatever the explanation this is likely to have been **Api's** outlying farmhouse - 'torp'.*

The Domesday Book records the manor as being held by the King. At that time there were sixteen villeins, four bordars and a mill rendering six shillings per annum.

The Willow Brook, known affectionately as the **'Willy Brook'**, a tiny tributary of the River Nene, flows through this delightful chocolate box village and passes under a picturesque hump backed bridge. The village was originally part of the manorial estate and has many quaint cottages huddled together and roofed with thatch or Collyweston slate.

The church of **ST LEONARD** was largely rebuilt about 1485 on the site of an earlier church and is mainly Perpendicular in style although the tower with battlements and spire dates from 1633.
Two stained glass windows in the south aisle were given by the *Brassey* family of **Apethorpe Hall** in memory of two sons killed in the First World War and both depict St Leonard (the Patron Saint) in manacles.

The crowning glory of the church is undoubtedly the south chapel of 1621 dedicated to the *Mildmay* family. It is very ornate and is thought by many to be the best of its period in England.
I visited the church during a very enjoyable walk from Kings Cliffe and was certainly most impressed when I first saw the chapel.

Opposite the church are stocks and a whipping post, parts of which date from 1780 and were once used to chastise local miscreants.
It is now a County Heritage Site.

In the grounds of **Apethorpe Hall** is a fine 17th century circular dovecote which was converted into a water tower when the Hall was being used as a school.

The village still has a public house, The Kings Head, which was built at the turn of the 20th century and has a highly crenellated and unsightly grain silo alongside the car park.
However there is no school and the children now have to travel to Kings Cliffe.

Included in the parish is the site of the deserted settlement of Hale.

HALE
(HALEFIELD)

DOMESDAY BOOK
HALA

It is recorded in the Domesday Book that Hale (open land) was owned by the Abbey of Ramsey and that there was land for one plough.

This settlement which centred on a minor tributary of the River Nene disappeared at the time of the plague between 1348-50 and had a church dedicated to **ST NICHOLAS** which has long since disappeared.

A large amount of medieval pottery has been found in the area but the site has been destroyed by modern ploughing.

The name has been perpetuated in the Grade II listed Halefield Lodge to the south of the village.

Today this is the home of Halefield Stud – a purpose built equestrian training centre offering a full range of facilities and services for the horse rider.

Earl of Westmorland

The Kings Head: Apethorpe

Apethorpe Hall

Apethorpe Hall (Grade I listed) which is built around three courtyards belonged to **Sir Guy Wolston**, Constable of Fotheringhay Castle in 1491 and contains architecture spanning the years from about 1500 to the early 20th century. The different styles of architecture do not in my mind blend together although they are attractive in themselves. The east front became the principal entrance in the 19th century.

It then passed through various hands until **Lord Mountjoy** sold the Hall and deer park in 1543 to **Henry VIII** who in turn sold it in 1550 to **Sir Walter Mildmay**. **Walter** was the youngest son of **Thomas Mildmay** whose family amassed great wealth by virtue of its involvement as Commissioners for 'Receiving the Surrender' of the Monasteries on the order of the King. **Walter** served as Chancellor of the Exchequer under **Queen Elizabeth I** and was founder of Emmanuel College, Cambridge.

He set about creating State Rooms in the south range in readiness for a visit from **Elizabeth I**.

There appears to be conflicting opinions about **Walter**, some thought he was good, others bad.

In the 16th and 17th centuries there were many royal visitors including **Elizabeth I, James I** and **Charles I**.

In fact royalty visited on at least twelve occasions between 1566-1636 making it the most popular House of the time in the County. The hunting in Rockingham Forest was a real attraction.

The Hall is reckoned to be one of the finest Jacobean houses in England.

There is a legend that **Lady Mildmay** now glides silently through the Hall scattering silver coins behind her.

In 1617 the Estate passed by marriage to **Sir Francis Fane** who later became the **Earl of Westmorland**.

Apethorpe remained in the family until the 13th Earl ran into financial difficulties in 1904 when it was bought by **Leonard**, later **Lord Brassey** a very rich and influential man who amassed a large fortune building railways.

After the Second World War much of the adjoining parkland was sold off and between 1949-1982 the Hall was used as an Approved School. In 1982 it was sold to a Libyan businessman who wanted to found England's first Libyan University but the shooting of **WPC Yvonne Fletcher** at the Libyan Embassy in 1984 put paid to these plans. The Hall remained empty for many years and was threatened with demolition.

English Heritage stepped in to save this precious building for the nation and proceeded to make it weatherproof with a view to a future sale. Unfortunately the economic slump arrived and English Heritage is now holding a massive 'white elephant' whilst still undertaking repair work.

In 2012 a substantial grant from the National Heritage Memorial Fund helped to ensure that the **Westmorland** archive, one of the most important family collections in Northamptonshire remained in the County.

The collection contains thousands of records based around family life at Apethorpe from the medieval period to the 20th century including letters signed by **Elizabeth I** and **Oliver Cromwell**.

The Hall and its grounds were used for filming scenes in 'Another Country' (1984) based loosely on the life of the spy and double agent **Guy Burgess** and Porterhouse Blue (1987) starring **David Jason**.

ARTHINGWORTH

Four miles south of Market Harborough
Population: 1801 – 207   2001 -229

DOMESDAY BOOK
ARNINGVORDE/ARNIWORDE
ERNIWADE/NARNINWORDE

*The village name is made up of three Old English elements, a personal name followed by 'inga' and worth - roughly translated into the 'Homestead of the People of **Earnia**'.*

The village is built mainly of red brick but its position standing on a hilltop site overlooking the small River Ise would have made it a favourite location for settlements during the Iron Age.
There are no fewer than nine tracks or roads from its centre which was in ancient times the hub of route ways.

At the time of the Domesday Book there was a recorded population of twenty two households and it was therefore quite large for that time.
The four different spellings relate to the areas held by four separate land owners including the royal manor of Rothwell and the Abbey of St Edmundsbury.
From the late 15th century until the 16th century the manor was held by the *Catesby* family.

By the early 18th century records show that there were forty five families in the village.
In 1851 it was reported that most of the population were engaged in agriculture or were 'in service' although seventeen ladies were said to be lace makers.

It gives me the impression of never having been a very prosperous village.

Although the Northampton to Market Harborough railway line which closed in 1981 was only one mile to the west of the village Arthingworth never had its own station.

The late 12th century Norman church of **ST ANDREW** has an embattled 15th century tower. Considerable alterations took place during the Victorian era including the introduction of a colourful organ and a stained glass East window. Unfortunately the restored chancel was never painted as the architect had envisaged owing to lack of funds.

Of particular interest is the grey and white marble monument in the south chancel to *Mrs Catherine Jekyll*, daughter of *Thomas* and *Elizabeth Rokeby* of **Arthingworth Manor** who died in 1775 aged only twenty seven.

The village has a popular public house, The Bulls Head, but no longer a shop or school.
Children now travel to the modern Primary school in nearby Braybrooke and the old school is now the village hall.

The remains of the mid 18th century Manor built of brick with two projecting wings are thought to be the fourth building on the present site.
The Arthingworth Estate comprising the old Manor House, new Manor House, four cottages, parkland, arable and pasture of about 678 acres was recently on the market for offers in excess of £8 million pounds.

Primroses

ASHBY ST LEDGERS

Four miles north of Daventry
Population: 1801-232   2001 – 166

DOMESDAY BOOK
ASCEBI
Ashby is a very common place name in England coming as it does from the
Saxon word 'aesc' - ash tree and the Viking word 'by' - village.
So common is it that most Ashby's have an additional descriptive adjective (e.g. Great, Cold, etc).
In this case the identifying addition comes from the dedication of the local church,
St Ledger *otherwise* **Leodegarius**

This very attractive village in the northwest corner of the County on the Warwickshire border
benefits by being somewhat off the beaten track although it still attracts visitors
by virtue of its beauty and historical interest.

The long distance footpath - the Jurassic Way
runs through the village increasing visitor numbers.

The most memorable feature of this Conservation village is the magnificent ironstone
Manor House alongside the parish church.

Like so many villages there is no longer a shop or post office but there is a
public house/restaurant called the Old Coach House Inn opposite which
is a picturesque row of six attractive thatched cottages which were provided for Estate workers.
The old school has been converted into a private residence.

.... ASHBY ST LEDGERS

The present Manor House was established between the 15th and 17th centuries and was altered and enlarged in the early 1900's for its new owner the *First Viscount Wimborne* by *Sir Edwin Lutyens*.

The Crown Estate which manages the Monarch's property interests bought the 2337 acre Estate but not the Manor House in 2005 for almost ten million pounds.
The land was put up for sale on behalf of the *Baker* brothers, a family who had owned it since 1982 having purchased it from the British Airways Pension Fund.

The site included a dairy farm, a country sports centre and Chapel Farm which one hundred and fifty years ago was the home of *Dr Thomas Arnold*, Headmaster of Rugby School.

Today there is an organic dairy farm and a game business marketed under the 'Ashby St Ledger' brand.

The Manor House was sold off separately by British Airways and passed through successive owners until it was bought in 1998 by *Viscount Wimborne's* grandson in an attempt to save it from total ruin.

Most of the buildings of 1605 are still there and *Lord Wimborne* has been reported as saying that it will cost about £10 million and will take years to preserve the House – it appears to be a race against time.

I was intrigued by the gateposts which are built with '**Beggars Seats**' where it is said a person needing to visit the rich man's house may have had to sit and wait.

The thatched village hall in what was once a barn has now been remodelled and modernised.

The lovely little 12th century church is well worth a visit and is unusually dedicated to **'THE BLESSED VIRGIN MARY and ST LEODEGARIUS'** - surely one of the longest names in the country.

As far as I could discover only three other English churches have the name **ST LEDGER** (a corruption of the name *Leodegarius*) they are at Basford (Notts), Hunston, (West Sussex) and Wyberton (Lincs). He was a political Bishop who lived in Burgundy in the 7th century and was declared a saint in 685AD.

The church is built of Northamptonshire ironstone with a late Norman tower although a notice warns visitors not to get too close owing to falling masonry.
Entrance is made through a very old south door and inside are some lovely 14th century box pews, hatchments and floor brasses commemorating five generations of the *Catesby* family.
The brass to *William Catesby* records his date of death as four days before he was executed after the Battle of Bosworth.

Among the greatest treasures are medieval wall paintings which possibly represent the finest Passion series in the country and draw visitors from far and wide. Other items worth seeing include a round undecorated Norman font, a rare three decker Jacobean pulpit, a musicians' pew at the west end and a beautifully carved rood screen from about 1500.

The Great War 'Roll of Honour' is quite unusual as the names are inscribed on a sketch of what appears to be a triumphal arch.

Buried in a small enclave to the side of the churchyard is *Ivor, First Viscount Wimborne* (1873-1939) who once owned the Manor and was an MP, Paymaster General and Viceroy of Ireland during the Easter Rebellion.

The Manor House: Ashby St Ledgers

Catesby family

The manor was gifted to **Hugh de Grandmesnil** by **William the Conqueror** and passed through various hands until acquired by the **Catesby** family about 1375. **William Catesby** inherited the Estate on the death of his father in 1470 and went on to become one of **King Richard III's** closest advisors holding the offices of Chancellor of the Exchequer and Speaker of the House of Commons.
In return he received a substantial grant of land making him richer than most other Knights.

William has been immortalised not only by **William Shakespeare (Richard III)** but in the famous satirical rhyme of **Collingbourne** which was nailed to the door of St Pauls Cathedral in London:-

'The Catte, the Ratte And Louell our dogge, Rulyth all Englande under a hogge'

Catesby was 'the cat', **Sir Richard Ratcliffe** 'the rat', **Francis Viscount Lovell** 'the dog,'
(he was commonly known as the Kings spaniel) and **Richard III** 'the hog', referring to his Coat of Arms.
For his trouble **Collingbourne** was hung, drawn and quartered in 1484 and within the next five years the four men named also suffered violent deaths. The manor was briefly confiscated after the execution of **William Catesby** after losing the Battle of Bosworth in 1485 but was later returned to his son **George**.

The manor passed down the male line to another **Sir William Catesby**. He was a staunch Roman Catholic and suffered for his faith with imprisonment and fines causing massive debts. In 1581 he was tried before the Star Chamber alongside **William Vaux** of Harrowden and **Thomas Tresham** of Rushton for harbouring the Jesuit priest **Edmund Campion** and spent most of the rest of his life in prison for various offences connected with recusancy.
At one time fines amounted to one fifth of his considerable Estate.
His son **Robert** was not so fortunate he also suffered financially because of his faith and in addition was forced to sell his own Estates. As a result he returned to Ashby to live with his mother and during his time there became involved in the infamous Gunpowder Plot – an attempt to blow up the Houses of Parliament.
The Gate House (see sketch), near the church is said to be where the conspirators met and hatched the plot.

Following the failure of the plot on November 5, 1605, **Robert** was eventually caught and killed at Holbeche House in Staffordshire. As a warning to others his head was exhibited outside Parliament.
Robert's mother lived on in the Manor House for another six years and there are some who believe that she was the brains behind the plot.
On the death of **Robert** in 1611 and then his mother the Estate was granted to **Sir William Irving** and finally passed out of the **Catesby** family after four hundred years.

SHLEY

DOMESDAY BOOK
ASCELE/ASCE/ASCEBI
The present name has a straightforward derivation from the Saxon words
'aesc' - ash tree and 'leah' - clearing in the woods.

Excavations in the area and the construction of the railway in the 19th century have revealed evidence of an Iron Age settlement in the form of a succession of circular huts bounded by a large ditch and also of Roman occupation with the discovery of fragments of a Roman pavement, urns and coins.

The site is close to the Roman road which ran between Leicester and Cambridge.

Four manors are mentioned in the Domesday Book divided up between *Robert de Tosny*, *Robert de Bucy* and *Countess Judith*.
In total there were twenty eight households and a mill rendering thirty two pence per annum.

The *Palmer* family of East Carlton were non-resident Lords of the Manor for over five hundred years.

In the 17th century the family built **Ashley Court** with a half-timbered overhang and a brown lower storey which was, until 1926 the home of the Rector who was also the village Squire.

They also built the Manor House to the north of the church which contains a room where the Lord of the Manor used to collect his dues.
It was refurbished in the 1860's by *E. F. Law* and its extensive barns and maltings were converted into seven houses in the 1980's.

Another 17th century house is the very attractive thatched **'Yeomans'** off Green Lane which may have been built on the site of a Saxon Manor House. It contains traces of a 13th century house.

Ashley is a delightful little village in a superb location overlooking the Welland Valley and shares its name with at least eight other villages in England.

It is regarded as a remodelled village because of the extensive demolition and rebuilding which took place between 1854-1858 when the wealthy Rector, the *Rev. R. T. Pulteney* commissioned the eminent architect, *Sir George Gilbert Scott*, to carry out restoration of the church and also to create a new plan for the village resulting in many attractive buildings.

I was not surprised to learn that the village is now a Conservation area with thirty one listed buildings and monuments.

At one time villagers were heavily engaged in basket making and made use of the large number of osier beds in the area.

17th C Yeomans : Ashley

A pump which used to supply these workers with water has now been resited outside number 48 Main Street.

The village once shared a station on the Rugby to Peterborough line with neighbouring Weston by Welland. Both the line and the station a quarter of a mile north of the village closed in 1951.

The station house with an old waiting room and ticket office has been converted into a private house.

One building the visitor must see is the Grade I listed ironstone and limestone church of **ST MARY** the **VIRGIN** dating back to the 13th century. It has a Decorative style tower with a broach spire.

My first attempt to get into the church was thwarted by workmen busy repairing the roof.
A return visit was very well rewarded.

Enter the church as I did to be amazed at the interior. The nave is superb and features a pink marble font but step through the ornate brass gates into the chancel with its beautiful barrel vaulted ceiling and alabaster reredos and 'wow'.

Victorian Font, Ashley

The interior is described by English Heritage as:-
'an outstanding example of the Victorian Gothic style at its height.'

The wall paintings are the work of *Arthur Bell* and were restored in 1973 by his great grandson.

I like the view of the church from the Main Street with the lovely lych gate in the foreground.

The churchyard is in good order and a yew tree was planted for the millennium in an area reserved for cremations.

History was made when a seven minute hurricane struck the village between five and six o'clock on the evening of 30th October 1669.
It created havoc in all directions and removed a large part of the roof of the Parsonage House.
Fortunately no loss of life was reported.

The Dissenters Meeting House in Westhorpe dates back to 1673 and was one of the oldest such houses in the County.

In the 18th century Dissenters would meet here in secret late at night and to avoid being discovered it was said that they would look up the chimney to check if dawn was breaking and then make a speedy exit.

It is reported that in their early years worshippers suffered considerable harassment from the Anglican Rector.

The chapel was closed in the 1950's and is now a private residence.

The shop and post office have also closed as has the handsome Gothic school opposite the church which was designed by *Sir George Gilbert Scott* and endowed by the *Rev. Pulteney* in 1858. It continued in use until 1966 when the children were transferred to Wilbarston school. It has two entrance porches one marked for boys and one for girls. The premises are now in private ownership.

Ashley once boasted five Inns but today only one - the 18th century George remains.

Every Easter Monday there is a Tug of War contest against neighbouring villages, Hallaton and Medbourne both of which are the other side of the River Welland in Leicestershire.

ASHTON

Seven miles south of Northampton
Population: 1801 – 292   2001 - 389

DOMESDAY BOOK
ASCE/ACESHILLE
*The name derives from
'aesc' - ash tree and 'tun' - farmstead.*

Village Sign : Ashton

Excavations about a mile from the village found evidence of a prehistoric site dating back to 2500BC and of Roman occupation with three Roman coins found in about 1948.
Other Roman sites have also been located.

The old village was built of limestone but there has been considerable modern development.

It lies just off the busy Northampton to Stony Stratford road but was once located in the midst of woods with Salcey Forest to the east and Whittlewood Forest to the south, separated only by the River Tove.

No major routes run through the village although the MI motorway between London and the north runs through the parish for about half a mile near the edge of Salcey Forest.

In 1066 Ashton was held freely by *Alden* however at the time of the Domesday Book the manor was held by *Winemar the Fleming* passing to *Philip le Lou* in 1315.

Ashton was annexed to the Honour of Grafton on its establishment in 1541 and most of the land became part of the vast holdings of the Grafton Estate.

The number of cottages gradually increased during the 19th century but the Grafton Estate and nearly all the houses in the village were put up for sale in 1913 with unsold lots offered in 1919.

Although many of the Duke's tenants bought the houses they occupied as they were reasonably priced others were not so fortunate and had to move away meaning more 'outsiders' arriving in Ashton.

The oldest surviving domestic building appears to be Rectory Cottage on the Hartwell Road which possibly dates from the 14th century.

The present Grade II listed Manor House was rebuilt in the late 16th century on the original foundations by the then Lord of the Manor, **Robert Marriott**, whose descendants went on to found the Hotel chain of that name.
Although the building with its original moat was threatened with demolition in 1958 it still survives as a private house.

The church of **ST MICHAEL** and **ALL ANGELS** dates back to 1298 when it was a small chapel - thought to be the present chancel with a small priest's door in the south wall.

The remainder of the building dates mainly from the 14th and 15th centuries.
The west tower was originally battlemented but in 1848 the tower which now houses five bells was rebuilt to become the saddleback tower which you see today.

Of particular interest to me was the rare oak effigy of a cross legged Knight thought to be **Sir Philip le Lou (alias Lupus)** Lord of the Manor 1315-1329 which is thought to be one of the oldest of its kind and a fine alabaster effigy of **Sir John de Harteshull** (1291-1368).

Sir John fought alongside the **Black Prince** at the Battle of Crecy in 1346 and is shown wearing the same armour as the **Black Prince** in Canterbury Cathedral.

Recent research has suggested that the two effigies may be resting on each other's tombs, both of which have recently been returned after restoration and conservation work.

In 1853 the Rector had the pulpit moved at his own expense to the south side of the nave in which unusual position it still stands

By removing some pews recently and designating part as '**Knights Hall**' it is hoped that better use will be made of the church by the villagers following the demolition of the old village hut which served as the village hall.

Chapels for both the Baptists and the Methodists were built in the 1850's but the Baptist chapel did not last long and was demolished and some of the furnishings were given to Hartwell chapel.

The Methodist chapel continued until about 1960 when it was sold to an adjoining householder.

I remember my father travelling by bus about four times a year in the 1950's to preach at the little Methodist chapel knowing that there would only be three or four people in the congregation.

Nevertheless he would be sorry to learn that it is now longer used for services.

Towards the end of the Second World War **Bernard Sunley** a local industrialist and benefactor invested heavily in the farms he bought and also built new cottages.

Sir John De Harteshull
1291-1368
Ashton

The village benefitted from his generosity including the provision of excellent sports grounds and a pavilion for the local cricket club.

The main West Coast railway line cuts the village in two with a massive embankment (the smaller part being known locally as Little Ashton) but although trains still rush by there has never been a station here.

The village still has a public house - the Old Crown Inn and a Primary school but no shop.

In the past the village has been mainly involved in agriculture but for a time was noted for its fine lace making.

On Tuesday 28th February 2012 the local newspaper the Chronicle & Echo reported that a few days earlier the villagers had woken up to find that the village signs had been changed to read 'Welcome to Ashton Kutcher' and the local public house renamed 'The Ashton Kutcher Arms' after a Hollywood Movie Mogul.

It was all part of a TV takeover orchestrated by a TV Channel Comedy Company in connection with the production of a video.

After the TV crews left the villagers returned to normal everyday life.

ASHTON

One mile east of Oundle
Population: 1801 – 112   2001 - 192

DOMESDAY BOOK
ASCETONE
*The name implies that this was a settlement
where ash trees grew.*

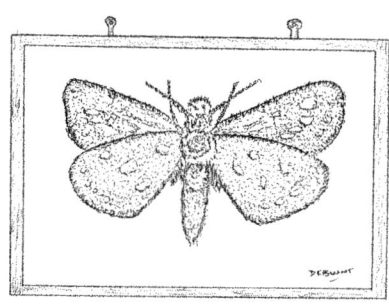

Chequered Skipper - Ashton. Nr Oundle

In Saxon times the village was set in a forest clearing; ash was a popular wood, its timber being used for furniture, tools and its branches for basket work. It was also a good source of fuel since it does not need to be seasoned before burning

The Abbey of Peterborough held the manor here at the time of the Domesday Book when Ashton was recorded as having fourteen households and two mills rendering forty shillings per annum (a lot of money in those days) and three hundred and twenty five eels.

After visiting the area in search of flora and fauna **Charles Rothschild** who founded the Society for the Promotion of Nature Reserves was so taken by what he found that he decided to purchase the Estate.

Ashton is unusual in that it is very much a model village having been rebuilt in 1900 for **Charles** the second son of **Lord Rothschild** on the site of an ancient settlement.

At the time model villages were the architects dream and resulted in **Port Sunlight** – home of Sunlight Soap and **Bournville** – home of Cadbury's chocolate.

Ashton is reputed to have been the first village in Britain to have a bathroom in every house

The village of Ashton and the Estate is now a Conservation area and comprises Grade II listed cottages.

This is fascinating little village of stone cottages with thatched roofs surrounding a fine Green overlooked by the local public house The Chequered Skipper formerly The Three Horseshoes named after a rare species of butterfly which local wildlife expert and scientist **Miriam Rothschild** tried to save from extinction.

The public house sign is unusual – not because it depicts a butterfly but because the butterfly is made up of painted nails.

The Chequered Skipper suffered fire damage in 1996 and was completely rebuilt to the design of the architect **John Robbins**.
The building had its Grade II listing reinstated.

In the summer months the Green is a popular spot to rest, have something to eat or drink or simply watch the peacocks or the children having fun.

It is most unusual not to find a purpose built church in a village but Ashton is one exception.

In 1706 a building was erected which served the dual purpose of a school and church room.
On the ground floor was the church whilst the upper floor was used as a school room (seems like a good idea to me).

Inside is a plaque and portrait of the founder, *Jemima Creed* a relative of the *Pickering* family of Titchmarsh.
I was unable to gain entrance but a quick glance through the clear glass windows revealed that the church room is now used as a rather untidy store.

In October 1952 the village hit the national headlines when two elderly local residents *George* and *Lilian Peach* were found bludgeoned to death in their cottage. There was no apparent motive for the crime and it remains unsolved.
Surprising arrests have been made many years after an event so even now someone may be brought to justice.

The village has the unusual honour of being the home of the *World Conker Championship* held annually since October 1965.

It is said that the competition started because a group of local men could not go fishing because of bad weather so they played conkers instead.
A small prize was given to the winner and a collection made for someone who had a blind relative.
The competition continued as a fund raising event on the village Green and increased in popularity.
A new location soon had to be found and this problem allied to inclement weather has meant that the contest has not been held for some time.

In 1990 to mark the Conker Silver Jubilee, twenty five young horse chestnut trees were planted in order that the young folk would have a good supply of conkers for the future.
Unfortunately lack of care and attention and adverse weather conditions have resulted in the loss of all the new trees planted.

I was interested to learn that the cricket pavilion at Ashton Wold is Grade II listed.

On a loop of the River Nene alongside the road to Polebrook is a three storey building with a Collyweston slate roof.
Originally it was a corn mill but today it stands empty and very forlorn and neglected.
Surprisingly there were once four mills in the parish, three for corn and one for fulling cloth.

As with most villages alongside the River Nene there are some lovely rural walks in the area.

Nearby was the abandoned village of Elmington which is now incorporated into the parish.

ELMINGTON

At the time of the Domesday Book there were two estates by the same name both held by the Abbey of Crowland.

The other Elmington is now located in the adjacent parish of Tansor.

As in so many instances the land was enclosed, tenants evicted and houses destroyed and little evidence now remains although the site is thought to be around Elmington Lodge.

HORSE CHESTNUT
[CONKER TREE]

Aston Le Walls

Six miles north east of Banbury
Population: 1801 – 225   2001 - 334

DOMESDAY BOOK
ESTONE

Estone simply indicates that this was east farm.
The unusual addendum can be dated back to Tudor times and refers to the existence of an old Roman Vallum
an earth made defensive embankment which once ran some twenty miles from here to Kirklington in Oxfordshire.

Geoffrey de Mandeville held the six hide manor at the time of the Domesday Book when there were twenty five households.

When compiling his detailed history of Northamptonshire in 1720 **Bridges** records that there were fifty two fishponds here in the 17th century.

The number has been queried as there is now very little evidence of their existence but they were thought to have been located to the north west of the church – some being on the site of the present sewage works.

The village stands on a hill with fine views over the neighbouring countryside of Oxfordshire and Warwickshire and just off the A361 between Daventry and Banbury.

The Welsh Road, or Lane, (see page 59) running across the northern edge of the village was on old Drovers Road which ran from Wales to London.

In the 1990's there were plans to widen this road but they were abandoned owing to the cost of replacing a disused railway bridge.

This decision worked in favour of the village as the Parish Council took on a twenty one year lease of the land in question and have created the Daisy Bank Pocket Park.

Trees and wild flowers have been planted alongside a pond, play area and picnic benches.

The railway bridge once carried the line between Stratford on Avon and Blisworth.

When the line was planned the S & MJR (Stratford on Avon and Midland Joint Railway) envisaged that Aston would be bypassed.

However owing to pressure by local farmers and landowners the company installed a short platform. The line and halt was closed in the 1950's but if the Government get their way there could be a new high speed rail link between London and Birmingham in the area in the future although the trains will not stop and will therefore be of no benefit to local people.

The church is dedicated to **ST LEONARD** of Noblac who was born around the year 466AD and lived to be ninety nine.

He lived a monastic life and became known as the Patron Saint of prisoners and women in childbirth – an unusual combination.

It is believed that the church was built about 1240. The piers, nave, large square font and tower arch are Norman although the nave roof is 15th century.

In the chancel is a pretty double piscina and a sedilia for three priests – one single and one double.

An interesting brass of 1609 shows *Alban Butler* with his two wives and fourteen children.

They were an old Northamptonshire family.

Extensive restoration was carried out at the beginning of the 20th century including rebuilding the tower. The church now needs to raise about £40,000 for the first stage of a five year plan of further restoration work.

Interestingly for such a small village there is a strong Roman Catholic influence.

The *Plowden* family who owned Aston le Walls Estates until 1920 built the Roman Catholic church in the early 19th century. The Roman Catholic Primary school was established in 1832 although the present school buildings with a Presbytery alongside are quite modern.

There is no longer a shop or public house, not surprising because I read that the sale of alcohol in the village is (or was) forbidden.

One of the oldest domestic buildings is the Manor House which has a hipped roof and a west front dating from about 1700.

A more recent arrival in the village is the Washbrook Farm Equestrian Eventing Centre created by *Nigel* and *Ann Taylor*. *Ann* was a member of the United States Olympic Team in Seoul in 1988. Aston welcomed the British Olympic Team before they left for Athens in 2004 and Beijing in 2008. Washbrook Farm is now one of the leading equestrian centres in the UK.

The parish includes the lost settlement of Appletree.

APPLETREE

*The name seems self explanatory
'the place of an apple tree'*

This small settlement lies on the western edge of the County and was once owned half by Aston and half by Chacombe Priory but was taxed with Aston le Walls.

It is first recorded by name in 1175 and was presumably included under Aston le Walls in the Domesday Book as I can find no separate mention.

In the 15th century nine people were listed as holding land in the common fields.

One claim to fame is *Alban Butler* (not the same one with the brass in Aston church) who was born in Appletree in 1710.

His once wealthy family had been reduced to near poverty because his father was instrumental in inviting *William of Orange* to England. A local benefactor arranged for *Alban* to be sent to France to be educated in the Catholic faith. In time he was commissioned as Catholic missionary to the Midlands.

His most famous work is his *'Lives of the Fathers, Martyrs and other Principal Saints'* which in its modern format runs to twelve volumes.

Today little is left of the settlement although it is still marked on Ordnance Survey maps.

AYNHO

Six miles south east of Banbury
Population: 1801 – 623   2001 - 632

DOMESDAY BOOK
AIENHO

*The name is thought to derive from **Aega,** a local tribal leader and 'hoh' meaning a cliff or projection of land – hence **Aegas** Ridge but I have also seen it as having derived from the old English - 'aegas hoh' meaning spring on the hill.*
Whatever the true explanation, there are some marvellous views across the Cherwell valley.

Finds of ancient skeletons, pottery and urns indicate that the Romans and the Saxons settled here long before the time of **William the Conqueror**. In 1086 the manor was held by **Geoffrey de Mandeville** who held other nearby manors. At Aynho there were forty households, a mill rendering ten shillings per annum and twenty acres of meadows.

By 1324 the village became a market town by grant of a Market Charter but the market did not last very long.

Aynho the most southerly village in the County is one of my favourites and is delightfully set in a superb location overlooking the Cherwell Valley.
Unfortunately only a stone's throw away is the busy junction of the B4100 and B4031 and the M40 Birmingham to London motorway with its constant roar of traffic

Nearly all the buildings in the old village are of local limestone, most were originally thatched but many have now been re-roofed in slate or tile.
Slate needing a less steep pitch meant that many house walls were raised to provide extra space.

The village, with its wide street is famed for the apricot trees growing in front of the cottages.

I was interested to read that in 1987 a group of ladies joined together to dance traditional English dances. They go by the lovely name of the: -
'Aynho Apricots'

I particularly like the church of **ST MICHAEL** and **ALL ANGELS** which is quite unusual at first glance and even more so on entering where it is more reminiscent of a Welsh chapel.
The walls are painted white and the body of the church is quite spacious with a gallery, box pews, a Georgian pulpit but no chancel.

The church, damaged during the Civil War, was rebuilt in limestone in 1723 - 1725 in the Grecian style. ***Thomas Cartwright*** contributed liberally towards the cost. Only the Decorative style 14th century tower of the medieval building still remains. Outside stands a Preaching Cross.

Interesting buildings in the village include the Jacobean Grammar school founded in 1654 by the ***Cartwright*** family and the Almshouses north of the school which were built in 1822.

The public house in the centre of the village was once an old coaching inn and used to be called The Red Lion. It has recently been massively refurbished with motel type accommodation in the courtyard and is now known as the Cartwright Hotel.

The village hall was built in 1920 reputedly from stones taken from the ruined plague house in Pesthouse Wood.

For a village of this size I was very surprised to learn that all the children of school age have to travel outside of the village for their education.

The two man stocks on the road to Deddington were in use until about 1850. It is recorded that in 1837, a labourer, ***Richard Howes*** was put in the stocks for being *'drunk and riotous'* on Coronation Day.

On the east side of the Oxford canal a little north of the B4031 is the site of an extensive wharf opened in 1788 which was used mainly for the transport of coal and stone.

Aynho once had a station on the Oxford to Banbury line and although the line is still in use the station closed in 1964.
There was also a halt on the line to Princes Risborough which is now closed.

'Defend the Faith'

Aynho Hall

Following a fatal car accident in 1954 the Estate was split up and for many years it provided luxury apartments for retired gentry. It has now been taken back into private hands but is still available for private hire for a limited number of exclusive weddings and events during the year.

To the surprise and somewhat disapproval of some local people a massive piece of grey sculpture in galvanised mesh in the form of clasped hands was positioned in front of the House in November 2009. It is, in my opinion, in completely the wrong setting and would be more suitable as a feature in open parkland.

Cartwright family

Richard Cartwright, *a barrister and member of the Inner Temple, acquired the manor of Aynho from the heavily indebted dramatist* **Shakerley Marmyon** *late in the 16th century.*
He bought the Hall and moved to Aynho in 1616 and built many village houses and a Grammar school.
In 1621 **Richard** *obtained a grant from the King to revive the weekly Tuesday market and Michaelmas Fair.*
The family initially supported the Parliamentary cause in the Civil War which caused the royalists to vent their anger and burn down the original Manor House in their retreat from defeat at Naseby.
By the 1660's their allegiance had changed and **Charles II** *paid compensation after his Restoration to the throne and Park House was rebuilt in 1662. It was enlarged and remodelled by* **Thomas Archer** *in 1707.*
William Cartwright *was instrumental in forming a local committee to achieve the publication of the History of Northamptonshire which had been left to gather dust after the death of its author* **John Bridges.**

Thomas *and* **William Cartwright** *were both MP's for the County in the 18th century.*
A succession of notable political and diplomatic personalities led the family into the 19th and early 20th centuries.
Several family members went into the church, one becoming Rector as recently as 1926.
Unfortunately a tragic car accident in 1954 killed the Squire and his 17 year old son and heir as they were returning from Eton and terminated the line resulting in the Estate being broken up. In the church are many memorials to the family although they are quite simple as the family were never particularly wealthy.
In the churchyard is a highly ornate wrought iron grave marker to **Marie Cartwright.**

BADBY

Three miles south of Daventry
Population: 1801 – 462   2001 - 645

DOMESDAY BOOK
BADEBI
Once again the name of the village derives from a tribal leader – 'Badda's burh' - fort.

Charters record that the land was given by a Saxon sheriff to the Abbey of Croyland (Crowland) around 726AD.

When *Canute* subsequently acquired Badby he transferred it to *Leofric* (husband of the famous *Lady Godiva*) who leased it to the Abbey of Evesham - a fact conveniently ignored in the Domesday Book which records ownership as Croyland Abbey. A fire at Croyland in 1091 destroyed any evidence.

By 1246 *Henry III* officially gave the manor to Evesham Abbey and when that was dissolved in 1539, *Henry VIII* gave the manor to *Sir Edmund Knightley* and his wife, *Ursula* of Fawsley.

In my view Badby is one of the most attractive Northamptonshire villages because of its location and buildings. I was not surprised to learn that there are at least twenty nine buildings considered of special architectural or historic interest to warrant inclusion in the list of special sites.

In the 18th century *Bridges* noted that *'at Badby there are several quarries of a fine blue rag stone, very hard and durable.........for building and pavements'.* I have no doubt that it found its way into some of the properties in the village.

The mainly 14th century distinctive medieval church of **ST MARY** is situated on one of the highest points in the village and has an embattled west tower with pinnacles which was rebuilt in 1707 in the Perpendicular style when its crowning glory, the spire, collapsed.

Interesting features include the clerestory with a magnificent line of ten windows added in the 15th century, a wide chancel, Victorian stained glass, 17th century altar rails and a small piscina built into the half pillar in the north aisle.
The church was heavily restored in the 1880's.
A kitchen and toilet were added as a 'north porch' in the late 20th century.

The area is popular with walkers as both the Knightley Way, Northamptonshire's first County footpath between Badby and Greens Norton (a distance of twelve miles) and the Nene Way which follows the course of the river start in the village.

In my cycling days Badby was often on my itinerary because it was a good place for a picnic on a pleasant day and also had a Youth Hostel for an overnight stay.

This was the only Youth Hostel in England and Wales to have a thatched roof.
Unfortunately it closed in 2005 and after modernisation was re-opened as a family home.
The Warden's House next door has had its corrugated roof replaced with much preferred thatch.

Although the village no longer has a shop or post office there is a village hall, a Primary school and a plant nursery with tea shop and two public houses - the Maltster Country Inn and The Windmill.

The United Reformed chapel which dates from 1873 started life as a Congregational chapel and is still in use.

It is said to be the birthplace of the *'Mite Scheme'* when in February 1986 a member of the congregation discovered that a sachet of sugar and salt which cost only five pence could save a child's life in the Third World.

In February 2007 the scheme celebrated its 21st birthday and is now supported by almost one hundred different organisations, most of which are churches and chapels.

Money raised is used to fund Oral Rehydration Therapy for severely dehydrated children and it is estimated to have saved three million lives.

Lantern House - Badby

ARBURY HILL

To the west of Badby is Arbury Hill which is thought by some experts to have been the site of an Iron Age hill fort and has for a long time been regarded as a fortified site. It was described as such in an Anglo Saxon Charter of 944AD. The hill at 734 feet is the highest point in the County but it is surrounded by other hills such as Blackdown Hill which is almost as high so appears to be less commanding. This 24 acre site shows evidence of Roman and Saxon occupation and is one of the County's greatest earthworks.

BADBY WOOD

Badby Wood owned by the Fawsley Estate, is ancient woodland covering one hundred and eighty one acres and in 1985 was designated a site of Special Scientific Interest (SSI).
It was imparked in 1245-6 creating a deer park for the Abbot of Evesham who had a Grange at Badby.
The park pale (the boundary created to keep the deer in) still exists in the form of woodland banks around much of the wood which consists mainly of native hazel and oak trees.

Bluebells carpet the woodland floor in May and June and cream teas are an annual event in the village during this time. As a young family Badby Woods was one of our favourite venues for a day out and is still a very popular spot for visitors.

An unusual building about half a mile south of the village is the quaint octagonal Lantern House (or Fawsley Lodge) which was built of local ironstone in the late 18th century possibly by *James Wyatt*. It stands at the entrance to Badby Wood was restored in 1981 and is now part of a large modern house.

BARBY

DOMESDAY BOOK
BERCHEBI

*The name is thought to be wholly Viking in origin - a derivation of the words 'berg' – hill
and 'by' – homestead. i.e. the house on the hill.'*

At the time of the Domesday Book the two hide manor was under the ownership of ***William Peverel***. There were nineteen households, woodland and six acres of meadow.

The village just squeezes into the north western edge of Northamptonshire and although within earshot of the busy M45 motorway it can only be reached on minor roads.

Barby Hill is nearly five hundred feet above sea level overlooking Leicestershire and Warwickshire.

Being in such an exposed situation it is not surprising that a windmill was built here.
Originally it was a post mill but in about 1830 a three storey tower corn mill was built and although the sails were blown off in the 1870's milling continued using steam.
Restored in 1998, it is now a private residence.

There is a project working to discover evidence of an Iron Age settlement in the area.

Prior to the establishment of the modern prison at neighbouring Onley, Barby also had prisoners.
During the Second World War these were initially Italian prisoners of war and when they were repatriated they were replaced with German prisoners of war many of whom were not repatriated until 1948 – some stayed in the area.

Like so many villages Barby once had a number of public houses and shops but growing prosperity and greater car ownership has changed people's lifestyles and shopping habits.

It is however, still large enough to support one public house, The Arnold Arms (after a former Lord of the Manor), a shop cum post office, village hall and a Primary school built in 1967 on the edge of the village.

There is a firm in the village which produces staircases, newels and spindles and specialises in architectural and fine carving with over sixty years' experience.
Their lists of clients include the National Trust, many listed buildings and the Royal Estate.

Fragments of a Saxon church can still be seen in the present church of **ST MARY** which was restored in the 13th and 14th centuries.
The square tower with a fine corbel of grotesque figures and a blue clock face was rebuilt in the 18th century.

I was very impressed with the stained glass windows many of them being the work of ***Kempe*** (with his trademark wheatsheaf in the corner) and his successor, ***Tower***.

The church is worth visiting for the windows alone but there is much more to see including the unusual 19th century eagle lectern in bronze, fragments of Celtic crosses above the chancel arch, Jacobean altar rails and a small Saxon window set in the south wall.

The organ dates from 1807 and according to the church leaflet there is a story that the Christmas Carol *'Once in Royal David's City'* was set to music on it when it was in private hands.

Once in Royal Davids City

Eagle Lectern
St Mary's Church
Barby

A list in the church gives details of an amazing number of projects completed since 2000 including new heating and lighting, new chairs and a new organ blower.

The Oxford and Grand Union Canal runs through the parish as once did the Great Central Railway although there was never a station here.
Two new canal marinas are currently being developed within the parish.

The village is mentioned in ***Tom Brown's Schoolda***ys of 1832 in connection with the 'Barby Run' from nearby Rugby School.

Just north of the village is the site of a former Manor House which is thought to have had a motte and earthworks but no bailey and is referred to by some as Barby Castle.

To the west of the village lies Onley which was joined to the parish about 1400 when that village became deserted.

ONLEY

*First mentioned in records of 1272 when it was called Onle (e) meaning **Ona**'s clearing or wood but was probably included under Barby in the Domesday Book.*

In the north west of the parish earthworks remain and some are well preserved although over ploughing has done some damage.
It is considered to be one of the most important sites of its kind in the country despite a lack of documentation.

The manors at both Barby and Onley were leased by ***William Catesby*** and in the early 17th century both manors were bought by ***Sir Giles Isham*** whose brother died at Onley in 1651.
Great importance attached to sheep farming in the area during the 1600's and the output of wool and meat were transported to markets in Coventry and London.

In 1729 Onley was described as a hamlet of seven shepherd's houses but a map of 1791 shows only five scattered farms.
In recent times the area has been repopulated and is now the location of three penal institutions, HM Prison Onley for young offenders, HM Rye Hill a Category C prison for adults and a mother and baby unit.

Onley Grounds and Onley Farm preserve the old name.

BARNWELL

Two miles south of Oundle
Population: 1801-240   2001 - 362

DOMESDAY BOOK
BERNEWELLE

The name is thought to be a derivation of two Saxon words 'beorna' – warrior and 'wielle'- spring.
Perhaps warriors used the spring when defending the settlement against invaders.

In the Domesday Book, Barnwell is recorded as having two manors, one held by the King and the other, which had a priest, two mills rendering twenty four shillings per annum and forty acres of meadow was held by the Abbey of Ramsey.
Unusually there is a record of two Market Charters – one dated 1270 and the other 1349.
Did they relate to the two parishes?
Whatever the reason they were short lived.

According to 18th century sources there were eight wells in the area.

This delightful village lies just off the main Northampton to Peterborough road and has many old limestone cottages some still with roofs of thatch or Collyweston slate.

The stream with its ancient stone bridge and wooden footbridges and ford runs through the main part of the village on its way to meet the River Nene.
This, together with the stone cottages on either side, is very reminiscent of Lower Slaughter in the Cotswolds and to me is one of the prettiest locations in the County.
A 'paddling' of ducks inhabit the stream which is lined with mature lime trees.

The Bridge : Barnwell

As recently as 1801 there were two villages here each with a church - All Saints and *St Andrews* but they were united ecclesiastically in 1821.

ST ANDREWS is still in regular use and has a beautiful spire with small broaches.
Externally it is mostly late 13th century with ornate dog tooth decoration.
The chancel was completely remodelled by
Sir George Gilbert Scott in 1851.

Near the altar is an elaborate monument to *Nicholas Latham* who in 1601 founded the Almshouses just opposite which has an entrance gateway also dated 1601 with the inscription:-

> *'Cast Thy Bread Vpon the Waterss'*

These Almshouses which were rebuilt in 1874 provided twelve poor people with accommodation, pension, clothing, washing and heating.
They even had two women to look after them.

The church of **ALL SAINTS,** or what remains, stands at the lower end of the main street and is now used for occasional worship.
It has a peaceful, well kept graveyard with lovely views over the fields.

The 13th century chancel with large Perpendicular style windows was left undisturbed when the church was pulled down in 1825 because it was the mausoleum of generations of the *Montagu* family, owners of **Barnwell Castle**, including the *4th Earl of Sandwich* who enjoyed gaming so much that he invented the 'sandwich' to save having to leave the table.

The most poignant monument is that to
Henry Montagu who tragically drowned in the Manor House moat in 1625 aged only three.
He is figured under an enormous obelisk like alabaster canopy.

Some stonework from All Saints church has now been incorporated into the wall dividing the Rectory from St Andrew's church.

On a knoll above the river occupying a site long used by fighting men are the handsome ruins of the Grade I listed **Barnwell Castle** with its high curtain wall flanked by two towers which is thought to have been built in 1266 by *Berenger le Mayne* who gave it to Peterborough Abbey.

At the Dissolution the Castle was bought by
Sir Edward Montagu who built a new Elizabethan house with beautiful stables in the outer courtyard.

The House which was restored and enlarged between 1890 and 1913 is gabled with mullioned windows and was the home of the
Duke and Duchess of Gloucester until 1995 when they moved to **Kensington Palace** and it was then let out on lease.

The 18th century public house is named quite naturally The Montagu Arms.

The village once had a station on the Peterborough/Northampton line but both closed to regular passenger services in 1964.

Remains of All Saints Church, Barnwell

The station built in 1845 is in the Old English style and is now converted into a private house but I am pleased to see that part of the wooden canopy and the platform edge remain.

There is still a shop cum post office but the Primary school closed in 2005 and children have to travel to nearby Oundle.

BARNWELL COUNTRY PARK

Just outside Oundle opposite the entrance to the marina and nestling in the Nene Valley water marshes is this delightful little Country Park which covers thirty seven acres and was established in 1970/1 on the site of several flooded gravel pits.
The Park is now a haven for wildlife including herons, kingfishers, grebes, ducks and much more and is a popular place for walkers, fishermen and ornithologists.
On the west side of the park are giant carved models of the evolution of a dragonfly from chrysalis to on the wing.

Visitors are provided with a large car park together with a Visitors Centre, toilets and a large woodland play area. On the edge of the Park is an impressive three storey stone water mill with a stone roof and a large wooden lucam (a gable like projection at the front of the building used to hoist goods) which has been converted into a restaurant.

BARTON SEAGRAVE

One and a half miles south east of Kettering
Population: 1801 – 159   2001 - 4185

DOMESDAY BOOK
BERTONE
The derivation of the name comes from the Anglo Saxon words meaning barley settlement.

In spite of its size the village centre retains much of its old world charm with some attractive ironstone cottages dating from the 18th century and a village Green.

Barton Seagrave has a long history and the impressive church of **ST BOTOLPH**, an East Anglian saint, is one of the oldest in the area. Much of the Norman style is maintained including its main door with tympanum, font and massive tower arches.
The present nave and chancel were added in 1878.

In the church which appears to be well supported are monuments commemorating the *Bridges* family including *John,* a Northamptonshire historian who was born at the imposing **Barton Hall.**

The church is well worth a visit and the key can be obtained from Church House (formerly the Rectory) next door.

On the north side of the church is a 17th century stone built tithe barn with a blue pantiled roof which is now a private dwelling.

It was once used for storage of flax, crops, etc. which provided a large part of the Rector's income in the 18th century.

Remains of the Castle moat can still be seen west of the church and Castle Way. Artefacts have been found which are now in the British Museum.

At the time of the Domesday Book the four and a half hide manor was held by *Robert de Mowbray.*

In the latter half of the 12th century the manor was split into two parts – Barton Hanred and Barton Segrave the latter being granted to *Nicholas de Segrave the Elder* from whence comes the Seagrave element in the village name.

Both the Grade II listed **Barton Hall** built in 1550 with stone from the old Castle for the *Humphrey* family who owned both Manors and the 19th century Grade I listed Orangery with its three saucer like domes built in the grounds in about 1820 have, since the 1930's, been owned by the Wicksteed Village Trust who run nearby Wicksteed Park - a very popular family day out.

The Hall was used as a Care Home for the Elderly but in 2012 it was decided to convert it into a fifty two bedroom hotel, wedding venue, restaurant, and spa.

Nearby is a stone built dovecote with a blue brick slate roof now incorporated into new housing.

Norman Doorway - Barton Seagrave

The Orangery: Barton Hall

The old school and school house have been replaced by modern buildings and are now in residential use. New enlarged school buildings which opened in 1957 were essential owing to the development of large new housing estates.

There is also quite a large Comprehensive school (now a Specialist Art College) nearby.

The new village sign was, like so many others, a millennium project by various local organisations.

To meet the needs of a fairly large population there are a variety of shops, a post office, community centre, garage and the 'Stirrup Cup' serving drinks and food. Further housing development is planned.

John Bridges
(1666-1724)

John Bridges was an English lawyer, antiquarian and topographer. He was born in Barton Seagrave where his father then lived. His grandfather was **Colonel John Bridges** of Alcester, Warwickshire whose eldest son of the same name purchased the manor of Barton Seagrave in about 1665.

His mother was **Elizabeth**, sister of **Sir William Trumball**, Secretary of State.

Bridges was bred to the law, became a Bencher of Lincolns Inn, was appointed Solicitor to the Customs in 1695, a Commissioner in 1711 and Cashier of Excise in 1715. He was elected a fellow of the Royal Society in 1708 and was also Governor of the Bridewell and Bethlehem Hospital.

In 1718 he was elected a Fellow of the Society of Antiquarians and in the following year began his history of Northamptonshire.

He travelled the County and employed several people to make drawings, collect information and transcribe monuments and records on his behalf. In this manner he spent several thousand pounds.

Bridges manuscripts fill thirty folio volumes with five quarto volumes of descriptions of churches collected for him and four similar volumes in his own handwriting. These went to the Bodleian Library in Oxford.

On his death in his chambers in 1724 they were left to gather dust until they were bought by **William Cartwright** of Aynho and a local committee was formed to arrange publication.

The first volume appeared in 1762 and the second in 1769 but the entire work was not published until 1791.

A copy of the work was deposited in the British Museum in 1883

BENEFIELD

UPPER & LOWER

Three miles west of Oundle
Population: 1801 – 354   2001 - 308

DOMESDAY BOOK
BENEFELD

*I like to think that the name simply comes from the two Saxon words meaning bean field but most etymologists agree that the name of the village derives from the Saxon meaning ``land of **Bera**'s tribe'.*

Today it is difficult to imagine this tranquil spot having a Castle but it is still possible to make out the mound of the 10th century wooden motte and bailey north west of the church.
At the time of the Domesday Book **Richard** held three virgates of land here at Benefield.

Only in the 15th century can I find the first mention of two villages, Nethethorpe (lower farm) and Upthorpe (upper farm).
In the Conservation area which stretches from Castle Mound to Brook Farm there are about forty two entries on a list of buildings of special architectural or historic interest.

Although the village is split into two, the only church is **ST MARY** the **VIRGIN** at Lower Benefield approached through a beautiful lych gate alongside which stands an impressive three hundred year old Holm oak (Ilex).

On entering I had to smile when I picked up a copy of the well presented little church booklet entitled *'III Bellys'*. The explanation given is that the Chronicles state that in 1552 Benefield possessed *'III Bellys'*.
No one seems to know what happened to them as the current six bells only date back to 1713.
The oldest possessions are the beautiful stalls with misericords thought to have come from Fotheringhay.

Lych Gate - Benefield

More modern items are the reredos added about 1897 by **Sir Ninian Comper,** a Scottish architect, and the slightly later rood and rood loft whilst unusual items include the very large funeral bier once used as an ambulance.

The font is of Caen stone and the floor is laid in encaustic tiles. A number of 'green men' can be found around the church which was largely rebuilt in 1847 for the **Watts-Russell** family of **Biggin Hall** except for the 14th century chancel.
On the north side of the nave is the family chapel which was furnished in 1925 in memory of **Captain Arthur Egerton Watts-Russell** of the Coldstream Guards.

There is no longer a shop or post office and the village hall which was much improved in 2009 was once the school which was built for 110 children in 1820 - the village population has since declined.
Originally the village had three public houses, today only one remains - The Wheatsheaf Inn at Upper Benefield which dates from 1659 and was a popular place for American Servicemen stationed at nearby Deenethorpe Airbase during the Second World War. The Inn which contains an impressive collection of airfield memorabilia including a silk escape map and photographs is today a popular Country House Hotel and Restaurant.

Opposite Yoke Hill Fisheries alongside the road to Weldon is a memorial which stands on the site of the World War II Air base (see Deenethorpe) to the men of:-

'the best damned outfit in the USAF'

The parish has included the hamlets of Biggin and Churchfield since they were transferred from Oundle in 1894.

BIGGIN

Biggin does not appear to be mentioned in the Domesday Book but the name implies a building, presumably a predecessor of Biggin Hall.

In the late 12th century *Abbot Benedict* built the 'New Place' or 'Biggin Grange'.
A park is first mentioned in 1327 when the Abbot of Peterborough had the grant of a deer leap here.
The deer park covered some 110 hectares around **Biggin Hall.**
Records show that there was some enclosure and depopulation here in 1518.

All that now exists is basically the Grange and the Hall which is a pleasant 18th century house with medieval origins.
Since 1822 it has been owned by the *Watts-Russell* family.
Here there is a seven acre lake full of water lilies in the middle of Oundle golf course.

CHURCHFIELD

This settlement had a Charter back in 964AD when it was known as Ciricfeld meaning 'open land by the church'.
It certainly had a chapel by 1189 but this has long since disappeared.

The Domesday Book does not appear to make specific reference to this community which today is one of
Northamptonshire's lost settlements.
In the 12th century Churchfield was held by the *Angevin* family but passed in 1289 to *Hugh de Gorham*.
It is thought that the settlement was always quite small and relatively insignificant.
Gradual desertion appears to date from 1403 and by about 1540 the whole area was laid down to grass and passed
to a large extent into the hands of the *Tresham* family who had large flocks of sheep in the neighbourhood.

Some limestone walls and part of a rectangular building thought to be a Manor was excavated
by Oundle school in 1960 but findings are said to be difficult to interpret.

The name and supposed site is preserved in modern Churchfield Farm on the minor road to Lyveden.

Watts Russell family

The manor of Biggin was originally held by the Abbey of Peterborough.
*At the Dissolution it was granted as part of her dowry, first to **Katharine Howard** and then to **Catherine Parr** the last wife*
*of **Henry VIII** before being acquired by **Jesse Watts Russell** in 1822.*
*Two years earlier **Jesse** inherited £335,000 from his father who had made his fortune in London*
firstly as a soap manufacturer and then as a successful city investor.He was one of the richest men in England at the time.

*Jesse had married **Mary Watts** of the Ilam Estate in Derbyshire in 1811 and changed their name in 1817 from **Russell** to*
***Watts Russell** to perpetuate the **Watts** name. They went on to have eight children.*

If you ever go to the Derbyshire Dales and visit Ilam you cannot fail to notice what appears to be a Queen Eleanor Cross
*in the middle of the road. This is a memorial to **Mary** who died in 1840.*

*When **Jesse** died in 1879 he left very little and the Ilam Estate and 1000 acres in Northamptonshire had to be sold.*
***Biggin Hall** is however still in family hands. One family member, **Ivo Watts Russell** born in 1954 was joint founder with*
***Peter Kent** of the English indie record label 4AD. He has also produced several records.*

BLAKESLEY

Four and a half miles north west of Towcester
Population: 1801 – 609   2001 - 492

DOMESDAY BOOK
BLACULVESLEI/BLACHESLEWE
BLACULVESLEA/BLACULUESLEI

*Some claim the name derives from the Black Ouse which flows through the village but many historians suggest an origin from **Blaecwulf**, a personal name and 'leah' a clearing and that the river took its name from the village of Blakeslee in the 14th century and the brook was then named the Blakeslee Ouse.*

This picturesque village is situated among a maze of minor roads with many old and attractive ironstone properties. In Saxon times the settlement was surrounded by Whittlewood Forest.
Until modern development Blakesley was unique in the County consisting of two almost completely separate units joined by a central Green.
By 1981 almost the whole village was designated a Conservation area.

The old girls' school built in 1876 from subscriptions organised by **Charles Bartholomew** of **Blakesley Hall,** a founder member of the RAC, was until recently used as the village hall, but in 2010 a new hall with a large car park was built overlooking fields on the Greens Norton road.
A boys' Grammar school was endowed by **William Foxley** in 1669 but lost its status in 1850 although the old building still survives as a private house near the church

The village is fortunate in that it not only has a public house, The Bartholomew Arms, (formerly The Red Lion) but also a Primary school and a shop cum post office. Among the facilities lost are two public houses, The Greyhound which closed in 1971, now a private house and The Boot which was demolished in 1906.
The old Methodist/Wesleyan chapel is now a car showroom.

Blakesley railway station on the Towcester/Stratford on Avon line was situated on the minor road to Woodend and operated between 1873 and 1952 for passenger trains and into the early 1960's for freight.

At Quinbury End just off the Maidford road are the renovated remains of a brick built six storey tower corn mill dating from 1832.
It is now much reduced in size and has been converted into a private house with a shallow curved blue/grey cap on the top.

Blakesley Hall was in fact located in the parish of Woodend and is mentioned in that entry.

A popular attraction is the Blakesley and District Agricultural Show which draws visitors over a wide area.
This show has been held annually since 1884 with the exception of the war years and the foot and mouth restrictions making it one of the oldest agricultural shows in the country.

BLAKEMAR BRIARS

Although now established in nearby Litchborough, the firm was set up in Blakesley in 1890 when **Thomas Martin** - the founder of the Blakemar dynasty - returned to his home village having trained and gained a good reputation with famous London Briar Pipe Makers. When **Thomas** died the business was taken over by his son **Richard** who was responsible for the move to Litchborough and for modernising the process.

One of **Richard's** most loyal customers was **Douglas Bader** the legendary World War II flying ace whose life story was told in the film *'Reach for the Sky'*. **Richard** died in 2003 but the firm is still managed by family members.

Church Street Blakesley

One of my favourite County views is looking towards the church from the village Green opposite the school. Built chiefly of ironstone **ST MARYS**, with an embattled west tower dates from about 1300 although the clerestory was added in the 15th century. The church was restored in 1873 and the chancel lengthened in 1897 by *Charles Bartholomew* in memory of his father.

The south chantry chapel now known as the Foxley chapel, houses a small statuette of the Madonna given by the Rector - *Canon Capron,* to mark his retirement in 1970 after fifteen years.

There is an interesting wall brass of *Matthew Swetenham* bow bearer to *Henry IV* who died in December 1416. Until quite recently there was invariably a flag flying from the tower, I understand that a previous Vicar was a Vexillologist - an expert on flags and related emblems - and that he was an authority on the subject in the Peterborough diocese.

The parish now includes the deserted villages of Foxley and Seawell.

FOXLEY

This was once a small settlement in the north east corner of the parish but its history is largely unknown.

It is not mentioned as a holding by name in the Domesday Book although it certainly existed then for its name was given to the Hundred which later became Greens Norton Hundred.

The earliest reference to Foxley as a settlement appears to be in 1190 when it was taxed with Greens Norton.

The main land owners were the *Foxley* family who also owned nearby Seawell and their main interest in the 16th century was sheep farming.

The one inch Ordnance Survey maps show a farm marked Foxley on the old Banbury Lane which probably indicates the location of the original settlement.

SEAWELL

DOMESDAY BOOK
SEWELL (E)
There are numerous springs in the area and it is thought that the name indicates the 'place of seven wells'.

This deserted village lay north of Blakesley.

In the Domesday Book it was listed as a three hide manor with thirteen households and a mill rendering twelve pence per annum. Little else is known until the 16th century when it is thought that the main landowners were the *Foxley* family of nearby Foxley who kept four hundred sheep in the area.

All that remains is Seawell Grounds Farm just off Banbury Lane. It is a working eight hundred acre mixed farm with an award winning pedigree herd of charolais cattle. The house is one of the imposing Regency style farmhouses built for the *Duke of Grafton* about 1840.

The previous house was the scene of the last robbery by the *Culworth Gang* before their arrest (see page 135).

BLATHERWYKE

Eight miles north east of Corby
Population: 1801 – 164   2001 - 55

DOMESDAY BOOK
BLAREWICHE
The name is interesting and is open to different interpretation.
The one I prefer is that Blarewicke is a worn down version of Blaecborn – blackthorn and 'wic' - dwelling.
Blackthorn is known to have been valued by the Saxons.

At the time of the Domesday Book **Northmann** held the manor of **Robert de Bucy** which had a mill rendering thirty pence per annum and six acres of meadow.

During the late 18th or early 19th century two stone coffins were discovered - one is thought to contain Roman female remains giving rise to the theory that this may have been **Boudicca** killed whilst fleeing from the Romans near St Albans.

Today Blatherwyke is a peaceful isolated one street village in a rural part of north east Northamptonshire with a lovely view of the ancient bridge over the Willow Brook as you drop down into the village from Kings Cliffe.

The bridge which has been restored or repaired a number of times has a date stone of 1656 and is carved with the *Stafford Knot* - the emblem of the **Stafford** family who once owned the manor, which passed to the **O'Briens** on marriage.

The village has declined in size over the years and there is no longer a shop, post office, school or public house. The former public house - The Horse and Jockey - on the road to Kings Cliffe has changed in use and is now Glebe Farm

There is a lovely peaceful walk by the lakes at Blatherwyke which are a haven for birds and wildlife. The lakes were dug by Irish labourers brought over from the **O'Brien's** Irish Estates at the time of the Potato Famine, as a source of water for the nearby Corby Steel Works and could be the largest manmade lake (as distinct from reservoir) in the County.
Today Blatherwyke Estate business is focussed on the delivery of premium quality, locally produced game and venison – all shot, butchered and dressed on their land.

Attached to the stable block of the former Manor House is a ruined chapel thought to have been established because of religious differences between the local clergy and the Lord of the Manor

Prior to 1448 there were two settlements - each with its own church. One near Glebe Farm was the church of **ST MARY MAGDALENE** but this was closed and has been lost.

The only existing church is dedicated to the **HOLY TRINITY** and was declared redundant in 1976 but thankfully is in the care of the Churches Conservation Trust. It is open occasionally to visitors - a guide book says on summer Sunday afternoons - but don't bet on it! I was fortunate to meet members of the Trust who were on a visit and looked around inside with them.

Norman West Tower: Blatherwyke

-54-

The church is hidden by surrounding trees and is reached along a grass track off the village street.
It has a simple Norman south doorway and west tower with a blocked doorway in the west wall.
The roof of the nave almost reaches the top of the tower. Inside there is a nave and an even wider chancel, an enlarged north aisle and a north chapel. It is a quite unusual arrangement.

Buried in the church is **Thomas Randolph** (1605-1635) poet and playwright, the adopted son of **Ben Jonson.**

The church also displays an unusual bequest by **Thomas Cole** that the profits from the sale of wood coppiced from his land nearby should be used to: *'provide six of the poorest men in the village with a plum pudding on Christmas Day'.*
I have not been able to discover when this practice ceased.
In the churchyard is a tombstone to
Anthony Williams, a black slave, who drowned in Blatherwyke Lake in 1836 whilst trying to save his Master's life.

Stafford

Stafford Knot - Blatherwycke

Stafford and *O'Brien families*

The **Stafford's** had owned Blatherwyke since the 15th century. **Sir Humphrey Stafford** who was born in 1427 was executed at Tyburn in 1486 on the orders of **Henry VII** for siding with **Richard III.**
Family lands were confiscated but **Sir Humphrey** (born 1461) eventually received a pardon from **Henry VIII** and was granted partial restoration
The Estate passed through a number of generations until in 1720 it was partitioned between two heiresses.
Susanna married **Henry O'Brien** the youngest son of an Irish Baronet who is thought to have descended from **Brian Boru,** (King of Ireland in 1002) (see Great Billing – page 193).
They got the Blatherwyke Estate whereas **Anne** who married the future **Lord Carbery** got the Laxton Estate.

Henry O'Brien who changed his name to **Henry Stafford O'Brien** immediately started to build a new mansion which is recorded as having cost £3838.2s.6d. At some time in the 18th century the Hall was enlarged, the old village moved and an extensive kitchen garden was built.

The church of the **HOLY TRINITY** became enclosed in the private garden of **Blatherwyke Hall** surrounded by a 400 acre deer park. The Hall remained in the family until 1948 although during the Second World War it housed Czech troops and then German prisoners of war. The last owner is reputed to have declared:- 'My family built this house, none other have lived here and none other ever shall, for I will pull it down' and pull it down he did.

Once gracing the gardens and now a reminder of the Hall and park there is a lone figure of Apollo Belvedere surveying the open fields spread out before him.
A section of the church is dedicated to family monuments and memorials.

BLISWORTH

Five miles south of Northampton
Population: 1801 – 730   2001 - 1786

DOMESDAY BOOK
BLIDESWORDE
This settlement appears to have started as a small hamlet among the trees of Salcey Forest.
*The name implies that this was a clearing in the forest owned by a person called **Blioe**.*

There was a settlement here long before the Normans arrived because during ironstone quarrying to the south east of the village there were finds of Roman coins, pottery and 'ornaments' some from wells and pits.

In the Domesday Book the three and a half hide manor was held by **William Peverel** and had eighteen households.
The mill rendered two shillings per annum.

Whenever I travel through Blisworth it is always a delight to see the long thatched cottage (originally three properties) at the Northampton end of the High Street. Unfortunately it is located right alongside a sharp bend but this means that on slowing down the motorist has more time to take in this idyllic scene.

The recent construction of a bypass on the busy Northampton to Towcester road has helped to restore a little peace and quiet to the heart of the village although it is still quite a busy little place with a shop, post office, Primary school, village hall and public house - The Royal Oak.

The underlying geology of limestone and ironstone meant that there was ample building material available locally and this is reflected in the older cottages and houses many of which have attractive banded stonework.

A large fire in May 1798 which started in what is now known as Crieff House destroyed with it eleven other houses and an assortment of other buildings together with a large amount of grain and many livestock.

The large building on the right at the bottom of the hill on the way to Towcester was built in 1879 as a steam mill and for storage purposes.
It was then used by the Co-op as a warehouse and by various other firms until it was refurbished and converted to residential apartments.
On the other side of the Grand Union Canal is the Old Sun, Moon and Stars which no one seems to want and has been standing forlorn and empty for a very long time.

About half a mile north of Blisworth the West Coast main railway line crosses the road to Northampton.
I used to thrill at the sight of those wonderful long distance steam engines pulling their string of carriages over the fine 30ft high railway bridge.
Nowadays it is still a busy line but the modern electric trains do not have the same appeal.

The once busy station has now closed and the Station Hotel currently operates as the Walnut Tree Inn and provides accommodation and meals with a mobile home park at the rear.

Today it is hard to imagine that the Hotel became so popular that pleasure gardens were created and many famous Music Hall stars came up from London to perform to the crowds.
Special excursion trains were run from both Northampton and Towcester.

Following the **Beeching** Report of 1963 the Branch Line to Northampton closed.

Blisworth was voted best large village and the overall winner of the Northamptonshire Best Village Competition in 2012.

In a commanding position overlooking the main street is the spacious church of
ST JOHN the **BAPTIST** which dates from the 13th century but has a Perpendicular style west tower built some two hundred years later.
Its most precious possession is a high rood screen with doors dating from the 15th century.

In the church is the altar tomb, with a top of Purbeck marble and brasses, of *Roger* and *Elizabeth Wake*. He was Sheriff of the County in 1483, fought for *Richard III* at Bosworth in 1485 and died in 1504.
The churchyard is well kept and in it you will find the base of an old cross.
Just off the main street is the Baptist chapel which was erected in 1825 and enlarged in 1871 with its own graveyard at the rear.
In March 2010 a large tapestry featuring the life and times of Blisworth was unveiled in the chapel where it can be seen on a Tuesday between 9.30 and 12 noon when the coffee shop is open.

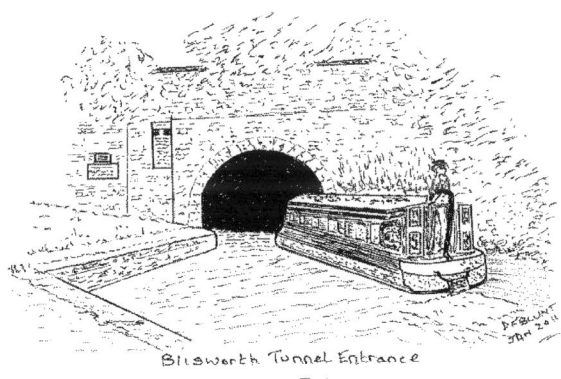

Blisworth Tunnel Entrance

GRAND UNION CANAL AND BLISWORTH TUNNEL

The village is situated alongside the Grand Union Canal and its chief claim to fame is its mile and three quarters long canal tunnel linking Blisworth with Stoke Bruerne.

The tunnel took ten years to build and was opened in 1805. It was once the longest navigable canal tunnel in the country and now ranks third in length in the UK after the Standedge and Dudley tunnels.
At its deepest point it is one hundred and forty three feet below ground level.

Barges had to be 'legged' through the tunnel by men lying on their backs on top of the barge and literally walking the barge through before the introduction of steam.
Canal cottage was where boatmen used to buy their candles before entering the darkness of the tunnel.

The Blisworth Hill Railway which ran from 1800-1805 was built to carry boat cargoes over the hill during the construction of the tunnel. Alongside the canal, is the home of Blisworth Tunnel Narrow Boats with boats for hire. Visitors flock here every August for the Canal Festival featuring decorated boats, trade stands, entertainment and refreshments.

Boddington

UPPER & LOWER

Seven miles north of Banbury
Population: 1801-576
2001 - 700

DOMESDAY BOOK
BOTENDONE

The name is thought to derive from a personal name **Bota** *and the Saxon 'dun' – hill - giving us* **Bota's Hill.** *The middle syllable first appeared in the 13th century.*

In the Domesday Book the manor at Upper Boddington was held (like so many others) by the **Count of Mortain**, half brother to **William the Conqueror** and had a priest, whereas, Lower Boddington was held by **Earl Hugh**, nephew of **William the Conqueror** and this too had a priest. Was the priest in fact shared by the two manors?

In medieval times both villages still had their own land and field system and by the 16th century the dominant landowner was **Earl Spencer**.

In 1873 a hoard of about 300 Roman coins all 'third brass' were found in a brown glazed red pot to the north of Upper Boddington. In addition Roman pottery has been found in the area.

Being on minor roads both villages are relatively free of traffic but in the past the **Welsh Road** ran through Upper Boddington meaning that the village saw a lot of passing trade.

Just outside Upper Boddington is Boddington Pool, a popular place for sailing boats and fishing. Car parking is provided for the visitor.

Manor Farm, part of which dates back to the 15th century was re-roofed after an aircraft crashed into it in November 1944.
A Wellington bomber had just taken off from nearby Chipping Warden when the port engine failed. The aircraft hit a tree and exploded.

The Carpenters Arms : Lower Boddington.

One of its engines crashed through the farm roof killing a mother and her two children - the family of a man based at Chipping Warden.
In addition seven trainee airmen were killed.

Upper Boddington has the Primary school, shop, post office, garage specialising in classic cars and the mainly 15th century church of **ST JOHN** the **BAPTIST** with its Perpendicular style west tower although there are earlier dated tombs in the church.
The first Rector is recorded as **Richard de Bamfield** in 1267.

I liked the East window but otherwise the glass is fairly plain.
The main treasure is an unusual 16th century chest six feet long carved from a single oak log encased in worked iron.

By 2010 the *'Bells for Boddington Appeal'* had successfully raised the money required to carry out vital restoration so that their sound may once again be heard over the village.

The churchyard is known for its variety of lichens including one County rarity.

Next to the church is the old Rectory built of ironstone with five bays and a rusticated doorway.

Once both the Upper and Lower village had a chapel but like so many places these have now been closed. Originally the Dissenters in Upper Boddington met at the bakehouse but had to relocate when Sunday baking started.

Two public houses serve the area:-
The Plough a 16th century thatched former Coaching Inn in Upper Boddington and
The Carpenters Arms in Lower Boddington which displayed a very large banner on my recent visit declaring:

'Beware of the Trains'.

There are no trains as yet but if plans go ahead in spite of local opposition there will be a high speed railway line very close by which will be of no benefit to the local population.

Apple Cottage which offers bed and breakfast accommodation in Lower Boddington is over three hundred years old.

DROVERS (WELSH) ROAD

The Welsh Road was a Drovers' road between North Wales and markets in the south east.

A 'Drovers road' or 'Drove way' which were between 40ft and 90 ft. wide were routes for droving livestock on foot from one place to another, such as to market or between summer and winter pasture.
In the United Kingdom where many original Drovers roads have been converted into single carriageway metalled roads, unusually wide verges often give an indication of its origin.

Drovers either on foot or on horseback accompanied their livestock travelling substantial distances.
They used dogs to help control the stock and these would sometimes be sent home alone after a drove, retracing their outward route and stopping at the same places, the Drover having paid for their food in advance on the outward journey.

Sometimes three or four hundred animals were moved at one time and feeding them over several weeks or months required expertise and authority.
Drovers in Tudor times had to be licenced and held a position of trust. They were often called upon by the gentry needing to transfer money to London – a sort of travelling bank.
On their return the drover would often carry large sums of money being income from sales.

The Drovers avoided Turnpike Roads wherever possible to avoid expenditure and also rivers which if in flood could cause considerable delay.

Boughton

Three miles north of Northampton
Population: 1801 – 344   2001 - 951

DOMESDAY BOOK
BOCHETONE/BUCHEDONE/BUCHENHO/BUCHETONE
It would appear that the name derives from 'buccaor' – 'he goat' i.e. a goat farm.

The village is recorded four times in the Domesday Book when part of the land was held by *Countess Judith* the niece of *William the Conqueror.*

The original village was near the old church on Boughton Green about half a mile to the east and was once famous for its fair which was held for three days in June of each year.
The first day was given to woodcrafts and agricultural implements, the second to festivities and horse racing and the final day saw the sale of horses and cattle – in its day it was the largest horse fair in the Midlands.

Eventually it lost support and was disbanded in 1916 after five hundred and sixty five years.

The infamous *'Captain Slash'* who was leader of a gang of trouble makers and notorious for his violent acts was arrested whilst attempting robbery at Boughton Fair and was subsequently tried and hanged in Northampton before a great crowd in July 1826.
Now he is said to haunt the old churchyard.

Boughton Maze was first mentioned in 1364 in the Boughton Fair Charter granted by *Edward III.*
It was a series of grass verges one foot wide alongside trenches and was circular with a thirty seven foot diameter and a single entrance.
The *'Treading of the Maze'* was a great feature of the Annual Fair. Sadly it was finally ploughed up by troops on exercise in 1916.

The old ruined church on Boughton Green dedicated to **ST JOHN** the **BAPTIST** is a mysterious yet interesting place with crumbling walls covered by ivy and undergrowth.
I remember attending an open air service there on one occasion.

The last wedding took place there in 1708 and the 14th century spire and tower fell in 1780.

The new church in the centre of the village also dedicated to **ST JOHN** the **BAPTIST** was built with stones from the old church on the site of a 14th century Chantry Chapel but has no churchyard.
It has little architectural interest or appeal for me except for the Perpendicular style tower.
The body of the church was restored and re-consecrated on the 6th March 1808.

Between 1764 and 1780 an extraordinary series of follies were built by *William Wentworth* the *2nd Earl of Strafford* who owned the Estate.

Some of these still remain including the castellated buildings of Bunkers Hill Farm, the crenellated archway known as 'The Spectacle' standing on a narrow lane just off the Moulton to Boughton Road and the giant Obelisk on the boundary with Northampton.

Alongside the main road between Market Harborough and Northampton (A508) can be seen the Hawking Tower. It looks like a small church with a large number of steps at the entrance but is in fact a two storey lodge.

The Estate eventually passed into the hands of the *Howard-Vyse* family who sold the whole village off at auction in 1927.
Although only a stone's throw away from Northampton's sprawling northern suburbs and just off the main road to Market Harborough, Boughton still retains much of its rural appeal.

There are some lovely old houses and thatched cottages near the church and some quite expensive houses on its perimeter.
One house I particularly like stands on the corner as you approach the village from the main road.
This charming detached Grade II listed stone and thatched cottage was built about 1650 and is within the village Conservation area. I have recently seen it advertised for sale at £399,000.

The Methodist chapel was built in 1804 and flourished between the wars but with attendance declining it closed in the 1970's.
The present village hall was built in 1967.

There were originally two public houses –
The Lion and The Old Griffin but these have been superseded by the present Whyte Melville public house which opened in 1928 and was once the home of *George Whyte Melville.*
He was a talented author who wrote over twenty novels predominantly based on fox hunting.
Copies of his books are on display in the pub.

Ironically he was killed in a riding accident in 1878 in the Vale of the White Horse during a hunt.

Some people say that his death inspired his friend *John Woodcock Graves* to compose the song - *'Do Ye Ken John Peel.'*

I was interested to see the new village sign dated 2001. It features my favourite view of the village looking up to the church from Butchers End (see sketch) but I was concerned to see that the sign is made of wood bark and wonder just how long it will last out in all weathers.
In addition to the church and the public house the village still has a Primary school built in 1841 but since enlarged and a shop cum post office.

On the edge of the village is a recently created Pocket Park, a very pleasant spot for a short walk, picnics, etc. and a party on Bonfire Night.

Church Street: Boughton

Boughton

Three miles north of Kettering

DOMESDAY BOOK
BOCTONE
The old name is probably from the old English 'boc-tun'
meaning beech farm although this is not universally accepted.

Boughton was recorded as having eleven households and two manors at the time of the Domesday Book, the larger manor which had a mill rendering twelve pence per annum was held by the Abbey at Bury St Edmunds.

The village has disappeared and what now remains is the Grade I listed **Boughton House,** parts of which date to about 1500. This has been home since the 16th century of the *Montagu* family and their descendants the *Dukes of Buccleuch,* the only Ducal seat in the County.

It is one of the great treasure houses of Europe and sits at the heart of the 11,500 acre Boughton Estate.

Foundations of earlier buildings were discovered when a bowling green was being prepared on the Estate.

The new House and garden construction meant the end of the village and cars now park and sheep graze where once villagers walked.

There is a lovely view of the House as you travel along the A43 north of Kettering.

The House and landscaped grounds with their statuary, fountains and walking trails are open to the public during the summer.

I particularly liked the stable block which houses collections of old fire extinguishers, laundry equipment, vacuum cleaners, heating appliances, lawn mowers and gardening and harvesting tools. Also on show is a fine 19th century yellow coach.

The House itself was never completed and visitors can see the unfinished wing which displays a portable Chinese tent made in the mid 18th century for the grounds of **Montagu House** in Whitehall thought to be the only one of its kind in Europe.

In 2012 a film crew spent a week at the House which will be the backdrop for several scenes in the screen version of *'Les Miserables'* which is based in 19th century France.

According to a spokesperson for the film company, Boughton was chosen: -

'as there isn't a house as French as Boughton
throughout the rest of the UK'.

The gardens recently received their first new feature for three hundred years.

It was designed by *Kim Wilkie* and is a seven metre deep pyramid named after Orpheus who travelled to the Underworld.

It is intended to echo the **Great Mound** which towers alongside it.

A ledge spirals downwards to a square pool at its base.

Montagu

West Façade : Boughton House

Montagu and Buccleuch family

Part of the manor of Boughton was acquired in 1528 by **Sir Edward** who was the second son of **Thomas Montagu** of Hemington in Northamptonshire and he set about making alterations to the existing house.
His success in the law had enabled him to establish the family foundations as landed gentry.

Sir Edward became an important political figure. He was Knighted in 1537, was made Chief Justice of the Kings Bench in 1538 and Chief Justice of Common Pleas in 1545.
During the reign of **Henry VIII** he was guardian to the young **Edward VI** and was well regarded following the Dissolution of the Monasteries and was able to buy the manors at Weekley, Warkton and Geddington and secured the remainder of the Boughton manor which had belonged to the Abbey of Bury St Edmunds.

He was also one of the Commissioners of **Henry VIII's** will but his involvement in the power struggle over the succession landed him in prison when **Queen Mary** came to the throne. It was a hard time for men of principle.
He lived at Boughton for about forty years until his death in 1566.
He was followed by another **Sir Edward** but it was his great, great grandson, **Sir Ralph** who inherited the Estate in 1683, who made **Boughton House** virtually what it is today – a grand French style palace:-
'The English Versailles'.
Ralph was chosen by **Charles II** in 1669 to be his Ambassador in France which was a plum job at the time.
His frequent visits to France and the Court and Palaces of **Louis XIV** whet his appetite for a French Palace of his own and on his return he set about transforming the aging Tudor house into his dream.
He courted the very rich but rather dotty widow of the **Duke of Albemarle** in the guise of the **Emperor of China** as she would only remarry a crowned Head of State.
He was obviously successful and her money helped to speed up the work being carried out at Boughton.
During the reign of **Queen Anne, Ralph** was created **1ˢᵗ Duke of Montagu.**
By the time of his death in 1709 the House was virtually complete.
It is a truly remarkable building containing a fine collection of furniture, paintings, silver, tapestries and porcelain.

In 1705 **Ralph's** son and heir, **John**, married **Mary Churchill**, one of the co-heiresses of the great **Duke of Marlborough.** His interest in Boughton was more geared towards the garden rather than the house.
He was given the name **'John the Planter'** due to his passion for creating avenues of trees which at one time totalled thirty five miles in length. Many of the elms have been destroyed by disease but the limes are still in good condition.

Following the death of **George**, the 3ʳᵈ **Duke** in 1790 the House passed through the marriage of his daughter the **Lady Elizabeth** to **Henry Scott, 3ʳᵈ Duke of Buccleuch**. Although the House was well cared for it was little changed or lived in from the mid 18ᵗʰ century – the **Buccleuch** family having other Estates in Scotland.

The House is now the Northamptonshire home of the 10ᵗʰ **Duke of Buccleuch** and his family.

BOZEAT

Five miles south of Wellingborough
Population: 1801-680   2001 -1941

DOMESDAY BOOK
BOSIETE/BOSIETA
*A likely explanation for the name is that it was a gate way - **Bosa's** gate.*
***Bosa** was a common Saxon name and a Saxon **Earl Bosa** held land in the area.*

Millennium Sign: Bozeat

Excavations in the area have revealed a considerable amount of evidence of Iron Age, Saxon and Roman settlements in the form of skeletons, pottery and building foundations.

By the time of the Domesday Book there were fourteen households and most of the land was held by **Countess Judith**, niece of **William the Conqueror**.

Some of the land was held by **Earl Waltheof**, a powerful Saxon Earl of Northumbria before the Norman Conquest and he became joint owner with **Countess Judith** when they married.

There are many wells in the village the most important being the communal town well which is supplied from a bank in Dychurch Lane.
Its upkeep is now provided for by a registered charity.

In my opinion Bozeat is somewhat uninspiring and is not a particularly attractive village.

The population has increased substantially in recent years with the result that it has a lot of modern housing, a number of shops a post office, Primary school and eating and drinking places including The Red Lion but little of a village atmosphere appears to remain.

In the 15th century there was a thriving weaving industry and many lace making workshops within the farming community.

The area I like best is around the church known as Burnt Close – so named as a result of a fire which swept through the area in 1729 causing considerable damage.
Rumour has it that **Widow Keech** left her baking unattended on the hearth as she was too busy gossiping with the neighbours.
A strong wind helped to spread the fire.

The village millennium sign depicts the church, windmill, cattle and birds and a boot on the supporting post indicates that the village was once heavily engaged in footwear manufacture which dates back to the middle of the 17th century.

For very many years it was regarded as a cottage industry as the shoes were made or mended in private houses or workshops attached to the rear.

The population of the village grew dramatically with the building of shoe factories prior to the First World War when the village could boast four factories, the last of which closed in 1982.

One such factory on the way out to Wollaston, the Drage Shoe Factory, was established in 1862 and has a large black boot painted on its side.
On closure it was turned into luxury flats.

The logo depicted in the ghost sign shows Drage *'Honest John'* painted on the wall in 1932 and then repainted in 2000 for posterity.

Another factory used to be housed behind The Nelson public house but that together with the public house has closed down.

The present church of **ST MARY** dates back to about 1130 and has a Norman tower which was rebuilt in the 1880's using much of the original stone.
The tower is topped by a heavy broach spire.

In the chancel which was restored in the late 19th century is a fine chancel screen although *Cromwell's* soldiers are thought to be responsible for the damage.

On Remembrance Sunday one person who is particularly remembered is *Lt. John Ahern* of the USAF who lost his life during the Second World War but saved his crew (who bailed out) and the village by piloting his damaged aircraft to open fields near Red Gables Farm.

The churchyard contains one or two fine trees but otherwise seems blank and featureless.
I was therefore very surprised to see proudly displayed on the church notice board that the churchyard had won the Conservation Churchyard Competition in 2009.

Standing high above the main street is the stark ecclesiastical looking edifice of the old Wesleyan Methodist chapel. I am told that it used to have quite a pleasant frontage but this has now been cut right back to provide car parking space for the occupants of the six or seven self contained apartments that now comprise the building.

The Independent Wesleyan chapel dated 1852 is still in use not only by its members but also by the mixed choir of about fifty voices who make up the *'Bozeat Windmill Singers'*.

An important event in the life of the village was the opening of the bypass on the A509 between Wellingborough and the M1 motorway.
This was witnessed by a great crowd on the 1st February 1989.
The traffic on this road grew dramatically and there have been a number of accidents.
As a result a new roundabout was constructed to replace a 'T' junction – making it much safer for motorists to enter and leave the village.

The village was in the headlines in March 2012 when a hot air balloon crashed into electricity wires. The balloonist and passengers had to stay suspended for many hours until rescue could be carried out. Fortunately no-one suffered unduly as a result of this accident.
The teenage pilot, *Adam Griffiths* has said that it will not stop him from flying balloons.

For their efforts in carrying out this unusual rescue the fire fighters from the Northamptonshire Fire and Rescue Service won a special recognition award at the first ever BBC 999 Awards in August 2012.

BRACKLEY

Eight miles east of Banbury
Population: 1801 – 1,495   2001 – 13,331

DOMESDAY BOOK
BRACHELAI
Bracca who came from nearby Halse lived between 550 and 650AD.
He came into possession of a 'ley' or clearing and built a small village – the Brackley of today.

This is a small yet delightful, mainly Georgian market town nestling on the side of a hill in the far south west corner of Northamptonshire separated from Buckinghamshire only by the River Ouse.
One of the town's features is the one mile long broad tree lined main street which swoops down to the Market Square.

In 1086 Brackley was a small agricultural village within the manor of Halse and Brackley Manor House remained in Halse for a further 200 years although as time went on Brackley outgrew its neighbour and became an important town.
In the old town at the top of the hill there was a Manor House on the site of a Norman Castle.
It was burned down by Royalists in 1645 and is commemorated in the road names of Manor Road and Manor Court.

The new town to the south by the River Ouse was in existence by 1173 and a market was granted at this time.

To prevent the Barons using tournaments as private battle grounds with fights and much loss of life *Richard I (the Lionheart)* named five official tourney sites in the country, one of which was on the outskirts of Brackley.

During the Middle Ages much of the land was owned by the *Earls of Bridgewater* and Magdalen College, Oxford.

The church of **ST PETER** with **ST JAMES** with its fine west tower occupies the site of its predecessor, the only original Norman remains of which are the superb south doorway with zigzag archway.

The worn statues over the west door are thought to be those of *St Peter* and *St Hugh*. Inside is some early 14th century stained glass and a window in the south chapel by *Kempe* dated 1901.

ST JAMES church in the town centre was founded about 1150 by the *Earl of Leicester* and was originally built as the chapel of the Hospital of *St James* and *St John*. It underwent a major restoration between 1869 and 1870 and is used by Magdalen College (founded in 1548) as the school chapel and is one of the oldest and largest school chapels in England. The Hospital itself has long since disappeared.

The attractive Georgian Town Hall topped with a charming little cupula is situated on an island in the centre of the town.
It was provided by the first *Duke of Bridgewater* in 1706 at a cost of £2000.
The lower storey which previously housed a market was later enclosed with round arched windows and was used as a Corn Exchange.
The building was sold to the town for just one shilling.

Town Hall : Brackley

Another attractive building is the tiny single storey stone Fire Station on the east side of the High Street. It is topped with a small brick arch with the words 'Fire Bell' carved in stone but with no bell.

The six Almshouses facing St Peters Street were founded in 1633 by **Thomas Crewe** of Steane who was MP for Brackley and Speaker of the House of Commons. They have now been converted into four apartments.

Opposite is The Crown Inn, a Georgian building which claims to have a history going back to **King John** (1199-1216).
The wide arched entrance would have been a welcome sight to travellers in the coaching era.

At one time the town had about thirty inns and was on a number of coaching routes to surrounding places such as Northampton, Oxford and London.

In more recent times Brackley had two railway stations, one at each end of the town, but both stations and lines had been closed by 1966.

Prior to the Reform Act of 1832 Brackley was a 'Rotten Borough' but afterwards it lost its MPs and never regained its former importance.
Furthermore in 1974 it lost its historic Borough status when it became a parish with its own Town Council within South Northants District.

Crown Hotel: Brackley

There was great celebration in the town during 2009 when a local firm involved in Formula One motor racing nearly folded but was saved at the last moment by **Ross Brawn** and as the 'Brawn Racing Team' went on to win the constructors and drivers championships. At the end of 2009 the team were taken over by Mercedes Benz.

Also in 2009 a collection of 15th century silver coins were found on nearby farmland by a man with a metal detector. They are thought to have been hidden during the War of the Roses about 1465. Some are on show at the British Museum and some were sold off at auction raising about £30,000 which was shared between the finder and the land owner.

ROTTEN BOROUGHS

A 'Rotten Borough' was one where there was a very small electorate and votes could easily be bought by land owners to affect the election results.
In Brackley there were only thirty three electors all being in the **Duke of Bridgewater's** pocket so the outcome of an election was never in doubt.

This situation continued until the Reform Act of 1832 when almost sixty such 'Rotten Boroughs' including Brackley and Higham Ferrers were disenfranchised.

Prior to that date Brackley sent two members to Parliament.

BRADDEN

Two and a half miles west of Towcester
Population: 1801 – 156   2001 - 179

DOMESDAY BOOK
BRADENE
The origin of this name appears quite clear from the Saxon 'brad- denu' for broad valley.

At the time of the Domesday Book there were two small manors with six households and two acres of meadows.

Although only a short distance from Towcester this is still a rather remote small village standing on a tributary of the River Tove where time seems to stand still.
It is mainly composed of mature houses built of mellow Northants stone, a remarkable number of which are of high status for such a small village.

One of the oldest domestic buildings was once a Dissenters Meeting House used as a secret or low profile meeting place for those who did not adhere to the teaching of the Church of England.
Baptisms took place at Cathanger Farm near Woodend, the home of *Thomas Lovell* one of the chapel deacons.
The impressive **Bradden House** is traditionally the site of a Manor House of the Knights Hospitallers of St John of Jerusalem, Crusaders who held land in the area and devoted their lives to reclaim the Holy Land for Christianity.

It was a popular cause and people gave them money and land to pay for the expeditions.

The Manor was in the possession of the *Ives* family until 1888 when it passed to the *Grant* family who built the present house and rebuilt the parish church of **ST MICHAEL** in about 1858 with the exception of the 13th century tower and the nave arcades.

Externally the church is quite attractive and unusual in that the stonework is built in bands of light and dark stone.

The pulpit is in memory of the *Rev. Cornelius Ives* who died in 1885 and was Rector here for sixty five years – a truly remarkable record.

When *Sir John Matthews* was Lord Mayor of London in 1490 the family had land in Bradden.

There was once a public house by the unusual name of The Sugar Loaf but this like the school and shop have now closed.

The now defunct red telephone box still stands and has found a new lease of life as the village notice board.

The Old Post Office : Bradden

Brafield

On the Green

Five miles east of Northampton
Population: 1801 - 284   2001 - 636

DOMESDAY BOOK
BRACHEFELD/BRAGEFELDE
BRACHESFELD
*Bragen was the Saxon name for Yardley Chase
and 'feld' was Saxon for 'open tract of land'
so the derivation appears obvious.*

Ring ditches, worked flints, pottery, animal bones, jewellery, iron nails and chains all found in the area indicate a settlement here going back to at least the Iron Age.
One of the four entries for Brafield in the Domesday Book records that *Judith* held some of the land but I noted that she also appears to have laid claim to other land held by *Odo* the *Bishop of Bayeux*.

The present village stands astride the main road between Northampton and Bedford resulting in a lot of traffic, fortunately many properties lie on a 'no through road' to the north.
Along this road you will find the Green from whence the village gets its suffix. This was added in Tudor times to distinguish it from the Brayfield in neighbouring Buckinghamshire.

The Green is a pleasant little oasis and incorporates a village pond away from the roar of the traffic.

When I visited recently following a spell of heavy rain the pond was making a great effort to flood the whole area.

There are a few good thatched cottages but unlike so many villages Brafield does not appear to have had a Manor House.

Set back from the road on the edge of the village is the church of **ST LAURENCE**.
It was pointed out to me by a church warden that it is dedicated to St Laurence and not St Lawrence.
The Norman west tower has rows of iron studs, gargoyles and is supported the largest buttresses I have ever seen. They were erected to support the tower which houses the bells.

The remainder of the church apart from the Norman south aisle is in the Early English style having been rebuilt or restored in the mid 19th century and further modernised in 1999.

What immediately struck me on entering was the well furnished chancel with its colourful east wall. On investigation I discovered that it was not tiles that covered the wall but plaster on which had been imprinted a design which had been picked out in maroon.

The population has increased dramatically in recent years with much modern housing and it is quite a busy little place with a shop and post office, petrol station, Red Lion Country Public House and Bistro, Working Men's Club, a Baptist chapel built about 1830 and even an undertaker.
The old school near the church was built by the Vicar in 1842 and is now used as a day nursery, the older children being taught elsewhere.

The village hall was built in Church Lane in 1955 in memory of *Charles Henry Sargeant*, a local landowner who died in 1951.

A popular venue for some is the Banger Racing at the old airfield on the Horton Road which goes by the grand name of the:-
'Northampton International Raceway'.

Large Buttresses at Brafield

BRAMPTON ASH

Three miles east of Market Harborough
Population: 1801-79   2001-59

DOMESDAY BOOK
BRANTONE

The name derives from the Saxon words 'brame' – bramble and 'tun' - farmstead.
The old name of brantone is fairly common and as a result many places with this name have adopted either
a suffix or prefix in this case the word 'ash'.

Countess Judith, niece of **William** the **Conqueror** seems to have held land everywhere at the time of the Domesday Book and Brampton Ash was no exception.

An unusually large number of a hundred and twenty nine people paid the Hearth Tax in 1674 but by 1801 the population had reduced to just seventy nine souls. Today it is even smaller.
Much of the land is now owned by the Brampton Ash Estate and there are remains of stone quarries in the area.

Being such a small village it does not have a shop, post office, chapel or public house.

The location of the church of **ST MARY** which now stands isolated on high ground alongside the main A427 Corby to Market Harborough road close to the Leicestershire border appears to indicate either movement or shrinkage of the village. A site map of 1839 shows the area already devoid of habitation.

The church has a medieval tower and an elegant broach spire which can be seen for miles.
Inside it is very light as there is no stained glass and no pews. It benefitted greatly under the will of a recently deceased organist and as a result has been able to install modern heating and lighting together with kitchen and toilet facilities.

Being the only public building in the village it is now ideally suited for various purposes including concerts, etc. although parking on the main road might be a problem.

In the chancel are a three seat sedilia, a piscina and a significant wall-mounted memorial to the **Norwich** family who once owned the Manor.

Norwich Family Memorial: Brampton Ash

A brass to an ancestor **Sir John Holt** (d.1418) was stolen in 1984 but a replica has been made and can be seen in the church.

This village is so quiet that nothing unusual ever appears to happen but it made national headlines in April 2006 when the bodies of **Fiona Marshall** and **Richard Flippance** were found after a severe fire at her home.

They died of stab wounds and her husband, **Alex Marshall** of Rushden, was arrested, tried for murder and received two life sentences.

BRAUNSTON

Four miles north west of Daventry
Population: 1801 – 909   2001 - 1675

DOMESDAY BOOK
BRANDESTONE

*The name derives from **Brant** or **Brand**
an Anglo Saxon Lord and 'ton' meaning village.*

Of the two manors mentioned in the Domesday Book, one was held by ***Walter d'Aincourt*** - the only reference I can find to him as far as Northamptonshire is concerned.
In his manor were seventeen households and a mill rendering two shillings per annum.

In spite of its present size this is still a picturesque village with brick and stone houses either side of a long wide high street which stands on a high ridge just off the A45 close to the Warwickshire border.

I love the view from the far end of the High Street with the majestic church spire rising to a height of one hundred and fifty feet above a variety of houses.
The elaborately decorated church of
ALL SAINTS can be seen for miles around and appears large and prosperous with a heavily crocketed spire and plenty of pinnacles.

With the arrival of the canal in the early 19th century the earlier church became too small for the growth in population so it was rebuilt in 1849 as:
'The Boaters Cathedral'
in 15th century style, the architect being
R. C. Hussey of Birmingham.

Among the new works are a font and pulpit fashioned from pink marble and alabaster although the clocks, bells, Norman font and chancel arches from the previous church have been retained.

Inside is a stone effigy of a 14th century Knight thought to be ***William de Ros*** who died in 1352 on a pilgrimage to the Holy Land.

The Windmill. Braunston

The Baptist chapel built in 1796 was demolished some years ago and whilst the Wesleyan chapel still stands it is in a sorry state.
Obviously it has not been used for years and nature is rapidly trying to obliterate it.

Near to the church is a picturesque 18th century tower mill. It is eighty feet high, built of red brick and has a red dome.

Originally it had sails and one of these caused a tragic accident in the 1880's.
Work was being undertaken on the sails when the wind suddenly turned them and threw a workman to his death in the churchyard below.
The mill was in use until the mid 20th century and has now been restored (but without sails) and converted to a luxury self catering apartment for up to six people.

One building which caught my eye is Southfields House, an old farmhouse with stables and a courtyard.

.... BRAUNSTON

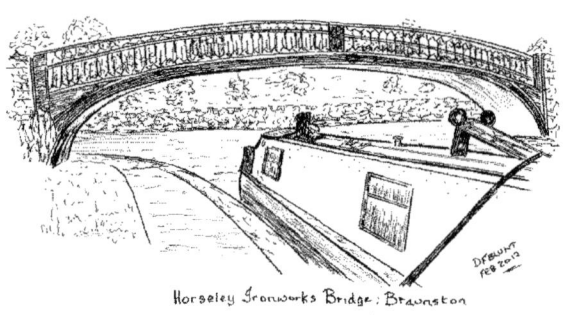

Horseley Ironworks Bridge, Braunston

Braunston Manor is a beautiful stone built Tudor residence set in ten acres and until recently offered four star accommodation, conference facilities, wedding receptions, etc. but at the time of writing is up for sale.

Located within the parish is the Grade II listed **Bragborough Hall** which is currently for sale with gardens, outbuildings, six Estate cottages and 346 acres of land.
The Hall dates back to the early 19th century although the architect is not known.
During the Second World War it served as an evacuation maternity Hospital for St Barts in London when it suffered bomb damage.

In the 19th century Braunston was a very busy place standing at the junction of the Coventry to Oxford Canal and the Grand Union Canal which emerges from a 2040 yard tunnel at this point.

There were once wharfs, moorings, workshops, working barges and numerous public houses but these have been replaced with quite a large marina packed with pleasure boats.
It is becoming a pleasant tourist attraction.

Each year since 2002 Braunston has held a Narrow Boat Rally and Canal Festival and over eighty historic boats add to the large number usually berthed in and around the marina.

Guest of honour in 2012 was **Gayle Hunnicut** whose association with Braunston goes back to 1970 when she starred in the thriller ' *Running Scared'* which was mainly filmed in the area.

I am fascinated by canals and always enjoy a visit to Braunston to see canal boats, bridges, tunnels, canal buildings and locks, etc.

I particularly like the white painted hump back canal bridge with fine sweeping approaches and balustrades of cast iron by Horsley Iron works which dominates the entrance to the marina.

The bridge was salvaged from the Buckingham Branch of the canal in 1962.

In the summer months there is often a canal barge moored here dispensing teas and refreshments, it is quite an unusual experience for this part of the country.
The barge goes by the rather unusual name of *'Gongooziller'* which I am informed is the term used by boat people to describe landlubbers who gaze at boats from the safety of bridges or the canal footpath.

The Boathouse alongside the canal was formerly The Mill House and has recently been redecorated and re-opened for business.
It is a delightful spot for a quiet drink or a delicious pub meal whilst *'gongoozilling'*.

For a great walk undertake the route of the Grand Union Canal from Braunston to Brentford.
I really enjoyed the days spent doing this walk which is quite easy and can be done in manageable stages by using the trains which run close to much of the canal to get back to the car.

Not only was Braunston served by two canal companies but for over sixty years had the benefit of two railway stations.

In 1890 the London and North Western Railway Company was granted permission to build a fourteen mile extension from Daventry to Leamington Spa. The station was situated just off the Daventry road near Canal Bridge 91 and was called Braunston (London Road) to distinguish it from the station on the Great Central Line which also served Braunston but was in fact sited just over the County border in Warwickshire.
Unlike the canals the railways and their stations have disappeared.

Before the arrival of the railway up to sixty mail and stage coaches rattled through the village each day and the village could boast twelve inns but life in Braunston has, like so many similar places, changed dramatically over the years.

Many businesses, shops and public houses have closed although a few still remain.

At the front of a building that was once a bakery and is now a private residence there is still displayed a large **HOVIS** advertising sign.
I like to see these old symbols of the past still on display.

The village still has a Primary school which was built in 1968 on the Barby Road.
The previous school now acts as the village hall.

Close to Braunston are the sites of two lost Northamptonshire settlements Braunston Cleves (or Fawcliff) and Braunstonbury.
At the time of the Domesday Book they were taxed with Braunston.

BRAUNSTON CLEVES (OR FAWCLIFF)

This lost settlement once stood north of Braunston on the south west slopes of Cleves Hill.
It is thought that it was part of the 11th century manor which belonged to **William Trusbott** and eventually came into the hands of Delapre Abbey.

The settlement is thought to have disappeared in the 18th century and there is now little evidence of its existence although the site is clearly marked on the Landranger Ordnance Survey Map.

BRAUNSTONBURY

The settlement stood to the south west of Braunston alongside the River Leam.
In the 11th century it was part of the manor of **William Trusbott** (see Braunston Cleves) but in this case the manor then went to the Abbey of Lilleshall in Shropshire.

At the Dissolution the lands went to the **Earl of Rutland** who had another manor nearby.

Today there is little evidence of the settlement except for ditches, banks, old brickwork and the odd farm building.

DFBLUNT
AUG 2012

BRAYBROOKE

Three miles south east of Market Harborough
Population - 1801 – 378   2001 - 338

DOMESDAY BOOK
BADEBROC/BAIEBROC/BRADEBROC

This name is confusing as it appears to be a corruption of the Saxon words 'brad' - broad and 'broc' - brook.
The river here, the Jordan, not the one mentioned in the Bible - is particularly small and narrow
perhaps the stream was prone to flooding?

At the time of the Domesday Book the land was held in part by the **Countess Judith** and the Abbeys of St Edmundsbury and St Mary of Grestain. The total recorded number of households at the time was twenty one.
In 1377, one hundred and sixty three people over the age of fourteen paid the Poll Tax and in 1674, eighty four people paid the Hearth Tax.

As in many villages the houses are a mix of old and new, some stone, some brick or whitewashed, the oldest dates from the 16th century.

The brown ironstone Bowden Bridge with its two massive cutwaters and low parapets over the River Jordan dates from 1402.
It is thought that the stream got its name because in the 19th century the local Baptists did not have their own baptistry and used its water for baptisms.
The Baptist chapel just around the corner is still used for services on alternate Sundays.

The main railway line from London to Nottingham and beyond passes through the parish but there has never been a station here.

The church of **ALL SAINTS** stands in a prominent position and is an attractive building with a 15th century tower and a graceful spire.

On gaining entry I was very surprised to see the chancel arch blocked up by unattractive panels and to find the south chapel looking so neglected because here is the splendid and rare oak effigy of **Sir Thomas Latymer** complete with shield and a dog at his feet.

Nearby is what must also have been a splendid monument to **Alfred Griffin** but this also is in a very sorry state.

In 1977 **Peter Gorham Webb** published his *'Portrait of Northamptonshire'* and mentioned the *'deplorable state of the south chapel.'*
Over thirty years later a restoration is still awaited.

River Jordan : Braybrooke

The church owns one of only two vamping horns in the County - the other being at Harrington although the six foot long 'Braybrooke Horn' is now on loan to Market Harborough museum.

There is evidence that in 1213 **Henry de Braybrooke** was given timber from the forest in Leicester to build a *'fair chamber'* near the village.
The manor then passed by marriage to the **Latymer** family and in 1303/4
Sir Thomas was granted licence to strengthen his Manor House and to embattle it.
Documents suggest that the moated house was constructed at this time.

The property and manor passed to the **Griffin** family in the early 15th century but after they moved to their new home at Dingley in the mid 16th century the buildings crumbled and were eventually destroyed.
The only remaining evidence of what is still known as Braybrooke Castle is a series of mounds marking fish ponds and a brew house.
A farmhouse stood on the site until 1960.

In the 18th century the main village occupation was weaving and the rush industry was important but suffered decline with the growth of northern mills. One small field where willows were grown for this purpose is still called 'Osier Beds.'

In 2009 the village hall was refurbished and re-opened at a cost of £90,000.

St Thomas de Latymer : Braybrooke.

The present school was opened in February 1972 for children aged 5-11 from both Braybrooke and Arthingworth but in August 2012 the local press reported that the school was in danger of closure owing to falling numbers.

The local public house is The Swan Inn originally called The Black Swan which was built in the 17th century and was extended in the 18th century.
In the 1950's **Graham Moffat** the fat boy of **Will Hay's** films was landlord.
The village sees quite a lot of walkers as three long distance paths, the Macmillan Way, Jurassic Way and Midshires Way all converge here.

VAMPING HORNS

Vamping horns are said to have been invented in 1670 by **Sir Samuel Moreland.**

He demonstrated the instrument to **King Charles II** who is said to have heard him quite clearly at a distance of 850 yards.

So impressed was the King that he not only ordered some for his ships but also three very large ones for his Castle at Deal.

Although originally intending to broadcast speech over quite a long distance they were also adopted for the use of church choirs in the same way as a microphone today.
People hummed to encourage the congregation to sing in tune.

The introduction of organs into churches at the end of the 19th century led to their demise.

It is said that there are only about six or eight remaining in the country.
This being the case Northamptonshire is very fortunate in having two - at Harrington and Braybrooke.

BRIGSTOCK

Seven miles north east of Kettering
Population: 1801 – 903   2001 -1329

DOMESDAY BOOK
BRICSTOC

*It is thought that the name derives from 'bierce' - Saxon for birch tree and 'stocc' - Saxon for stump or log
likely to refer to an enclosure surrounded by birch logs i.e. a clearing in the forest.
Others think that the name could denote a stockaded bridge,
for an ancient bridge existed in Anglo Saxon times over the stream now known as Harpers Brook.*

The village with its delightful stone cottages and a 16th century Manor House is a much more peaceful place since the opening of the bypass on the A6116 Thrapston to Corby road.

Brigstock began as a Saxon settlement and became one of the largest villages in Rockingham Forest.
The Domesday Book records Brigstock as a three and a half hide royal manor with twenty six households, a priest (no mention of a church) and a mill rendering five shillings per annum.

At one time the forest was so dense that the church bell was rung three times a day to guide the traveller.
Deforestation began about the time of **Charles I** who needed vast amounts of timber for his navy.

There is still a mill which was in use until 1910. Remains of the water wheel can still be seen although the mill is now a private dwelling.

The Charter for a weekly market was granted by **Edward IV** in 1466 but it appears that the market had gone by 1623.

The ancient Market Cross on the square is a County Heritage Site and was erected as a symbol to the reigning monarch, **Elizabeth I**.

Various dates are inscribed – 1586, 1705, 1778, 1887 and 1953 the latter being the date of the Coronation of **Queen Elizabeth II**.
The other dates may represent memorials to other Queens. Did the villagers decide to save money on new monuments? The Cross is still used as the focal point for the annual May Queen ceremony.
This is, in my opinion the most attractive part of the village in spite of the fact that the open space is largely taken up with parked cars,

In the 17th and 18th centuries the area had a bad reputation because of the high number of licensed premises and a larger number of people who couldn't hold their drink. Nowadays two licensed premises The Green Dragon and The Old Three Cocks (an old coaching inn) remain.
Fotheringhay House in the High Street is said to have been built partly from materials taken from **Fotheringhay Castle** where **Mary, Queen of Scots** was beheaded in 1587.

Between the two World Wars and into the 1950's the village had a very good silver band.

I like the story of the little drummer who not being able to see over his drum, one day marched alone towards Thrapston when the rest of the band turned right over the bridge to Grafton.

Market Cross : Brigstock.

Brigstock was early in the field of education as its first school was endowed in 1620 by *Nicholas Latham* (Parson at Barnwell) who was the son of the Keeper of Brigstock Great Park. The actual building which stood on the site of the present War Memorial in Hall Lane no longer exists but the modern school carries his name.

Whilst enjoying a very pleasant walk close to the village I came across a comfortable seat which provided a welcome spot for a picnic.
Alongside me was an unusual stone with a plaque identifying it as the Bocase Stone.
It is about three feet tall and is thought to mark the location of a large oak tree which was blown down about the time of *Charles I*.
Here local men are said to have met to improve their skill in archery and to hold court.

The church of **ST ANDREW** is one of the oldest in the County and has a mixture of styles, Norman, Saxon and Tudor. Its chief object of interest is the low Saxon tower and semi circular attachment to the west side almost like an East Anglian round tower, similar to that at Brixworth.
The tower top and spire with low broaches is in the Decorative style. The tall Saxon arch in the tower is thought to be one of the finest in Europe.

At the west end of the north chapel is a medieval screen said to have come from the former Cistercian Abbey of Pipewell.

Buried in the church are members of the *Lyveden* family including *Robert Smith (Vernon),*
1st Baron Lyveden (1800-1873) MP, Under Secretary of State for War at the time of the Crimean War.

A notice inside the church acquaints visitors with the fact that bats love the church and have made it their home and that is obvious from their droppings.

In School Lane is the Congregational chapel of 1798 with simple arched windows but some 19th century alterations. Other chapels are now closed and have been put to other uses.

The Bocase Stone, Nr Brigstock.

An unusual building is the imposing four storey factory built in stone in 1873 as a clothing factory and known locally as 'The **Matchbox'.**
A bell under the pedimented gable summoned the workers. It was part of the Wallis and Linnell Company until 1979 when it was converted into offices.

Brigstock International Horse Trials which have attracted top class riders and thousands of visitors to the area in recent years was cancelled for 2012 owing to the sale of the host property Fermyn Woods Hall. In 2013 the event will be moved to Rockingham Castle.

GATEWAY TO ROCKINGHAM FOREST

Just outside the village off the A6116 is one of the largest Country Parks in the County with picnic areas, walks, nature trails and a children's playground. It was opened in 1986 on the site of former sand pits.

It is adjacent to Fermyn Woods with its impressive Hall which dates back to the 14th century.

The Hall which is currently up for sale for £5.8 million was originally built for the Head Archer of the Brigstock parish of the forest but later was used by *Sir Christopher Hatton* (see Kirby) as a shooting lodge after which it passed to the *Lyveden* family.
The deer attracted both outlaws and members of royalty particularly *King John* who stayed at the Manor House several times and held court there on 27th February 1207.

In World War II the Hall housed London evacuees for whom it must have been the most dramatic change from their life in the big city.

BRIXWORTH

Six miles north of Northampton
Population: 1801 – 718   2001 - 5162

DOMESDAY BOOK
BRICLESWORDE

*The origin of this name is **Bricels** - a local Saxon leader - and 'worth' being a clearing or enclosure.*

Its high location overlooking a vast swathe of delightful English countryside indicates a place of some importance in the past and this is endorsed by the finding of a substantial amount of Roman material and the site of a Roman settlement.
When these buildings were destroyed much of the material was recycled, particularly in the church - who said that recycling was a new phenomenon?

Brixworth is probably better known than most Northamptonshire villages because of its historic Saxon church which dates back to 680AD.
It was built by the monks of Peterborough and is the best and largest of the fine group of seven 7th century churches still standing.

ALL SAINTS is also unusual in that it is one of only four churches in the area to have a stair turret attached to the outside of the tower.

In my opinion it is certainly one of the most inspiring churches in Northamptonshire and worthy of a very long and leisurely visit and of its Grade I listing.

Simon Jenkins in his excellent book - *'England's 1000 Best Churches'* gives **ALL SAINTS** three stars.

The church houses a reliquary thought to be the larynx bone of *St Boniface* but nowadays it is only on public view on very special occasions.

As one travels around the area the spire can be seen over quite long distances.
In 1980 villagers celebrated the 1300th anniversary of the ancient church – the oldest historic building in Northamptonshire.

The village briefly became a market town following the grant of a Market Charter by *Henry III* in 1268.
Remains of a 14th century ancient butter cross where trade was conducted and the village stocks are to be found on the Green below the church.

By the time of the Domesday Book the rather large nine and a half hide manor was held by the King and had twenty nine households and a priest (churches were not usually recorded).

The two mills rendered thirty three shillings and four pence per annum and there were eight acres of meadow. In addition there was woodland rendering one hundred shillings per annum being part of the Kings Forest.

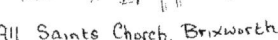

All Saints Church. Brixworth

As you climb the hill from Northampton there is on your left, a twenty one foot high stone cross erected in 1908 to the memory of *Viscount Charles Cavendish* who fell off his horse and broke his neck whilst following the local Pytchley Hunt. His memorial says that he was:-

'a good man, a gallant soldier and a true sportsman'

In my teens I did a lot of cycling in the area and this cross was a welcome stopping place for a breather whilst struggling up the incline.

When the railway came to Brixworth in 1851 it changed the lives of the population.
Soon after iron ore was found and brick built cottages sprung up to house the workers.
There are still some quarries in operation in the area but whereas the stone was once transported by rail it is now moved in large lorries.

Brixworth is the home of the famous Pytchley Hunt with grand neo-Georgian kennels built in 1966 near the site of the former railway station.
At the entrance are two houses each bearing a stone marked 'PH 1966.'

Two large industrial estates have sprung up in recent years to the north of the village and many modern houses have been built resulting in a large increase in population.
Current plans to erect many more houses in the village are causing considerable unrest to the present residents.

Today Brixworth is a mix of the very old and the very new. To meet local demand there are a number of shops, public houses, restaurants, a Primary school, library and a community centre with a coffee shop.

One business you would not expect to find is 'The Vineyard' which was planted in 2002 and produced its first wine in 2005.
Some of the first 4,500 bottles were shipped to France. Visits can be made by appointment.

Brixworth Workhouse which covered thirty three parishes opened in 1837 at a cost of £5,800 to accommodate two hundred and sixty five inmates and was quite a notorious and unhappy place.
On 2 June, 1890 a letter was written to the Northamptonshire Mercury expressing disgust at the behaviour of the Poor Law bullies at Brixworth. The Workhouse which still stands, functioned for over a hundred years but today is used as business premises.

One of the old buildings in the village carries the inscription:-

'This school house was built with the school money in the year 1811 by the Trustees who were Walter Strickland, Edward Wayte, William Wood and John Ekins.'

Brixworth Hall was built in Tudor times but was demolished in 1954 and the grounds are now the location for a small modern housing estate.

Just outside Brixworth off the bypass is Pitsford Water (see Pitsford page 335).

BRIXWORTH COUNTRY PARK

The Park opened in 1990 and at the Brixworth entrance is a visitor centre, car park, the Willow Tree cafe, toilets and a children's play area.

It is the starting point for a number of walks and cycle tracks including the seven and a half mile circuit of the western end of the reservoir.

This is also the base for Northamptonshire Sailing Club particularly in the summer and you can often see yachts skimming across the water.

BROCKHALL

Four miles east of Daventry
Population: 1801 – 70   2001-31

DOMESDAY BOOK
BROCOLE
The old name clearly indicates a derivation from Saxon words 'broc'- badger and 'hol' – hole.

I have seen Brockhall listed as a deserted village but from what I have been able to discover it does not appear ever to have ever been much larger than it is today. There is no school, shop or post office although embedded in a row of attractive cottages near the church is a Victorian post box.

In 1086 when the land was owned by the **Count of Mortain** it was recorded that together with nearby Muscott there were just six households with Muscott almost certainly being the larger of the two. It is thought that the land was enclosed in 1605 although **Bridges** in 1720 wrote of twelve houses here.
Brockhall is now virtually deserted and comprises a church, a small group of cottages and a Hall in the centre of parkland and is situated down a lane marked 'Brockhall only' midway between Daventry and Northampton.
You pass through some lovely woodland on the way, unfortunately, however, the M1 goes straight through parkland below the Hall and the noise of the traffic disturbs an otherwise peaceful setting.

The attractive Georgian Rectory on the edge of the village has recently been advertised at a guide price of £1,600,000.

The small church of **ST PETER** and **ST PAUL** was started in the 12th century although the west tower and west bay were added later.
On display is a royal Coat of Arms which dates from the reign of **George III.**

The church was largely rebuilt in 1874 and consists of a chancel, nave, and south aisle with a decorated tomb recess, west tower, vestry and south porch. Inside are many memorials and a number of hatchments of the **Thornton** family.
An attractive modern feature is the altar frontal produced by **Mrs G Myles** in 1982 at the time of the Falklands crisis to represent peace.

Brockhall Hall
and the Thornton family

Alongside the church is the Jacobean Grade II listed Brockhall Hall sitting in thirteen acres of grounds.
*It was built in the early 17th century together with the Manor House by the **Eyton** family but was sold to **Thomas Thornton** of Newnham in 1625.*
*He supported **Oliver Cromwell** but was later pardoned by **King Charles II.***
*The **Thornton** family remained in residence until 1978 when the male line became extinct after the death of **Colonel T. A. Thornton.***
One member of the family was both Squire and Rector for sixty three years and there is a window in the church in his memory.

During the Second World War the Hall and its grounds were used by the American Office of Strategic Studies, an early predecessor of the CIA. Personnel were trained to be parachuted behind enemy lines. In the church is a plaque to the memory of the many servicemen of OSS and airmen of Harrington (who provided the aircraft) who gave their lives during these operations.
The Hall which is said to be haunted by a white lady has now been converted to luxury apartments.

Thornton

Brockhall Hall

BROUGHTON

Two miles south west of Kettering
Population: 1801 – 374   2001 - 2047

DOMESDAY BOOK
BURTONE
*The name derives from
the Saxon 'broc' - brook and 'tun' – farm.*

For years the village stood on the main A43 road between Kettering and Northampton. Fortunately it no longer has to contend with heavy lorries following the opening of the bypass in 1984.
In recent years there has been a lot of uninspiring modern development but near the church there are still a number of attractive stone built cottages.

Two manors of Broughton are mentioned in the Domesday Book. One being part of the royal Manor of Rothwell and the other held by the *Countess Judith.*
Even at that time it appears that there were a comparatively large number of households.

Although no church is mentioned one must have existed round about this time as evidenced by Norman features including the arch over the south door of the present church of **ST ANDREW**.
This is built of brownish yellow ironstone although the broach spire is grey and dates mainly from the early 14th century.

Worthy of note is the lovely 14th century font with an elaborately carved octagonal bowl and pedestal with traceried panels and angle shafts described by *Arthur Mee* as - *'the chief treasure of the church'.* The chancel was rebuilt in 1828 and the church restored in 1854.
A recent improvement is the installation of toilet and kitchen facilities in 2002.

Inside is a marble bust to *Harold Kynnesman* who was the Treasurer to *Queen Elizabeth's* army during an ill fated Irish rebellion, he was subsequently executed.

Yeomans House : Broughton

Externally a prominent feature of the tower is the 17th century church clock which is thought to be one of the oldest in England but to me the large russet faced clock seemed to dominate the overall appearance of the tower and spire.

Nearby stands one of the oldest and most attractive buildings in the village, an impressive gabled Jacobean house thought to date from about 1580.

Another building of note is the tall thatched Yeoman's House built about 1620 although it is now half its original size due to road widening.

Like most villages of a similar size Broughton once had a number of public houses, but only two now remain - The Red Lion and The Sun, both situated on the main road.
A further public house - The Buccleuch Arms - in honour of the *Buccleuch* family who still own much land in the area is now in private use.

The village still has a Primary school, village hall, working men's club, Baptist chapel, shops and a post office.

BUGBROOKE

Five miles south west of Northampton
Population: 1801 – 611   2001 - 2773

DOMESDAY BOOK
BUCHEBROC/BUCHEBROCH
*The name of Bugbrooke possibly comes from the Saxon
words 'buce' - buck and 'broc' - stream
a spot where stags gathered.*

Village Sign -- Bugbrooke

This large village has a mixture of quite attractive 17th and 18th century houses and a somewhat more motley assortment of uninspiring modern properties. It stands astride the B4525 Banbury to Northampton road resulting in a lot of through traffic.

The Grand Union Canal passes the western end of the village and the public house -The Wharf - with its canal side garden is a favourite haunt for canal people, walkers, motorists and villagers alike. Other public houses are The Bakers Arms and The Five Bells.

Owing to its size the village also has shops, a garage, village hall, medical centre and pharmacy and both Primary and Secondary schools although according to stories I have heard the Campion school (Secondary) was built back to front.
I was informed that this was the first purpose built Comprehensive school in the County but it is certainly not very attractive or inspiring.

The plain ironstone Baptist chapel was founded in 1808 and since 1969 has been the home of an independent religious group 'the Jesus Army' who also own Bugbrooke (New Creation) Hall on the road to Litchborough.

Quakers Cottage just off the High Street was once the Quaker Meeting House and the centre of Non-conformity in the village.
At one time it had the third largest congregation of Quakers in the County.

Set in a pleasant location surrounded by trees on the road to Litchborough is the church of **ST MICHAEL** and **ALL ANGELS** which prior to the 19th century was dedicated to *St Mary.*

The present church grew from an earlier small chapel and has a fine early 13th century south arcade set on Norman columns.
Its 14th century west tower built of marlstone and ironstone strips has a recessed spire and houses five bells and a sanctus.
Pinnacles were added about 1890.

The fine 15th century wooden rood screen with its canopy is one of the few remaining in the County.
It must have looked spectacular when it was brightly painting with much gilding.

Of the lovely stained glass, one window I particularly liked can be seen in the south aisle.
It was donated by *Frank Hawthorn* of **Pattishall Hall** (now **Cornhill Manor**) in memory of his daughter *Bluebelle* who died in 1912 at the age of twelve. The figures include an image of his daughter on the right hand side.

The chancel was rebuilt in 1890 and the top half of the spire was rebuilt in 1940 after it had been struck by lightning. A modern north porch with toilets was added in 1998.

A clearer view of the church can be obtained from the open space at the rear with the Hoarestone Brook flowing through it.

The name of the stream is thought to be a corruption of horse-stone as an old packhorse route crossed the brook by a single slab bridge just outside the village.

This delightful little oasis which was planted with native trees in 1999 was opened in May 2000 to celebrate the millennium by *Sir Michael Harrison* when a time capsule was buried in the area by children from the local Primary school.

Over the years Bugbrooke has seen much activity and was one of the first places in England to house a soap factory which was located in outbuildings attached to the pet store.

The factory was set up by the first Baptist minister, *John Wheeler,* a candle maker, who dipped candles in hot wax and converts in the brook thus gaining the local name of *'John the Dipper'.*

BUGBROOKE MILL

A mill on the site goes back to at least 800AD and was mentioned in the Domesday Book when it was the third highest rated mill in England.

By 1086 when *William the Conqueror* undertook his great survey, one hundred and fifty five manors in Northamptonshire had a watermill and three manors, Finedon, Harrington and Evenley each had four. Obviously water power was well used.

Windmills first appeared in England from about 1180 but the use of water to harness power was at its peak just before the Industrial Revolution.
It is estimated that at one time there were 10,000 watermills country wide.

Bugbrooke Mill on the River Nene is now one of only two mills still in use in Northamptonshire (the other being at Wellingborough).

The *Heygate* family have farmed the area since 1562 and first became involved in flour milling in the late 19th century.
The business in its present form was established by *Arthur Robert Heygate* and family members are still actively involved. Over 200,000 tons of wheat is milled each year mainly for bread production.

The mill is a major employer in the area and it is not unusual to see one of the firms many lorries on the road when travelling around the area.

Old School Buildings: Bugbrooke.

BULWICK

Six miles north east of Corby
Population: 1801-389   2001 - 152

There is no mention of Bulwick in the Domesday Book, presumably it was included elsewhere or settled later. Did the original settlement produce beef? It may have done as the original name was 'bula-wic' - bull farm.

The village whose name is usually pronounced 'Bullick' is pleasantly situated just off the busy A43 road between Stamford and Kettering.

There is now a much more peaceful atmosphere since the days when traffic wound its way down the village street prior to the building of the bypass in 1986. Before it was opened villagers organised a fun run along the bypass and the opening was celebrated with the ringing of church bells and a good old booze up at the pub!
Leave the bypass and venture into the village and you will not be disappointed.

Most of the houses are built of stone and part of the village is now in a Conservation area with a number of buildings of special architectural or historic interest.

Although not mentioned in the Domesday Book it is known that in the reign of **Henry II** (1154-1189) *'there were two hides of land in Bolewyck and one in Henewyck in the hands of **Vitalis Lovet.'***

At that time the part of the village on the west side of the Willow Brook, was known as Henwick but it seems that this part all but disappeared as a result of the Black Death and land enclosures in medieval times.

In the 12th century the manor was held by **Reginald Fitzurse**, one of the four Knights who murdered **Thomas á Becket** in Canterbury Cathedral. The Knights fled to Scotland but were later excommunicated by the Pope and ordered to make a penitential pilgrimage to the Holy Land from which it is said none returned.

By 1293 Bulwick had a weekly market courtesy of a Charter granted by **Edward I.**

Queens Head Inn : Bulwick

On a bank amongst cypress trees in the centre of the village is the church of **ST NICHOLAS** which dates from the 12th century.
It has an embattled west tower surmounted by a well proportioned recessed spire rising to a height of one hundred and fifteen feet (34 metres).
The East window dates from the late 13th or early 14th century but was filled with stained glass in 1877 in memory of *Anne*, daughter of *Sir John Trollope* and wife of *Thomas Tryon*.

Carbery House, an 18th century building was once The Carbery Arms - named after the **Laxton** family.

The present public house - The Queens Head, named after **Catherine of Braganza,** wife of **Charles II** is believed to have once been three cottages and has the date stones 1675 and 1683.

Close by is the village hall and the local store **'The Pickled Village'** specialising in pickles of all sorts. The public house and shop are let by the Bulwick Estates which have been in the hands of the **Tryon** and **Conant** families since 1619.

Very young children are well catered for at Simba's Den Day Nursery opposite the church but the Primary school which was built in 1831 for eighty children closed in 1990 – an indication of just how much the village population has declined.

This is a very popular area for walking and cycling and consequently sees many visitors particularly during the summer months.

Tryon

Thatched House: Bulwick

Bulwick Hall and the Tryon family

Peter Tryon was a Flemish weaver who having fled Holland due to religious persecution by the **Duke of Alba**, arrived in England in about 1560 with £60,000.

His son **Moses** bought the manors of Harringworth and Bulwick in 1619 and their family rebuilt the mansion in Bulwick in 1676 when a seven bay flat roofed loggia with a balustrade was added.
The lovely gardens were also laid out at this time.

One of the most eminent members of the family was **William** who became Governor of the State of North Carolina in 1765.
On the death of **Guy Thomas Tryon** (who has a memorial in Northampton Roman Catholic Cathedral) in South Africa in 1901 the Estate was inherited by his sister **Mrs Conant** whose descendants still live in Bulwick.

Many members of the family served in the armed forces and a number died in battle as witnessed by the number of memorials in the church.
These include a bronze plaque to the memory of **Vice Admiral Sir George Tryon** who died with three hundred of his men when his ship the HMS Victoria collided with HMS Camperdown in the Mediterranean in 1893.

His son, **George** (born 1871) was elected MP in 1910 and was elevated to the peerage as the **First Baron Tryon** in April 1940 but died just six months later.
No fewer than five family members gave their lives in the First World War.

I like the story about the Lord of the Manor who in 1890 witnessed a boisterous crowd leaving the village public house opposite the church on the Sabbath day. He was so outraged that he promptly had the hostelry closed, a situation that lasted for sixty six years until 1956.
I wonder what the reaction would be to such a situation today?

BURTON LATIMER

Four miles south east of Kettering
Population: 1801 – 669   2001 – 6,740

DOMESDAY BOOK
BURTON/ BURTONE

*Burton derives its name from the Saxon 'burrh' -
a fortified place and 'tun' - farmstead.
The addition took place in the late 13th century when the
manor was held by **William le Latymer** although at that
time there was another manor called Burton Plessy.*

1970's Weetabix Advert

When preparing land for the newly built wind farm evidence was found of earlier settlements including artefacts from the late Iron and Early Roman era. Other finds have been discovered in excavations elsewhere.

At the time of the Domesday Book two manors here were recorded as having two slaves, thirty nine villagers and twenty one smallholders.
In Navisland Hundred there were two mills rendering sixteen shillings per annum and in Warden Hundred there were two mills rendering twenty six shillings per annum.

One manor was held by *Guy de Raimbeaucourt* and the other by the *Bishop of Coutances*.
The two manors were united in the 18th century when both halves were purchased by
John Harpur but the title 'Lord of the Manor' was not unified until the 19th century.
Since 1974 the two manors have been perpetuated in the names of the two Burton Wards on Kettering Borough Council.

To the west of the church is an attractive two storey thatched Manor House which is thought to stand on the site of an earlier Manor House of the *Plessys*.

Underground passages leading towards the church were discovered during alterations in the early 20th century.

The term Burton Latimer alias Plessy, is found in church and legal records right up to the 19th century.

Latimer Hall in Kettering Road, home of the *Harpur* family since 1662 stands on the site of the former Latimer Manor House.
It was built in the early 17th century and although it has been altered over the years still retains some Jacobean features.

During the war it was used by the Nuns of the Good Shepherd from London who cared for orphaned children.
Later it was used as a Land Army Hostel.
Both Manor Houses are now private residences.

Although agriculture was the main source of labour in the area, by the early 19th century carpet weaving became a major employer.
One local factory is said to have had four hundred employees out of a population of about a thousand.

The town expanded rapidly with the coming of the railway in 1857 and the large scale production and distribution of boot and shoe footwear.

Prior to the arrival of the railway Burton was on a stage coach route.
Public houses such as The Waggon and Horses, The Dukes Arms and The Red Cow were stopping places.
They did not change horses at these establishments although they had stabling for visitors or for those going further afield on the Mail Coach - a sort of modern day car park.

There is a record that in October 1812 following a stop at The Red Cow the Leeds to London stage *'The Royal Mail'* was robbed of sixteen letter bags somewhere between Burton Latimer and Higham Ferrers with no-one being any the wiser.

Subsequent findings of the empty mail bags led to the arrest and eventual execution of the culprits, **Kendall** and **White** on Northampton Racecourse in August 1813 before a large crowd.

The Waggon (note the spelling!) and Horses is still in use but the Red Cow in High Street closed for business in 1956.

It was used for about forty years as commercial premises but was eventually demolished in January 2009 for redevelopment.

The fairly recent bypass on the busy A6 road has relieved some of the traffic through the centre of Burton Latimer although it is quite a busy place with shops, a school, health centre, library, doctors, public houses, etc. but no railway station although the main line still passes close to the town.

The Station House is now a private residence.

There are a number of attractive older properties most of which are to be seen in Church Street but in the main the village is predominantly red brick housing and modern residential estates.

Burton Latimer was one of the first villages in the UK to have a Grammar school. This was endowed with £47 per annum arising from ten acres of land and a house which were bequeathed in 1589 by *Elizabeth Margaret Burbank*.

The school was built in 1622 to teach boys Greek and Latin. It can be seen in Church Street and is my favourite building in the town.

It is an oblong one storeyed building with mullioned windows on each side of a doorway above which is a big ogee-sided gable containing the arms of the donors.

Today it is a private residence.

At one time it was the town's Infant school but closed in 1960 when new premises were provided.

When at the junction of Churchill Way and High Street look down to admire the millennium mosaic by *Paul Smith*.

Major employers in the town are Alumasc who make brewing and car products and Weetabix the manufacturer of cereal products who took over the site of one of the old mills in the 1930's and whose premises you cannot miss when travelling by train.

The church of **ST MARY** the **VIRGIN** is a large very fine stone building of the 12th century when it was thought to be cruciform in style.

Of particular interest are the murals on the north wall, depicting *St Catherine,* which are considered to be the best in the country and also the paintings of the Patriarchs over the arcade arches which date from about 1600.

The west tower and spire were rebuilt in 1866 with battlements when the rest of the church was restored. The restored chancel screen is over five hundred years old and the north door has two large double doors studded with nails and dated 1510.

Other denominations are well catered for.

The Methodist chapel built in Duke Street in 1890 had new school rooms added in 1930.

The ironstone Baptist church was established in 1744 by *John Yeoman* a landowner and carpenter. He became the first Pastor and carried out baptisms in the river. The chapel was once called the Baptist meeting house giving rise to Meeting Lane.

A new hall dedicated to the founder was built in 1993. When the Council wanted land from the chapel to build a sheltered housing scheme the chapel acquired a new manse.

The housing scheme is named Yeoman's Court.

Of more recent date is the *St Nicholas Owen* Roman Catholic church which opened on the 2nd March 1972. It was the first Roman Catholic church in the town for over four hundred years.

St Nicholas Owen was a Jesuit lay brother and martyr. As a carpenter he used his skills to construct secret hideouts for Roman Catholic priests fleeing persecution including one in **Harrowden Hall** near Wellingborough.

For his faith he was thrown into the Tower of London where he died in agony in 1606.

He was canonised in 1970.

BYFIELD

Seven miles south west of Daventry
Population: 1801 – 842   2001 - 1252

DOMESDAY BOOK
BIFELDE/BIVELDE

The name Byfield appears to derive from a combination of the Saxon words 'bye' - a habitation and 'felde' - a field to distinguish a populated area from surrounding waste or uncultivated land.

A Roman villa and a kiln were discovered in 1851 in a field off the Byfield/Marston road.
Further discoveries have been made both there and elsewhere of pottery, roof tiles and burnt stones.

At the time of the Domesday Book there were two manors. The larger eight hide manor was held by *Earl Hugh* of the King.
There were twenty households and a Knight.

The village consists of three parts, Church End, High Street and Westhorpe and being situated on an old turnpike road, now the A361 Daventry to Banbury road, it became a busy trading area and once had its own cattle and horse market.

The area to the north of the village is still extremely busy with traffic from five roads converging onto a double roundabout.
There is still a Primary school, shop, public house - The Cross Tree, a petrol station and garage and a village hall.

The remains of the old Market Cross stand on a mound together with the War Memorial at the junction of Banbury Lane and the High Street.

I never knew that Northamptonshire had War Memorial Competitions but Byfield proudly displays the fact that they have won the competition on many occasions.

The fine church of the **HOLY CROSS** originally dedicated to *St Helen* or *St Helena*, mother of the Roman Emperor *Constantine* was started in 1242 using mostly local stone. It is an impressive building and is well worth a visit.
Over the years the church has been added to and altered. Its fine lofty tower with battlements and recessed spire rises in five stages to a height of one hundred and forty feet (43 metres).

The tower has housed bells since 1552 and now has eight – the last two being added in 1991.
As you enter the south porch you cannot fail to notice the four huge gargoyles which used to be placed on turrets on the four corners of the tower but were considered unsafe and a danger to the public and were removed in 1952.

The colourful stained glass windows are mainly the work of *Kempe* who in the 19th century was responsible for a large number of stained glass windows in Great Britain and America.
He had wanted to be a priest but due to a speech impediment devoted his life to glorifying God in worship through his windows and decorative art.

A simple wooden cross hanging on a wall was brought back from France by the mother of a local boy, *Corporal Walter Smith (M.M.)* of the Machine Gun Corp.

During my visit I was given many interesting facts about the church including the story of the *Rev. Charles Weatherall* who was appointed Rector in 1819 and appears to have been difficult to get on with and had many disputes with his Curate. He was more interested in living it up in London than spending time on his duties in the parish. Eventually he was declared bankrupt and imprisoned but still returned to his post and remained Rector until 1867.
There he rests immediately in front of the altar.

When researching for an earlier book the congregation was engaged in raising funds for restoration and improvement work including a new lighting system. On my most recent visit the money had been raised and the work completed.

The village magazine *'The Byword'* published by the church of the Holy Cross and issued free to all residents in the village makes interesting reading and gives information regarding many village activities and village organisations.

I was impressed with the facilities offered in the area now known as Brightwell Fields.

Originally it was simply a playing field the size of a football pitch and was given to the village in 1944 under the will of **Thomas Brightwell** in memory of his son, another **Thomas,** who was killed in France in 1918.
The Recreation Ground was doubled in size in the 1980's by incorporating redundant land purchased by the Parish Council from British Rail.

Byfield station was served by the East/West railway line between Towcester and Fenny Compton until closure during the Beeching era.
In its heyday the station staff were keen gardeners and regularly won competitions for the best kept station garden on the line.

Opposite the playing fields is the Independent chapel of 1829 which is now a private house and the Conservative club in the old school which has an interesting round turret at the entrance.
This is, I understand, to house the spiral staircase giving access to the upstairs rooms.

On the Boddington road near the water tower a prisoner of war camp was established in 1944 firstly for Italians and later for Germans.
It was derequisitioned in 1949.
Currently plans are being considered for a recycling plant on the site.

For those who enjoy walking there is a very pleasant walk across the fields to nearby Aston le Walls and back via Boddington reservoir with its popular sailing club.

Conservative Club Byfield

TURNPIKE ROADS

A Turnpike is literally a defensive frame of pikes that can be turned to allow passage of horses, but in this context refers to a gate across the road to stop carts until a toll was paid as authorised by an Act of Parliament.
The erection of these gates was considered to be the most successful way to raise money for the maintenance and improvement of the roads.

During the first seventy years of the 18th century a comprehensive network was created across Britain and a total of 450 miles of Turnpike Roads criss crossed Northamptonshire alone.
The first Turnpike road in the County was what we now call the Watling Street between Old Stratford and Dunchurch. This operated from 1706 -1821.

One sixth of English roads were Turnpike roads but many lanes remained the responsibility of the parish and were toll free.
Enclosure of old open fields often created newer, straighter roads rather than the more chaotic older routes.
Most Turnpike Trusts were wound up by an Act of Parliament between 1873-78.

Canons Ashby

Eight miles south of Daventry
Population: 1801 – 40   2001 - 50

DOMESDAY BOOK
ASCEBI

The common Saxon name 'ascebi' simply meant 'farmstead by an ash tree'.
However, soon after the Normans secured a foothold, they founded a Priory here and the name changed.

This village which now consists of the House, church and a few other properties was once an important place. The original settlement lay to the north of the present House. During ongoing excavations in the area remains were discovered of a Castle, thought to be a Norman motte and bailey.

In the Domesday Book sixteen households were recorded but by 1377 eighty two people over the age of fourteen paid the Poll Tax.

The population declined between 1489-1492 when the Prior of the Abbey enclosed the land, evicted twenty four people, destroyed houses and converted the land to pasture.
By 1524 only twenty one taxpayers remained and this figure had reduced to just nine by 1535.

The Black Augustinian Priory founded here by **Stephen de Leys** for thirteen Canons in about 1150 must have been a very grand place.

In 1253 the Augustinians were granted a licence to enclose a well to provide water for the Priory evidence of which can be seen in the curious stone structure with arched entrance to the north east of the village.
The Priory eventually owned the whole of the parish. Regrettably most of the monastic buildings were destroyed at the time of the Dissolution of the Monasteries.

All that remains is the west end of the Priory church of **ST MARY** with its impressive north west tower.

When I think of monks I imagine them as quiet, devout, law abiding members of society and I have no doubt that this was true of the majority.
However, from what I have read about Canons Ashby the monks here were very different.

An Episcopal visitation in the 15th century reported that the monks preferred to visit the local Inn instead of attending services, dressed badly and generally misbehaved.
They were probably egged on by visiting Oxford students. Perhaps the Priory should have been closed even earlier than it was.

The church is noteworthy because it is one of only four in England since the Reformation privately owned by the Lord of the Manor and because the fabric is the only part of a monastic building surviving in the County.

I remember visiting in the 1950's when part of the church was being used as a cattle shed.

During the Civil War a group of Parliamentarians took refuge in the church where they were attacked but were saved by a relief force from Northampton.
At the Dissolution of the Monasteries the Estate was acquired by **Francis Bryan** and a year later it passed to **Sir John Cope,** a wealthy Banbury lawyer who, in 1547, grazed 2,000 sheep in the parish. In 1551 the Estate passed by marriage to the **Dryden** family.

The church receives many visitors as it is now cared for by the National Trust in conjunction with Canons Ashby House across the road.

St Marys Church - Canons Ashby

Dryden

Canons Ashby House
and the Dryden family

The **Drydens** came from Cumberland in 1551 after **John Dryden's** marriage to **Elizabeth**, daughter of **Sir John Cope**. He felt the need to improve the House in keeping with his new status.

His son, **Erasmus** a staunch Puritan and prosperous London grocer continued work on the House and purchased a Baronetcy in 1619. He was High Sheriff in 1620 and MP for Banbury.

His son **John** followed him into Parliament as MP for Northamptonshire 1640-1653 and 1654-1655.

Probably the best known of the **Dryden** family is another **John**, grandson of the First Baronet, who was born at Aldwincle (Northants) in 1631 and went on to become Poet Laureate to **King Charles II** in 1670 and is said to have regularly visited Canons Ashby. He converted to Catholicism in 1686 and lost his post as Poet Laureate after the Glorious Revolution of 1688-9 possibly because he refused to denounce his faith.

Sir Henry Dryden inherited at the age of nineteen in 1837 and was Squire through most of the Victorian era.

As a young man he referred to himself as the 'last of the Black Canons' - a reference to the earlier Priory.

Perhaps he likened himself to the monks who drank copious amounts of beer as he was often taken to be a tramp.

Henry inherited his father's interest in local history and archaeology; he was known as the 'Antiquary' and protected the House from change. He married late in life and had one child – a daughter – upon which he lost no time in sacking two of the female kitchen staff as there were 'too many women in the house'.

They were quickly reinstated by his wife. **Sir Henry** died in 1899 but left a vast treasure store of antiquarian interests including local history and archaeology.

When **Queen Mary** visited in 1937 the House still had no water or electricity.

The last Baronet, **Sir Arthur**, died in 1938 and the Estate passed to a nephew who took the name **Dryden**.

Towards the end of the 20th century the House had become in danger of collapse and was 'at risk'.

There followed a national campaign to save the building and the National Trust accepted ownership and commenced restoration. It is now presented as it would have been at the time of **Sir Henry**.

This Grade I listed building is a tranquil 16th century Elizabethan Manor House set in beautiful gardens thought to be on the site of the guest house of the Priors and built of stone from the old Priory.

The House with its stunning Jacobean plasterwork and tapestries in the grand rooms and the domestic detail of the servants' quarters and kitchen is well worth a visit but you don't have to visit the House to enjoy a drink or a meal in the National Trust restaurant at the entrance.

CASTLE ASHBY

Seven miles east of Northampton
Population: 1801 – 123   2001 - 134

DOMESDAY BOOK
ASEBI
*The name 'asebi' - common in Saxon times
simply meant 'ash tree by a farm.'*

The manor was held by **Hugh** of the **Countess Judith** in the 11th century and is recorded in the Domesday Book as having eighteen households and a mill rendering six shillings and eight pence per annum.

However there were settlements here long before 1066 as findings have been made locally of a quantity of Iron Age pottery, flints, Roman pottery and coins.

Castle Ashby is situated on minor roads on the south side of the flood plain of the River Nene between Northampton and Wellingborough.

The Castle part of the name dates from 1306 when **Langton, Bishop of Coventry** obtained a licence from the Crown to embattle his mansion at Ashby.

The church of **ST MARY MAGDALENE** lies immediately adjacent to the east garden of **Castle Ashby House** and even today feels much like part of the private garden.

The north porch has a late Norman doorway embellished by zigzags, lozenges and dogtooth carving but elsewhere the style of architecture is mainly Decorative or Perpendicular but was restored in 1870.

In the church and churchyard are many monuments to the family of the **Marchioness of Northampton** including **Spencer, 2nd Marquess** (1790-1851) who took over the Northampton seat in Parliament from **Spencer Perceval**, son of the **Earl of Egmont**, the only British Prime Minister to have been assassinated.

Castle Ashby Gateway.

The village was moved from east to west when the south side was cleared to get rid of: - *'a receptacle for idle persons....and a harbour for strumpets'* and the north side was cleared to create a landscape on which **Capability Brown** could work.

Most of the existing Estate cottages date from the 1860's onwards.

The Estate grounds which are often open to the public include a garden tea room, plant centre, gift shop and farmyard are quite extensive and include popular fishing lakes.

On the road between Cogenhoe and Grendon stands a very unusual building featuring a tower with a conical roof, which was the Porters Lodge or Station Lodge being the nearest point to Castle Ashby Station on the Northampton to Peterborough line.

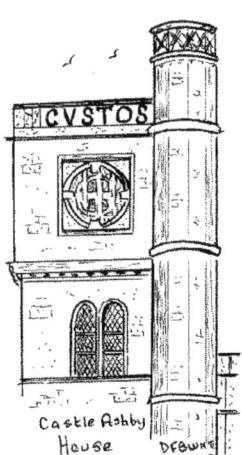
Castle Ashby House

A damaged goods train at Castle Ashby on the 18th October 1877 resulted in the worst passenger accident on the line.

Both up and down trains were forced to use the same section of track resulting in a head on collision between two passenger trains one carrying judges, lawyers, witnesses and journalists from the Quarter Sessions in Northampton.

Four people lost their lives.

When the line was closed in 1964 the track and some buildings were removed and what now remains is the old goods shed which has been converted into a popular restaurant.

After your meal you can retire to a restored passenger coach for coffee and a chat.

The village no longer has a local shop, post office or school but the Rural Shopping Yard with craft workers, country clothing, gift shops and restaurant attracts visitors from far and wide.

Until recently The Falcon which was founded in 1594 was a very popular restaurant and inn but recently it closed its doors to the public and its future seems uncertain.

Tout bien au rien
'All well or nothing'

To the south of the village is the small hamlet of Chadstone.

CHADSTONE

DOMESDAY BOOK
CEDESTONE

In 1086 the population was recorded as fourteen households. The manor was held by **Drogo de la Beavriere** but it is said that he fled the country after murdering his wife.

About 1284 the small settlement which lies on a 'no through road' on the Castle Ashby Estate was combined with neighbouring Castle Ashby.

In the early 18th century there were six houses but foundations of other houses have been discovered.

The Old Rectory, a Grade II listed building belongs to the Castle Ashby Estate and was once the home of the Vicar of the local church.

Castle Ashby House and the Compton family

*The **Compton** family grew in prominence when land at Castle Ashby was given to the family by **Henry VIII** in 1512.*
*Sixty two years later **Elizabeth I** permitted **William, Lord Compton** to demolish the old House and replace it with the present one. Sir **William** also married to his advantage. He purchased other manors including Yardley Hastings and six others nearby to form the nucleus of one of the County's greatest Estates.*
*Dating from 1574 and built of Weldon stone the House in the shape of an 'E' is essentially Elizabethan and Jacobean in style but was modified in the 17th century by **Inigo Jones** who added the south wing.*
The lettering around the parapet of the east wing is in Latin and is taken from Psalm 127:- (in English)

'Except the Lord build the house they labour in vain that build it,
except the Lord keep the house the watchman waketh but in vain'.

Other Biblical extracts in English are featured elsewhere on the property.
*The House is approached via an impressive gateway on the Bedford Road and stands at the end of an avenue, three and a half miles long, which dates back to the time when **William of Orange** visited in 1695.*
*Other royal visitors include **Queen Victoria** and **King James I**.*

***Henry Compton** (1632-1713) the younger son of the 2nd **Earl of Northampton** was ordained in 1666, became Bishop of Oxford in 1674 and Bishop of London in 1675. Although suspended from office in 1686 for refusing to discipline a clergyman for anti papal sermons he was the only cleric to sign the invitation to **William of Orange**.*
*Eventually **Henry** was reinstated Bishop of London and crowned **William III** and **Mary II** in 1689.*
***Charles Compton, 9th Earl of Northampton** was MP for the town between 1784-1796 when he entered the House of Lords.*
He was created Marquess of Northampton in 1812.

*Castle Ashby House surrounded by 200 acres of parkland designed by **Capability Brown** has recently passed to the son of the 7th **Marquess** to continue the family tradition of managing the Estate.*
*The **Compton** dynasty survives to this day but the present Marquess now lives at **Compton Wynyates** in Warwickshire and **Castle Ashby House** is used commercially, hosting many different functions.*

CATESBY

UPPER AND LOWER

Four miles south west of Daventry
Population: 1801 – 95   2001-76

DOMESDAY BOOK
CATESBI

The ancient name of Catesbi appears to derive from the Viking word,
Kati *- perhaps a local tribal leader and 'by' - meaning village or farmstead.*

At the time of the Domesday Book the four hide manor had a population of twenty four households and a priest although this probably included Newbold. There were two mills rendering sixteen pence per annum.

The division between Upper and Lower Catesby which lie on minor roads south west of Daventry probably came about with the establishment of the Cistercian Priory at what is now Lower Catesby in 1175. The authorities obviously thought that Catesby was going places with the grant of a Market Charter in 1246.

Today both are so small and so quiet that it is almost impossible to believe that one hundred and seventy two people were assessed for payment of the Poll Tax in 1377.
The population dropped quite dramatically after that date.
Upper Catesby with just a few dwellings, developed around an old church dedicated to **ST MARY** which served both villages. This church was damaged during the Dissolution and has long since disappeared with little remaining except for the old burial ground with a few headstones and one giant tomb.

One of the wayside cottages in Upper Catesby took the columns of a doorway once built into the Priory entrance.

In 1491 the Prioress ordered the destruction of fourteen houses, evicted sixty people and converted land at Lower Catesby to pasture.
It is thought that the village once lay opposite the site of the Priory to the north of the present church dedicated to **ST MARY** and **ST EDMUND** which was built by *Gillett* of Leicester on the site of the old Priory chapel in 1861/62 for the *Attenborough* family who owned the Estate.

The church is now situated in the middle of a field surrounded by a ditch and at the time of my visit was being carefully guarded by a magnificent herd of Highland cattle.

Inside are the painted Royal Arms of ***King Charles II*** and some relics of the old Priory including the piscina and ornate sedilia.

The Jacobean pulpit with a canopy has lovely carvings and there is a superb golden eagle lectern.
It is claimed that the bell in the bellcote is one of the oldest in Northamptonshire.

If you ever go to a service in Catesby on a very cold day, go early and claim one of the front seats – these are the only ones with heating!

Tomb at Old Churchyard: Upper Catesby

In the vicinity of the church are some rather extraordinary red brick stables with a turret and some stone built cottages or farm buildings reminiscent of a row of Almshouses

Catesby House is a fine building standing on the hillside between the two villages and was built between 1863 and 1894 using some stone from both the old Priory and the old church at Upper Catesby. It was once the home of *John Parkhurst* the lexicographer, publisher and author.

The owners did not want the proposed Grand Central Railway spoiling their land and as a result the line which opened in 1897 goes underground for about two miles.
The ventilation shafts are a visible reminder of this line which eventually closed in September 1966.

The tunnel at 2,997 yards long was the longest on the old Great Central Railway and has been closed off to the public but still visible is the 159 yard long Catesby viaduct built of Staffordshire blue bricks.
There is no shop, school or public house but between Upper and Lower Catesby is a sign directing you to the Hayfields Luxury Dog Hotel.
The long distance footpath the Jurassic Way passes through Lower Catesby.

The parish now includes the deserted village of Newbold.

NEWBOLD

Although not specifically mentioned in the Domesday Book it is thought that this lost settlement was, in 1086, taxed with nearby Catesby.
The land became part of Catesby Priory and it appears was imparked by the Prioress at the same time as at Catesby in 1491 leaving little evidence of its existence.

CATESBY PRIORY

A Cistercian Priory for ten nuns was founded in 1175 at Lower Catesby possibly by *Robert de Esseby* who, with his grandson *Sasfrid* held the manor under *William Peverel* at the time of the Domesday Book.

It was originally endowed with the church at Upper Catesby the chapel at Hellidon and the two mills.

From what I have read it seems that initially this was a relatively poor Priory until *Edmund* the Archbishop of Canterbury placed his two sisters there at the wish of his deceased mother.

One of the sisters – *Margaret Rich* became Prioress and on the Archbishop's death was given his pall and a silver tablet engraved with a figure of Our Lord which he had always carried around with him.
Miracles soon became associated with these relics and Catesby became a place of pilgrimage and healing. There are many such stories associated with the church and in fact healing services are still held from time to time

The Priory grew in stature and appears to have become a grand place because when the monasteries were being demolished by *Henry VIII* in 1536/7 the Kings Commissioners are said to have been so struck by its admirable condition that they asked for the Priory to be reprieved.

Unfortunately the request was not granted and the destruction was soon implemented and all property granted to *John Onley.*

CHACOMBE

Three miles north east of Banbury
Population: 1801-438   2001 - 659

DOMESDAY BOOK
CEWECUMBE
*Until recently the spelling varied between
Chacombe and Chalcombe -the name comes from
Ceawa - local leader and 'cumb' - valley.*

Them Bells .. Them Bells

Nestled close to the Oxfordshire border in a well wooded valley with hills on three sides, it is thought that there was a settlement here at the time of the Iron Age followed by the Romans and Saxons and that it once had an important cloth industry.

The Domesday Book records that the four hide manor was held by **Godfrey** of the **Bishop of Lincoln** and that there were thirty three households, three mills rendering sixteen shillings per annum and nine acres of meadow.

On low lying land to the west of the village once stood an Augustinian Priory dedicated to St Peter and St Paul founded by **Hugh de Chacombe**, Lord of the Manor in the late 12th century.

In 1535 **Sir John Tregonwell** reported to **Thomas Cromwell** - *"at Chacombe the Prior is newly come and is competently well learned in Holy Scripture. He is bringing into some order his Canons who are rude and unlearned. I am only afraid that he is too familiar and easy with them".*

Little else is known of the history of the Priory and it was suppressed in 1536.

The present building known as the 'Priory' dates from the 17th century and contains part of the medieval chapel of the monks and in the grounds are gravestones and old fish ponds.
This very impressive building overlooking a lake with a mass of yellow water lilies in the summer is now in private hands and is not open to the public but can easily be seen and appreciated from the Banbury Road.

Bumps and hollows in Berry Close around the mound are part of the remains of the abandoned part of the medieval village.
The mounds were raised so that the Bagley Bell Founders could cast their bells in the pits.
Bell Cottage probably stands on the site of the famous Bell Foundry (1600-1785) which cast more than four hundred and forty bells for churches in England including six bells in Chacombe church although two of the bells have since been recast.

Other houses in the village such as the Old Forge and the Old Farmhouse and Weavers bear witness of their former use.
The village hall is a relatively new building having been provided in 1981.

Older buildings include the Primary school built in 1868 but much enlarged and improved.
Unfortunately there is a possibility that the proposed high speed rail link between London and the Midlands will cut through this site and that another school may have to be built although there is no suggestion that Chacombe will have a station. For a time the village had a halt on the line between Culworth and Banbury but it was closed by British Rail in 1956 and the line taken up in 1966.

The village boasts a Music Festival in memory of **Sophie** the 19 year old daughter of **Stephen** and **Cherry Large** who died in a car accident in 1998. The converted **'Sophie's Barn'** provides rehearsal space for musicians and actors.

An unusual event to be witnessed in Chacombe is the Northamptonshire Soap Box Derby.

It has been held in the village annually since 2007 and involves daredevil drivers in a variety of handmade go-karts negotiating a course with pot holes and corners along the Thorpe Road Course ending in the centre of the village at The George and Dragon public house which has a date stone of 1734 and is unusual in that a twenty foot deep well covered with toughened glass is part of the bar.

Tucked away down a little lane behind the public house and in an idyllic setting is the church of **ST PETER** and **ST PAUL** which dates back to the 13th and 14th centuries.

In 1982 a 14th century wall painting of the martyrdom of *St Peter* was discovered after the removal of some loose stones from a blocked up window.

It is thought to be one of only two such paintings in England (the other being at Ickleton in Cambs).

Above the painting was a large stone which has been identified by the five consecration crosses on its surface as a medieval altar. The stone has now been restored to its original use.

On the night of the infamous bombing raid on Coventry during the Second World War (14/15 Nov 1940) stray bombs fell on Chacombe demolishing part of the Priory grounds.

Stained glass windows in the west end of the church were shattered and a local person collected and labelled segments of the glass which turned up fifty years later in a Deddington antiques shop.

It is said that Chacombe church representatives were almost unique in the diocese as they put in an insurance claim for war damage.

The missing stained glass has been replaced by plain glass but some original glass remains.

In 1786 a Methodist chapel was built in the village. This is still in use and holds shared services with the Anglican community.

George & The Dragon Inn Sign ~ Chacombe

Cherwell Valley Golf club is located on both sides of the road as you approach the village from Middleton Cheney so be aware of golf balls or golf buggies.

The Jurassic Way passes through Chacombe and there are also a number of bridle paths radiating into the countryside.

Gladys
Duchess of Marlborough
(1881-1977)

Gladys, Duchess of Marlborough was a colourful local character. She was the second wife of Charles Churchill 9th Duke of Marlborough whom she married in 1921 and was acclaimed the world's most beautiful woman - the toast of Paris.

Unfortunately her lifestyle caused her to be evicted from Blenheim Palace where she used to sit for meals with a revolver by her side.
Gladys became an eccentric recluse at Grange Farm, Chacombe where she was known simply as Mrs Spencer.

Apparently she moved about at night, slept during the day, barricaded herself in and would not let anyone visit.
A friend supplied her with food which she hauled up into the house on ropes.

Eventually she was admitted to St Andrews Hospital in Northampton where she died in 1977 and is buried in Chacombe churchyard.

CHAPEL BRAMPTON

Four miles north west of Northampton
Population: 1801 – 170   2001-470

DOMESDAY BOOK
BRANTONE

At the time of the Domesday Book this was only a single village with the name from the Saxon meaning Bramble Farm. The settlements 'Church and Chapel' were officially divided in 1670.

The ***Count of Mortain*** is recorded as holding the manor in 1086 - just one of approximately a hundred manors he held in the County.
Other significant holders of the manor have been the ***Treshams*** of Rushton and the ***Hattons*** of Holdenby.

The ***Spencers*** became involved in the manor in the mid 18th century. Today Chapel Brampton is an attractive ironstone village on the A5199 with Althorp Estate housing of 1848, a Primary school but no shop.

I have never known there to be an ancient chapel here in spite of its name.
It has been suggested that this was a manorial chapel which has long since disappeared.

From 1637-1824 the present Spencer Arms was an ale house known as The Stags Head.
The name was changed in 1825 when it became a public house (as opposed to an inn where lodging was provided).
Like most of the village at the time the public house was owned by the ***Spencer*** family of nearby Althorp House.

Chapel Brampton is unusual for in the immediate area are three public houses I've no doubt that its proximity to Northampton is a major factor.
In addition to the historic Spencer Arms in the village there is now The Windhover a quite attractive new building made to appear older near the old level crossing on the road to Northampton and The Brampton Halt, part of the old station buildings on the road to Pitsford.

The station closed in June 1950 although the line remained open for some years afterwards.
This is now the base for the volunteer run Northampton and Lamport Railway which started preservation in 1984.
It operates trains during the summer months and Christmas on a short section of restored track.

The line has recently been extended to The Windhover public house where it is hoped to erect a small halt. The whole of the old track bed from The Windhover to Market Harborough is now a wonderful leisure opportunity for walkers and cyclists.

At the junction of the main road and the Pitsford road is an unusual looking building with a large central door and fanlight above and to the right a large multi paned rectangular window.
This was once the home of the blacksmith and agricultural implements manufacturer - a very important job in Victorian times.

'Merry Tom Lane' just north east of the village is reputed to have been named after one of the *1st Earl Spencer's* favourite hunters killed whilst jumping a brook. It is said that the horse was buried where it fell complete with saddle, stirrups and bridle. The whole area is still very much given over to horse riding.

Sedgebrook Hall on the Pitsford Road set in thirteen acres is well known locally as a place for luxury weddings, conferences, etc. This Country House Hotel with 102 bedrooms and a Banqueting Suite also has a Health and Leisure Club with a gym, all weather tennis courts and sauna.

CHARLTON

Four miles west of Brackley
Population: 1801 - 297
2001 – 438   (with Newbottle)

DOMESDAY BOOK
CERLINTONE

The 'tone' indicates a farmstead here and the remainder probably implies that it was worked by the ceorls – people who achieved freeman status and were able to work on land granted to them.

Of the two manors listed in the Domesday Book the one and a half hide manor held by the **Count of Mortain** was recorded as *'waste'*.

A Charter for a market was granted in 1250 but like so many of its day did not last very long.

This is a medium sized village near the Oxford border in the south west of Northamptonshire and is unusual in that it has no parish church - this being located about half a mile away in the hamlet of Newbottle. The reason for this is that Charlton unlike Newbottle had no single powerful Lord to build a church near his Manor. To all intents and purposes the two settlements are treated as one.

In the centre of Charlton must be one of the grandest cottages in the land – home of **F. E. Smith,** the *1st Earl of Birkenhead*.
He was a lawyer and rose to become Lord Chancellor of England and was a close friend of **Sir Winston Churchill.**

He moved here to a small hunting lodge in 1907 and extended and transformed it into an imposing house right on the village street with gardens at the rear stretching down to a small lake.
His tomb designed by **Lutyens,** a leading 20th century British architect, is in the cemetery to the west of the village.

Almost opposite this grand house is the attractive thatched Rose and Crown which dates back to 1670 - the last of four public houses which used to exist in the village.
There is still a shop with post office, a village hall with many active groups and a Primary school founded in 1872 but with a modern extension.

The Independent chapel from 1827 is in decline with an uncertain future.

Through the generosity of **Mr F. Myers** who lived at the Lodge the village was provided not with just one village pump but a number at intervals along the main street.
Four of these blue brick arched constructions can still be seen although some have been put to other uses including a storage bay for plastic recycling bins.

RAINSBOROUGH CAMP

A mile to the south of the village is an oval Iron Age hill fort on the edge of a plateau 480ft above sea level.
There are extensive views to the north and north west over the Cherwell Valley.

Excavations reveal that in the early 4th century BC it was re-fortified. In the 18th century the inner bank was heightened and the ditch deepened.
The site was extensively excavated between 1961-65 when evidence was found of activity here between about the 5/6th centuries BC and the 4th century AD.
Many items were found during excavations and these are now in the Ashmolean Museum in Oxford.

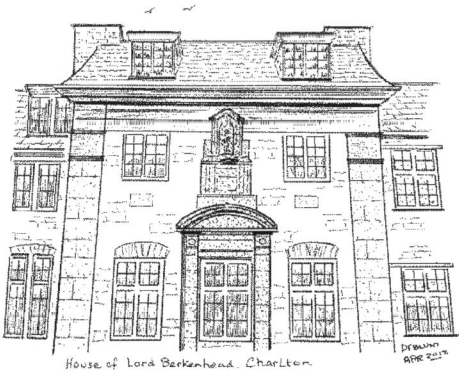

House of Lord Berkenhead, Charlton.

CHARWELTON

UPPER AND LOWER

Four and a half miles south west of Daventry
Population: 1801 – 185   2001 - 185

DOMESDAY BOOK
CERWELTONE/CELVERTONE/CERVELTONE
The village grew up as a' tun' – farm on the River Cherwell which rises in the village.

The villages were recorded together at the time of the Domesday Book when the land was divided between four manors, one of which *'was waste'* with a population of eleven.

It has been suggested that the manor held by Thornby Abbey actually refers to Upper Charwelton which lies off the A361 Banbury to Daventry road.

The small hamlet to the south east, known as Lower (now Church) Charwelton suffered badly when the Black Death and enclosures by *Thomas Andrewes* decimated the population and the village declined.

By 1547 there were in excess of two thousand sheep in the area but few people.

In addition when the line of the main road altered a few of the remaining inhabitants moved up the road (about half a mile away).

Certainly by the time *Bridges* compiled his *'History of Northamptonshire'* in the early 18th century he wrote that Church Charwelton was *'in great measure depopulated at this time.'*

By 1847 it was recorded that the whole settlement had been abandoned. All that remains is the isolated church and **Charwelton House,** an ironstone Manor Farm House with a hipped roof and a fine array of outbuildings – some in a very sorry but rather picturesque state.

The remote and peaceful location of the church and Manor House in Lower Charwelton is one of my favourite places in the County.

Here you will find **HOLY TRINITY** church with its Decorative style west tower dating mostly from the 14th and 15th centuries.

The church has been restored over the years especially the chancel between the years 1901/04.

There are a number of monuments and brasses to the family of *Thomas Andrewes* who purchased the land here in 1417.

On the west wall is a carved wall tablet commemorating the *5th Sir Thomas Andrewes* and his two wives, *Mary* and *Frances*. The memorial depicts them and their twelve children including the empty cots of two who died in infancy.

Old Barn : Church Charwelton

Packhorse Bridge - Charwelton

The south porch has two storeys – presumably overnight accommodation for any visiting preacher.

The oak pews with their fine poppy heads came from the church of All Saints in Warwick which was demolished in 1967/8.

There were four bells but a fifth bell was added recently which together are said to provide one of the best peals of bells in the area.

Motorists on the main road see little of either Upper or Lower Charwelton apart from the local public house – The Fox and Hounds.

Charwelton was served by the Great Central Railway which arrived in 1897 and closed in 1963. The line and station have now been completely demolished although you can still see evidence of the line with embankments and brickwork.

I understand that the station had many similarities to the Rothley and Quorn preserved station on the Great Central Heritage Line.

The old school which closed in 1935 was given by the *Knightleys* of Fawsley who also gave the village hall which was officially opened on the 2nd November 1922.

Today there is no longer a shop or post office and the delightful little old Methodist church now housing the Chapel of the Good Shepherd is used for some Anglican services and is usually open during the day. Over the porch is the clock from the old school. The building is in very good order having been refurbished with comfortable seating as a millennium project.

An interesting and historic feature alongside the main road is the three foot wide Grade I listed Packhorse Bridge built of ironstone over the River Cherwell about seven hundred years ago.

It has two Gothic arches and one cutwater and is described as one of the finest surviving packhorse bridges in England and is the only bridge of its kind in the County.

The River Cherwell once started its journey towards the Thames at Oxford in the cellar of the former Cherwell Farm close by the road to Hellidon. Today it starts its journey from a pool close to the replacement house.

A landmark to the west of the village is the 118 metre (387 ft) tall British Telecom Tower.
It is one of the few British towers built of re-inforced concrete.

CHELVESTON CUM CALDECOTT

Three miles north east of Rushden
Population: 1801 – 266   2001 - 541

DOMESDAY BOOK
CELVESTONE

The names given to these two places are both Anglo Saxon in origin and mean
Ceolwulf's farmstead in the case of Chelveston and 'cold' or 'inhospitable cottage' for Caldecote.
I am sure that the properties in that small hamlet cannot be so described today.

Recent excavations have revealed a large number of Iron Age and Roman sites in the parish.

After 1066 the settlement of Chelveston cum Caldecott was part of the manor of Higham Ferrers given to **William Peverel**, **William the Conquerors** son, who held other manors in Northamptonshire and over a hundred and forty in total.

It was confiscated after the War of the Roses and in 1486 **Henry VII** granted it to **Sir Charles Somerset** (later **Earl of Worcester**).

These two villages combined in name, stand about half a mile apart on the minor B645 which was until quite recently the main road between Higham Ferrers and St Neots – now better served by the new A14 road nearby.

There is no longer a shop or post office and the Primary school closed in 1967 but in the centre of the village is the public house - The Star and Garter.

For many years Baptists met at the home of **William Richard Gross**, a farmer in Caldecott and the first chapel was built as an extension to one of his properties. The present chapel building dates from 1924 but closed through lack of support in the early 1980's and is now a private house.

Since the mid 18th century the Lords of the Manor were the **Disbrowe** family and the last was **Lt. Col. Henry Disbrowe CBE** who inherited the title from his mother.
He also inherited an Estate in Derbyshire and as a result he sold off the family's Estate properties in Chelveston by auction in July 1919.

The church of **ST JOHN** the **BAPTIST** is actually in Caldecott and is mostly 13th century.
Its sixty foot tower stands on the north side and is linked to the side of the church by a fragment of the lost north aisle.
I was very surprised on entering the church to see how wide, light and empty it was. There are plenty of windows all but one with clear glass and many of the pews have been removed to leave an open space towards the back of the church where there is now provided a modern open kitchen.
In the spring the churchyard provides a wonderful display of snowdrops which attracts visitors from far and wide.
Modern pictures of the *'Stations of the Cross'* are the work of the nuns at Turvey Abbey in Bedfordshire.
The small Lady Chapel was refurbished in 1968.

In 1995 drums containing nearly 900kg of depleted uranium were found dumped in a farmer's field by woodland near to the Caldecott / Newton Bromswold road. The farmer sold three of the drum loads to a local scrap metal dealer who in turn sold them to a dealer in Sheffield.
On arrival alarms were triggered at the weighbridge and an investigation was set up and specialists were sent to clean up the mess which included corroded drums and tops.

USAF CHELVESTON

During the Second World War Chelveston saw a lot of activity. In 1940 grass runways and three hangars were constructed as an RAF base but in early 1942 it was turned over to the USAF and concrete runways were constructed.
The first B17's of the 301st Heavy Bomb group arrived in August of that year.

Until the end of the war in 1945 the airfield was used by heavy bombers including Flying Fortresses of the 305th Bombardment Group (Heavy) known as the *'Can do group'*.
20th Century Fox films used Chelveston for the opening sequence of the film
'Twelve O'Clock High'.

The base continued in a standby role until its closure in the early 1970's when much of the site was broken up and removed.

On the edge of the village of Caldecott is quite a large housing complex once used by servicemen stationed nearby. At the time of writing the whole estate was deserted and the site offered for sale.

On the outside wall of the church tower is a memorial to men of the base and on the 26 May 2007 a granite memorial in the village centre was dedicated. Fifteen US veterans and thirty nine family members attended the service.

PLAQUE ON MEMORIAL

This monument in local stone and polished granite is dedicated in gratitude to the memory of the men who served with the
305th Bombardment Group flying from the Chelveston airfield one mile SE of this site during World War II.

The group flew 480 missions and 769 men were killed with many more wounded in action.
This pole was the wind sock mast which probably dominated the roof of the main hangar.

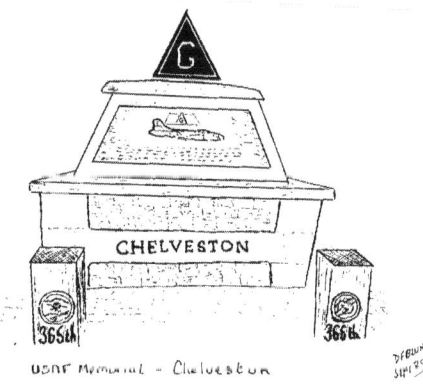

USAF Memorial - Chelveston

Chipping Warden

Five miles north east of Banbury
Population: 1801 – 294   2001 - 529

DOMESDAY BOOK
WAREDONE

It is thought that the old name derives from two Saxon words 'weard' - watch and 'dun' - hill - a local lookout point (Warden Hill nearby). The addition appeared in the 13th century when the Manor obtained a grant of a weekly market - 'chipping' from the Saxon - 'cieping' - for market.

There is evidence of both Iron Age and Roman settlement in the area. Arbury Banks or Camp, an Iron Age fort lies on the flat summit of a low hill south west of the village and the site of a Roman bath house was discovered on a valley side close to the River Cherwell.

Ploughing in the area has revealed extensive stone foundations, coins and large quantities of Roman pottery of the 1st - 4th century.

The manor itself has quite a long history going back to **Guy de Raimbeaucourt,** a Baron from northern France in 1086, but the Manor House with a small central tower, east of the church is apparently part of a 16th century house.

This very attractive ironstone built village is situated in a mainly agricultural area on the A361 and not surprisingly is in a Conservation area.

Just off the main road is a very colourful village sign incorporating various aspects of local history including the church, drovers and sheep which frequently passed through the area, thatched cottages and an aircraft.

During World War II there was an airfield just outside the village and some of the old buildings can still be seen. This was the base of No 12 Operational Training Unit.

The site now contains some large storage facilities and brings much needed employment to the area in the form of clerks, store men, lorry drivers etc.

A Wellington bomber crashed into Warden Hill on 5th March 1943 on its return from a night training sortie.

There is a memorial on the hill to the five airmen who died - only one crew member survived.

On the main road and still in use is an old Coaching Inn, The Rose and Crown and not far away is The Griffin Inn.

There is still a Primary school and village hall but no local retail shop as such but some goods can be purchased from a small building behind The Griffin Inn.

The Wesleyan chapel of 1884 has been converted into a private residence.

Market Steps : Chipping Warden

A particularly attractive and tranquil scene can be found around Hogg End.
Here is the church and a lovely row of stone built cottages plus the fairly sizeable stump of the old market cross which stands proud above a square base with six quite steep steps - a reminder of the days as a busy market town.

A Market Charter had been granted in 1219 but the *Bishop of Lincoln* who controlled the Market at nearby Banbury obtained letters from *Henry III* revoking the Chipping Warden Charter as he was losing business in his market.

The large ironstone church of **ST PETER** and **ST PAUL** with its very prominent water spouts and an embattled tower with pinnacles is mostly of the Decorative and Perpendicular style of the 14th century.
It is a lovely church with an impressive East window by *Christopher Whall* (protégée of *William Morris*) which shows the 'Adoration of the Magi' together with scenes from the lives of the Patron Saints.

The church has two wide aisles, an old battlemented reredos and also a lofty 15th century clerestoried nave of six bays.

It is worth while taking a short stroll to the south of the church to see the lovely old Court House with thatched cottages next door and the Court House stables opposite.

From this point you can start a very pleasant local walk to nearby Edgcote as part of the local Battlefield Trail - one of a number of walks in the area.
In the 19th century mass burial pits were found in the area and they are believed to have been victims of the nearby Battle.

Donkey Stable : Chipping Warden

To the east of the parish and on the west side of the River Cherwell is the deserted settlement of Trafford.

TRAFFORD

In the Domesday Book *Robert* held of *Earl Hugh* one hide and one virgate of land in Trafford.
There were six households, three acres of meadow and a mill rendering six shillings and eight pence per annum.

In the 13th and 14th centuries the manor was owned by the *Trafford* family whose name lives on in the present Trafford House which is marked on some Ordnance Survey Maps.

By the 16th century the land was being used for sheep production which suggests that the area had been depopulated by that date.

CHURCH BRAMPTON

Four miles north west of Northampton
Population: 1801 – 173   2001 - 251

DOMESDAY BOOK
BRANTONE
Originally it was only a single village with the name meaning Bramble farm from the Saxon.
The settlements (Church and Chapel) split about 1474 as the population grew.

In the Domesday Book only one manor of Brantone is mentioned. It was part of a large area held by the **Count of Mortain** including nearby Creaton and East Haddon.

There was a population of twenty two households and a mill rendering twenty eight shillings per annum.

Church Brampton has some delightful old stone cottages many built by the **Spencer** family in 1848 for workers on the nearby Althorp Estate and in my opinion is more attractive and somewhat more peaceful than its neighbour Chapel Brampton which lies only a short distance away.

As you approach the village from Harlestone you will see, set up on a high bank, the church of **ST BOTOLPH** which is mostly Perpendicular in style and dates from the 14th century.

The massive west tower is Decorative in style and has battlements and pinnacles above a corbel table of tiny heads and monster gargoyles.

Inside is a very ornate font but what really caught my eye were the lovely stone angel corbels overhead playing a variety of musical instruments.

In the chancel which was rebuilt in 1860, these angels are accompanied by even more angels but this time in wood.

Just outside the church is a fragment of an old Grade II listed Preaching Cross.

Close by is a group of ten Grade II listed gabled Almshouses built by **Earl Spencer** in the mid 19th century. They are Tudor in style and are the work of **John Wykes**.

The Memorial Cross on the edge of the churchyard was given by **Reginald Loder** of **Maidwell Hall** in honour of the village having the highest number of volunteers of any village in the County in the First World War.

Brampton Heath Golf Centre off Sandy Lane boasts a magnificent 18 hole heathland course and a 9 hole academy course.
The Centre is also a renowned venue for parties, weddings and functions.

Primary school children are educated in Chapel Brampton but shoppers now have to travel further afield.

Brampton stables were started by **Derick Ward** in 1970 and proved so successful that they moved to their present quarters on a typical Northamptonshire farm in 1978.

This is very much horse riding territory and when driving in the area the motorist has to be very wary of the number of riders either in the road or on the grass verges.

CLAYCOTON

Six miles east of Rugby
Population: 1801 – 116   2001 – included in Lilbourne

*This settlement does not appear to have been recorded until 1175 and the name is thought
to have derived because the 'coton' (cottage) was situated on heavy clay soil.*

It would appear that in 1086 Claycoton was taxed with nearby Lilbourne and hence does not appear in the Domesday Book.

It was certainly settled prior to 1086 as a medieval coin hoard of four hundred and thirty five groats dating from the 5th century was discovered in the 19th century.

From old maps it appears that the village had a large roughly triangular Green south of the church but this has all but disappeared.

Today Claycoton is quite small with a few attractive buildings on the border of Northamptonshire and Warwickshire very close to the new major A14 trunk road from the Midlands to the docks at Felixstowe. It does not appear ever to have been very large or important.
I particularly liked the black and white Manor Cottage and Fawn Cottage.

Overlooking the village is the church of
ST ANDREW which has an unbuttressed Decorative style west tower and a very short recessed spire.
There are fine tall Decorated style windows in the chancel.

The church stood unused for thirty five years and was threatened with demolition in the 1970's but is now a private residence although the surrounding graveyard still has public access.
It has three bells dated 1615, 1619 and 1810 which are apparently in situ although I read that the bell ropes have been removed for safety reasons.

The parish chest has been rehoused at the parish church in Courteenhall.

Some years ago a 'witch pot' was found hidden in the inglenook of an old house thought to date from from 1850 and was featured in the BBC's website
'A History of the World in 100 Objects'.
The pot would have been placed behind the chimney to prevent witches and evil spirits from entering.

In 2010 the Grade II listed Manor House in Claycoton, believed to have been built in the late 18th century in the Jacobean cruciform style was for sale for £1,450, 000.

The village has no school and no shop and the public house - The Fox closed in 2002 and is now a private house.

St Andrews Church - ClayCoton

CLIPSTON

Four miles south of Market Harborough
Population: 1801 – 737   2001 - 613

DOMESDAY BOOK
CLIPESTONE
*It is thought that the name originates from **Klyppr** a
Scandinavian personal name
and 'tun' - farmstead.*

The Old School - Clipston

At the time of the Domesday Book reference is made to four manors one of which belonged to the Abbey of St Edmundsbury and another was part of the large royal manor of Rothwell.

The area was settled well before 1086 as evidence has been found recently of four small Roman settlements in the locality.

Today Clipston with its wide streets and fine Green is a medium sized village but with rather more history than many of a similar size.
It gives the impression of being a much more important place at one time.
The River Ise rises in the parish and eventually flows into the River Nene below Wellingborough.

It is interesting to note that the population of Clipston has hardly changed over two hundred years and currently stands at about 620 persons.

In the High Street is an impressive looking building especially for a village and the notice board outside indicates that this is now Clipston Endowed Primary school.
Over the front door it states that:

> *'this free Grammar school and Hospital
> were built and endowed by
> Sir George Buswell, Bart in 1667
> 'for the maintenance
> of a Graduate School Master and for twelve
> poor persons forever'.*

There is a monument to **Sir George** on the north side of the chancel in the church.

It is interesting to note that initially only boys living in Clipston, Kelmarsh, Oxendon, Marston Trussell and Hazelbech were taught at the school for free.
The School Master had to be single, a graduate of Oxford or Cambridge and a member of the Church of England.
The Hospital for twelve men occupied two wings (I wonder what **Sir George** had against women!) The girls had to wait until 1862 for a school.

Close by on the Green is a War Memorial erected in 1921 with a semi circular seat.

I was very impressed with the large Baptist chapel reputed to be one of the most historic of its kind in the country with services first held in 1752 although there is evidence of a Baptist chapel in Clipston in 1718.
Most of the present building was erected in 1803 with the grand façade added in 1864.
Doors have now been added to provide access to the ground floor but I was interested to see that the stairs up to the balcony are open to the elements.

It is said that the **Rev William Carey** often visited Clipston and had meetings there to discuss the formation of the Baptist Missionary Society.

A plaque outside the church indicates that **Catherine Short** who, with her sister **Dorothy**, went to India in 1793 with **William Carey**, worshipped in the chapel for the last twenty years of her life until her death in 1827.

Also commemorated is *Thomas Jarman* a well known composer of religious music who is buried in the Baptist burial ground. His best known and much loved tune is named *'Lyngham'* which is generally used for that great voice raising hymn:-

'Oh for a thousand tongues to sing'.

The church of **ALL SAINTS** with its low broach spire was probably started during the Norman period but little remains of that era except two doorways, one being the entrance door, the other being the entrance into the south chapel and a font which was found in the churchyard in 1885 when restoration was taking place. It was subsequently taken back inside where it now remains resulting in the church now having two fonts.

They must have had a problem here with the congregation in 1794 as records show that *Nathaniel Mott* was employed as Verger to carry a white wand during services to keep people awake and also to keep the Sunday school children in order.

A tombstone which interested me was that of *Arthur Arnold Stanley Wartnaby,* Commander RN, born in 1898.
He served in HMS Tiger in the First World War and HMS Fiona in the Second World War but was accidentally killed in January 1955.

The church clock was donated in 1887 by a
Mrs Hanbury to commemorate *Queen Victoria's* Jubilee.
A crowd gathered to witness the blessing by the Bishop when the clock struck twelve.
For some reason it failed to perform so the Clerk had to climb the tower and strike the tenor bell twelve times with a hammer.

The old white cottage opposite the church is named **Prince Rupert's** cottage - I wonder – is he reputed to have stayed there prior to the nearby Battle of Naseby.

There are still two public houses, The Red Lion near the attractive triangular Green and The Bull's Head on the Harborough Road.
When looking for a pub lunch on a cold January morning I chose the attractive looking Bull's Head which claims to be a 17th century Inn although records appear to show that it had not been in continuous use as a public house.
It now has some accommodation in a stable block to the rear of the premises.

Clipston and Oxendon station were served by a rail service between 1859 and 1960 on the Northampton to Market Harborough line but passenger numbers were never very high.
The track way is now part of the Brampton Valley Way for walkers and cyclists.

The present parish includes the two deserted settlements of Calme and Nobold.

CALME

I cannot find Calme specifically mentioned in the Domesday Book of 1086 but it is thought to have been the manor held by the Abbey of St Edmundsbury which had five households.

The only other information I have been able to glean is that the site was probably in the area of Twantry Farm on the gated road to Marston Trussell where a skeleton and a spear thought to be from the 15th century was dug up in the 19th century. I am unaware of the reason for depopulation of the area.

NOBOLD

Little is known of the history of this now deserted village whose name does not appear in records until about 1284 when there were thirty five virgates of land divided between three manors.
It is thought to have been located about one mile west of Clipston with which it was taxed and to have survived until land enclosures in 1776.

Human skulls have been found in the area to the west of Clipston suggesting the existence of a church and graveyard but I have found no supporting evidence.

CLOPTON

Four miles east of Thrapston
Population: 1801 – 88   2001 - 134

DOMESDAY BOOK
CLOTONE/DOTONE
This village is sometimes called Clapton
but Clopton is nearer to the original spelling recorded in about 960AD which meant Hill Farm.

The Roman road between Godmanchester and Leicester entered the County just to the south of the village and the line of it is now a short stretch of modern road marking the Clopton/Titchmarsh parish boundary.

At the time of the Domesday Book there were two manors with twenty eight households and a Knight presumably attached to the Abbey of Peterborough one of the land owners.

The village which lies close to the Huntingdon border on the minor B662 road certainly appears to have shrunk over the centuries particularly in the area around the church immediately north of which are a large area of earthworks indicating the presence of earlier buildings.

Just off the Thrapston to Oundle road is Woodside Pet Hotel which offers 'superior accommodation' to cats and dogs but as far as the villagers are concerned there is no longer a shop, post office, chapel, school or public house.

A mill was mentioned here in 1397 and there were also brickworks in the parish but these like almost everything else apart from the church and a few other buildings have long gone.

The former Church of England Primary school is home to World Mandate Ministries and is used to run ministry schools and courses. The movement was founded in 2001 by the **Rev Elaine Roberts** an ordained evangelist with the Elim Pentecostal church together with her husband **Peter**.
Residential accommodation is available for students and church retreats.

The church of **ST PETER** with a saddleback roof on the west tower was rebuilt in 1863 by **Richard Armstrong** in late 13th century style after years of decay and a fire.
The upper part of the north aisle is the burial place of the **Dudley** family who for many years from 1390 owned **Clopton Manor**.

A member of the **Dudley** family is said to have murdered **Richard de Hazelbeere** because of a dispute over the rightful ownership of the Manor. **Dudley's** ghost - known as '**Skulking Dudley**' – a hunched, ungainly figure is said to have made frequent visits to the scene of the crime until his spirit was put to rest, so it is said, by the Bishop of Peterborough in 1905.

The old Manor was demolished and the current stone building built in the neo classical style dates from 1907.
At the north end of the Manor is the Grade II listed **King John House** which was originally the stables of the former Clopton House.

The wide roads around the village were the result of road widening in the 1980's as a result of siting Cruise Missiles at Molesworth two miles to the south east.

Violets

COGENHOE

Five miles east of Northampton
Population: 1801 – 184   2001 – 1439 (including Whiston)

DOMESDAY BOOK
CUGENHO
The unusual name appears to come from
'cucken' - to spy and 'hoh' - hill.

Pronounced locally as 'Cooknoe,' the village is situated on a hill overlooking the Nene Valley and must once have been an excellent look-out point.

There is considerable evidence that people have lived in this area for centuries.
One of the earliest settlements was to the east of the village and these were followed by the Celts and then the Romans who had a corn drying mill and later the Saxons.
Finds have included skeletons, iron and lead objects, coins, pottery and building stone.

A mill rendering thirteen shillings per annum is mentioned in the Domesday Book.
After the Norman Conquest the village was moved further up the hillside.
The area around the old mill site on the River Nene is an excellent location for country walks, fishing, bird watching and boating. There are today a number of residential caravans and chalets so it becomes quite a busy place in the summer.

Iron ore was mined in the area during the mid 19th century but the company was closed in 1888.
The area has been turned into a very pleasant Pocket Park.
Further employment in the form of shoe making followed although the factory closed in the late 1940's. In the 1950's a major employer was *York's* coaches but they were taken over by *Bowen's* coaches leaving only a small presence in the village.
Nowadays this is very much a commuter village with little of interest in the long Main Street except for the village sign featuring the church and plaques commemorating past industries, farming, shoe making, brick making and coach travel on its square base.

Old School & War Memorial : Cogenhoe.

In my opinion the most attractive part is the area around the Green just off the Main Street where there are a number of older properties including the Elizabethan Rectory and the parish church.

The building of the present church of **ST PETER** started about 1225 and was completed by 1280 in a mixture of ironstone and limestone although the tall Perpendicular style west tower was built towards the end of the 14th century.

An effigy of a cross legged Crusader is thought to be *Nicholas de Cogenhoe* who is credited with building the present church.
He was Lord of the Manor and at one time a Knight of the garrison of Northampton Castle.

The church which claims to hold the earliest population censuses in England was extensively restored in 1869-70 when the north chapel was rebuilt on its original foundations, the chancel and aisles were re-roofed and a new East window was put in the chancel.
A new heating system, modern altar and comfortable chairs have been installed recently.

There is still a Primary school, a public house - The Royal Oak, a Working Men's club, a shop and post office.

Unfortunately the small Baptist chapel in the Main Street closed in April 2010 due to falling attendances.

COLD ASHBY

Eight miles south west of Market Harborough
Population: 1801 – 379   2001 - 255

DOMESDAY BOOK
ESSEBI

At the time of the Domesday Book it was simply called Essebi - ash tree by a village or homestead, but once again the name was added to in order to avoid confusion with other settlements with the same name including a number in Northamptonshire. Did the height above sea level give rise to the word 'cold' appearing?

At the time of the Domesday Book Ashby had sixteen households and four manors, two of which were held by **William of Keynes** of the tenant in chief the **Count of Mortain** having previously been held by **Aethelgifu the widow**.

The main manor was held both before and after the Norman Conquest by the Abbey of St Mary in Coventry but was given to the Cistercian Abbey of Pipewell when that was founded in 1142 and remained in their hands throughout much of the medieval period. The monastic farm is thought to have been of considerable size.

When **Bridges** wrote his famous history of the County in 1720 he said that at that time the building still stood *'in the fields'* (possibly Grange Field).

Situated just off the B5199 Northampton to Welford road near the Leicestershire border and close to Junction 1 of the main A14 this is thought to be the highest village in Northamptonshire, situated at seven hundred feet above sea level on the crest of some hills although both Badby and Staverton near Daventry make similar claims.

One feature which caught my eye was a small well restored in 1991. I have no doubt that the water is unfit for human consumption but it provides a suitable environment for a number of goldfish.

Victorian Lych gate : Cold Ashby.

Mill House stands on the site of an old steam mill. The engine is thought to have been installed at the east end of the building and was still there at the beginning of the 20th century.

From Honey Hill a mile away there are on a good day some excellent views over Warwickshire and Leicestershire.

The modest Grade II listed church of **ST DENYS** is approached through a grand Victorian lych gate dated 1883 in fine white and red Ancaster stone by **John Hanley** of Chester.
The lych gate was restored in 2000.

The north doorway is possibly Norman and let into the doorway of the vestry are carved stones from what was once thought to be a Saxon arch.
The tower was added in the 15th century.
There are no aisles but the nave does have a clerestory.

One of its bells is inscribed 1317 and is thought to be one of the oldest in the County and to have come from Sulby Abbey.

The village contains an assortment of houses few of which have any appeal for me.

I did however like the little Victorian school in the centre of the village which has been converted for residential use.

Although there is no longer a village school there is a public house - The Black Horse and on the Stanford road is the twenty seven hole Cold Ashby Golf Club set in two hundred acres which is a popular venue for weddings and parties.

In winter the golf course is transformed into a winter fun park and two portable ski lifts are set up so the hilly terrain can be used to its full advantage.

TRIGONOMETRICAL STATION

The stations are typically concrete posts set up on high ground.

Sometimes known as triangulation stations, trig beacons, trig points, trig stations or simply trig - they are fixed points from which to take readings leading to a survey of the area by means of a theodolite or reflector.

The 11,678 such stations are located so as to provide a network of triangulation.

The first observations for the retriangulation of Great Britain were made at the Trigonometrical Station here by *Sergeant T F Mullinger* of the Royal Engineers on the 18th April 1936.

The deserted medieval settlement of Elkington lay to the west of the village.

ELKINGTON

DOMESDAY BOOK
ELTETONE/ETENDONE
*The name is thought to derive from the name of a local leader **Elta** followed by 'ton' - a hill or fortress.*

Elkington is referred to in the Domesday Book as part of one of the four manors of Cold Ashby.
In 1066 it was held by *Leofric* and in 1086 by *Alfred of Watford* of *Geoffrey de la Guerche*.
The family name of Elkington is thought to have originated from this settlement.

The whole village and church was given to Pipewell Abbey in about 1142 and the Poll Tax of 1377 showed there to be thirty nine taxpayers but by 1412 it was reported that pestilence had reduced the population to three or four Pipewell Abbey servitors.
There does not appear to be any records of a settlement here after 1420.

All arable land had been converted to pasture by the time of the Dissolution after which the land was divided up.
Only one house is thought to have survived at the Dissolution but it would appear from old records that the settlement then increased in size for a time before finally becoming deserted.
It is reported that in 1547, four thousand sheep grazed here.
Today all that is left is little more than a few farm buildings although I am informed that outlines of the settlement can be seen from the air close to Bridge 28 on the Leicester Section of the Grand Union Canal.

The Jurassic Way passes through the settlement.

Trigonometrical Station: Cold Ashby

Cold Higham

Four miles north west of Towcester
Population 1801 – 271   2001 - 289

DOMESDAY BOOK
HECHAM

The name is a corruption of 'heah' – high and 'ham' - homestead. As the village stands on high ground it is thought that this gave rise to the adjective element (cold) as in Cold Ashby.

Two manors are recorded in the Domesday Book each having a priest, which I find a little surprising and a total of nineteen households.

The village is to be found on the old Banbury Lane just a stone's throw from the busy A5 (old Roman Watling Street).

The church of **ST LUKE** with its comparatively large churchyard for the size of the village has a 13th century west tower with a splendid saddleback roof thought to be the original.
There is Norman work in the nave.

The tower arch was originally narrower than it is now as the arch is too wide for the imposts.
In the south chapel lies a 14th century carving of a cross legged Knight wearing plate armour said to be *Sir John de Patteshull*, Lord of the Manor who died in 1350.

Apart from the church there is little else of note but I do like the lovely little well maintained village hall near the church which was the local school until its closure in 1969.

The Old School : Cold Higham

In this part of South Northamptonshire are found the sites of a number of lost or shrunken settlements - many ending with the suffix 'cote', one of which - Potcote - is located in the parish.
I can find no direct reference to the three settlements listed below in the Domesday Book so presumably they were taxed with Cold Higham or elsewhere if they existed before 1066.

FOSTERS BOOTH

The name is thought to derive from the hut or booth of a forester - the area being part of the ancient royal forest of Whittlewood.

I have included this small settlement with a few properties either side of the Watling Street (A5) under Cold Higham although that part to the east of the Watling Street actually lies within the parish of Pattishall.

GRIMSCOTE

From historical records it would seem that Grimscote has had the largest centre of population in the parish at least since the 17th century and that it was once even larger than it is today.
It does not appear to have had a church but has a chapel which has now been converted into a private house although it has undergone considerable alteration.
If you are interested to see a medieval hollow road this is the place to go.
I did not expect to find a rare Victorian letter box in situ.

POTCOTE

On modern maps the now very small settlement of Potcote approached from Cold Higham and Potcote Farm approached from Greens Norton lie some distance apart - the former in the parish of Cold Higham and the latter in Greens Norton.
The manor and most of the land came to the *Greene* family of Greens Norton before 1428 and they destroyed four houses, enclosed 304 acres of the land and expelled thirty people in 1499.
In 1551 lands here and nearby were grazed by 2,000 sheep owned by *John Hickling.*

COLLINGTREE

Four miles south of Northampton
Population: 1802-153   2001-963

DOMESDAY BOOK
COLENTREV
*Some people will tell you that the Domesday name simply means ' the place of **Columbus**' but I have also read that the name derives from a Saxon tribal leader **Cola** and the Saxon word for tree - 'treow'. If this is true the tree was maybe a religious site or place of meeting.*

This village just off the A508 has a few older properties near the church but otherwise has proved popular for modern development by virtue of its close proximity to Junction 15 of the M1 London to Leeds motorway.

Most of the older properties were once thatched but the only thatch left is on the village public house - The Wooden Walls of Old England - which was once called 'The Ship' and has been serving the village since 1615.

Of much more recent origin is the Hilton Hotel just outside the village which always appears to be very busy.

There is no longer a village shop, post office or library although the library sign opposite the pub is still in situ and the Methodist chapel erected in 1820 is now a private residence.

The church which dates from the late Norman period is dedicated to **ST COLUMBA** who founded a monastery on the Isle of Iona just off the Scottish Isle of Mull.
It has a tall medieval tower but only one aisle as the north aisle was demolished in 1808 as it was in a poor state of repair.
The nave arches on the north side have been filled in except for the slim windows making a rather unusual interior.

The church is the proud owner of three ancient *Books of Homilies* dated 1551, 1567 and 1623.

In the chancel are stained glass windows in memory of *Pickering Phipps* (a brewing magnate) and his family and to the *Sears* family (boot and shoe manufacturers) who used to live in the now demolished Manor House and are buried in the churchyard.

Opposite the church is the old village school dated 1861 but the present generation of children have the benefit of a new school close by.

There was drama in the village on 9th April 1941 when the Luftwaffe dropped a line of nine bombs across the village from the A508 (now the A45) to alongside Maple Farm.
Fortunately they all fell on open ground and none exploded.

Wooden Walls of Old England: Collingtree

COLLYWESTON

Four miles south west of Stamford
Population: 1801 – 294   2001 – 425

DOMESDAY BOOK
WESTONE

I was interested to discover that 'colly' is a term implying 'awry', out of square or crooked and can be traced to Elizabethan times when Westone was popular with the royals.
Was it to do with the curve of the Collyweston slate roofs?
It also became associated with deliberately untidy dress - 'all collyweston'.
Another suggested derivation is that it was originally Colyn Weston - Colyn being the French abbreviation of
***Nicolas** when **Nicolas de Segrave** was Lord of the Manor.*

This attractive village on the main A43 Stamford to Kettering road is situated in a prominent position overlooking the River Welland.

Most of the stone built houses stand on a downward slope leading to the valley below and the whole of the village to the west side of the main road is a Conservation area.

A Roman Sanctuary about one and three quarter miles south of the village which seems to have been occupied between the 1st to the 4th centuries was excavated in 1954.
Roman pottery and roof tiles have been found elsewhere.

Ralph de Limesy held the manor of the King in 1086 - the only manor I can find him holding in the County.
There was a mill rendering twenty shillings per annum, twenty two households, twelve acres of meadow and some valuable woodland.

To the west of New Road is the site of the old Manor also known as the Palace which was occupied in the 15th century by **Ralph Cromwell**, Lord Treasurer to **King Henry VI** and later by **Lady Margaret Beaufort**, mother of **Henry VII**.

It was given to **Anne Boleyn** by **Henry VIII** and passed down to the **Tryon** family.

Collyweston

The Manor House was demolished in 1640 and all that remains are the terraces, fishponds and a barn with an attached dovecote dated 1578.
A 17th/18th century high stone wall with a very handsome 18th century stone sundial encloses the site.

The trees in the grounds, which are open to the public, are now subject to a Preservation Order and much of the area around is owned by the Burghley Estate Trust.
The present Manor is dated 1696.

Dominating the village is the fine embattled west tower of the church of **ST ANDREW** which was rebuilt about 1440 on the instructions of *Lord Ralph Cromwell.*

The impressive tower which surprisingly only houses two bells is built of Barnack stone with clasping buttresses and four big crocketed pinnacles - very similar to that at nearby Easton on the Hill. It has unfortunately been struck by lightning twice - in 1931 and again in 1960.
The pews with their poppy heads and the choir stalls with their pelicans are obviously well maintained but the church is in urgent need of repair.
A sad sight was the choir vestry or Lady Chapel, formerly the *Tryon* chapel - where instead of memorials and monuments I saw a much neglected area.

The church clock is thought to have been removed from the old Palace when it was demolished.

An unusual reminder of the past is at the old forge on the main road where there is an oversized horseshoe displayed on the gable end of the former blacksmith's shop.

The village school has closed as have some of the public houses including The Engine, next door to the church, and The Blue Bell opposite.
Both The Engine and The Blue Bell still have the frame work of the old pub sign but now without its illustrated name board.

Next to the old Engine public house is a house with a sundial bearing the cryptic wording -
'I Ray for No Man'
(possibly means that the sun shines irrespective of man)

One public house that still seems to do good trade is The Collyweston Slater Bar and Restaurant on the main road.

I was pleased to see that a community shop has recently opened in the village with a part-time manager supported by volunteers.
It seemed to be well supported on my recent visit.
Two long distance footpaths - the **Jurassic Way** and the **Hereward Way** pass through the village to the north.

COLLYWESTON SLATE

Collyweston is known principally for its limestone slate for roofing which has been quarried in the area since Roman times and is very much in evidence around the villages in this part of the County today.
Once *'anybody who was anyone'* in Collyweston rented a strip of ground, quarried it in winter and farmed it in summer. There are said to be the sites of thirty six old quarries around the village.

Blocks of limestone were dug out of the ground in the winter months and were laid out with the bedding planes vertical and kept watered to prevent them drying out.
They were then split into thin layers with a cliving hammer by hand, often helped by frost action.

Extensive use of the slate was made locally but it can also be seen at London Guildhall, Nuffield College, Oxford and several Cambridge colleges and even a mansion on Long Island in New York. 14,000 slates are said to have been supplied to Rockingham Castle in the 14th century.
Large scale production ended in 1967.
The reason, so I was informed, is that we no longer get the extreme frosts and attempts to split the stone by artificial means have not succeeded.

A limited amount of slate is produced by two small firms primarily for repairs.

Church of St Andrew: Collyweston

CORBY

Six miles north of Kettering
Population: 1801 – 611   2001 - 53174

DOMESDAY BOOK
CORBEI/CORBI

Corby may be a new town but the name goes back more than a thousand years to the time of the Viking invasions.
*Originally it was **Kjori's** Farmstead - **Kjori** being a Danish tribal leader.*

Corby's Danish heritage has been recognised in the naming of one of the towns largest modern estates - Danesholme.
The settlement appears to have started life as a little hamlet in the midst of Rockingham Forest.
Its centre was probably where the old town lies near **The Jamb.**
Unfortunately many of the older properties in this area were demolished after 1958.
This is a far cry from the busy town of today.

When ***William the Conqueror*** decided to carry out his land survey in 1086 it was recorded that in the royal manor of Corby *'many things are wanting.'*

The population of Corby has grown quite dramatically since 1801 when the population was 611.
Corby was designated a new town in 1950 and new estates grew up all over the town to meet the influx of workers. Today the population stands at well over 55,000 and is still rising.

The beginning of industrialisation came with the handloom weaving trade, followed closely by the opening of brickworks in the early 19th century.

The Romans were aware of the iron ore deposits almost two thousand years earlier as various finds indicate that they had ironworks during their stay in the area.

The presence of ironworks is mentioned in the Domesday Book but it was not until the 1850's and the building of the railway that the extent of the deposits in this region were realised.

This re-discovery resulted in the establishment of the Lloyds Ironstone Company in the 1880's which became Stewarts and Lloyds in 1920 but it was not until 1933 that work began to tap resources under the surface.

Originally iron ore was smelted in the West Midlands and the first blast furnace did not appear in Corby until 1910.

During the depression in the 1930's Corby was the site of one of the biggest iron and steel making complexes in the world and this attracted a large force of workers mainly from Scotland.
Even today Corby still retains a strong Scottish tradition.
Over 4000 men worked for Stewarts and Lloyds during the Second World War.

In spite of the steel industry's importance during the war years only a few bombs were dropped by solitary planes and there were no casualties.

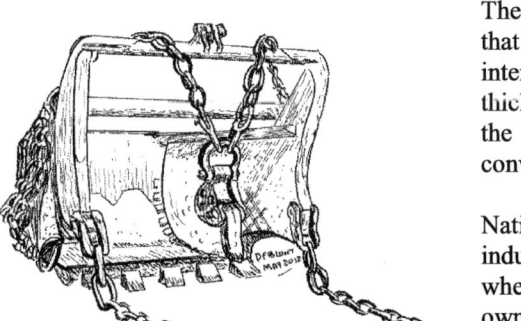

Dragline

The reason is thought to be that oil and latex were intentionally burnt to create thick black clouds that hid the glowing Bessemer converter furnaces.

Nationalisation of the industry took place in 1945 when it came under the ownership of British Steel.

The Works began closure in the 1980's resulting in Corby having to find alternative employment for thousands of steel workers.

Corby started to look like a ghost town, however in recent years a considerable number of new and diverse companies have made their home in the town partly with help from the European Economic Community.

The town lost its railway station on the Leeds to London line in 1966 but a new railway station opened in early 2009 connecting Corby once again with London and proves to be very popular.

Henry de Braybrooke (Lord of the Manor) was granted the right to hold two fairs by *Henry II* in 1226. The fairs have disappeared but the customs are retained. A bizarre event in Corby happens every twenty years - the next occasion being in 2020. It stems from a Charter granted to Corby by *Queen Elizabeth I* in 1585 and contained six valuable rights to landowners at that time.
The *Queen* is said to have granted the Charter in appreciation for being rescued by villagers when she became lost whilst hunting with a party in Rockingham Forest.
A more likely explanation is that money was paid to the *Queen* in return for the Charter which is now incorporated in the Pole Fair.
The fair starts with the reading of the Charter at three main entrances to the town, Church Street, The White Hart and The Jamb, followed by a carnival.
Anyone failing to pay a toll is carted away to the stocks. The most recent Fair held on 6 May 2002 attracted great crowds from miles around.

Another popular attraction is the Highland Gathering when Pipe Bands from far and wide, including Corby itself celebrate the town's Scottish roots. The bands play in competition during the day which concludes with a march past of the massed pipers. The fairground provides plenty of fun for the children.

In 2012 the centre of the town is undergoing complete transformation.
Already in place and well over budget, is a large glass building by the name of 'The Cube' which houses a new library and theatre.

Some of the original public houses still stand including The Cardigan Arms, the Nags Head and The White Hart.

The Knights Lodge public house and restaurant which existed as a Foresters Lodge in 1585 is still a popular venue although said to be haunted.

The church of **ST JOHN** the **BAPTIST** (previously *St Peters*) on the edge of the old village dates back to the early part of the 13th century although the broach spire is of the 14th century. Inside are fragments of medieval glass and a 12th century font with dogtooth pattern.

In many instances there appears to be no logical reason for a change of name but in this case it was changed to avoid a clash of Patronal Feast Days with *St Peters* at nearby Deene - the Rector had been responsible for both churches.

The church was struck by lightning in 1801 and the spire crashed through the nave. It took several years before restoration could take place

To meet the demands of a growing population a number of new churches have been built and the town now has a modern shopping centre with pedestrianised areas, civic centre, small hospital, theatre, swimming pool and a variety of schools and colleges for all ages.

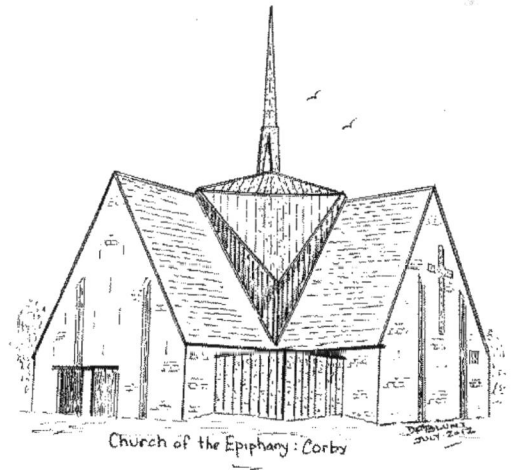
Church of the Epiphany : Corby

COSGROVE

Eight miles south east of Towcester
Population: 1801-575   2001 - 480

DOMESDAY BOOK
COVESGRAVE
It was originally called Covesgrave
a village near a clearing.

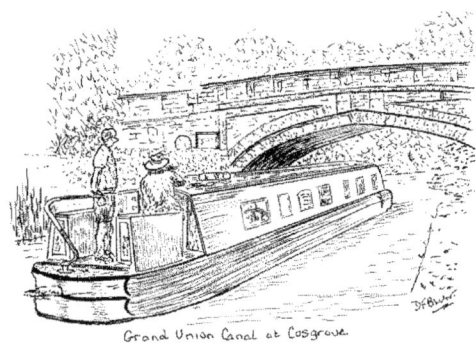
Grand Union Canal at Cosgrove

Four manors are recorded in the Domesday Book.
In total there were twenty five households,
'a Frenchman' (what the significance is I have no idea) and a priest.
The two mills rendered thirteen shillings and eight pence per annum respectively.

Situated in the south of the County bounded by the Rivers Ouse and Tove, settlers have been attracted here since Roman times.

The village was once set amongst the trees of Whittlewood Forest although you would not know it from the landscape today.

Although only a few miles from the sprawling new town of Milton Keynes, Cosgrove retains some of its old English village charm.
This may be attributed to the absence of a through road and its location on the River Ouse and the Grand Union Canal.

The river and the canal certainly attract many visitors and provide for some good walking, bird watching and relaxation opportunities.

I have enjoyed many a walk in this area and on one occasion remember being accompanied by a large number of Red Admiral butterflies as I strolled along the canal bank.

This is an area I always enjoy visiting as I am fascinated by canals and its architecture and activities.

One interesting feature is the 'Cattle Creep' a horseshoe shaped culvert where the footpath passes under the canal near The Barley Mow Inn.

This was originally constructed so that cattle could transfer from field to field.
Today it maintains communication between the two parts of the village either side of the canal.

Two canal bridges are also of interest.
One is the historic 101 foot long iron trunk aqueduct which was built in 1811 to join the two halves of the Braunston to Brentford canal where they had to cross the River Ouse.
It is still in use today and one gets an unusual feeling when walking across on the tow path with a canal boat alongside.
To celebrate its bi-centenary the bridge was given a £300,000 birthday makeover and repainted in its original colours.
The red wheel plaque also commemorates the site as one of historical interest.

The other bridge with particular appeal is **'Solomon's Bridge'** (Bridge No 65) in the Gothic style built in the 1790's at the insistence of local landowners - the ***Biggins*** family.
It is one of only two ornamental bridges over the Grand Union Canal and is very charming.

Parts of the aisleless church of **ST PETER** and **ST PAUL** are over a thousand years old but it was subject to considerable restoration in the 19th century.

The attractive tower with a gilded copper weathercock and an elegant round copper faced clock stands high above the houses at the top end of the village.

The 15th century nave has wavy oak roof timbers which were discovered as recently as the 1930's when old plasterwork was removed.

Walkers on the Grafton Way, an eleven and a half mile footpath between Cosgrove and Greens Norton (opened in 1975) are actually directed through the churchyard.

Near the church is **Cosgrove Hall** built in the early 18th century on the site of an earlier house and once owned by the *Furtho* family.

The Hall is not open to the public and was formerly the headquarters of a company selling English reproduction furniture
At the entrance are some very dilapidated gates and what was once a charming 'L' shaped black and white thatched cottage rapidly falling into ruin and now a very sorry sight.

South east of the Hall and church there were many finds during the construction of the canal including an urn of silver coins.
Excavations in the area in the 1950's and 1960's have revealed a well preserved bath house, the main buildings of a Roman villa and a temple.

One building of particular appeal is **Cosgrove Priory** which is situated along a private lane just to the north of the village.
It was built in the 17th century by the *Rigby* family on the site of a medieval Manor House and was once the home of *Admiral Robert Moorsom* who was in charge of HMS Revenge, was wounded at the Battle of Trafalgar and carried the great banner at *Lord Nelson's* funeral.

There is a memorial plaque to *Admiral Moorsom* and his wife in Cosgrove church where they are both buried.

When I last visited, the Priory was the UK Headquarters of the Pericom Group an IT Company.

At one time there was a water mill close by but it was demolished in the mid 20th century.
Today the area is said to be haunted at full moon by the miller's daughter who threw herself into the mill race and drowned when her lover, a local shepherd, was falsely accused of sheep stealing and was deported to Australia.

In a field behind the old National school and surrounded by iron railings is *St Vincent's Well*, one of the genuine Holy Wells, safeguarded by Act of Parliament and said to have great healing properties.

The village still has one public house, The Barley Mow, a village hall and a school but the shop closed some time ago although the villagers could, in an emergency, use the shop at the nearby Leisure Park.

COSGROVE LODGE PARK LEISURE CENTRE

The huge sand and gravel pits used for various road and rail projects resulted in the establishment of the popular Cosgrove Lodge Leisure Park, this being one of the largest inland caravan and leisure parks in England.

It is set in 180 acres of beautiful parkland featuring twelve lakes and two rivers and is open daily between March and October.
The Grand Union Canal embankment runs along one side of the park.
Facilities include Holiday Homes and exclusive Lodges with their own private fishing platform, space for touring vans, water skiing, outdoor heated swimming pool, a lakeside café and shop.

COTTERSTOCK

One and a half miles north east of Oundle
Population: 1801 – 136   2001 - 149

DOMESDAY BOOK
CODESTOCHE

There are a number of plausible explanations for the derivation of the name. Could it derive from the Saxon words 'cother' - assembly and 'stoc' - place? i.e. a settlement of public gatherings

Cotterstock's history reaches back to Roman times. In the summer of 1736 a Roman villa with a large mosaic floor was discovered during ploughing north west of the village together with pottery, coins, bones and building material. Another mosaic and some pavements were discovered close by in 1798.
They are now scheduled as Ancient Sites.

When the Domesday Book was written the three hide manor was held by three Knights of the Abbot of Peterborough Abbey.

This small village is peaceful and quiet and seemingly off the beaten track although it is quite close to the busy A605 to Peterborough.
There is a delightful walk along either side of the River Nene to Oundle.

What is remarkable about Cotterstock is that it was once the seat of one of the largest, if not the largest, College of private foundation of a charity nature throughout the kingdom.

It was founded in 1338 by *John Gifford*, Rector and Canon of York for a Provost, twelve Chaplains and two Clerks who said daily mass for the King and Queen, their children and the good estate of the founder and his brother.

John Gifford became very powerful and was Steward to *Queen Isabella* and then the Kings Clerk. He died of the plague in 1349.

Unfortunately the College suffered as a result of the Dissolution and all that remains is the superb tall chancel and the ornate three seat sedilia of the 12th century church of **ST ANDREW** which stands proudly on the hillside overlooking the River Nene.
The west tower features a statue of the Patron Saint above the door. The elaborate 15th century porch has crenellations and carved beasts.
Also look out for the gargoyle with its mouth being held open by a hand – it looks as if toothache might be the problem!
Inside there are more carvings.

Under a carpet in the chancel is a fine monumental brass to *Robert Winteringham* who was Provost of the College between 1365-1398.
The church was heavily restored in the 1870's when plaster was stripped off the internal walls.

The mill built during the 19th century was once a wharf serving the town of Oundle, sadly it was destroyed by fire in 1968 but has undergone rebuilding and is now a private dwelling.
I was surprised to find no mention in the Domesday Book of a mill here.

Another interesting and charming building is **Cotterstock Hall** which was originally built in the early 17th century although it was altered in 1658 by *John Norden.*
It is said that *John Dryden* was a frequent visitor and whilst in residence wrote his Fables.
The Hall was used for the 2012 horror film, *'The Woman in Black.'*
Filming took place over three days in 2010 but because the building is kept in such good order by the current owner they had to adorn the lawns with masses of weeds and place ivy up the walls.
The set was then recreated at Pinewood Studios.

The village cross has had various locations but has stood on its present position at the end of the road leading to the church since 1897 but there is no school, shop or public house.

Behind the Green is Dovecote House the former Manor House with a date stone of 1722 - named after its early 19th century dovecote.

COTTESBROOKE

Eight miles north west of Northampton
Population: 1801 – 290   2001 - 144

DOMESDAY BOOK
CODESBROC/COTESBROC
*In my opinion the most obvious derivation of the name is from the
Saxon 'cot' - cottage and 'broc' - brook or stream - 'cottage by the stream'.*

Two manors are recorded in the Domesday Book with twenty two households, a priest and a mill rendering twelve pence per annum

In the northwest corner of the parish is what is said to be the site of a cell of Premonstratensian (White) Canons founded in about 1150 by
St Norbert of Laon, France.
The order lasted until the Dissolution in the 16th century.
However some believe this to be not the site of a monastic house but rather a grange or farmstead attached to **Sulby Abbey** as the land was given to that Abbey by **Wm de Buttivilla** about 1150.
In any event there is in the area a *'Monks Well'* in a field sometimes called *'St Norberts'*.

The layout of the village was altered about the middle of the 18th century when the area around the Hall was imparked and landscaped.
Today Cottesbrooke is a delightful little Estate village with some lovely old world properties and lies somewhat off the beaten track which helps to maintain its tranquillity.

In a well kept churchyard with some fine cedar trees stands **ALL SAINTS** church which dates from about 1220 and was a long cruciform church although the north transept has been pulled down.
Its 18th century furnishings include a complete set of box pews, some of which are said to have come from Brixworth workhouse, a three decker Georgian pulpit with a canopy rising to the roof and a raised family pew with its own fire grate.
Considerable restoration took place in the mid 20th century.

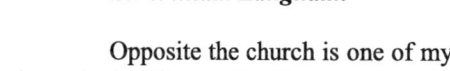

Free Standing Urn
Cottesbrooke Church

For safe keeping church plate and an 18th century font and cover are kept at **Cottesbrooke Hall** and may be viewed by appointment.

There are a large number of monuments including one to **John Rede** who died in 1604 featuring ten kneeling infants and also to the **Langham** family who once owned the Hall. Some destruction took place on the memorials when **Cromwell's** army was based in the area at the time of the Battle of Naseby.
Cannon balls now in Northampton Museum were found in surrounding fields.
In the body of the church are a number of memorials by the fashionable late Georgian sculptor **John Bacon.**
The largest is the free standing urn erected in 1851 after the death of **Sir William Langham.**

Opposite the church is one of my favourite buildings - The Grange.
It is a grand old edifice with a fine facade and four bold stacks each with three chimneys.

Near the entrance to **Cottesbrooke Hall** is an old Victorian post box set in the wall.
This was eventually restored after local protests about its replacement by a modern box.
It is good to know that the voice of the people is still heard and acted upon sometimes.

The Langham Hospital and school on the road to Brixworth was built in 1651.
I remember doing election duty there one year and it seemed like a place where time stood still and everyone knew everyone else.
The school has now closed and there is no shop or public house.

Langhams
of Cottesbrooke

Cottesbrooke Hall

Cottesbrooke Hall and the Langham family

John Langham who had made his fortune as a London turkey merchant came from Guilsborough and bought Cottesbrooke from the Saunders family in 1635. He sat in Parliament from 1654 until 1660 when he was created a Baronet. This did not prevent him from being imprisoned in the Tower on two occasions for refusing to publish an act for the abolition of the Monarchy. A number of his descendants became Members of Parliament.

The Hall was designed by Francis Smith of Warwick for the 4th Baronet, Sir John and was built between 1702-1712 with the main vista aligned with the ancient Saxon tower of Brixworth church in the distance. Later additions by Robert Mitchell included bow windows in the Adam manner.
It is an architecturally magnificent seven bay Queen Anne House standing in extensive parkland with a Georgian bridge and is reputed to be the pattern for Jane Austen's 'Mansfield Park'.
The Woolavington collection of sporting pictures including paintings by Stubbs, Ben Marshall and many other artists are among the finest of its type in Europe.
The family had a town house in London which has given its name to a London district and the Langham Hotel now stands on the site of Langham House which was built by the 10th Baronet.

During the tenure of Mr Herbert Hay Langham the Hall was visited by the Empress of Austria.
It is reported that the she filled her stay at Cottesbrooke with excellent days of hunting in the company of Earl Spencer and others in the hunting fraternity.

The Grade I Listed building remained in the family until 1911 when financial worries caused Sir Herbert to sell the Estate to R.B. Brassey and the Langhams moved to County Fermanagh.
Since 1937 it has been the home of the Macdonald Buchanan family.

They employed Lord Gerald Wellesley (later the 7th Duke of Wellington) to make alterations to their home including changing the entrance from the front to the other side of the house.
The Hall, with its beautiful interior and magnificent gardens with its three hundred year old cedar trees is occasionally open to the public in the summer months.
At the end of June each year the Estate is home to a large three day plant finders fair.

Cottingham

Two miles west of Corby
Population: Cottingham 1801 - 471   2001 - 912

DOMESDAY BOOK
COTINGEHAM

There appears considerable dispute over the original meaning of the name but I am happy to accept that it simply means a farmstead (ham) of Cotta's people.

The Abbey of Peterborough held the seven hide manor in 1086 when there were forty three households, twelve acres of meadow and a mill rendering forty pence per annum.

During excavations in the 1960's evidence was found of a Roman industrial site to the north of the village. Certainly Romans passed through the area as it was on the route of the Roman road between Leicester and Godmanchester.

This is a lovely little village just off the busy A427 Market Harborough to Corby road overlooking the peaceful scenery of the Welland Valley.
Most of the older buildings are of pale ironstone.
In the Northamptonshire Best Village Competition in 2012 Cottingham was proclaimed winner of the medium village category.

An unusual structure is the large three storey brick building with a date stone of 1872 standing at the top of the hill on the Rockingham Road.
It has carved faces protruding from the front and for many years it was owned by the *Wallis* Clothing Company but like the similar factory in Brigstock is no longer in commercial use and has now been converted into three apartments.

Former Clothing Company Factory : Cottingham.

One feature of Cottingham that the visitor cannot ignore are the steep hills and half way up the steepest is the church of
ST MARY MAGDALENE built of ironstone which although dating from the 13th century was constructed mainly in the 15th century.

The present very fine tower has angled buttresses and an octagonal spire with low broaches and pinnacles.
The capitals on the top of the pillars of the north arcade have fascinating medieval carvings of ladies and knights.

Also worthy of note is the 13th century Easter Sepulchre and the rare parish chest made at Watford in Northamptonshire in about 1520.
The church was restored in 1880 when the galleries were removed and the chancel rebuilt.

The Jurassic Way - a long distance footpath through the County actually goes through Cottingham village.

There is still a Primary school between the two villages, known as Middleton cum Cottingham, a shop and post office, two public houses - The Royal George and The Spread Eagle and the fifty three bedroom Hunting Lodge Hotel which now attracts wedding parties, etc. and was once the stable block of the 17th and 18th century Manor House.

The Methodist church in Corby Road was built in the 19th century and is still in use.

COURTEENHALL

Five miles south of Northampton
Population: 1801 – 139   2001 - 88

DOMESDAY BOOK
CORTENHALE/CORTENHALO
There have been numerous spellings of the name which simply derives from 'corta's halh' - nook of land.

Courteenhall was first documented in the Domesday Book as being divided into two manors, both of which were held by
William Peverel.
One had fourteen households plus a priest but no population was given for the other.

William gave the major part of his holding to Lenton Priory on its foundation at the beginning of the 12th century and it was held by them until its Dissolution when it was incorporated in the newly created Honour of Grafton.

In 1571 *Queen Elizabeth I* leased Courteenhall to *Richard Ouseley* at a rent of thirty pounds.
He then complained about the ill repair of both the Manor House and the farm buildings.

The Estate was purchased by *Sir Samuel Jones* in 1647. He died in 1672 and his will provided for the building of a free Grammar school which today is used as the village hall.
He is remembered with an impressive marble monument in the church.
His Estate was inherited by a relative of
Sir William Wake, 3rd Baronet of Piddington.

Excavations have revealed that the old Manor House was situated in what is now a wide expanse of open parkland between **Courteenhall Hall** and the church.

In spite of being only a stone's throw from the busy junction 15 on the M1 motorway and close to Northampton the size of the population has in fact diminished over the past two hundred years as a result of emparkment.

It is now a tiny remote village at the end of a narrow lane which terminates at the church gate.

There is no longer a school, public house, shop or post office but in the main street there still stands one of the old iron water pumps.

With a history going back over nine hundred years the church of **ST PETER** and **ST PAUL** was probably built on the site of a Saxon church.

There is evidence of Norman workmanship but the present building was reconstructed in the 13th century and the embattled tower was added in the 15th century.

The visitor cannot miss the many memorials to the *Wake* family who were either buried in or near the church.

Other items which caught my eye were the open book in marble in the north wall containing the Apostles Creed and the Lord's Prayer and a small marble figure behind a glass panel in the south wall in memory of two *Wake* children who died in infancy.

Wake Family Crest.

'Watch and Pray'

Courteenhall Hall Stable Block.

Wake family

The family descended from the **Hereward** who at the time of the Norman Conquest was a prime leader in English resistance to the Normans. In 1070 he plundered Peterborough Abbey to fund his fight against the invaders.

The family originated from Lincolnshire and first came to Northamptonshire in 1265 when they inherited the manor of Blisworth. Through marrying wealthy heiresses they acquired a vast amount of land.

The **Wake** family have provided High Sheriffs since the 12th century as well as an Archbishop of Canterbury in the early 18th century plus a Major General in the British Army and an Admiral in the Navy.

Roger Wake (born 1452) married into another noble family - the **Catesbys** - and went with his father in law, **Richard Catesby** to fight for the King at the Battle of Bosworth in 1485.

The Battle did not go well for the King and **Catesby** was beheaded whereas **Roger** was imprisoned and had his lands forfeited - these were later restored by Act of Parliament. After the Battle of Bosworth the family fortunes declined and land at Collingtree, Blisworth and in Lincolnshire was sold off.

The family continued to live at Piddington and Hartwell but like their predecessors married wealthy heiresses and inherited Courteenhall by marriage in 1672, it has remained their home ever since.

About thirty generations all succeeded through the male line from father to son all of whom were Northamptonshire or Lincolnshire Squires.

The present Hall which cost just £10,000 was built in the late 18th century for **Sir William Wake, 9th** Baronet and sits in a fine parkland setting designed by **Humphrey Repton** and is protected by a 'ha ha' to stop the sheep who graze the pastureland from venturing into the gardens.

During the Second World War the **Wake** family moved into the magnificent Palladian style stable block next door and the Hall was tenanted by the St Lawrence College of Ramsgate. It then became a Church of England residential community centre but by 1953 the House was in a very bad state and was threatened with demolition. Fortunately the building was repaired and refurbished allowing the family to resume occupancy in 1953.

Joan Wake, daughter of the 12th Baronet died in 1974 and was a notable local historian and archivist who founded the Northamptonshire Record Library.

The Hall is currently the home of the 14th Baronet and his family.

For many generations the family have used the name **Hereward** (which is thought to date back to the 11th century) and in a talk at Blisworth in 2003, **Sir Hereward** is reported as saying 'My father, when a boy, used to say the Lord's Prayer thus - 'Our Father who Art in Heaven, **Hereward** be Thy Name'.

CRANFORD

ST ANDREW & ST JOHN

Four miles east of Kettering
Population: 1801 – 419   2001 - 414

DOMESDAY BOOK
CRANEFORD
*The name from the Saxon simply means
the place where cranes or herons are seen.*

As far back as the Domesday Book in 1086 two separate villages and two manors were recorded.

The manor of St Andrew appears to have been held by **Robert Daundelyns** or **Dorlands** until 1360 when it was sold to **Henry Pyel,** afterwards Archdeacon of Northampton.

The manor of St John was held by the **Bishop of Coutances** and was said *'to be waste'.*

It was not until April 1935 that they were merged into one parish but both kept separate churchwardens and church councils until 1954.

The two villages are linked by a footpath across some glorious English parkland and are to all intents and purposes one village divided by the Alledge Brook.

Until recently the main Kettering to Huntingdon road ran alongside the Green at Cranford St John but since the opening of the main A14 trunk road just a short distance away the village sees a lot less traffic.

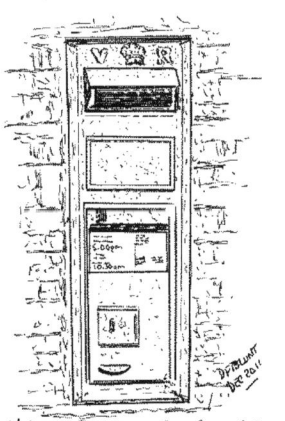

Victorian Post Box : Cranford St Andrew

Cranford Hall and the Robinson family

Sir John Robinson *(d.1680) was the son of the Archdeacon of Nottingham who made his fortune as a merchant in London.* **John** *helped to secure London for* **Charles II** *and was created a Baronet in 1660.*

The title then passed to **James** *who inherited the Estate in Cranford.*

The Grade II listed early Georgian Hall of mellow Weldon stone was built in 1720 but slightly altered in the 19th century and remains the seat of the **Robinson** *family who still live there although it is now a popular venue for short breaks, weddings, lunches, dinners, product launches and exhibitions.*

When a turnpike road (the present A604) was being constructed in the 18th century Roman coins, pottery and animal bones were found indicating a Roman settlement. Similar findings were made in the surrounding area.

ST ANDREWS church was declared redundant in 1966 but is used occasionally for services in the summer and is now in the care of the Churches Conservation Trust.

It is basically a late Norman church with 13th century west tower and 12th century north arcade.

The north transept was added in 1847 to provide a family pew for the *Robinson* family of the nearby Hall and has its own outside door and contains many family memorials.

Buried in the church is *Maud Fosbroke* who was nursemaid to *Henry VI*. The *Fosbrokes* were great landowners in the 16th century.

Their connection with Cranford ceased when their six daughters all became co-heiresses and the Manor was sold and the Estate divided up.

When I visited recently repairs were necessary on the porch as a notice indicated that the lead on the roof had been stolen - unfortunately not an unusual situation.

To the west is a circular dovecote thought to have been built in the mid 15th century.

Its outside walls were probably once whitewashed. Call at Dairy Farm, a 17th century thatched Jacobean Manor House for access.

En route to Dairy Farm is a rare Queen Victoria red pillar box set into a wall.

The public house - the thatched 18th century Woolpack has recently been closed and has been converted into a most attractive private house.

ST JOHN'S church which is still in regular use dates back to the 12th century although the tower and chancel are of slightly later date. It is notably lacking in monuments. At the beginning of the 18th century the local historian *Bridges* recorded that *'the stump of the spire was standing'* although there is no evidence of it today.

The village has been the venue for the annual Kettering Vintage Rally and Steam fair for the past twelve years. The Rally started out as celebration of the millennium and has proved more and more popular over the years.

Cranford St John has the shop, post office, Primary school and public house - The Red Lion whereas Cranford St Andrew has an excellent coffee shop in the Old Forge and the village hall.

In 1866 an attractive station was opened on the Kettering to Huntingdon line but this closed in 1956 although some buildings remain.

DOVECOTES

Cranford Dovecote

Dovecotes may have been introduced by the Romans based on the fact that pigeon rearing was common in Italy.

However as there is little firm evidence for this it seems likely that it was the Normans who first introduced the dovecote into England and as a result domesticated the rock dove from which the feral pigeon of today is descended.

For centuries doves and pigeons were a valuable source of meat, manure and feathers for mattresses and cushions.

In the Middle Ages only Manorial Lords could keep these birds so the few remaining medieval dovecotes in the County are usually connected with Manor Houses or Parsonages.

The law relaxed after about 1600 so many lesser owners had dovecotes until their use declined after the 18th century.

Dovecotes were built in a variety of shapes although most are circular and share common characteristics. All had small doors and windows to prevent shadows from frightening the birds and all had a roof opening usually covered by a glover to protect the inside from the weather.

Nesting boxes were located around the walls with a ledge for the birds to land on and to collect the eggs. In the centre of the circular dovecote was a revolving wooden pole with a ladder (called a potence) to enable people to reach the nesting boxes. Good examples of circular dovecotes can be seen at Cranford St Andrew, Denton, Furtho, Wadenhoe and Warmington which are all County Heritage Sites.

A number of others in different forms can be found around the County.

CRANSLEY - GREAT AND LITTLE

Two miles south west of Kettering
Population: 1801 – 217   2001 - 283

DOMESDAY BOOK
CRANESLEA/CRANESLEG

The derivation of the name Cransley is subject to some dispute although the 'cran' obviously comes from the Saxon word for crane and this is supported by the name of the village pub 'the Three Cranes' and the cranes which appear in a stained glass window in the church.

Only a short distance separates the two villages which are located just off the A43 between Northampton and Kettering.
Great Cransley is the older of the two although the first element was not added until Tudor times.
Today Little Cransley has been absorbed into nearby Broughton.

The Grade I listed church of **ST ANDREW** is over seven hundred years old and is well worth a visit. Records date back to 1226 when the Rector was *Ralph of Cransley*. Particularly noticeable is the large blue clock face on the north wall of the embattled west tower with its recessed spire.

I was impressed with the clerestory with its six matching windows on either side with wooden angels supporting the roof and the beautiful stained glass window known as the '*Churchill window*' which was presented to the church by the men of 384 Bombardment Group of the US Airforce who were stationed nearby.

The window has a pictorial record of six historical occasions associated with the history of Britain and America.
In the bottom right hand corner *Winston Churchill* is seen holding his trade mark cigar during his meeting with *President Roosevelt* in 1941.

The old Manor which is now known as **Cransley Hall** dates back to the 16th century although the south and east fronts date from 1708-9.
The enlargement of the Hall grounds and the erection of a small park and fishponds in the 19th century led to the closing of the old road to Broughton and the creation of the existing road.

A motte to the north west of the church (now on private land) suggests a wooden construction of a castle or something similar.

For many years Cransley Iron Works provided employment for villagers in the ironstone quarries which were served by a number of tramways to transport the stone.
These have now disappeared and there is no longer a shop or a school but the village pub - The Three Cranes still serves the village.

During the Second World War the Lord of the Manor witnessed rowdy workers fighting in the road on a Sunday which so upset his daughter that he ordered the pub to be closed on a Sunday.
This closure lasted for twenty years.

CREATON

Eight miles north west of Northampton
Population: 1801 – 421   2001 - 488

DOMESDAY BOOK
CRAPTONE/CRETONE

Owing to the different names featured in the Domesday Book there is some doubt as to the origin of the present one but a likely derivation is that the prefix relates to a personal name or an ancient Celtic word 'craig' meaning rocky hill.

Creaton with its pleasant village Green lies on top of a ridge on the B5199 to Welford and used to be in two parts Great and Little, or Magna and Parva in the Domesday Book.
When the main road to Welford became a turnpike road, **Highgate House** at Little Creaton which dates from 1663 was a Royal Mail posting station.
Today it is a busy Conference centre.
The two villages were amalgamated in 1884.

The simple little church of **ST MICHAEL** and **ALL ANGELS** stands close to the village centre on a mound which rises from the hillside.
It dates back to the 12th century although in 1857 the whole church was restored, the south transept removed and a south aisle built.
There are no outstanding monuments or carvings although there is a Jacobean pulpit and an unusual three panel reredos.
Approach is made via an attractive lych gate at the entrance erected in 1930 in memory of a
Mr Wroughton of Creaton Lodge who was killed in a riding accident.

The United Reformed chapel near the church came into being in 1694 when the Anglican Vicar *Richard Hook* was excommunicated because he would not conform to the terms of the
Act of Uniformity of Worship passed in 1662.
The original building has been replaced and the chapel is still in regular use.

Quite a number of old wells are apparent as you drive through the village.

Lych-gate Creaton.

The Manor House is dated 1603 and one of the old cottages 'Morningside'' is said to have a doorway from the demolished **Holdenby Palace**.

Although a former public house, The Chequers has been converted into a private house, there is still another public house - The Bricklayers Arms on the main road. The village seems to have almost everything else that it needs.
In addition to the church and chapel there is a shop, post office, a popular Primary school and 'Ducklings' pre-school. The village hall was built in 1935 to commemorate the Silver Jubilee of *George V* and *Queen Mary*.

Creaton Sanatorium was opened on the 23 June 1910 for the treatment of tuberculosis.
It was taken over by the NHS in 1956 and turned into a Hospital where I remember visiting sick friends. It eventually closed on 30th September 1979 and the site was redeveloped for housing and is known as Highfield Park.

LITTLE CREATON

DOMESDAY BOOK
CRETONE/CRETONE

Little Creaton which lay about one mile south of Creaton is recorded in the Domesday Book as having two manors.
One held by *William de Cahagnes* of the
Count of Mortain had four households and in the other was a Frenchman with two oxen.
I can find no information about its size until the early 18th century when *Bridges* writes of eight surviving houses.
Today the area is all but deserted except for the area around Highgate House which on my last visit was proudly displaying a sign that said it had 'The Chef of the Year'.

CRICK

DOMESDAY BOOK
CREC
*The name comes from the Anglo Saxon
'cerrig' - meaning a crag.*

When *William* carried out his great land survey in 1086 the four hide manor was held by *Geoffrey de la Guerche* of the King.
There were seventeen households and a priest.

Crick is an ancient village lying close to the gap carrying north - south communication routes from the Roman Watling Street to the modern M1 with Crick being the northern end of the motorway for a while. Not surprisingly Roman coins, pottery and building stone have been found in the area.
Between these times the railway and canal shared the same route, adding to the prosperity of the village which in 1880 housed forty five weavers, thirty seven farmers and ninety one tradesmen.

Daventry International Rail Freight Terminal (DIRFT) with large distribution warehouses for Tesco, the Post Office and *Eddy Stobart* to the west of the village and alongside the M1 and M6 motorways has replaced the more ancient trades and occupations. The village has recently been bypassed but prior to that traffic on the busy A428 Northampton to Rugby road en route to the motorways trundled through the village which has considerably increased in size in recent years.

There is now a Primary school, a number of shops, a garden centre, a chapel and three public houses.
The Red Lion is the oldest public house being built in the 17th century as a coaching inn.
The Royal Oak is today much larger than it was as the original 1790's premises were much altered around the time of the Second World War.
The Wheatsheaf was first recorded in 1770 and by the early 20th century was a staging post for the Royal Mail on its journey through the County.
It was also a meeting point for the Pytchley Hunt.

The church of **ST MARGARET** of **ANTIOCH** with its west tower of red Warwickshire stone and broach spire is in fine Decorative style although a church may well have existed before the stone building of 1077, the presence of a priest being recorded in the Domesday Book.

The church contains and still uses the *Elliot* pipe organ built for the Chapter Royal at St James Palace in 1842. It was restored in 2011.
Also of interest are the windows, corbels and the oldest feature a Norman font which rests on three crouching Atlas figures.

The most famous Rector was *William Laud* before he became Archbishop of Canterbury although he does not appear to have visited the church often. His portrait in the church is believed to have been painted by a pupil of *Van Dyck*.

Buried in the church is *George Smith* (1831-1895) philanthropist, who brought in regulations for canal barges which regularly used the Leicester Arm of the Grand Union Canal nearby with its 1400 metre long Crick tunnel which was opened in 1814.
One of the country's largest canal waterway rallies takes place here every year.

The Ex-Servicemen's Club south of the churchyard in Victorian Gothic style of diapered brick with a turret was built in 1847 originally as a school for boys. A school for girls was opened at about the same time but was vacated when the present Primary school was built in 1915.

Now known as the 'old school' the building remains virtually unchanged on the outside but inside it contains a developing village facility with an IT centre, meeting rooms, archives, etc.

CROUGHTON

Three miles south west of Brackley
Population: 1801-301   2001 - 998

DOMESDAY BOOK
CLIWETONE/CREVELTONE/CRIWELTONE
There have been many spellings for this village over the years - even the Domesday Book gave three.
It seems most likely however that the origin was 'creowel' - fork and 'tun' - farmstead
a farm where a single street divided or forked.

During the laying of a pipeline in the area in 1991 evidence was found of a Roman Villa with a fine mosaic of the late 4th century.

By the time of the great Domesday Survey there were four manors with a recorded population of eighteen households and a mill rendering two shillings per annum.

Although there are a few attractive buildings in Croughton I find it generally quite uninspiring.

It lies on the B4031 close to the Oxfordshire border with an RAF base (formerly USAAF) close by - its spherical communications domes clearly visible from the main Brackley to Oxford road.

One interesting and attractive feature of the village is the Primary school with a thatched roof in the main street although there is now a modern extension for today's pupils.

At its peak in 1850 lace was made in great quantities in the village and was either sold at Banbury Fair or was sent to agents in London.

Today a few residents are engaged in small businesses locally on the small industrial estate or in agriculture.

The village still has a Reading Room, village shop cum post office, petrol station, and a popular public house,
The Blackbird Inn and
The rather delightfully named 'Puddleducks' Play School.

Of the two non-conformist chapels the Free Methodist is thought to have closed around 1920 and the Wesleyan Methodist in the 1980's having been used for some years by American servicemen from the nearby base.

What immediately struck me as I entered the church of **ALL SAINTS** which dates back to Norman times were the beautiful 15th century very low benches. There is also a Jacobean pulpit.

The unbuttressed squat west tower was repaired after it suffered fire damage on Monday 14th September 1922.

The most famous feature of the church and what draws the most visitors are wall paintings said to originate from 1280-1300 and although they have suffered badly in the past some parts are still quite discernible.

The south wall depicts scenes from the life of the *Virgin Mary* and the north wall mainly scenes from the Passion of *Christ*.

These paintings were only rediscovered in 1921 after being covered with whitewash during the Reformation. They must have been quite spectacular in their day.

Primary School: Croughton

CULWORTH

Seven miles north east of Banbury
Population: 1801 – 532   2001 - 488

DOMESDAY BOOK
CULEORDE

Culworth is an ancient site.
Stone Age people walked here on an old track way
and a Roman coin was found in Banbury Lane.
The Culeorde of the Domesday Book is thought to
derive from 'cula' and 'worth' - meaning enclosure.

In the Domesday Book Culworth is recorded as a small manor with fifteen households however the Domesday Book also refers to another place also in Culworth parish, listed as Brime.

This was once a busy, important place with the grant of a market and an annual fair to *Richard de Coleworth* in 1264 which may be connected to the provision of a Market Place between the two settlements of Culworth and Brime.

Located at the junction of two Drovers roads there would have been many travellers, those going towards Northampton would proceed along the Banbury Lane leaving those heading for London to carry on southwards.
You don't see many cattle in Culworth nowadays!

It is still a busy yet very attractive village with a long street of banded limestone and ironstone cottages just off the Northampton to Banbury road (B4525) so called Banbury Lane.

Culworth still has a village Green where the old cross has been rebuilt as a War Memorial.

Village Cross : Culworth

ST MARY'S church dates back to the 13th and 14th centuries with its first Rector, *Richard de Coleworth* recorded in 1267.
It was considerably restored in the 19th century.
There is a beautifully carved pulpit, some interesting Victorian stained glass and a fine 19th century bier. I liked the impressive wooden eagle on the lectern which dates from August 1880.

The wall behind the altar is decorated with the Ten Commandments, the Lord's Prayer and The Creed. Look out for the wonderful faces which feature on the corbels around the church.
The millennium tapestry depicts families and buildings in the village.

Near the church door is a restored tombstone in memory of *Charles Bacchus* a black servant boy who died in 1762 at the age of 16.
The inscription reads - *'He was loved and lamented by the family he served'.*

Close to the church is the ring work of a small 12th century motte and bailey castle built in the reign of *King Stephen*.

It is said that *Charles I* stayed with *Sir Samuel D'Anvers* at Danvers House at the west end of the village for four nights before the battle at nearby Cropredy Bridge. Accommodation must have been good because I read that *Charles I's* son also stayed there prior to going into battle.
The present house is thought to have been built with materials from the former mansion.
Charles's Pebble on a grass verge by the old cross is said to be where *Charles I* reviewed his troops and mounted his horse.

Near Danvers House is a cottage where one of the earliest Moravian ministers held services in 1748. When they tried to open the house for public meetings there was local opposition and as a result they acquired premises in nearby Eydon.
The chapel in Culworth did not open until 1809 but the simple little red brick building has now been converted into a private house.

Other buildings of note include the elaborate Gothic Rectory built in 1854, the 17th century Old Manor and Danvers Free school built about 1795.

Between March 1899 and September 1958 Culworth had a station just outside Moreton Pinkney on the Great Central Line. It did not prove to be very popular with the village folk which is not surprising as it was two miles away.
Even more surprising is that Culworth was not provided with a station when the Great Central Branch line to Banbury was later laid just outside the village.

The village has a Care Home and a farm shop but no longer has a general store or post office although I was surprised to see an Art Gallery and an Oriental Rug Shop.
There is still a good Primary school, a public house, The Red Lion, together with a village butcher who also provides a mobile butchers shop to many of the villages around.

One of the first projects I have heard about concerning the Diamond Jubilee of
Queen Elizabeth II was the installation of a Jubilee Clock at Culworth. It was built entirely by hand by **Martin Rowling** and marked the end of a seven year project. The prominent black and white clock was unveiled on the east wall of the forge at a well attended ceremony on 9th June 2012.
The inscription on the dial reads reads –
'If my time you cannot tell, hark to hear the hourly bell' although the words and figures are laid out in an unusual manner.

Today the parish includes what is often listed as a deserted village - Brime.

BRIME

DOMESDAY BOOK
BRIME

In 1086 this had a population of just eleven households plus a priest and has been identified as one of Culworths two manors coming under one owner by about 1300.
I can find no evidence of evictions or desertions in the area to explain the loss of this settlement or of the existence of another church so perhaps it has just been swallowed up by Culworth.

Does a priest in Brime indicate that what was once called Brime is now part of the village?

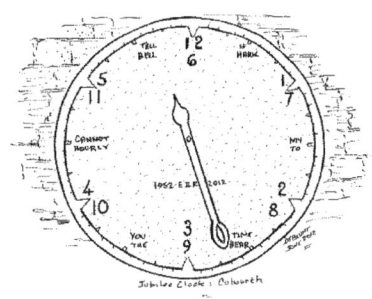

Jubilee Clock : Culworth

CULWORTH GANG

For nearly twenty years in the late 18th century the notorious **Culworth Gang** terrorised the countryside for miles around, attacking stagecoaches, robbing travellers and plundering houses.

Most of the gang were arrested and tried at Towcester Assizes in 1787. Some were deported but four gang members were publicly hanged on Northampton Racecourse on Friday 3rd August 1787.
Such was the public behaviour and vast crowds that thereafter executions were transferred to the 'New Drop' at the back of the County Gaol.

I remembered that in my days of running a Holiday Company for the Over 60's I was invited to give **'The Gang'** a slide talk. To my surprise when the members arrived and took their seats the men sat on one side and the women on the other side.

They did not even get together when the afternoon finished with tea and biscuits!

DAVENTRY

Twelve miles west of Northampton
Population: 1801 – 2582   2001 - 22376

DOMESDAY BOOK
DAVENTREI

The earliest form of the name appears to be from the Celtic 'dwy – afon-tre' the town of the two avons which perfectly describes its position between the Leam flowing west and the Nene flowing east (avon meaning river). However the town's Common Seal dated 1595 shows a rather crude drawing of a Dane felling a tree. The old pronunciation was Danetree and some think the name derives from Dafa - a Saxon tribal leader and 'treo' - tree. The tree could have been a focal point for meetings.
Some are of the opinion that the Danes planted the tree on Borough Hill to mark the centre of England.

History goes back to prehistoric days when **Borough Hill** a little east of the town was a stronghold for Ancient Britons and for men of the Stone and Bronze Ages. Being 600 feet (180 metres) above sea level it was an ideal place to defend and became one of the largest and certainly one of the highest fortified camps in the heart of England.
Many relics have been found in the area.

Even in 1066 when the eight hide manor was held by *Countess Judith*, Daventry was of considerable importance - it was recorded that there were thirty three households, a priest and twelve acres of meadow. In 1108 the monks of the Cluniac Order (an offshoot of the Benedictines) moved their Priory here from its early base at Preston Capes.

The Priory dedicated to St Mary of La Charite and St Augustine was sited adjacent to the parish church.

By the 14th century the number of monks had grown to fourteen and the Priory was well endowed with land and churches.

Cardinal Wolsey asked for a gift of land from the Priory in about 1520 to endow his new College in Oxford. His request was refused but *Wolsey* got what he wanted - and more - as the Estate was granted to him by *Henry VIII* when the Priory was dissolved somewhat earlier than similar institutions. The remaining parts were demolished in 1826 and nothing remains to be seen today.

During the Civil War the Royalist Army are reputed to have camped on **Borough Hill** the night before the decisive Battle of Naseby in 1645 whilst *Charles I* enjoyed more comfortable accommodation in The Wheatsheaf Inn which has now been converted to residential use.

In 1925 the newly created BBC built a Broadcasting Station on Borough Hill.
Daventry was chosen because it was the point of maximum contact with the land mass of England and Wales. *'Daventry calling'* became a familiar sound over the wireless throughout the country.
The mass of masts were a familiar sight in the area but the station closed in 1992 and only one mast remains near Dodford. Aircraft are frequently seen overhead because just four miles south of the town is a directional radio beacon (VOR) identifier DTY for aircraft.

The Moot Hall - Daventry

The unusual looking church of the **HOLY CROSS** on the edge of the Market Place was built between 1752-8 by *David Hiorne* of Warwick at a cost of £3,486. This was a Georgian replacement for the former conventional church of the Priory.

At the time of the Gothic revival in the 19th century Georgian ecclesiastical architecture was held in low esteem and there were many who criticised the design.

This is the only 18th century town church in the County and has a chancel, nave, aisles and a west tower with octagonal spire and a musical clock.

Inside there are painted galleries and pillars and an impressive pulpit. A porch was added to the broad west front in 1951. It is certainly visually different but I like both the appearance of the church from the Market Place and also the interior.

In March 2012 the local evening newspaper reported that *'the church could be forced to close unless £129,000 is raised locally before the end of the year'*. Serious repair work is necessary and English Heritage who have offered some financial support have put it on their 'at risk' register.

The oldest church in Daventry built in 1773 and still in regular use is the delightful United Reformed church hidden away in Foundry Place. A Grammar school built in New Street in 1600 now houses a Roman Catholic congregation.

One building of note is the fine 18th century Grade II listed **Moot Hall** on the Market Square which sadly is also on the *'at risk'* register.

It is a three storey building in sand coloured ironstone with a grand façade housing a broken pediment at the front with a clock and has a delightful little domed shaped cupola on top.

Over the years it has been used as Council Offices, the Mayor's parlour, a women's prison, a museum and Tourist Information Centre and even an Indian Restaurant.

I hope it can be saved as Daventry can ill afford to lose such an attractive building.

There is not a lot else of real architectural interest.

On the Market Place where markets have been held since before 1200 stands a Gothic Memorial Cross of 1908 in memory of *Edmund Charles Burton* a respected local solicitor and churchman. Nearby is the ironstone National school (Abbey Buildings) which dates from 1826.

In the days of horse drawn travel Daventry was a popular staging post between Coventry, Warwick and Northampton and would have up to eighty coaches a day. There were many Coaching Inns of which two remain - The Dun Cow and The Saracen's Head. In addition and to meet the needs of the population there are now a wide variety of supermarkets, shops, public houses, restaurants, banks and leisure facilities.

The red brick Workhouse with a classical style pediment was built about 1838. At the side is a simple Gothic chapel with a small apse whereas at the rear is a modern NHS Hospital.

I wonder just how many people realise that the town is mentioned in the works of *William Shakespeare* when in *Henry VI* part one reference is made to *'the red nosed innkeeper of Daintree'*

Recently Daventry has grown considerably and now encompasses the former village of Drayton.

DRAYTON

In the Domesday Book Drayton was probably included under Daventry although they appear to have been approximately equal in size.

The earliest mention of a manor was in 1531 when *Nicholas Woodhull* held the land. I have an interest in the area as my maternal grandparents were born there.

DAVENTRY COUNTRY PARK

The Green Flag Award winning Country Park is centred on the old reservoir which is one of two in Daventry - the other being Drayton reservoir.

When full it covers twenty seven acres and is fed by many streams from the north and west.

The Country Park has a children's play area, car parking, toilets, refreshments and even some gym equipment.

The riverside walk makes for a very pleasant stroll on a crisp morning or sunny afternoon.

DEANSHANGER

Seven miles south east of Towcester
Population: 1801 – 685 (but listed as Passenham)   2001 - 2900

Although not mentioned specifically in the Domesday Book
(when it was part of the parish of Passenham) it still has a long history.
It went by the name of Daneshanger meaning a clearing in the wood where the Danes lived.

When Roman buildings south of the village were excavated in 1957 evidence was found of a tiled floor timber framed structure on stone foundations together with outbuildings.

At one time there was a Gilbertine monastery here and it is reputed that after a fall out with *Henry II* in 1170 *Thomas á Becket* sought refuge there disguised as a peasant and performed one of the first of over seven hundred miracles that is said to have led to his canonisation.

This large village lies on the main A422 Stony Stratford to Buckingham road with an Upper school recently renamed the *Elizabeth Woodville* school on the left just prior to entering the village from the north.

It is not the prettiest of villages although there are some attractive properties including the 1823 Carpenters Charity Almshouses overlooking the Green which were renovated in 1974.

The church of the **HOLY TRINITY** in Victorian Gothic style was built by *B. Ferrey* in 1853.
It is a surprisingly simple church for what is now quite a large village and comprises a nave with bellcote, north aisle and chancel but with modern cloisters at the rear.

The churchyard was being mown the last time I visited but sadly the area around the War Memorial looks to be in need of some tender loving care.
Near the church and still in regular use is the fine Methodist chapel built in 1892 and opposite is the Deanshanger District Conservative Club of similar date.

In 1820 there was a flourishing ironworks in the village producing prize winning agricultural implements and such was their success that they became engineers of world renown.
Despite a major fire in 1912 the business continued until it went into liquidation in 1927.

Carpenters Almshouses : Deanshanger.

A business for the production of iron oxide then grew up on the site.

Whenever I visited Deanshanger in my cycling days immediately after the Second World War I could not fail to notice that everything, roofs in particular, had a coating of a red/pink powder from the iron oxide production.

The factory eventually closed in the 1990's when production was transferred to China.
Most of the buildings were decontaminated and demolished over the next few years.

I can imagine that the closure of the factory was met with great relief by most villagers even though it meant less local employment.

In an area which the owners, the Ready Mix Concrete Company, hoped to mine but were refused planning permission, has sprung up a Pocket Park.
Here a thousand trees have been planted to provide small woodlands around the site which includes a large pond containing legally protected Great Crested newts.

In 1801 according to statistics Deanshanger was recorded as a hamlet in Passenham parish although by the 16th century it is likely that Deanshanger had outgrown Passenham.
Certainly in the past two hundred years Deanshanger has grown to such an extent that its now dwarfs its neighbour.

Two of the Keepers cottages in Whittlewood - Hanger Lodge and Shrobb Lodge are located within the current boundaries which date back only to 1951 when the south eastern portion of the ancient parish of Passenham was transferred to the newly established civil parish of Old Stratford.

To meet the demands of the large population there are Nursery, Primary and Secondary schools, public houses including The Beehive and The Fox and Hounds, a number of retail outlets, an ambulance station, health centre, library, village hall and playing fields.

What surprised and pleased me was the number of seats dotted around the village, some of which have only recently been donated by village organisations.

Today Deanshanger is a parish in its own right and includes the very small hamlet of Puxley to the north.

PUXLEY

DOMESDAY BOOK
POCHESLAI/POCHESLEI

Puxley had two very small estates mentioned in the Domesday Book whereas nearby Deanshanger (which is now many times bigger) is not mentioned by name – how times change!

This small hamlet which was once described as an 'unnucleated village' lies just to the north of Deanshanger towards the southern edge of the County.

From records the village which was never large appears to have been depopulated in 1489 by *Sir Nicholas Vaux.*

As I travelled along a rough minor road expecting to find little but a farm and a few houses I discovered it to be quite a busy little place.

True there are not too many houses but opposite Grange Farm are a number of large barns guarded by a very substantial security fence.
In addition there is the busy Greenacres livery yard with stables and a riding centre with many horses and horse boxes in the fields and the Green Acres Day Nursery.
Needless to say there were quite a few cars and farm vehicles around.

DEENE AND DEENETHORPE

Five miles north east of Corby
1801 – 399   2001 - 103

DOMESDAY BOOK
DENE
The Saxon name is simply 'denu' or 'den' - a valley.

In 1086 this was one of just two manors in the County held by the Abbey of St Peter of Westminster (the other was Sudborough) and as a result was visited many times by the Abbot of Westminster and his entourage.

Deene is a tiny unspoiled one street limestone Estate village just off the A43 Corby to Stamford road with its larger and less attractive neighbour, Deenethorpe, on the hillside on the opposite side of the Willow Brook. Over the years Deene has shrunk in size but Deenethorpe has increased.

The Grade I listed **Deene Hall** is largely 16th century and incorporates a medieval Manor House built around a courtyard with important rooms added during the reign of *George III.*
Stained glass windows in the Grand Hall were damaged following the air crash nearby during the Second World War but these have been restored.

The Hall was used to billet troops during the war and they left it in a sorry state. It has since been restored and is open again to visitors who are shown rooms regularly used by family and friends. A lovely little chapel was incorporated when the nearby parish church closed.

There are some pretty gardens with long borders, specimen trees and topiary teapots. The Hall stands in a large park where visitors may picnic beside the lake where the village once stood.

ST PETER'S church at Deene is inescapably the *Brudenell* church and is somewhat isolated on the Estate overlooking a lake. The west tower dates from the late 12th century and is topped with one of the earliest recessed broach spires known. Inside it is in the Victorian tradition with a marble pulpit, a decorated chancel, a very ornate piscina and a three seat sedilia. The church was restored on the instructions of the widow of the *7th Earl of Cardigan* in 1868-69. The south chancel is filled with impressive family monuments.

When the church was in use, villagers from Deene sat on one side of the nave and those from Deenethorpe on the other. Sadly since 1980 the church has been 'redundant' and is cared for by the Churches Conservation Trust.

The former public house, The White Hart was once called The Sea Horse Hotel.
It is a large impressive 17th century building with a distinct oval window.
The old school dates from 1872 and is now the village hall. The pupils were specially clothed by the *Brudenell* family.

401ST USAF BOMBARDMENT GROUP

During the Second World War there was an USAF base behind Deenethorpe. It was built in 1943 and was one of the last wartime airfields to open in the County. The base was used by the 401st Bombardment Group who flew 254 missions over Germany and Occupied Europe in gigantic B17 bombers between 1943 and 1945 and were accredited as having the best bomber accuracy and one of the lowest loss ratios among USAF bomber groups.

One morning in December 1943 a fully laden Flying Fortress crashed into an unoccupied cottage on the edge of Deenethorpe. On impact the bomber caught fire, fortunately all ten crew members escaped and the only casualties were a calf and fourteen chickens. All villagers but one were evacuated before the bomber exploded but not one of the thirty two houses in Deenethorpe escaped damage.

The ground crew had a memorable war in that they travelled to the UK on the Queen Mary and departed after hostilities on the Queen Elizabeth.
A granite memorial was dedicated in 1989 to - *'The Best Damned Outfit in the USAAF'*.
It stands with the Union Flag and the Stars and Stripes flying proudly together on the Weldon to Benefield road at the edge of the airfield

Brudenell

Deene Park

Brudenell family

By the 15th century the family owned several properties in the Midlands and it was **Robert** (1461-1531) who established the family at Deene in 1514. He was a distinguished lawyer and invested his large fortune in land and was well connected at Court serving **Lady Margaret Beaufort**, **Henry VII's** mother in her capacity as the Kings Deputy in the turbulent northern counties.

Robert attended the coronation of **King Henry VIII** with whom he found favour being Knighted in 1516 and later appointed Chief Justice of England.

He was succeeded by his son, **Thomas** and then by **Sir Edmund** (1521-1585) who entertained **Elizabeth I** in 1566 when plans for her to stay at Burghley House were thwarted due to **Sir William Cecil's** daughter contracting smallpox.

By marriage the family became related to the **Treshams** and the **Montagus**.

In 1626 **Thomas Brudenell** (1578-1663) was convicted of recusancy and two thirds of his possessions and rents were forfeited to the King. Although this was partially rescinded later their religious faith represented a serious threat to the family fortunes as it did to the **Treshams**.

During the Civil War disgruntled Parliamentary troops came to Deene Park and ransacked the home of the absent Royalist **Sir Thomas**, burning, discarding and stealing papers and furnishings. Many of the books now to be seen in the Bow Room were stolen by the Cromwellians and to his fury the **1st Earl** was made to pay to get them back. Although **Sir Thomas** owned Estates in eight counties his fortune was drastically reduced in paying the ransom of £5,000 for the release of his 18 year old heir who was sent abroad to complete his education but had been captured at sea by Spanish privateers and eventually jailed in Spain.

The best known member of the family is **James**, (1797-1868) the **7th** and last **Earl of Cardigan** who inherited **Deene Park** at the age of 40 and has gone down in history as having led the Charge of the Light Brigade into the jaws of defeat at Balaklava in 1854 and also introduced the 'cardigan' into the English language.

He is reported as having had many mistresses including a scandalous affair with a woman, twenty seven years his junior who he eventually married after the death of his first wife.

The family are still resident at Deene Hall which contains a collection of Crimean memorabilia and the stuffed head of the **7th Earl's** charger 'Ronald' upon which he rode into battle.

DENFORD

Two miles south of Thrapston
Population: 1801-267   2001-250

DOMESDAY BOOK
DENEFORD
Most likely the name comes from the ford in the valley – 'denu.'

The Domesday Book records Denford as having thirty seven households, two mills rendering fifty shillings and eight pence per annum and two hundred and fifty eels.
It was obviously quite a large and valuable manor.

Today it is a delightful stone village although somewhat spoilt by the many vehicles that negotiate the narrow bends on the road to and from Thrapston.
Twelve buildings in the village are registered as having special architectural or historical interest.

The village stands on the River Nene which to the west is popularly known as the 'Nen' and to the east as the 'Neen'.

As you leave the village en route to Thrapston there is a lay-by alongside a very pleasant riverside location – a lovely spot for a picnic and a spot of meditation as the river flows peacefully onwards.
Here you will find a village sign, a railed War Memorial and a wide variety of ducks not to mention some inquisitive swans.

There are some pleasant walks in the area particularly near the River Nene alongside which stands the church of the **HOLY TRINITY**.

It has a fine 13th century west tower with a recessed broached spire behind a parapet with pinnacles and is Early English in style.

Restoration has taken place on the buttresses and the lower part of the tower and its broached spire was restored.

In the 19th century brick and tile kilns provided much local employment but like so many villages today the residents are for the most part employed elsewhere.

The village school which opened in 1870 has now closed as has the Methodist chapel which was built in 1872 but the local pub with the unique name of 'The Inn at Denford' is still open for business although there is no longer a shop or post office.

Ducks & Village Sign : Denford

DENTON

Six miles south east of Northampton
Population: 1801 – 378   2001 - 767

DOMESDAY BOOK
DODINTONE

In the Domesday Book it was recorded as Dodintone (the same as Great Doddington)
but over the years evolved to be known as Denton.
Up to two hundred years ago it was also known as Little Doddington
(i.e. a daughter village to Great Doddington).

This is an area rich in archaeological finds.
A number of prehistoric and Roman sites have been recorded and finds have included Iron Age and Roman pottery, part of a bronze toilet set and shaped arrow heads.

The village lies just off the road between Northampton and Bedford (A428).
One of the earliest bypasses in the County has diverted the stream of heavy lorries and cars from village streets and as a result it tends to get bypassed but leave the main road to see the most attractive part around the church with some lovely old properties including The Red Lion public house.

Alongside the public house is Holly Cottage in the garden of which is a circular dovecote with ornate cupula dating back to the 17th century.

Nearby is an old horse trough which today seems to double up as a very convenient car wash.
Further along the village street is Lower End where you will find Manor Farm with attractive banded stonework.

The Baptist chapel erected in 1878 was converted to a private residence in 1996 and was recently up for sale at a guide price of £365,000.

In Vicarage Lane is **Compton House** built for the son of the *5th Marquess* of *Northampton* by *Wade* in 1893 in elaborate brick and stone Jacobean style.
Nearby is a dentist, a modern Primary school and the village hall.

In the centre of the village stands the church of **ST MARGARET** with its unbuttressed 13th century west tower.
The body of the church was rebuilt in 1827/8 although the chancel is dated 1629.
The church does not have aisles and has pointed windows, very much like a chapel.
Unfortunately the most important window is partly obscured by a screen which it is hoped will be repositioned at some future date.

I was warmly welcomed when I visited the church on a Friday morning when a Coffee Morning was being held. This is a church well worthy of a visit if only to see the interior which is filled with murals completed in 1976 by the noted Northamptonshire artist *Henry Bird.*
The murals feature the faces of many local people.
Is this the only church with a mural in the cloakroom?

A millennium project was the installation of a fine window depicting the church and dovecote.

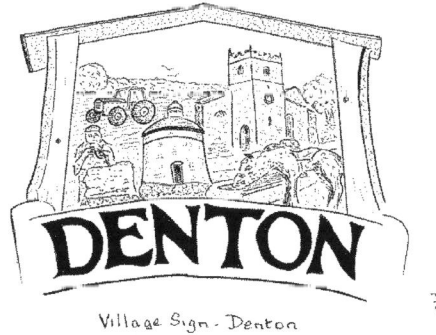

Village Sign - Denton

DESBOROUGH

Four miles north west of Kettering
Population: 1801-831   2001 - 8073

DOMESDAY BOOK
DEREBURG/DESBURG/DEISBURG

*The name 'borough' obviously derives from the Saxon word 'burh' meaning fortified place
but of the rest there appears to be some dispute although some historians think it may derive from
'dis' a 'sacred fortified place' or 'dear' (deer).*

There has been a settlement here since the Bronze Age and several relics from this period have been found. The most famous is the decorative bronze **'Desborough Mirror'** which is thought to date from the 1st century BC and is now displayed in the British Museum.

A replica can be seen in the excellent award winning Desborough Heritage Centre (free admission) located at the top of Station Road.

Also found in the area is evidence of a number of Anglo Saxon cemeteries and a Roman settlement.

At the time of the Domesday Book the Lord of the Manor was **Robert de Todeni**.

The manor passed through many hands until it was acquired by the **Poulton** family who were Lords of the Manor for over thirteen generations.

Desborough is now a small unspectacular industrial town about mid way between Kettering and Market Harborough but is considerably quieter traffic wise with the recent opening of the A6 bypass.

It was famous both for its boots and shoes and its corsets. The corset factory on the original main road was built in 1905 for the Co-operative Wholesale Society. The name is picked out in white brick on the parapet fronting the building and the letters C.W.S on the face of the chimneys.

As factories go I think that this is quite an attractive building and is still in commercial use.

Although shoe manufacture has virtually ceased in the town a few old shoe factory buildings still remain and some have been converted into apartments and offices but others are now left in a sorry, derelict state.

The town has grown quite dramatically over the past two hundred years but very little is manufactured here today although a major employer is Rigid Containers and there is a small industrial estate on the edge of the town.

Even the railway station has been closed although trains still rush past on the main line from St Pancras to the north.

The original station building closed in 1968 and is now a private dwelling and the surrounding area now houses a fairly large supermarket

There is a reasonable variety of other shops although I imagine that most of the population find Kettering or Market Harborough more in keeping with their shopping requirements.

For very many years the Ritz Ballroom had a very good reputation and was a popular place to visit. When it closed the building became very unsightly but it has now been completely refurbished and modernised.

In October 2011 it re-opened as a state of the art Banqueting, Conference and Wedding venue with three bars and function rooms with a capacity of 500-600 guests.

Two buildings close to the church are worthy of note - the 18th century Church House and Desborough House, a 19th century building with classical facade and graceful Doric pillars which now houses an Ex- Servicemen's Club.

The oldest building is the Grade I listed church of **ST GILES** built around 1225 most likely on the site of an older church.
This is a fine building occupying a commanding position and having a good 15th century embattled tower and broach spire.
Like many other churches the spire was struck by lightning but this one has been particularly unfortunate in being struck three times in 1818, 1843 and 1873.

The layout of the church is quite unusual with a one bay nave and wide transepts because originally the site was restricted by roads on either side. It is quite a light and airy building and one in which I was greatly impressed.

The decorated Tudor canopy above the rood screen staircase displays Tudor roses and the emblem of the powerful *Stafford* family - the **'Stafford Knot'**.

I was told that you can find thirty six different carved heads in the building including several 'Green Men' and one man with an apparent toothache.

Buried in the church is ***Fernando Poulton*** (1536-1617) a legal historian who is thought to have been involved in the Gunpowder Plot.

The church is used by both the Church of England and the Methodist community and a window in the church commemorates the inauguration of this union on 7th September 1969.
Most church members hold joint membership of both churches.

Other churches in the town still in use include the Baptist church near the old station, the United Reformed church and the Catholic church in the old Methodist chapel.

Desborough Baptist Church

At the end of North Street is a rusticated 18th century pillar surmounted by a stone sphere and often referred to as the 'old Market Cross' but it is thought to be a gateway pillar from **Harrington Hall** which was demolished about 1745.

Of the seven inns on historic maps only two survive today. Both are still public houses but only one has its original name. They are The George and The Oak Tree (formerly The Kings Arms).

The town saw some activity during the Second World War when an airfield with three tarmac runways and a number of hangars was established in the area in 1943 from which Wellington Bombers operated.
It did not have a long life and closed in 1945 but you can still see some of the old buildings and the tarmac.

DINGLEY

Two miles east of Market Harborough
Population 1801-143   2001-209

DOMESDAY BOOK
DINGLEI/DINGLE/TINGLEA

Like so many villages, Dingley has been recorded with many different spellings. The origin appears to derive from the Saxon word 'dingle' for deep hollow or clearing following the name of a local leader.

In spite of its present size Dingley is recorded in the Domesday Book as having four manors with twenty eight households.

Today it is just a small and very quiet village although it lies on the A427 between Market Harborough and Corby.

Dingley Hall

*In the Middle Ages the **Knights Hospitallers** had a house here which was dissolved at the time of the Reformation.*

*On the site now stands **Dingley Hall** which was built for **Sir Edmund Griffin** younger son of the **Griffins** of Braybrooke and is thought to date from 1550-60 when English domestic architecture was rare.*

*__Edmund__ was Attorney General under **Edward VI** and **Philip** and **Mary**.*

The gardens were laid out in 1680 when it is thought that the village was displaced and rebuilt.

It was a Courtyard House although the west wing was pulled down in 1780-2.

The Hall became derelict after the Second World War despite being Grade I listed and the east wing was partly demolished in 1972.

Parts of the remaining buildings have now been converted into private residences

In the grounds of the Hall stands a stone gazebo which may have been constructed by stone left following demolition of part of the Hall.

The village is no longer large enough to support a public house, school or a shop but surprisingly does have the Dingley Lodge Hotel.

When driving through the village recently a number of posters were advertising 'horse racing in Dingley'.
The racing is in fact 'Point to Point' meetings which take place monthly between January and July and consist of six or seven races over a three mile course.

Water Pumps: Dingley

Before we had the benefit of water plumbed into our homes people had to fetch water from outside.
Northamptonshire was well (!!) blessed with many natural springs.
Evidence of well heads and pumps can still be seen in various locations including at the top end of Church Lane in Dingley where there stands a pair near the main Harborough road, one is encased in cast iron.

It is not usually difficult to find the church in any village but Dingley proved to be an exception. After walking up and down Church Lane on two occasions without a soul to ask, I actually saw a gentleman who pointed me in the right direction, through a blue gate in the wall. Eventually I found it and it was well worth the search.

The church of **ALL SAINTS** stands in a delightful churchyard with its magnificent yew hedge close to **Dingley Hall**. It has a 15th century tower and evidence of Norman work on the south side of the nave and chancel.
The south porch is about 600 years old with a carved angel in prayer over the door.
The rest was remodelled in the 17th century.

On one of my visits workmen were busy re-erecting the very ornate weathervane which had been restored and regilded.

There are a number of monuments to the **Hungerford** family of Dingley Hall.
Buried in the churchyard is **Ethel, Countess Beatty** (1874-1932) wife of **Earl Beatty** (Battle of Jutland) who for a time owned the Hall.
He is buried in **St Pauls Cathedral**.

DITCHFORD

Three miles east of Wellingborough

I can find no reference to Ditchford as a settlement in the Domesday Book but a mill was recorded in Dichesford in 1235, the name meaning a ford by the 'dic' - possibly a subsidiary course of the River Nene.

Ditchford gets a page of its own simply because I did not know where else to put it being 'in the middle of nowhere' on the boundary of three parishes, Irthlingborough, Irchester and Rushden.

I have also seen it referred to as *'three miles from anywhere'* and *'the one man village of England'*. You cannot call it either a village or a hamlet and it rarely appears on maps.

In my opinion the only memorable aspect of Ditchford is that it used to house a knackers' yard and the area around was always pungent with the smell of rotting carcasses until Health and Safety got involved.
Ditchford became the first place in the UK to process feathers for sale to blenders of agricultural foodstuffs. Gladly the smells have gone and now it is home to De Molder Enterprises and the Hornigold Haulage Co.

Surprisingly there used to be a station here as an Act of Parliament decreed that a station had to be provided when the line crossed a turnpike road and that every train stop there if necessary.
It is hard to imagine that this was once an important road and that Ditchford was so popular for fishing and boating during the depression in the 1920s and 1930's that it became known as **'Ditchford on Sea'**.

Ditchford is famous as the locality of reputed **'treacle mines'**. The origin of this fantasy is obscure although the station sidings were primarily to serve a nearby ironstone quarry.
Treacle mining is the fictional mining of treacle (similar to molasses) in a raw form similar to coal. It has been a standing joke for a century or more and there are supposed to be many treacle mines in Britain.

There is even an internet site under the heading *'All things treacle'*.
I understand that the treacle master has been informed that Ditchford has been omitted.

For most of its life the station was without water which had to be brought in each day by train.

The Station Master had the power to stop any train so that his family could travel to Wellingborough. Its remoteness meant that it saw little business and the line closed to passengers in 1924 but remained open to railwaymen and their families and freight until 1950.
The buildings were not demolished until 1967.

Tragic news was made in 1849 when **Thomas Abbott** wandered across the line and was killed by a passing train. He was an umbrella repairer and it is said that several umbrellas were scattered around the scene.

A three arch causeway or raised walkway to avoid floods gives pedestrian access to Ditchford Bridge which probably dates from the 14th century and is fourteen feet wide with massive cutwaters.

When crossing over the bridge recently there was quite a lot of activity with fishing and the Nene Valley Ski Club not to mention the odd muntjac deer.

The bridge is first mentioned in the Comptus Rolls of Peterborough Abbey in 1292 as Dikford Bridge. The Abbey had manorial holdings in the area.

DODFORD

Three miles east of Daventry
Population; 1801-208   2001 - 160

DOMESDAY BOOK
DODEFORDE
The origin of the name is in dispute.
*Is this the same **Dodda** after whom Great Doddington*
and Denton are named? - or a waterweed called 'dod'
which grew along the nearby Nene meadows.

Dodford lies in a quiet hollow just off the A45 and has a number of attractive older properties and one of the longest drive through fords in the County.
There are considerable earthworks to the north side of the stream which indicates that the village was once much larger.
For the most part the Roman road (A5) Watling Street forms the eastern border of the parish.
It is not therefore surprising to learn that Roman coins have been discovered in the area.
It was certainly mentioned in an Anglo Saxon Charter of 944 and had a priest and twenty one households at the time of the Domesday Book when the three hide manor was held by the
Count of Mortain
The manor was acquired by **William de Keynes** in 1222 and he enclosed much of his land including a deer park. After three hundred years it was passed to the **Knightley** family of Fawsley.
In 1916 at The Wheatsheaf Hotel in Daventry the Fawsley Estate put the manor at Dodford up for sale.

The church of **ST MARY** the **VIRGIN** is a Grade I listed building founded by the Normans and there is evidence of their work in the circular font and in the south wall. Subsequently a north aisle was added with a clerestory on the north side only. The chancel was rebuilt in the 19th century.
The aisle is full of very interesting monuments to the **Cressy's** and **de Keynes**, including a Purbeck marble effigy of a crossed legged Knight thought to be **Sir Robert Keynes** dated 1305 and a fine alabaster altar tomb of **Sir John Cressy** who died in 1443.The windows were undergoing restoration on my last visit.

The village no longer supports a shop, public house or school.

DRAUGHTON

Seven miles south of Market Harborough
Population: 1801-171   2001 - 68

DOMESDAY BOOK
BRACSTONE/DRACTONE
The old spelling indicates that this is
a settlement on the slope of a hill.

Draughton is recorded in the Domesday Book as three separate manors but no population is recorded for two of them as they are thought to have belonged to larger manors at Lamport and Rothwell. There has obviously been a settlement in the area since the early Iron Age.
On the eastern boundary of the parish during the preparation of land for a wartime airfield (Harrington) evidence was found of a number of huts and pottery of the Iron Age period - thought to be the homes of a small group of iron workers.
Roman pottery and a coin of **Hadrian** suggest that the Romans also spent some time here.

The village lies about five hundred feet above the valley floor to the south and is a small village with little of note in quiet countryside east of the Northampton to Market Harborough road.

The church of **ST CATHERINE** has a flat topped west tower of the late 12th century with a small round arched west window.
The chancel was added in 1885 and the font of 1800 appears to symbolise Eve being tempted by Satan in the Garden of Eden.
The East window of the south aisle is the work of **Kempe** dated 1895.

Although there was never a station here the Northampton to Market Harborough railway line ran in the valley between Maidwell and Draughton until its closure in the 1970's.
All that remains is the trackbed which is now the Brampton Valley walk (a popular walking and cycling route) and an old ironwork footbridge minus its wooden flooring.

There is no shop, post office, chapel or public house.

DUDDINGTON

Five miles south west of Stamford
1801-298   2001 - 181 (including Fineshade)

DOMESDAY BOOK
DODINTONE
*The name is thought to derive from **Dodda** a local name and 'tun' - homestead or village.
It is interesting to note that this village shares the same name (Dodintone) in the Domesday Book
with Denford and Great Doddington although they are widely separated in the County.*

The King held the manor in 1086 when there were twelve households, a priest and a mill rendering four shillings per annum.

Duddington is set in the north east of the County near Stamford and was originally situated within the old Rockingham Forest. A 14th century bridge spanning the River Welland marks the boundary between Northamptonshire and Rutland. It is hard to imagine that it once carried a main road.
Alongside the bridge is a picturesque water mill with its mansard roof dating from 1664 which was built by **Nicholas Jackson.** It has been restored and is now used as offices. On the opposite side of the road is the 18th century Mill House.

This is a very attractive stone built Conservation village with some lovely old thatched properties and much more peaceful since the busy A47 and A43 bypasses were constructed.
Hemmed in amongst the buildings and trees and very difficult to photograph is the 12th century church of
ST MARY with a very solid looking main door dating from about 1220 still with its original iron-work.
In the nave are box pews and six Norman arches.

The church is unusual in that the 13th century tower stands at the east end of the south arcade because having previously extended the nave there was no room for a tower between the west end and the neighbouring Tithe Barn.
The short broach spire was added at a later date.

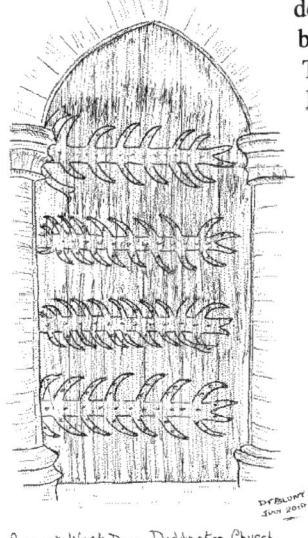

Ancient West Door. Duddington Church

There are some traces of medieval paintings and many floor slabs commemorating the **Jackson** family who were major landowners in the area from 1667.
Frank Jackson, the last member of the family died about ten years ago and a great nephew who inherited lives in Australia. As the Trust expires in a few years time it is possible that the Manor, the Mill and the rest of the Estate could soon be sold.

When I visited the church recently the porch was covered with beautiful pink roses.
Previously it was being used as a temporary newspaper collection point owing to the closure of the village shop.

Adjacent to the church is Church Farm which from 1770-1834 served as the parish Workhouse.
Alongside is a two cell 18th century dovecote with eight hundred nesting boxes.
The large building next door is the Manor House with an early 17th century gable. It was held by the **Burghley** and **Cecil** families between 1585 and 1798 and more recently by the **Jackson** family.

The former school which was opened in 1893 is an ornate building with a Coat of Arms. There were separate entrances for boys and girls. There is still a public house - The Royal Oak but the former Crown is now a private residence.

EARLS BARTON

Seven miles east of Northampton
Population: 1801-725   2001 - 5353

DOMESDAY BOOK
BARTONE/BURTONE

Barton is a common place name from two Saxon words 'bere' - barley and 'tun' - farmstead.
The Earl in the name first appeared in 1261 and was probably a reference to the
*Earl of Northampton, (**Simon de Senlis**) who owned the manor.*

Standing on a hill and sandwiched between the old Northampton/Wellingborough road and the new dual carriageway Earls Barton enjoys extensive views over the Nene Valley. The Domesday Survey lists the **Countess Judith**, niece of the Conqueror, as both landowner and mill owner.

It certainly seems to have been an important place with three mills rendering twenty eight shillings and eight pence per annum and three manors, one of which 'Widethorpe' was probably in the area now known as Dowthorpe End.

The history of Earls Barton however goes back to well before 1066. A large number of pits and ditches containing Iron Age and Early Roman pottery were discovered in 1966 and the church tower dates back to the Saxons.

The village has in the past been variously known as Barton on the Hill and in the 13th century as Barton Pynckney when it was named after the then Lord of the Manor.

The present Manor House is thought to originate from the late 1500's to early 1600's.

The two date stones of 1714 and 1737 refer to alterations.

Until the wool manufacturing industry moved north in the 14th and 15th centuries sheep rearing and woollen cloth making were important.
Rush mat weaving, chair bodging, basket making and lace were crafted locally.

The village also has a long association with the footwear industry. In the 13th century shoes were made with leather from Northampton and by 1801 most of the population of seven hundred and twenty five were employed in shoe workshops.
The village had a tan yard until 1984.

Today the population has risen to over five thousand, many are still employed in shoe making at **Barkers** in their new factory opened by *H. M. the Queen Mother* on the 7th May 1987.
The considerable rise in population is reflected in the large number of new properties.

Some older properties including 17th century ironstone buildings still remain in the centre of the village around the church which is called The Square but is certainly far from square. This area surrounded by shops, churches, schools, library, restaurants etc. always seems to be very busy.

South Door - Earls Barton Church

Overlooking The Square and well worth a visit is **Jeyes** Pharmacy which is run by descendants of *Philadelphus Jeyes* of **Jeyes** fluid fame.

This is said to be the only pharmacy in England housing a Building Society. The adjoining block of three Victorian cottages house a museum of village life, a 'book nook', 'card cottage', miniature fun fair, exhibition, gift shop and Dolly Lodge not to forget the Apothocoffee shop next door.

A very popular event in the village is an Annual Steam Rally featuring steam engines dating back to the 1900's together with miniature and stationary engines. The 15th Annual Event in August 2012 drew more than 10,000 visitors.

For over a thousand years the eighty foot west tower of the Saxon church of **ALL SAINTS** which is situated on a grassy mound in the centre of the village has been a symbol of the faith of our Saxon ancestors and has drawn visitors from far and wide. The exceptional tower which can be seen for miles around has no buttresses but some attractive decorative pilaster strips which convey the impression of half timbered framework.

It has been photographed many times and in 1972 featured on a four pence stamp which at that time was the cost of a first class mail - how times have changed.

The building has examples of ecclesiastical architecture from every period.

Apart from the tower what particularly caught my eye was the Norman nave and doorway in the south porch, the lovely highly decorated 15th century rood screen depicting saints and butterflies, the 16th century Jacobean carved oak pulpit, the 20th century stained glass and the modern **Chris Fiddes** painting *'Christ of the Streets'* although the latter was not to my taste.

The church which is usually open most mornings and afternoons during the summer months was featured in the film *'Kinky Boots'* in 2005 and is well worth a visit.

All Saints Church - Earls Barton

To the north and partly in the churchyard you can still see evidence of the existence of a Norman castle motte.

Both the Wesleyan chapel in Doddington Road dated 1870 and the Baptist chapel opposite the church are still used for religious worship.

For those wanting a little peace and quiet there are some very pleasant walks along the River Nene and around the lakes created by sand and gravel extraction.

One area of the village is currently known as Dowthorpe End - the name being linked with the long lost settlement of Thorpe.

THORPE

This hamlet is thought to have been located about a mile south east of Earls Barton near the banks of the River Nene.

Of the three mills held by the *Countess Judith* in 1086 two were probably located here. Two watermills are recorded as being in the hamlet in 1580.

By 1261 it was known as Barton Thorpe and later as Thorp juxta Barton.

I have not been able to establish the reason for the desertion of the site but a map of 1772 shows the area as being completely deserted except for a mill.

EAST CARLTON

Three miles west of Corby
Population: 1801-84   2001- 270

DOMESDAY BOOK
CARLINTONE

In Viking times 'karla' was used to indicate a freeman i.e. a man who was no longer a serf.
So Carlton was probably his dwelling place.

East Carlton is an interesting and somewhat unusual little village situated just off the A427 between Market Harborough and Corby.

In 1660 there were two very close manors, East Hall and West Hall. The site of West Hall is thought to be to the west of the church but East Hall (now East Carlton) has been considerably enlarged on the park side as a result of the influx of workers from the nearby steel works.

The church of **ST PETER** was originally built in 1228 as a Chapel of Ease for the nearby parish of Cottingham.

When East Carlton became a parish in its own right the church was rebuilt in 1788 in the Decorative Gothic style but without its original two naves and is consequently much smaller than the previous building.

The west tower with a band of carving below its parapet and four fine pinnacles is particularly attractive.
Inside there is a lovely double decker pulpit and neat box pews.

The south chapel is dedicated to the *Palmer* family and all the stained heraldic glass in the chancel, chapel and south aisle is in memory of family members a number of whom served as Members of Parliament.

In 1668 *Sir Geoffrey Palmer*, Bart. endowed a small group of Almshouses.
Some two hundred years later a descendant, *Charlotte Palmer* decided that they needed to be rebuilt and more amply endowed.

The original Almshouses stood where coaches are now parked and the new ones are those you see on your left as you approach the entrance to the park. They are now private dwellings.
Above the door is a stone tablet inscribed:-

> *'Hospital of the Blessed Jesus*
> *in Carlton and rebuilt and more*
> *amply endowed by Charlotte Palmer.*
> *Anno Domini 1868'*

East Carlton was one of only two *'Thankful Villages'* in the County following the Great War - the other being Woodend in South Northants.

To commemorate the safe return of all seven men who served, the villagers decided to buy a surplus army hut and convert it into a village hall which in 1936 was extended to become 'Coronation Hall'.

In 2001 the hall was demolished and the original army hut moved to a resident's garden where it is devoted to memorabilia of both World War and depicts *King George VI* and *Elizabeth* his wife, above the door.

Fifty nine houses were built on the edge of the park for managers and white collar workers.
Since the steel works closed the housing has been used as private residences.
It is said that part of the stone wall which surrounds the park was re-used stone from the old Hall.

As in so many small villages there is no longer a shop, post office, school or public house.

Palmer
of Carlton

East Carlton Hall

East Carlton Hall and the Palmer family

*The **Palmer** family acquired the whole manor at the time of **Henry IV**.*
*The most famous family member was **Geoffrey** who was born in 1598 to be 'a great man of his line'*
He was a lawyer at the Middle Temple and one of the original members of the Long Parliament.
He was imprisoned for rebelling against the Protectorate and on the Restoration was made Attorney General
and created a Baron. He died in 1670 and has a grand alabaster monument in the church.

*It was **Sir John** (5th Baronet) who had the present Grade II listed East Carlton Hall built in 1776*
It is built of red brick and ironstone with a symmetrical facade and is a truly grand building with
Italianate details and French style pavilion roofs but certainly appears out of place in its present setting.
*It was restored and enlarged in 1870 by **E. F. Law**.*
Many members of the family have been MP's and a number High Sheriffs in either Northamptonshire
or Leicestershire. East Carlton was the family seat from some 500 years until in 1933 when they moved to
Carlton Purlieu Hall in Leicestershire.
The Hall was purchased by the Corby Steel Corporation in 1934 as a hostel for its unmarried batchelor staff and in
1978 was sold to Corby District Council and has now been converted into residential apartments.

EAST CARLTON COUNTRY PARK

This is a very pleasant and open area of parkland once part of the East Carlton Estate with splendid views overlooking the Welland Valley.
One hundred acres were given over to the Country Park and it is now a very popular area receiving about 400,000 visitors a year. It is particularly popular with family groups because of the large open spaces for play and picnics, children's play areas, ice cream kiosk, toilets and walking trails.

The former stable block of the Hall and its immediate area now house a cafe, craft shops and the Corby Heritage Centre with artefacts of the famous Corby steelworks including massive steel ingots and parts of the gigantic walking dragline excavator.
An unusual feature on the approach to the park which is open all year is a Petanque Court which was funded by the National Lottery.

EAST FARNDON

DOMESDAY BOOK
FERENDONE/FAREDONE

*The name Farndon is simply a corruption of 'fearn'
from fern or bracken and 'dun' - hill.*

At the time of the Domesday Book when the
manor was held by the *Countess Judith* the
settlement was known simply as Farndon.
The 'East' was added in the 17th century to
distinguish it from the Farndon near Woodford
Halse.
A find of a scatter of Roman pottery in the area is
an indication of early settlement although earth
works may be connected with Civil War activity
during the Battle of Naseby.

Situated just south of Market Harborough on the
Northamptonshire/Leicestershire border it is
basically a one street community with stone and
brick built houses on both sides of the very steep
hill. Although a minor road there is a lot of traffic,
some of which travels too fast down the hill.

One building which caught my eye is situated in
Back Lane. It is worth a detour to see this
Jacobean Manor House built in 1664 partly in
stone and partly in brick with two storey
mullioned bay windows at each end.
Like so many villages the shop, public house and
village school have all closed recently but there is
a fairly modern village hall.
The Jurassic Way passes through the top of the
village.

Overlooking the whole village is the church of
ST JOHN the **BAPTIST** which is Decorative and
Perpendicular in style and has a 14th century west
tower with battlements and pinnacles.
Originally it had had both a north and south aisle
but the north aisle fell into disrepair by 1631 and
was demolished. The north side of the nave was
then rebuilt and as a result the tower, nave and
chancel are out of alignment.

The church certainly appears to be well supported
financially for on display are embroidered
tapestries recalling all those who helped finance a
Bell Fund Appeal in 1938, a Windows Appeal in
1989 and the Chiming Clock Appeal of 2009
although the clock was not working when I last
visited.

I was very interested in the painted glass panels on
two window cills being the millennium
contribution of the Sunday Club.
These depict the four seasons and the four
churches in the Benefice at that time. Since then
the number of churches in the Benefice has risen
to seven. There is a peal of six bells the oldest
dating from 1587.

Just outside the village on the road to Clipston the
Naseby Battlefield Project have provided a car
park and viewing platform at the spot where it is
thought that *Prince Rupert of the Rhine*
marshalled his Royalist troops before joining
battle with *Fairfax* at nearby Moot Hill at the
commencement of the Battle of Naseby on the
14th June 1645.

Jacobean House - East Farndon

JUDITH STONE

This can be found NNW of the village on land
sloping gently east. It is shown marked with its
present location on a map of 1856.

The stone is, in fact, a large irregular block of
granite (possibly Scandinavian) about one metre
high and one metre wide. Where it came from and
why it is there is a mystery.
Perhaps it is a reminder that at the time of the
Domesday Book the land was owned by
Countess Judith of Huntingdon.

EAST HADDON

Six miles north west of Northampton
Population: 1801-259   2001 - 651

DOMESDAY BOOK
EDDONE/EDONE/HADONE
Haddon derives from the Saxon words heath, heath land and 'dun' - hill,
to distinguish two villages of the same name East and West were first mentioned in the 13th century.

East and West Haddon are listed separately in the Domesday Book. In East Haddon the land was divided into three manors all held by the **Count of Mortain** who held about ninety other manors in the County.
There were thirty nine households and a priest and a mill rendering eight shillings per annum.
It was quite a sizable settlement.

Today East Haddon is a quiet, pretty village just off the A428 with a mix of modern housing and lovely old thatched cottages.

Occupying a prime position in the middle of the village is the church of **ST MARY**.
The building dates back to the Norman period and still has pillars and a lovely sculptured font from that era.

The church was remodelled during the 14th century and the top of the tower with arched lights and pinnacles was added in 1673.

It is thought that the church has the world's first recorded peal of five bells which rung in the New Year in 1757 and was recorded in the Northampton Mercury, a sister newspaper of the current local paper the Chronicle and Echo.

Other churches may, of course, dispute this claim.

Having been in use for about four hundred years the bells were eventually removed from the tower in 2009 to undergo restoration at a bell foundry in Loughborough and were rehung in 2010.

The churchyard with its mass of little white daisies in season has been cleared of gravestones and those removed were placed in back to back rows at the rear of the church.

There is now a virtually uninterrupted view of the church from the main street.

A short distance from the church is the new cemetery where **Annie Pritchard** (1860-1892) murder victim of **Andrew George McRae** (a famous murder case in local history) is buried.
Her headless body was found near Althorp Station.
The inquest took place in The Red Lion and the court case lasted five days.
McRae was hanged in Northampton gaol.

Stable Block: East Haddon

.... EAST HADDON

The five bay **East Haddon Hall**, a Grade I listed property north of the church, was built in 1780-1 for the *Sawbridge* family who gave money to rebuild the church and built various Estate cottages.

The big 18th century gates at the entrance are from Stoke Doyle Manor. Alongside the gateway is an impressive thatched sandstone stable block with a date stone of 1669 and a vertically placed oval window above the porch.

Opposite the church once stood the post office, to the rear of which is the old round water tower with a conical tiled roof which was built of stone in 1890. It rises some twenty five feet to the eaves. When in use water was pumped to the tank in the roof from the brook which passes under the road.

In the 1800's there were more than a dozen pumps and a couple of wells from which the villagers could draw water. Although villagers now have mains water one of the old pumps remains at the corner of St Andrews Road under a coned thatched roof supported by six pillars, it is a lovely little feature of the village.

Village Pump : East Haddon

I could not understand why there should be a St Andrews Road in the village when the church is dedicated to *St Mary* but research revealed that the *Andrew* family had a manor in East Haddon prior to their move to Gotham in Nottinghamshire.

Another little gem I discovered was the Haddonstone Jubilee Garden just opposite the church. This lovely little oasis is open to all and features many of the stone products of the company but they are very attractively set out.

The firm which has its headquarters in the village was established in 1971 to produce high quality decorative cast stonework. Their products have found their way into palaces, stately homes, hotels and National Trust properties.

The local shop closed recently but there is still a Primary school which was built in 1790 and still uses the original classroom which has been refurbished. Opposite the church is the village hall outside of which is a replica of an old turnpike milestone which was once located just outside the village.

The Red Lion has a good reputation for its food and was voted into the Michelin top ten UK Country Pub lists in 2012.
I'm not into cooking but if I was I might be interested in attending one of the day or evening classes or gourmet weekends organised by the Shires Cookery School in the grounds.

The old Methodist chapel on Holdenby Road which was erected in 1811 is now a private house and has a most unusual porch with the pediment supported by two figures.

Water Tower : East Haddon

EASTON MAUDIT

Six miles south of Wellingborough
Population: 1801-135   2001 - 88

DOMESDAY BOOK
ESTONE

*Easton Maudit takes its name from the **Maduit** family who bought the estate at Easton in 1131
the Easton was simply the East Farm. The spelling 'Maudit' is quite modern.*

Of the two manors mentioned in the Domesday Book, one was held by *Countess Judith* and the other was *'waste'*. Prior to that, the area was settled during the Iron Age as evidenced by discoveries of pottery, flint axes and iron slag. Roman coins and pottery have also been discovered locally.

The village does not experience much traffic as it lies on minor roads just off the A509 between Wellingborough and Olney.
This is still very much an Estate village with most of the farms and houses owned by *Earl Compton.*
Just off the main street is a short terrace of two storey stone cottages which abruptly ends with a very unusual single storey building with a thatched roof supported by knotty tree trunks.
The wide overhang provides a porch to each of its three sides.
By the gateway pillars into the grounds of nearby **Castle Ashby House** is a second thatched cottage with a similar veranda and rustic columns.

The church of **ST PETER** and **ST PAUL** with its 14th century tower with flying buttresses, a beautiful 15th century spire and handsome pinnacles beckons from miles around.

In the 18th century when *Thomas Percy* was Vicar he had frequent visits from his friends *David Garrick*, *Dr Samuel Johnson* and *Oliver Goldsmith.* A plaque in the church marks where they used to sit.

Unusual Cottage at Easton Maudit

Other items which caught my attention were the Minton floor tiles throughout the church and the strainer arch similar to the ones at Finedon and Rushden.
The north chapel contains two large tombs which survived the church restoration of 1860.
One is the tomb of *Sir Christopher Yelverton* (1535-1612) Lord of the Manor, Speaker of the House of Commons and the other is the rather more elaborate tomb of his son *Sir Henry Yelverton* (1566-1629) MP and Attorney General.

In 1636 when *Charles I* visited the village the *Yelvertons* were granted permission to disafforest the manor together with parts of the land in Bozeat and were licenced to impark five hundred acres.
The decline in the population had started and was noted by *Bridges* in his history in 1720.

The Manor House lay to the east of the village but was demolished in 1801. All that remains is an area planted with Cedars of Lebanon.

What always fascinates me in Easton Maudit is the very old and hollow gnarled trunk of an elm tree which measures about 20ft in circumference.
It is supported by a very substantial steel pillar and brackets - if only trees could talk!
Both *John Bunyan* and *John Wesley* are believed to have preached the gospel beneath its canopy.
The old school and school house are closed and are now private residences.
The famous TV personality *Derek Nimmo* lived in the village and is buried in the churchyard.

EASTON NESTON

One mile east of Towcester
Population: 1801-114   2001- 74

DOMESDAY BOOK
ESTANESTONE/ADESTANESTONE

*The Domesday Book records the name as Estanestone namely a farmstead belonging to a person called **Eadston** or **Aethelstan.** It was not split into two names until about 1610.*

In 1086 Easton Neston was recorded as having two small manors and part of a mill rendering four shillings per annum. The other part appears to have been held by the manor at Hulcote.

The population declined when in 1499 the owner *Sir Richard Empson*, lawyer and councillor to *Henry VII* obtained licence to *'impark four hundred acres of land and thirty acres of woods as well as a free warren, a fishery and licence to build walls and towers of stone within his manor and crenellate the same'.*

Sir Richard feathered his own nest as *King Henry's* tax collector but his good fortune collapsed on the death of *Henry VII* in 1509.

He was brought to trial for treason and was sentenced to be executed on Tower Hill.

One of the jurors was *Sir Richard Fermor* who purchased Easton Neston Estate and by 1541 only the Manor House remained. The remaining inhabitants had been rehoused in Hulcote.

Today all that remains of the village of Easton Neston is the House and church in beautiful parkland off the busy A5 (Watling Street).

The church of **ST MARY** with a Perpendicular style west tower is situated in a quiet location near the House and has a fine south aisle and west window of the late 13th century.

The chancel has a blocked priest's doorway and there are wall paintings in the eastern end of the north aisle and over the arch together with a monument to a pet dog called 'Pug,' a two decker pulpit and box pews.

In the Estate grounds is Towcester Racecourse with a great Coade stone archway providing an impressive entrance from the A5. Coade stone was manufactured in London between 1769 -1840 and was actually fired clay but was marketed as artificial stone since at that time it was the preferred material for artificial decoration.

In recent years a new Grandstand has been built and racing has proved very popular - admittedly on many occasions there is free admission to the Racecourse - I wonder whether this is the reason for the popularity.

The Racecourse buildings now regularly hold conferences, exhibitions, meetings and even weddings.

Fermor

Easton Neston

Easton Neston House and the Fermor and Hesketh families

Richard Fermor, a London merchant bought Easton Neston from **Thomas Empson** in the early 16th century.

A descendant, another **Richard** was created a Baronet in 1641. His son **Sir William**, who was MP for Northampton 1670-9 became **Lord Lempster** in 1692 and built the present mansion to the designs of **Nicholas Hawksmoor** a protégé of **Sir Christopher Wren** between 1700-02.

His son **Thomas** was made **Earl of Pomfret** in 1721 and his wife, the **Countess of Pomfret** was a dominant personality in society and an early enthusiast of the 'Gothick' revival.

The House came into the **Hesketh** family through the marriage in 1846 of **Sir Thomas George Hesketh** the 5th **Baronet of Rufford** in Lancashire to **Lady Anna Maria Fermor**,
sister and heiress of the 5th and last **Earl of Pomfret**.
In 1935 the 8th **Baronet** was created **Lord Hesketh**.

Until the 1950's when the 3rd **Lord Hesketh**'s father and grandfather died, the upkeep of Easton Neston was largely paid for by the fortunes of his grandmother and great grandmother who were both American heiresses.
Nevertheless it was quite a surprise and subject to much local media interest when the decision to sell came after a fire in July 2002 badly damaged the north wing of the house.

In 2005 the 3rd **Lord Hesketh** sold the House and 600 acres for £15 million to **Leon Max** the Russian born owner of the Californian based Max Studio retail chain.
Following restoration and improvements the House is said to look better than it has ever done with splendid interiors.

In recent years tragedy has struck the family in motoring accidents. The **Dowager Lady Hesketh**, wife of the 2nd **Baron** lost an eye in 1972 and her second son **Robert** was killed in 1997. Monuments to the **Fermor/Hesketh** family can be seen in both the church and churchyard.

Margaret Thatcher is said to have used Easton Neston House as a 'bolt hole' after her tearful resignation as Prime Minister in November 1990.

The parish now includes the hamlet of Hulcote and the lost settlement of Showsley (Sewardsley).

HULCOTE

DOMESDAY BOOK
HALECOTE/HULECOTE
The name means 'hovel like cottage' somewhat unfortunate given the nature of the hamlet today.

The manor was held by **de Hulcote** family between 1242 and the early 16th century when it passed to the **Empsons.**
This is the Estate village to Easton Neston and comprises a small group of delightful houses along two sides of a Green built of chequered brick with pointed Gothic windows.
The ecclesiastical look of the cottages has caused it to be known by some as the *'chapel village'*.
The old school house bears the date 1816 so it is possible that this was the date when the present houses were built.
Hulcote lies on a quiet 'no through road' just north of Towcester. The original Manor House is said to have stood in a field called Hall Close.

SHOWLSEY/SEWARDSLEY

*The name derives from 'leah', a clearing and possibly **Siward** the main landowner at Easton Neston in 1066.*

In 1179 this small settlement was listed as Sewardeslega and once had a small Priory of Cistercian nuns founded by **Richard de Lester** who was Lord of the Manor in the reign of **Henry II.**

In 1459-60 finances were so poor that the House was appropriated by the Cluniac Abbey of St Mary de la Pre in Northampton.
The Priory was eventually suppressed in 1536 when there were only four nuns and a Prioress.

Today the existing settlement with little more than a farm and a few outbuildings is known as Showsley by which name it appears on today's maps.

EASTON ON THE HILL

Two miles south west of Stamford
Population: 1801 -579   2001 - 956

DOMESDAY BOOK
ESTONE
Originally this was another 'est tun' - east farm and the addendum does not appear until the 18th century.

The two manors mentioned in the Domesday Book appear to have been held at least in part by the Abbeys at Peterborough and Saint-Pierre-sur-Dives in France. The mill rendered twenty shillings per annum.

This is a delightful hill village overlooking the Welland Valley and has a good mix of attractive stone buildings dating from the 16th to the 19th century within the Conservation area.

I particularly like the view of Church Street looking up towards the church.

Unfortunately the modern development outside the village centre is not particularly attractive.

A dominant landmark at the north end of the village is the 12th century church of **ALL SAINTS** with a fine 15th century Perpendicular style ashlar faced west tower with clasping buttresses, battlements and tall crocketed pinnacles, very similar to the church at Collyweston.

Its height from the ground to the top of the pinnacles is one hundred feet (30.5metres).

In June the south porch is covered with a charming mass of white roses.

Old School: Easton on the Hill

Inside the church is very light and airy owing to the lack of stained glass but there are some medieval paintings including a 'Doom' or 'Last Judgement' over the chancel arch.

Other points of interest include the many box pews some of which carry the name of the family that once used them and are lined for warmth, the 16th century parish chest and two 15th century gargoyles which were found on the ground when the tower was struck by lightning in August 1915.

Opposite the church is Easton House which now houses the Chartered Institute of Purchasing & Supply.

Near the **Priests House** is the 18th century Glebe House which has a white sundial above the front door with the words - *'Fear the Lord Always'*.
It was once occupied by the Rector's son, ***Captain Lancelot Skynner,*** Master of the vessel **La Lutine** which sank in 1799 off the coast of Holland. His memorial is in the church.

The ship's bell was recovered and used at Lloyds of London to signal with one stroke when a ship was lost at sea. Nowadays because of a fault it is rarely rung other than to mark a royal death.

For anyone interested in date stones this is the place to visit - you see them all over the village.
One house in particular - Number 11 Church Street has four date stones although only those from 1607, 1674 and 1792 are legible.

In the 19th century Easton on the Hill like so many other villages had a windmill. It still exists today a little way off the Stamford road but it is in a sorry state with no sails and its shell covered in foliage. Tragically in 1876 twenty year old *Miss Stancer* was struck on the head by one of the sails and was killed instantly.

An ironstone quarry in the area which employed many local men only operated for about fifty years around the time of the First World War and was never a great success possibly because the nearest ironworks were in Scunthorpe about sixty miles away.

There are still three public houses, one is The Bell in the centre of the village and the other two are on the main road - The Oak Inn and The Exeter Arms.
Public houses no longer in existence include The Slater's Arms (in the Lane), The Retreat (in Stamford Road), The White Horse and The Crown Inn in Stamford Road with a crown plaque on the wall.

The Methodist chapel in Church Street was built in 1874 on the site of an earlier chapel but this is now a private residence.

There is still a convenience store, post office and a modern Primary school - the Easton Garford school named after *Richard Garforde* who bequeathed funds in 1670 for education and religious teaching in the village.
The old school built in 1868 with an ornate spiral tower, cupula, clock and bell now serves as the village hall.

As you leave the village en route to Stamford in a quiet little spot is a distinctive four faced monument to the Polish paratroopers who were stationed in the area during the Second World War before taking part in the Battle for Arnhem.

The Priest's House : Easton on the Hill

On the 23rd February 1941 during the Second World War two bombs fell on the village and blew off the roof of The Firs, 15 High Street, killing one person and injuring another.
The pitched roof was never replaced and it has a flat roof to this day.

THE PRIESTS HOUSE

The oldest house in the village, commonly known as the Priests House, is shrouded in mystery. It appears to be 16th century in origin but no one seems to have any evidence as to when it was built.

It is thought that it may have been part of another building (possibly a Rectory) and was used by visiting priests. It certainly appears to have been used in the past as a school but also as housing for pigs and cattle and storage of hay.

The building was renovated by the eminent architect *Sir Thomas Graham Jackson* in 1867 and saved by the Peterborough Society from demolition in 1963.

Since then it has been in the hands of the National Trust and is used as a local museum and meeting room. It is certainly worth a visit. If closed a key can be obtained locally.

ECTON

Five miles east of Northampton
Population: 1801 - 474   2001 - 439

DOMESDAY BOOK
ECHENTONE
*The possible derivation of the name comes from **Ecca** a local leader or landowner and 'tun' - farmstead.*

A large number of finds locally of pottery, flint tools, coins and jewellery from the Bronze and Iron Age and the Saxon and Roman era indicate that this area alongside the River Nene was inhabited many centuries before **William I** ordered his land ownership survey in 1086.
The discovery of a large number of kilns indicates that the manufacture of pottery was important to the area.

The Domesday Book records forty one households, two mills rendering fourteen shillings and thirty two acres of meadow.
It was obviously quite a valuable manor.

Bondi held the manor prior to the Norman Conquest when it passed to **Ralph** who held it of **Henry de Ferrers** who also held Estates elsewhere.
Ownership descended through the Duchy of Lancaster to the **Montgomery** family who held it until 1574 when it was sold to **Thomas Catesby.**

The Reading and Recreation Room in High Street was erected by the **Sotherby** family to commemorate the 60th year of the reign of **Queen Victoria** in 1897 and was converted into two houses in the 1960's.

Mrs Sotherby also provided money for the War Memorial erected in 1917 at the top of the High Street near the school, before the First World War ended. It is thought that it was originally a memorial to her husband **Major General Lionel Sotherby** who was killed in 1915.

At the end of the war the names of others from the parish who were killed were added.
The unusual design of the Memorial led it to become known as *'The Shrine'*.
The Memorial suffered mindless vandalism in the 1970's but has now been restored.

As the village of Ecton lies at right angles to the busy A4500 Northampton to Wellingborough road the traffic roars straight past leaving the village a delightful and peaceful oasis with many lovely old ironstone cottages some of which stand side on to the long winding High Street.

In the early part of the 20th century there were at least four shops but sadly all have gone - the last one closing in 1989.

Ecton was one of the first villages in Northamptonshire to be protected by a Conservation Order under the Civic Amenities Act 1967 thus recognising its unique character.

The large church of **ST MARY MAGDALENE**, a Grade I listed building was built of ironstone in the late 13th and early 14th century.

The west tower is prominent and rather unusual because the lower part was built of sandstone and then a century later a paler limestone top was added which does not harmonise with the mellow stonework of the rest of the building.

Inside are 19th century box pews and pulpit and a defaced 14th century font which was discovered being used as a cattle trough.

Ecton and its church see many American visitors because buried in the churchyard to the left of the north porch arc **Thomas** (1702) and **Eleanor** (1711) aunt and uncle to **Benjamin Franklin** who helped draft the Declaration of Independence, signing it in 1776.

The Three Horseshoes public house built on the site of an old smithy which was owned by **Thomas**.

The Reading Room: Ecton

Ecton House a Grade II listed Rectory stands north of the church and was originally built by the **Montgomery** family around 1500 and remodelled in the Gothic style by **Eyre Whalley** about two hundred years later.

In recent years it has been used as a Retreat and Conference Centre for clergy but it closed in 2003 and has been converted into luxury apartments.

On the old main road stands a public house with the unusual name, The Worlds End.

An Inn was mentioned as long ago as 1678 when it was called The Globe - but the present building probably dates from about 1765 and has been extended somewhat in recent years.

Was it so re-named because it was way out in the country at one time or was it because after the Battle of Naseby it is said to have been used as a compound for the injured and captured Royalist prisoners and many came to meet their end whilst in residence.

Not surprisingly some people claim to have seen a ghost in the clothes of a man but with the face of a skull.

Being located near to the River Nene there are some lovely walks in the area including one to Cogenhoe on the other side of the Nene Valley during which the footpath crosses the 18th century Packhorse Bridge which spans the original meandering course of the river.

Ecton Hall

*In 1712 the Estate was acquired by the **Isted** family who enclosed some land to extend their park resulting in the loss of some properties in Lower Ecton.*

*The façade of the Hall is dated 1756 but other parts are much earlier. The gazebo is attributed to **Ambrose** who developed the Estate during his fifty years of residence in the mid 18th century.*

*The last member of the **Isted** family died in 1881 and the Estate passed by marriage to the **Sotherby** family who continued to improve the property.*

***Major General F E Sotherby** inherited in 1887 and became very active in local affairs.*

His initials 'FES' can be found on the Reading Room and on other village properties.

*The last Lord of the Manor was **Lt. Col. Herbert Sotheby** who died in 1954. His heir, **Commander Sotheby** decided to sell the contents of the Hall and treasures which had taken years to collect were disposed of in just a few days and many villagers lost their employment.*

By the 1960's the Hall was almost a ruin and was threatened with demolition but following alterations it was brought back into use in the 1980's as luxury apartments. The present Ecton Hall has been described as:-

'a foremost example of the early Gothic revival in the County'

EDGCOTE

Six miles north east of Banbury
1801-66   2001 - 57

DOMESDAY BOOK
HOCECOTE
*It is thought that the name refers to **Hwicca's** 'cot'
the cottage of a Saxon tribal leader.*

The Romans built a villa at Blackgrounds on the north bank of the River Cherwell a quarter of a mile east of Edgcote. Excavations in 1849 revealed the site of a bath house (36ft x 18ft) plus bones and coins of the 3rd and 4th centuries AD. This is believed to be the site of the large Roman station of *Brinauis* and has been placed on the 'at risk' Register by English Heritage citing threats of ploughing and a risk of collapse.

At the time of the Domesday Book Edgcote had a two hide manor held by *Walkelin* of the *Bishop of Coutances*, a mill rendering ten shillings per annum and twenty five households but is now so small that it does not feature on some maps.

There was partial depopulation in 1502 when forty people were evicted and two hundred and forty acres of arable land was enclosed and converted to pasture. Nine houses were destroyed but eighteen families remained.
About 1760 the rest of the village was depopulated by the Lord of the Manor for a landscaped park west of his house but two new farms and seven cottages were erected elsewhere on the Estate.

Today Edgcote consists only of an old Rectory, a few Estate cottages and a pleasing composition of the Manor flanked by stables on one side and the church on the other. It is, nevertheless a very pleasing and peaceful location.

The church of **ST JAMES** dates from the 13th century. Interestingly there is no division between the nave and chancel but there is a two storey vestry although the upper floor is missing.

The wide manorial pew has a window like that of a private house looking on to the front courtyard of the Manor.

The church is well worth a visit if only to see its many beautiful and elaborately carved tombs including four by *Rysbrack* of the *Chauncey* family who were Lords of the Manor for some 240 years. There is also an interesting memorial stone to *Bridget* who died in 1730 on which is written:-

'under this marble stone lies whatsoever was mortal of Bridget Chauncey of whom no man was worthy.'

It is thought she may have been a nun.
There is also a brass of *Arden Bayly* who was Rector for forty nine years during the 19th century.

The Grade I listed **Edgcote House** with a hipped roof and a three bay pediment was rebuilt in ironstone between 1747 and 1752 at a cost of £20,000 for *Richard Chauncey*. It replaced an earlier building where *Charles I* and his two sons are said to have spent the night before the Battle of Edgehill in Oct 1642 during the Civil War.
There was an earlier battle at Edgcote itself.

BATTLE OF EDGCOTE MOOR
26th July 1469

This was one of the battles which took place between the House of Lancaster and the House of York during the War of the Roses.

The *Earl of Warwick* (the Kingmaker) had endeavoured to put the Yorkist *Edward IV* on the throne and hoped this would ensure that he had an important part to play in matters of state. However he became disenchanted with the King's government following the Battle of Towton and furthermore felt humiliated by *Edward's* marriage, in secret, to *Elizabeth Woodville* in 1464.

As a result he rose up in open rebellion in 1469.
A battle was fought at Edgcote near a crossing of the tributary of the River Cherwell and pitted followers of the Lancastrians represented by *Richard Neville*, *16th Earl of Warwick* against those of the Yorkists of *Edward IV* under *Wm Herbert, Earl of Pembroke*. The battle resulted in a Lancastrian victory and the Yorkists suffered great slaughter of whom it is said 168 knights, squires and gentlemen perished. *The Earl of Pembroke* and his brother were taken prisoner and were put to death by the rebels.

EVENLEY

Two miles south of Brackley
Population: 1801-369   2001 - 537

DOMESDAY BOOK
AVELAI/EVELAI/EVELAIA
*Its name derives from the two Saxon words
'efn' - even or smooth and 'leah' - grove or clearing.*

The Red Lion: Evenley

The village stands in an elevated position on the County boundary with Oxfordshire.

Finds of pottery and significant hoards of coins of *Nero, Domitian, Severus Alexander, Probus, Carausius, Constantine* and others indicate that the area was well settled prior to 1086 when it was recorded as one of the few places in the County having four water mills. The number of households recorded numbers fifty one so it was quite a large settlement at the time of *William I.*

Today this is a pleasing village, the most notable feature of which is the large, almost square village Green which is bounded by lovely little rows of two storeyed stone cottages many of which have striped roofs by utilising black and red tiles.
This is an idyllic spot and superb for a leisurely game of cricket on a lovely sunny afternoon.

Among the other buildings around the Green are the old village school built in 1834 and now used as the village hall, the shop cum post office and The Red Lion Hotel. I read that the last man in England to be hanged for sheep stealing was apprehended in this very public house.

On the north side of the village is the church of **ST GEORGE** built between 1864 and 1865 by *H. Woodyer* for *Mrs P. S. Pierrepoint* of **Evenley Hall** in memory of her husband. It stands on the foundations of the previous 12th century church which was gutted by fire. The west tower with its stair turret is in Early English style and has a distinctive shingled broach spire.

When I visited the church recently workmen were busy repairing the leaking nave roof and doing some work on the tower walls.

The chief monument is to *Sir Creswell Levinz* (1627-1701) Attorney General, who is buried in the church. He was a colleague of *Lord Jefferies* at *'The Bloody Assizes'* and also Defence Counsel for the Seven Bishops. This fine monument together with others was moved to the base of the tower when the church was rebuilt.

The Georgian **Evenley Hall** set back from the A43 in parkland dates back to the 1740's.
A devastating fire in 1897 was not helped by the fact that the water froze in the hoses as they tried to douse the flames.
Considerable restoration was necessary.
During the Second World War it was used by the Yorkshire Regiment until 'D' Day when evacuees from London arrived.
In 1941 ownership passed to the National Children's Home. Since then it was briefly used by the County Council and is now a private house.

West of the parish is the lost village of Astwick.

ASTWICK

This small abandoned settlement was probably listed under one of the manors of Evenley in the Domesday Book where it is not specifically mentioned.
It was located between Croughton and Evenley and is still marked on some Ordnance Survey maps.
Some land belonged to Brackley Hospital whose property passed in 1484 to Magdalen College, Oxford.

It is recorded that in 1510 there were at least fifteen houses and as late as 1720 *Bridges* described it as 'a village of six houses' and also said that 'Astwick appears to have been formerly a large town as may be seen from the ruins which are called the Old Town.'
About a hundred years later the site was abandoned.

EVERDON

GREAT AND LITTLE

Three miles south east of Daventry
Population: 1801-585   2001 - 325

DOMESDAY BOOK
EVERDONE

At the time of the Domesday Book - Everdone – 'hill of the wild boar', was just one village and was owned by the Benedictine monks of Bernay. Little Everdon appeared later in medieval times as a daughter village.

The **Bishop of Bayeaux** held the manor after the Norman Conquest of 1066.

Bernay Abbey in Normandy appears to have had a cell in the village probably consisting of a small colony of monks sent over from France to look after the estate.

This cell is said to have been located on the site of the present Manor House but no trace of it remains.

It was suppressed during the reign of **Henry V** (1413-22) and the Estate given to Eton College which was founded by **Henry VI** in 1440.

The College appointed Rectors in Everdon until 1923.

In the heart of the village is the warm brown stone 14th century church of **ST MARY** with its heavily buttressed west tower, wide nave and tall arcades.
It is huge for the size of the village and it is thought that it was possibly financed in part by the monks from Bernay in Normandy.

Although many of the windows are filled with old clear glass which makes the church very light take the time to admire the East window in the south aisle and see if you can spot the pelican in the north west window of the nave.

Also high up at the west end is what I took to be a minstrels gallery but I have since learned that it was provided at some uncertain date to give access to the church roof.

A particular treasure is the 14th century carved oak rood screen said to be one of the best in Northamptonshire.

On a lovely sunny day it was a real joy to sit on the well placed bench near the south porch with its beautiful doorway and gaze across the meadows towards the lost hamlet of Snorscomb and imagine the inhabitants walking through the fields to church where it is said that the south aisle was reserved for them.

The poet **Thomas Gray**, author of an
'Elegy written in a country churchyard'
often stayed in the village with his uncle
William Antrobus who was the local Vicar between 1729-1744.

The Great Fire of Everdon took place on the 13th April 1786 when a plumber working on the church tower accidently set fire to the roof and the blaze spread to some twenty houses plus outhouses and workshops but thankfully with no loss of life. Unfortunately only two or three houses were insured.

In the late 19th century the population was considerably larger than it is today although the number of properties has remained constant indicating that there was much overcrowding.

This is a pretty village with many old cottages surrounded by rolling countryside.
The biggest difference in appearance today is that most properties now have roofs of tiles instead of thatch.
There is no longer a shop or post office and the local school has closed and is now a Field Study Centre consequently you often see school parties in the area.

Opposite the church is the only public house, The Plough Inn. The old 'Plume of Feathers' is now a private house but still has the public house sign above the door.

On the road to Farthingstone is Everdon Stubbs seventy acres of deciduous woodland managed by the Woodland Trust. It is famous for its magnificent display of bluebells in the spring.

Wild boar once roamed the area but now there are foxes, badgers, chiff-chaffs, woodpeckers and owls. It is a site of Special Scientific Interest.

I remember years ago visiting Everdon Stubbs with my young family at bluebell time.
Everyone was enjoying the experience until I felt something brush my trouser leg.
On looking down I saw it was a rabbit absolutely riddled with myxamotosis. Its head was swollen and its eyes bulging and covered with slimy excretions. It was a horrible sight. I hurriedly called the family together and left the scene.

On reflection I should have put the rabbit out of its misery but at the time I was more concerned that my children did not see the poor animal.
Up until that time I used to enjoy rabbit pies but the myxamotosis epidemic put me and many other people off the delicacy.

The current medieval bridge which crosses a tributary of the River Nene stands on the site of a bridge recorded in 944AD.

Also within the parish is the hamlet of Little Everdon and linked to Everdon by a very little used track is the deserted village of Snorscomb.

LITTLE EVERDON

This tiny but rather select hamlet is located about half a mile north of Everdon. It is a very quiet place with a number of old attractive properties alongside Everdon Hall with its livery stables and horse trials.

In 1720 *Bridges* noted that there were seventeen houses - not too different from today - although earthworks in the area suggest that it was once a larger settlement.
One of the County's long distance footpaths - the Nene Way passes through the area.

SNORSCOMB

DOMESDAY BOOK
SNOCHESCUMBE

There does not appear to be agreement as to the derivation of the name but one widely accepted view is that this was the valley of someone called **Snoc**.

It is very hard to imagine today but this deserted village one mile south of Everdon once had a thriving community and even had a Charter in 944.
In the Domesday Book it was held by the **Count of Mortain** and was divided into two small manors.
The larger manor was held by **Philip Lovell** at the time of **King John** but was depopulated when land was enclosed and nine houses were pulled down on the order of **Richard Knightley** of Fawsley about 1520 as a result of which he was prosecuted - a process that cost him a lot of money in lawyer's fees.

What now remains consists of little more than a large house and a few farm buildings although Snorscomb and Snorscomb Mill are still featured on Ordnance Survey maps.

EYDON

Eight miles south of Daventry
Population: 1801-484   2001 - 422

DOMESDAY BOOK
EGEDONE
*The original version of this name may derive from someone called **Aega** who was a tribal leader in the area - the same personal name as in Aynho.*

Wakelyn Manor House: Eydon

In 1086 the two hide manor was held by **Hugh de Grandmesnil** when there was a recorded population of fourteen and a mill rendering two shillings per annum.

The Lordship of the Manor passed through various hands including **John of Gaunt** and then to the **Beauforts** and eventually to **King Henry VII**

To the north west of the village there is evidence of shallow surface quarrying which probably dates back to medieval times but the site has been damaged by modern cultivation.

I love visiting this small and very attractive village in the quite remote western edge of Northamptonshire surrounded by undulating wooded countryside.

Eydon contains many fine houses but no longer has a school, shop or post office although I have seen mobile butchers and fish merchants in the village.
Even the coach firm set up by **Geoff Amos** in 1954 ceased trading in August 2011.

There is still a public house, The Royal Oak which dates from 1692 and gives its name to a group of Morris Dancers formed in 1985 to dance at the village fete.
They now perform further afield with dances from the Cotswold villages.
Legend has it that cock fights used to regularly take place in the pub.

I was not surprised to learn that much of the village is in a Conservation area with almost a quarter of the houses being listed buildings.
Additional building work is now closely monitored.

One house I particularly like is the ironstone **Wakelyns** Manor House situated near the Green with its impressive and fairly large porch.
The House was once a public house –
The Blackamoors Head and later the Mens Club Reading Room. **King George V** is said to have taken tea and bread and butter in the Reading Room when he visited troops in the village during military exercises that took place all over the South Midlands in 1913.

The Great Central Branch Line from Woodford Halse to Banbury had a small halt at Eydon Road to serve the village.
This opened in 1900 but lasted little over fifty years. You can still see evidence of the line and its bridges as you travel in the area.

The church of **ST NICHOLAS** is mainly medieval in structure but was significantly restored in 1865 by **R. C. Hussey**.
The earliest part is thought to date from the 12th century and workmanship of this period is still evident in the northwest pillar of the north aisle and the font.
The low west tower was added during the 14th century and has two bells, the oldest of which is dated 1603 and is still in use today.

The tower itself has four unusually tall, yet small, corner towers very much like chimney pots and some delightful gargoyles.

During the restoration of 1865 a south aisle and porch together with a vestry in the north aisle were added.
There are some lovely stained glass windows.

In 1980 the Methodist church closed and the congregation joined **ST NICHOLAS** which has reminders of the Methodist church in the form of a small font, chair, plaque, hymn board and communion table.

The churchyard contains the remains of the Preaching Cross which has a new shaft and top.

I have visited the churchyard when it was ablaze with a profusion of wild flowers.
On my most recent visit there were still a few wild flowers but not so many and I wonder if the grass was mown at the wrong time of the year.

Opposite the south porch is an archway and gates linking the church to the Hall.

There were two fires in the village on the 13 August 1651 and 28 May 1905.
Both were quite disastrous as many of the houses and barns were roofed with thatch.
Some of the stone still shows scorch marks.

The Grafton Hunt moved its kennels to just outside Eydon during 2009.

As a reminder of days past when local villains were punished within the village there are old stocks and a whipping post on the Green which were restored in the 19th century.

The last person to undergo punishment here was a veteran of Waterloo who regularly got drunk when he got his pension.
This is now a County Heritage site.

Stocks & Pump
Eydon

Eydon Hall

*The Grade I listed Eydon Hall was built in the Palladian style for the **Rev. Francis Annesley** (1789-91) and has five bays and a basement plus two storeys.*
*It was then owned by **Colonel Henry Cartwright**, MP for South Northants 1858-68 who died there in 1890.*

*Then followed a period of neglect until 1927 when it was saved by American money under the ownership of **Lord Brand** who then passed it to his daughter **Lady Ford**.*

In 1982 the Hall was put on the market for £1.5 million.
*It returned to the market in 2004 with an estimated price of £11 million but to the surprise of the property industry it was said to have been sold in just two weeks for considerably more, to the current owner **Tim Stamper** founder of the computer games company 'Rare'.*

A public footpath runs through the delightful parkland but at sufficient distance as to not be seen from the Hall.

FARTHINGHOE

Five miles east of Banbury
Population: 1801-338   2001 – 418 (inc Steane)

DOMESDAY BOOK
FERNINGEHO
Prior to the Domesday Book it was just a hamlet possibly deriving from Saxon words meaning 'ridge of the dwellers in the bracken'.

Earl Aubrey held this four hide manor in 1086 when there was a population of thirty three including a priest.
The village is built on a grid system giving a good example of medieval planning as shown on a map dated 1805. However in 1841 another map shows part of one street had been abandoned and this has now been built over.

Most of the older properties are located off the busy A422 between Banbury and Brackley in a Conservation area first designated in 1978 which is just as well as the traffic on this road is very heavy and continuous - a bypass is badly needed.
This did not stop a very proud peacock from sauntering slowly along the road completely oblivious (or simply ignoring) the line of cars impatiently queuing up behind.

Alongside the main road is the church dedicated to **ST MICHAEL**. The lower part of the tower is Norman but the top part has an inscription dated 1654 being the year in which the tower was repaired by **John Egerton**. The one handed clock is quite unusual. Was it installed like this or did someone steal one of the hands?
Inside is a fine Norman tower arch as wide as the nave. The clerestory dates from the 15th century.
I was particularly interested in the monument to **George Rush** who died in London in 1803 and is thought to have once been Lord of the Manor.
It is unusual as it shows him as an old man in robes, nightcap and slippers.

Abbey Lodge to the west of the church is the oldest and to my mind the most interesting house and is thought to date from the 14th and 15th century. It is said to have been the Lodge of the Abbot of Leicester.

There is a public house and restaurant - The Fox - with accommodation created in 2009 as a result of the conversion of an old barn.

Also popular with visitors is the Farm Shop and Tea Rooms in a recently converted medieval barn at Limes Farm alongside the A422. It is owned by the **Deeley** family who I understand, can trace their family back to land at Purston in 1066.

The Victorian Gothic Primary school near the church seems to be very popular if the number of cars waiting outside for the finishing bell is anything to go by. Its popularity may be owed to small class sizes and a high adult to child ratio.

The railway once provided connections to Bletchley and Oxford but by 1963 had closed to all traffic and the station buildings were demolished. A cutting on the old line has now been converted into a Nature Reserve.

The old chapel has been converted into a private residence.
In recent years the parish boundary has been altered to include the once independent parish of Steane - page 375.

The parish also includes the lost village of Great Purston although its near neighbour Little Purston is in the parish of Kings Sutton.

GREAT PURSTON

DOMESDAY BOOK
PRESTONE

As in the case of Little Purston this is likely to have been a priest's settlement although no priest is mentioned in the Domesday Book. At that time there were six households.
The settlement declined when three landowners combined to enclose the land, destroy six houses and expel forty three people in 1494. You can still make out areas where buildings are likely to have stood.

It is now little more than a grand Manor House with a hipped roof, a farm and outbuildings and is approached by a narrow 'no through road'. It is worth making the detour as you will find a large number of assorted coloured and very fascinating alpacas. I could have watched them all day.

FARTHINGSTONE

Five miles south east of Daventry
Population; 1801-230   2001-179

DOMESDAY BOOK
FORDINESTONE
*Often referred to as Farraxton, the original name
derives from a personal name* **Fordein**
and the Saxon word' tun'- farmstead.

The **Count of Mortain,** one of the County's largest land owners at the time of the Domesday Book held the two manors here. There were fifteen households and a Knight.

This little village lies off the beaten track between Towcester and Daventry with some delightful old houses built of local stone. Its centre is dominated by the church of **ST MARY** which is approached through an attractive lych gate. The church has a simple north doorway dating from about 1200 but was extensively renovated in the 1920's by the *Agnew* family (owners of Punch Magazine).

Of the lovely stained glass windows all except the East window are in memory of members of the *Agnew* family who were looked on as local Squires. The windows in the south wall of the nave are in memory of **Enid Jocelyn** who died in 1921 aged 22 years and two brothers who died in the Great War.

Of particular interest are the beautifully carved poppy head pews. It is said that the wood carver objected to the new fangled pipe organ being introduced and showed his displeasure by carving a monkey bashing some cymbals, a demon playing a drum and an owl playing a pipe.

The Kings Arms opposite the church is a picturesque neo Tudor building built before 1845 but reconstructed after a fire in about 1870.
It has certain ecclesiastical characteristics including crosses and gargoyles peering down from on high which is not surprising as I was told that material was re-used from a nearby church reconstruction.

The *Agnews* provided a little oasis known as 'Joymead' in the centre of the village in memory of their daughter. This is still in use today as an ideal play area for children and an excellent venue for wedding receptions, garden fetes, etc.
Nearby is the Old Rectory which has a porch with a plaque inscribed:

> **ICW 1842**

North east of the village, south of Castle Dykes Farm is evidence of a Norman motte castle with three baileys and the buried remains of a Bronze Age barrow. In 1712 workmen digging for building stone found a room with a vaulted stone roof and another room beneath with rudely carved human figures carved on the stones.

A popular location close to the village is the eighteen hole Golf Club and sixteen bedroom Hotel. Opened for the first time in 1972 it was based upon the design by *M. Gallagher* using the existing natural wooded landscape.

The Baptist chapel has recently closed and the members have joined the nearby congregation in Weston.
There is no longer a shop and the school which closed in 1962 is now the village hall.
The building next door is known as Pension Row and is very unusual in design with brick door frame, giant arches and walling faced with crocks and plaster.
Another unusual sight is the Air Navigation Beacon on Maidford Road which looks like a UFO. It is wide and low and could easily be missed when passing by car owing to the roadside hedge.

FAWSLEY

Four miles south of Daventry
Population: 1801-29   2001 - 32

DOMESDAY BOOK
FELEWESLEIE/FAELAU/FALEWESLE
FALEWESLEIE/FELESLEWE/FELVESLEA

In the Domesday Book the name of the village was listed with a number of different spellings but all appear to have derived from the Saxon words 'feula' - fallow and 'leah' – clearing i.e. meadow of the fallow deer.

Fawsley, which stands in the midst of parkland just off the A36 was once a thriving community but is now just a deserted medieval village with little remaining although its history reaches back to Saxon times when it was part of a royal estate.
In 1086 the entire Estate belonged to the King with about fifty households.
A market was granted in 1224.
It then passed through various hands before being sold in 1415 to *Sir Richard Knightley* who enclosed the land to keep sheep by which time almost half the population had been lost to the Black Death.

The village lay south and east of the Hall but by 1547 there were 2,500 sheep and very few people. Eventually it seems that the sheep population rose to 10,800. There are still sheep but nowhere near as many today.

In the 1760's and 1770's the landscape gardener, *Lancelot 'Capability' Brown* transformed the Estate including designing ornamental gardens, parkland and the double lakes which are thought to cover the site of the former village.

I still enjoy visiting the area and have had many enjoyable walks in the locality.
When I had a young family Fawsley provided a very good day out. It was not too far and there were plenty of places to picnic, play and walk without spending unnecessary money.

The church of **ST MARY** with its west tower dates from the 13th century and escaped the flooding of the old village.

It now stands isolated on a grassy knoll overlooking the beautiful curving double lake with only cattle and sheep for company.
Entry is made by crossing a small bridge over the 'ha ha' (provided as a barrier to animals) and through a very narrow north doorway.
The tower has only four bells but this does not appear to hamper the ringers who have won a number of five bell contests in neighbouring churches.

The high sided box pew in the south aisle enabled the *Knightley* family to be hidden from the congregation but via a large squint they could witness what was happening at the altar.
The church is primarily a mausoleum to the family containing a considerable number of magnificent monuments including a fine 16th century alabaster free-standing tomb featuring effigies of
Sir Richard Knightley and his wife, *Jane*.
Also worthy of note is the East window of the north aisle featuring *Washington* heraldic shields brought from Sulgrave Manor in 1830 and the unusual stone Bible on the window ledge in the north wall. The church is a very popular wedding location and is still used occasionally during the summer and for concerts, etc.
Fawsley Hall with its Great Hall with vaulted oriel windows overlooking the lakes, dates from the 16th century.

Towards the end of the 19th century it was used as a convalescent home and was the brief holiday home for *Joseph Merrick* - better known as
'The Elephant Man.'
The Hall was used by the army in both the First and Second World Wars and suffered accordingly.
In the 1950's and 60's it was loaned to a timber company as a workshop and continued to deteriorate. Its sorry state was featured in an exhibition at the V & A entitled:
'The decline of the English Country House'

In 1975 it was bought by a wealthy couple,
Mr & Mrs Saunders who with the help of a consortium have restored it as a high class Hotel. It is now one of the country's top ten venues for weddings.

Fawsley Hall

Knightley of Fawsley

Knightley family

The **Knightleys** came to England with **William the Conqueror** and settled in the village of Knightley in Staffordshire from where came their name. They arrived in Fawsley in 1415 when **Sir Richard** (d. 1442) bought the Estate and the family continued in residence for over 500 years. Although the direct line failed again and again there was always a cousin or nephew waiting to carry on the succession.

Sir Edmund, (1488-1542) a lawyer, was born at Fawsley and went on to become a 'Commissioner to the Survey' before the Dissolution - a post which appears to have favoured a number of influential people.
With the death of **Sir Edmund** his widow took up residence in the **Dower House** which stood in a remote part of the Park about three quarters of a mile east of the Hall. It is reputed to be the oldest brick building in the County.
Today it is just a fine old ruin. It is not surprising given its remote location and ruinous condition that some people have reported ghostly events in the vicinity.

The family became very unpopular because of their deliberate policy of evicting tenants in order to turn land over to sheep farming which was far more profitable. It is said that the sheep population on their land rose to over 10,000. Not only did they arouse the anger of their tenants but also managed to arouse mistrust in those they could least afford to offend. **Sir William Parr** wrote to **Thomas Cromwell** in 1533 saying that 'considering the grudges borne to me by the **Knightleys** it would be of small comfort to me if any of them next year were Sheriff of Northamptonshire. **Parr** himself became Sheriff that year and a **Knightley** did not hold the office again for 20 years.
The family however grew rich and continued to develop sheep farming at the expense of their tenants and are said to have at one time held forty one manors.

Sir Richard (1533-1615) was Knighted in 1565. He was an eminent lawyer and a prominent member of the Puritan faction in Parliament. It is said that copies of the famous Martin Marprelate tracts attacking Bishops were printed at Fawsley in secret on a printing press which was moved from location to location to avoid detection.
He was finally arrested and fined £2,000 by the Star Chamber. Some years later he was more heavily fined.
In 1587 he was commanded by **Elizabeth I** to be present at the execution of **Mary Queen of Scots** and entertained **Elizabeth I** at Fawsley the following year.
John was created a Baronet in 1789 and the 3rd Baronet was **Rainald** who was MP for 40 years and was raised to the peerage in 1892. He died childless in 1895 and the Barony became extinct.
His wife, **Louisa**, the last family member, died in 1913 and in order for the will to be proved the contents of the House were sold by auction in 1914 and the House then stood empty.

In 1921 **Sir Charles** sold off some 20,000 acres on outlying Estates.
The last **Knightley** Baronet died in 1938 and the Estate was inherited by **Viscount Gage** by virtue of his marriage to **Rainald's** sister although by that time the House had become derelict.

FAXTON

Two miles east of Lamport
Population: 1801-54 (included Mawsley)

DOMESDAY BOOK
FEXTONE
The name appears to come from the
Scandinavian Fakr and the
Anglo Saxon 'tun' - meaning Fakrs farm.

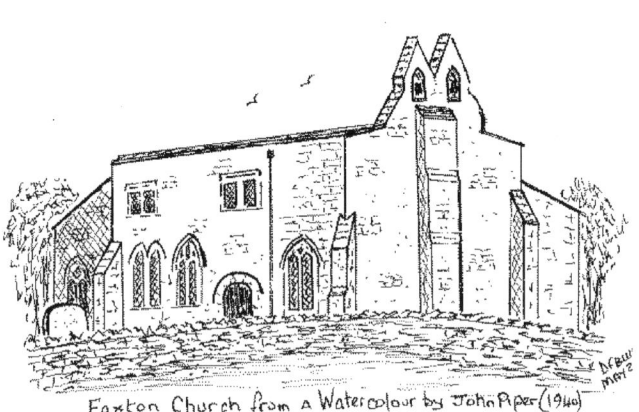

Faxton Church from a Watercolour by John Piper (1940)

It is incredible to think that at the time of the Domesday Book when the manor which included Old and Walgrave was held by the King, the population for Faxton alone was approximately sixty to eighty people and it was worth more than nearby Kettering.

Although the village was quite isolated it suffered badly at the time of the plague when it is recorded that a family relocating to Faxton to avoid the disease instead brought it with them and wiped out much of the settlement.

A map of 1746 shows thirty two cottages here but the 1841 census which probably included Mawsley recorded one hundred and eight inhabitants and the *Rev. Vere Isham* started a school in the village.

An aerial photo of the 1950's shows about fifty dwellings (many of which may have been empty) but the population declined and the last villager left in 1960 after the demolition of the church.

The site is marked on modern Ordnance Survey maps but today you need to walk along narrow farm tracks to reach the site of Northamptonshire's most recent deserted village.

Faxton Grange on the Lamport/Old road is more than a mile south west of the original village.

During my teens it was quite exciting to cycle over to Faxton with friends and picnic among the eerie surroundings of a derelict church and empty houses. In later years it was a good place to take the family for picnics and to play in the remote and rather unusual setting.

A church was built in the 13th century dedicated to **ST DENIS.** This incorporated part of a 12th century chapel and had a chancel, clerestoried nave and four bays but was unusual in that it had no tower or spire and over the western gable was a 15th century bell cote with just two bells.
The church closed for worship in August 1940 and gradually deteriorated before it was finally demolished in 1958. All that remains is a memorial stone although some of the fittings were transferred to churches in Kettering and Lamport.

Faxton's most famous resident was *Sir Augustine Nicholls* (1559-1616), Lord of the Manor and Circuit Judge of the Common Pleas under *James I* in spite of the fact that *James* called him *'the Judge that would give no money'*.

I read that *Augustine* was poisoned by four women who thought (wrongly) that by killing the Judge they would save a relative from execution.
A memorial to him was positioned inside the church but was smashed during the demolition. The pieces were then stored in the stables of Lamport Rectory until in 1965 the Victoria and Albert Museum (where it is now housed) agreed to accept it for restoration which took three years.

FINEDON

Three miles north east of Wellingborough
Population: 1801-886   2001 - 4188

DOMESDAY BOOK
TINGDENE

*There have been many spellings of the name but it appears that all originate from the Saxon words
'denu' - valley and 'thinge' – assembly i.e. a valley where people assembled.
The initial letter 'f' replaced 'th' around the 18th century.*

Of the two manors mentioned in the Domesday Book the largest by a long way was held by the King. It had previously been held by *Queen Edith* wife of *Edward the Confessor*.

This was one of the largest manors by way of population in the County and furthermore one of the very few places to have had four water mills. These rendered fifty seven shillings per annum. By 1294 there was a weekly market and the village started to flourish.

Like so many towns and villages Finedon also had a great fire. This happened on 12th March 1738 and in its wake destroyed sixteen houses together with large quantities of hay and corn.

The name recorded in the Domesday Book and the later version 'Thingdon' was used until the 19th century when Finedon became the commonly accepted version.

Finedon stands at the crossroads of the A6 and the A510 roads and consequently sees a lot of traffic.

Today the town is a real mish mash of some very attractive older properties and modern development.

You have to get off the main roads to really appreciate the most attractive area which has some lovely old ironstone buildings including the Gothic **Thingdon Cottage** – dated 1862 and the nearby row of gabled Almhouses dating back to 1847.

The boys' school was built in 1595 at the bequest of *Richard Walter* who died in 1588.

The beautiful large church of **ST MARY** the **VIRGIN** with grey stone dressings and battlements was built about 1300 in ironstone in the Decorative style. Inside there is a Norman font and a nave with a great strainer arch built about 1400 to strengthen the side aisles.

The present parish priest is the *Rev. Richard Coles,* a former member of the pop group *'The Communards'*.

Buried in the church and churchyard are members of the *Dolben* family, one of whom was an Archbishop of York.

The present *Finedon Hall* is thought to be of Elizabethan origin and its Gothic cum Tudor appearance is due to alterations carried out by *William Mackworth Dolben* between 1835-1859.

By the 1970's the building was deteriorating and the then owner *Geoffrey St Clair* illegally demolished the top of the tower.

This was restored by Tingdene Homes to something like its former glory but without the ornate gables.

The property has now been converted into residential apartments.

Old Water Tower: Finedon

.... FINEDON

William Mackworth Dolben who had a passion for strange buildings was also responsible for a number of other properties in the town including the present mock Gothic Bell Inn of 1872.

It is thought to stand on or near the site where an Inn has allegedly stood since 1042.

Above the doorway an inscription reads:-

> *'ER 1042 (Queen Edith) TINGDENE HOPSTELRIE VR 1872'.*

The Bell Inn, Finedon

There is a statue of *Queen Edith* neatly positioned in the stonework.

The Volta Tower, another folly, was also built by *William Mackworth Dolben* to commemorate the loss of his eldest son who drowned when a Man of War of that name capsized off the coast of West Africa in 1863.

The tower was circular and one hundred feet high but collapsed on the 16th November 1951.
At the time it was the home of *Mr & Mrs Northen* and although *Mr Northen* was outside the house at the time his wife was inside and died from her injuries.
Subsequent enquiries revealed that no mortar at all had been used in the construction of the tower.
A farm and a bungalow now stand on the site but the tower is still depicted on the town sign near the roundabout on the A6.

The obelisk sited at the cross roads nearby was erected in 1789 by another member of the *Dolben* family, *Sir English*.

The Town Hall on Berry Green was built in 1868 and has two storeys with Gothic trefoil headed first floor windows. The local library currently occupies the ground floor.

As you enter Finedon from Higham Ferrers you cannot fail to notice the tall highly decorative octagonal former water tower built in brick in 1904. It must make an interesting and highly unusual home for the current occupants.

A well known building standing on the Wellingborough Road is the attractive three storey factory of red brick and blue and white decorative trimming. Together with the white arched banding on many of the windows it makes it in my opinion a fine looking building.
Until the 1970's it was occupied by *Arthur Nutts* shoe factory and many people still refer to it as **'Nutts Factory'.**
Following closure the building was converted into use for residential apartments although much of the original façade has been retained.

The former Quaker Meeting House was built in 1690 and is the oldest existing non-conformist place of worship in the County.
Today it houses the Finedon local History Society.

The town has a small range of shops, schools, bars and restaurants, although the once popular Tudor Gate Hotel currently stands empty and is becoming derelict. A large scale development is planned to the south.

FINESHADE

Seven miles south west of Stamford
(No population statistics)

This settlement which I cannot find mentioned in the Domesday Book lies just off the main A43 Kettering to Stamford road.

There was once a structure here belonging to the *Engayne* family known as Hymel Castle although it was probably nothing more than a motte and bailey. It is believed to have been demolished about 1200 to make way for an Augustinian Priory (St Marys).

Over the following years the *Engayne* family endowed various lands to the Priory until it owned a significant Estate.

However, although the Prior, *Richard Harrington* and six fellow Canons, unlike so many of their kind, agreed to the demands of the King and acknowledged the supremacy of the Monarch in 1534 it was dissolved in 1536 and the Priory and lands sold to *Sir Robert Kirkham* who turned the House into a home.
Extensive alterations including a fine dining room were made in 1750 by trustees of *William Payne King*.
The *Monkton* family owned the house for six generations until 1920.

During the Second World War the buildings housed prisoners of war who left it in a deplorable state.

Eventually the Abbey buildings were demolished in 1956 and all that remains are the stables and ancillary buildings now re-used for other purposes including residential accommodation.

The site is still marked on Ordnance Survey maps as Fineshade Abbey but today it is Fineshade Woods - a large remnant of the former Rockingham Forest which draws the visitor.
Here you will find car parking, toilets, retail outlets and the Top Lodge Cafe.

Apart from the forest trails it is the red kite that attracts interest. These were fairly recently introduced and have thrived and any motorist in the area cannot fail to see one or more of these magnificent birds soaring over the countryside. The red kite was extinct in England by the start of the 20th century but in 1995 the RSPB introduced them back to Fineshade Woods where they have been closely monitored and protected.
They are not artificially fed as they are at some sites but survive by their own ability and instincts.

The re-introduction of these magnificent birds has been a great success and it is estimated that there are now between 800-900 in the area.

FLORE

Seven miles west of Northampton
Population: 1801-821   2001 - 1221

DOMESDAY BOOK
FLORA/FLORE

*Could the name derive from the Latin 'flora' - flowers or the Saxon 'flor' - floor,
both are possible as the soil is fertile and there is evidence of a Roman Villa nearby.
I understand that the village was called Flower until 1685 and has an indigenous plum - the Flore plum.
Mythology has it that the Romans named the settlement after seeing plum trees in bloom.*

Flore, with some lovely old properties at its centre, many of which are listed, lies on a gentle slope overlooking the Nene Valley. Unfortunately the village stands on the busy A45 road between Northampton and Daventry and there have been many calls for a bypass - it is badly needed.

Most modern houses are on the edge of the village and although there are some newer ones in the centre for the most part they blend in with the older and generally more attractive thatched stone cottages.

Of the lovely old properties my favourite is the majestic 17th century rich brown Northamptonshire ironstone **Flore House** with high pitched gables. It was built in 1612 but much altered in 1820 and 1901.
Other interesting properties include the early 18th century Manor House near the church with a hipped roof and the attractive Grade II listed thatched Manor House in Kings Lane.

Flore had a weekly market under a Charter of 1333 but although that has now gone the village retains its floral traditions with May Day festivities and still supports a shop, post office, day nursery, garage, garden centre with farm shop and tea room.

The Primary school was originally built in 1852 and has increased in size to meet demand.
Another building once used as a school is now the headquarters of Flore Scout troup.
That school was provided for twenty poor boys in accordance with the will of **Richard Capell** when he died in 1835.
The excellent Brodie Lodge playing field was given to the village in 1963 and is now run by a charitable trust.

Unfortunately the little Salvation Army chapel on Ram Bank which was built in 1907 is no longer used for worship and is now a hairdressing salon

Two public houses, The White Hart and The Royal Oak are still open for business but others including The Queens Head, The Bakers Arms and The Chequers Inn are now private residences.
On your right as you approach the village on the main road from Northampton is the modern Holiday Inn offering meals and accommodation.

The Nene Way is a long distance footpath through the County passing through the south of the village.
The village hall on the main road was renamed the Flore Millennium Hall in 2000 and outside is the War Memorial around which are a number of flagpoles.
When passing I always look to see which flags are flying but can rarely identify many!

13th Cent Priests Door · All Saints Church. Flore

-178-

The flags are displayed as part of Flore's unique Commonwealth Flag Project and Disaster Relief Scheme which started about three years ago.

Correspondence from Flore to all Commonwealth and Overseas Territories has so far resulted in 90 of the 91 countries joining the scheme and they have sent flags to be flown in Flore on their respective National Day, the Queens Birthday and other important dates.

The family of *Cecil Rhodes* founder of the former Commonwealth country of Rhodesia lived in Flore from 1760 until the 1960's.
Gravestones of members of his family can be seen in the churchyard.

The fine church of **ALL SAINTS** is superbly located on the edge of the village with wide open views across the meadows. Snowdrops in the churchyard in the spring are a joy to behold.
The church was built partly in the 13th century but mainly in the 14th century although a Saxon font and Romanesque carvings suggest an earlier church once existed on the site.

The spectacular 13th century priest's door with its ornate carvings is regularly photographed.
The chancel screen dates from about 1500 but the chancel itself was built at an angle to the nave.
This feature known as a *'Weeping Chancel'* is often found when churches have been extended.
Look at the dark roof timbers which in 1963 were covered in decorative panels.

The west end of the church was re-ordered in 2005 to include a meeting room, kitchen and cloakroom. These changes with new carpets, comfortable seats and a light interior give an inviting appearance and make it more adaptable in catering for a variety of needs.
Alterations were partly financed from proceeds of the very highly successful Annual Flore Flower Festival and Open Gardens when the village attracts hundreds of visitors who pass through the church to admire the floral decorations and more recently an exhibition by Danetre Quilters.

In 2012 the church celebrated the 50th anniversary of this Festival - a record only beaten it is thought by Walpole St Peter in Norfolk.

In the church is a memorial window and a wooden cross in memory of *Lt. Bruce Capell* aged twenty two who was awarded the Military Cross for his bravery on the battlefield in the First World War. His father designed the War Memorial on the High Street. The cross was brought back from Flanders by a fellow officer.

One other church remains in use – the United Reformed church in Chapel Lane which was built in 1880. The older church stands next door and is used as the church hall.

Flore Primary School

The parish includes the lost village of Glassthorpe.

GLASSTHORPE

DOMESDAY BOOK
CLACHESTORP

There was a settlement here at the time of the Domesday Book when there were two small manors and six households were recorded. Part of the settlement spread into the neighbouring parish of Brington.
It never became very large and reduced further in size in the 16th century with land enclosures.

By 1720 it is recorded as being *'long depopulated'* but its name lives on in Glassthorpe Hill two miles east of Flore.
A Wellington Bomber is recorded as having crashed into the hill during the Second World War.

FOTHERINGHAY

Three miles north east of Oundle
Population: 1801-307   2001 - 123

DOMESDAY BOOK
FODRINGEIA

*I could not find common agreement on the origin of the name – there are apparently so many possibilities but a generally accepted explanation is that it was the Island of the people of **Forthere**.*

Fotheringhay is a delightful village with much history and is well worth a visit.

Few small villages can claim to have so many tragic royal associations but today this quiet one street community has a peaceful atmosphere in an idyllic setting by the River Nene although it does attract many vistors because of its past.

As you approach the village from Tansor there is a wonderful view of the church from the picturesque 18th century stone bridge over the River Nene.
It is one of my favourite County views.

The Collegiate and the parish church together must have been at one time a spectacular place although they were cut off from each other by stone screens.

The York Window : Fotheringhay

What is today known as the church of the **BLESSED VIRGIN MARY** and **ALL SAINTS** is in fact the parish church end of the Collegiate church founded in 1411 by *Edward, 2nd Duke of York*. Work on the College ceased when *Edward* died at the battle of Agincourt on Friday 25th October 1415.

When *Edward* was buried in the partially built quire of the new Collegiate church the building work ceased for a time but was eventually continued by *Richard, the 3rd Duke of York* whose two sons became Kings of England, *Edward IV* and *Richard III*.

Richard the 3rd Duke lost his life at the Battle of Wakefield in 1460 and with his wife *Cecily* (1415-1495) are among a number of other royal persons who were buried in the Collegiate quire.

The College which was established to pray for the souls of the founders and their families, consisted of a master, twelve fellows, eight clerks and thirteen choristers

When the College was dissolved under *Henry VIII* the Collegiate buildings and the choir were completely demolished but the nave, not being legally part of the College, was, I am glad to see, left virtually untouched.

Elizabeth I visited in 1573 and found the graves of her ancestors in disarray so she ordered the building of the two identical imposing monuments which can today be seen alongside the altar.

When driving in the area you cannot fail to notice the superb octagonal tower but it is well worth making a detour to look inside and see the superb fan vaulting under the tower.

None of the old glass has survived and its disappearance is one of Fotheringhay's unsolved mysteries. The plain glass causes the building to be very light inside and I liked the heraldic glass including the York window showing connections with the House of York.

If you are interested and have the time you will find that there are a number of panels providing a wealth of information on the history of the site, the Castle and its royal connections.

An unusual discovery was made in 1989 when a secret room beneath the north porch was discovered with its floor covered with broken glass, pipes, coins and human bones.

Some items have been built into the East window of the upper room over the porch and others are on display in the nave.

At the time of the Domesday Book the manor was owned by *Countess Judith*, niece of *William the Conqueror*.

Her daughter *Maud* married *Simon de Senlis* who in 1100 is said to have built the first Castle here originally of earth and timber which gave way to stone in the 13th century.

After many different owners it came into the possession of *Edward III* who gave it to his son *Edmund Langley* who was destined to become founder of the powerful House of York.

During the reign of *Henry VIII* the Castle was granted to each of his six wives in succession.

The Castle is most famous for the birth of *Richard III* in 1452 and for the trial and execution of *Mary, Queen of Scots,* who was brought here in 1586 after eighteen years in captivity.

Her trial took place in the Great Hall on the 14/15 October and she was beheaded there on the 8th February 1587.

It is reported that it took three blows to sever her head and when the executioner grasped her auburn hair it proved to be a wig and her head fell to the ground showing her grey hair although she was only forty four. Her little dog then appeared from beneath her skirt and refused to leave her side.

Mary's heart and viscera were removed and buried secretly and her embalmed body lay in a lead coffin in the Castle for six months until it was considered safe for her to be taken by night for burial in Peterborough Abbey. It was *Mary's* son, *James I* who had her remains transferred to Westminster Abbey some twenty five years later.

The Castle which does not appear to have been used after *Queen Mary's* death fell into ruins and was pulled down about 1622.

Stones were used to build many of the local cottages and walls in the area.

All that remains of this very important historical site is a mound, the outlines of a moat and a quite insignificant piece of masonry alongside the River Nene.

I spent a most enjoyable time sitting on top of the mound under the summer sun looking out over the landscape and at the river below with its pleasure craft slowly cruising along among the ducks.

A large deer park was located in the north east part of the parish in 1230 when *John, Earl of Huntingdon* was given permission to construct deer leaps.

Twice in the following years he was granted deer from Rockingham Forest.

It is thought to have been disparked in the 17th century.

A very popular eating place is the *Egon Ronay* recommended early 19th century Falcon Inn.

Of the two previous inns - The Old Inn which has disappeared and The New Inn now known as Garden Farm with its 15th century gateway were once used for the overflow of visitors to the Castle.

A village hall was built in 2000 but there is no longer a shop and the old school is a very attractive private residence.

In 2000 an old village pump thought to date from about 1640 was rediscovered in undergrowth near a former inn connected with the *York* family in medieval times.

This was restored in 2002 for the Golden Jubilee, returned to its previous location and is now visible from the street.

The area is well worth a visit not only for its picturesque beauty and history but also for the delightful countryside and riverside walks.

FURTHO

Seven miles south east of Towcester
Population: 1801-9

DOMESDAY BOOK
FORHO
*The name is derived from the Old English 'ford hoh'
which describes a ford by a spur of land.*

Church & Dovecote : Furtho

The **Count of Mortain** who held many manors throughout the County also held the land here in 1086. At that time there were just three small holdings and fifteen households.

The **de Furtho** family became Lords of the Manor in 1254 and remained in residence until 1640.
Edward enclosed the land, diverted the road between Stony Stratford and Northampton and depopulated the village.

When the family left the Estate was taken over by the **Banastre** family of Passenham.

Later the manor was purchased by **Edmund Arnold**, an eminent lawyer.
He directed that after his and his wife's death the income from the manor of Furtho should be given to *'pious and charitable uses'* with particular focus to be given to poor children's apprenticeships in *'honest trades.'*
The charity still exists for 'the relief of poverty' and preference is given to *'those who are comfortable to the doctrines of the Church of England.'*

The church of **ST BARTHOLOMEW** probably dates from the 13th and 14th centuries but was rebuilt about 1620 a time when church building in the County was rare.
It is a simple little church with chancel, nave and west tower.

There has never been a school in Furtho and no evidence of a non-conformist chapel.

During the Second World War the church was used for the safe storage of archives from the Northamptonshire Record Office.
Unfortunately a bomb fell in a nearby field and shattered the windows on the north side.

Although no longer in regular use having been declared redundant in 1989 it is still structurally sound having been extensively restored in 1991/2. The building is still consecrated and is under the care of the Churches Conservation Trust.

Apart from the church which lies at the end of a single track road off the A508 between Old Stratford and Northampton the only other medieval manorial building is the 15th century circular dovecote restored in 1917 with a conical roof and three hundred nests.

Since 1949 it has been under the care of the Northamptonshire County Council and is now a Scheduled Ancient Monument.

This is a lovely peaceful spot which I came across quite unexpectedly on one of my walks in the area. I have since enjoyed further visits taking the opportunity to enjoy the peace and quiet for a time of sketching with one of my grandsons.

GAYTON

Five miles south west of Northampton
Population: 1801-247   2001 - 512

DOMESDAY BOOK
GAYTON
*The name possibly derives from the words
'geit' and 'ton' meaning Goat Farm*

This is one of the few villages in the County where the name has not changed in spelling or pronunciation since 1086 when the manor was held by *Sigar de Chocques* (the only one he held in the County).

There were forty households and a priest, probably about one hundred and fifty people in total.

However there is evidence that there were people in the area long before that as excavations in 1840 revealed a bronze Cupid, coins mostly from the 4th century and remains of a possible Roman temple.

In more recent years there was much ironstone mining in the area and also three brickyards on ground sloping to the River Nene but these have been filled in with domestic rubbish.

This pleasing village high above the Grand Union canal where there is a large marina has many old attractive buildings. This is an excellent area for countryside and canal walks with some unusual features and sights on the way.

One point of interest is Turnover Bridge No 47 especially constructed so that horses could change sides of the canal without unhitching the tow rope. A mass of daffodils on either side of the road from Blisworth make a wonderful display in the spring.

The layout of the village is unusual with five minor roads meeting at the Green on which the villagers have erected a millennium sign and a seat. It was here where the pound once stood an area for impounding stray cattle.

Nearby is the village hall, a playing field and a Primary school dedicated in 1900 to the memory of *Captain Cecil Eykyn* of the 42nd Royal Highlanders, the Black Watch.

The village hall owes its origin to *Isabel Ratledge* sub postmistress who bequeathed her estate to provide a public hall for the village. It was opened in May 1957 and has been progressively developed to meet modern requirements.

Rather surprisingly the village with only about five hundred inhabitants has two public houses, The Eykyn Arms and The Queen Victoria. Even more surprising - they are almost side by side.

The church of **ST MARY** is mainly 14th century although part of the west tower is Norman.

Owing to its ruinous state it was much restored in 1815 although the height of the tower was reduced. Among the many interesting items is a monument to *Francis Tanfield* with his large family - several children being wrapped in shrouds and a rare wooden effigy thought to be *Philip de Gayton* (d.1316) lying in full armour with a dog at his feet.

The six excellent carved 14th century misericords are thought to have come from the dissolved **St James Abbey** in Northampton.

The churchyard has some lovely spring flowers but in 2010 part of the land was used for the building of a much needed toilet block.

In 2011 the village was declared the winner in the best Northamptonshire small village category.

The Grade I listed cruciform Manor House opposite the church was built in the 16th century for the *Tanfield* family. It is a very interesting and attractive house with pointed gables and mullioned windows and is said to be one of only four such buildings in the country. An unusual feature on the Dower House in Deans Row are the barge boards with biblical texts.

Grand Union Canal at Gayton

GEDDINGTON

Four miles north east of Kettering
Population: 1801-663   2001 - 1504

DOMESDAY BOOK
GEITENTONE/ GADINTONE
*The name derives from a Saxon personal name **Geiti** and the Saxon word – 'ington' - homestead.*

It is hard to imagine today but Geddington was once set in the heart of Rockingham Forest.
In the Domesday Book the manor was held partly by the Crown and partly by the Abbey of St Edmundsbury.

In medieval times it became very important with the granting of a Market Charter and the building of a royal Hunting Lodge at a cost of £17 for **Henry I** which was situated on a rise north of the church.
It was improved by **Henry II** who made it more comfortable and it became a place of great prominence when in 1188 a *'Great Council'* was held here to discuss *'the organisation of a Crusade to the Holy Land'*
The wooden building was in use for over a hundred and sixty years but nothing remains today.

The hunting proved very popular with royalty and it is said to have been visited by six Kings including **Edward I** and his wife **Eleanor of Castile** who bore him fifteen children.

When she died at Harby in Nottinghamshire in 1290 her body was taken to be entombed in Westminster Abbey stopping overnight at Geddington. Wherever she rested **Edward I** ordered a cross of the finest workmanship to be erected in her memory.
Geddington now draws visitors from far and wide to admire and photograph the famous cross which still stands today and is a fine centrepiece to the village.

I particularly like the view of the church from near The Star public house with the Cross in the foreground but wherever you stand in this area the view is superb.
It is no wonder that the centre of the village is designated a Conservation area.

The best route into the village is over the 13th century bridge of five arches (one dated 1784) with three cutwaters over the River Ise.
Traffic has taken its toll and it is now much restored. The bridge is quite narrow and further restricted by bollards to prevent larger vehicles crossing.
There is a ford alongside which can be quite deep at times. I got the impression that the locals tend to use the ford rather than the bridge (they seem to think it is fun) whereas I always use the bridge.
I have never seen anyone stranded but I suppose that it does happen sometimes.

In the days before tarmacked roads this was an important crossing point over the river on the route between Oxford and Stamford.

Near the bridge is a playing field and Centennial Garden funded and created by the parish council to celebrate the centenary of the council in 1994.
The garden and land was leased to the parish council by Boughton Estates.

Queen Eleanor Cross. Geddington

A bypass was built in the early 20th century to divert traffic on the Kettering/Stamford road from the centre and many a motorist has been caught by the speed cameras discreetly located at both approaches to the village.

At its historic heart is the church of **ST MARY MAGDALENE** which has evidence of a Saxon nave and a west tower with a recessed spire in the Perpendicular style.

On my recent visit I was allowed access to the church by workmen who were repairing beams in the chancel roof – maintenance and repair being an ongoing problem with buildings of such age.

Memorials including brasses to *John Mulsho* and the *Tresham* family were transferred from St Faith's church at Newton in the Willows when it closed in 1972 to become a Field Study Centre.

The modern seating in the church which has been sponsored looks far more comfortable than the old wooden pews a few of which have been retained.

When local boy *Sir Robert Dallington*, who became Gentleman of the Bedchamber to *Prince Charles* (later *Charles I*) died in 1636 he left £300 for distribution of bread to the poor inhabitants of the village known as the *'Bread & Bun Dole'*.

Some quite severe rules and regulations were attached to this gift as displayed in the church porch and it is still considered to be a symbol of respectability to those who receive their weekly allowance of a loaf of bread today. They even have the choice of a brown or white loaf.

A list of current recipients was pinned up in the church porch on my last visit.

I wondered how £300 given in 1636 could still be providing funds for today's distribution.

It transpires that the charity initially invested the money in land at Loddington and the income derived there-from has allowed the charity to continue although in a modified form.

The goods were originally dispensed by *Lady Montagu* of **Boughton House**.

The attractive old school building near the church is still in use but has been extended to meet the growing population.

Until November 1948 the village was served by a station on the Kettering to Melton Mowbray line which suffered under the *Beeching* cuts.

This was never a very busy place except for the 20th June 1945 when a series of special trains were laid on to transport the ground staff from nearly USAF Deenethorpe to Gairloch in Scotland on the first leg of their journey home after the Second World War.

QUEEN ELEANOR CROSS

The one at Geddington was built shortly after 1294 in local Weldon stone and is a structure of great beauty and quite elaborate.

Rising from seven steps to a height of nearly forty feet it was restored in 1892 and is the best preserved of the three remaining Crosses out of a total of twelve originally built.

Situated at its base behind locked doors is a spring which once supplied drinking water for the village.

According to a magazine issued by the village blacksmith - *David Townsend* - a custom dating from the 18th century used to take place annually in the village on Easter Monday.

The locals caught squirrels in Geddington Chase and then turned them loose near the Cross.

People then threw stones at the squirrels and they attempted to escape up the Cross.

I'm glad this ancient custom has stopped although squirrels can be a nuisance.

I am sure that *Edward I* would not have been happy with this practice.

GLAPTHORN

Two miles north west of Oundle
Population: 1801-315   2001 - 264

The village is not mentioned in the Domesday Book but by 1185 it was recorded as Glaptorn.
The suffix clearly comes from thorn or thorn bush and possibilities for the prefix include
*'glaep' - sloping and **Glappa** - a personal name.*

Glapthorn is an ancient village belonging to a group of forest villages including Southwick, Bulwick and Nassington which once lay within the medieval forest of Clive or Cliffe – a sub division of Rockingham Forest.

In 1512 **Robert Brudenell** acquired the manor of Glapthorn beginning a long family association with the village although there has never been a grand Manor House.

Upper and Lower Glapthorn are in two contrasting parts separated by a brook and a road and just to the north west of the attractive market town of Oundle. In the area there are many old limestone buildings and Glapthorn is no exception although there are many new properties.

The church of **ST LEONARD** with an unbuttressed west tower housing three bells mostly dates from the 13th century and was once a Chapel of Ease for Cotterstock.
There is an old wall painting of *St Christopher* on the north wall of the north aisle.
The lack of monuments indicates that there is unlikely to have been any wealthy patrons or inhabitants.

The octagonal font is of the late 14th or early 15th century and there is also a Victorian iron bier for conveying the dead to the church.

The churchyard is well maintained and volunteers were at work there on my recent visit.

At one time there were two public houses, The Crown and The Royal Oak - today there are none and no shop but there is a school which is located on the edge of the village.

Along the Benefield Road are Glapthorn Cow Pastures with excellent walks at any time of the year. The woodland had been designated a Site of Special Scientific Interest and is a Nature Reserve under the Wildlife Trust for Northamptonshire.

A tradition of May singing around the village was started by a previous Head Teacher, *Mr Martin Palmer* in 1975.
The children call on doors and sing 'May' songs. The boys carry May sticks and the girls posies of flowers finishing at the church where the children lay the flowers at places special to them.
They collect money for the *Joe Homan* Trust which is used to sponsor the education of children in India.

St Leonard's Church Glapthorn

GLENDON

Three miles north west of Kettering
Population: 1801- 48 2001 - N/A

DOMESDAY BOOK
CLENDONE/CLENEDONE
The name is thought to derive from the Old English 'claenan cun' meaning clean hill.

Although it had fourteen households at the time of the Domesday Book this is one of Northamptonshire's shrunken villages and today consists of little more than the Hall, Bunkers Hill Farm a few outbuildings and some isolated properties.

The farm keeps alpacas and they probably outnumber the residents!

Most of Glendon which lay to the east of the Hall disappeared in the 16th century when nine out of the twelve houses were destroyed as a result of Estate expansion and land enclosure for sheep by *Robert Malory.*

Sixty two people lost their homes but no action was taken against the land owner until twenty seven years after the evictions. The area is now landscaped and little evidence remains.

Only two or three houses were recorded by *John Bridges* in his history of 1720.

ST HELENS church is said to have comprised *'a body and a chancel'* and is thought to have dated from 1254 but fell into ruins in the 18th century.

The site featured in a 'Time Team' TV documentary in 2006 after local resident *Martin Hipwell* uncovered a skeleton while building a house for his mother.

To their surprise they found evidence of a considerable number of burial sites over different levels the most important of which was that of a mid teenage Roman girl. Alongside was a pottery urn inside of which was another glass vessel said to contain charred figs. Little evidence was found to suggest the site of the church.

It is thought that the old village lay under the present **Glendon Hall** and the church under some of the farm buildings.

The Hall itself is a patchwork of styles dating back to the 17th century. The stables east of the Hall date back to the late 17th and early 18th century with the Coach House Barns constructed in 1862.

Some of the glass in the Hall is thought to have come from the old church and the porch from Pytchley Hall which was pulled down in 1824.

Violet Lane used to carry the road to Thorpe Malsor but travel down there today and after about one and a half miles you come to a complete dead end, the road having been closed with the building of the major trunk road the A14 between the M1 and the docks at Felixstowe.

Since April 1935 Glendon has been merged into the parish of Rushton (see pages 360/361).

GRAFTON REGIS

Five miles east of Towcester
Population: 1801-183   2001 – 248   {figures includes Alderton}

DOMESDAY BOOK
GRASTONE
The name Grafton derives from the Saxon words 'graf' - grove and 'tun' - farm.

It would be only too easy to speed past Grafton Regis without realising it was there and unaware of its historical importance.

The public house – the 16th century thatched White Hart and the village hall, which was once the Primary school, and a few stone houses stand on the east side of the busy A508 road from Northampton to Stony Stratford; most of the houses are situated off this road but there is no longer a school, shop or post office.

In the 15th and 16th centuries houses were often destroyed to create pastureland but in the case of Grafton Regis houses to the west of the main road were demolished in the 20th century to provide easier access to the newly built M1.

Arms of Elizabeth Woodville

In 1066 the manor of Grafton was held by *Godwin* who had estates in Furtho and Cosgrove but the village was transferred to the ownership of the Abbey of Grestain in Normandy in the 12th century.

The *Woodvilles* who had lived at Grafton since the 12th century acquired the manor in 1440.
Excavations in 1964/5 at the supposed site of the **Woodville Manor House** approximately three hundred metres west of the village revealed medieval buildings arranged around a cloister and floor tiles bearing the family crest which are on display in a cabinet in the church.

The Manor was sacked and burned by the Parliamentarians on Christmas Day 1643 during the Civil War.
The Royalists lost many troops but the Parliamentary casualties were light.

It was later rebuilt incorporating much of the earlier remains and is now used as a private Hospital for people with brain injuries.

The royal connections stem from the meeting of *Elizabeth Woodville* and *Edward IV* (a Yorkist). She was a widow and waylaid the King as he hunted in Grafton Woods to petition him for the return of her dead husband's Estates.
The couple are said to have married at Grafton Regis in secret in May 1464.
Did the royal wedding have anything to do with the grant of a Market Charter just one year later (much later than most such Charters)?

Their daughter *Elizabeth of York* married *Henry VII* (a Lancastrian) and brought about the union of the Houses of Lancaster and York following the War of the Roses.

Their son *Henry VIII* stayed at Grafton Manor many times for the hunting and enlarged the manor, extended the park to the west of the village and added the word '**Regis**' to the name.

In 1529 when *Henry VIII* was seeking a divorce from *Catharine of Aragon* in order to marry *Anne Boleyn* he had a meeting at Grafton with *Chancellor Thomas Wolsey* and the Pope's envoy *Cardinal Campeggio.*

This was to be the last meeting between *Henry* and *Wolsey* but it did not go at all well as *Henry* went ahead with his marriage whereas *Wolsey* was stripped of all his titles and publicly humiliated.

After the Restoration the Estate reverted to the Crown and *Charles II* granted the rights to his son *Henry Fitzroy, 1st Duke of Grafton*, by his mistress *Barbara Villiers*.

The royal connections continued when *Prince Charles* visited the village on the 4th September 2000 when a peal of five bells celebrated his planting of the **Woodville Oak**.

At the top of a lane running down to the valley and the Grand Union Canal stands the church of **ST MARY** the **VIRGIN** which was built mainly during the 12th to 14th centuries although it has a Norman font. It consists of an embattled west tower, nave, north aisle, chancel, and south porch.

Although not in a very conspicuous position but nevertheless well worth seeing is an altar tomb with a deeply incised alabaster top in memory of *John Woodville* (1415) great grandfather of *Elizabeth Woodville*, lying with a lion at his feet.

The church and churchyard contain a considerable number of monuments in memory of the *Fitzroy* family, descendants of *Henry Fitzroy*.

The delightful East window in Munich glass is dedicated to *Barwick John Sams* who was Rector for a remarkable 47 years until his death in 1885.

A brass plate in the chancel is in memory of his son *Charles Dawson Sams*, *R.N.R.* who at the age of forty one lost his life when the **'Bokhara'** was wrecked off the Pescadores on 10th October, 1892.

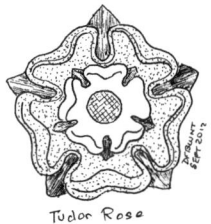

Tudor Rose

WOODVILLE FAMILY TREE

Richard Woodville 1st Earl Rivers 1416-1469 married **Jacquetta** of Luxembourg 1416-1472

↓

Elizabeth 1437-1492 ....and 12 siblings

Married 1) in 1453 to John Grey, 2nd Baron Ferrers of Grosby 1435-1461 ...... 3 siblings

Married 2) in 1464 to **Edward IV** 1442-1483 (Yorkist)

↓

Elizabeth of York 1466-1503   **Edward V** 1470-1483   **Richard** 1473-1483 ....and 7 siblings

Married in 1486 to   ----- Princes in the Tower----

King Henry VII 1455-1509 (Lancastrian)

↓

Arthur Tudor	**Margaret** Tudor	**King Henry VIII**	**Mary** Tudor......and 3 siblings
Prince of Wales	1489-1541	1491-1547	1496-1533
1486-1502			

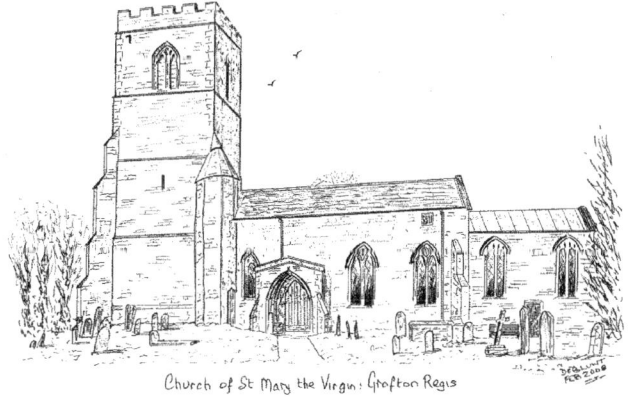

Church of St Mary the Virgin: Grafton Regis

GRAFTON UNDERWOOD

Four miles east of Kettering
Population: 1801-227   2001 - 134

DOMESDAY BOOK
GRASTONE

The name Grafton - as also in Grafton Regis - derives from the Saxon words meaning 'farm in a woodland grove'. As in many other places an addition was made - underwood – a reference to the surrounding wood to distinguish the village from those with similar names.

Whereas most of the manors in the County were held by people who held other lands in Northamptonshire this is the only one I can find to be held by **Robert T. Blunt**. In 1086 there were nineteen households and a priest.

In 1343 **Simon Simeon** who had earlier bought the manor obtained licence to enclose his woodland and five years later to empark it but was not allowed to make a deer leap.
About a hundred years later when the manor was held by **Henry Greene** he obtained leave to empark further land to make a larger park.

The manor was disafforested in 1639 but there is still a good amount of woodland to the north of the village. Much of the area was disturbed when the airfield was built in 1941.

Most of the limestone cottages in this picturesque small village are 17th or 18th century, some with thatched roofs, others with Collyweston slate.

Until recently the whole village was owned by the **Duke of Buccleuch** but many properties are now in private ownership.

What makes the village so attractive is the Alledge Brook, a tributary of the Nene, which runs along the main street and is crossed by several bridges. It is a popular place for ducks and visitors alike.

The area has changed little over the years and was made subject to a Conservation Order in 1977.

Even the K6 red telephone box designed by **Sir Giles Gilbert Scott** is listed.

Unfortunately the old school and school house erected in 1853 by the then **Duke of Buccleuch** are no longer used for educational purposes.
The shop and post office have also recently closed.

Main Street : Grafton Underwood

Among the older properties are the former public house, The Dukes Arms which dates from 1645 and is now a farmhouse and the Manor House which dates from 1653

Sunday afternoon teas and an annual street fair every summer are very popular and attract many visitors.

Overlooking the main street is **ST JAMES** church which is a mixture of various architectural styles and periods. The older parts are the tower and nave which are late Norman, although the tower has a Perpendicular style recessed spire.

In the vestry is a record of **Thomas Carley** (1757-1825). He was born without hands yet went on to be the local School Master and Parish Clerk. He learned to write by holding a pen in his teeth and managed to write beautiful copper plate writing.

Buried in the church is **Richard, 1st Baron Gowran** who was a Royal Navy Captain at the Battle of Vigo Bay and died in 1727.

Grafton Underwood Airfield

The airfield home of the 384th Bombardment Group was to the north of the village
on land owned by the **Duke of Buccleuch.**
It was built by **George Wimpey** and Co in 1941 and was originally planned as a satellite airfield for RAF
Polebrook. The base covered 500 acres and housed up to 3000 personnel.

The first American airmen arrived on 14th May 1942 and started training on RAF Bostons
as their own aircraft had not arrived. Eventually heavy bombers arrived in the form of B17's,
the famous and highly successful 'Flying Fortresses'.
This is the airfield from which both the first and last bombing raid by the USAF took off during the Second World
War. These large bombers were a frequent sight and sound over this previously tranquil village.

The base suffered appalling losses and by the time their sixth mission was completed the 384th had lost thirty five
out of its original thirty six aircraft. Replacements were constantly arriving.
On a mission to Hamburg the base experienced its 'Ghost Squadron' when all seven of the B17 Flying Fortresses
sent out failed to return. The airfield closed in 1959.

On the Brigstock Road is Grafton Park Wood
which was used during the Second World War by American servicemen.
If you look hard enough you may still see the remains of various buildings including the theatre.
Today it is a popular place for picnics and walks.

I was present in 1971 when a granite memorial was unveiled on the Geddington road
on the site of the main runway.
The ceremony which was arranged by local dignitaries and attended by representatives of the USAF
concluded with a display from one of the remaining and serviceable famous
Flying Fortresses - it was quite a memorable occasion.

GREAT ADDINGTON

Three miles north of Irthlingborough
Population: 1801-200   2001 - 319

DOMESDAY BOOK
EDINTONE
*This name is of old English origin and means 'where **Edda's** people live.'*

Today the two villages we know as Great and Little Addington are good examples of mother and daughter villages where the larger village became overpopulated and set up a daughter settlement nearby.
Both are likely to have existed at the time of the Norman Conquest as four manors with a total of three mills are recorded.

An ancient burial ground known locally as **Shooters Hill** was used by both the ancient Britons and the Romans and Roman graves, weapons and ornaments have been found there.

Central to the village which overlooks the River Nene is **ALL SAINTS** church dating mostly from the late 13th to early 14th centuries with a west tower with battlements and cross slits.
A Norman church existed on the present site but only the south porch with zigzag mouldings remain.
Over the years many feet have trod the path if the well worn entrance steps are anything to go by.

The interior is quite plain but I did like the lovely old round stone font with wooden cover, supported by a large central pillar with four smaller pillars on the outside.
There is also an unusual piscina on the side of what appears to be a window seat.

Tucked away in what now seems to be little more than a store room is a lovely plain tomb chest with an alabaster figure of **Henry de Vere** who died in 1516 leaving three daughters.

He was cousin to **Henry VII** and fought at the Battle of Bosworth in 1485.
There are other memorials to the **Tyley** and **Lambe** families.

A plaque on the outside of the churchyard perimeter wall states that the church clock is a memorial to those killed in the First World War and the Memorial Hall opposite to those who lost their lives in the Second World War.

The most impressive building is the Manor House opposite the church although it is almost completely hidden behind a very tall stone wall.
Glimpses can be seen from the road particularly of the multi gabled roof.

This stunning Jacobean building with landscaped formal gardens and grounds was once the home of the **de Vere** family who became famous in the diamond industry.
It has recently been sold for £2.7 million.

The village still has a Primary school and a public house – the 18th century Hare & Hounds although this also appears to double up as the local shop.

I think that this is a good idea where no other shop exists and wonder why more villages do not adopt similar arrangements.

At one time the Northampton to Peterborough railway ran close to the river but the station burned down just before the Second World War although trains still ran until 1964.

Norman Doorway
All Saints Church: Great Addington

GREAT BILLING

Three miles east of Northampton
Population: 1801-267   2001 – 8642
(inc Lt Billing, Ecton Brook and Bellinge)

Cory - Elwes

DOMESDAY BOOK
BELLINGE

*In 1086 there was only a single settlement once again named after a local man - 'the people of **Bydel** '.*

Finds in the area indicate that the land here was settled by the 6th century.

The largest of the three manors recorded in the Domesday Book was held by **Gilbert the cook** of the King. There were twenty three households and a mill rendering twenty shillings per annum. The three hide manor held by **Gunfrid de Chocques** had a mill rendering two shillings per annum.

Two separate settlements appear in the 13th century - Billing Magna and Parva Byllinge.

The Great and Little are of relatively recent origin. The old village of Great Billing west of the present church was decimated by the Black Death, abandoned and rebuilt in its present location.

In spite of its proximity to Northampton there is still a village atmosphere with a 12th century church, old Rectory, Methodist chapel, attractive houses, school, a village pump and a horse trough.

The church of **ST ANDREW** with its Norman nave is situated away from the current village centre.

The tower is late 13th to early 14th century but the upper part was rebuilt after the spire fell in 1759 doing great damage although the spire was not replaced. Repairs were paid for by **Lord Cavendish**. The unusual tower and nave parapets are from the demolished Billing Hall.

Buried in the church with a lack lustre monument erected in 1700 is *Henry, 7th Earl of Thomond* (1691).
I was not surprised to read that **Pevsner** refers to it as *'shockingly inept'*.
I read that the architect became insane and died the following year.

Billing Hall
and the Elwes family

*The original Hall was built in 1629 by **Baron Dundalk** and became the County seat of the **Earls of Thomond**, descendants of **Brian Boru, High King of the Irish**.*

*The **Elwes** family arrived from Lincolnshire in 1779 by which time the Hall had been rebuilt in the Palladian style for **Lord John Cavendish**.*

*The history of the village became inextricably linked to the **Elwes** family who were notable Roman Catholics.*

At one time they owned the whole of the village except for one house and five cottages.

*The most famous member of the family was **Gervase** (1866-1921 who inherited the Estate in 1902 by which time he had become a renowned singer. During the Second World War he visited troops in France to raise morale.*

A plaque in the High Street commemorates 'a beloved Squire' who 'With his whole heart he sung songs and loved Him that made him.' He died in a rail accident in the USA.

Another family member was an enthusiastic breeder of horses and won the Derby twice.

The Hall was demolished in 1956 although some outbuildings have been converted into residential use.

*The **Elwes** family are still remembered in the name of the village public house - The Elwes Arms, two roads with the family name and a former school which was converted into a Roman Catholic chapel in 1874.*

Roman Catholic Church
Great Billing

GREAT BRINGTON

Five miles north west of Northampton
Population: 1801-772   2001 – 482 (inc Althorpe)

DOMESDAY BOOK
BRININTONE/BRINTONE
The name is thought to mean Bryni's 'tun' - the home of Bryni.
Together with Little Brington this is a good example of a mother and daughter village.

William Peverel and **Robert, Count of Mortain** both had small manors here at the time of the Domesday Survey. Presumably one was what is today known as Great Brington and the other as Little Brington.

Great Brington enjoys relative peace and quiet as it lies on minor roads just off the A428.

The church of **ST MARY** is a large and well proportioned building of Northamptonshire ironstone and dates back to the 13th century although there is mention of a priest in the Domesday Book which probably indicates an earlier church.
The fine baptismal font of Purbeck stone is thought to be a survivor of that church.

Entrance is via the south porch with its attractive internal glass doors.

The nave arcades are very high with six bays on fluted pillars above which is the 15th century clerestory with six windows one side and four on the other.

What is most striking on entering the church is the sheer number of magnificent and quite prominent pew ends. According to the church handbook there are a total of one hundred and eight one poppy heads fashioned over five hundred years from about 1405.

I also like the East window by **William Morris** which represents the *'Adoration of the Lamb'* and the huge Jacobean Poor Box with three locks.

An unusual feature on the exterior of the church is the fine tomb of an anonymous cleric - who was he and why is his tomb just there by the south porch?

What attracts most visitors is undoubtedly the **Spencer** chapel opening off the north aisle.
This contains splendid memorials to the **Spencer** family (from nearby Althorp) from the 16th, 17th and 18th centuries.
There are many who believe, contrary to official reports, that the late **Princess of Wales** was laid to rest together with her forebears in the church at Great Brington.

The memorial stone to **Robert Washington** (1544-1629) great, great, great grandfather of **George Washington** who became the first President of the USA draws many American visitors. The **Spencer's** and the **Washington's** were related by marriage and two sons of **Lawrence Washington** lived in the area in around 1600.

Henry Chichele who was born in Higham Ferrers and went on to be the Archbishop of Canterbury was Rector here between the years 1400-1408.

Medieval Cross Outside Brington Church.

Charles I is said to have taken communion in the church in 1647 during his time of imprisonment.

Outside the church, on the Green is the weatherworn shaft and steps of a medieval cross.

Next door to the church is the really impressive old ironstone Rectory with its fascinating little cone topped tower. It is now a private residence.

In the 19th century much of Brington and the neighbouring villages of Harlestone and Brampton became part of the Althorp Estate. The majority of the population lived under Estate roofs.

Great Brington is set in a Conservation area with just a few modern houses blending in with the older stone and thatched roof cottages.

Primary school children are educated at neighbouring Little Brington but Great Brington does have a popular public house - The Fox and Hounds (Althorp Coaching Inn) and next door is the village shop cum post office with a Reading Room close by.

Today's parish includes Little Brington, (see page 274) Althorp (see page 24/25) and Nobottle.

NOBOTTLE

DOMESDAY BOOK
NEUBOTE
As in the case of Newbottle the name simply means new buildings.

Nobottle was first recorded in the Domesday Book with a total of nine households when *William Peverel* held the land here under the King.
There was a mill rendering seven shillings per annum.
I cannot find any more information until 1673 when eleven people paid the Hearth Tax and in 1720 *Bridges* writes of twelve houses.
In 1841 it was recorded that ninety nine people lived in eighteen houses.

The Midshires Way passed through this small village which borders the Althorp Estate who own much of the property.

A popular six hundred yard Rifle Range here was closed by the Ministry of Defence about twenty years ago.

Althorpe Coaching Inn

GREAT DODDINGTON

Two miles south of Wellingborough
Population: 1801-311   2001 - 1061

DOMESDAY BOOK
DODINTONE
The name in the Domesday Book - Dodintone - is also found for the villages of Denton and Duddington.
*In this case it means **Dodda's** farmstead. The daughter village of Little Doddington is now known as Denton.*

A settlement here is thought to date back to the Iron Age since traces of hut circles and storage pits have been found in addition to Saxon and Roman pottery.

The mill at Barnards was later held by the *Earl of Northampton* probably on the site of the present picturesque mill at Hardwater Crossing just south of the village.

Hardwater Crossing - Nr Great Doddington

Countess Judith, niece of *William the Conqueror* held the four hide manor which had a population of twenty three households and two acres of meadow although I could find no mention of a mill.

By the 13th century there were two manors - Greens Manor owned by the *Tregoz* family and Barnards Manor owned by *Wm de Champayne* and then by the *Daundelyn* family.

The existing Manor House is a fine example of a Tudor ironstone Grade I listed property and was built by 1510 by *John Barnard*.
A descendant of the same name is believed to have inherited the house and lived here with his wife *Elizabeth*, the granddaughter of *William Shakespeare*.
The property has recently been advertised for sale at a cost of £1,150,000.

The bridge across the river at this point is single track but nevertheless I always slow down to take in this idyllic English scene.

People can often be seen sitting on the river bank drawing and painting the scene as was my pleasure on one occasion.

Unfortunately the mill experienced tragedy for, in 1329, whilst closing the sluice gates, the miller fell into the water and drowned.

It is said that *Thomas á Becket* fled here in 1164 after the clash with *Henry II* at Northampton Castle before his exile in France. The mill was at the time owned by the nuns of Delapre Abbey.

The corn mill ceased working in about 1930 and is now in private ownership as a delightful waterside dwelling.

Great Doddington is basically a long winding narrow hilltop settlement between Earls Barton and Wellingborough overlooking the Nene Valley and the Summer Leys Local Nature Reserve.

The long distance footpath the Nene Way is diverted away from the river at this point to pass through the picturesque village which has a Conservation area with many pleasing 17th century stone houses with thatched or red tiled roofs.

Hidden among the trees is the church of
ST NICHOLAS.
It is partly Norman in style although the lower part of the tower is 12th century but the rest of the church is early 14th century. The tower top has the date 1737 (possibly referring to repairs).

There is a Jacobean pulpit with wrought iron hour glass dated 1618 and four carved misericords.

The village still has a Primary school, general stores, social club, United Reformed chapel with the datestone 1899 and the very popular public house and restaurant on the edge of the village - the thatched Stags Head with a date stone inscribed:- ' IC 1686.'

DODDINGTON THORPE

I must admit that I was struggling to find out anything about this deserted medieval settlement apart from a Grid Reference (SP 871656) until I contacted the local Parish Council.

Thanks to them I learned that the settlement is largely unrecorded but Bottom Thorpe (locally pronounced 'Tharps') the local name for a field suggests that it was probably known as Doddington Thorpe.

In the 14th century a person is recorded with the name *Johannes de Thorpe de Doddington*.

The area is now entirely ploughed up and earthworks have been destroyed.

A silver groat of *Elizabeth I* (dated 1560/1) has been found at the site although the settlement is thought to have been destroyed by the end of the 14th century possibly on account of the Black Death.

SUMMER LEYS NATURE RESERVE

The Wildlife Trust for Bedfordshire, Cambridgeshire, Northamptonshire and Peterborough purchased this Reserve thanks to funding from Natural England and the Department of Communities and Local Government through the River Nene Regional Park.
The Reserve was formed by sand and gravel extraction in the Nene Valley and was at one time owned by Hanson Aggregates UK.

Summer Leys is situated to the south of Great Doddington and is an important refuge for breeding birds including lapwings, plovers, widgeon and shovellers.
The appropriately located bird hides make good vantage points. The area is very popular with walkers and bird watchers alike and is one of the best bird watching sites in the area.

GREAT HARROWDEN

Two miles north of Wellingborough
Population: 1801-95   2001 - 74

DOMESDAY BOOK
HARGINDONE/HARGEDONE/HARDGINTONE
It appears that this was an area of pagan worship since the name comes from 'hearg' - shrine and 'dun' - hill.

Great and Little Harrowden are recorded separately in the Domesday Book. The manor here was held by *Walkelin* of the *Bishop of Coutances*. There was a Knight and twenty eight households and a mill rendering eight shillings per annum.

This small village stands astride the main Kettering to Wellingborough road.
Obviously there has been a population shift in this area for Little Harrowden now has the much larger population.
The original village appears to have been located immediately south west of the church but the whole site has been destroyed by ploughing.

At the time of the millennium it had just seventy nine residents and their names are recorded on a brass plaque in the church - a valuable record for future historical researchers.

Alongside the main road stands the church of **ALL SAINTS** which is built of ironstone except for its tower of grey ashlar. In the west wall of the nave the remains of a Norman window and the responds of the Norman tower arch can be seen.

The church dates from the 12th century although the chancel was reconstructed in 1845.
The spire which collapsed in the 18th century was not replaced when the tower was rebuilt in 1822.

A 14th century 'Doom' painting high above the chancel arch was discovered in 1896 and was restored in 1963. It is reckoned to be one of the finest 'Dooms' in the country.

Other items of interest include a brass in the chancel in memory of *William Harrowden* (d.1434) and his wife who owned the Manor.

The present **Great Harrowden Hall** was built in the early part of the 18th century by the new owner *Thomas Watson Wentworth* to replace the 15th century mansion. It is the only 'Great House' in this part of the County.

On the opposite side of the main road is the old Manor House dated 1648 – a fine old two storey ironstone building with a projecting three storey porch.

Great Harrowden Hall

Vaux of Harrowden

Vaux family

The family are of Norman origin and settled in Northamptonshire in the 14th century after acquiring the manor of Great Harrowden through marriage.

*They supported the Lancastrian cause in the War of the Roses but after defeat at the Battle of Northampton in 1460 fled into exile to France with **Queen Margaret of Anjou** to whom **William Vaux's** wife was a maid of honour. She remained constant to her Queen when others forsook the Lancastrian cause.*

***William** died at the Battle of Tewkesbury in May 1471 and the family fortunes were destroyed.*
*However in 1485 on the accession of the Lancastrian **Henry Tudor (Henry VII)** the family lands were restored and the title **Baron Vaux of Harrowden** was created for **William's** son, **Sir Nicholas Vaux (1460-1523)** in 1523 just before he died. He was succeeded by his son **Thomas**.*
*The family remained prominent at Court until 1533 when **Henry VIII** severed ties with Rome in his desire to marry **Anne Boleyn**. **Thomas** retreated from Court and did not participate in the Pilgrimage of Grace in 1536.*
*Unlike many other noble families the **Vaux's** did not benefit from the Dissolution of the Monasteries.*
***Thomas Vaux** died of the plague in 1556 and was succeeded by his eldest son **William**
(3rd **Baron Vaux** -1535-1595) who escorted **Elizabeth I** from Hatfield to her coronation in London.*

*The **Vaux** family were staunch Roman Catholics and refused to accept Protestant doctrines and as a result were frequently punished with fines, confiscation of property and imprisonment.*
The situation was made even worse because they colluded with other prominent Roman Catholics and provided secret hiding places for fleeing priests.
*In 1572 a spy reported that **William** had employed a priest and provided a chapel with 'splendid fittings'.*
*Eventually he was convicted of recusancy together with his brother in law **Sir Thomas Tresham**
and afterwards was tried in the Star Chamber for harbouring the Jesuit priest **Edmund Campion** and for contempt of court. He was imprisoned in the Fleet prison and fined £1000 (about £205,000 at current prices).*

*On **William's** death in 1595 he was succeeded by his grandson **Edward (1588-1661)** who inherited the title just before the age of seven. When he died the Harrowden Estate passed to the **Earls of Banbury** and was bought by the **Hon. Thomas Watson**, son of **Baron Rockingham** of Rockingham Castle in 1695.*

*A descendant of the **Vaux's** through the female line **George Charles Mostyn, (1804-1883)** had the **Vaux** barony revived in 1838. His grandson **Hubert**, 7th **Lord Vaux** purchased Harrowden from the **Fitzwilliams** in 1893.*
*He left the Estate virtually untouched apart from the building of a chapel dedicated to **St Hubert** in 1905 being a copy of the Chantry Chapel at Higham Ferrers.*
*On his death in 1935 it passed to his daughter and then to her eldest son, **Father Gabriel**, a Benedictine monk who took his seat in the House of Lords in 1962 – the first Benedictine monk to do so for 400 years.*

In 1975 the Hall was saved from almost certain demolition when it was purchased by Wellingborough Golf Club and it remains their Headquarters.

GREAT HOUGHTON

Three miles east of Northampton
Population: 1801-214   2001 - 636

DOMESDAY BOOK
HOHTUNE
*The name derives from the Saxon
'hot' - ridge and 'tun' - farmstead.*

In 1086 one manor was held by the **Bishop of Bayeaux** and the other by **Robert** of **William Peverel.** There were a total of forty two households and a mill rendering eight pence per annum.

Great Houghton is fortunate in that although it is close to the busy town of Northampton it is just off the A428 Bedford road and has little through traffic.

The small attractive village stands on a ridge overlooking the River Nene. There are several early cottages, a fine old Rectory, a converted school house and other stone built dwellings.

Owing to an increase in population a daughter village was established nearby now known as Little Houghton.

Opposite the church is the village public house, The White Hart although there is no longer a shop or a state school but there is an Independent day school for girls and boys from three months to sixteen years and a hair and beauty salon

In common with most villages in the Middle Ages, Great Houghton possessed a parish church but it fell into disrepair and by 1753 it was decided that it should be demolished.
The following year it was rebuilt in *a 'plain, decent and commodious manner without unnecessary ornament'.*

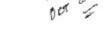

Tower & Spire : St Marys Church, Gt Houghton

The new church of **ST MARY** the **BLESSED VIRGIN** with an aisle less body of three bays was built in 1754 to the design of **David Hiorne** of Warwick who also designed the church of the Holy Cross at Daventry - another unusual building for this area.
When restored by **E. C. Hakewill** in 1878 the Georgian windows received their two light divisions.

The church has a fine square west tower with an arrangement of Tuscan columns at the top supporting a delicate spire.
In a religious census of 1851 the Rector **Chas Hutton** referred to the church as the:-
'ne plus ultra of ugliness'.
The new style was held in low esteem at that time.
It is quite unusual but I like it - it is so different from the hundreds of other churches in the area.

There is an interesting window in the south wall which was commissioned by the Head of the Preparatory School next door to celebrate the 25th Anniversary of the Queen and of the school.
The window features Concorde, North Sea oil and chemistry - important developments over that twenty five year period.

GREAT OAKLEY

Two miles south of Corby
Population: 1801-189

DOMESDAY BOOK
ACHELAU
*The name Oakley simply implies that this was
a clearing among the oaks*

A total of twenty one households were recorded in the Domesday Book when the manor was held by *Lanzelin* of the *Countess Judith.*

There is evidence of a settlement here well before the Norman Conquest as stone foundations of a Roman building have been excavated one and a half miles north east of the village.

The peaceful twin villages of Great and Little Oakley stand on the perimeter of what was once Rockingham Forest but are now the edge of the busy town of Corby.

Approach Great Oakley across the fields and you will come upon the church of **ST MICHAEL** situated in a superb, quiet location.

It has a small 17th century west tower with arched lights and battlements and a big nave roof of Collyweston slate which reaches on the south side down to the eaves of the aisle.

The church contains relics from the demolished **Pipewell Abbey** including medieval floor tiles, choir stalls with carved heads at the ends, four misericords, one with an old man with scythe and hourglass.

In the churchyard are a number of tombs to the *Capell-Brooke* family - one of whom was *Sir Arthur, 2nd Baronet* who was co-founder of the Royal Geographical Society.

Alongside the church is **Great Oakley Hall**, a three storey building which was built about 1555 in local Weldon stone for *Thomas Brooke*, his wife and eighteen children.

The *Brooke* family became sole Lords of the Manor and descendants of the family still live in the Hall today.
I have heard many stories about accidents and mysterious happenings around windmills but one of the most tragic tales I have come across concerns the mill at Great Oakley although I can find no reference to a mill here in the Domesday Book.

In 1865 a son of the miller was helping with the work at the mill when he was suddenly taken ill and died a few days later. His grief stricken father left the boy's coat hanging on the mill door and it stayed there until the father died twenty six years later. The mill was demolished in 1895.
The miller's younger son went on to become a local benefactor, founding Corby brick works and an ironstone quarrying company in the area.

The former school was built by *Sir William Capell Brooke* but was closed in 1957.

Nearby (actually at Oakley Hay) is the popular Spread Eagle public house and restaurant dating from 1759, a former coaching inn on the Kettering to Uppingham Turnpike.

GREAT OXENDON

Three and a half miles south of
Market Harborough
Population: 1801-211   2001 - 307

DOMESDAY BOOK
OXENDONE/OCEDONE
Originally this would have been a place where oxen grazed – hence the name.

Ulf held the manor of **Countess Judith** following the Norman Conquest when there was a total of eleven households.

Great Oxendon lies to the north of the County on the A508 Northampton to Market Harborough road.

The position of **ST HELENS** church on a hill between the two settlements of Great and Little Oxendon is thought to have been chosen so as to be seen by both communities but some historians are of the opinion that this marked the site of the original village but I have not found any evidence of this.

The church has been here since Norman days and its tall slim oddly proportioned west tower with battlements and pinnacles has small windows belonging to that era.
In addition there is a tub shaped Norman font with vertical zig-zags and Jacobean altar rails.

It is recorded that in 1968 during heavy incessant rain the church roof collapsed and that the Vicar preached his Harvest Festival sermon from under an umbrella.
The church was then closed until 1976 when it was re-opened following repairs.

Buried in the church is *John Morton* (1671-1726) a former Rector and author of
'The Natural History of Northamptonshire.'

Although there is no longer a school, shop or post office there is still a pub - 'The George at Great Oxendon' on the main road which seems to get great reviews.

During the era of the Northampton/Market Harborough Branch Line the village had a railway station which it shared with neighbouring Clipston. The line and station which stood near Station Cottages closed in the 1960's.

St Helens Church - Great Oxendon

All that remains is the trackway which is now part of the Brampton Valley Way and the twin tunnels referred to by engine drivers as the 'Rat Holes.'

The trackway no longer experiences the sights and sounds of passing trains but rather the chatter and laughter of walkers, cyclists and horse riders.

The walk between Market Harborough and Northampton I have undertaken a number of times and it now has a much better surface than when it was first opened.

A house with the name plate 'Tunnels End' perfectly describes its location.

GREAT OXENDON TUNNEL

The twin bore Oxendon tunnel which is 418 metres (a quarter of a mile) long was designed and built by *George Stephenson* and was opened in 1859.

It was part of the line between Northampton and Market Harborough and was used to transport the huge amounts of ironstone that were found in Northamptonshire in the mid 19th century.

Approximately half way through there is a vertical air shaft which casts a circle of light onto the tunnel floor.

Inside are a number of doorways which have been bricked up - these were called refuges and were used to stand inside to avoid passing trains.
If walking the Brampton Valley Way remember to take a torch as the Great Oxendon tunnel is very dark and its surface fairly uneven.

One mile north of Great Oxendon and still regularly marked on Ordnance Survey maps is the lost village of Little Oxendon.

LITTLE OXENDON

DOMESDAY BOOK
OXEDONE

At the time of the Domesday Book this settlement was taxed separately from Great Oxendon although it does not appear to have been either a large or wealthy settlement.

It appears that it was in the parish of Little Bowden (in Leicestershire), was a Chapelry of that church and that the Chapel was still standing in 1525.

In 1467 the manor was owned by the non resident *Boyville* family who sold it to *Andrew Palmer* in 1515.

The Black Death took its toll on the population but the real reason for its decline appears to have been land enclosures in the 16th century.

When digging for stone in 1863 a farmer found evidence of roads covered with loose stones, also pavements and the remains of a building of considerable size thought to be a church or a chapel and coins of *Elizabeth I* and *William III*.

Charred wood indicated destruction by fire.

I have read of the suggestion that the village was destroyed at the hands of Parliamentary troopers after the Battle at nearby Naseby in 1645 but can find no evidence.

All that is left today is a farm and associated buildings.

GREATWORTH

DOMESDAY BOOK
GRENTEVORDE

According to my research it appears that etymologists believe the name to be spelt incorrectly in the Domesday Book as the name is thought likely to originate from 'greot' - gravel and 'worth' – enclosure.

The two hide manor was at the time of the Domesday Book held by **William** fief of the **Bishop of Bayeaux**. There were at the time seventeen households.

Today the village which stands among minor roads is much larger. It stands on a hill some five hundred feet high just to the south of an important Drove road called the Welsh Lane which was used for taking stock from Wales to London.

The picturesque older part of the village with thatched stone cottages lies within a Conservation area.
There are three streams running into three rivers, the Cherwell, the Tove and the Ouse.

I like the location of the simple little church of **ST PETER** which was described by **Arthur Mee** as *'a little wayside church'*.

It dates from the 13th century although the nave has been rebuilt in the style of the earlier church.

The windows are filled with coloured geometrical glass which I found to be rather appealing.
In 2005 after restoration the three old bells supplemented by three new bells were rehung in the tower.

Dominating the churchyard is a giant sycamore tree flanked by two hornbeams.
Old gravestones are heavily covered with lichen.

The present Manor House near the church is in a commanding position overlooking the agricultural landscape. It stands on the site of its predecessor which burned down in 1793 and contains fragments of the old House.

Pineapple finials: Greatworth

Most striking are a pair of large elaborately carved stone pineapple finials marking the entrance to the previous building.

The old Manor was at one time owned by the **Pargiter** family and it was **Robert's** daughter **Anne Aimee** who married **Lawrence Washington** of Sulgrave establishing the **Washington** connection and there is a commemorative plaque in the church.

I have been unable to find out why the houses on the west of the street known as Westhorpe were until 1935 administered by Marston St Lawrence, a mile and a half away down a steep hill.
It must have been a real nuisance to bury the dead of Westhorpe in the graveyard at Marston St Lawrence when Greatworth graveyard is only a few hundred yards away.

RAF Greatworth to the north of the village was a Communication base between 1950 and 1988.
It was later used for a time by the USAF but is now a trading estate using some of the old base buildings.

The village still supports a public house - The Inn, a shop and post office, social club, Primary school and a Wesleyan chapel which was rebuilt in 1860.

It is interesting to note that the present parish of Greatworth includes two settlements that were once important enough to be parishes in their own right.

HALSE

DOMESDAY BOOK
HASOU

Halse, three miles north west of Brackley is recorded in the Domesday Book as a manor having one of only three churches in the County (the others being Guilsborough and Pattishall).
The church appears to have been dedicated to *St Andrew* but what happened to it and when is a mystery.

In 1377 one hundred and seven people were recorded as paying tax although this is thought to have included old Brackley. Over the years the population has declined and today it is little more than a Manor Farm a delightful little green Mission Hall and a few houses.

Originally it was the mother settlement of Brackley and therefore more important than its neighbour.
Brackley Manor House remained in Halse until about 200 years after the Norman Conquest.

STUCHBURY

DOMESDAY BOOK
STOTESBERIE
It is thought that the name derives from the birthplace of a Saxon nicknamed 'stut' meaning gnat or midge.

This deserted village which lay about two miles west of Helmdon is recorded in the Domesday Book as having a population of ten households which increased when a cell of Cluniac monks from St Andrews Priory in Northampton was set up in 1110.

The village flourished as shown by the Poll Tax of 1377 when there were fifty nine taxpayers suggesting a population of about 250.

Stuchbury was once an independent parish with a church built by the monks dedicated to St John which stood in a field between Stuchbury Hall and Stuchbury Lodge.

The Priory is thought to have cleared the land ready for sheep farming in the late 14th century although the monks stayed until the Dissolution in 1537 when the Estate was re-granted to *Lawrence Washington* of Sulgrave Manor who grazed 1,000 sheep there in 1547.

Eventually the remaining houses and church were demolished so that by 1674 there were just four houses about the same as today including Stuchbury Hall Farm and Stuchbury Lodge.

The parish was abolished in April 1935 and merged with Greatworth.
The sunken single track 'no through road' which leads to the Hall would have been the main street into the old village.
It must have been quite an important and prosperous place in its heyday.

GREENS NORTON

Two miles north west of Towcester
Population: 1801-615   2001 -1587

DOMESDAY BOOK
NORTONE

*Originally just Nortone from the Saxon for North Farm
but the appendage refers to the **Greene** family who held the Manor
from the early 14th century to 1506 when the last member of the family, **Thomas**, died.
In a survey of 1801 Greens Norton was also referred to as Norton Davie.*

In 1086 the manor was held by **William** the **Conqueror** having previously been held by **Edward** the **Confessor**.

There were forty four households and two mills rendering fifteen shillings per annum.

But why is honey worth four shillings mentioned? Surely other manors had bees but I can find little reference to them.

Today Greens Norton is a pleasant, attractive village close to Towcester, containing old houses and cottages built of local yellow stone but apart from the church, the 'Chauntry'e House' and Bengal Manor it has very little outstanding architecture.

There is a considerable amount of new building and with Towcester getting ever bigger how much longer will it be before it loses what it still has of its rustic charm?

This was the family home of the **Greene**'s for six generations from 1355 when the mansion was bought by **Sir Henry Greene**, Lord Chief Justice of England. The daughter of the last **Greene** (**Thomas**) was the mother of **Catherine Parr**.

She was the sixth wife of **Henry VIII** and is said to have lived in Bird's House in Bengal Lane but according to experts on the subject this seems unlikely although her family tree is proudly displayed in the church.

My favourite house is Chauntry'e House opposite the church built in 1496 by **Matilda Greene** to house six priests to pray for the dead.

The village, which once had a number of lacemakers, still seems to have a lot going for it with a public house, The Butchers Arms, rebuilt after a fire in 1937, a village shop and post office, Medical Centre, Primary school, church and Methodist chapel built in 1866 and a master butcher - **Julian Hunt** - specialising in rare breeds with an old slaughterhouse next door.

Prior to 1866 the Methodists worshipped in the building which is now the village shop and post office which still has some of the original chapel windows.

The old Dame school still stands at the head of School Lane but is now a private residence although for a time it was used as the village Reading Room.

The tall slender spire of **ST BARTHOLOMEW'S** church once known as **St Lawrence's** is a landmark for miles around.

A church has existed here since Saxon times and there is still some evidence of their work in the eastern wall of the nave and in the tower.

The list of Rectors goes back to **Nomina Ignota** in about 1050.

Chauntry'e House, Greens Norton

The west tower had its upper parts repaired about 1718 when the structure was considered unsafe and the elegant spire with an embattled collar at its base was rebuilt in 1807 and again in 1957.

The chancel was rebuilt in 1890-1 and is commemorated in a stained glass window given by *Elizabeth Whitton* of Blakesley.

Alabaster effigies of *Sir Thomas Greene* (who died in 1457) and his wife *Philippa* lie on a modern raised platform whereas nearby is a table tomb with brass plates inset in Purbeck marble in memory of their son, also *Thomas,* who died on 9th September 1462 and his wife *Matilda*.

Another interesting memorial is the simple wooden cross brought back by the family of *William Geoffrey Walford* who died in Belgium in 1918 while serving with 62 Squadron RAF.

Other features include a round stone font and a large iron bound wooden Tudor chest with handles and three locks.

Bengal Manor dates back to 1698 and stands just outside the village at the end of a long narrow lane.

It is featured in the lovely stained glass memorial window in the church to *Brigadier Guy Peyton* who lived in the Manor until his death in 1958.

The window features many interpretations of his life including cricket, writing and books, his family and the four seasons.

One sport depicted, fox hunting, would almost certainly not be allowed in such a window today.

The village is a good starting point for a number of walks. One (the Knightley Way) starts here en route to Badby whilst to the south is the Grafton Way - a long distance footpath to Cosgrove.

There is also a pleasant little walk to the Country Park on the site of an old brick yard about a quarter of a mile from the village centre.

Between 1952 and 1983 Greens Norton had a Youth Hostel and as a result was regularly visited by cyclists and walkers (motorists were not allowed to use Youth Hostels in the early days - not that there were many cars around).

The YHA sign can still be seen on the side of the now deserted building.

However during the war strangers of a different kind were housed there firstly Italians and then German prisoners of war.

These men were sent to work on local farms and some courted local girls and a few decided to stay on in the country after the war ended.

The present parish includes three deserted/ shrunken settlements which were not mentioned in the Domesday Book and which first appear by name about 1200. In all three instances the land appears to have belonged to the *Greene* family who inherited the royal manor of Greens Norton.

CASWELL

The name implies that this was the spring or stream where cress grew.

The whole hamlet appears to have been lost in 1509 when five houses were destroyed and 300 acres turned to pasture by *Sir Nicholas Vaux* - it is recorded that *'twenty four people here were left weeping.'*

The site on the edge of Greens Norton was taken over by the Plessey Company in the 1940's after the firm had to move from Ilford due to bombing.
It is now a Science and Technology Park.

Caswell House is a former family farmhouse built by the *4th Duke of Grafton* in 1839.
The building and its stables are Grade II listed.

DUNCOTE

*The name is thought to refer to **Dunna's** cottage.*

Situated just off the busy A5 (Watling Street) there are very few properties and the only building of note is Duncote Hall which is now a Residential Nursing Home.

FIELD BURCOTE

This was the place of the Peasants cottage

Now little more than a farm built about 1840 by the Grafton Estate and a few outbuildings at the end of a 'no through road' from Duncote.
The *Greene* family are recorded as destroying four houses in 1499 and converting 200 acres to pasture.

GRENDON

Eight miles east of Northampton
Population: 1801- 480   2001 - 477

DOMESDAY BOOK
GREDONE/GRENDONE
*The Domesday spelling derives from the Old English
'gren' - green and 'dun' - hill.*

The Half Moon. Grendon

Air photography of the area has revealed a remarkable series of pre-historic crop mark sites and there have been finds of Roman coins and both Roman and Iron Age pottery.

The *Countess Judith* held this three hide manor at the time of the Domesday Book when there were three mills along the Nene rendering three shillings per annum and thirty acres of meadow.
She in turn granted it to *King David* of Scotland as part of a Knights Fee - he was bound to grant her service as one of her Knights.

Later the manor was bequeathed to two sisters and the area divided into two parts - Over Grendon (Top End) and Nether Grendon (Bottom End).
They were reunited in the 16th century when the *Earl of Northampton* acquired the Estate.

The village which occupies a commanding position overlooking the Nene Valley is not particularly attractive but does have a few fine ironstone properties some with thatched roofs.

On a recent visit one was being rethatched with straw which I was told is expected to last 25-30 years. Reeds are much more expensive but last considerably longer.

The people of Grendon have jokingly been called *'Moonrakers'*. It is claimed that they come out of The Half Moon public house, which is still open, the worse for wear and seeing the moon reflected in Grendon Brook they try to rake it out thinking it to be a large cheese!

Another public house was The Crown Inn but this is now a private residence and there is no longer a shop or post office in the village.

The old school dates from 1850 but was extended in 1976 to accommodate children from some nearby villages when other small schools closed.

Opposite is the old chapel building which closed in 2004 and is now in use by a pre-school playgroup.

The church of **ST MARY** with its embattled nave stands on a 'T' junction in the centre of the village. It has a Perpendicular style tower with bands of brown and grey stone and a clock with a date of 1862.
Just inside the door is a square lead lined Victorian font on four columns.

In a glass frame is displayed a silk damask funeral pall from the 17th century made in either France or Italy. It used to be attached to the front of the wool curtain which now hangs over the chancel door having been restored in 1998.

Featured on a nearby wall are the hatchments of the *Compton* family which were displayed outside the house of the deceased and then brought into the church for safe keeping.

Also on show are the workings of an old tower clock which was made in 1690 but was taken out of service in 1960.

If you look up as you walk under the chancel arch you will see two corbels featuring what is thought to be a husband and wife glaring menacingly at each other - I wonder why?

The chancel contains a three seat sedilia and an Easter sepulchre over which a vigil was once kept from the eve of Good Friday through to Easter Sunday.

Parts of **Grendon Hall** date back to the 16th century but most of the present building with its hipped roof was constructed under the direction of *Lt. General Hatton Compton* (Deputy Lieutenant of the Tower of London) of nearby Castle Ashby who inherited the Estate on the death of his father in 1661.
The stables and an oblong dovecote to the north both date from the 18th century.

During the Second World War the Hall was used for the training of members of the French Resistance.

After the death of the owner, *Miss Mundy*, the Hall was sold to Northamptonshire County Council and on the 29th July, 1946 was opened by the then *Princess Elizabeth* as a Youth Centre (only the second of its kind in the country) and as such still runs numerous residential and non residential outdoor activity courses for young people.

The Parsonage to the south west of the church is a picturesque Tudor building with an odd lantern and cupola is now a private house.

As a result of gravel extraction in the Nene Valley there are a number of lakes known locally as Grendon Lakes which are a popular place for leisure and water sport activities.

One interesting story about Grendon concerns a horse called Grundon trained by *Mr Bletsoe* at **Grendon Hall** which won the Grand National in 1901. The course was thick with snow and whilst other horses suffered with balled up hooves Grundon prevailed with a pound of butter lubricating each hoof.

The parish contains the lost settlement of Coton

COTON

I have been unable to gather much information about this deserted settlement which seems to have been located to the west of Grendon Hall.

The settlement was recorded in the 13th century and in 1970 excavations found a scattering of medieval pottery and what appears to be building foundations.

GRETTON

Four miles north of Corby
Population: 1801-675   2001 - 1240

DOMESDAY BOOK
GRETONE

Opinions differ as to its origin but to me the name has a simple explanation it was 'Big Farm' or 'Great Town'
indicating that it must have been a good sized settlement.

It was written in the Domesday Book that
'very many things are wanting' to this manor
which at the time was held by the King.
However the settlement had twenty one
households, a priest and a mill rendering three
shillings. In addition reference is made to twenty
acres of meadows as well as woodland and
ironworks (very similar to the Domesday Book
entry for Corby).

On an escarpment overlooking the Welland Valley
the village was once set in the midst of
Rockingham Forest and was originally the third
largest village in the forest.

Today it is still quite large with a mix of lovely
old and not so lovely new building and is well
served by public houses including The Blue Bell,
The Talbot and The Hatton Arms, parts of which
are thought to date from the 12th century.
The Blue Bell apparently had its licence renewal
refused in 1840 owing to the *'bad character'* of
the landlady and the *'bad reputation of the*
House'.
What was actually happening I do not know
and can only guess.

It must have been quite serious as
twenty licences were being held
in the village at that time.

A number of former public houses including The
Fox and The Crown are now private residences
whereas The Old White Hart now houses the
village shop.

In addition to the public houses, church and
Baptist chapel licensed in 1825, there is a Primary
school complete with prominent tower, a shop and
post office, hairdresser, art studio, recreation
ground and pocket park, coffee shop and village
hall.

It is a very interesting place to explore with some
lovely architecture including the single storey
National school south east of the church which
was built in 1853.

The church of **ST JAMES** was built as an
aisleless early Norman church. The west aisle and
the north aisle were added after 1130.
On entering I could not help but notice the unusual
shape of the East window. The chancel walls have
a pronounced inward slope and the window has
been designed to mimic the slope. It is almost
unique amongst 14th century medieval East
windows. The ironstone west tower is one of the
tallest in the County.

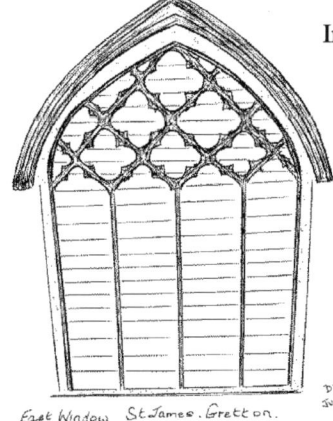

Inside there is a 15th century font and
pulpit and Georgian box pews.
The chancel floor is raised four steps
higher than the nave to
accommodate the **Hatton** family
vault beneath the choir stalls.

East Window St James . Gretton .

A board displays the names of over ninety people who were associated with improvements in this area in 2003.

The *Hattons* used to own nearby **Kirby Hall** and the church contains memorials to the family including *Christopher, 1st Viscount Hatton* (1632-1706) Governor of Guernsey.

In 1670 he and his wife and family were living in the Governors official residence in Castle Cornet when its keep and some living quarters were destroyed by an explosion. His wife and mother were killed but his life was saved by *James Chappell* a black servant.
In gratitude *Sir Christopher* is said to have granted *James* a healthy pension and made him landlord of The Hatton Arms then known as The Lords Arms.

Stocks & Whipping Post
Gretton.

A reminder of the past is a three man stocks and a two man whipping post standing on the Green near the church. Sometimes I think that they should be brought back into use.
Although the use of stocks and whipping posts fell into disfavour following the reforms of
Robert Peel in the 1830's there is a record that in 1857 a local man was the last to face the penalty when he failed to pay a fine for drunkenness.
In such circumstances a stocks warrant was requested and a policeman had to stand guard whilst they were in use.
It is now a County Heritage Site.

The site of the old Manor lies immediately north and north east of the church on the summit of a slope overlooking the Welland Valley.
It is believed that when it was demolished much of the building stone was used elsewhere in the village. Many Roman coins and pottery have been dug up on the site.

The imposing Gretton House dates back to the mid 18th century but a small part is believed to be a remnant of a 16th century farmhouse.
During the Second World War it was requisitioned by the War Office as a Military Hospital and then used by Stewarts and Lloyds as a Convalescent Home for its workers. Today it is a home for the mentally handicapped.

At the corner of Kirby Road and Corby Road is the '**Jo Stone**' said to be where farmers struck a bargain.

Gretton once enjoyed the benefit of a rail service but this has long gone although the line still remains. It is now used occasionally for freight traffic or occasional excursion trains.

Between Gretton and Rockingham stands the lost settlement of Coton (not to be confused with the village of the same name near Guilsborough).

COTES OR COTTON

This lost village which does not appear in the Domesday Book is thought to have been sited close to the River Welland.
The name suggests a single farmstead possibly a secondary settlement of Gretton.

The first reference appears in 1225 and between 1229-1300 there was a Hospital dedicated to St Leonard but the area seems to have been deserted by the mid 15th century and is now arable land.

Guilsborough

Eight miles north west of Northampton
Population: 1801-531   2001 - 660

DOMESDAY BOOK
GISLEBURG

There was an extensive Roman settlement in the area and parts are still visible.
*The village was possibly a fortified place named after a local leader **Golda** or **Gyldi.***

In medieval times the manor of Guilsborough probably included Hollowell and Coton

The village with its wide streets stands at five hundred feet overlooking two reservoirs with sailing and fishing, just off the A50.
It is set in an attractive area of Northamptonshire with many old and interesting buildings and gives the impression of having been a much more important location in the past.
Like so many places it has suffered from modern development including a large not particularly attractive Secondary school on its perimeter.
The upper storey of the oblong two storey block is faced with stone from Guilsborough Hall which was demolished in 1959.
The Church Mount estate now occupies this site.

There is a Primary school overlooking the Green a village hall, a shop with a coffee bar and post office (formerly the Doctors Surgery) and a new Doctors Surgery.

One feature of the village which has been lost is the Zoo which closed in 1991. It was opened in 1971 in the grounds of Guilsborough Grange, an attractive Regency House on the West Haddon Road. From small beginnings it grew to four hundred animals and birds and was a popular tourist attraction.

Of particular interest is the old cob barn which stands isolated on the village Green.
It has a thatched hipped roof and orange coloured mud and straw walls and is thought to have been used to store coal for the poor of the parish.

In the Domesday Book mention is made of a church in Guilsborough which is unusual as secular buildings were not as a rule included.

There is no trace of a Saxon church but evidence of a later church thought to have been dedicated to **St Wilfred** can be seen in the present basically 13th century church which has the unusual dedication to **ST ETHELDREDA.**
She founded a religious community and built a magnificent church on the site of which now stands Ely Cathedral.

The two saints appear side by side in one of the stained glass windows in Guilsborough church.
The west tower and spire are Early English in style but the low broach spire is dated 1618.

This is a lovely church and memorials include one to **Adelaide, Countess Spencer**, wife of the **4th Earl** who died at Guilsborough Hall in 1877.
Buried in the graveyard extension is **Thomas Orde Hastings Lees** (1846-1924) Chief Constable of Northamptonshire (1875-1881).

Opposite the 17th century thatched Ward Arms (pub and restaurant) is Guilsborough's most impressive non ecclesiastical building, the Jacobean Old Grammar School built of Northamptonshire ironstone.

It was founded by **Sir John Langham** of Cottesbrooke a London turkey merchant and grocer in 1668 to provide free education for fifty boys living within a radius of four miles.
Fees in 1825 were twenty five guineas a year.
Although the Grammar school closed in 1839 and decayed somewhat over the next twenty years it was restored by the **Rev. Robert Isham** of Lamport in 1858 but closed again in 1909.

During the two World Wars it was used for Prisoners of War and Army accommodation and was converted into private dwellings in 1972.

Guilsborough Witches (from Old Print)

The parish now includes the lost settlement of Nortoft.

NORTOFT

DOMESDAY BOOK
NORTOT

Two small manors at Nortoft are recorded in the Domesday Book. They are thought to have been located to the north of Guilsborough. The common fields were enclosed in 1588 by common agreement.

General Fairfax is said to have camped here in 1645 prior to the Battle of Naseby.
Today this is now a lost settlement although the name is perpetuated by Nortoft Lodge and Nortoft Grange.

GUILSBOROUGH WITCHES

The history of Guilsborough records suspected witches as far back as 1612 when two Guilsborough women, *Agnes Brown* and her daughter *Joan*, were hanged in Northampton for bewitching *'unto bodily harm'* *Mrs Elizabeth Belcher* and her brother in law.

As late as the 1880's there was supposed to be a witch family in the village.

In the village hall hangs a tapestry depicting the 'local witches' and one scene depicts one of the so called witches, the aforesaid *Agnes Brown,* recruiting two other people whose name seems to change depending upon the version being read and then riding on a sow's back to visit a powerful old witch in neighbouring Ravensthorpe.

HACKLETON

Five miles south east of Northampton

DOMESDAY BOOK
HACHELINTONE/BACHELINTONE
*It is thought that the name derives from a local tribal leader **Haecel** who had a farmstead ' ingtun' here.*

Salcey Forest at one time extended to Hackleton, it has a current boundary at nearby Piddington. Although Hackleton is mentioned in the Domesday Book it was once a hamlet in the parish of Piddington and hence has no parish church.

Over the years following the opening of the Northampton to Stoke Goldington Turnpike in 1709 Hackleton, which is comprised mainly of Victorian and modern housing, outgrew its neighbour.
Today it is quite a busy place with plenty of traffic, a shop, post office and public house –
The White Hart, a Primary school and the *Dudley Winterbottom* Memorial Hall.

The Baptist chapel is dedicated to the memory of *William Carey*, Charter Member of the Baptist Missionary Society who was at one time a cobbler in the village. In 1793 he went to India as a missionary and never returned.
The chapel still houses the pulpit from which *William Carey* gave his first sermon in the village.

The Grade II listed 'The Grange' is a beautiful stone Georgian building which dates back to 1763.

The present parish of Hackleton includes Horton, Piddington and Preston Deanery all of which were once parishes in their own right and still have a parish church.
They are mentioned elsewhere in this book.
Horton – page 243
Piddington – page 332
Preston Deancry – page 341

Hannington

Seven miles north east of Northampton
Population: 1801-144   2001 - 207

DOMESDAY BOOK
HANINTONE/HANITONE
*The name derives from **Hana***
possibly a local leader and 'ingtun' - farmstead.

Hannington is a small quiet village approximately halfway between Northampton and Kettering, just off the A43 but I was surprised to see so much new building activity.

Evidence exists from the Bronze Age of occupation in the area just to the north of the present village and settlement remains have been found south and south west of the church and Manor House.
It never seems to have been a large place.

The Millstone was once a public house and The Red Lion or Half Way House on the main Kettering to Northampton road has been standing empty for some years.
The Primary School closed back in 1931 and there is no longer a shop or a post office.

Today there is a Pocket Park but little of historical interest apart from the small church of
ST PETER AND ST PAUL which is late 13th century and has a slender west tower, chancel, nave and north porch

The church stands on the site of an old monastery said to have belonged to the Gilbertine order of monks. They were the only order to admit both men and women and this is probably the reason why the nave has a central column running through the middle from east to west - one side for men and one for women.
It has been suggested that there was once a central barrier between the two parts.
As far as I am aware this unusual arrangement is only to be found in one other parish church at Caythorpe in Lincolnshire.

In the chancel are recesses for a piscina, sedilia, aumbrey and Easter sepulchre and further recesses can be seen elsewhere indicating that the church was well equipped for all the traditional acts of worship.
Thomas á Becket is said to have taken refuge here in 1164 after his escape from Northampton Castle whilst evading ***Henry II's*** troops.

In 1562 ***Thomas Godwin*** became Rector and he then went on to become Dean of Christ Church, Oxford and eventually Bishop of Bath and Wells.
His son, ***Francis*** (who was baptised at Hannington) wrote the first science fiction novel in the English language with some amazing predictions called -
'The Man in the Moone.'

Church of St Peter & St Paul: Hannington

HARDINGSTONE

Two miles south of Northampton
Population: 1801-712   Population - NA

DOMESDAY BOOK
HARDINGESTORP/HARDINGESTONE
*This was once a small village thought to have been named after a local leader - **Hearding**.*

The King held the larger of the two manors at the time of the Domesday Book when the two mills rendered fifty shillings per annum.

Today Hardingstone has almost been swallowed up by the southern sprawl of Northampton but still has some semblance of a village.
There is a modern Primary school, a variety of shops, a post office, village hall and two public houses, The Sun and The Crown Inn.

The ironstone and brick buildings are typical of many Northamptonshire villages.
Many of the brick terraced houses in the High Street were built by the ***Bouverie*** family who lived in nearby Delapre Abbey.

On the B526 to Northampton stands the old Hardingstone Union Workhouse which dates from 1839 and was built of ironstone in the late classical style with seventeen bays and a pedimented higher centre.
The building was partly demolished in 1972 but has now been refurbished and adapted as modern apartments.

At the heart of the village stands the parish church of **ST EDMUND** which dates back to the 13th century although it was mentioned in documents dating from 1107.
It has an unbuttressed 13th century tower with a double stepped arch towards the nave and was restored in the 1860's by the ***Bouverie*** family of Delapre Abbey.
The chancel contains fifteen identical oval memorial plaques to family members.

In what is my image of a typical old village churchyard lies the body of an unknown hitchhiker who on Bonfire Night in 1930 was the murder victim of ***Alfred Arthur Rouse*** who hoped to fake his own death. The victim's remains were found in a burnt out car and his grave is marked by a simple wooden cross. The murder and the arrest of the culprit made national headlines at the time. ***Rouse*** was found guilty and hanged in Bedford Gaol on the 10th March 1931 having confessed to his crime shortly beforehand.

'Awards for All' has recently granted £4,500 to fund a village sign.

Hardingstone Workhouse 1839

HARDWICK

DOMESDAY BOOK
HERDEWICHE/HARDEWICHE
The name derives from the Saxon words 'heorde' - flock and 'wic' - farm.

Hardwick, with or without a final 'e' is a fairly common place name in England.

Villages of this name can be found in the neighbouring counties of Buckinghamshire, Cambridgeshire, Lincolnshire, Oxfordshire and Warwickshire together with a deserted medieval village in Rutland.

This tiny hamlet sits hidden and almost unnoticed on minor roads close to the busy A43 and appears to have changed little in generations.

It is quite possible that the population today is smaller than it was in the Domesday Book when the two manors, one in Hamfordshoe Hundred and one in Orlingbury Hundred were held by *Alan* of the *Countess Judith.*

There were recorded fourteen households which with an average of 4.5 occupants each would have given a population of about sixty people.

The manor descended to the *Grimbauds*, then the *Seymours* and subsequently into the hands of the *Greenes* of Greens Norton through marriage to a *Seymour* heiress.

In 1567 it was sold to *Thomas Nicholls* whose son *Sir Francis Nicholls* is buried in the church and was Governor of Tilbury Fort at the time of the Armada.

The church of **ST LEONARD** dates back to the 13th century but the embattled west tower was added about a hundred years later.

Considerable reconstruction took place in 1866.

The Manor House, a picturesque gabled building which appears to date back to the 14th century is now a farm where you can 'pick your own' fruit but for generations it was the home of the Knights Templar.

The lovely little Victorian village school and school house alongside the church is now used as the village hall.

As expected in such a small village there is no longer a shop, post office, public house or chapel.

Old School, Hardwick

HARGRAVE

Five miles east of Higham Ferrers
Population: 1801-188   2001 - 236

DOMESDAY BOOK
HAREGRAVE

*Its name appears to derive from the Saxon words 'har'
meaning boundary or 'hara' meaning hare and 'graf'
meaning grove although some would suggest
that the name might mean an army camp.*

This was once the site of Roman occupation so maybe the army camp theory can be accepted. Several stone coffins from that period have been unearthed including one of the largest stone coffins in the County measuring seven feet long and over two feet wide. It can be seen just outside the north door of the church.

Although mentioned in the Domesday Book this manor of *William Peverel* does not appear to have been very large. Today this small quiet village is only just inside Northamptonshire on the Bedfordshire and Cambridgeshire border but it once had a thriving clay pit and brickworks.
The clay pit is now a pond and the brickworks are in ruin and said to be haunted.

The track of the long vanished Kettering to Cambridge railway line is still partly visible in farmland on the outskirts of the village.

The picturesque church of **ALL HALLOWS** or **ALL SAINTS** as it is now more commonly known dates mostly from the 13th century, the first Rector being *Henry de Rand* in 1236.
The slender west tower with its broach spire was rebuilt between 1868 -1870.
The font is exceptionally high and the base is said to have been a Roman altar.

An interesting feature is the flat stone in the church carved with lines believed to have been used for playing the game 'Nine Men's Morris.'

Millennium Sign
Hargrave.

I particularly liked the circular stair turret attached to the tower and the small two person pews in the very narrow north and south aisles.
The nave which has a very tall tower arch is separated by a rood screen from the chancel which has a wooden barrel ceiling.
On the north wall is a large medieval painting said to be of *St Christopher* but it is difficult now to fully appreciate the image.
A little gem is the small oak poor box which was carved out by a villager in 1597.

On a lovely spring afternoon the churchyard was a scene of activity with friends of the church giving it a tidy up. With its lovely spring flowers it looked all the better for it.

The idyllic looking thatched black and white cottage nearby was once The Nags Head public house. Behind it a large thatched building was intended to be a function room but it would appear that the proposals to develop the property became a 'white elephant' - this has now been converted into a private house.
There is no longer a public house, shop, post office or school although the old striped brick school building still stands. The small Methodist chapel in Brook Street closed in the 1960's.

In 2005 *Duncan Farrington* from Bottom Farm decided to take a risk and invested £12,000 in the hope of making a business selling cold rapeseed oil. The business expanded from 120,000 bottles a year to 6000 every few days.
The product marketed under the name 'Farringtons Mellow Yellow' is regularly used by some of the best known chefs.
At the entrance to Hargrave on the main A45 is Three Shires House, once the home of an eccentric farmer called *Dunham*. When his wife died suddenly in 1837 he quarrelled with the local priest who then refused to allow her to be buried at Hargrave. As a result he had her body bricked up in the house and placed his daughter's body beside her when she died in 1843.
It was only when the farmer himself died in 1861 at the age of eighty five that his surviving son had both the bodies buried in the churchyard at nearby Covington in Cambridgeshire.

Harlestone

UPPER & LOWER

Three miles north west of Northampton
Population: 1801- 437   2001 - 420

DOMESDAY BOOK
ERLESTONE/HEROLVESTONE/HEROLVESTUNE
*It is generally accepted that the name derives from **Herewulf's** 'tun' - farmstead.*

In the west of the parish a large Roman building was excavated in the late 1920's. A hoard of eight hundred and fourteen Roman coins were discovered together with pottery indicating that the site had been occupied from the 2nd to the 4th centuries. Further finds were made in the same area in 1970. Evidence has also been found of several ancient quarry pits.

Four manors are mentioned in the Domesday Book one of which ' *was waste.* '
The others had a total of ten households plus a priest. The manor held by the **Count of Mortain** had a mill rendering two shillings per annum.

Two separate villages developed in the Middle Ages of which Lower Harlestone, whilst containing some delightful ironstone cottages is quite a busy place as it lies on the main Northampton to Rugby road, whereas Upper Harlestone is off the beaten track and is in my opinion a far more pleasant and attractive village as a result.

Both villages are on the Estate owned by the **Spencer** family of nearby Althorp.

Standing in a prominent position on a bend on the main road is the local public house - The Fox & Hounds (previously known as The Dusty Fox).

ST ANDREWS church with an unbuttressed west tower and finials like chimney pots stands between the two villages and is mainly in the Decorative style with the exception of a late Perpendicular clerestory and the East window.

The renowned architect **Sir George Gilbert Scott** was involved in the restoration of the church in 1853 and it has recently re-opened following further repair work.
Inside are a late Norman font and a lovely black carved pulpit said to have come from Fotheringhay.

The attractive lych gate was a gift from the **Duchess of Grafton** in 1903 to commemorate **Queen Victoria's** Diamond Jubilee.
Near the church in Lower Harlestone is a Primary school, whereas Upper Harlestone has a shop and the Village Institute.

Lych Gate : St Andrews Church Harlestone

Stable Block : Harlestone

On the site of the present golf course once stood the Hall which was demolished in 1940 although the large Palladian stables remain just above the church.

Some people claim that **Harlestone Hall** built in the early 18th century by the *Andrewes* family was the setting for *Jane Austen's* **'Mansfield Park'**.
It is known that she lived there for some time.

The *Spencer's* were resident here between 1876-78 when their home at Althorp was closed for large scale alterations.

There is an excellent walk through the fields, across the fine golf course and around the ornamental lakes between the two villages.

Alongside Dovecote House in Upper Harlestone is a round dovecote thought to date from the early 15th century with a conical roof, small cupula and nesting places for about four hundred pairs of birds.
These were once a regular feature of village life and provided a welcome addition to the diet.
The key can be obtained from the Estate Office.

Near the dovecote which was restored in 1995 is a large blue and white enamel sign indicating that this was once the home of the Dovecote Laundry.

Just outside the village on the A428 Northampton/Rugby road is a large Garden Centre. Alongside is a large car park which is well used by visitors to Harlestone Heath.

HARLESTONE HEATH

In my youth the woodland was commonly known as 'Harlestone Firs'.
I well remember as a school boy being taken by coach through the Firs and being dropped off near some cottages (now demolished) and setting off on foot to nearby fields for a spot of potato picking and a very exciting sum of pocket money!

The three hundred acres of woodland is part of the Althorp Estate and has always been popular with walkers, particularly those with dogs.

Within the woodland is a Timber Merchant providing a range of products such as fencing panels, posts, etc.

Boxing Day is usually an occasion for a large number of visitors to witness the 'Meet' of the local Pytchley Hunt.

The Heath was first mentioned in 1287 and later became a Racecourse.

HARPOLE

Four miles west of Northampton
Population: 1801-546   2001 - 1547

DOMESDAY BOOK
HORPOL
The Saxon name comes from 'horh' - muddy or dirty and 'pol' - pool or lake
i.e. a muddy pool on the surrounding Nene water meadow.

Harpole has a long history going back well before the Norman Conquest.

The Nobottle road which cuts through the north of the parish was once the Roman road to Bannaventa.
Evidence of a Roman Villa south west of the village was discovered in 1846 and 120 years later during roadworks additional artefacts were discovered.

The settlement is a fairly rare example of the estate being held by the same man both before and after the Norman Conquest.

Bisceop held it freely in the time of Edward the Confessor but under **William Peverel** in 1086. There were twenty six households and a priest.

Old records show that at one time the village was split into two parts Upper and Lower Harpole, situated at either end of the High Street.

The present village combines the two and is quite large.

Located just off the busy Northampton to Daventry road with easy access to junction sixteen of the M1 motorway it is a popular location for commuters.

Villagers have a lot of social clubs to join, a Primary school, a shop and post office, a bowls club and two public houses the 'Live and Let Live' and The Bull together with The Turnpike at the junction with the main A45.
The Bull holds a clay pipe smoking competition every Shrove Tuesday but I don't know how the tradition started.

Central to the village are some attractive ironstone properties but these have been somewhat overwhelmed by the urban modern development.

In the 1860's Harpole had quite a thriving cottage boot and shoe industry but nowadays there is little local work and people have to travel into Northampton or further afield.

By 1863 a small local Co-op store was set up and this grew to the extent that by the 1920's the Co-op had about twelve properties in the village selling everything from bakery, drapery, coal, grocery and butchery.
Most of these establishments have now been incorporated in a new store built in 1970.

Lamp Standard : Harpole

At the very heart of the village is the lovely coloured sandstone church of **ALL SAINTS** with parts dating back to the 12th century which has a 13th century west tower with battlements and pinnacles.

Its chief treasure is a marvellously carved 12th century font.

Norman remnants also include the south porch and heavily studded priests door - the actual door is now affixed to the inside wall of the church to avoid further deterioration.

The nave is unusual as there are four pointed arches on the south side but only three opposite. The north chapel contains a sepulchre thought to be of the founder *Norman de Salceto.*

The present Baptist church is the third such meeting place for local Baptists although today it is part of the Jesus Army Fellowship based in Bugbrooke.

Methodists were in the village as far back as 1769 when it is recorded that the great Methodist evangelist *John Wesley* preached to a *'thirsty multitude'*.

The first Methodist chapel was built in 1836 and was extended sixty years later.
Following the Second World War the congregation dwindled and by the 1970's the future of the chapel was in doubt.

It was then decided to spend money on new facilities rather than waste money on the old.
In 1987 a new chapel was built and the congregation has since increased.

A big event in the village calendar is the annual Scarecrow Festival held each September since 1997.

Local inhabitants and some businesses create one or more scarecrows based on a chosen theme and these are displayed throughout the village to raise money for local charities and the local church.

This event draws visitors from a wide area and for those who can't walk or simply do not want to there are open top bus tours around the displays.

I wonder - is this the modern equivalent of the Harpole Patronal Feast and Fair which took place on November 1st each year between the 1700's to 1964. Some local folk would like to see this 'Feast and Fayre' revived.

Harpole has quite a history of charitable giving including the gift of a coat to the oldest man in the village and a gown to the most deserving woman.

The custom has now died out but the money is now used to give cash at Christmas.

The Grade II listed **Harpole Hall** in Glassthorpe Lane with a massive Doric porch dates from the early 19th century

It was built for the *Manning - Watts* family who were Lords of the Manor, and acquired their money from brewing and agricultural enterprises.
A sheltered housing scheme for the elderly in Garners Way is named in their honour.

By its very name 'Glassthorpe Lane' it is assumed that at one time this led to the lost village of Glassthorpe which lay in the adjoining parish of Flore.

HARRINGTON

Five miles south east of Market Harborough
Population: 1801-140   2001 - 154

DOMESDAY BOOK
ARINTONE

Although the spelling has changed over the years the name of the village still sounds the same today as it did in the Domesday Book. This would have been the farmstead named after a local leader.

Harrington is a quiet picturesque village standing on a hill overlooking the Ise valley with a long winding main street bordered by lovely limestone cottages.
It is a delight to visit in the early spring when the verges and gardens are full of snowdrops and aconites.

The five and a third hide manor was held by the Abbey of St Mary of Grestain and at the time of the Domesday Book it had twenty nine households and was one of the only three places in the County having four water mills.

From 1288 until the Dissolution of the Monasteries it was the site of a Manor House belonging to the Knights Hospitallers of St John of Jerusalem.

It was then leased to the **Saunders** family and then passed to the **Stanhope** family and **Sir John** who was created **Lord Stanhope** of Harrington in 1605 built a large mansion. The extensive terraced gardens were hailed as 'remarkable' and gave rise to the area being called **'The Falls'**.

The building was demolished about 1745 and the gardens are no more but you can still see evidence in the great grassy banks and carefully preserved fishponds.

The earthworks are sufficiently important to be marked on current editions of the one mile Ordnance Survey maps.

Some little distance out of the village on the road to Thorpe Underwood in a lovely peaceful spot stands the church of **ST PETER** and **ST PAUL** which until the early 18th century was dedicated to **St Botolph.** Dating from the 12th century it is constructed in ironstone and is unusual inasmuch as the tower of grey ashlar with ironstone buttresses is attached to the south transept having been built in 1809 on the site of an earlier tower.

Items of interest are the Vamping Horn dated 1672, displayed in a glass case (the only other one in the County belongs to Braybrooke church), the impressive alabaster monument dated 1588 erected in memory of **William Saunders** who was Lord of the Manor and the six embroidered appliqué wall hangings on the nave pillars featuring village life between 1066-2000.

Many of the dead from both sides in the Battle of Naseby were reputedly buried side by side in the churchyard.

The thatched Tollemarche Arms, originally called The Red Cow, takes its name from the **Rev Hugh Tollemarche**, Rector of Harrington for fifty eight years who died in 1890 aged eighty seven. He objected to the villagers attending the public house on a Sunday so bought it and installed his coachman as landlord and instructed him not to open on the Sabbath. Today The Tollemarche Arms opens seven days a week.

The old Sunday school building of 1828 is now the village hall but there is no longer a school, shop or post office.

The parish now includes the lost settlements of Newbottle and Thorpe Underwood.

NEWBOTTLE

DOMESDAY BOOK
NEUBOTE

Although in the Domesday Book the name is spelt slightly differently to the village of the same name near Brackley it means the same – 'new building'.

In 1086 the land and mill belonged to the Abbey of St Mary of Grestain. Once again land enclosures took their toll and by 1547 three hundred sheep were being kept here.

Newbottle Bridge near Thorpe Underwood is thought to be the site of this deserted village but there is no trace of the existence of this settlement above ground.

THORPE UNDERWOOD

This small hamlet *'near the forest'* was a secondary settlement to Harrington and never appears to have been very large.
Records show that in 1492 twenty four people were expelled from *'the mansion place'* was this simply a large house?
Nothing now remains to be seen of the settlement.

Harrington Airfield

During the Second World War there was a large airbase to the south of the village.
It straddled the minor road between Lamport and Rothwell where there is now a memorial to the American Airmen - *'Carpetbaggers'* - from the base who lost their lives during the Second World War.
'Carpetbaggers' flew night bombing operations from this secret base and parachuted agents, many of whom were trained at Brockhall, to assist the underground resistance fighters.

Some 2800 sorties were flown and over a thousand people dropped behind enemy lines.
Now a War Museum is housed in some of the remaining site buildings.

The airfield was the only one in the County during the Second World War to be built by USAF engineers for the RAF but later was occupied by the USAF only. It had the distinction of the most westerly operational base of the Eighth Air Force and at 530 feet above sea level was also the highest airfield used by them.

The 801st USAAF Bombardment group with their Liberator bombers arrived in March 1944.
Between 1959 and 1963 this was a base for three 'Thor' intermediate range ballistic missiles.

Harringworth Viaduct.

HARRINGWORTH

Six miles north east of Corby
Population: 1801-404   2001 - 247

DOMESDAY BOOK
HARINGEWORDE
It is thought that the name derives from the Saxon words 'haer inga worth' meaning
'the dwellers at the enclosure at the stony place.'

Countess Judith held the five hide manor in 1086. There was a mill rendering five shillings per annum and forty seven households possibly numbering 160 -180 people, so not much smaller than it is today.

This is a delightful little village with many 16th and 17th century thatched and stone properties.

It is dominated by the impressive eighty two arch railway viaduct straddling the River Welland.

Some people may not like the presence of the viaduct but I am very impressed with it and to me its adds an additional dimension to the village.

The former station stood on the hill to the left as you leave the village on the Gretton road but the old signal box has been acquired by the Nene Valley Railway and has been moved to Wansford.

The church of **ST JOHN** the **BAPTIST** has a 12th century west tower topped by a 14th century broach spire and a ring of six bells.
Look out for the carved heads, including one with its tongue sticking out.
At the entrance to the churchyard is a thick walled Roman coffin excavated on the edge of the village in 1932 and now making a very unusual flower planter.

The church has a wide nave and chancel but what caught my eye was the fine example of ironwork from about 1700 surrounding the **Tryon** family vault which occupies two bays of the north aisle.
The **Tryons** lived at Bulwick Park from 1676 and the vault was used as a burial place for the family from the latter part of the 17th century until the year 1833.
There are many reminders of the family in the form of monuments, memorials and hatchments even the church clock which was given by **Thomas Tryon** in 1879.

Other features of interest are the late 12th century font, the fire hook for removing burning thatch and the three seat sedilia with a missing upright which now houses a tapestry featuring the *'Tree Of Life.'*

Harringworth has one of the best kept Market Crosses in the County which rightly has a Grade I listing. It dates back to the time when *William la Zouche* was granted an annual fair and Tuesday market here in 1387.
The steps were repaved and the Cross and the topmost stone of the shaft renewed in 1837.

The White Swan Inn which has won awards recently for the quality of its food is said to be one of the oldest public houses in the County and dates from the early 16th century.
I was amused to see that the large Inn sign also refers to it by another name -'The Mucky Duck'.

Unfortunately the village no longer has a shop or post office but does have horse riding stables.

The old Manor House to the north east of the church, contains parts of the former medieval Manor House of *Lord John Zouche* who fought at Bosworth in the War of the Roses.

The family held the Manor from the 13th century until it passed to the *Tryon* family in about 1617.
One of the original fishponds still exists.

The present Manor House which is situated south of the church dates from the late 17th century and has five bays, two storeys and a hipped roof

The old school provided for seventy children in 1825 by one of the *Tryon* family is set back a little from the road and is used as a village hall now that children are educated elsewhere.

The parish includes the hamlet of Shotley.

SHOTLEY

This tiny hamlet is located half a mile east of Harringworth.

I cannot find any reference to the settlement prior to 1430 although there are indications of an earlier and larger presence.

In the 1860's the owner of Shotley Cottage sought permission to erect a Congregational chapel in Harringworth but this was refused.
Not to be outdone he decided to have a chapel built in his own garden and there it stands to this day although it ceased to be a place of worship in 1961.

The long distance footpath the Jurassic Way runs through the hamlet.

HARRINGWORTH VIADUCT

The viaduct spanning the Welland Valley was built entirely of about twenty million locally made red and blue bricks.
It is about three quarters of a mile long and was completed in July 1878 for the Midland Railway Co. on the line between Kettering and Manton.
The viaduct has eighty two arches of forty foot span. The foundations of the piers and abutments are concrete.

Navvies, many with their families, came from all over the country seeking work and two settlements were built comprising almost fifty huts at the Seaton end and twelve huts at the other end.
Four hundred men were engaged on the work and the Railway Mission built a Mission Hut for each settlement. Although the work brought money into the area it also brought in more than its fair share of drunks and poachers.

The line is not now in regular use but you occasionally see the spectacular sight of a steam train hauling coaches across the immense structure on special excursions to the delight of steam enthusiasts.

HARTWELL

Seven miles south east of Northampton
Population: 1801-387   2001 - 1815

DOMESDAY BOOK
HERTEWELLE
The name means what it says - simply the harts well.

At the time of the Domesday Book this was a single manor held by **William Peverel** under the **Bishop of Bayeaux.** There was a priest indicating the existence of a church or chapel.

The original village was, until about 1527 located about a mile south of the present one in an area around what is now Chapel Farm where there was once a Chapelry connected with the ancient parish of Roade.

After the medieval village was abandoned the main focus of the settlement became the modern village of Hartwell.
It was here that the church of
ST JOHN the **BAPTIST** was built in 1851
by *Vickers* and *Hugall*.
The builders incorporated aspects of the former Norman church in the new building which now consists of a nave with double bell cote and chancel and ornately carved doorways.
It has been suggested that one of the two bells came from the demolished church.
As a result of the relocation of the village there are very few old buildings but many new houses.

The Wesleyan chapel was erected in 1814 and rebuilt in 1889. The last service was held in the summer of 2004 when the site was converted into residential use. The chapel had become too expensive for the small congregation who now hold joint services with the Anglicans in the church opposite.

The village has the benefit of a general stores, post office, community centre opened in 1991, Conservative club with a White Hart sign on the wall and a public house - The Rose and Crown.

The school which has a history going back to 1861 was the first new Primary school to be built in Northamptonshire after the Second World War.
It was officially opened by the Bishop of Peterborough on the 17th February 1962.

The M1 Motorway between Junction 14 and 15 passes west of the village and east of Salcey Forest.

During the Second World War Italian prisoners were billeted at Park Farm and German prisoners worked locally. The Grafton Estate owned virtually all the houses in the late 1800's but most houses were sold in the early years of the 20th century although considerable modern building has been completed since.

SALCEY FOREST

The Forest has a very long history and was once much larger than it is today.
Following the Norman Conquest it was set aside for a royal hunting forest, its main purpose being to provide and protect animals such as boar and various species of deer, fox and hare for the benefit of the King.

Salcey also provided a considerable amount of timber for various building projects including churches in Northampton and Northampton Castle.
During the 15th century it also provided vast quantities of oaks for the Royal Navy.
Hunting continued until the 18th century.
During the 2nd World War the forest housed the stores for the No 72 Maintenance Unit RAF Roade.
Thirty eight buildings were scattered in the forest - the hard standings can still be seen today.

In 1971 Salcey was designated a site of Special Scientific Interest (SSI) which gives protection to the ancient woodland.
Today the 1,250 acres of Forest Enterprise woodland offers some good walks not only on the ground but high above the trees on a unique tree top walk way.
It is a popular tourist attraction and has a large car park, toilets and a cafe.

HASELBECH

Six miles south of Market Harborough
Population: 1801-118   2001 - 87

DOMESDAY BOOK
ESBECE
The derivation of the name hazel is obvious but not the 'bech' - this derives possibly from beche '- hill did hazels once grow on the hill?

Gable at Haselbech.

There is certainly a steep incline on the road from Cottesbrooke. Haselbech is a very small village located on minor roads with little more than the Hall, church and a few expensive properties.

In 1086 there were nineteen households and a single manor. By the 16th century much of the land was in the hands of the *Tresham* family who in 1598 enclosed the common fields, evicted tenants, destroyed houses and introduced sheep.

The area cleared lay to the south west and north west of the now isolated church.

The population has further declined in recent years resulting in a change from an Estate village to a community of owner occupiers.

In spite of its size there are a number of listed buildings including the former Rectory (1768) and the Manor Farm, below which stands the old school which following closure was converted to a private residence.

There is no shop, post office or public house.

The church of **ST MICHAEL** dates back to the 13th century but the west tower with its quatrefoil frieze, battlements and only stumps of the pinnacles dates from the 14th century.

I was very interested in both the south porch where the uprights are not as upright as they should be and with the fancy crest above the window on the outside of the south chapel.

Inside are some lovely old pews, a Jacobean pulpit with back panel and tester and a beautiful two seater sedilia close to the altar but why are the stocks in the south chapel?

The churchyard is very well kept and there is an unusual set of gravestones, one a roundel, one of box type with very attractive lichen and the other with a rounded top - all are memorials to the *Ismay* family of **Haselbech Hall.**

Haselbech Hall

The Hall was built just prior to 1678 for the Wyke family. The present park around the Hall was laid out about 1773 and involved stopping up the road to the east of the church.

Fire gutted the property in 1917 and it was rebuilt for Captain Bower Ismay at which time the Jacobean gables were added.
The gatehouse was originally two cottages which were knocked into one and used as a Hunting Lodge.
A carved plaque on the Hall has the same design as those found on the Ismay tombs.

Bower Ismay was the brother of Bruce Ismay, the Managing Director of the White Star Shipping Line who survived when his ship the Titanic sank in 1912 with the loss of 1,500 lives.

In 2009 film crews descended on Haselbech to film scenes about the life of Churchill as the Hall is thought to resemble Chartwell in Kent.

HELLIDON

Four miles south west of Daventry
Population: 1801-340   2001 - 180

The settlement is not mentioned in the Domesday Book but by 1189 it was called Elliden.
The name 'dun' – hill - is obvious but the remainder is subject to speculation.

There is evidence of dwellings earlier than the Norman Conquest with the discovery locally of a Saxon axe head of the Neolithic or early Bronze Age and a Roman Cinerary Urn.

By the 13th century there appears to have been two manors - one held by the *Gifford* family and the other by the *Baskervilles.* The latter is thought to have been on the site of the present Manor House.

Over the past two hundred years the population has declined quite dramatically.

Today this quiet little village is reputedly one of the highest in Northamptonshire.
It lies close to the Warwickshire border on the route of both the Jurassic Way and also the Salt Way, the latter being used for transporting salt from the mines in Cheshire to south east England.

The area does not appear to have been short of water as the rivers Leam, Cherwell and Nene rise in or near the village and there were said to be at least twenty eight wells.

The delightful Decorative style church of **ST JOHN** the **BAPTIST** lies at a high point on the edge of the village overlooking the lower levels.
The list of Vicars in the church only goes back to 1607 although the tower is thought to date from about 1350 but was much altered in 1845-7 when the pinnacles were removed.

On entering I was very impressed with the heavily timbered roof and with the colourful array of attractive kneelers.

The stonework on the uprights of the porch are quite deeply scarred - said to have been caused by soldiers sharpening their swords before the Battle of Edgehill in 1642.

Of particular note are two memorial windows, the one for the First World War featuring the faces of four men from the village who lost their lives and the other for the Second World War giving thanks for the safe return of all the servicemen.

As a millennium project a tapestry map of the village was made on which are placed in position cross stitch miniature representations of eighty two properties.

During the Second World War when the four church bells were silent, bees made over a cwt of honey in the clock and as a result it became affectionately known as **'The Honey Church'**

The churchyard is very well kept with a lovely display of wild flowers in the spring.

Pots of Honey

Hellidon House with a five bay frontage and a porch of pairs of unfluted Doric columns dates from the late 18th century.

Until the 1950's the village used to be the centre of an ironstone quarrying industry and had an industrial railway which conveyed ironstone to the Great Central line at Charwelton.

A one and three quarter mile tunnel on the Great Central Line which took about two years to build passes under Hellidon.
Four men who were killed during tunnel construction are buried in the churchyard.

There has been a windmill here since the end of the 13th century but the present tower mill was built in 1842 and was last used for grinding corn in the early 20th century and was converted to a dwelling in 1978.

About the same time a vineyard was planted which passed through the hands of two owners until bought by the *Hillier-Birds* in the mid 1980's when it was in a neglected state.
It was said to be the highest vineyard above sea level in Britain and produced its first wines in 1996.
I read that on the ground floor is a shop offering a range of wines and ciders but try as I might I did not find it. The area now appears quite neglected although I did see one or two vines peeping out amongst the weeds and thistles.
Only time will tell what the future holds for this undertaking.

Popular with visitors is the Hellidon Lakes Golf and Spa Hotel - a four star establishment set in 220 acres of peaceful grounds with a 27 hole golf course and a ten pin bowling alley.

There is no longer a shop, post office or school but the public house, The Red Lion, with a beacon outside is a popular watering hole for walkers on the Jurassic Way.

The non-conformist chapel which dated back to the early 19th century was closed in 1966.

JURASSIC WAY

This is a clearly designated and signposted eighty eight mile long distance footpath that connects Banbury in Oxfordshire with Stamford in Lincolnshire.

For most of its route it passes through Northamptonshire entering the County in the south west near Warkworth and passing through Hellidon, Ashby St Ledgers, Sibbertoft and Rockingham before leaving in the north east corner near Easton on the Hill.

The route is based on evidence found by archaeologists in the 1930's and 1940's of a prehistoric trackway which stretched across Middle England between the Humber and Severn estuaries.

This was thought to have followed the great watershed created by Jurassic limestone escarpments - hence the Jurassic Way.

HELMDON

Six miles south west of Towcester
Population: 1801- 421   2001 - 938

DOMESDAY BOOK
ELMEDENE
It is thought that as Helmdon lies on an upper
tributary of the River Tove that the 'don'
came from the Saxon 'denu' - meaning valley.
The prefix is from the Saxon name **Helma.**

Helmdon Viaduct

The **Count of Mortain** held the manor in 1086 as he did many other manors throughout the County. At the time the mill rendered twelve pence per annum.

By the 15th century Helmdon had three manors but no Squire. Overbury was the principal manor and was associated with Worcester College, Oxford, the others being Middlebury and Netherbury.

Five roads converge near the centre of the village but none see a vast amount of traffic except possibly when the Grand Prix is held at Silverstone and motorists make a detour in order to avoid traffic jams near the circuit.

Where the roads converge is the War Memorial alongside which is an American Memorial set up in honour of the American Servicemen who lost their lives when their plane crashed at nearby Astwell Castle Farm in 1943.

This is quite a long village with a pleasing mix of old and new properties.

Of particular note is Priory Farm on the Sulgrave road which has an extremely large barn.

Helmdon has long been recognised as a valuable source of stone for building.

Limestone quarries on each side of Weston Road sprang up from about the 14th century and during the 19th century they were very busy supplying Helmdon stone for neighbouring towns and for the construction of the railway.

The stone was also used for a number of stately homes including Easton Neston, Stowe and Blenheim.

The quarries resulted in an increase in population.

Lacemaking was also a thriving industry in the village from the early 18th century but nowadays many people have to travel much further afield for work.

The Welsh Lane, an old Drovers' route runs across the south of the village.

Close by once stood one of Helmdon's two railway stations. The top one on the Great Central Line was known as Helmdon (for Sulgrave) and opened in 1897.

The other station in the centre of the village was known as Helmdon on the S & M J Railway.

The old station yard is now the depot for a local coach company.

One reminder of the days of the old Great Central Line which closed in 1966 is the nine arch viaduct which spanned the S & M J Railway - the *'nibble and clink line'* - between Towcester and Banbury across the infant River Tove.

Near the lower station and as a reminder of past days you can see the old post office and the 'Hygenic Bakery' dated 1903 (were the others not so hygienic?)

The village no longer has any rail link or shop but still has The Bell Inn and a Primary school with a modern extension plus a Reading Room given by **Charles Fairbrother** in 1887 in memory of his parents who had lived in the village.
Originally this was a place where men could go as an alternative to the public house.
Newspapers and books were provided.
It was not until the First World War that women were allowed to use the premises except to attend an annual dance. Nowadays the building is used by everyone as the village hall.

There used to be three other public houses,
The Chequers, The Magpie and The Cross, these last two are now private houses.

When I last visited Helmdon the local Baptist chapel had been closed on account of subsidence and plans have been submitted for its demolition and the construction of two modern dwellings.

Helmdon has won a number of 'Village of the Year' competitions and in 2011 was again voted the Winner in the Medium Village Category.

The church of **ST MARY MAGDALENE** which stands high above the village was built mainly in the 13th and 14th centuries although it was preceded by a Saxon church.

The list of Vicars goes back to **Walter de Kancia** who died in 1283.
Prior to the Reformation the church was dedicated to **St Nicholas.**

The west tower was rebuilt in 1823 after a lightning strike. In the long and tall Decorative style chancel can be seen both serious and comical carvings, an aumbrey and a three seat sedilia.

An Early English style piscina near the north door was found under some old pews during restoration in 1875/6 and was placed in the wall where it now sits.

I was particularly interested in a stained glass window dated 1313 commemorating **William Campiun** a stonemason, which shows him wielding his hammer.

Campiun Window
Helmdon Church

It was re-leaded in 1976/7 and is one of the very few English medieval windows to depict an artisan using the tools of his trade.
The striking East window represents the birth, crucifixion, resurrection and transfiguration of **Jesus.**

Kitchen and toilet facilities were recently installed in the south porch.

In the churchyard is a magnificent yew tree said to be about two thousand years old but a certificate in the church indicates that it is 'only' seventeen hundred years old.
Some old boughs had to be cut off as a result of a blizzard in April 1908 but it is still, nevertheless, a majestic tree.

.... HELMDON

Astwell Castle

The parish now includes the deserted village of Astwell and the shrunken village of Falcutt.

ASTWELL

DOMESDAY BOOK
ESTWELL(E)
The name simply means east spring.

In the Domesday Book Astwell is recorded as having seventeen households and a mill but today it is one of Northamptonshire's deserted medieval villages with few residents and little of note except a fragment of the 'castle' or former Manor House.

Astwell and Falcutt Manors came together in the *Lovett* family in the late 15th century and it was *Thomas Lovett* who created a deer park in 1547
In its day Astwell was one of only three fortified manors in Northamptonshire.
Today it is in private hands and is not open to the public.

Selina, Countess of Huntingdon, founder and patron of Calvanistic Methodists was born here in 1707.
During her lifetime she established sixty four chapels and used much of her fortune to maintain them.
By 1791 she is said to have spent over £100,000 in works of private and public charity.

The hamlet is still recorded on Ordnance Survey maps.

FALCUTT

In 1220 it was known as Faucot (e) and is thought to relate to the nature of the building material (variegated) of the original dwellings.

Today Falcutt consists of a Manor House and a small number of other properties on the southern edge of Helmdon village.

It is not mentioned in the Domesday Book and is not marked on a map of 1500 but there is recorded in 1491 the fact that money was donated for the reparation of the chapel.
This is thought to have been demolished about 1655.

There is evidence of a village still existing in 1720 but no population is stated.
In 1841 there were recorded as being eighty two residents - it is very difficult to imagine that today.

For many years Falcutt (together with nearby Astwell) was part of Wappenham parish but since 1935 they both form part of the parish of Helmdon.

HEMINGTON

Four miles south east of Oundle
Population: 1801-100   2001 - 65

DOMESDAY BOOK
HEMINTONE/HININTONE
*Originally this would have been **Hemma's** farmstead.*

The Abbey of Ramsay held one of the two manors at the time of the Domesday Book - the other being held by three Knights of the Abbey of Peterborough.
In 1279 the Abbots of the two Abbeys reached agreement about their overlapping interests in the parish and Hemington was assigned to the Ramsey Abbey cellarer.

In 1511 Ramsey leased the whole manor to *Edward Montagu* for seven pounds per annum. He thereafter became responsible for maintenance of the houses and the Estate and built the Grade I listed Manor House now known as **Beaulieu Hall**

What remains of the Hall was restored in the 20th century with Collyweston slate roof tiles.
A 16th century fireplace was removed to Boughton House.

Apart from the village hall dated 1924 there appears to be no other community facility.

This very small village lies in the north east corner of the County on minor roads and has declined in size over the years possibly because of the lack of larger roads.

Earthworks near the church suggest that at one time houses stood on either side of the road to the now isolated church.
The village is thought to have been re-sited by the 17th century as evidenced by a map of 1716.

On the edge of the village is the church of **ST PETER** and **ST PAUL** with a 15th century Perpendicular style west tower. The rest dates from 1660 but was Gothicized in 1873.
It has ten splendid 13th century stalls with intricately carved misericords in the chancel which come from Fotheringhay College. The *Montagu* arms can be seen over the west door.
What struck me as I entered were the white washed walls and the abundance of candles - they were everywhere.

A small school in the village was endowed by the *Rev. Latham* in 1619 with a teacher paid eight pounds per annum. *Rev. Latham* was Rector of Barnwell at the time and endowed similar schools for both boys and girls at Oundle, Barnwell, Brigstock and Weekley.
At Hemington the school appears to have been located in a house rather than a special school building. Nothing now remains but *Latham* is still remembered locally by a Charitable Trust which dispenses a small sum annually for educational needs.

Church of St Peter & St Paul : Hemington

HIGHAM FERRERS

Four miles east of Wellingborough
Population: 1801-726   2001 - 6086

DOMESDAY BOOK
HECHAM
*This was originally 'high ham' - literally a farmstead or village that stood on a hill thus describing its location overlooking the Nene Valley. The family name **Ferrers** was added about the 12th century in honour of **Wm de Ferrers**, **Earl of Derby** who owned the Estate.*

William Peverel held the six hide manor in 1086 when Higham Ferrers was an important market town. In addition to a recorded population of twenty nine households it had a priest and a mill rendering twenty shillings per annum.

A Castle was built in the late 11th century just north of the present church but was demolished in 1523 and the stone granted by **Henry VIII** to **Sir Richard Wingfield** for the construction of the Tudor wing on Kimbolton Castle.
Accounts show that there was a dovecote in the grounds in 1313 and there is still a dovecote today although this is thought to date from the early 17th century. It comprises of three uncovered walls with nesting boxes and can be seen in the Recreation ground to the north of the church.

The first Charter of 1251 was a far sighted act of the Lord of the Manor, **William de Ferrers** in order to promote the prosperity of the area. The Castle and manor were granted by **Henry III** to his son **Edmund Crouchback, Earl of Lancaster**.

They remained with the **Lancaster** family until they went to the crown at the time of **Henry IV**.

The Manor was the home of **Laurence Washington** and his wife **Elizabeth**, for forty years from 1530. Since 1910 the Manor has been part of the Duchy of Lancaster.

Higham Ferrers stands on the old A6 road between Bedford and Kettering but the recently constructed bypass means that the town now has considerably less through traffic.

As you explore you appreciate that this was once a much more important place.
Just off the Market Place is the finest collection of ecclesiastical buildings in the County, largely attributed to or associated with **Henry Chichele.**

The centrepiece is the very grand church of **ST MARY** the **VIRGIN** which was built between 1250-1280 and is certainly one of the best parish churches in the area and is well worth a visit.
Its most notable feature, visible for miles around, is the richly crocketed spire rising to a height of one hundred and seventy feet (52 metres).

The spire and part of the tower fell down in 1630 but was reconstructed immediately with the original stone. The west front contains an interesting recessed porch with twin doorways and 13th century sculpture.

Church of St Mary the Virgin: Higham Ferrers

On entering the church you cannot fail to be impressed by its overall size with two wide naves and three rows of arches making it a complete square.

Hanging on the north wall is some military armour bought by the Borough to fulfil a Government demand to defend the town should this become necessary.

The present rood and loft was installed in 1920 and was the work of *Sir Ninian Comper*.

The choir has a complete set of carved misericords which were used by members of the College founded in 1422 for twenty members by *Henry Chichele.* Brasses in the church commemorate members of his family although he is buried in Canterbury Cathedral.

Henry VIII dissolved the College and all that now remains is the gabled front with its Tudor windows and doors, above which are empty niches which once held statues of Patron Saints.

The ruins alongside the main street are now preserved by English Heritage and access can be obtained through the gate to the left of the site.

Medieval fishponds nearby provided a source of food for the College.

Fortunately the Bede House founded by *Archbishop Chichele* still stands near the church as it has done since 1423. It is an oblong building with bands of ironstone and grey stone on the north and west sides. The Bede House was designed for twelve poor men of the parish over the age of 50 years and everyone had their own locker and cubicle which was divided by a screen (much like today's NHS!).

The word 'Bede' means prayer and the men had to adopt a monastic lifestyle and pray for the King and their benefactor.

There are still Bedesmen today who hold their Feast Day on the 21 December and attend the church for a service followed by a social but the Bede House was vacated in the 17th century and is now used for functions.

. Bede House : Higham Ferrers

Of particular appeal is the Chantry chapel with its fine perpendicular style architecture and superb tall crocketed pinnacles and carved battlements.

It continued to be used as a Grammar school for three hundred years after the Dissolution and has now reverted to church use.

Henry Chichele was not the town's only benefactor. Almost opposite his College are a group of six Almshouses endowed in 1866 by *George Newman* which were provided for six widows or spinsters resident in the town who also received eight shillings a week for ever (not a bad income at that time!).

Among the many other splendid buildings is the delightful little Town Hall standing on its own south of the Market Place. It was erected about 1809 with a central Venetian window.

The top floor houses the Council Chamber with its Town Charters, mace and other such antiquities dating back to the days when this was a Rotten Borough.

Until the late 1930's the Town Hall was also used as a court and a lock-up.

ROTTEN BOROUGHS

A 'Rotten Borough' was one where there was a very small electorate and votes could easily be bought by the land owners to affect the election results.

This was one of the smaller Rotten Boroughs returning just one MP to Parliament until the Reform Act of 1832 which disenfranchised fifty seven such Boroughs including Brackley and Higham Ferrers.

.... HIGHAM FERRERS

Also to be seen on the Market Square is the old Market Cross where a cone of stone replaces the original stepped base.
A market was recorded in the Domesday Book of 1086.

In the early 19th century the working population of the town was almost solely engaged in making shoes or pillow lace, now little remains of either industry.
Similarly the railway which brought business and people to the town has also gone.

A great fire on the 21st March 1882 destroyed many properties and rendered one hundred and thirty two people homeless.

The centre still retains a little market town atmosphere with a variety of shops, inns, schools, clinics, churches, a library and some attractive buildings.

Henry Chichele

Henry Chichele must surely be Higham Ferrers most famous son. He was born in 1362 the youngest of three sons of **Thomas** and **Agnes Chichele**.
Thomas was a yeoman farmer and Mayor of Higham Ferrers in 1373. They lived at 67 High Street.

Henry, said to have been an outstanding scholar at a very early age, was introduced to the Bishop of Winchester **William of Wykeham** who was working in the Castle on plans for New College in Oxford.

Henry's achievements impressed the eccliastical authorities for after spells in Salisbury and St David's he was appointed Archbishop of Canterbury in 1414 a position he held until his death in 1443 aged 81 and thus became the longest serving Archbishop of Canterbury.
He is buried in Canterbury Cathedral in a 'cadavar' tomb which has the inscription:-
'I was pauper born, then to primate raised,
Now I am cut down and served up for worms,
Behold my grave'

He was renowned chiefly for his educational foundations particularly the College in Higham Ferrers and two at Oxford including All Souls College.

Chichele College, Higham Ferrers

HINTON IN THE HEDGES

Two miles west of Brackley
Population: 1801-177   2001 - 179

DOMESDAY BOOK
HINTONE
According to etymologists the name comes from' higna tun', Saxon for monks farm.
There is another village named simply Hinton near Woodford Halse.

In 1086 the two hide manor was held by **Arnold** of **Geoffrey de Mandeville** and had seventeen households and a mill rendering two shillings per annum.

Today it is a quiet backwater served only by minor roads to the west of Brackley with a small triangular Green and a rare wooden clad village pump at its centre.
I was informed that restoration is planned as a **Queen Elizabeth II** Diamond Jubilee project. Other pumps in the village are surrounded with bricks.
Hinton once lay on the Banbury to Brackley turnpike road but today the main road is some distance away.

The recently refurbished Crewe Arms public house is named after the **Crewe** family of nearby Steane. Apart from the church this is the only meeting place as there is no longer a shop, school or village hall.
The playing field was given to the village by **Captain Norris** of Steane in 1979 for *'children of all ages'*.

A pair of two storey Almshouses were built for aged widows by **Thomas Crewe** in 1633 and display an almost undecipherable inscription in Latin above the door. They are currently in use but no longer considered suitable for older people

During the Second World War a small airfield was built which is still in use today in a small way for gliding, parachuting and private aviation.

The mainly Early English style limestone church of the **HOLY TRINITY** stands in a quiet churchyard at the end of a drive off the village Green. It has a Norman west tower and font although traces of Saxon masonry have been found locally suggesting an earlier church.

There is an unusual tomb of
Sir William de Hinton (born 1284) dressed as a medieval Knight who, with his wife rest head to toe in a straight line.

Old Well - Hinton in the Hedges

HOLCOT

Six miles north east of Northampton
Population: 1801-343   2001 - 399

DOMESDAY BOOK
HOLECOTE
The name comes from the Saxon 'holh' - hollow and 'cot' - cottage i.e. 'the cottage in the hollow'

Two manors are mentioned in the Domesday Book. One was attached to the royal manor at Brixworth and the other was held by **Hugh** of the ***Countess Judith.***
Twenty three households were recorded.

Holcot is a quiet little village some way off the Kettering to Northampton road overlooking Pitsford Reservoir. It still has its town well and restored fish ponds together with the site of a medieval wash pit although the shop, post office and school have now all closed. There is however a popular public house - The White Swan and a riding school with livery stables.

The church of **ST MARY** and **ALL SAINTS** stands on a slight rise in the centre of the village.
It has Decorative style windows and arcades plus a 14th century embattled tower with four large gargoyles. There are many wall paintings although they are quite indistinct.

In 1844 the north door was walled up for reasons unknown and on the wall today is a drawing of *'the man with a hat'* in lead dated 1666 which was removed from the roof during repairs.

The church is well worth a visit to see some fine stained glass - the window I most liked is above the altar at the east end of the south aisle and is thought to be the only example of ***Frampton's*** work in Northamptonshire showing **Christ** debating with Elders in the Temple.

On the south side of the churchyard is the stump of a 15th century limestone cross and alongside the road is the old school room built in 1843 but now used for small meetings and functions.

The car park just off the reservoir causeway on the Brixworth road is a very popular place for walkers, bird watchers, fishermen and picnickers. Ducks and waterfowl are drawn to this point in great numbers to partake of the food provided by the visitors.

When water levels are low it is still possible to see the remains of a bridge which once carried a minor road over a small tributary of Pitsford Brook which was dammed to form the reservoir.

Since 1997 a popular Steam Fair has been held just outside the village each year which attracts large crowds.

HOLDENBY

Five miles north west of Northampton
Population: 1801-119   2001 - 100

DOMESDAY BOOK
ALDENESBI/ALDENESTONE
It is thought that the name derives from the Viking name
Halfdan *and the Saxon word - 'by' - for settlement.   i.e. this was **Halfdans** village*

The Domesday Book listed just one manor in Holdenby held by the ***Count of Mortain*** with fourteen households but there is evidence to suggest that there was a second manor or settlement here - one sited near the present church and the other near the site of the present village.

Two villages existed until just before 1580 when the settlement around the church was removed and the present village was rebuilt. Holdenby is sometimes spelt and pronounced Holmby.

Today it is basically a small Estate village built around **Holdenby House.**
When the original House was completed in 1583 it was the largest in England.

The little Primary school is now the home of the Moulton College Schools Centre for visiting groups. Courses are linked to the National Curriculum and aim to provide both teachers and pupils with an educational and exciting experience of the countryside.
There is no shop or public house.

The largely 14th century church of **ALL SAINTS** is now so remote and isolated that for years I have travelled on the minor road between Northampton and East Haddon without realising where it was.
It can be reached either from the grounds of Holdenby House when they are open or down a grass track from the village which is not really suitable for a motor car particularly in bad weather.

The church is built of local ironstone and contains a number of memorials and brasses to the *de Holdenby* family who had owned this manor for three generations when *Sir Christopher Hatton* decided to build a grand mansion.

The church was declared redundant in 1972 when the parishes of Holdenby and East Haddon were united ecclesiastically and is under the care of the Churches Conservation Trust although it has an occasional service and is often open on a summer Sunday afternoon.

Old Gates - Holdenby

.... HOLDENBY

The chancel was rebuilt in 1843 to the design (so it is said), of *Sir Henry Dryden* of Canons Ashby who was an amateur architect.

Much of the church now dates from the restoration by *Sir George Gilbert Scott* in 1867/8 although the rood screen, tower screen and reredos were previously in Holdenby House.

When visiting Peterborough Cathedral recently I was interested to see Holdenby church featured in one of the stained glass windows but I have not been able to find out why.
The Cathedral also has in its Treasury, the communion plate once held at Holdenby consisting of an Elizabethan cup and cover, a paten dated 1570 a bread holder of 1718 and a flagon of 1720.

The wall surrounding the churchyard contains a quantity of stones from the old mansion.

A popular attraction at the House are falconry displays. These are organised by Icarus Falconry a family run business situated in the Estate grounds since 2002. The collection includes a variety of hawks, falcons and owls.

For the past five years Holdenby has hosted the Northamptonshire Food Show.
The two day event includes many food and drink exhibitions, live cookery demonstrations, family entertainment and falconry displays and attracts thousands of visitors.

Holdenby House.

Holdenby House

Holdenby House was built between the years 1570-1583 by **Sir Christopher Hatton** *who, in 1587, at the age of forty seven, became Lord Chancellor.*

It is recorded that he refused to sleep a night in his grand mansion until **Queen Elizabeth I** *had slept there and remarked that he meant to leave this 'shrine, I mean Holdenby, still unseen until that Holy Saint may sit in it to whom it is dedicated' - he waited in vain.*

The original House was reputed to have been the largest of its kind in England but all that now remains are indications of landscaping and two curious stone archways dated 1583 which stood to the east of the old House and led into the two courtyards of the main House.

The cost of building Holdenby House and Kirby Hall at virtually the same time financially ruined **Sir Christopher** *and he died in 1591. The House was sold to* **James I** *in 1607 and for four months in 1646 imprisoned the captured* **Charles I** *before* **Cornet Joyce** *came with a body of Parliamentary troops and carried him away by coach (see Althorp).*

During the Civil War the House was a Royalist headquarters but in 1651 it was bought by **Adam Baynes**, *Captain of the Parliamentary Army who demolished most of the old House except for a small domestic wing and let the once magnificent gardens become neglected.*

The property became a romantic ruin until it was inherited by **Lady Clifden.**

In 1873 she set about restoring the building by using the original kitchen wing and adding two side wings in the same style. The result being that the present House is only about one eighth the size of its predecessor.

The Grade I listed building is open to the public at various times of the year and often has special week-ends including birds of prey displays.

Holdenby House has been used in a number of films including 'Friends and Crocodiles' in 2005 and 'Great Expectations' in 2011 when it was transformed over four days to become the derelict mansion of spinster **Miss Havisham** *- Satis House.*

The House descended down the female line to the **Lowther** *family who date back to 940AD*

HOLLOWELL

Seven miles north west of Northampton
Population: 1801-227 2001 - 353

DOMESDAY BOOK
HOLEWELLE
*The derivation of the name is as it sounds
hollow well - or deep well.
There are numerous springs in this part of the County.*

Although Hollowell is mentioned at least four times in the Domesday Book the major portion of land appears to have been held by the *Bishop of Lincoln.*

In a survey of 1801 Hollowell was listed simply as a hamlet in Guilsborough Hundred although even then it had a population of two hundred and twenty seven. Hollowell which is located just off the A5199 about midway between Northampton and Welford was constituted as a separate parish from Guilsborough in 1850.

The church of **ST JAMES** is quite modern having been built in 1840 by *Kempthorne* at the expense of the *Rev. J. D. Watson,* Vicar of Guilsborough.
The simple but heavily buttressed church is built in the Lancet style with polygonal apse and small bellcote and a high pitched roof below which is a wheel window. The churchyard is well kept.

The *Rev. J. D. Watson* also provided the money for a school in the village which has now closed although the premises are used as the village hall.
There is no public house or shop but the village is well known in the County as the location for the annual Hollowell Steam Fair and Traction Rally.
This was started in 1986 to raise funds for the repair to the church roof and became so popular that it is now one of the largest of its kind in the region.

The delightful little round bus shelter on the main street with conical thatched roof topped by a square clock tower and weathervane featuring a traction engine was donated to the village by the Steam Rally organisers to mark the millennium.

Properties of note are the old Manor House which dates from 1665 and the ironstone building of 1698 known as the Vicarage since it was purchased as such just before the church was built.

Hollowell reservoir covers one hundred and forty acres and has an active sailing club, coarse fishing and thriving wild life and is linked by a tunnel to nearby Ravensthorpe reservoir.
I enjoyed a leisurely walk around the reservoir but although this is apparently an official right of way I got the impression that walkers were not too welcome - maybe I just chose a bad day.

The parish includes the small hamlet of Teeton.

TEETON

DOMESDAY BOOK
TEAHE
The high ground here was used as a look out and this fact may have given rise to its name 'taecne' - beacon.

At one time Teeton had a Chapel of Ease (church without a graveyard) but this has long since disappeared.
There were ten households at the time of the Domesday Book so things have not changed much in this area.

It is thought that Teeton was simply the Estate for Teeton Hall which was held by the *Breton* family from the 13th century until it was sold to *John Langton* a London merchant in 1718.
Today this is a very small hamlet with a few people.

The most impressive building is the present Grade II listed Manor House which was rebuilt in 1771.
The datestone of 1870 on a rear gable is probably the date of restoration or remodelling work.

HORTON

Six miles south east of Northampton
Population: 1801-79
2001 – 1568   (inc Piddington and Hackleton)

DOMESDAY BOOK
HORTONE
The name comes from the Saxon words 'horh' - muddy and 'tun' - farmstead - simply 'muddy farm.'

The village which always seems to have been small is on the B526 road to Newport Pagnell and must once have been surrounded by forests.

Until the building of the MI motorway this was on the main road and the old coaching route between London and Northampton.

At the time of the Domesday Book Horton was divided into several small manors one of which *'was waste'* and there were eighteen households.

The whole lordship was acquired in about 1620 by *Sir Henry Montagu* (who later became the *Earl of Manchester)*. Another member of the family, *Charles*, (1661-1715) originated the Bank of England in 1694 and was Prime Minister in 1697.

Horton Hall was rebuilt in the 17th century and the grounds landscaped resulting in a number of evictions. The Hall which was once the home of the *Montagus* and later the *Pickering Phipps* family (local brewers) was demolished in 1936.

Some interesting architectural features remain including the impressive entrance to the present village between a pair of Victorian Lodges leading to the red brick Georgian stables and an attractive little coachman's house.

Unusual and modern upmarket housing is very evident.

During the railway era there was a station to the north of the village on the Northampton to Bedford line. Why it should have been named Piddington station when it was nearer to both Horton and Hackleton I do not know.
The line and station has now gone and the station buildings have been converted to a private residence with an industrial site next door.

The French Partridge dating back to the 16th century was originally a coaching inn on the main road but today it operates as a Boutique Hotel and Holistic Spa.

There is no shop, post office or school and the younger children are educated at nearby Hackleton. The village does have a splendid cricket ground and the club celebrated its centenary in 2008. It was quite appropriate therefore that *Alan Lamb* the England cricketer chose to live in the village in the 1970's.

In the grounds of what was once the Horton Estate stands the church of **ST MARY** which dates from the 13th century. Upper parts of the pinnacled west tower with its one handed clock are early 18th century although it was almost entirely rebuilt in 1862/3 by local architect *E. F. Law.*
It is now in such a dangerous condition that it is closed to all visitors.
As a result I was unable to see the alabaster tomb of *William, Lord Parr* of Horton 1546 who was present at the *'Field of the Cloth of Gold'* and his wife. He was uncle to *Catherine Parr*, Queen of England. The property is currently subject to consultation with the Church Commissioners to decide whether or not the building should be closed permanently as *'there is not a viable congregation to sustain regular acts of public worship.'*
In the churchyard there is a touching gravestone of a little boy holding a teddy, pointing to a sunflower and the name, *'Benjamin'.*
Sadly *Benjamin Pouncey* died in 1989 aged five.

Tombstone at Horton Church

IRCHESTER

Three miles south east of Wellingborough
Population: 1801-528   2001 - 4807

DOMESDAY BOOK
HIRECESTRE/IRENCESTRE

*It is well known that the appendix 'chester' is indicative of a Roman settlement and certainly a small settlement
existed here in the 3rd and 4th centuries - some Romano British finds have been made.
The prefix may be associated with the discovery of iron or may simply be a person's name.*

River Nene Near Chester House

Irchester, with its roots firmly in the Iron Age is situated just off the A45 between Wellingborough and Rushden.

To the north of the parish close to the River Nene lies the 17th century **Chester House** where excavations have revealed evidence of both Iron Age and Romano/British periods including coins, pottery and graves.

This was the site of a walled Roman town and was the junction of a number of Roman roads.

The House was badly damaged by fire in 2010 but there are plans to restore the property and develop the area into a heritage attraction.

In reading the Northamptonshire entries in the Domesday Book I was intrigued to see a record of *'a Frenchman with a plough'* in Irchester.

The mill at that time was rendering sixteen shillings per annum but was:-
'in dispute between the King and Wm' **(Peverel)**.

In spite of its long history there is not much visible evidence today of the past.

The population grew from the 19th century when ironstone quarrying began alongside the Irchester to Little Irchester road. Since the quarries closed in the 1960's the area has been transformed into Irchester Country Park.

The population has increased almost tenfold in the past two hundred years and this has resulted in much building during the Victorian era and many properties of more recent date. There is very little of any real age or architectural interest.

The town, (or is it still a village?) has all the usual features including schools, chapels, shops, post office, public houses and restaurants but no station although the main line between St Pancras and the north passes close by. The War Memorial contains the names of nine local residents who lost their lives in an air raid on 20th May, 1941.

One of the few attractive buildings is the church in the High Street and having obtained the key I entered via the priest's door straight into the chancel. Most of the priest's doors I have come across have obviously not been used for very many years or have been bricked up.

The church is dedicated to **ST KATHARINE** who was put to death in 307AD for professing Christianity. After converting her gaolers the Emperor ordered her to be put to death by a special instrument consisting of wheels set with knives (Katharine Wheel) but this was miraculously destroyed and she was then beheaded.

In the popular devotion of the Middle Ages, fifty seven churches were dedicated to her in England alone.

The story of *St Katharine* is thought to have been brought back to England by the Crusaders and if so would imply that the church in Irchester was probably re-dedicated following repairs and re-consecrated towards the end of the 13th century.

The Decorative style west tower has alternating bands of ironstone and limestone. This is topped with a graceful spire and delightful weathervane soaring 156 feet (49 metres) high, a landmark for miles around which features, so I am told, a Katharine Wheel but you would need extremely good eyesight or powerful binoculars to see it.

What can be seen is the beautiful window installed in 1926, dedicated to *St Katharine* and depicting scenes from her life. Also of note is the East window which was installed in 1890 in joint memory of *T. A. Macan* and *R. W. Arkwright* by members of the Oakley Hunt.

The five lights depict the principle events in the life of *Jesus*. The Jacobean pulpit with rich carving dates back to 1611. Even older is the bread oven in the Sanctuary which was used for baking bread for use at Communion.

Almost opposite the church is a public house with the unusual name – 'The 19th' - as in golf terminology. The Manor House next to the church is not, in my opinion very inspiring.

One walk I did directed me through the cemetery extension which at the time looked like a festival site with red and white ribbons absolutely everywhere. I later discovered that Health and Safety had been at work and declared many of the tombstones to be unsafe and hence taped off.

I don't know what has happened since but on a recent visit not a single ribbon was to be seen.

In the parish is the lost settlement of Knuston.

KNUSTON

DOMESDAY BOOK
CNUTESTONE

The original settlement appears to have been located north and north west of the Hall.

Twelve taxpayers were recorded here in the Domesday Book so it must have been a reasonably sized place.

Two mills rendered twenty shillings and eight pence per annum respectively.

Knuston had no church of its own but was a dependant Chapelry of Irchester and taxation records include both places. The Chapel of *St Leonard* at Knuston is mentioned in a Deed in 1348 in which a Vicarage was created at Irchester. The chapel had completely disappeared by 1591.

Unfortunately in 1500 eight houses in the area were demolished during land enclosures but *Bridges* in 1720 recorded twenty families in the village.

The population further declined following more land enclosures and imparkment.

The great House was developed to become the rather grand **Knuston Hall** which is situated in parkland leading down to an artificial lake and containing architecture of the 17th, 18th and 19th centuries.

The Hall passed through various owners until 1865 when it was bought by *Sir Robert Arkwright*, great grandson of *Richard Arkwright*, inventor of the Spinning Wheel.

H. E. Bates, a local author is thought to have based his country mansion in his novel '*Spella Ho*' on Knuston Hall.

During the Second World War the Hall was used as a temporary hospital and as a transport depot.

In 1949 the Hall was bought by the County Council for £12,000 and today it is a residential adult educational facility run by the Authority.

IRCHESTER COUNTRY PARK

This 220 acre park adjoining the B570 is open to the public and has play areas, walks, refreshments, toilets, car park etc. and is a popular tourist attraction.

The Park opened in 1971 and had been planted with a variety of trees providing a good area of woodland.

The area once went by the name of 'Wembley Pit' after stone was quarried for the original Wembley Stadium in 1924 and you can still see the evidence.

Ironstone quarrying in the area ceased in 1940 but on show are some of the industrial engines and rolling stock at the Narrow Gauge Railway Museum in the Park. During the summer months the museum is open to the public.

IRTHLINGBOROUGH

Four miles north east of Wellingborough
Population: 1801-811   2001 - 7033

DOMESDAY BOOK
ERDIBURNE/ERDINBURNE
There was a settlement here well before the Domesday Book in 1086.
In 780 AD the village was known as Yrlingaburg, thought to derive from a personal name
plus 'burh' - fortified place or fort.

The two manors recorded in 1086 were held by the Abbey of Peterborough.
There were twenty three households and two mills rendering a total income of twenty three shillings per annum.

The town overlooks the valley of the River Nene which is spanned by two bridges.

I prefer the one which dates from the 14th century and has ten ribbed arches but although this was restored in 1925 it was found to be inadequate for the volume of traffic on the busy A6 between Kettering and Bedford. The traffic now uses the not unattractive 20th century bridge alongside.

The area has grown considerably since the 19th century when industrialisation including boot and shoe manufacture and the railway brought prosperity.

The railway ran from Northampton to Peterborough and was opened in 1845 but the station was located some distance from the town on the opposite side of the river and passengers had to cross an old packhorse bridge to get there.

In 1966 the line closed following *Beechings'* infamous report and part of the trackway is now used as a footpath to Stanwick Lakes.

Until the year 1774 the ecclesiastical history of Irthlingborough was one of two parishes each with its own church, one of which - the church of **ALL SAINTS** has long since been demolished but was the site of an excavation in 1965 when evidence was found of Roman settlement.

When *Sir William Cecil* of Burghley heard of the demolition of the church he is said to have *'requested'* the lead from the roof for his grand house at **Burghley** and what *Cecil* wanted he got although this time it cost him ten pounds.

It has been suggested that the other church dedicated to **ST PETER** was originally a Chapel of Ease dating back to the Norman era since when it has been much altered and enlarged.

Great changes took place in the 14th century when *John Pyel* (1310-1382) purchased the Manor of Erdiburne in 1353 from *Sir Simon de Drayton*.
John was born in the town and became a man of great standing and wealth and traded in the City of London where he was an MP and a Sheriff.

In 1375 he obtained a Royal licence to found the College of *St Peter* for six secular Canons. Unfortunately he died before completing this task but his widow continued with the project.
When the College was dissolved in the reign of *Henry VIII*, *William Alcoke* was retained as Vicar of the parish church and the other Canons were granted a pension of six pounds per annum.

The building has great architectural appeal and beauty and although situated in the town centre it overlooks the Nene Valley.

It is large and unusual with a very tall and dominant west tower which I particularly like.
The amazing four stage tower in ironstone and grey stone is topped by an octagonal lantern which rises to a height of one hundred feet (30.5 metres).

The lantern is an unusual feature among churches in Northamptonshire and it is thought to date back to the days before the Nene Valley was bridged or drained.

There was only a river ford between Higham Ferrers and Irthlingborough across the boggy marshes and fog was a real problem.
Fires would be lit in the lantern during poor weather to guide the traveller to safety.

In 1887 the tower was found to be leaning to the south east so was dismantled brick by brick and rebuilt to the original design.
The work was completed in 1893 at a cost of £2,760.

The interior of the tower was once divided into three storeys, two of which had fireplaces and were used as residential accommodation for the College.

The church is well worth a visit and has many interesting features including the stained glass windows and the eight misericords or monks stalls which are still in use by the choir today.

The medieval alabaster memorial to **John** and **Joan Pyel** was once richly and lavishly emblazoned as was the ancient tomb under a canopy of marble which is the memorial to **Sir Thomas Cheney**, **Kt**. who was responsible for rebuilding the Lady Chapel after it collapsed in the late 15th century.

St Peters Church
Irthlingboro

DFBLUNT
AUG 2010

As one would expect for a town of over seven thousand people it has a fairly busy High Street with various public houses, shops, banks, cafes and a library but boot and shoe manufacture has virtually ceased.

There is also a very large school site incorporating Nursery, Infant and Junior schools.
The Secondary school is on a separate site.

In spite of the history surrounding the church, Irthlingborough is almost totally lacking in buildings of beauty, historical or architectural interest.

I was surprised to learn that in 1914 Irthlingborough was a centre of film making with the production of six films by an American Movie magnate, **Charles Weston**, including 'The Battle of Waterloo' in which one hundred lancers from Weedon Barracks recreated the cavalry scenes.
It could have become the UK's answer to Hollywood.

.... IRTHLINGBOROUGH

More recently in 1974 Irthlingborough has featured in the TV series *'Hunters Walk'* when parts of the High Street were used and again in 1977 when much of **H. E. Bates,** *'Love for Lydia'* was filmed in the town.

The old chapel in the High Street is now a business centre and an old chapel in Meeting Lane is boarded up and is in a sorry state.

The Methodists who moved to a new building to seat 600 people in 1897 in College Street then extended the premises again in 1960 still meet regularly for their services.
Churches elsewhere in the town serve the Baptists, Salvation Army and other Christian communities.

The Market Cross dates from the 13th century -
the town having held markets since before 1200.
In 1925 it was restored by HM Office of Works and was moved to its present location in the centre of the town in 1966.
The Cross has a square base and a series of seven octagonal steps. Its shaft is thirteen feet long and is said to have been used as a standard 'pole' for measurement of agricultural land in the open fields system of shared land from about the 10th century until the early 19th century.

The immediate area around the Cross has been considerably improved in recent years.

Close by is The Bull which was rebuilt in the 1930's in mock Tudor style and is now shuttered up. Is this another of the many public houses that has finished its life's work?

A real bonus for the town was the building of the grand football stadium by lower league standards, just off the busy A6 road - the brainchild of *Max Griggs* of *Dr Marten Boots* (see Rushden).
Unfortunately things started to go wrong when funds dried up.
It was built as the home of the combined Rushden and Irthlingborough football clubs and hosted Football League matches between 'Rushden & Diamonds' and their opponents.

Unfortunately the 'Diamonds' as they were known went into liquidation in 2011 and the ground was for a season the home of one of their bitter rivals - Kettering Town Football Club until they too suffered financial difficulties.
I am waiting with interest to see what happens with the ground and stands.

When travelling out of town towards the Addingtons it is a surprise to come upon a sizeable estate of houses on Crow Hill which is part of Irthlingborough although some little distance away. Nearby is an area very popular with older children and teenagers, the Frontier Adventure Centre, which provides a whole range of outdoor activities.

ISHAM

Three miles south of Kettering
Population: 1801-247   2001 - 743

DOMESDAY BOOK
HISHAM/ISHAM
*It appears obvious that the River Ise
is the basis of the name.*

The area was settled long before the Norman Conquest as evidence has been found of Iron Age and Roman settlements in the form of coins, pottery, flint tools and animal bones.

Of the three manors mentioned in the Domesday Survey one of them is recorded thus:-
'Eustace occupied this land by force, wronging the Church of Ramsey'

The other manors were held by *Walkelin* of the *Bishop of Coutances* and *Ralph* of *Guy de Raimbeaucourt.*
Two mills are recorded each rendering ten shillings per annum.
In the 12th century two and a half hides in Isham were held by *Henry de Isham* of the fee of *Daundevill* which probably makes the family among those who have dwelt longest in the County. The family, who went on to hold the manors at Pytchley and Lamport, transferred their right to Isham to a member of the *de L'Isle* family by marriage.

Isham is situated on high ground on both sides of the main A509 road between Wellingborough and Kettering and separated from Burton Latimer by the Ise Brook a tributary of the River Nene.
In spite of the heavy traffic it is still a very pleasant place

Prior to 1841 when they were united into one benefice the parish was divided into two - Isham Superior and Isham Inferior, situated on higher and lower ground respectively.
According to parish records the Rector of Isham Inferior was removed in 1662 for *'contending for the upper Parsonage'* when *Mr Galston* was presented to both by the Bishop of Lincoln and the King.

The two Rectories were recorded by *John Bridges* in his history which was written at the beginning of the 18th century.

In the garden of Manor Farm opposite the church is the 17th century rectangular dovecote of the former Elizabethan Manor House which was demolished in 1824.
The dovecote built of limestone has five hundred and eighty nesting holes.

The church of **ST PETER** stands in a very prominent position on the main road and was constructed between the 13th and 15th centuries although there is some evidence of earlier building including two bays with Norman capitals in the nave.
It is unusual in that in addition to having an embattled west tower it also has a bellcote but without a bell at the east end

There is a fine Jacobean pulpit with a high back canopy. The west tower is Decorative to Perpendicular in style with a top frieze of cusped lozenges and battlements and grotesque gargoyles. They watch over village affairs from each corner of the medieval tower.

Until its closure Isham shared a station with Burton Latimer on the line between Leicester and London.

There are two public houses - The Monk and Minstrel previously known as The Red Lion on the main road and The Lilacs in Church Street together with a shop and a garage.
The Lilacs has a pub sign depicting a lilac rabbit. This breed of rabbit is known to have originated in a number of locations at about the same time.
The first English breeder is said to have been *H. Onslow* of Cambridge who exhibited in 1913 at the London Exhibition. The rabbits are said to be reasonably docile and make good pets and at maturity can weigh up to eight pounds.
In the 1950's the breed became almost extinct and they are still fairly rare.

The Primary school dates from 1840 but has been enlarged and the Methodist chapel built in 1861 which is still in regular use started out as an Independent Wesleyan chapel.

ISLIP

Two miles west of Thrapston
Population 1801 - 440   2001 - 763

DOMESDAY BOOK
ISLEP/SLEPE
As the River Ise is some distance away the name must derive from another source
– possibly the Saxon 'slaepe' meaning slippery place.

The royal manor of Brigstock held land in the area at the time of the Domesday Book but there must have been a settlement here long before the Norman Conquest.

Evidence was discovered during ironstone workings in the 19th and 20th centuries of a Saxon burial site and various Roman remains.
These ironstone workings continued until the furnaces closed in 1942.

Close to the footpath which leads due west from the village is a sixteen foot tall brick built ventilation shaft chimney which used to vent the Islip Iron Company's mine some one hundred feet below.
Men around Islip were heavily involved in mining and quarrying for furnaces both here and in Corby.

This is a picturesque village standing on high ground on the west bank of the River Nene close to Thrapston.
It once stood on the main A6116 to Corby but a degree of peace has returned since the building of the bypass.

Most of the buildings in the High Street, some of which are thatched, are of Northamptonshire limestone.

The church of **ST NICHOLAS** is of Perpendicular style and although it has some 12th century parts it dates mainly from the 15th century.
Its pinnacled west tower is ornate with clasping buttresses and is topped with a recessed and crocketed spire which was damaged by lightning during a storm in 1900.
A large number of gargoyles with long spouts in their mouths can be seen around the roof area.

The nave is particularly tall with tall ogee hooded arches and the roof is supported by angel corbels.
In the chancel are two fine looking and well preserved brasses although they are not covered.

These represent *John Nicholls* and his wife *Annys* who had twelve children - the memorial was placed there by an American descendant, *Matthias Nicholls* who went on to become Mayor of New York in 1671.

Unfortunately the original brass plate disappeared and was replaced by American descendants at the beginning of the 20th century.
They also donated the chancel screen.
Another American connection is *Dame Mary Washington* (1624) who is buried in the church. She was the great, great, great aunt of *George Washington*, first President of the USA.

An interesting property near the church is St Nicholas House, timber framed, half brick and half stone. It is believed to be the oldest domestic house and its site can be traced back to the 13th century.

Islip House by the 12th century 'nine arch' bridge is Georgian and has bonded wine vaults beneath. It was the home of *Thomas Squire* who was largely responsible for making the River Nene navigable between Thrapston and Peterborough. Completion of the work was celebrated with a 'Grand Opening 'in November 1737.

The old school in School Lane was opened in 1862 but was closed in 1992 and the younger children travel to nearby Aldwincle.

Two public houses remain, The Rose and Crown in Mill Road dating from 1691 and The Woolpack of 16th century origin which houses the Rockingham Forest Visitors Centre.

In the days of horse power the village had two factories producing horse collars which were stuffed with rushes plucked from the nearby river. Production ceased in 1960 and one of these buildings now houses Islip Working Men's Club. Now there is very little local employment and most people work elsewhere.

There is no longer a general store or post office but I was surprised to see one shop, that of a beauty therapist.
The 'Old Shop 'in Mill Road is now a private residence.
In the High Street is the village hall and the recreation ground with its ornate gate donated by the *Stopford - Sackville* family of **Drayton House** to mark the end of the First World War.

This is a fine area for walking with many signposted paths particularly around the Nene Valley and the lakes towards Aldwincle and beyond.
The Nene Way (a long distance footpath) actually goes through the village.

One footpath takes you past the old mill nestling in a picturesque position by the River Nene.
It continued to grind corn up to 1960 and is now a private residence in need of some tender loving care.

The Mill - Islip

KELMARSH

Five miles south of Market Harborough
Population: 1801-131   2001 - 80

DOMESDAY BOOK
KEILMERSE/CAILMARC/CALME
*I cannot find positive agreement as to how the name
derives – was it a personal name
given to a marshy area?*

In 1086 there were two manors, one part under the royal manor of Rothwell and the other held by **William Peverel**. In 1377 eighty people over the age of fourteen paid the Poll Tax indicating a sizeable community.

It is thought that the population declined between 1727-32 when the present Hall replaced its predecessor and some clearance took place.

The older settlement appears to have been north of the present isolated church.

Today, Kelmarsh is a small, largely Estate village in the Northamptonshire Uplands on the A508 Harborough to Northampton road.

On approaching Kelmarsh from the south there is a sign pointing to the tea shop at the Nagarjuna Buddhist Centre in the old Rectory. It is part of a complex promoting Buddhism and meditation. Don't feel afraid to visit - you will get a very warm welcome with no pressure and enjoy a cup of tea and a cream cake in the 'World Peace Café.'

It is recorded that in 1849 **Lord Bateman** owner of the Grade I listed **Kelmarsh Hall** was so incensed by the bad behaviour of his tenants that he called them all together and ordered them to attend church regularly and conduct themselves in a proper manner.

As part of his attempt to make the locals better citizens he provided them with a school so that the children could learn to read and write. The school has closed but the building on the Harrington road still stands and has a plaque above the porch.

The former Kelmarsh Arms has been converted into a private house but on the gable above the door can be seen the former name.

A fire on the 4th May 1943 started in a thatched roof and destroyed thirteen houses and rendered forty four people homeless. No one was injured but many possessions were lost. The cottages were rebuilt in their present form in 1948.

A short distance from the village on the Clipston road is **ST DENYS'** church with a massive 15th century west tower, clasping buttresses and a broach spire. Most noticeable are the round pink marble columns alongside the north aisle and the very ornate font standing on pink marble pillars. Pink marble from Rome also features prominently in the chancel which was rebuilt in 1874 in high Victorian style by **Mr & Mrs Naylor** of the Hall.

In the north chapel there is a colourful yet somewhat macabre monument to **Sir John Hanbury**, one time Lord of the Manor who died in 1639.

Finally take time to see the hammer beam roof adorned with golden angels.

I could not help but be intrigued by the massive memorial in the churchyard in pink marble with large corner finials. This is the grave of **Christopher Naylor** 1814-1899 (and presumably family members). Also buried in the churchyard is **Claude Granville Lancaster**, MP for Fyle and former owner of the Hall.

Kelmarsh had a station on the Northampton to Market Harborough line. After withdrawal of services in 1960 the Royal Train was sometimes parked on the line and although the track and station buildings have been removed the trackway remains and has been turned into the Brampton Valley Way and is very popular with walkers, cyclists and horse riders.

This is a very pleasant and easy walk which I have completed a number of times. As you approach Kelmarsh you have the choice of using the 332 yard tunnel (mind the puddles) or climbing over the hill and undertaking a long detour.

At the site of the former station is a relic of the Second World War because it was here that aviation fuel was stored. The area is still very well protected but is now used for domestic supplies.

Lancaster

Gate Way to Kelmarsh Hall

Kelmarsh Hall

*The red brick Palladium style Kelmarsh Hall with a three bay pediment and symmetrical wings was built between 1727-32 to the design of **James Gibbs** for **William Hanbury**, a noted antiquarian.*
Gibbs designed many famous buildings such as St Martin's in the Fields church in London but Kelmarsh is one of only a few of his country houses still standing.

Richard Naylor, a Liverpool banker and horse racing enthusiast purchased the Estate in 1864 mainly for its hunting potential. The Orangery to the south of the house was built in the late 18th century.
*It used to stand near **Brixworth Hall** and was re-erected at Kelmarsh in the 20th century.*

George Granville Lancaster thanks to a fortune founded in iron and coal bought the Estate in 1902.
*His son **Claude** inherited in 1924 and it then passed to his sister **Cicely** in 1977.*
When she died in 1996 the Kelmarsh Trust took over custody of the Estate.

*Ronald Tree and his wife **Nancy** rented the property between 1928-1933. He used his position as the first American Master of the Pytchley Hunt as a launch pad into British politics eventually becoming MP for Market Harborough.*
*After the couple divorced in 1948 **Nancy** returned to Kelmarsh as wife of the then owner **Colonel Claude Lancaster** but the marriage was short lived.*
*As a reminder of **Ronald Tree's** use of the Hall there is today in a hallway, a large, interesting wall mounted map of the area covered by the Hunt. Although the entrance lodges and gates were designed by **James Wyatt** in 1778 they were not then built. The original drawings were only discovered during the 1960's in Northampton Public Library when a decision was made to implement the original design.*

*The gardens at Kelmarsh Hall are largely inspired by **Nancy Lancaster** and received a top honour from English Heritage in 2010 being designated a garden of 'exceptional national historic significance.'*
A Visitors Centre and tea room have recently re-opened following refurbishment.

The Estate is now run by a Preservation Charity who regularly hold a series of fund raising events: - car rallies, heritage shows, crafts fairs, game and country fairs, etc. The Hall and grounds are also available for weddings. Snowdrop weekends are very popular in February.

KETTERING

Seven miles north of Wellingborough
Population: 1801-3011   2001 - 51,063

DOMESDAY BOOK
CATERINGE

Names ending in 'ing' derive from the Saxon words 'inga' or 'ingas' meaning 'the people of '
The prefix I like is that it derives from 'cyta' - Saxon for kite.

This ten hide manor with thirty two households and two mills rendering twenty shillings per annum was held by Peterborough Abbey in 1086.

Objects of Bronze, Roman and Anglo Saxon times have been found locally suggesting a settlement was in existence well before the Domesday Book when the town was known as Cateringe.

From the 17th century Kettering was the main centre for weaving in the County and grew quite rapidly with the arrival of the boot and shoe industry in the 19th century. In 1851 there was just one boot and shoe factory but by 1901 there were 57 factories and 28,653 inhabitants.

Sadly boot and shoe manufacture in the UK has virtually ceased with the flood of cheaper foreign imports and many of the old factories have been demolished. Fortunately some factory façades remain thus providing a link with the past although most have been converted to apartments.

Much of the land on which the town is built was part of the Estate of the ***Rockingham*** family and the ***Dukes of Buccleuch*** owners of nearby **Boughton House.**

Kites were once common birds of prey in early medieval times and in more modern times they have been re-introduced with great success in the area and can regularly be seen soaring and gliding overhead in the skies north east of Kettering.

The town has a noticeable absence of historic buildings although the little row of Almshouses at the top of Station Road built by ***Edmund Sawyer*** is still in use. They were originally known as **Sawyers Hospital** and accommodated six poor or aged widows who were nominated by the local landowner the ***Duke of Buccleuch***.

Kettering has had a market since 1227 and just off the Market Place is the town's oldest and grandest building the church of **ST PETER** and **ST PAUL**. It is the third church to have been built on the present site. The most notable aspect of the church is its tower and crocketed recessed spire rising to a height of one hundred and seventy eight feet (55 metres) - a landmark for miles around.
The north porch is probably from a previous church as it is slightly out of line.
The font is from the demolished church at Faxton.

This is a light and airy church with a nave, two aisles and two chapels – the Lady Chapel and the chapel of St John sometimes called the **Sawyer Chapel** with a bronze monument to
Edmund Sawyer.
As there is a peal of twelve bells it is not surprising that the tower has three light bell openings.
The ornate west gates are a memorial to generations of the ***Roughton*** family of medical practitioners.

Before the mid 16th century the Patronal Feast Day on 29th June was purely a religious church festival and holiday for the population. It has changed dramatically over the years to become the Fun Fair of today.

Kettering has a long history of non - conformity and it is therefore not surprising that events took place in the town that have found a place in the history books. On the 2nd October 1792 a meeting was held in the Mission House in Lower Street, Kettering at which were laid the foundations of the **Baptist Missionary Society.** A plaque on the front wall of the premises records this fact.

One of the founders was *William Carey* who volunteered to be its first missionary setting sail to India where he died in 1793.

The Mission House with a modern extension at the rear is now a Home for the Elderly.

The first General Secretary of the BMS was *Andrew Fuller* and the impressive looking Baptist church built at the top of Gold Street in 1861/2 with a classical facade and a big pediment now carries his name.

A Heritage Room at Fuller Baptist church can be visited to discover the links between *Fuller, Carey* and other prime movers in the formation of the BMS.

Just around the corner in Newland Street is the church's modern coffee shop which appears to be a very popular place for shoppers and visitors alike.

At the lower end of Gold Street is another non-conformist church, the Toller Independent chapel (now the United Reformed church) built in 1723 but restored in 1875.

In addition to churches of all denominations there are a wide selection of shops, a library, the prestigious *Alfred East* art gallery, pubs and restaurants and an indoor Shopping Mall.

Schools cater for students of all ages.

The Workhouse with a three bay pediment was built in 1837 and has now been incorporated into St Marys Hospital whereas on the Rothwell Road is a large General Hospital.

Due to the efforts of the Kettering Civic Society the railway station platforms dating from 1857 still contain some fine Victorian ironwork with a wealth of 'pierced grill' cast iron said by many to be the finest in the country.

Fuller Baptist Church, Kettering

A regular train service is provided between London St Pancras and the north.

The town's most popular tourist attraction is undoubtedly Wicksteed Park at the top of the hill on the London road.

WICKSTEED PARK

Charles Wicksteed bought the land in 1913 and gave it to the town in 1921.

He donated much of his wealth which was derived from engineering to charitable causes and in this case it was a park to provide sport and recreation particularly to the children of Kettering.

The Park and *Charles Wicksteed* very much led the way in the provision of play equipment and leisure facilities for the young. Still a popular feature is the water chute which is 80 years old and was designed by *Charles* and is the oldest in the UK.

The narrow gauge railway is almost as old and has been giving rides to both young and old for over 75 years. It carries around 200,000 passengers a year.

In addition there is the largest free playground in the UK with some of the most modern equipment.

The Park and much of the surrounding area are administered by the Wicksteed Trust.

It is said that *Charles* often used to visit the Park in his two seater car with his pet dog Jerry in the passenger seat. Unfortunately when visiting in 1928 Jerry disappeared without trace.

In the Park is a statue of a dog with the inscription

To the memory of Jerry 1920-28
The constant companion of
Charles Wicksteed'.

Wicksteed Park was a popular place to visit when my family were growing up although the nature of the rides (with Health & Safety Rules) has changed dramatically.

KILSBY

Five miles north of Daventry
Population: 1801-703   2001 - 1221

DOMESDAY BOOK
CHIDESBI
The name possible derives from the Saxon 'childe' - for son - possibly of the Lord of the Manor and 'bi' - meaning settlement.

The village was probably founded between 890-920AD and during the Middle Ages it was an important sheep trading centre standing on the cross roads of two important Drovers Roads.
In 1086 the two hide manor was held by the Abbey at Coventry.
There were twenty one households.

Whenever I visit Kilsby I can't help wondering why so many roads both major and minor, meet in the centre of the village not to mention the M45 and the M1 which are only a stone's throw away.

An interesting little fact I read is that the A361 which terminates in the village and runs from Ilfracombe in Devon is said to be the longest three digit road in Britain. (I have not attempted to check that claim).

The church is now dedicated to **ST FAITH** but once went by the name of *St Denys* and then *St Andrew.*
The first Rector was *Hugh de Cambio* in 1220, before that Barby was the mother church and the two villages still share a Rector today.

The church has a fine tower with a low recessed spire and is mainly of the 13th and 14th centuries but was heavily restored in the 19th century.

It consists of a nave, north and south aisles, a chancel and a north chapel retained as a burial place for the *Cowley* family who were local benefactors.

The south aisle has a lovely window depicting *Simeon* and the infant *Christ* in the Temple.

What caught my attention and which I cannot recall seeing elsewhere in the County in such numbers were the texts painted above all the windows and door arches.

The Congregational chapel (now United Reform) with its pedimented gable dates from 1764 and is one of Northamptonshire's earliest Independent chapels as it is thought to have been founded secretly around 1663.
During the Second World War the gallery was partitioned off to provide schooling for evacuee children. The little coffee shop run by chapel volunteers made an enjoyable stop during a recent visit to the area.

Kilsby was caught up in the Civil War when in August 1642 a small troop of Royalists rode into the village and shot dead a number of the inhabitants, the first casualties of the conflict.

United Reformed Church : Kilsby

Two weeks later *Charles I* actually raised his standard at Nottingham.

Ironically, three years later at nearby Naseby the Civil War was virtually ended in favour of the Parliamentarian *Oliver Cromwell*.

Sheep farming and work relating to wool brought prosperity to the area and many villagers were employed in the weaving of worsted or the making of woollen 'Tammies' a sort of English cousin of a Highland bonnet.

Many families prospered and built sandstone and ironstone cottages.

With the rise in population in recent years there has been a considerable amount of modern development but the older part of the village is well worth a visit.

Facilities include a shop and post office, village hall and modern Primary school.

Of the two public houses, The George which once stood alongside the Daventry/Lutterworth turnpike now stands in a cul de sac and is said to have been rebuilt at the same time as the famous railway tunnel.

Kilsby Tunnel Portal

KILSBY TUNNEL

The railway tunnel is about 2400 yards long and was designed and engineered by *Robert Stephenson* famous son of the equally famous *George Stephenson*.

I am informed that it is the 18th longest tunnel on the British railway system and took much longer than expected to build because quicksand was encountered.

During part of the construction *Robert* lived in the village in what is now the Grade II listed house known as Cedar Lodge on the Main Road. I understand that in the garden is a concrete model of the tunnel mouth which he built for the guidance of his foremen - this too is Grade II listed.

The last of the 30,000,000 bricks was laid on the 21 June 1838 and the tunnel opened to commercial traffic a few days later. Passengers had to wait until September 17th.
High speed trains between London Euston and the north regularly thunder along the line.

When travelling in the area it is easy to see the two high sixty foot diameter ventilation shafts with crennelated tops poking out of the ground. During the construction of the tunnel three navvies fell to their deaths down one of the ventilation shafts and their ghosts are said still to haunt the area.

The work must have woken the village from its rural charm as over a thousand navvies lived in the village or in a shanty town on its edge. There was drunkenness, petty theft, cock fighting and good old punch ups. At one time soldiers were sent over from Weedon Barracks to quell a riot.

KINGS CLIFFE

Seven miles south of Stamford
Population: 1801-876   2001 - 1137

DOMESDAY BOOK
CLIVE
Clive, as in the Domesday Book simply means 'steep slope or cliff'.
The addendum was added in about 1300 when the Estate passed to the ownership of Norman Kings.

This is a lovely 'Cotswold' type village and it is well worth taking a walk around to see some delightful old and historic buildings of local Barnack or Weldon stone and Collyweston slate roofs. It was one of the three bailiwicks of Rockingham Forest.
The village stands on a slope overlooking the Willow Brook in a sparsely populated area to the north east of the County.
The area is also good for walking particularly around the riverside.

The village is one of the most historic places in Northamptonshire as its history goes back to at least Saxon times when the settlement consisted of a few mud huts. The Old Warren occupies the site of a Norman castle used by *King John.*

In 1086 the King held the manor which had fourteen households and a priest, together with a mill rendering twelve pence per annum.
The royal connection stimulated prosperity and by 1249 there were three weekly markets and a large annual three day fair

Over the years the village has suffered a number of fires, the worst being the great fire recorded in 1462 which destroyed most of the village (about one hundred houses) including the Royal Manor House or Hunting Lodge nothing of which remains above ground.

This resulted in the village being rebuilt on its present site to the north of the church.
After the fire Kings Cliffe went into decline since it did not have a resident Lord of the Manor and became an 'open' village and a real magnet to people who, for whatever reason, had been evicted from their own village.

For over three hundred years until the early 20th century it was noted for wooden ware and was known as the *'wooden spoon village'.*

In 1874 the village had no less than ten listed woodturners. The tradition lived on in the name of the former inn - The Turners Arms.

The church of **ALL SAINTS** was built from the late 12th century onwards. It has a chancel, clerestoried nave, transept and north and south porches and a Norman crossing tower.
The stunted broach spire was added in the 13th century. The rest of the church dates mainly from the 15th century.
Some of the stained glass, carved pew ends, pulpit and reading desk are said to have come from Fotheringhay. In the chancel is a priest's door, a piscina and a large three or four person sedilia.

At the time of the Civil War the Parliamentarians are said to have stabled some of their horses in the church and to have caused damage to the village on their departure possibly because the Rector at the time was a Royal Chaplain and undertook clandestine work for the King.

The Georgian Rectory south east of the church was once Mill House.

Visitors still come to Kings Cliffe because of its association with *William Law* (1686-1761) who was born here. He was a renowned religious thinker and Christian writer and had great influence on *John* and *Charles Wesley*.
Although he never became Rector of Kings Cliffe he had a great influence on the area.
His tomb in the churchyard is in the form of a very large writing desk.

In the Bridge Street area are several charitable and educational buildings by the *Rev. William Law* these include Laws Library dating from the 17th century, Widows Almshouses dated 1749 and the Spinsters Almshouses of 1754.

Another local benefactor was *John Thorpe* who provided Almshouses in Park Street.

Kings Cliffe had a Youth Hostel between 1939 - 1965 which attracted many cyclists and walkers to the area.

In olden times rivers or streams had to be crossed on foot by means of pieces of wood or stepping stones or even Clapper Bridges.

The one at Kings Cliffe was renovated and renamed **Leycesters Bridge** in 1999 in memory of a villager who had recently died at sea.

This is now the focal point of the Annual Duck Race each August Bank holiday which raises money for charity. In 2012 the event attracted up to 1,000 plastic ducks.

Two non-conformist chapels, the Methodist which opened in 1828 and the Congregational which opened in 1846 are now in private ownership.

There is still has an Ex Servicemen's club, two schools, a bakery, an art studio and even a publisher of specialist railway periodicals.

The remaining public house is the 17th century Cross Keys. Other public houses such as The Old Red Lion with an old AA sign outside indicating it is eighty seven and a half miles to London and the 18th century Wheatsheaf are closed.

The railway came to Kings Cliffe in 1879 when the Seaton to Yarwell Junction line was constructed but failed to be profitable and the station line closed in 1968.

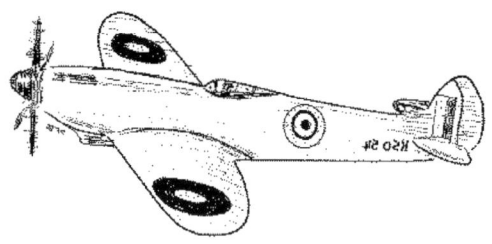

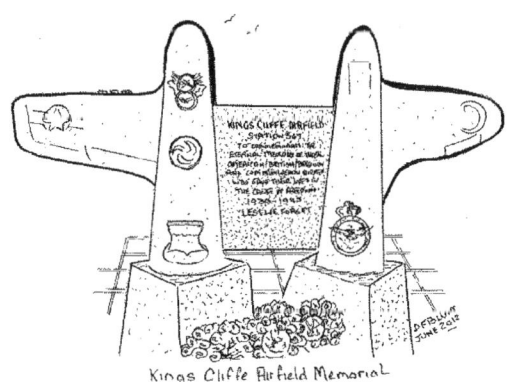

Kings Cliffe Airfield Memorial

Kings Cliffe Airbase

A grassed airfield on the site of a former deer park was opened in October 1941 to the south of the old Roman road to Peterborough.

Initially it was used by RAF Spitfires before being occupied by the USAF 20th Fighter Group.

The renowned US band leader *Glenn Miller*, with his 40 piece American band played his last ever concert here on the 4th October 1944.

The concert lasted over an hour and it is said that there were over 2,500 people in attendance.

Just over two months later on the 15th December whilst flying to a concert in France his plane disappeared over the Channel.

The 20th group vacated the airfield in October 1945 and it then became a temporary base for German prisoners of war awaiting repatriation.

After they left in 1947 the land was sold.

Today there is a Memorial alongside the road which commemorates the American, Belgian, British and Commonwealth airmen who lost their lives flying out of the base.

KINGS SUTTON

Four miles south east of Banbury
Population: 1801-1021   2001 - 2069

DOMESDAY BOOK
SUDTONE/SUTONE
The name derives from Saxon words meaning
south farmstead.
The prefix to the name is of more recent origin.

Penda, the last pagan King of Mercia is believed to have had a royal household at Kings Sutton.
His reputed grandson *St Rumbold*, was born to a Saxon Princess in the 7th century and according to legend is said to have declared at his birth
'I am a Christian' and asked to be baptised.
He died aged only three days.
I find it difficult to understand how an infant could have the power of speech and *George Walker*, a writer from Bodicote gives a possible explanation that he lived until adulthood and that the three days probably referred to his 'life after baptism.'

At the time of the Domesday Book Kings Sutton had a market rendering twenty shillings per annum and was a royal manor but was alienated in 1155 and did not continue to be such an important centre although it remained a significant place in the Hundred which gave it its name.

In addition to the 17th century *St Rumbolds Well* a new well (bog spring) near the station opened in 1749 and attracted tourists seeking a cure from their ailments.

The village fell out of fashion when Leamington Spa, Bath and Tunbridge became the places to go and came to an abrupt end when a fire in 1785 caused by a careless washer woman destroyed about forty houses.

This quite large village has many modern and uninspiring properties but in the central area and around the church there are some lovely old buildings.

Although situated quite close to Brackley and Banbury because of its location on minor roads it is quiet and peaceful.

It was a real delight during a recent countryside walk to rest awhile and take in the delightful vista whilst partaking of a quiet drink (non alcoholic!) in the Square outside the two hundred year old White Horse. I would include this setting, looking towards the church, as one of my favourite twelve views in the County

Nearby are two other public houses, The Three Tuns and The Butchers Arms, and also a post office and stores, supermarket and a new (millennium) village hall with adjoining Health Centre.
The Baptist chapel with the Manse next door is still in regular use and has a modern extension and a well maintained graveyard to the rear.

Standing at the heart of the village is the magnificent church of **ST PETER** and **ST PAUL** which has one of the finest spires in the County.
It was built in about 1400 and at one hundred and ninety eight feet (61 metres) high is a landmark for miles around.
The west tower has a crown of thorns, splendid gargoyles, superb pinnacles and delicate flying buttresses.

Problems have been experienced with the pinnacles in the past as a result of weather damage and lightning resulting in a number of rebuilds.

The greater part of the chancel is Norman and there is other evidence of their work in the nave and in the rough plain font but the church is predominantly of the Decorative style.

Of particular interest is the richly designed oak rood screen to the design of *Sir George Gilbert Scott* who restored the church in 1866.

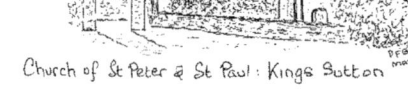
Church of St Peter & St Paul : Kings Sutton

Close to the church is a tall house known as Lovells, a couple of pretty thatched cottages and the Manor House which dates from the 17th century with its gables and mullioned windows.
One of the most important buildings in its day was the 16th century timber framed Court House which was extended in the 18th century.
Today it is a private residence.

Punishment sometimes resulted in being impounded in the stocks which are still preserved behind an iron fence nearby.

Whilst many men would be engaged in agriculture a large number of girls and women were employed in the lace making industry in the 19th century.

Kings Sutton station on the London to Banbury line has been in continuous use since 1850 and although now an unmanned halt it still gets plenty of use and is one of only six places in Northamptonshire connected to the Railway network.

A Literary Festival is held in the village annually which attracts book lovers from a wide area.

Whilst researching for this book I came across this little traditional rhyme published by **Halliwell** in 1760 which I thought was well worth including.

Kings Sutton is a pretty town
And lies all in a valley;
It has a pretty ring of bells,
Besides a bowling alley:

Wine and liquor in good store
Pretty maidens plenty;
Can a man desire more?
There ain't such a town in twenty.

BLACKLANDS

In the north west of the parish is the identified site of a large Roman settlement known as Blacklands.

Roman money was discovered prior to 1712 and in 1825 a cinerary urn was uncovered together with Roman pottery of the 2- 4th century.

Blacklands got its name because of the dark colour of the soil.

The parish includes the deserted villages/hamlets of Astrop, Little Purston and Walton Grounds (Gt Purston is located in the parish of Newbottle).

AISTROP

Now attached to Kings Sutton and generally regarded today as part of that village.

In late medieval times Upper & Lower Aistrop shared one land unit. The date of the enclosure of the common fields around the two is unknown though thought to be before the 18th century.
A spring was 'discovered' at Astrop in the mid 17th century and was found to be rich in minerals so much so that doctors recommended their patients to take the waters as it was said to be beneficial for many ailments. The village became a fashionable spa and *St Rumbolds Well* can still be seen at the foot of the hill on the Newbottle road.

LITTLE PURSTON

DOMESDAY BOOK
PRESTETONE
The name is a corruption of preston
meaning a priests settlement.

I was very surprised to note that both Great and Little Purston in the north east of the parish existed at the time of the Domesday Book.
Little Purston was recorded as a half hide manor in 1086 and it is not thought to have ever been much more than a single farm.
There is now not much habitation but you are likely to see plenty of sheep, horse eventing and alpacas.

WALTON GROUNDS

DOMESDAY BOOK
WALETONE/WALTONE

Referred to as **Walton Grounds** in the Domesday Book when it had three small manors and a total recorded population of ten it is still known as such today where the farm buildings are given over to seed research and production.
It appears that in 1487 *John Goylyn* destroyed five houses, expelled 80 people and enclosed two hundred acres of land. A few years later the process was repeated by *Richard Fermor* but he was prosecuted for his trouble. Although there is record of a chapel here this appears to have been in ruins by the 16th century.
The site has been destroyed by modern ploughing.

KIRBY

Four miles north east of Corby

DOMESDAY BOOK
CHERCHEBERIE
The old name simply means 'by the church'

A small manor held by **Robert** with six households, woodland and six acres of meadow at Kirby is recorded in the Domesday Book.

Maps of 1584 and 1587 show much of the village which was never very large still existed including a church just south west of the Hall.

It is thought that depopulation took place between 1685-6 when formal gardens were laid out.
All had disappeared when **Bridges** wrote in 1720.

This is now one of Northamptonshire many lost villages and all that remains apart from the Hall is a slight mound in the gardens where once stood the church.

Kirby Hall was started in 1570 for **Sir Humphrey Stafford** a distant descendant of the **Earls of Stafford** on the site of the old Manor House but he died in 1575 before work was completed and the Estate was bought by **Sir Christopher Hatton**.

He set about providing a home fit for the Queen although there is no record of **Elizabeth I** visiting this grand house much to his disappointment.

It was however visited by royalty no less than eight times between 1605-1705.

The Hall which started to decay following the death of **Charles** the **3rd Viscount**, has seen better days and only part of that which now remains is roofed.

It has the feeling of a building that has not been finished rather than one which has succumbed to the ravages of time.
Nevertheless it is a magnificent Grade I listed romantic ruin - well worth a visit.

The Hall is owned by the **Earl of Winchilsea** but is now cared for rather than restored by English Heritage and is open to the public during the summer months - the audio tour helps to bring the building back to life.

This Elizabethan Country House has been used on a number of occasions as the setting for films including **Jane Austen**'s *'Mansfield Park'*, *'A Christmas Carol'* in 1999 as well as **Steve Coogan**'s *'Tristram Shandy'* and *'A Cock and Bull Story'* in 2005.

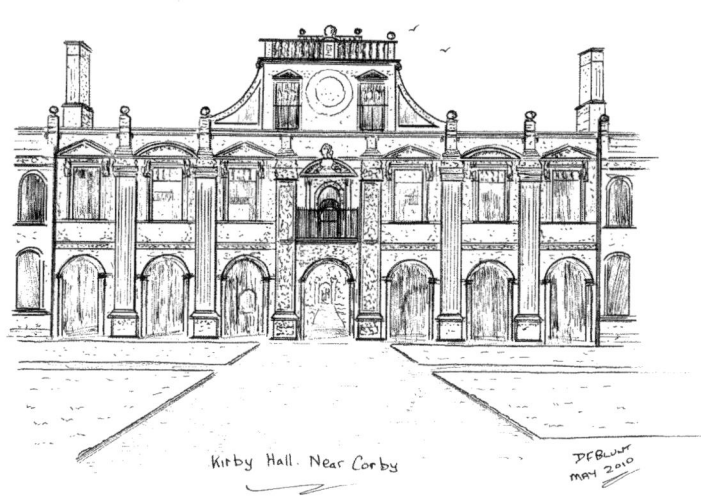

Kirby Hall. Near Corby

DFBLUNT
MAY 2010

Hatton family

The **Hattons** came originally from Cheshire - one branch setting up in Northamptonshire at the time of **Sir Christopher's** great grandfather who inherited the Holdenby Estate through marriage.

Sir Christopher bought the Kirby Estate when **Sir Humphrey Stafford** died in 1575 having already inherited land and property at Holdenby. He was one of **Queen Elizabeth I's** 'handsome young men' and rose to the position of the Queen's bodyguard and Lord Chancellor by the age of forty seven in 1587 when he was nicknamed 'The Dancing Chancellor' because of his love of the ballroom. He acquired a considerable fortune and took upon the almost simultaneous tasks of rebuilding the house at Holdenby and enlarging the **Stafford** house at Kirby.

I can't imagine why he wanted two very grand houses not more than twenty five miles apart. Perhaps by doing so he thought it would enhance the chances of **Queen Elizabeth I** making a visit but in this quest he failed.

Because of the favour shown to him by **Elizabeth I**, **Mary Queen of Scots** accused him in 1584 of being her lover.

Duties at Court meant that he did not have time to supervise the work at Kirby and in August 1579 he is said to have asked **Sir Edward Brudenell** of nearby Deene to check on the building work.

In spite of his high office he spent heavily on his properties and when he died in 1591 he was heavily in debt.

To maintain his dwindling wealth **Hatton** began to invest in some of the voyages of **Sir Francis Drake** and helped fund **Drake's** acts of piracy in Spanish America.

It is said that he made a profit of £2,300 on one particular voyage - a large amount in those days.

Although there were rumours of a secret marriage **Hatton** appears to have remained single and as he died apparently childless the Estate passed to a relative, **William Newport**, who took the name **Hatton**.

When he also died childless in 1597 the Estate went to a distant relative who was also named **Sir Christopher Hatton** (1605-1670). He was an ardent Royalist and benefitted in wealth and status during the reigns of **James I** and **Charles I** who created him **Lord Hatton** and Comptroller of the Royal Household

When Parliament prevailed he fled to France leaving his wife to run the Estate. On his return from exile following the Restoration he preferred to develop his antiquarian interests rather than manage the Estate.

He was succeeded by yet another **Christopher** (2nd Baron – 1632-1706) who was created a Viscount in 1683 and was made Governor of Guernsey. He recouped the family fortunes and refurbished Kirby Hall inside and out.

The great gardens created in the late 17th century have now been recreated as they may have appeared at that time.

Because of its remote location the Hall was thought to be a useful 'bolt hole' for **King George III** in the event of a Napoleonic invasion.

Charles Hatton the 3rd Viscount so enjoyed life at Kirby that he was accused of neglecting his appearances in the House of Lords. The male line died out when he died in 1762.

KISLINGBURY

Four miles west of Northampton
Population: 1801-482   2001 - 1221

DOMESDAY BOOK
CESELLINGEBERIE/CIFELINGEBERIE
The spelling of the name has changed many times over the years but the most likely explanation is that it originally derived from three Saxon words 'ceusel' - gravel, 'inga' - people of and 'burh' - fortified place.

Little is known of Kislingbury until the Domesday Book where two manors are recorded.

One was held by the **Count of Mortain** and the other by **Gilbert de Ghent.** The manor was then confiscated by the Crown but returned to **Gerard de L'Isle** in 1326. It then passed through various hands until the early part of the 17th century during which time the Kislingbury Town and Estate Charity was formed.

When **John Mansell** acquired the Estate about 1611 he proceeded to sell off parcels of land to local farmers.

The village stands on the River Nene to the west of Northampton and has certainly seen much change over the years with sand and gravel extraction creating many lakes and ponds.

A little more than one hundred years ago most villagers worked in their immediate area, the majority in agriculture but nowadays it is mainly a commuter village. The close proximity of Northampton and Junction 16 on the M1 motorway makes it a popular village for commuters.

It is surprising that the village has not grown more in size although when I last visited I saw many placards protesting about the encroaching suburbs.

At the moment the village still maintains an element of village life and I particularly like the area around Church Street where there are a number of 17th and 18th century properties.

There is still a village school, a shop and a butcher, a fine playing field, village hall, two public houses, the Olde Red Lion and the thatched Sun Inn and The Cromwell restaurant and public house (formerly three cottages) as you approach the village from Northampton.

It is claimed that the Parliamentary troops under **General Fairfax** were stationed in the area prior to the Battle of Naseby in 1645 and that **Oliver Cromwell** himself joined them on the 13th June of that year.
If this is correct they must have got a move on to be at Naseby some twelve miles away as the crow flies ready for battle on the morning of the 14th June.

I can just imagine the sight of an army of some 10,000 soldiers, 2000 horses and artillery, etc trooping across the ancient bridge that still crosses the River Nene on their way to battle.

The bridge has, of course undergone some repairs over the years but how long will it be before a new bridge is needed as it is heavily used and only one vehicle can cross at a time.

In the immediate area a considerable amount of money has been spent on flood defences - the area was until very recently very prone to flooding.
One building near the church has a stone indicating the flood level in 1663 when some houses were flooded up to a depth of four feet.

Kislingbury Mill

ST LUKE'S church was built of Northamptonshire ironstone in the first half of the 14th century, mostly Decorative in style and very fine especially the chancel with a five light East window which depicts a Second World War scene and was presented to the church by the *Dunkley* family in memory of their son who was killed at El Alamein in 1942.

The west tower is Decorative in style with a recessed spire and two tiers of lucarnes and was restored in 1717.

The Grade II listed Rectory said to be one of the finest in the County was built about 1710 of ironstone and has a hipped roof and finely moulded window frames.

The Rectory barn has a cupula and in it are over thirteen hundred nesting places for pigeons

The long distance footway the Nene Way following the course of the River Nene passes through the village.

Recorded in the Domesday Book is the existence of two mills rendering forty shillings per annum.

The present three storey mill and the mill house in Mill Road were erected during the last quarter of the 19th century.

It was used for grinding corn but ceased operations in the 1920's. Today the premises are occupied by a local firm who manufacture specialist fireplaces.

Nearby and still in regular use is Kislingbury Baptist chapel built in 1828 on the site of a converted barn which previously had been used as a chapel.

The village also had a Wesleyan chapel which was built in 1826 but closed in 1923 and is now a private dwelling.

Great tragedy struck the village in 1895 when the Choir Supper was being held in the school and some of the party drank contaminated water causing an outbreak of typhoid during which ten people died and this resulted in a clamour for a safe drinking supply.

A new pumping station was opened on the Berrywood Hill in 1898 and those willing to pay had water pumped to their homes whereas others had to rely on a number of standpipes in the village.

LAMPORT

Seven miles north of Northampton
Population: 1801-148   2001 - 207

DOMESDAY BOOK
LANGEPORT

*The name implies that this was once a trading centre
(a market place) along the Saxon trading route between
Rothwell and Northampton.*

It is hard to imagine that this very small linear village was once an important trading centre.
It is located midway between Northampton and Market Harborough and although it does have a public house it no longer has a school, shop or post office.

I am pleased to see that the recently built properties have been designed to blend in with the older houses.
Of particular appeal are the polychrome houses with bricks in three shades of colour laid out in a diaper pattern. These date from the 1850's when Victorian Gothic revival was well under way.

The village is dominated by **Lamport Hall** the home of the Isham family for about four hundred years.

Swans figure on the Coat of Arms of the *Isham family* and a pair of white swans which guard the main gate to the Hall are a familiar sight to motorists on the A508. The local public house is called The Swan.

Just north of the village is the location of the level crossing on the Northampton to Market Harborough railway line which on closure was transformed into the Brampton Valley Way.
Here stands the only surviving station building on the line. It has decorated stone gables and still appears very much as it would have done in the railway era.

Swan at Lamport

ALL HALLOWS CHURCH stands alongside a minor road close to the Hall, and has a low medieval west tower but the remainder of the church was reconstructed in the 17th and 18th century. Inside is the *Isham* family vault built in 1672 and housing generations of the owners of **Lamport Hall**.

Included in the parish is the small hamlet of Hanging Houghton.

HANGING HOUGHTON

Population: 1801-117 2001-N/A

DOMESDAY BOOK
HOHTUNE

*The name implies that this was settlement on the side of
a hill - very appropriate as it stands high above the
Brampton Valley.*

This small settlement which has diminished in size over the years lies to the west of the main A508 Northampton to Market Harborough road on the side of a slope to the valley below. I doubt that many people bother to venture down the 'no through road' - it still retains its quiet peacefulness. There is very little more to see than a couple of farms and a few cottages.

It was certainly important enough to be listed four times in the Domesday Book when there were thirty households indicating a population of between 110-120 people. No trace remains of the houses which are thought to have been located to the north side of the village.
The school house with seven bays and two storeys was built in 1772 according to the will of *Sir Edmund Isham*. Today it is a private residence.

Lamport Hall

Isham

Isham family *and* Lamport Hall

Although the family dates back to the time of the Norman Conquest they did not arrive in Lamport until 1560 when **John**, *a London adventurer and mercer and 4th son of* **Euseby Isham** *of Pytchley, bought the manor from* **Sir William Cecil** *for £610.* **John** *built up a considerable fortune by property speculation, lending out capital and by marrying into money. On arrival in Lamport he started sheep breeding and sold to merchants far and wide. He also built a new Manor House in 1568 assisted by his son,* **Thomas** *whose only son John (1582-1651) was both Knighted and created a Baronet in the early 17th century but then lost much of his wealth when the* **Stuart** *dynasty floundered.*

Nevertheless there was sufficient capital left for **Justinian** *(1610-1675) who succeeded him to commission* **John Webb**, **Inigo Jones'** *principal assistant to enlarge the House. Work started about 1655 and resulted in a fine two storey classical building. The stables which are regularly used for craft fairs and exhibitions date from 1680.*

In the 1730's the **Ishams** *commissioned* **Francis** *and* **William Smith** *of Warwick to add a north and a south wing thus increasing the overall size of the west façade from the original five bays to thirteen.*
Further alterations have been made over the years and it is now one of the County's finest Grade I listed buildings.

The 10th Baronet, **Charles** *(1819-1903) was responsible for the twenty foot high alpine rockery in the gardens and for introducing garden gnomes into England in the mid 19th century*
One gnome remains, a very little chap by the name of 'Lampy' who is said to be insured for a million pounds.

A free standing arched doorway leading into the garden was added by **Sir Giles Isham**.
It was transferred from the entrance of the church of **ST DENIS** *in nearby Faxton when it was demolished in 1958 together with memorials to the* **Raynsford** *and* **Isham** *families both previously connected with Faxton.*

After being used as a Prisoner of War Camp during the Second World War, the Hall suffered dry rot which resulted in very high restoration costs. In 1974 **Sir Gyles Isham** *the 12th Baronet created the Lamport Hall Preservation Trust and on his death in 1976 bequeathed the Hall, its contents and land to the Trust with the aim of providing historic and artistic education.*
The Hall with its collection of family portraits spanning 400 years and a fine collection of furniture is regularly open to the public during the summer as are the grounds which occasionally host garden parties, craft fairs, open air theatre productions,etc. The Hall along with a number of other locations in the County was used in the film
'Cock and Bull Story' starring **Steve Coogan**.

LAXTON

Seven miles north east of Corby
Population: 1801-214   2001 - 160

DOMESDAY BOOK
LASTONE
*Possibly once known as Lax's 'tun',
the farmstead of Lax.*

William held the one and a half hide manor of the King following the Norman Conquest.
There were at the time thirteen households.

This is a lovely little Estate village just off the A43 midway between Kettering and Stamford built in about 1800 around the Green with picturesque stone cottages mostly in pairs with barge boarded gables.
Many of the cottages which are named after flowers were originally thatched.
The woodland adjoining Laxton is a remnant of Rockingham Forest and there are some rewarding walks in the area.

Almost hidden away among the trees is the church of **ALL SAINTS** which was built in the Early English style and has a late 13th century west tower and a short spire with low broaches although the church was practically rebuilt in the 1860's by *Lord Carbery* - a talented amateur carver.
I particularly like the superb cast iron carved gargoyle water spouts in the form of dragons which he is said to have designed.

Cast Iron Gargoyle : All Saints : Laxton

The oldest part of the church is thought to be the Norman spiral designs on the capitals of the south doorway.

Nearby is the Grade II* listed **Laxton Hall** which is set in ninety seven acres of land and beautiful gardens. It was built about 1811 but subsequently altered after the *7th Lord Carbery* succeeded to the title in 1845. The stables have a cupola and a bell dated 1805. In the grounds is the now unused school which was built for forty children in 1807/8.

Between 1924-1968 it served as a school for a religious Dominican Order. It now houses a residential Care Home for the Polish community and is not open to the general public.

Spanhoe Airfield

About midway between Laxton and Harringworth lies the site of Station 493 - a former USAF airfield.
The airfield opened in January 1944 and was the last war time airfield to be built in Northamptonshire.
It was mainly used by Dakota (C47) aircraft for troop movements.
Because of its relative short history it is not as well known as those bases in the County such as Kings Cliffe and Chelveston.
Nowadays much of the airfield has disappeared under quarrying.

An obelisk to the men of the 315th Troop Carrier Group of the 9th Airforce stands at the entrance to the site on the road from Harringworth.

LILBOURNE

Four miles north east of Rugby
Population: 1801-234   2001 – 363 (inc Claycoton)

DOMESDAY BOOK
LILLEBURNE/LINEBURNE
*The name derives from **Lilla**'s 'burna' – stream.*

Lilbourne is situated in a remote north western corner of Northamptonshire on the fringe of three county boundaries within a triangle bounded by three busy roads, the M1 the A14 and the A5.

The village is first mentioned in the Domesday Book when there were three manors and a total of twenty eight households – a figure thought to include nearby Claycoton which appears to have once been part of Lilbourne.

In medieval times the road system with its merchants and its sheep trade made Lilbourne a wealthy and busy trading point.
It is hard to imagine it today.
The market held under a Charter of 1219 in a field known as 'The Butts' was larger than the one in nearby Rugby but it did not have a long life.

To the north west of the parish was a Roman settlement called **Tripontium** *'the place of three bridges'* over three waterways, the Avon, the Swift and a tributary of the Swift later named the Avon.

Some distance away from the present village is **ALL SAINTS** church one of the oldest in the district. Its earliest construction goes back to the 13th and 14th centuries although two Saxon doorways have been discovered.
The unbuttressed squat west tower has a Perpendicular style arch towards the nave.
The tower houses five bells but they are said to be in a poor condition and funds are being raised for restoration.
There is a sanctus bellcote over the nave gable.

Externally it looks as though some use was made of the rubble from the derelict motte and bailey Castle across the road.

This Castle alongside the River Avon is thought to have been destroyed in the 13th century although a mound can still be seen.
Today the church, Castle remains, Victorian Rectory with its fancy chimneys and diaper pattern brickwork and Glebe Farm are all that remain of the former village which was relocated on the hilltop.

During the First World War Lilbourne was the site for one of the earlier airfields when No 73 Squadron RAF was stationed there.

Lilbourne once had a railway station on the London and North Western Line between Rugby and Market Harborough although it was situated some distance away - in fact - just over the River Avon in neighbouring Leicestershire.
This closed in 1966 but you can still make out part of the route.

Also gone are the three public houses The Bull, The Bell and The Chequers and also the village school, shop and post office but the old Methodist chapel now houses an Evangelical church.
The main focus of village life is now the thriving village hall. On a more sombre note Lilbourne is home to Britain's first green burial site - Greenhaven.

Evangelical Chapel — Lilbourne

LILFORD

Four miles north east of Thrapston
Population 1801-97   2001 - 101

DOMESDAY BOOK
LILLEFORD
*The old name implies this was simply **Lilla**'s ford.*
The settlement lay about mid way
between Thrapston and Oundle.

At the time of the Domesday Book when the land was held by **Walter** of the **Countess Judith** this must have been quite a large and prosperous settlement being worth eight pounds with a mill rendering twenty four shillings per annum.
In addition there were forty households indicating a population of between 140-160 people.
The records of population and taxation always appear to have included the daughter hamlet of Wigsthorpe.

Lilford is a typical example of brutal aristocratic enclosure. Twelve houses and a Vicarage were demolished by order of **Sir Thomas Powys** the Lord of the Manor in 1755 in order to create a 240 acre park and rebuilt in nearby **Wigsthorpe** which today consists of little more than a few houses dotted around a large farm and its outbuildings.

The parish church of **ST PETER** which stood south east of the Hall was subsequently demolished as superfluous and some of the stone re-erected as picturesque ruins on private land alongside the river at Thorpe Achurch.

Lilford Hall

parta tueri

Powys
Lord Lilford

Lilford Hall and the Elmes and Powys families

*The Manor and Hall at Lilford was in the possession of the **Elmes** family between 1473-1711 when it was acquired by the **Powys** family who remained in residence until 1949.*

*It was the **Elmes** family who built the Jacobean part of the Hall in 1635. A prominent member of the family was **Robert Browne** who broke from the established church to found his own church on Congregationalist principles but returned to the Church of England late in life.*

*The **Powys** family were responsible for the Coach House and Stable Block and replaced the interior in the Georgian style. The most impressive colonnade of thirteen chimneys connected by arches was added in the manner of **Vanbrugh**.*

Lilford Hall and Park were the subject of an article in an issue of Country Life in January 1900.

In the 1980's the Hall was a location, together with Rockingham Castle, for the TV series:-
'By the Sword Divided' - a story of conflict during the Civil War when members of the same family were divided in their loyalty between King and Parliament.

During the Second World War the Hall served as nurses quarters for the USAF hospital in the park and when hostilities ceased was for about five years a Polish school. It then stood empty for nearly thirty years before it was taken over by a private company who opened it, after a facelift, as a business centre and venue for various events, craft exhibitions,etc. but these failed and the grounds were closed to the public in 1990.

*It is now the home of the **Micklewright** family, only the third family in over five hundred years to have lived there permanently.*

LITCHBOROUGH

Eight miles south west of Northampton
Population: 1801-302   2001 - 300

DOMESDAY BOOK
LICEBERGE

*Early spellings imply that this may have been known as
the 'hill of the dead' from 'beorg' - burial mound and
'lice' - stream or body.*

It is thought by many that this was the site of the
Celtic garrison town **Lycanburgh**.

John Bridges the County historian wrote that it
was one of the last of four Roman garrisons in
England to be taken by the Saxons in 571AD,
certainly the ancient fortifications of Castle Dykes
and Stow Heath are nearby and some evidence has
been found of Celtic settlement.
At the time of the Domesday Book this was the
only manor in the County held by the Abbey of
Evesham having previously been held by
Leofnoth. There were fourteen households.

Litchborough is a delightful stone built village on
the B4525 between Northampton and Banbury - in
my young days as a cyclist we always knew this
road as the **Banbury Lane.**
Today the village is in a Conservation area
although it is a pity that a road passes through its
centre and it gets a lot of traffic.

Standing by a small green just off the main road is
the church of **ST MARTIN** with its embattled
west tower. Construction started in the 12th
century almost certainly on the site of quite a large
earlier building. Over the north porch is a quaint
group of heads showing *'Joy and Horror'* - a
demon sits with its fingers in the eyes of the head.

It is said that the church was attacked during the
Civil War and that *Cromwell's* soldiers were
responsible for destroying much of the stained
glass but you can still see many interesting
examples of the craftsmen's art including a very
rare sundial in the south window of the chancel -
only two others are known to exist.
Over the years the early glass has become badly
corroded inside and out and some restoration work
involving a new technique called 'isothermal
glazing' was started as a millennium project.

The church contains memorials to the *Grant*
family who lived in the attractive **Litchborough
Hall** opposite between 1740 and 1971.

The churchyard has a conservation policy and a
map in the south porch explains how the area is
managed as a wildlife habitat.
It is said that under the terms of an ancient
tradition the Rector has the right to graze six sheep
and four goats in the churchyard but I have never
seen this right exercised.

Opposite the church is The Red Lion public house
which has recently reopened after refurbishment
but there is no longer a shop, post office or a
village school. I was pleased to see that when the
old school which is now a private residence was
extended in 2007 the architect kept very much to
the original Victorian Gothic style.
In 2009 a new village hall was built at a cost of
£500,000 to replace an old wooden hut which had
served the village for more than eighty two years.

The small Baptist chapel which celebrated its one
hundred and fiftieth Anniversary in 2012 is still in
regular use although poorly supported.

Two businesses which you would not expect to
find in the village are the manufacture of
Blakemar Briars which moved from nearby
Blakesley in 1961 and Hoggleys brewery which
every week produces about 3,000 pints of award
winning real ales and stouts.

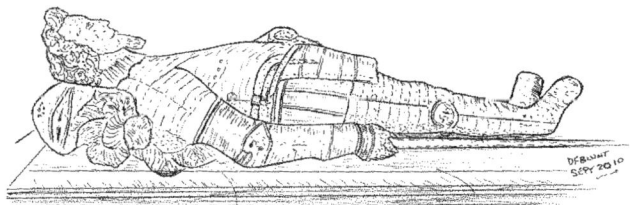

Tomb of Sir John Needham : St Martins - Litchborough

LITTLE ADDINGTON

Two miles north of Irthlingborough
Population: 1801-212   2001 - 275

DOMESDAY BOOK
ALIA EDINTONE/EDINTONE
This is a daughter village of Great Addington although it must have existed in 1086
*as it is listed as 'alia edintone' - the place of **Edda**'s people.*

The manor was held by **Hugh** of the Abbot of Peterborough Abbey in 1086 when there were fourteen households and a mill rendering twelve pence and two hundred eels.

The beautiful medieval church of **ST MARY** dates from the late 13th to mid 14th century.
It has a massive west tower with unusual use of ironstone and limestone, battlements and a recessed short spire.
I liked the west doorway of the tower with its mouldings and carving around the arches.

Inside the church is a pre-Reformation pulpit and rood screen with doors and a room over the porch.

As the village does not appear to have had wealthy landowners the church lacks internal ornamentation.

I was surprised to see that the churchyard was half given over to allotments and learned from a villager that the area was deemed too large for such a small population and only part of the churchyard was consecrated.
I cannot recall coming across any similar situation.

In the centre of the village is a delightful little Green overlooked by a lovely thatched cottage.

Unfortunately when I last visited the area the village sign had been vandalised and was missing its decorative top.

Little Addington House was built of local stone with a Collyweston slate roof in 1858 originally as the Rectory but it is now a private residence.

A focal point in the village and apparently very popular is the public house - The Bell, built in 1762 on the loop road.

I had to smile when I saw that the Sunrise Care Home was to be found at Amen Corner - very apt!

The Methodist chapel which closed in the 1960's is now a private house and there is no longer a shop or school - young children are educated at nearby Great Addington.

During the Second World War there was a prisoner of war camp in the area on a site which now houses an industrial estate.

The Nene Way passes through the village.

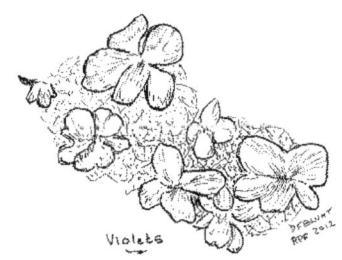

Violets

LITTLE BILLING

Three miles east of Northampton
Population: 1801-64

DOMESDAY BOOK
BELINGE/BELLICA
*The name implies that this was the settlement of the people of **Bydel**.*

Only one Billing is mentioned in the Domesday Book although there were three manors, one of which was held by **Gunfrid de Chocques** when there was a priest, twenty households and a mill rendering two shillings per annum.

The two separate settlements of Great and Little Billing appear in the 13th century by the names of Billing Magna and Parva Byllinge.

The present village has been virtually absorbed into the eastern expansion of the County town which has a new housing estate called Bellinge to continue the link with the past. Unfortunately there is a sewerage farm nearby and the smell arising therefrom is often most unpleasant.

Little Billing Priory was a grand mansion immediately to the north of the church which belonged to the **Longeville** family for nearly four hundred years from 1315.
By 1789 it was in a bad state and was partly demolished. Some 14th and 16th century remains were incorporated into a new building in the 1880's. This Grade II listed building known locally as 'the Castle' is now the home for the Priory Day and Resource Centre with day care for dementia patients, training courses and meeting rooms.

In the church of **ALL SAINTS** the north chapel and chancel both open now into the nave, the north aisle having been removed.
The north tower is thought to date from 1849.
Of particular interest is the tub shaped Norman font with its Latin inscription.

Between 1845 and 1964 Little Billing had a railway station on the line between Northampton and Peterborough. My very first train journey as a very young child was the short distance between Northampton and Billing to visit the Aquadrome. It was an exciting occasion and I well remember getting off the train at Billing station and walking what seemed to me to be half way back to Northampton to get to our destination.

BILLING AQUADROME & MILL

Today Little Billing is best known because of the popular Aquadrome which was formed out of old sand and gravel workings by **Mr A. J. Mackaness** during the late 1930's.
The area has been developed and now covers an area of at least 270 acres. Here you will find caravans, both static and mobile, tents in the summer, picnic and play areas, shops, restaurants and bars and boats.
It is a favourite holiday location for many people.

The mill which is mentioned in the Domesday Book was granted to the monks of the Abbey of St James in Northampton in the 12th century and remained in their possession until the Dissolution in 1538.
The present mill which is a very popular location for both diners and drinkers was built in the early part of the 19th century and was worked commercially until the Second World War.
Much of the machinery has been restored.
Since 2009 the Aquadrome which is now owned by Hoseasons has been the home of the Northampton Hot Air Balloon Festival when thousands gather to see these amazing objects take flight. The 2012 Festival was the 23rd of its kind in Northamptonshire.

D F BLUNT
AUG 2010

LITTLE BRINGTON

Five miles north west of Northampton

DOMESDAY BOOK
BRININTONE/BRINTONE
*The name derives from **Bryni**'s farm.*

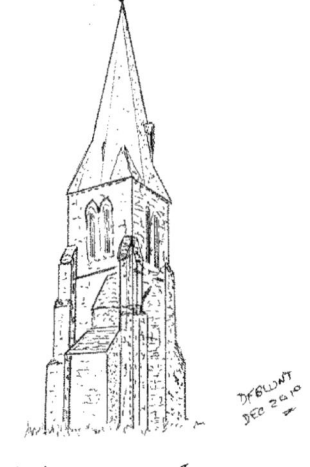

Little Brington Tower

Little Brington stands on an old Roman road between Duston and Bannaventa (see page 433) and three quarters of a mile south of its sister village Great Brington.
This road with its long straight stretches so typical of a Roman road has quite a bad record of traffic accidents.

Alongside this road stands the solitary tower and broached spire of the church of **ST JOHN** which was built for the *4th Earl Spencer* of Althorp in 1856 as a memorial to his first wife *Elizabeth Georgina Poyntz*.

By the end of the First World War the church had become unused and neglected and was eventually partially demolished.

Before completion however, the Air Ministry asked that the tower and spire be spared as they appeared on RAF maps and were used as landmarks by their pilots and so they remain to this day.

In the centre of the village which has some lovely thatched cottages and stone walls is a cone shaped building with a thatched roof which was once the village well.
In 1848 a number of semi detached Estate houses with gables and patterned chimneys were built.

The Baptist chapel in red and yellow chequered bricks was built about 1837 and is now used as offices.

Little Brington has the Primary school which serves both Bringtons, a public house and restaurant, the popular Saracens Head but no shop or post office.

In 1606 when *Lawrence Washington* of Sulgrave fell upon hard times and was obliged to give up his Manor House, his good friend and neighbour *Lord Spencer* built him a house in the village of Little Brington named Washington House where he is said to have lived during the remaining years of his life.
The House was later occupied by his brother *Robert* and his family.
Unfortunately it was destroyed by fire in 1956.
The replacement building carries the datestone 1961 and an inscribed stone from the former building which reads:-

> *The Lord Giveth*
> *The Lord Taketh*
> *away, Blessed be the*
> *Name of the Lord*
> *Constructa*
> *1606*

LITTLE HARROWDEN

Two miles north of Wellingborough
Population: 1801-284   2001 - 881

DOMESDAY BOOK
ALIA HARGINDONE

As in the case of Great Harrowden it would appear that this was an area for pagan worship
since the name comes from 'hearg' - pagan shrine and 'dun' - hill.

In the Domesday Book, both Great and Little Harrowden were held by **Walkelin** of the **Bishop of Coutances** and are recorded separately, but the land in Little Harrowden was taxed with that of its neighbour.

The Bishop's lands had been taken and redistributed before a Northamptonshire Survey in the 12th century and changed hands many times throughout the centuries.

The village which lies just west of the Wellingborough to Kettering road is one of the longest and narrowest parishes in the County.

At its heart is the church of **ST MARY** the **VIRGIN** which dates from the Norman era but over the past three hundred years its appearance has changed dramatically.
The Decorative style west tower was demolished in 1967 although the spire fell down in a storm in 1703.
It is now topped by a simple single bell turret housing the smallest of the original four bells.

From the outside the church does not appear to be very unusual or inspiring.
However as you approach you are faced with a superbly moulded Norman doorway and on entering it is a delightful little church.

On Main Street is the Wesleyan chapel dated 1882 which closed in the early 1970's owing to a decline in attendance, it is now a private house.

There are still two public houses, The Lamb in Orlingbury Road and another with the unusual name - The Ten O'Clock which has a 'pretend' clock on the wall overlooking the car park.

It is believed to have its origins in the early days of the postal service when the pub was the stopping point and ten o'clock was the time of the arrival of the foot post in the village.
Alternatively it could so easily be that ten o'clock was throwing out time!

In 1890 a family of fifteen lived under the one roof consisting of the landlord, **Mr Hobbs**, his wife, three sons and ten daughters.

In addition to the public houses there is a Primary school, a village hall and a Working Men's Club and quite a large block of sheltered housing for the elderly but since 2010 no shop or post office.

Ten-O-Clock : Little Harrowden

LITTLE HOUGHTON

Four miles east of Northampton
Population: 1801-389   2001 - 367

DOMESDAY BOOK
HOHTUNE
A daughter village of Great Houghton meaning farmstead on a ridge

The area has been settled since pre-historic times as five stone hand-axes and other flint tools and arrowheads have been found locally.
A Celtic coin was also found together with evidence of a later Roman settlement.
Before 1086 the manor was held by *Ulf* but was then transferred to the *Countess Judith.*
There were twelve households and a mill rendering thirteen shillings per annum.

Little Houghton with some lovely old properties stands just off the main road between Bedford and Northampton and is more peaceful since the bypass was built in 1979. Before then it was a tortuous route for traffic through the narrow main street, alongside which stands the church of
ST MARY with its 13th century embattled west tower. Although largely rebuilt in 1873 by *Charles Buckeridge*, the south doorway dates from around 1200.
The organ was installed in 2000 but it was originally built in 1846 by *William Hill* of London and this rare and important instrument served in three other churches.

A great fire in 1333 claimed most of the properties in the village leaving the church as one of the few remaining buildings. The second conflagration in 1780 destroyed a further eight or ten houses and left others with reddened stonework.
The grandest domestic building is undoubtedly Little Houghton House which dates from 1780.

The village retains its butcher's shop where two animal heads – a ram and a bull - adorn the front.
There is also a garage, village hall, shop cum post office, modern Primary school and a public house which used to be called The Red Lion.
Today it goes by the name 'The Four Pears' after four sets of friends (i.e. four pairs) rescued it from closure in 2011.

The former White Lion public house and the Reading Room dated 1704 have both been converted into private dwellings.

Near the village shop are the two man stocks and whipping post. Their last occupant was *William Baucutt* who, in the late 1800's, was lodged there for drunken behaviour and beating his wife.
They were lifted and restored in the early 1990's

According to a report in 1830 a drunken customer (was this the same *William Baucutt*) of an unnamed hostelry announced that the local Vicar had generously bequeathed a field containing an abundance of turnips for the poor of the parish.
Everyone cheered and drunk the Vicar's health and the next day started to clear the field until the irate Vicar complete with stick and servant appeared on the scene.

CLIFFORD HILL

Clifford Hill, about half a mile north of the village is one of the largest mottes in the country although I cannot find any evidence that a castle was built here.
On the north side it sweeps down to the ford which crosses the river - a strategic crossing point. The motte is presumed to date from the 11th or 12th centuries and was even taller than it is now as in the 17th century the Lord of the Manor, *William Ward,* levelled off the top to make a bowling green. The project was not very successful as the bowls kept rolling down the hill.

John Clare the poet is said to have spent a great deal of his time walking in this area whilst an inmate at the County Asylum - now St Andrews Hospital.
In one of his poems he refers to Clifford Hill:-

'At the foot of Clifford Hill, Still I hear the clacking mill
And the river's running still. Under the trysting tree
O there's something falls so dear On the music of the ear,
Where the river runs so clear, And my lover met with me.'

LITTLE OAKLEY

Two miles south west of Corby
Population: 1801-113   2001 - 147 (inc Newton)

DOMESDAY BOOK
ACHELAU

*Little Oakley got the name, 'clearing in the oaks'
because of its position within Rockingham Forest.
The Domesday Book records only one settlement.*

This is a one street village far removed from the
hustle and bustle of nearby Corby with a church
but very little else - no school, shop, post office or
village hall. The old school built in 1852 and the
former public house, The Dukes Arms are now
private houses.

The church of **ST PETER** has a fine early
13th century chancel and a 15th century
Perpendicular style west tower with clasping
buttresses, tall bell openings and battlements.

It was restored in 1867 but was declared redundant
in 1975 when it was taken over by the Orton Trust
as a training base for stonemasons.

Tools of the Trade

Today little Oakley is a very quiet place but there
was an unusual event in the church during the
reign of *Queen Elizabeth I* when fifteen local men
caused a riot over a dispute between the new Lord
of the Manor *(Wm Montagu)* and a new priest
who had been appointed by the Crown. The rioters
supported the priest but unfortunately one man
from Little Oakley was killed and another injured.

The Manor House, now Manor Farm, west of the
church probably dates from 1550-60 and is gabled
with mullioned windows with arched lights.
A date stone indicates some rebuilding in the
18th century

LODDINGTON

Three miles west of Kettering
Population: 1801-183   2001 - 477

DOMESDAY BOOK
LODINTONE

*The name simply indicates that this was
Lodda's 'intun' - farmstead.*

This was part of the royal manor of Rothwell at
the time of the Domesday Book.

Overlooking the village in early English style is
the ironstone church of **ST LEONARD**.

The 13th century west tower with four gargoyles
along the east and west end is topped by a superb
broach spire. I particularly like the elaborate west
doorway to the church with an unusual gable over
the door thought to have sheltered a statue at one
time, possibly *St Leonard* himself. An hour glass
stand minus the glass by the pulpit was a reminder
to the Vicar not to give too long a sermon.

In 1893 a beautiful stained glass window was
installed south of the altar by *William Morris* in
memory of the Rector's son.

The most imposing house is **Loddington Hall**
opposite the church, with its impressive 18th
century gates. It is mainly Jacobean in style dating
from about 1615 and was built on an 'E' plan with
a large north extension dated 1893.

After the Second World War the Hall became a
Special school but more recently it has been
converted into twelve luxury apartments.

The village hall was presented by *Major A. Steele*
in 1928 in memory of his mother.

There is still a Primary school and a public house
and restaurant - The Hare - but the former chapel
is now a private residence.

Unusual Gable West Door Loddington

LONG BUCKBY

Eight miles north west of Northampton
Population: 1801-1600   2001 - 4000

DOMESDAY BOOK
BUCHEBI

*Opinions differ as to the name. Is it of Saxon origin deriving from 'bucc' - male deer (where deer are found) or was it the village of **Bukkr**, a Viking personal name?*

Long Buckby west of the road between Northampton and Rugby lives up to its name as its main street stretches about one and a half miles.
The prefix 'Long' is first recorded in the time of **Elizabeth I**.

Buckby appears in two entries in the Domesday Book and had a total of thirty eight households indicating a sizeable population for the time of about 160-180 although the value of the manors does not appear to have increased between 1066-1086.
The tenants in chief were **Gunfrid de Chocques** and **Alfred the butler**. By the mid 12th century the manor was held by **Sahir de Quincey** and it is he who is said to have built a Castle here.

The original village is thought to have been sited to the west of the present one in the area known as Salen but residents moved to the new centre around the Market Place when in 1280 **Henry de Lacy, Earl of Lincoln and Salisbury** was granted a weekly market and two annual fairs.

It is around the Market Square that you will find shops, banks, restaurants, a library, post office and Primary school. The area is normally very busy but particularly so on August Bank Holiday Monday when the annual Buckby Feast takes centre stage.

In the 18th century the village was a noted centre for wool combing and worsted weaving but when trade declined at the end of that century it left much of the population in deep poverty.
It was therefore a godsend when footwear manufacturing arrived in the 19th century bringing much needed employment to many people.
At its peak there were twelve factories of varying sizes, one factory supplied riding boots for the Royal Horse Guards.

Many other people were employed as out workers but unfortunately that trade too declined in the mid 20th century with the arrival of cheaper foreign imports. One of the larger employers was '**Cooks**' in Station Road. When manufacturing ceased the premises were taken over by a potato crisp manufacturer but in recent years the building has been converted to residential use.
Another former factory - that of the Castle Shoe Company can still be seen in King Street to the west of Market Square whereas workshops can be discovered around East Street and the Church Street areas.

A short distance south of the village is Buckby Wharf where the Grand Union canal, A5 trunk road, the West Coast main railway line and the M1 motorway all run parallel to each other within a very short distance.

At various times the Wharf has been the home of a brick works and various other trades but the remaining buildings are now converted into dwellings.

Old Kings Head : Long Buckby

Long Buckby Station built in 1880 is not linked directly to the West Coast main line as it is on the Northampton to Rugby loop line but it is still well used which results in some car parking problems for commuters.

In the heyday of railways there were about ninety stations of varying sizes in the County but today this is one of only six stations still in use.

The small wayside station sprang into prominence in 1977 when the *Queen* and other members of the Royal family disembarked here en route to nearby Althorp House for the burial of *Princess Diana* - the station at Althorp having been closed many years ago.

With the population drift the ironstone church of **ST LAWRENCE** now stands on the edge of the village approached along a pathway lined with pollarded limes. The tower dates back to the 12th or early 13th century and is thought to be the oldest part of the church. Battlements and gargoyles were added later. It is recorded in 1883 that *'the coating of plaster that disfigured the tower was removed'*

The roof of the nave was raised to provide for a clerestory and new pews added during work carried out by *Sir George Gilbert Scott* in 1861.

The sanctuary has a piscina and a three seat sedilia.

Buried in the churchyard with a memorial in the church is *Eliza Gardner* (1840) the Curate's wife who was *'frightened to death'*.

Her death was instantaneous and arose from a violent attack made on her home by three or four drunken men with a view to disturbing the sleeping inhabitants in the dead of the night.

The attack was considered so serious that the youths appeared before Northampton Assizes facing a possible charge of manslaughter.

The judge considered that *Eliza* was quite poorly anyway and as a result the youths were let off with a fine and told to behave themselves for the next three years.

Also buried in the churchyard is *Stanley Unwin* who in the latter part of the 20th century became famous as the inventor of a peculiar form of language called *'Unwinese'*.

Non-conformity has been a strong feature of this village over the years and it is recorded that in the mid 19th century the three chapels between them attracted more than four times the congregation of the Church of England.

Boot Maker

Two quite large chapels are still in use - the Congregational chapel in Market Place which dates from 1771 and the Baptist chapel of 1846 built in classical tradition.

The little Mission church near the A5 was built in 1875 as a Chapel of Ease but closed in the 1960's.

Not many people outside of the County may ever have heard of Long Buckby but worldwide they see evidence of items originating from the village.

The items referred to being the Maclaren baby buggy first made in 1965 and originally manufactured by the million from a factory near the station.

One of the first ever 'buggies' is now on show at the Long Buckby Museum on Station road which is open occasionally at weekends.

Just to the west of the village is **Murcott** which I have listed as one of Northamptonshire's lost settlements.

The location is marked by the imposing Georgian Mill house which dates back to 1760 and today offers 4* bed and breakfast accommodation.

LONG BUCKBY CASTLE

South west of the church is the site of Long Buckby Castle. Little is known of its history, but recent excavations suggest that about 1150 *Sahir De Quincey*, later *Earl of Winchester*, who held the manor until 1264, built an oval ringwork defended by a timber wall on an earth bank surrounded by a ditch.

The Castle is thought to have lasted little more than fifty years and today is a pleasant little rural oasis and is scheduled as a Heritage Site.

Lowick

DOMESDAY BOOK
LUDEWIC/LUHWIC
*The name possible derives from **Luha's** 'wic' - farmstead.*

Two manors are recorded here in the Domesday Book, one held by *Edwin* and *Algar* of the ***Bishop of Coutances*** and the other by *Sibold* (the only one in the County I can find held by him). Together they had fourteen households and in addition there was a mill rendering sixty four pence per annum.

In 1385 *Richard III* granted a Charter for a weekly market.

In most instances these were obtained by manorial Lords to enhance the status of the village.

Lowick is a delightful village of mainly stone cottages which has managed to keep its charm and identity, helped in some way by the construction of the bypass between Thrapston and Corby in the early 1980's.

It would be easy to speed past on the dual carriageway but the sight of the tower of **ST PETER'S** church seems to draw the traveller closer and there is certainly much to be seen.

Unfortunately the church is in urgent need of funds to repair the roof and visitors are faced with a large panel inviting them to buy part of the roof at a cost of £10 per square foot. Obviously you don't actually own your piece as the text on the panel explains.

It is a very good Perpendicular style church built chiefly at the expense of the *Greene* family of nearby Drayton.

The west tower which rises up in four stages with a superb collection of carved pinnacles above the battlements was probably completed after 1470. On top is an unusual, but nevertheless superb octagonal lantern with its own eight pinnacles.

The church contains a series of 16th century medieval stained glass windows and some splendid memorials to the *Greene* and the *Stopford - Sackville* families of **Drayton Hall.**

The earliest tomb commemorates *Sir Ralph Greene* (d.1417) and his wife *Katharine*. This was once coloured and gilded and had a canopy, the cut off supports of which can still be seen. It is unusual in that the figures are holding hands rather than being in an aspect of prayer.

One quite moving monument is the white chest tomb of *Charles Sackville* with his mantle draped over the end, his shield leaning against it and his coronet on a cushion on the ground.

The former school was founded between 1717-1725 by *Sir and Lady Germaine* for twenty poor children. It was formerly called the *'Green Coat School'* on account of the costume that had to be worn by its pupils.

There is an engraved scroll above the front door.

The building is used as the parish hall but known as the Germaine Rooms.

In my opinion this is one of the most attractive churches in the County.

-280-

It is said that the book *'Middlemarch'* by **George Eliot** was written at least in part in the old Rectory in the village and that it is mentioned in the book itself.

Opposite Mordaunt Close on Drayton Road is a stone surround and trough for a still flowing outlet from a spring.
The stonework carries the date 1830.
The village no longer has a school, shop or post office, but the popular public house and restaurant is delightfully named 'The Snooty Fox.'

Legend has it that a wounded soldier from the Battle of Naseby was brought back to the village on his white horse whereupon it dropped down dead from exhaustion at the point where the pub, originally named The White Horse, now stands.

Young children are fortunate in having a lovely little play area and a recreation ground alongside the minor road to the lost village of Drayton which lies in the parish.

DRAYTON

There is little else to see other than the impressive Drayton House, south west of Lowick.
It stands on the site of a medieval village called Draiton (sloping land by a farmstead) which does not appear to be mentioned in the Domesday Book. The only access to the area today is via a private road or a public footpath and so is unnoticed by most people.

Depopulation appears to have taken place when the House was extended and the grounds expanded in the 16th-18th centuries.

Drayton House and the Sackville family

*The Estate has been owned since the 14th century by various branches of the same family including the **Greenes**, the **Mordaunts** and at the present time the **Sackvilles**.*
*Its history goes back to 1328 when **Simon de Drayton** was granted licence to crennelate his house and the core of that house still survives.*
*In 1361 **Simon's** son conveyed Drayton to **Sir Henry Greene**, Chief Justice of the Kings Bench who added to the House in the 15th century.*
*Then followed the **Mordaunts** in the early 16th century who undertook further alterations and additions.*
*When the **Earl of Peterborough**, still of the **Mordaunt** family, died in 1697 his daughter the **Duchess of Norfolk** who had divorced the Duke took up residence with her lover **Sir John Germaine** who she married in 1701 - their monuments are in Lowick Church.*

*The last of the major changes to the House took place at the beginning of the 18th century including the addition of the delightful twin cupulas. In 1770 the House passed to the **Sackville** family who changed only two rooms in the Adam style and it is still the family home.*
I particularly liked the superb 18th century ironwork and the entrance gate piers with urns.
The House is certainly most impressive but I would have preferred it without the tall grey wall with battlements and arrow slits which date back to its early days.

There is a public right of way through the grounds skirting the House which is not usually open to the public but groups can visit by prior appointment.

LUDDINGTON IN THE BROOK

Five miles south east of Oundle
Population: 1801-104   2001 - 50

DOMESDAY BOOK
LULLINTONE

*The name is thought to derive from **Lilla**'s 'ington' - farmstead - the same personal name appears in place names from Lilbourne and Lilford although historians have not discovered the identity of **Lilla**.*

This tiny village lies off the beaten track to the north east of the County on the Cambridgeshire border. Luddington is often omitted from maps and there are few signposts. It is almost as though the villagers don't want anyone to find them.

At the time of the Domesday Book the manor was held by *Walter* of the Abbey at Peterborough.
A total of seven households were recorded.
Since 1888 the parish has included land which at the time of the Domesday Book was recorded under the County of Huntingdon.

It never seems to have been very large and developed as labourer's dwellings on both sides of the Alconbury Brook until the landlord - the *Duke of Buccleuch* and *Queensberry* had a new road and new cottages built above the flood plain in 1863.
Until that time the main street and houses lay along the bed of the winding brook and flooding was a real problem. Luddington was literally, *'in the brook.'*

John Bridges, the County historian described it as *'low and dirty.*
On the edge of the village and accessed along a farm track off the road to Thurning is the 13th century church, topping a low grassy knoll close to the brook.

The church was originally dedicated to **ST ANDREW** but since 1791 has been dedicated to **ST MARGARET**
It has a very plain west tower with a short broach spire but has a superb display of gargoyles - some quite large and amusing including a man's head with one eye open and one eye shut.
Points of interest inside are the linenfold patterns on the pew ends and a plain five hundred year old octagonal font.

Apart from the church the village seems to lack all public amenities apart from a rare VR letterbox on the wall of the former red brick bakehouse - quite possibly because the post office forgot it was there.

Gargoyles at Luddington Church

LUTTON

Five miles west of Oundle
Population: 1801-155   2001 - 145

DOMESDAY BOOK
LIDINTONE/LUDINTONE
Once known as Luddington in the Wold now Lutton to distinguish it from Luddington in the Brook nearby.
*The origin of Luditone is thought to be **Luda's' ington' - farmhouse.***

The two manors at the time of the Domesday Book were both held by monastic institutions, one by Peterborough Abbey and the other by Ramsey Abbey.

On the 30th September 1895 the Huntingdonshire part of the parish was added so that it is now totally within Northamptonshire although on the very far north eastern edge of the County.

The village has reduced in size over the years and there are extensive earthworks indicating former houses to the south east of the present village.

The church of **ST PETER** which has a Perpendicular style west tower built around 1430 with clasping buttresses and battlements stands in a superb position at the 'T' junction.

In the chancel which dates from the late 13th century is an unusual Easter sepulchre of 1450.

The bells date from 1604.

According to church history there was a Saxon church on the site in about 800AD and a shaft of a Saxon cross has been built into the north wall of the tower.

The unusual *Apreese* memorial which was erected in 1633 features three praying men in black garments. The family once owned the 17th century Manor House.

Also remembered in the church are *Lt. Vergens* and *Lt. Ashton* and their crews who lost their lives on the 6 February 1945. Their two planes were returning in bad weather to Polebrook from operations over Germany but collided over Lutton and crashed some two hundred yards apart.

In 1960 a hoard of 183 silver coins dating from 1557 – 1644 were found in a field to the south of the Manor House.

The village no longer has a shop, post office or public house but does have a number of attractive properties. One opposite the church which caught my eye was a substantial old house with tall slender, crooked, chimneys.

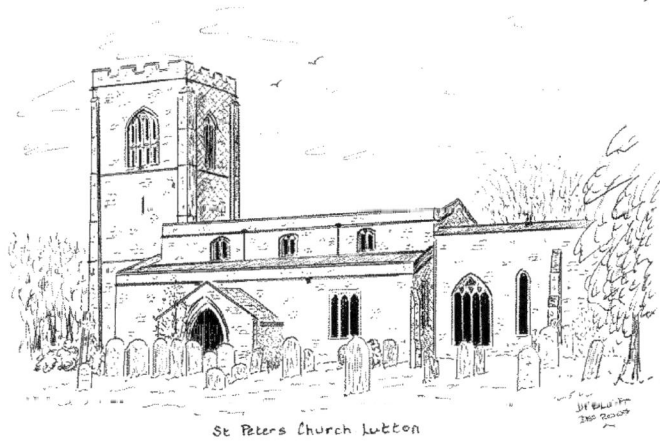

St Peters Church Lutton

LYVEDEN

Four miles south west of Oundle

The settlement is not mentioned in the Domesday Book.
*In 1175 there was a village here called Louenden meaning **Leofa's** valley.*

Lyveden, in the parish of Aldwincle St Peter is south west of the picturesque market town of Oundle and three miles east of Brigstock.

Although it is hard to imagine today there was a pottery making centre here in the 13th century.
Ten potters were mentioned in the Court Rolls of 1406.
The settlement started to dwindle in the 15th century and was eradicated in the 16th century when **Thomas Tresham** emparked the land surrounding his Manor House.
By 1583 there was pasture for 3,000 sheep, a figure which had almost doubled by 1597.
Although now virtually devoid of inhabitants the area is worth a visit for two Houses - the **Old Bield** and the **New Bield** both of which have Grade I listing

Old Bield just off the Brigstock to Oundle road belonged to the **Treshams** of Rushton who came to live here when their grand house at Rushton was confiscated after the Gunpowder Plot.

The Manor House dates from the 16th century but all that remains of the original three wing building is the south range. At the time of writing it is up for sale with a guide price of £2,100,000.

In 1595 after serving a period of twelve years imprisonment for harbouring priests **Sir Thomas** began work on the New Bield, possibly as a 'secret house' which was the custom in the 16th century but it was unfinished at his death in 1605 and has never been completed.
Today it is a magnificent roofless shell of a large mansion and lies some distance south of the Old Bield.

The Bield is full of symbolism and represents the Passion in the shape of a cross and together with the superb landscaped gardens is a remarkable survival of the Elizabethan age.

The New Bield and its gardens are now under the ownership of the National Trust and as such are regularly open to the public. Take a picnic because there are very limited refreshment facilities.
There is a delightful little walk among the woods alongside the New Bield. Do the walk at bluebell time for a really magnificent spectacle.

Lyveden New Bield

Tresham

Maidford

Five miles north west of Towcester
Population: 1801-228 2001 - 179

DOMESDAY BOOK
MERDEFORD

I have not been able to establish with any certainty how the village came by its name - many possibilities have been suggested - was it once the site of a nunnery?
Or was it simply where young women used to collect water or maybe gather for some other purpose?

This small village has a long history as it is mentioned in the Saxon Geld Roll and again in the Domesday Book as the settlement of Merdeford Manor when there were thirteen households and a priest. A total of forty seven households paid the Hearth Tax in 1673 - a figure very similar to that mentioned in *John Bridges* history of 1720.

At one time employment was traditionally associated with the land and this was followed in the Middle Ages by limestone quarrying but the quarries have long gone. In the 18th and 19th centuries it became a centre for silk stocking and pillow lace making.
Nowadays there has been a change of lifestyle and it is very much a commuter village.

The Manor House with its large blocked up medieval window adjacent to the church
(now known as Manor Farm), together with its adjacent barn is thought to have been an outlying settlement connected with the Augustinian Priory at Canons Ashby.

Old Chapel : Maidford

Evidence of medieval fishponds can still be seen in the grounds.
There are several springs impregnated with iron and mineral salts in the area.

The church of **ST PETER AND ST PAUL** dates back to the 13th century and has a west tower with a fine saddleback roof.
The first Rector was appointed in 1219.
Two windows of note are the brightly coloured East window of the chancel featuring a picture of *Christ* and the East window in the south aisle which shows *Jesus* on a boat on a stormy sea with his frightened disciples. The latter window is in memory of *Arthur William Grant* who lived at the Manor and died in September 1878.

A group of copper beeches was planted in the churchyard as a memorial to the men of the village who died in the First World War.
These have grown so large and together with the other trees make the churchyard very dark.

The red brick Wesleyan chapel dates from 1858 but has now closed as has the village school which is now the village hall and although there is a small garage on the main road there is no longer a shop or a public house.

The most notorious resident was probably *Thomas Tew* who was born in the village in the 17th century. He operated as a pirate around Bermuda and got the name the *'Rhode Island Pirate.'* He died in 1695 in the Arabian Sea.

During World War II Maidford was home to the entertainer *Roy Hudd* who was born in Croydon in 1936. He was just one of thousands of Londoners who were evacuated to safer areas.
When he returned to London it is said that he was made fun of because of his Northamptonshire accent.

MAIDWELL

Seven miles south of Market Harborough
Population: 1801-208   2001 - 325

DOMESDAY BOOK
MEDEWELLE
This is another puzzling prefix as in the case of Maidford - the suffix is from the Saxon 'wielle' - for spring.

Unusual Gateway : Maidwell

The three manors here were recorded as having twenty nine households possibly meaning about 120-140 people - quite a sizeable population at the time. One of the manors was held by *Ansgar the chaplain* - the only one I can find him holding in the County.

There are some attractive properties on either side of the busy A508 Northampton to Market Harborough road but it is more interesting and quieter as you leave the main road en route to Draughton which crosses the route of the Northampton to Market Harborough railway line. This opened in 1859 and closed in 1981.
A footpath between the two villages crosses the old line (now the public footpath known as the Brampton Valley Way) over which is a fine example of a Victorian foot bridge but now minus its timber steps.

The village is somewhat unusual in that in the Middle Ages there were two churches and two Manor Houses, one of which stood near Manor Farm and the other behind the church.

The church of **ST PETER** was demolished in the 16th century and the site is occupied today by St Peters Close.
The existing church of **ST MARY** was originally built during the Norman period and the south doorway and the unbuttressed west tower with rounded shafts at the angles contain some work of that era.
The chancel was rebuilt in 1891 in the Victorian style when the clerestory was removed resulting in quite a dark interior although the church contains several windows by *Kempe* dated between 1892-1906.

The painted tomb of **Lord and Lady Dundalk** was transferred to St Marys when the neighbouring church was closed.

The churchyard and the little shed it contains are crying out for some tender loving care as is the church roof.

Reginald B. Loder was Squire of Maidwell between 1888-1931 and the village hall carries his name. The unusual stone gateway to what is now called 'Wyatts' has a stone inscribed 'Gateway restored by *Reginald B. Loder*.'

Oliver Wyatt - a renowned plant breeder, purchased **Maidwell Hall** in 1933 to establish a school with boarders with him as the Headmaster.

Whilst at Maidwell he raised a new variety of Clematis with blue flowers which goes by the name *'Maidwell Hall'*
The Hall has a porch dating from 1637 but was gutted by fire and rebuilt in 1902.
It is now used as a private school for boys and girls aged 7-13 years.

The village retains a public house and restaurant - The Stags Head which stands on the main road opposite the garage.
There has been a public house formerly known as The Goat on this site since 1766.

The Primary school stands opposite the church and had a grand looking extension added in 2000.
It was rated in an Ofsted report for 2009 - 2010 as outstanding.

MARSTON ST LAWRENCE

Six miles east of Banbury
Population: 1801-371   2001 - 209

DOMESDAY BOOK
MERESTONE
The name derives from 'mersc tun' - marsh farm and was subsequently given the addition of the dedication of the Parish Church to save confusion with other Marstons.

As a result of extensive examination throughout the area by *D. J. Barrett* in the 20th century there have been a large number of prehistoric and Roman finds including washed flints, coins, bones and pottery which obviously pre date the Norman Conquest.

Robert held the manor of *Earl Hugh* in 1086 when there were forty three households and a mill rendering eight shillings per annum.
It was obviously quite well populated for the time.

This village which lies in rolling countryside in the south of the County half way between Brackley and Banbury has some attractive stone cottages and the Grade II Listed **Marston House** at the rear of the church.

Within the grounds of the House is a lake surrounded by lawns and shrubs with a bridge dated 1759 over its south end.
The Estate was given to the *Blencowe* family by *Henry VI* and they lived there until 1955.
It now houses a commercial enterprise.

Much evidence of the *Blencowe* family can be seen on the memorials, hatchments and stained glass of the church of **ST LAWRENCE** which has a Perpendicular style west tower dating from the 11th century and a spacious interior with comfortable seats in place of pews.

The three well worn sedilia seats in the chancel look very strange being close to the floor as the chancel floor was raised and retiled in the 19th century. Opposite is a worn Easter sepulchre.

What most impressed me was the beautiful Jacobean dark oak screen dated 1610 which is now situated in the tower arch

One Rector, the *Rev. Charles Chauncey*, was reported as being *'opinionated and arrogant'* and fell foul of the ecclesiastical authorities in England. Was this the reason he sailed to America in 1638? He was eventually appointed President of Harvard University a position he held until his death in 1671.

The churchyard contains a Yew tree which has been certified as being over fifteen hundred years old but at the moment looks to be in need of some tender loving care.

Although the village no longer has a shop, post office or school it does have a well used village hall and a public house - the six hundred year old Marston Inn which was once three cottages seized by *Oliver Cromwell* and used to raise money for his army prior to the Battle of Edgehill after which it was given to the *Belcher* family.
It then became a butcher's shop before becoming a hostelry over 150 years ago.

MARSTON TRUSSELL

Three miles west of Market Harborough
Population: 1801-212   2001 - 163

DOMESDAY BOOK
MERSITONE
The name is thought to have derived from 'mersc' - Saxon for marsh and 'tun' - farmstead.
Welland meadows are prone to flooding even today.

The area was settled well before the Norman Conquest as considerable evidence of prehistoric or Roman settlement has been discovered in the vicinity of the Welland Valley.

At the time of the Domesday Book Marston Trussell was linked with Thorpe Lubbenham as a single manor held by *Hugh de Grandmesnil.*
There were forty two households indicating a population of about 140-160 people so it was quite a large settlement.

The Estate was leased from *Henry II* by *Osbert Trussell* in the 12th century and it is from him that the name suffix derives although the family died out in the 14th century.
The Hall then became the seat of the *Barwell - Ewins - Bennett* family.

The village of Marston Trussell lies just off the A4304 Market Harborough to Lutterworth road on the Leicestershire border.
The two counties are separated at this point by the River Welland.

One lasting impression of my first visit to the church of **ST NICHOLAS** which is located in a lovely position on the edge of the village is the unique north porch.
It is thought that the arched doorway timbers may have come from a Danish ship stranded in the Welland when the river was navigable.
The other timbers are thought to have come from the nearby Castle, the remains of which went to repair Holdenby House.

I visited the church on a cold damp January morning and had a surprisingly warm welcome as I entered. The overhead heaters were going full blast because the roof was leaking like a sieve and attempts were being made to stop church furnishings etc. getting damp. Seats were protected with plastic sheeting and everywhere there were receptacles collecting drips.

The church has a tall Perpendicular style west tower with clasping buttresses, ironstone and ashlar battlements and pinnacles.
Merchant marks can still be found on some stones.

Inside a carved oak chest said to date from the time of the Magna Carta is still in use.

North Porch. St Nicholas Church. Marston Trussell

-288-

The *Mark Brewster* memorial commemorates a remarkable 16th century adventurer. He was a wool merchant but in earlier days operated as a pirate in the Baltic. He came to live in Marston Trussell and was a great benefactor to the church.
However the Russians got to know of his whereabouts and had him taken to Moscow where he was executed for his crimes in 1612.

The five bells mostly dating from the early 1600's were recast in 1959 and rung for the first time since *Queen Victoria's* Jubilee.
Nowadays they appear to be rung quite often by the Peterborough Diocesan Guild of Bell Ringers and you can see certificates of special peals, including weddings, birthdays, commemorations, anniversaries, retirements, Mothering Sunday and half muffled on Remembrance Day.

The old Manor House near the church was demolished about 1870.

When the present **Marston Trussell Hall** with a battlemented porch was built, some houses opposite were demolished and the road to Sibbertoft which ran directly in front of the Hall was relocated to leave a very pleasant open view across to the lake in the distance.

The splendid 17th century gate piers and wrought iron gates were originally made for the house of *Sir Erasmus Norwich* at Brampton Ash which was demolished in the 18th century.

After the Battle of Naseby in June 1645 a group of fleeing Royalists were trapped in an enclosure called Pudding Field east of the church.
Here they were massacred and thrown into a shallow pit afterwards known as 'Cavaliers Grave,' the area was named Slaughterford and as a result is said to be haunted.

This is a small village with little more than the church and the Hall for interest.
The school is dated 1857 but is no longer in use and recently the local public house, The Sun Inn and restaurant was closed.
Being nosy I looked into the windows and discovered the place had been stripped bare except for a whole lot of zimmer walking frames - is there a story there somewhere?

The parish now includes two of Northamptonshire's lost villages, Hothorpe and Thorpe Lubenham.

HOTHORPE

DOMESDAY BOOK
UDETORP

At the time of the Domesday Book when the land was held by the Abbey of St Edmundbury, Hothorpe with one sokeman and half a plough had one of the smallest recorded populations in the County but by 1377 there were fifty seven people recorded as paying the Poll Tax and *Bridges* in 1720 recorded twenty houses.

This long lost settlement lay close to the River Welland which marks the boundary between Northamptonshire and Leicestershire.
It was once a Chapelry of Theddingworth.

Little remains today although **Hothorpe Hall** which was built in 1801 by *John Cook* is still marked on Ordnance Survey Maps and is now advertised as a versatile Midlands Events Centre catering for meetings, functions, weddings and short breaks.
The land was laid out as a Park in 1830 when villagers were moved to Theddingworth.

THORPE LUBENHAM

DOMESDAY BOOK
TORP

This was once the secondary settlement of nearby Lubenham (in neighbouring Leicestershire) from which it takes its suffix to distinguish it from other Torps.

This settlement lay to the south of Lubenham in Leicestershire but on the Northamptonshire side of the River Welland.
At one time it was a Chapelry of Lubenham.
I cannot find any independent reference to Thorpe Lubenham before 1316. Manorial ownership was disputed in 1406 and was passed on to non resident heiresses of Glendon and Newbottle.
Desertion of the village is thought to have occurred sometime before 1674.

The Hall was rebuilt outside of the park in the 18th century replacing a moated, possibly timber predecessor.
Previous owners of the Hall often invited the Queen and her family to the Hall during the 1960's.

MAWSLEY

A settlement is thought to have existed here before 1086 and was most likely taxed with Faxton.
I have seen it listed as a deserted medieval village which vanished at the time of the Black Death although the exact location seems to be unknown. However the Mawsley of today covers such a wide area that some part most likely stands on the site of the original settlement.
The village lies just off the A43 and has only recently started to appear on Ordnance Survey and AA maps.

It is not often that a deserted settlement is brought back to life but here the Authorities seem to be going over the top! First planned as a new village by Northamptonshire County Council in 1993 construction began in 2001 and when completed it is expected to have about one thousand homes.
As modern building goes the village is quite acceptable but lacks a heart although it did win a recent Daily Telegraph 'Best New Build Village' title.

It has a 'Village Centre' which houses conferences, wedding receptions, parties, quiz nights, coffee mornings, day nursery etc. and also a new Primary school and health centre. A public house is planned.
The village does not yet have its own church but is now part of the parish of St Andrew at Great Cransley where some services are held.
The congregation also meets regularly in the 'Village Centre' and in private homes on other occasions.

MEARS ASHBY

Seven miles north east of Northampton
Population: 1801-339   2001 - 442

DOMESDAY BOOK
ASBI
Yet another Ashby, ash tree by a village, but it became Essebi Mares in the 13th century
Robert de Mares *held the Manor from 1242.*

There have been settlements in this area for a very long time. The Romans preceded the Saxons and left their mark in the form of pottery, building stone and tiles. In 1086 there were twenty two households when the four hide manor was held by **Countess Judith** and the land belonged to Earls Barton.

This is a lovely old village, particularly in the area around the church. The village centre is relatively peaceful with a number of small fields and paddocks although it is surrounded on four sides by quite busy roads. What a joy it was to see the young lambs prancing about amongst the spring flowers alongside the Swanspool Brook which adds to the attractiveness of the area.

There are a number of fine old ironstone buildings including **Mears Ashby Hall**, a lovely gable fronted Elizabethan building dated 1637. To the east of the Hall and standing on a sloping bank is a rectangular dovecote with slightly battered walls some three feet thick and topped with a small wooden lantern.
The Manor House west of the church dates from the early 18th century and the steeply gabled old Vicarage by **Buckeridge** from the 19th century.

.... MEARS ASHBY

At Duchess End on the approach from Wilby there is at a panel which tells the story of tragic events over the village on 31st March 1943. On that fateful day two B17 Flying Fortresses - *'Two Beauts'* and *'Ooold Soljer'* from the 8th USAFF 303rd Heavy Bomber Group set out on a raid but collided overhead and fifteen servicemen lost their lives. Two primed bombs exploded and others dropped harmlessly.
Fortunately the village survived whether by luck or brave heroism on the part of the pilots I do not know.

The church of **ALL SAINTS** is superbly located at the heart of the village and has an embattled squat west tower, massive nave and steep pitched chancel.
The south door and part of the chancel date from around 1200, the rest is mostly 13th to early 14th century.
Among the interesting items to be seen inside are the magnificent Norman octagonal font, the remnant of an old Saxon 'Wheel' Cross from about 1000AD and the vast 'Doom' painting over the chancel arch which was restored in 1984.
The village still has a Primary school and a public house – The Griffins Head, a stone built village hall but no shop.

MIDDLETON

Two miles west of Corby
Population: 1801 – 411   2001 – 328

The settlement does not appear in the Domesday Book but by 1197 was referred to as Middelton or Middle Farm (between Carlton and Cottingham) so was presumably included under one of those manors.

Middleton which stands between Cottingham and East Carlton Country Park has some pretty 17th and 18th century houses. The supply of water to the village does not seem to have been a problem as there are the remains of at least six wells and a handsome horse trough with the inscription:-

'THP 1844'

The *Palmer* family lived at nearby **East Carlton Hall** so presumably they were the donors.

The Manor in the High Street is now the Manor House Care Home.

Primary school children attend the Church of England School which stands between the villages of Middleton and Cottingham.
The present Red Lion public house stands on the site of the original thatched building which was destroyed by fire. There is still a shop and café but I was sad to see the state of the old Congregational church which was built in 1844. It now looks so unloved and neglected.

A long distance footpath, the Jurassic Way runs through the village and attracts many visitors.

Water Pump. Middleton

MIDDLETON CHENEY

Three miles east of Banbury
Population: 1801-1153   2001 - 3753

DOMESDAY BOOK
MIDELTONE
The name obviously derives from Middletun - middle farm.
*It became Middleton Curcy in 1224 when the Estate was owned by **John de Curci**,*
*although some would say the suffix is derived from the Domesday Lord, **Ralph de Chenduit**.*

The village which is the largest in the South Northants district is located just inside the County boundary with Oxfordshire. Although most of the heavy traffic between Banbury and Brackley now uses the A422 bypass the main street through the village is still very busy.

Originally there were two hamlets, Upper (or Church) Middleton and Lower (or Nether) Middleton but today it is one large and not particularly attractive village overall although it does have some lovely old stone cottages, dating back to the early 17th century by the church.

The Domesday Book records three manors, one of which had a junior priest indicating some form of Christian community although the first known priest appears to have been **Radulphus** of Middleton in 1180.
In 1296 a report stated that the chapel was in a poor state of repair.

The present church of **ALL SAINTS** dates from 1302 and is in the Decorative style and is one of my favourites in the whole of the County.

The church was extended at the end of the 1400's and it was then that the superb collection of seventy stone figure heads were carved and installed both inside and outside the church.

The west tower is lofty and embattled with eight pinnacles and is topped by a tall and graceful spire in the Perpendicular style which rises to a height of 153 feet (48 metres) and dominates the skyline for miles around.

The spire appears to have suffered three lightning strikes so I hope that a good conductor is now firmly in place.

Externally the church is magnificent but it is well worth gaining access to see the treasures inside.
What most impressed me were the stained glass windows and I was not surprised to learn that many of them are the work of the talented and famous **William Morris** and his company.
Pevsner says that the windows:-
> *'make it a place of great enjoyment,*
> *the Holy of Holies of Morris Glass'.*

One of the most dramatic windows features **Shadrach, Meshach** and **Abednego** in the fiery furnace.
The East window is also worthy of particular note as it features saints, angels, flags of the tribes of Israel etc. and at the top a panel representing the
'Adoration of the Lamb'.
The church underwent restoration by **Sir George Gilbert Scott** in 1865 during which the pulpit and ceilings were painted.

All Saints Church : Middleton Cheney

Note also the rare opus sectile stone marquetry panels at the west end of the nave.

As I approached the church I could not fail to notice the large and imposing neo Gothic tomb of members of the **Horton** family.

William Horton of London purchased a large part of the **Chetwoode** family Estate in 1799 thus becoming Lord of the Manor. The family became considerable landowners and had extensive interests in the manufacture of silk stockings. **William's** daughter, **Mary** did an enormous amount of good work for the poor of the village and was responsible for the building of the Almshouses in 1863 originally for workers on the Horton Estate.
Money was bequeathed for the building of Horton Hospital in Banbury with the proviso that there would always be at least one bed available for a resident from Middleton Cheney.

One of the first battles of the Civil War was fought here on 6th May 1643 when over two hundred Roundheads were killed of whom, according to church records, forty six were buried in the churchyard the next day. It is said that the present War Memorial was erected over their grave.

This being quite a large village it has a reasonable number of shops, a care home and sheltered housing scheme, a library and both Primary and Secondary schools.

Near the church are a Baptist chapel of 1806 and a Methodist chapel built in 1867 which are both in regular use.
In the 1840's a large number of the Baptist community were encouraged to emigrate to Australia with their previous Pastor.
The Baptist chapel runs a pre-school play group which goes by the unusual name of the 'Ma-Mites' - very appropriate indeed.

One unusual event took place in the village on Bank Holiday Monday May 7, 2012, when eighty five teddy bears took part in the 'Teddy Olympics' by parachuting from the church tower to raise money for charity. The event resulted in a total of £242.00 being donated.

There are two public houses on the main road, The Dolphin Inn, near the War Memorial and The New Inn. Another public house which went by the name of The Red Lion was being completely gutted and refurbished in 2012 probably in preparation for use as a private residence.

On leaving the village en route towards Brackley there is a sign directing you to the Pudding Pie Cookery school.
Here you can hone your cookery skills and even gain a **Duke of Edinburgh** Award if you are so inclined.

OVERTHORPE

A very short distance to the west of the village is the small hamlet of Overthorpe.

It is a civil parish within Northamptonshire and in 2011 had seventy houses and two hundred and forty two inhabitants many of whom appear to live or work at the Carrdus School based at **Overthorpe Hall**.

I have no doubt that the many scholars can make a lot of noise but during school holidays you can hear a pin drop.

Horton Tomb: Middleton Cheney.

MILTON MALSOR

Four miles south of Northampton
Population: 1801-327   2001 - 713

DOMESDAY BOOK
MIDELTONE/MILDETONE
In the Domesday Book the village was simply known as Middletone - middle farmstead

The first record of this settlement would appear to be in the Domesday Book when there were two manors held by **William Peverel** and **Geoffrey Alselin.**
There was a mill rendering thirty pence per annum and the population included a priest.

In the 12th and 13th centuries one manor was held by the **Malesoures** family and it is from them that the village got its suffix.

In a survey of 1801 the village was referred to as Middleton Malzor. The name was formally changed to Milton Malsor on the 21st July 1960 to avoid complications with about forty other Miltons in the United Kingdom.
There are still two manors – one in Rectory Lane (formerly Plucks Lane) and one known as the Manor House west of the church which dates from the 18th century.

The village is fortunate in that it is located just to the east of the busy Northampton to Towcester road and therefore gets little through traffic although access to the main road is difficult due to the awkwardly placed bends.

Much of the village with the village Green at its centre is now in a Conservation area

There has been a considerable amount of new housing but a number of attractive older ironstone properties with thatched roofs remain.

A 16th century dovecote stands in the garden of the house on the wall of which is a blue plaque indicating that **James Harrington**, author of *'The Commonwealth of Oceana'* 1656 lived here as a young man between 1614-1621.

The Greyhound : Milton Malsor

At the Restoration he was thrown in the Tower because of his strong Republican views and when he died in 1677 he was buried in *St Margaret's* church, Westminster, alongside *Sir Walter Raleigh*

A feature of the village is the unusual tower and spire of the church of the **HOLY CROSS**.
The unbuttressed west tower with battlements and pinnacles is topped with an octagonal lantern above which is a very short crocketed spire.

The oldest parts of the church are the solid round pillars in the north aisle and a late Norman font with original lining.
I particularly like the round Catherine Wheel window at the East end.

As a millennium project a large tapestry was worked featuring village life and this now dominates the wall of the south aisle.

Money is currently being raised to build an extension to include kitchen, cloakroom and meeting room which when completed will be dedicated to *St Helen* reviving the original dedication of the church.

During the 19th century pillow lace was made in almost every cottage and there was even a school where youngsters were taught the craft.

One unusual activity was the manufacture of brass pins in a small factory close to the Baptist chapel one of only three such factories in the County - the others being located at Long Buckby and Hardingstone. The business had closed by 1925.

The Baptist chapel is dated 1827 but there were Baptists in the village at least forty years previously. The chapel, which was built on the site of two cottages, has a baptistry and box pews but the old Methodist chapel built in 1865 is now a private house.

Although not a particularly large village there are two public houses - The Compass and The Greyhound, the latter was once a malt house where *Thomas Cockerill* sold his own home brew. In 1806 he expanded his brewing business and built a brewery next door – the Hope Brewery where beer was brewed for about a hundred years. It has now been converted into offices.

The Greyhound itself with a small pond in the garden was refurbished in 2008 and looks most inviting when travelling along the road to Towcester.

There is still a Primary school a shop, village hall and the Holly House Care Home.

Just outside the village is the Counties Crematorium which was opened and dedicated in July 1939 by the Lord Bishop of Peterborough.

Headlines were made in May 2012 when the wife of a wealthy businessman stabbed herself to death in their £700,000 mansion in the village.

Common Dandelion

MORETON PINKNEY

Eight miles south of Daventry
Population: 1801-420   2001 - 364

DOMESDAY BOOK
MORTONE
The name derives from the Saxon 'mor tun' meaning farm by a marshy place.

The manor of Morton with twenty two households was held by the *de Pinkneys* between 1084 (after the Norman invasion) until 1346 but from my research it would appear that the village did not get the suffix 'Pinkney' until the 16th century.

One member of the family, *Robert*, was a signatory of the Magna Carta in 1215.

The Manor changed hands many times and the last owner of the full Estate was *Lennox Fitzroy*, the *7th Earl of Grafton*.
He married *Ann Balfour* in 1847 and lived at **Wakefield Lodge** near Potterspury but when he died the Estate was broken up.

The road between Northampton and Banbury twists and turns as it goes through the village but it does give the motorist time to have a look at the several small greens and attractive cottages with high pitched roofs and striped brickwork.
A number of wells are visible from the road.

In the 19th century Moreton Pinkney had the reputation of being *'a very rough place'*.
According to the Rector, the *Rev T. Mozley* -
' in no part of England have I seen so primitive a state of society'.

Of particular notoriety were the *Prestidge* family. *John*, his three sons and a nephew were hauled before the Court and as a result two were imprisoned for two years each and the other three were transported for life.
The women, particularly *Laura Prestidge*, seem to have been little better.

Today Moreton Pinkney is such a quiet little village that it is almost impossible to imagine it at the time when it had two railway stations.
To the north was the station on the Stratford on Avon and Midland Junction Railway and to the south on the Great Central Line although this was called Culworth to distinguish one from the other.
Hunting was so important in the area that a special gated crossing was provided near one of the stations for local huntsmen for which the Master of Foxhounds held the key.
Both stations and lines closed in the 1950's.

The school also closed in 1973 after one hundred and fifty years and is now a private residence.
Above the school house porch is a stone marked:-

> *'Deo Gloria 1822'.*

The small Baptist chapel which was built in 1827 was closed in 1987 ending 150 years of non-conformity in the village and has been converted into a private house.

-296-

On entering Moreton Pinkney from Weston the road passes under an iron footbridge.
I always thought that this was provided so that the Lord of the Manor could have a secret romantic liaison with a lady on the other side of the road.

However, on talking to a villager recently I learned that when the Manor House, which was built between 1859-1870, was sold it was divided into apartments and the footbridge was erected so that the tenants could more easily carry their tools across the road to tend their gardens on the other side. I much prefer the first explanation.

During the Second World War the film giant Twentieth Century Fox moved their operations to the Manor for safety.

Almost hidden away from view behind the houses is the church of **ST MARY** the **VIRGIN** which has a simple Norman doorway and west tower dating from the 13th century.

Buried in the church is *Edward Bagshaw* (1662) a member of *Charles I* Parliament.

There is a fragment of an Anglo Saxon cross shaft in the south east corner of the churchyard.

At about 5.00 p.m. on one cold January evening in 1893 the church tower burst into flames.
Local residents tried to douse the fire while a boy was sent to Banbury (ten miles away) for help - no motor cars or telephones in those days.

The fire engine did not arrive until 9.00 p.m. owing to the 'heavy' state of the roads and the firemen were still there the following morning.

Some places are memorable and Moreton Pinkney is one such on account of the fact that one afternoon when enjoying a time of sketching in the churchyard I was suddenly attacked by a swarm of wasps. (I had not noticed that I had parked myself under a tree full of rotting plums).
I unceremoniously fell backwards off my chair and ruefully surveyed the damage both to my sketch and myself.

Originally there were three public houses,
The Crown on Brook Street,The Dun Cow and The Red Lion on Upper Green. The latter was renamed 'Rose of the Shires' after the late *Princess Diana*.
Now there is only the Rose of the Shires which has been closed for a number of years but recently some of the outbuildings have been demolished
The building dates from the 17th century and when I last ate there still had old ceiling beams and other period features.
There are plans for a complete renovation and refurbishment to provide a public bar, coffee lounge and Restaurant.
In addition a row of five terraced houses are to be built in local Northamptonshire stone.
Near the rebuilding site is the village hall but there is no longer a shop or a post office but at Home Farm they are busy producing chemical free chestnut, oyster and shitake mushrooms for sale at local farmers markets.

When I did the walk from Moreton Pinkney across the fields to Canons Ashby and back I was pleasantly surprised with the wealth of butterflies, birds and bees accompanying me on my travels.

MOULTON

Four miles north east of Northampton
Population: 1801-843   2001 - 3388

DOMESDAY BOOK
MOLTONE/MULTONE/MULETONE

In Saxon times mules were a common beast of burden and it has been suggested that the name of the village derives from 'muleton' - a farm where mules are kept, but others believe it could derive from the Old English 'mul' - a stream or 'mola' - a mill, which was mentioned in the Domesday Book.

Moulton Park was first a Carthusian Monastery then a Royal Park known as the '**Kings Park of Northampton**'. It is mentioned separate to the village of Moulton in the Domesday Book.

The present village which promotes itself as the 'home of *William Carey*' lies north east of Northampton and in spite of its close proximity to the town the heart of the village is now a Conservation area and contains the oldest and most attractive properties.

By reason of its size the village centre with its shops, public houses and library gets a lot of traffic and as a result there is now a one way circuit of the area - one of the very few County villages to require such a traffic calming measure.

One of my favourite views is looking down Church Street with the church of
ST PETER and **ST PAUL** at the far end.
The present church built of ironstone dates mostly from the late 13th century and replaced an earlier one which was ruined in 1265 during the Barons War. Some Saxon remains including the shaft of a cross were found nearby.

In 1645 the lead was stripped from the roof and spire by Parliamentary troops to be used, so it is said, to make bullets to be fired at the Battle of Naseby.
Subsequently the spire was removed leaving the 73 foot (23 metres) embattled tower.
Two of the twelve bells are unusual as they are dedicated to *Dr William Carey*, the pioneer missionary who lived and worked in the village.

The new church centre opened in 2000 and plans are now in hand to carry out an upgrade of the interior of the church. Funds are currently being raised to replace the existing pews with comfortable seats, provide better lighting, heating and facilities for serving refreshments

The Methodist chapel which was built in 1835 with steeply pointed windows and a steep gable is now home to the Moulton Theatre Group.
One place of non-conformity which is still in use is the Baptist chapel dating from the mid 17th century named in honour of *William Carey* who was for a time their Pastor.
It is in excellent condition following recent refurbishment and modernization.

Manfield Hall opposite the library was originally a Primitive Methodist chapel built in 1864 and was used as such until the 1920's and then became Manfield House. It now houses the Moulton Evangelical chapel.

MOULTON COLLEGE
The College developed from a Farm School which opened in 1913. I was the first Bursar there in the late 1950's when we only had about sixty full time residential students studying basic animal husbandry, horticulture, poultry, etc. and it was known as the Northamptonshire Institute of Agriculture.

In 1992 it became independent of the Northamptonshire County Council.
Nowadays it has over eight thousand students studying a wide variety of subjects and is one of the largest Specialist colleges in the UK.

Church Street: Moulton

Popular with visitors to fetes and garden parties in the area are the Moulton Morris Men who were founded in 1972 and frequently perform at many local charity events including the Moulton Village Festival which is held in May each year.

The event with its music and dancing, stalls, competitions, exhibitions, etc. regularly attracts thousands of visitors from miles around and raises funds for the church and local charities.

The *Jeyes* family (famous for the invention of the disinfectant which carries the name) lived just west of the village at Holly Lodge which was built in 1861.

The frontage is a copy of the design for the *'Spectacle'* a *Wentworth* folly (see Boughton).

The gateway is a remarkable piece of ironmongery as twelve items of farm implements make up the gates designed by *Philadelphius Jeyes* himself.

They were made by local traction engine builders - *Allchins* - and it is not unusual to see them being photographed.

WILLIAM CAREY 1761-1834

William Carey was born in Pury End, Paulerspury on the 17th August 1761.
Williams's parents, *Elizabeth* and *Edmund* were relatively poor. *Edmund* was a weaver before becoming schoolmaster at a charity school in Paulerspury which *William* attended until the age of twelve.

Originally *William* wanted to become a gardener but had to give up this ambition owing to an allergy.
As a result he found employment as an apprentice shoemaker in Piddington.
It was here that he met *Dorothy Plackett* and they married in Piddington Church on the 10 June 1781.

William's friendship with a fellow apprentice named *John Warr* led him to leave the established church and attend an Independent Meeting House in Hackleton. In 1783 at the age of twenty two he was baptised in the River Nene in Northampton near the present Castle Station.
John Newton and *William Cowper* of Olney were great influences on *William's* early Christian life and it was in the Baptist Church in Olney where *William* was commissioned to be a Minister.

In 1785 *Carey* went on to become Schoolmaster and Pastor at Moulton where he continued to make shoes to supplement his small income. At the same time he started to study languages.
In May of 1792 in Nottingham he preached possibly his most memorable sermon in which he uttered the words which will be forever attributed to him: - *'Expect Great Things from God - Attempt Great Things for God.'*

Within a few months following meetings at *Widow Wallis'* house in Kettering
(now a residential Home for the elderly) he became instrumental in the formation of the
Baptist Missionary Society together with *John Ryland*, *John Sutcliff* and *Andrew Fuller*.
He volunteered to be its first missionary and travelled with his family to India where he died in 1834.

NASEBY

Six miles south west of Market Harborough
Population: 1801-538   2001 – 525

DOMESDAYBOOK
NAVESBERIAE/NAVESBERIE
*Originally the name derived from the Saxon words **Hnaefe** – a personal name and 'burh' - fortified place, but was later altered by the Vikings to **Nafni** - a personal name and 'by' - village.*

William Peverel held the seven hide manor in 1086 when there were twenty one households and a priest indicating some form of early church.

Although the name of Naseby is known nationally by virtue of the important Civil War Battle here in 1645 it is still a small almost remote village of about five hundred inhabitants.

The village stands at six hundred feet on the Northants uplands and it is here that you will find both the sources of the Warwickshire Avon and the Ise, the northern tributary of the River Nene.

The spring in the garden of the Georgian Manor Farm is marked by a large conical iron jug inscribed *'Source of Avon 1822.'*

The village is comprised mostly of red brick cottages built by **Lord Clifton** in the 1870's for his estate workers. He demolished almost all of the old thatched cottages although recently some new houses with thatched roofs have been built and these are gradually blending in with the older properties.

In 1203 **King John** granted the village a Royal Charter to hold a weekly market and the cross was erected opposite the church on what was the Market Place (now called Newlands).
It was a thriving market town in the early Middle Ages although its population declined after the Black Death.

By the 1820's the Cross had been reduced to a stump and **John Fitzgerald**, the Lord of the Manor had it removed to a new site at the junction of the Hazelbech and Harborough roads but owing to the increasing danger there from passing vehicles its shaft and the base were moved again to the Green in 1993 by Naseby Parish Council

The local public house, The Fitzgerald Arms was named after a former Lord of the Manor.
At one time it had a reputation for good food but sadly it was gutted by fire in March 2010 as a result of faulty wiring used for the illegal cultivation of cannabis and the person in charge had his licence revoked.
The building is now in a sorry state and its future is uncertain.
The other public house - The Royal Oak in Church Street is still open for business.

The church of **ALL SAINTS** is in a lovely setting in the village and is quite impressive from the outside. Unfortunately the inside is due for some tender loving care.
The origins of this ancient church which has a Norman font reaches back to the Saxon era although the present building dates back to the 13th century. In the 15th century the tower was raised and a low spire built on which was mounted a large copper ball capable of holding sixty gallons of ale. The present tower and lofty crocketed spire was built in 1860 and the copper ball was saved and can be seen in its church resting place at the west end of the north aisle after spending some years just outside the church door.
It is said that the towers of forty churches can be seen from Naseby tower on a clear day.

Cromwell's table reputedly to be from a public house opposite the church (now Shuckborough House) where the Parliamentary leader supped the evening before the Battle of Naseby was presented to the village by *Lady Annly* in 1909.

Some dispute this claim and say that *Cromwell* had a victory meal at the table after the Battle. Take your pick! If only wood and stones could speak!

The rather elaborate War Memorial featuring a lion (based on a *Landseer* lion from the foot of **Nelsons Column**) was originally planned for the churchyard but now has pride of place on the Green in Newlands.

The village still has a shop and post office and a Primary school where one of my son in law's father was Head Master for many years.

The school was built in 1843 although a schoolroom existed elsewhere from 1811.

Nearby the old Post House has been converted into a Bed and Breakfast Guest House.

A millennium project was the rebuilding of the village hall in 1999 at the highest point of the village.

Naseby Battlefield Monument.

BATTLE OF NASEBY
14th June 1645

After months of skirmishes the rival armies of **King Charles I** and **Prince Rupert of the Rhine** with 10,000 men and the new Model Army with 14,000 men under **Cromwell** and **Sir Thomas Fairfax** met in the fields to the north of the village.

The resulting Battle proved to be a decisive victory for the Parliamentarians and paved the way for a more democratic form of government.

Five thousand prisoners were marched to Northampton and many more were imprisoned in the church.

The King never recovered from this defeat and was eventually executed.

There are two monuments in the parish.

The *Fitzgerald* Monument on the road to Market Harborough was built in 1823 on the site of an old windmill about one mile from the actual battlefield although the plaque states that :-

'the battle was fought on this field'.

The County monument erected in 1936 in a fenced enclosure in a field on the way to Sibbertoft is said to mark the spot from which *Cromwell* led his charge.

This too is thought to be in the wrong place.

Interestingly I am informed that the parish records make no reference to the Battle of Naseby.

It is quite remarkable that until recently there was very little for the visitor to see at the site of one of the most important dates in English history unlike, for example at Bosworth Field.

With the fairly recent formation of the Naseby Battlefield Project there are some signs of rectifying the omission.

Informative panels and view points with car parking have already appeared at some important locations and work has already started to prepare and build a three million pound museum and visitor centre at Mill Hill to the north of Naseby which it is hoped will attract 25,000 people a year.

To the great regret of many people plans are afoot to erect six wind turbines up to 415 feet high next to the Battlefield site.

NASSINGTON

Five miles north east of Oundle
Population: 1801-441   2001 - 670

DOMESDAY BOOK
NASSINTONE

The name derives from three Saxon words, 'naess' – headland – 'inga' - people of, and 'tun' - farmstead.
i.e. farm of the headland dwellers.

Remains of Roman occupation and early iron workings have been found nearby.

An archaeological dig in 1942 near the River Nene revealed parts of an old Anglo Saxon cemetery with about fifty graves, grave goods, jewellery and drinking cups (some examples are in the Peterborough museum).

One skeleton was said to be nearly seven feet long.

It was a Royal village with its own church in Saxon times and remained in the hands of the Crown many years after the Norman Conquest.

King Canute is said to have visited his manor here sometime after 1017.

The Domesday Book records the existence of twenty six households, a priest and two mills rendering thirty shillings and eight pence per annum.

Although this is a remote corner of the County and somewhat off the beaten track it is nevertheless quite a large settlement which was of great importance in medieval times.

The village is today located on a small promontory above the River Nene higher up the hill than it was in Saxon times and is famous for its picturesque grouping of quintessentially English houses and church which are built of the local mellow grey limestone. The village is well worth a visit.

One building in the main street which I consider to look out of place in this delightful setting is the three storey Walnut House - the third storey incorporating a hipped roof.

Dominating the main street is the lovely church of **ST MARY** and **ALL SAINTS** which replaced an earlier church but still has a partly Saxon nave and a portion of a Saxon cross believed to date from the 10th century which is on view.

The west tower is topped with a magnificent crocketed spire which was struck by lightning on the 14th May 1905 necessitating major repairs.

As in so many churches during the time of *Cromwell* the stained glass and wall paintings suffered badly but some murals at the northern end and above the chancel arch have been uncovered but not restored although the church was restored in 1885.

Modern seating has now replaced the old fashioned and uncomfortable pews.

In the past there was employment locally in agriculture, brickmaking, gravel extraction and ironstone quarrying but nowadays many of the villagers have to travel further afield for work.

There is still a shop and post office, a butcher and a wine shop but the former Methodist chapel of 1875 is now in commercial use and the old schoolroom is now the village hall but there still seems to be a good community spirit.

The present school with a lovely green cupula dates from 1894 although it has since been enlarged.

With the closure of the Congregational chapel of 1839 it has been converted into an attractive private residence. Nearby is The Queens Head Hotel and Restaurant with an inviting picnic area alongside the River Nene to the rear.

Another public house still open for business is the white painted and listed 17th century Black Horse which boasts a fireplace from Fotheringhay Castle but other public houses such as The Three Horseshoes, The Plough and The Boat have all closed.

Nassington once had a station on the branch line between Yarwell junction and Seaton but in October 1912 it suffered a devastating fire which completely destroyed one side.
Had it not been for the prompt arrival of
Colonel Proby's private steam fire engine from Elton Hall, it is likely that the whole of the building would have been reduced to ashes.
Like so many villages the station and line have closed.

I refer to Sulehay under the village of Yarwell but I understand that there is traditionally a grudge stemming back to the 19th century between Nassington and Yarwell concerning extra parochial areas of New and Old Sulehay which lies close to both villages.
I am not taking sides on this dispute.

PREBENDAL MANOR

By the early 12th century the manor and its lands were held by the Bishop of Lincoln who chose Nassington as a base for a Prebendal Manor of the Diocese of Lincoln which would exercise the ecclesiastical authority over the surrounding villages for the next six hundred years.

The present Manor with its fine square 15th century dovecote is a 13th century Grade I listed building, the oldest Manor House in Northamptonshire and one of the longest continually occupied houses in the country.
It is claimed to be the site of the manor of **King Canute.**

The property was sold in 1875 by the Ecclesiastical Commission to the **Earl of Carysfoot** who rented it out to local farmers. After being sold again in 1968 it was extensively restored and renovated.

Although now in private hands the House with its dovecote, Tithe Barn Museum and medieval fish ponds is open most Sunday and Wednesday afternoons in the summer and on other occasions for special events.

DF BLUNT
AUG 2010

Prebendal Manor. Nassington

NETHER HEYFORD

Six miles west of Northampton
Population: 1801- 386   2001 - 1584

DOMESDAY BOOK
HEIFORDE/HAIFORD

In medieval times there was just one settlement here known as Haiford - a possible derivation being 'a ford over which hay was carried'. As the two settlements developed they were distinguished by different descriptions and eventually settled for Upper & Lower (Nether) Heyford.

The village of Nether Heyford is situated west of Northampton in the valley of the River Nene and is bordered by the Grand Union Canal.
Not surprisingly a mill was recorded here in the Domesday Book rendering sixteen shillings per annum.

There has been quite rapid expansion in recent years due to better travel and the close proximity to Junction 16 of the M1.

Street names can often give a clue as to former buildings or uses. Furnace Lane is no exception as it serves as a reminder of the former existence of three blast furnaces which produced iron from local ironstone between 1857 and 1891.
Remains are still to be seen between the canal and the railway and the entrance house still exists.

This is a delightful little village and a particular treasure is the large five acre village Green which is one of the largest in the country. Until 1924 the right to graze cattle here was much sought after.

Overlooking the Green is the village hall which opened in May 1960 and is the centre of activities of all kinds and for all ages and the *Bliss* charity school. This was founded for the two villages in 1673 at a cost of £400 under the will of *William Bliss*, a wine merchant and former resident.
It was to be free for all children in the two villages but interestingly was also available free to any child with the family name living within five miles.
There is a large *Bliss* Family History Society with many members in the USA.

The school was rebuilt in 1880 in the Victorian style and with the new extension at the rear still educates younger children.

It is a pity that more of the old buildings were not preserved as there is now a motley collection of properties surveying this lovely scene.

There are however several attractive period houses in Church Street which winds round from the church to the Rectory.

Villagers still have a shop, a baker, a hairstylist and two public houses, The Foresters Arms on the Green and the Grade II listed Olde Sun Inn, a 17th century public house with various nooks and crannies and a fascinating collection of memorabilia.

The Baptist church overlooking the Green was built in 1826 and is still in use but the old Primitive Methodist chapel is now a private residence.

Much of the church of **ST PETER** and **ST PAUL** dates from the 13th century in the Decorative style including the west tower.
The interior is quite dark but what first caught my eye were the modern light coloured pews which seemed to me to be quite out of place.
Look out for the carved corbels of stone heads, shields and angels in the roof of the aisles.
In the north east corner of the chancel, covered with a rug, is an old brass depicting *Sir William Mauntell*, Lord of the Manor and his wife holding hands - how often is this seen on an ancient brass plate? *Sir William* fought in the War of the Roses and died in 1487.

There is a magnificent Tudor monument in brightly painted alabaster on the south aisle of the church to **Sir Francis Morgan**, Judge of the Kings Bench who is said to have pronounced sentence of death on **Lady Jane Grey**, (the Nine Days Queen) but who, in great torment, took his own life shortly after with the lament –

*'Take away the **Lady Jane** from me'.*

The Manor House of the **Mauntells** and the **Morgans** was in Upper Heyford but by the end of the Civil War was in decay and uninhabited.
The vast Estate was sold and split up.
The present Manor House is thought to have been built by **William**, the **3rd Marquis of Powys** about 1740 using stone from the old house.
In the early 1900's it was the home of the brother of **Philadelphus Jeyes** of Northampton.

During the Second World War soldiers were billeted at the Manor and there was a communications room for use between Bletchley Park and Weedon. In 1975 the land was sold for housing development and the house converted into residential apartments.

The area near the old Roman Watling Street is rich in Romano British history.
For the past sixteen years archaeologists and students have been excavating a site on a hillside overlooking the Upper Nene valley just to the south west of the village.

Finds have included a villa with twenty to thirty rooms located between two roundhouses which are thought to date from the 2nd century together with brooches, rings, and fragments of glass vessels and the figure of a gladiator.
Unfortunately the site is on private land and not open to the public except by prior arrangement.

The Nene Way, a long distance footpath along the River Nene passes through the centre of the village

UPPER HEYFORD

DOMESDAY BOOK
ALTERA HAIFORD

Although Upper Heyford has a specific mention in the Domesday Book it was valued with the manor in Lower Heyford.

Today it consists of just a few houses and buildings either side of the A45 Northampton to Daventry road.

Bliss Charity School: Nether Heyford

NEWBOTTLE

Four miles west of Brackley
Population figures included under Charlton.

DOMESDAY BOOK
NIWEBOTLE
The name derives from two words
'niwe' and 'bool' meaning new building.

The small hamlet of Newbottle stands close to the Oxfordshire border and is one of Northamptonshire's many shrunken villages now consisting of little more than the church, the Rectory, the Manor House, a large stone dovecote, a couple of cottages and a few farm buildings.

At the time of the Domesday Book when it was recorded as a single manor the land was owned by *Hugh de Grandmesnil* and had thirty one households and a Knight, indicating a population in the region of about a hundred and twenty.
It was quite a large and prosperous community although the population figures almost certainly included nearby Charlton.

In 1301 there were twenty three taxpayers whereas Kings Sutton (now with a population of over 2,000) had just forty one.
In 1488 *Lord Grey* owned the Manor, destroyed six houses, evicted thirty eight people and enclosed three hundred acres as pasture for 1,000 sheep and the depopulation had begun.

Even the Manor House which probably dates from the time of *Henry VIII* but was added to in later years is much smaller than its predecessor.
The original House was severely damaged by a fire in 1795 following which the remains were converted into the present property.

All the houses in Newbottle including the Grade II* listed Manor House and a number of properties in nearby Charlton are owned by the Newbottle Estate which covers about 1,400 acres and includes a farm with arable land and Aberdeen Angus cattle.
Brackley Butchers is owned by the Estate and is an exclusive outlet for the beef produced.

The church of **ST JAMES** was started by the Normans and still has a Norman font.
Apart from the west tower the church was rebuilt in the 14th century and contains a lovely decorated rood screen and an East window in memory of *Lady Cartwright* who was buried at Aynho in 1892 and whose family once owned the Estate.
The church was re-roofed as recently as 1984.

The churchyard is famous for its many varieties of lichen and for its mass of snowdrops in the spring.

Newbottle Woods nearby is a popular place for walkers, cyclists and horse riders.

Newbottle, together with its near neighbour Charlton are usually regarded as one unit, Newbottle has the church but Charlton seems to have everything else.

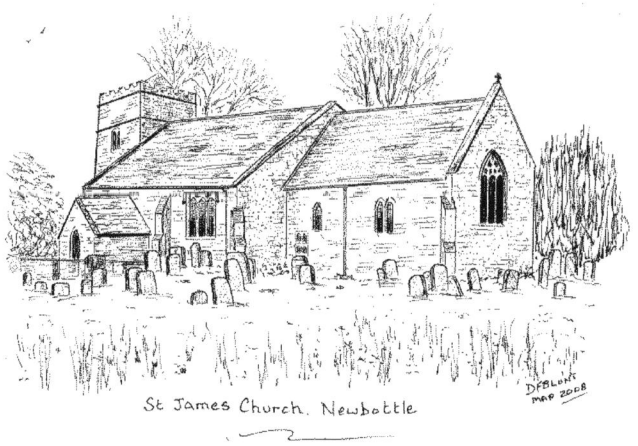

St James Church, Newbottle

Newnham

Two miles south of Daventry
Population: 1801-437   2001 - 608

*The name simply means new homestead
from the old English – 'ham'.*

This is a charming village with a number of little Greens and some lovely thatched cottages.
It attracts many visitors as the Nene Way which for the most part follows the river deviates slightly at Newnham to run through the village.

In researching for this book I have come across the name **Chelverdescote** a number of times although the actual location of this lost village appears to be unknown. There is a body of opinion which suggests that Newnham which is not mentioned in the Domesday Book is in fact **Chelverdescote** by a different name. Others believe that it was located on the border of Fawsley and Badby parishes.
Perhaps later discoveries will solve this dilemma.

The church of **ST MICHAEL** and **ALL ANGELS** was formerly a chapel of the parent church at Badby both of which were owned by the Abbey of Evesham until the Reformation so perhaps the manor of Badby also contained Newnham when the Survey was carried out.

The 15th century tower porch open on three sides is unique in Northamptonshire and very unusual elsewhere. It must have been a cold place for the bell ringers in the past.
The Victorians considered the tower to be in need of strengthening and installed large cast iron tie rods and anchor plates.

The pulpit dates from the 18th century but above it is a 15th century brass plate to the memory of *Letitia Catesby* which was placed there for safety when that of her second husband *Robert Catesby* who died in 1467 was stolen.

The Romer Arms : Newnham

The school which was once situated alongside the church has been relocated and the old school is now used as the village hall.
On a recent visit the only shop was empty and displaying a sign indicating that it was closed.
I wonder if it will ever re-open?
The chapel with a date stone of 1909 is now a private residence.

Established by the *Marriott* family of Newnham House over two hundred years ago is **The Nuttery**, 2.3 acres of hazel coppice underplanted with snowdrops and daffodils. It is open to the public and is in the care of the Woodland Trust.

Newnham Hall a quarter of a mile north east of the village dates from 1820 and is set in one hundred and twenty acres of parkland.
In 1898 the Hall was owned by *Romer Williams* after whom the local public house is named. He kindly offered to finance the rebuilding scheme when the previous public house on the site,
The Baker's Arms burned down and his Coat of Arms is depicted on the pub sign.

Outside what was once The New Inn which is now a private residence is an old lamp standard on which is a plaque celebrating the centenary in 2008 of the Newnham Hill Climb which started from that point.

At the summit of Newnham Hill is a windmill which has stood here since 1660 and has recently been repaired and reconstructed.

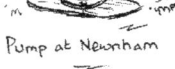

Pump at Newnham

NEWTON BROMSWOLD

Three miles east of Rushden
Population: 1801-101   2001 - 62

DOMESDAY BOOK
NIWETONE
In Saxon times this was simply 'newetone' - new farm. Bromswold first appeared in 1605 - it being the name given to a stretch of woodland on the border of Northamptonshire and Huntingdonshire.

At the time of the Domesday Book there appears to have been two manors - one in Northamptonshire and the other in Bedfordshire. Subsequent boundary changes have placed the whole parish within Northamptonshire. Before 1066 the Northamptonshire manor was held by *Alwin* on behalf of the Lord of the Manor, *Burgred*. After the Conquest it was granted to one of the King's chief ministers - *Geoffrey de Mowbray*, *Bishop of Coutances.* He installed one of his stewards into the holding.

Newton Bromswold is today one of the County's smallest villages and being so tiny it is surprising to find that the village still has a public house, The Swan, which was rebuilt after a fire in 1930.
However there is no longer a school or a shop. The village claims association with the American family of *Washington* by virtue of the fact that one of the grandchildren of the owner of the Manor in the 17th century (*Needham Langhorne*) married into the *Washington* family.
The little church of **ST PETER** completed in 1272 has a Decorative and Perpendicular style west tower and spire. It is most unusual in such a small church to find that there are six stone seats for priests, one of which seems to have doubled up as a piscina. I have not been able to establish the reason for this.

The north window of the north aisle which features a mitred saint thought to be *St Hugh* is considered to have some of the finest medieval glass in the Midlands.
The only glass similar to this is at All Souls College, Oxford.
In the churchyard there is the base of the old village cross which now serves as a dog bowl.

NEWTON IN THE WILLOWS

Four miles north of Kettering
Population: 1801-104   2001 - inc in Little Oakley figures

DOMESDAY BOOK
NEUTONE/NEWETONE
The name simply implies this was a new town or new settlement.

Three manors are recorded in the Domesday Book one of which was likely to be Little Newton

The village is accessed down a 'no through road' about a mile west of Geddington.
Originally there were two villages, Great and Little Newton each having its own chapel.
In 1449 they were united but both chapels remained in use until **ST LEONARDS**
at Great Newton fell into decay.
All traces have now disappeared and the manor barn now stands on the site.

.... NEWTON IN THE WILLOWS

The other church dedicated to **ST FAITH** stands alone in the tranquil meadows and appears cut off from the outside world.

It is a 14th century building with a 15th century tower and broached spire.

Last used for worship in 1958 it was declared redundant in 1971 when it was acquired by a Trust and is now used as a Field Study Centre.

The East window has been blocked up presumably to accommodate the change of use.

The ancient monuments and memorials were moved to the nearby church in Geddington.

Newton has seen many changes and more than its fair share of turmoil but today it is a sleepy backwater but nevertheless well worth a visit.

In the late 16th or early 17th century the powerful *Tresham* family built a mansion complete with dovecote in Little Newton and depopulated the village in preference for sheep.

They adopted the church for personal use of family and Estate workers.

What few houses remain are modern and look prosperous.

NEWTON DOVECOTE

The dovecote standing in a field north east of the church is thought to have been built about 1593 and is the only relic of the former mansion of the *Treshams*.

It is rectangular in shape and unusual in size measuring 53'9' x 23'7" and the roof ridge about 35' and with the familiar trefoil emblem is evidence of *Treshams* ownership.

Built of limestone under a roof of Collyweston slate it is said to be the largest in Britain and has nests for about 2000 nesting pairs – an enormous number considering the population at the time. I wonder what the family had for dinner!

This is certainly the largest dovecote I have ever seen and I am not surprised to learn that it is Grade I listed.

The Newton peasants who were normally law abiding citizens were angry about the loss of their land and livelihood. On the 8th June 1607 about a thousand of them from the area (known as **Levellers**) gathered under *John Reynolds* who called himself *Captain Pouch.*

He had a leather pouch which followers thought contained either money to pay them or a magic charm that would protect everyone that followed him but when he was captured all the pouch contained was a few crumbs of green cheese.

Unfortunately the Levellers suffered brutal retaliation and some of the leaders were hung, drawn and quartered.

Outside the churchyard is a memorial stone set up in 2008 to mark the 400th Anniversary of the Midland Revolt.

I thought it to be an unusual place to site such a stone.

Surely it should be within the churchyard particularly bearing in mind that during the rebellion forty peasants were killed here and others imprisoned in the church prior to facing the courts.

The Mansion passed through various hands until purchased by the *Montagu* family in 1715.

Within a short time the House was demolished and the gardens abandoned.

In recent years a new venture has been established close to the village with separate access from the Geddington road. Here there is a large car park with a farm shop, gift shop, children's play area and an excellent buttery serving hot and cold drinks snacks and hot meals. It is just the place for a little outing or for refreshment whilst walking in the surrounding countryside.

Elizabethan Dovecot : Newton in the Willows

Northampton

Population 2001 Town 189474

DOMESDAY BOOK
HANTONE/NORTHANTONE
*The name comes from the Old English and appears to imply that this was a Home Farm
a place of importance to the surrounding area.
The prefix was added about the time of the Domesday Book
due to the growing importance of the other Hantone – the modern Southampton.*

I have lived and worked in Northampton all my life and the town has had a very great influence on my comings and goings and life's experiences.

Much could, and has been, written about my home town but for the purpose of this book I have decided for the most part to concentrate on those places and areas which have most concerned or interested me.

Its history is thought to date back to at least the 6th century and appears to have grown in importance by the 8th century although to the south of the town at Hunsbury Hill is the site of an Iron Age hill fort which is now a Scheduled Ancient Monument.

At the time of the Domesday Book the town had a market and a population of about fifteen hundred living in about three hundred houses which was quite a reasonable size in those days. Borough status was granted in 1189 by *King Richard I.*

The town became significant when the Normans under *Simon de Senlis, 1st Earl of Northampton* built town walls and a Castle which stood in the area now occupied by the Railway Station - it was until quite recently called Castle Station to distinguish it from Bridge Street and St John's stations which no longer exist.

The Castle was a popular place for royalty drawn to the area for hunting.
It is recorded that *King John* stayed there about thirty times and moved the Treasury to Northampton Castle in 1205.

The town prospered, Northampton became the third largest town in the country and was home to Parliament for two hundred years.

A University was established in 1261 by scholars from the University of Cambridge. It flourished briefly but was dissolved by *Henry III* in 1265 as it was thought to pose a threat to the University of Oxford. The town had to wait more than eight hundred years for its present University.

In 1164 the Castle experienced what one modern historian has called one of the most dramatic and revealing encounters in medieval history when *Henry II* and *Thomas á Becket,* Archbishop of Canterbury, who were once good friends, faced each other concerning vital matters of church and state. The discussion did not go well and *Thomas* whilst resting at the nearby Priory of St Andrew decided to flee to France dressed as a humble priest but not until he had taken a drink, so the story goes, from the well alongside *Becket's* Park and known as *Becket's Well* to this day.
The present well was rebuilt in 1845 on the site.

Beckets Well: Northampton

The Castle declined and by the 14th century there were reports that many parts of the town were in ruin. The town also suffered from the Black Death 1348 -1350 and lost almost half of its population.

In 1662 the town walls and Castle were slighted on the orders of *Charles II* because of the support given to the Roundheads during the Civil War but enough of the Castle was left to allow it to be used as a gate and a Court.
Further demolition came as a result of the building of the railway and station in 1879.
Eventually what was left was removed and all that remains of the once great fortress is a postern gate erected in a wall near the station with an informative plaque.

To the south of the town centre was the Abbey of Mary De-La-Pre (St Mary in the Meadow) one of only two Cluniac nunneries in England which dated back to 1145 and was founded by *Simon de Senlis* the second *Earl of Northampton.*

On two occasions the Abbey played a role in national events.

Following the death of *Queen Eleanor of Castile*, wife of *Edward I* at Harby in Nottinghamshire on the 28th November 1290 her body was conveyed in solemn procession to London.

One of the stops along the way was Delapre Abbey where the Queen's body remained whilst the King lodged at nearby Northampton Castle.

The procession then continued south towards London halting at the top of the hill so that a place could be set aside for the location of a magnificent stone monument, one of the twelve crosses commissioned by *Edward* to commemorate his wife and her final journey.

It is a fine monument although regrettably not in its original state - the top having been lost sometime before the 2nd Battle of Northampton during the War of the Roses.

On the 10th July 1460 a Yorkist (*Edward IV*) army led by the *Earl of Warwick* approached from the south and was met by the Lancastrian *King Henry VI* and his army encampment.

Watched by the Archbishop of Canterbury and the Bishop of London from the safety of the *'headless cross'* - *Queen Eleanor's* Cross - the battle took place during the afternoon in the water meadows beside the River Nene near to the Abbey and resulted in a swift and disastrous defeat for the Lancastrians.

In 1538 *Henry VIII* dissolved the Monasteries and Abbeys in England and Delapre and its lands were bought by the *Tate* family.
Over the next two hundred years they transformed the former Abbey into a comfortable country house and Estate.
In 1764 the Estate was bought by the *Bouverie* family in whose hands it remained until 1946 when it was sold to the Northampton Corporation (now Northampton Borough Council).

The Abbey housed the Northamptonshire Records Office until its move to Wootton Hall in 1991.
At the moment part of the remaining buildings are being used as a tea room operated by the Friends of Delapre Abbey and some restoration is being carried out on the fabric.
The future of the Abbey is subject to ongoing discussion and fund raising but the restored gardens are well worth a visit.

Northampton was one of the first towns to establish a Hospital with the founding of the Hospital of St John in Bridge Street although the exact date of foundation and the name of the founder is uncertain.

St John's Hospital · Northampton.

The little chapel of *St John* still stands and is currently in use as a restaurant.

Other religious establishments in the town included St Andrews Priory founded by *Simon de Senlis.*

The most prominent and most central church in the town is **ALL SAINTS** which acts as a traffic island just off the Market Square.

The medieval church except for the west tower and the crypt was largely destroyed in the Great Fire of Northampton on the 20th September 1675, when over six hundred houses in the town were also burnt down.

The Welsh House of 1595 on the Market Square with a Welsh inscription above the door is one of the few buildings which escaped the fire.

The church was rebuilt almost immediately and is regarded by many as the finest example of church architecture of the period outside of London.

The lovely little green topped cupula was added in the 18th century. Above the portico is a statue of *Charles II* in Roman toga and full bottomed wig.

He provided a thousand tons of timber from the royal forest of Whittlebury to help in the rebuilding and remitted the payment of chimney money for seven years.

A statue was erected in gratitude and annually on the 29th May - Oak Apple Day - it is garlanded with oak leaves (a reminder of the time when *Charles I* was fleeing from defeat at Worcester in 1650 and hid in an oak tree).

The portico with its Ionic columns is said to be the place where *John Clare*, the great Northamptonshire poet used to sit and work when allowed out of the asylum.

The church had a lucky escape on the night of 15th July 1941 when a Stirling bomber crashed at the top of Gold Street.

The only civilian casualty was a cyclist who was blown off his bike and broke a leg.

The crew bailed out safely except the pilot whose parachute failed to open and his body was found on the Racecourse.

It is a fine church and is used for civic ceremonies, Remembrance Day parades, etc. and has a popular coffee shop.

During the last few years and in an attempt to make the area more attractive the local council have had laid a Mediterranean type Piazza in front of the portico. I think it makes the area more attractive although many consider it to be a waste of money.

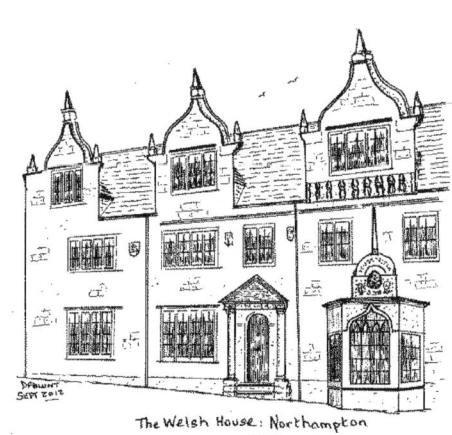

The Welsh House : Northampton

Another fine building is the nearby Grade I listed Sessions House. It was built in 1678 after the Great Fire as the County Assize Court. It was also used four times a year for Quarter Sessions.

When the Court moved in 1993 the building remained empty until 2010 when a new Visitor Centre was opened. The Court Rooms and the old prison cells and dock can still be seen by visitors.

Possibly the most important church historically is the Grade I listed **HOLY SEPULCHRE**, affectionally known locally as 'St Seps' in Sheep Street. My mother and father married there on the 3rd August 1929.

This round church was founded about 1110 by *Simon de Senlis, Earl of Northampton* who took part in the First Crusade to the Holy Land.

Churches of this type were favoured by the Knights Templar as they were intended to be a copy of the church in Jerusalem.

This is the oldest building in the town, survived the Great Fire of 1675 and is the largest and best preserved of the four remaining round churches in the country but this is the only one of the four not built by either the Knights Templar or Hospitallers.

Later in the 12th century *Simon* gave the church to St Andrews Priory. 'Seps' is also known as the 'Soldiers Church' and the Regimental Chapel to the Northamptonshire Regiment and its successors has recently been restored.

My favourite church is **ST PETERS** close to Castle Station.

Like St Sepulchres church it was built by *Simon de Senlis* in the 12th century.

Archaeological excavations over the years revealed that in Saxon times this site was of great importance and the location of an earlier Saxon church.

The present church is almost entirely Norman and is considered by many people, including myself, to be one of the finest examples of Norman architecture in the country.

The arcade was shortened at the west end when the tower collapsed and was rebuilt in the 17th century.

The Sessions House : Northampton 1676.

Although no longer used for regular worship it is carefully maintained by the Churches Conservation Trust and often houses concerts, etc. to raise funds for its preservation.

It is thought to be the last resting place of **St Ragener,** Northampton's forgotten saint who was killed in 870 at the Battle of Hoxne between *Edmund*, King of East Anglia and marauding Vikings.

St Peters Church. Northampton

Two other town churches deserve mention.
Near the General Hospital is the cruciform church of **ST GILES** with a central Norman tower although this was rebuilt following its collapse during a storm in 1613.
The Norman west doorway is a fine reconstruction.

Of much more recent date and standing on high ground near the Racecourse with a magnificent 170ft tall spire is the 19th century church dedicated to **ST MATTHEW** which was designed by the eminent architect *Matthew Holding*.

The church attracts many visitors to view two famous pieces of modern art namely the
Henry Moore sculpture - *'Madonna and Child'*
and the *Graham Sutherland* portrayal of
The Crucifixion. This was unveiled in 1946 and is reminiscent of the artist's memorable tapestry of *'Christ in Glory'* in Coventry Cathedral.

Unfortunately during my lifetime I have seen a number of churches demolished including **ST PAULS** in Semilong, **ST ANDREWS** at the bottom of Regent Street and **ST EDMUNDS** in Wellingborough Road.
On the opposite side of the road is the former Workhouse built by *Sir George Gilbert Scott* in the classical style in 1837. Most of the building has now been demolished but the façade is currently preserved for incorporation into a new development.

Many non-conformist chapels have been lost including Princes Street Baptist, Gold Street and Regent Square Methodist and the Mayorhold Mission where my parents used to worship.

The five 'village' churches in the town, Abington, Kingsthorpe, Weston Favell, Duston and Dallington have all now been encompassed by the ever increasing town suburbs but they are still worthy of merit.

The most impressive of the five in my view is the church of **ST JOHN** the **BAPTIST** in Kingsthorpe with its fine west tower dating back to the 14th century and recessed spire.

The Weston Favell church of **ST PETER** has evidence of Norman work including the entrance doorway and the lower part of the tower.
It once had a spire but this was destroyed by lightning in 1726.

The Duston church of **ST LUKE** with its central tower is a beautiful building with strong evidence of Early English and Gothic architecture.
I particularly like the piece of modern art entitled the *'Dancing Madonna'*.

The Dallington church of **ST MARY** was built in the 12th to 14th century. The *Raynsford* Chapel was added in 1679 in the Gothic style and contains memorials to the *Raynsford* family who had Dallington Hall built in the 18th century.

The best location must go to the church of **ST PETER** and **ST PAUL** which stands within the grounds of Abington Park alongside a large house which was once part of Abington Manor.

Schools in the town have also changed although the three schools I attended are all still used for educational purposes. My first school was St Georges in St George Street before I moved on to Kingsthorpe Grove Infants and then Junior school. After success at the 11+ examination I moved on to the Northampton Grammar school in Billing Road. That school has changed out of all recognition and is no longer a Grammar school but still has a very good reputation.

As a youngster, apart from the Church Youth Club and with no TV, the cinema was one of the few places to go in an evening and there was plenty of choice.
Those holding fond memories include the Coliseum in Kingsthorpe Hollow, Cinema de Luxe in Campbell Street and the Temperance Hall in Newlands all of which have been demolished.
Of those still standing the Picturedrome is now a Pub, the Essoldo in Grove Road has residential apartments, the Ritz is a Methodist church and the Savoy on Abington Square is the home of the religious group known as the Jesus People.

Fortunately the delightful little Victorian Theatre in Guildhall Road has survived but the grand New Theatre in Abington Street was demolished in about 1960 at a time when our heritage was not considered to be particularly important.

Opposite was the long frontage of the school of Notre Dame which also should have been saved from demolition. The school was founded by two sisters in the mid 19th century and was used until 1975. Tucked away behind the present row of shops is a tiny nuns cemetery. Stories are told of nuns coming back to the area after dark.

It was towards Abington Street that thousands of youngsters gravitated after church on a Sunday evening in the 40's and 50's to join in the '**Bunny Run**'. It was an opportunity to meet old friends and make new ones and many relationships and marriages can be traced back to those evenings.

In those days Abington Street had two way traffic and got very crowded.
It is now pedestrianised and in 1986 was adorned with the 'Cobblers Last' a twelve foot high bronze statue by *Graham Ibberstone* recording the main industry of the town with two children symbolising the town's regeneration.
Another statue in Abington Street commemorates the life of one of the scientists who discovered the double helix structure of DNA, *Francis Crick*, who was born in the town and with the help of American *James Watson* unlocked the key of life in 1953.

Apart from these two examples of modern art the town is almost bereft of statues apart from those on the façade of the Town Hall.

One you cannot miss as you travel through Abington Square is that to *Charles Bradlaugh* who was MP for Northampton between 1880-1891 and was imprisoned in a cell beneath Big Ben at Westminster for refusing to take the oath of allegiance to the Queen.

In my view there have been many other people associated with the town who better deserve recognition.
These include *Malcolm Arnold* who was born here in 1921 and composed the film score for the 'Bridge Over the River Kwai' in 1958 and has an Academy named after him in Northampton.

Cobblers Last
Abington Street.

Margaret Bondfield born in the town in 1873 went on to become the first woman Cabinet Minister in the UK.

Joan Hickson (well known for her TV and film role of Miss Marple) was born in Kingsthorpe and *Philip Doddridge* although born in London in 1723 was the Pastor of the Independent Congregation at what is now called Doddridge United Reformed Church for twenty two years and wrote numerous books and hymns and established an Academy in Sheep Street,

Public houses as watering holes have never appealed to me although I do like to look at old stone properties and admire their architectural beauty.
Those worthy of a visit in my view include The Wheatsheaf in Dallington village, The Cock Hotel in Kingsthorpe, The Trumpet at Weston Favell and The Squirrels at Duston - all originally village public houses before the rapid expansion of Northampton.

The general lay out of the main roads through the town has changed very little with Gold Street, the Drapery, Mercers Row, the Horsemarket, Sheep Street and Derngate being constant reminders of the town's history.

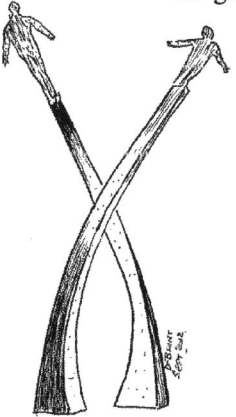

D.N.A. Sculpture
Abington Street.

One feature of the town which deserves special mention and over the years has been an important place in the life of the town is the Market Square which was described by the author **John Morton** in 1712 as 'the finest in England, a fair, spacious and open space.'

Unfortunately 'new development' in the 1960's and 1970's meant the loss of many old buildings including the lovely old Emporium Arcade and the Peacock Hotel, both of which should have been saved.
Also gone is the fountain which stood at the heart of the market until being demolished in 1962.
It certainly had a lot more appeal than the water jets that have recently been installed as part of a modernisation project which have been having problems ever since.

Did **John Betjeman** have Northampton in mind when he wrote:-

'I do some mild developing.
The sort of place I need
is a quiet country market town
that's rather run to seed.
A luncheon and a drink or two,
a little savoir faire
I fix the Planning Officer,
the Town Clerk and the Mayor.'

In my youth the market was filled with stalls on a Wednesday and Saturday and people would flock there from miles around. On other days it was used as a giant car park. Nowadays the market is half its size and is usually fairly quiet although efforts are being made to bring it back to life.

The Gothic Town Hall in St Giles Square which dates back to 1864 with its modern extension is a fine building. The façade is richly decorated and contains in pictures a wealth of information about the town from the trial of **Thomas á Becket** in 1164, the foundation of Northampton Grammar school in 1541, the Great Fire of Northampton in 1675 not to mention statues of monarchs who have visited the town - **Queen Elizabeth I** in 1564, **Charles I** in 1634 and **Queen Victoria** in 1844.

I am pleased that the lovely old Becket and Sargeant School in a narrow road off Gold Street has so far managed to escape the bulldozers.
The school was founded in 1738 for thirty girls who used to attend a special service in All Saints Church wearing their distinctive blue dresses.

Northampton is fortunate that it possesses a good number of open spaces. The largest is the one hundred and eighteen acre Racecourse which in spite of its name no longer stages horse racing.
In its heyday a tavern known as the Kingsley Park Hotel was built to cater for the racing fraternity but shortly afterwards racing stopped following the death of a spectator and in 1904 the tavern became known as The White Elephant - a name by which it is still known today despite attempts to change it.
Opposite the White Elephant crowds used to witness public hangings between 1715-1818 including members of the notorious Culworth Gang (see page 135).

Of the other open spaces, Abington Park is very popular particularly in summer when a band can often be heard playing in the Bandstand on a Sunday afternoon.
The Park was given to the town by **Lady Wantage** in 1892 and opened to the public in 1897.

Within the park is the Manor House (sometimes referred to as an Abbey) which was for some time the home of **Susannah**, favourite daughter of **William Shakespeare** who died in 1670 and is buried in the church.
The building now houses a museum.

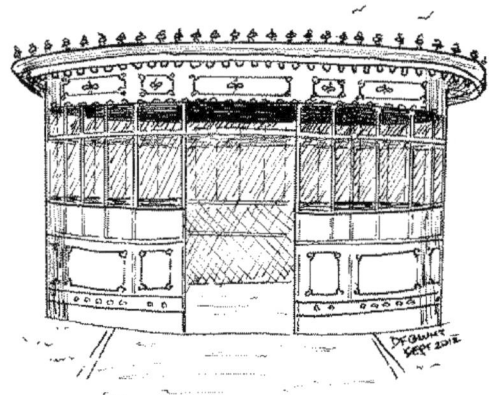

Victorian Tram Shelter: Cock Hotel.

Victoria Park has recently received a makeover with the establishment of a new marina on the River Nene. Plans are in hand to add additional facilities including shops and a restaurant.

With the expansion of the town in the 19th century transport was needed to enable citizens to travel from home to work and for leisure. This arrived in 1881 in the form of a three foot, six inch gauge horse tramway which operated between the Town Centre, the Kingsley Park Hotel, St James and Kingsthorpe. The horses were replaced by the electric tram in 1904 when thousands flocked to the streets to witness the opening. By 1914 there were nearly six and a half miles of track.

By 1933 it had all gone in favour of motor buses but a few reminders of the era of the tram still exist in the form of tram shelters in various locations. The one opposite the Cock Hotel in Kingsthorpe has recently been repainted although I must admit I don't like the pink colour - I am sure that the original tramcars must have been deeper in colour.

For many years talks have taken place about the re-introduction of trams such as has been done very satisfactorily in Manchester, Sheffield and Nottingham but nothing so far has happened much to my disappointment.

The trams were a great asset to the many thousands of townspeople engaged in the manufacture of boots and shoes in the 19th and 20th century as they travelled to the many quite large factories in the town.

Manufacture has virtually ceased following the arrival of cheaper footwear from overseas.

Many of the old factories have been converted into residential apartments whereas others have been demolished.

One fine shoe factory building that still exists is the old Headquarters of the Barratt Shoe Co. on Primrose Hill. This is an attractive red brick structure with elaborate embellishments.

For those interested in sport there is a first class County Cricket team, a Premiership Rugby Union side and a Football Club in Division Two of the Football League

The Rugby Club originated as a boys' improvement class founded by the *Rev Wathan Wigg*, Curate of *St James* church, hence the name 'Saints'. In the case of the Football Club the nickname 'Cobblers' is more obvious, Northampton once being an important shoe town.

In 1965 Northampton was designated a New Town which led to a considerable expansion in population initially on the east side of the town but there are now major developments to the west.

In 2010 the official population of the town was stated as 186,000.

The re-development of the main shopping complex - the Grosvenor Centre has been under discussion for about ten years but remains unresolved although the Council has recently approved the demolition of the Fish Market in order to build a new bus station.

This will replace the present Greyfriars Bus Station which was listed in The Guardian as the third most hated place in England.

What of the future? - only time will tell - Councils come and Councils go and all promise to change things for the better.

Fishmarket : Northampton

NORTON

Two miles east of Daventry
Population: 1801-362   2001 - 363

DOMESDAY BOOK
NORTONE
*The name simply means north farmhouse and unlike
many Nortons in the County
has not been given a prefix or suffix.*

This is quite an attractive, mainly stone built village, lying somewhat off the beaten track to the west of the Roman Watling Street.

The **Count of Meulan** held the manor of the King in 1086 - his only land holding in the County. There were thirty three households, a priest and a mill rendering ten shillings per annum so it was a reasonably sized settlement.

Norton has at its centre quite a large public house The White Horse and opposite are a row of houses with a stone plaque inscribed:-

Norton Charity 1853

Nearby is the village hall which from 1844 was the local school until its pupils were relocated to larger schools elsewhere and there is no longer a shop.

The church is situated in a superb position and it was a delight in the lovely spring sunshine to walk the rather long curved path through the carefully maintained churchyard with its abundance of flowers to the south porch.

The church of **ALL SAINTS** is well worth a visit. Dating from the 13th century it has a battlemented tower and medieval arcades of six arches on each side of the nave although the pillars on the north side are a different pattern to those opposite.
On entering I could not fail to notice the large organ loft with plaques behind carrying the words of the Lord's Prayer, the Ten Commandments and the Creed. The large round font which has carvings of four heads is quite unusual.

Old Gateway - Norton Hall

The most amazing aspect of the church however are the monuments about which much could be written.
One that particularly caught my attention was that to **Lady Elizabeth Seymour** second wife of **Richard Knightley** of Norton who died in 1602. She was the daughter of **Prince Edward, Duke of Somerset** and niece of **Jane Seymour**.

Other monuments include **Beriah Botfield** who died in 1813, **Nicholas Breton** and his wife and **Dudley Knightley** son of **Richard Knightley** by his second wife **Lady Elizabeth**.

Dudley - *'having received a musket shot in his neck in the defence of Ostend in Flanders came to Norton and in a short time the bullet fell down wherewith a fever took him and he died on the 11 April 1602'.*

In addition to these monuments are a number of hatchments of various members of these important families and also quite a comprehensive family tree.
It is a pity that some of their money has not found its way into church funds to help with maintenance.

Hanging on the north wall of the aisle is the unusual sight of farming implements including a billhook, a large two handled saw and wooden yokes.

To mark the millennium a map of the village, a copy of the Electoral Roll at that date, a photograph of the villagers and a book about the village has been placed in a glass case - all useful tools for future historians.

In the churchyard are a number of table top tombs but none as large as that of the *Botfield* family, surrounded by railings - it is simply enormous but is now falling to rack and ruin.

One tombstone which did intrigue me is quite small and simply has the inscription *'Whacker' Man of the Road*. I wonder what the story is behind the inscription - was he a travelling man whose real name no one knew?

Norton Hall was owned by the *Knightley* family of Fawsley during the reign of *Elizabeth I*.
A local legend has it that the village was moved away from the Hall on the order of the then owner *Beriah Botfield* who did not want the villagers knowing who was visiting him and gossiping about him.
Sadly the Hall was blown up by the army after the Second World War as it was in poor condition and too expensive to restore.
All that remains are the coach house, blacksmith's shop, stables, ice house and an entrance gateway alongside the church gate.

A recent addition to the village is *'Jacks Patch'* a recreation area opened in 2008 in memory of *Jack Yates* who owned the land for many years and was Parish Councillor for over sixty years.

The parish includes the deserted villages of Thrupp and Muscott.

THRUPP
DOMESDAY BOOK
TORP
I was interested to see that all references to this now deserted village refer to it as Thrupp Grounds - a name which still appears on Ordnance Survey maps.
Much of the land was acquired by the Cluniac monks at Daventry who had it enclosed in 1489 destroying eighteen houses and a chapel and evicting one hundred people.
In 1518 it was described as *'ecclesia in desolocionem'*.
The chapel was dedicated to *St John the Baptist* and stood in a field called 'The Priory'.

Today there is a popular public house and restaurant alongside the Grand Union Canal but no evidence of the existence of the earlier settlement.

MUSCOTT
DOMESDAY BOOK
MISECOTE
The name may come from the old English 'musa-cote' meaning mice dwellings or simply humble cottages.

In 1547 the manor was bought by *Sir John Spencer* of Althorp who enclosed some acres for sheep farming.

Muscott which is reached on a very narrow and little used track still appears on Ordnance Survey maps.
Today a farm house and associated farm buildings occupy the area and apart from the gateway of a pre-Reformation house very little else can be seen of this lost settlement.
Excavations in 1958 in view of the impending destruction of the site by farming revealed evidence of a 13th and 14th century complex and derelict roads.
It appears that it was once quite a sizeable village.

Farm Buildings : Muscott.

OLD

Seven miles north east of Northampton
Population: 1801-369   2001 - 308

DOMESDAY BOOK
WALDA
*The present spelling is quite recent
and some older citizens still call it Wold from the Saxon 'weald' - meaning woodland or high heathland.*

At the time of the Domesday Book this was a manor belonging to the royal manor at Faxton and assessed together with Walgrave.

The village stands among minor roads just north of Pitsford Water. It contains several attractive properties including the early 18th century Rectory with a hipped roof, a fine gabled farmhouse with the date 1768 and the Brewery House.

There is still a public house, The White Horse, alongside which a track takes you to Grange Farm and the church of **ST ANDREW** which dates from the late 13th century but was extensively restored during the late 19th century.

The church has a Perpendicular style west tower with two light transomed bell openings, a quatrefoil frieze, battlements and a very ornate Perpendicular doorway. The best feature is the nave roof with its carved angel corbels.
Chairs have replaced pews to provide more flexibility of usage.

In 2000 after seven years work by the 'Old Kneelers Group' the church received much publicity when fifty kneelers and an altar kneeler were formally presented.

A very useful acquisition to the village is the stone faced bus shelter built in 2000 which was funded by the Daventry Millennium Fund, the parish charities and the Parish Council of Old.

After fund raising for ten years the villagers were rejoicing in March 2010 when the first turf was cut to start work on a new village hall incorporating kitchen and bar facilities, meeting rooms, full disabled access and sports changing rooms. The new hall opened in November 2010.
Sadly many other community buildings such as the shop, old chapel and the school have closed and have been put to other uses.
Just outside of the village on the road to Walgrave is an estate of quite sizeable modern houses which goes by the name of Cherry Hill. Old was voted the best small village in the Northamptonshire Best Village Competition in 2012 and runner up to the overall winner, Blisworth.

Church & Pub, Old.

OLD STRATFORD

Seven miles south east of Towcester
Population: 1801 - estimated 150   2001 - estimated 260

Being located on the Watling Street and therefore known in Roman times I was amazed that I could find no reference (Stony or Old) to a Stratford in the area at the time of the Domesday Book.
I can only assume that it was assessed with Furtho or Passenham or some other neighbouring community.

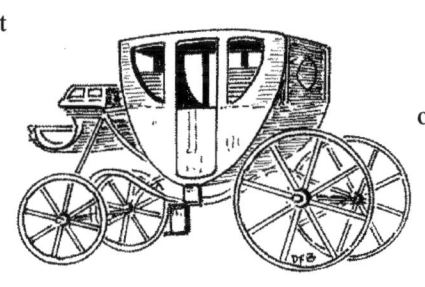

In 1278 the settlement had the name West Stratford implying a western expansion across the River Ouse of the older settlement of Stony Stratford in Buckinghamshire. Early 17th century maps name the village as Old Stow.

There was a lot of activity here during the coaching era and beyond but today with the construction of the MI motorway which takes much traffic off the A5 together with the dual carriageway bypass the area is considerably more peaceful although it still gets a fair amount of local traffic.

Now virtually part of the sprawling city of Milton Keynes, Old Stratford is still technically part of Northamptonshire - the County border being the River Ouse which flows between Old and Stony Stratford and in fact the village started as a fording point over the river in other words a 'street-ford.'

A toll bridge over the Ouse is first mentioned in the 13th century
The bridge itself was partly destroyed during the Civil War and fell into disrepair.

In 1834 Northamptonshire and Buckinghamshire shared responsibility for the building of a new bridge and for tolls to be collected for the next 21 years.

Until the creation of the civil parish of Old Stratford in 1951 the village had no separate administrative identity.
It now has its own parish council.

There has never been a parish church here. Worshippers in the mid 19th century would meet in a schoolroom and although residents petitioned for a church the project did not go ahead.
Instead it was decided to restore the ancient church in Passenham which lies in the new parish.

There was a chapel attached to the Hospital of St John on the causeway leading to the bridge at Stony Stratford but there is no longer any evidence of its existence.

In the late 19th century a light railway was built between Deanshanger and Wolverton via Old Stratford.
This remained in service until 1929 but the Old Tram Shed lasted until 1999 when it was demolished for housing.

There is still a public house - The Swan - the only one of four originally serving the village and a Primary school although until as recently as 1966 the young children had to travel to nearby schools.

ORLINGBURY

Four miles south of Kettering
Population: 1801-268   2001 - 395

DOMESDAY BOOK
ORDINBARO
The prefix is taken from a personal name
Ordin *and the suffix from 'berg'*
Saxon for hill or mound - i.e. ***Ordins*** *hill.*

The ***Count of Mortain*** held the manor here in 1086 when there were just three households as against seventeen households plus a priest at nearby Wythmail.

The village lies within a triangle of main roads linking the towns of Kettering, Wellingborough and Northampton.

Clustered around the Green which remains the heart and focal point of the village is a medley of old and new buildings, some of local stone with ironstone as decorative masonry.
These include the three major listed buildings, the Hall rebuilt in about 1709, the old Rectory of 1703 and the church.
It is a delightful village scene and typically English.

Opposite the entrance to the Rectory is a square dovecote which dates from 1700 and was probably a rebuild of an earlier one on the same site.
Originally it had seven hundred and sixty nesting boxes. The key is available locally.

Because it had fallen into such a bad state the church of **ST MARY** was completely rebuilt in 1842/3 in the early Victorian Gothic style by ***Richard C. Hussey*** of Birmingham and was paid for by the Rector and ***A. Young*** of the Hall.

The tall crossing tower with filigree battlements and pinnacles which were lowered by ten feet in 1970/1 is a landmark for miles around.

The church is magnificent to look at from across the large Green but on entering I found it to be somewhat disappointing - I expected more.
It is almost a barn like structure with no aisles.

What did appeal to me however were the beautiful stained glass windows in the chancel and the lovely rose window.

I was also impressed with the modern stained glass window in the nave given by the ***Ormerod*** family in memory of ***June Ann Ormerod*** (1928-1993) a well loved and respected doctor.

The window depicts the church tower, sheep etc. with the text :- *'I will lift up mine eyes to the hills.'*

Two deserted medieval settlements lie within the parish boundary - Badsaddle and Wythmail.

BADSADDLE

*The settlement was not mentioned in the Domesday Book but in a 12th century survey was referred to as Bates Hasel meaning **Baefti's** hazel or hazelclump.*

This long deserted settlement never appears to have been much more than a hamlet and today there is little evidence of its existence apart from a wood and a farm of that name.
Henry Green bought the manor in 1348 and the area was emparked about 1570 but after complaints was later disparked.
An effigy of *Jack (*or *Jock) of Badsaddle* who it is claimed killed the last wolf in England can be seen in Orlingbury church.

WYTHMAIL

DOMESDAY BOOK
WIDMALE

It has been suggested that the name derives from the old English words for 'place against a ridge' but many disagree with this explanation.

Wythmail Park Farm and Wythmail Park Wood are current reminders of this long lost settlement.
In the Domesday Book there were seventeen households and a priest who may have been associated with Orlingbury.
I can find no evidence that there was ever a church here although a manorial chapel was mentioned in 1357 and may have been connected with Orlingbury

The Manor was acquired by *Lord Vaux* of Harrowden who also held nearby Badsaddle.

A park was created in 1614 from the common fields and by 1720 when *Bridges* compiled his history only one house remained. All traces of the settlement have been obliterated by modern farming methods although I am told that earthworks can be seen from the air. Excavations at the site in 1954 revealed evidence of a reasonably sized croft from the 13th or 14th century.

ORTON

Three miles west of Kettering
Population: 1801- 83 2001 - 74

DOMESDAY BOOK
OVERTONE
The name derives from two words meaning farm on a slope or bank.
The settlement is sited on a fairly steep hillside.

In 1086 it was part of the royal manor of Rothwell and was not recorded as a separate manor.
Information on the history of the settlement is very hard to come by but in a survey of 1801 Orton was referred to as a Chapelry of Rothwell and not recorded as an independent parish.

The church of **ALL SAINTS** has a short unbuttressed Norman west tower with late medieval top with battlements and pinnacles and a Norman arch towards the nave.
It was closed in 1964 and is now used by the Orton Trust (formed 1968) with the aim of encouraging the traditional stonemasonry skills used in the restoration and conservation of historic buildings.

Little remains of the village except for the church, Manor Farm, and a few cottages.

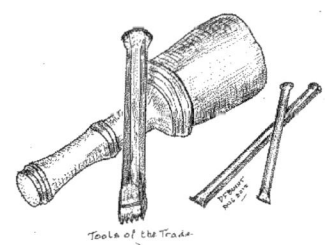

Tools of the Trade.

OUNDLE

Ten miles east of Corby
Population: 1801-1956   2001 - 5345

DOMESDAY BOOK
UNDEL/UNDELE

The name appears to have come initially from a Saxon tribe who lived in the area soon after the Romans left - the name being 'undulas' from the Saxon word 'undal' meaning undivided.

Oundle is unusual for Northamptonshire inasmuch as it never saw industrial developments on the scale of the boot and shoe industry and engineering which were common elsewhere. Brewing was of considerable importance until the 20th century and former buildings are still visible.

It is always a delight to visit this attractive market town whose Market Charter dates back to 972AD. In the Domesday Book the market was valued at twenty five shillings per annum.

When the market is operating the central area becomes a very busy place but thankfully owing to the construction of a new bypass in 1985 the town no longer has to contend with a very high volume of heavy through traffic.

The six hide manor was held by the Abbey of Peterborough and had thirty six households, fifty acres of meadow and a mill rendering twenty shillings per annum and two hundred eels. From *King William's* point of view, a valuable manor.

On an island in the middle of the Market Place stands the Market House with the Town Hall above. It was built in 1825 in the Tudor style using stone from a redundant church in Barnwell. This is a fine building with stout gables and a charming oriel window on its west end. Oundle has many superb buildings, including dignified houses of the 17th and 18th century, ancient inns and a fine church.

The town is surrounded on three sides by the River Nene which is crossed by two important bridges. One is the ancient narrow bridge (single track with traffic lights) when approaching from Thrapston and the other is the north bridge which was rebuilt and widened in 1912-14. It has eleven arches and carries a stone tablet found during repairs in 1835 and reads:-

In the yere of our Lord 1570 thes arches wer borne dovne by the waters extremytie in the yere of over Lord 1571 they wer bvlded agayne with lyme and stonne.
Thanks be to God.

The centre of the town is dominated by the magnificent church of **ST PETER** nearly the whole of which is of the 13th century. The original crossing tower has been removed and replaced by the present two storey tower with battlements and pinnacles. This is topped by a magnificent octagonal crocketed spire which rises to a height of two hundred and ten feet and is the tallest in Northamptonshire and can be seen for miles around. The date 1634 at the base of the spire indicates its rebuilding.

One of the most notable features of the interior is the massive stone pillars of the nave. This is a wide, light church with modern seating, the only pews being in the Lady Chapel. The 15th century lectern in the shape of a brass eagle is similar to one in Southwell Minster.

St Peter's Church: Oundle

The pulpit dates from the 15th century and was painted black when **Cromwell** was causing havoc but in 1966 eight layers of paint were stripped off and the pulpit was repainted in bright colours considered to be as near as possible to the original. Memorials include those to **William Loringe** (d.1628) and to the **Rev. John Shillibeer** Headmaster of Oundle Grammar school and Rector of Stoke Doyle where he is buried.

The Catholic Church was built in 1879 and stands as a traffic island facing Stoke Hill and Benefield Road. It was designed in the Gothic style by **Arthur Blomfield**. Opposite is the Old Court built in 1877. Today the Court has gone and the building houses the excellent Oundle Museum.
I visited recently and was most fortunate to see the superb Biggin quilt worked by **Mrs Mary Selby** and completed in 1893 when she was sixty two years of age. Because of its age and value it is rarely on show to the public.

The Congregational chapel of 1864 has, since 1980, housed the **Stahl** Theatre Company owned and managed by Oundle School and run by the drama department. Two other churches have found a change of use. The former 19th century Methodist church in West Street now houses a restaurant and the former Baptist chapel of 1852 has been converted into flats.

Oundle is probably most famous for its public school which was founded under the will of local boy, **Sir William Laxton**, grocer and Lord Mayor of London in 1556.
Oundle School has been a vital part of the town ever since and occupies most of the most striking and larger buildings.
There were 60 -70 boys by the mid 17th century but this number has increased to 840 boarders and 240 day students by early 2000 making it the third largest independent and boarding/day school in England. Girls were first admitted in 1990 and now represent about 40% of the pupils.

The London and North Western railway which on regrouping in 1923 became the London Midland and Scottish Railway opened a station to the north end of the town in 1845 on the Northampton/Peterborough line.
Regular passenger services ceased in 1964 although specials to Oundle School ran until 1972.

The former station is a grand stone building with numerous gables and tall chimneys but is hidden behind trees and other properties. **John Betjeman** described it as 'one *of the finest examples of domestic rail station architecture in England.'*

On the opposite side of the road is the former Riverside public house which has been boarded up for many years and now looks a sorry sight.

A number of public houses are still in business. The most famous is the Grade I listed old coaching hostelry The Talbot Inn which is said to contain materials from Fotheringhay Castle and to be haunted by the ghost of **Mary, Queen of Scots**. A hostelry has existed on this site since 638AD but the present building dates from 1626.

In North Street is Lathams Hospital, a pretty set of four Almshouses founded and endowed in 1611 by **Nicholas Latham**, Rector of Barnwell St Andrews where he provided other Almshouses. He also founded Lathams Blue Coat School for thirty poor men's sons in 1620.
The school no longer exists but the building forms part of Lathams Hospital.
Glapthorn Road Hospital was built as a Workhouse in 1837 by the young **George Gilbert Scott**. It is in late classical style with the usual raised octagonal centre and has a separate chapel with lancet windows.

Oundle with its good assortment of shops and restaurants is a great place to visit. There always seems to be plenty going on and some very attractive buildings and shops to explore.
Take away the cars and you can imagine that you have turned the clock back many years.

The Talbot Hotel : Oundle.

OVERSTONE

Five miles north east of Northampton
Population: 1801-173 2001 – 659

Pytchley Gates - Overstone Hall

There are numerous streams in this part of Northamptonshire and it is thought likely that the name comes from 'ofer' - river bank and 'tun' - homestead.

The majority of today's villages are mentioned in the Domesday Book but Overstone is one exception. Was it perhaps included with Sywell at that time? The two villages are close together geographically and nowadays it is easy to miss where one starts and the other finishes.

By 1167 a village was recorded north west of **Overstone Hall** but all that remains are a few earthworks. Part of the original village is thought to be under the ornamental lake.

Overstone had fifty three tenants in 1398 and forty two in 1520 but the population then dropped particularly with land enclosure in 1727.

By the early 19th century the village and its church were demolished and the village itself rebuilt on its present site straddling the main road.

The church of **ST NICHOLAS** which was erected in 1849 now stands alone in a field in Overstone Park between the Hall and the present village

It is a fairly plain building although the East window is of German stained glass.

Inside are wall plaques from the old church.

I have travelled through Overstone many times but until recently had not ventured off the beaten track to see the church which was built of Kingsthorpe stone by Estate workers. *Lady Wantage* had the church restored and enlarged in 1903.

There is still a shop, post office and a village hall. Although there is no public house in the main street, Overstone Manor public house and restaurant carries the village name but is actually located on the far side of Overstone Park off the Sywell/Ecton road. The park is enclosed by some three miles of stone wall behind which have been built some quite expensive properties.

In my youth Overstone Solarium - a forerunner of today's Leisure Parks - was a great visitor attraction.

In addition to parkland and woods there was a large outdoor swimming pool, boating, fishing, crazy golf and tennis not to mention a narrow gauge railway.

The caravan site remains but they are now more numerous and luxurious.

The local Primary school is housed in an attractive building of stone, tile and a half timber upper part and stands alongside the village street.

It was built at the request of *Lady Wantage* in 1895 for seventy children at a cost of £1700.

The impressive classical stone gateway at the northwest corner of the grounds originally stood at the entrance to Pytchley Hall which was demolished in 1824.

It was moved to its present location as the main gate to Overstone Hall some nineteen years later but was virtually rebuilt in 1973 following a car accident and again in 2008 when yet another car caused considerable damage.

Overstone Hall

*The Grade I listed **Overstone Hall** with 119 rooms was built in 1860 for the opulent banker **Samuel Jones (Lord Overstone)** to the design of **William Milford Teulon**. It is certainly ornate but **Pevsner** in his 'Buildings of England' (Northamptonshire) was not impressed and states that it 'defeats description and appreciative analysis.'*

*It is reported that **Lord Overstone** hated it and refused to live there. The Hall was inherited by his only daughter (**Lady Wantage**) in 1883 but on her death in 1921 the house and grounds were sold.*

For a short time it was used as a Training College for the Conservative and Unionist Party and was then converted to a private school and was used as such until 1978. In 1980 it was bought by the New Testament Church of God, the largest black led church in Britain, to provide accommodation and offices for the National Church and to house a Bible College.

Unfortunately there was a spectacular fire in 2001. At present it stands isolated - a splendid Gothic ruin whose future is in doubt.

PASSENHAM

Eight miles south east of Towcester
Population: 1801-685 (but this included Deanshanger)

DOMESDAY BOOK
PASSONHAM/PASEHAM/PASSEHAM
*The name implies that this was **Passa's** meadow.*

Passenham was a royal manor at the time of the Domesday Book with a mill rendering thirteen shillings, meadows and sixteen households.

The mill was in use for generations but ceased operations in 1920 and is now a private residence. Opposite is a field containing earth mounds which to me indicate the site of earlier occupation and fragments of Roman pottery from the 5th century found in the area indicate a Roman presence.
The area was at one time heavily wooded to the north and was within the boundaries of the then royal forest of Whittlewood.

At one time Passenham on the southern edge of the County and only separated by the Great Ouse from the sprawling city of Milton Keynes was an important place and included in the parish was nearby Deanshanger which would appear from old records to have become the centre of population by the 14th century.

Now Deanshanger has a population of almost three thousand whereas Passenham is a small, quiet place consisting of a church, old Rectory, old mill and two magnificent tithe barns with massive stone walls, a fine Manor House dating back to the 17th century and very little else.

The church with its unusual dedication to
ST GUTHLAC was first mentioned in 921 AD when *Edward the Elder* stationed his army here. *Guthlac* was a Mercian nobleman who became a hermit in the Fens in the 7th century. After his death in 714 his shrine became the nucleus of the great Abbey at Crowland, Lincolnshire.

The church lost its spire which collapsed about one hundred years ago. The present church with its west tower dates from the 13th and 14th centuries although the chancel was rebuilt in 1626.

The crowning glory of the church is the chancel with its painted wagon roof, choir stalls with misericords and wall paintings of Old Testament Prophets and New Testament Evangelists. Elsewhere the olive green box pews, west gallery and superb pulpit caught my eye.
The rebuilding and re-fitting, which is of a high quality, was carried out in 1626 on the instructions of *Sir Robert Banastre*, Comptroller of the household of *James I*, who bought the manor in 1624 where he stayed for forty years during which time he rebuilt the Manor House.

Unfortunately *Sir Robert Banastre* who did so much good for the church appears to have had a darker side.
He was known as *'wicked Bobby Banastre'* and his name was used to frighten naughty children.
His ghost is said to have been seen driving his coach and horses madly in the area and the village has a reputation for being haunted with many stories of ghosts and other unearthly happenings.

The parish of Passenham was abolished in 1951 and the area divided between Deanshanger and Old Stratford.

Common Dandelion

Pattishall

Four miles north west of Towcester
Population: 1801-551   2001 - 1501

DOMESDAY BOOK
PASCELLE
*The name indicates that this was a hill belonging to a person named **Pasca** or **Paetti***

In Saxon days a considerable number of small communities were established on either side of the Roman road (Watling Street) now the A5.
The road now forms part of the boundary between Pattishall and its neighbour Cold Higham.

In the Domesday Book reference is made to a church in Pattishall - one of only three churches in the County.
The others being Guilsborough and Halse.

There are some attractive old stone houses in the narrow streets which lead to the village Green but a lot of typical new buildings.
I must admit that it does not rank very highly on my list of most attractive villages.

A few properties caught my eye including the Upper Vicarage and Festal Grange (1878) near the church.

The village grew in the 19th century with the boot and shoe trade.

To commemorate the millennium an attractive and informative parish signpost was erected which represents 2000 years of history and features the church, the old Watling Street and Drovers Road, rural crafts including shoemaking and the village hall and modern day activities.

Originally the parish had about nine public houses but in Pattishall today there is only The Red Lion on the A5 which dates back to 1637.
Nearby was another pub called The George and Dragon dating from 1637 which although still in use is now an Indian Restaurant/Takeaway.

The church of the **HOLY CROSS** stands on a small limestone plateau in the centre of the village and dates from Saxon times although the chancel was rebuilt by the Normans.

Within a century of the Domesday Book two priests are recorded as serving Pattishall in a church which had been substantially extended and embellished.
In the 16th and 17th centuries however, the church is reported *'as falling into decay with broken pulpit steps, chancel in a bad condition and windows requiring repair'*. In addition there was *'only one surplice for the two priests'*.
This caused considerable friction as **Priest Powell** was High Church and **Priest Burkett** a Puritan.
A Curate was appointed to spy on **Burkett** with the result that **Burkett** to whom many of the congregation had turned was excommunicated.
There were, however, still two priests in the parish in the early 1800's.
I was pleased to see a variety of wild flowers in the churchyard.

Unfortunately the Baptist chapel established in 1838 closed in 1945 and has been converted into residential use although the little chapel clock still overhangs the front door.

As I walked around the village my eye caught the unusual sight of a black GR post box in a wall near the junction of The Crescent and Church Street.
A school was founded in 1684 by **Thomas Young** with free places for fifteen boys.
The new school was built in 1855 which became the Infant's school. This has been modernised and extended to meet today's requirements.

The present parish includes the hamlets of Astcote, Dalscote and Eastcote.

ASTCOTE

DOMESDAY BOOK
AVIESCOTE

Aefic was a monk of Evesham Abbey and it is thought by some that this place was - Aefic's cottage.

Gildre held the manor of Astcote at the time of the Domesday Book when there were nine households.
At one time Astcote which lies just off the A5 had three small shoemaking factories - almost every house must have had someone working there.

It now consists of private houses, a few farms and a small Methodist chapel which was built in 1874 and is still in use.
In a religious survey of 1851 the report on Astcote Methodist chapel states *'this chapel is about to be disposed of by the trustees on the account of the few that attend'*.
I wonder what happened to cause this 'new' chapel to be built.

A former public house, The Dun Cow is now in private hands.

DALSCOTE

*This small hamlet was not mentioned in the Domesday Book and the earliest reference I can find is that in 1203 it was called Derstanescote meaning the cottage of one called **Deorstan** or **Deorlaf**.*

This is thought to be the site of a larger settlement with finds locally of post medieval pottery.
Today it is so small that you hardly notice it at all.

EASTCOTE

*Like Dalscote this village does not appear in the Domesday Book and the earliest reference I can find was that in 1277 it was known as Edeweneskote meaning **Eadwine**'s cottage.*

Eastcote is still basically a farming village.
During the First World War an Internment Camp was built but in 1916 the nature of the Camp was changed to a Concentration Camp to cater also for prisoners of war.

The natives of the village were said to be
'very nice, they bring us cigarettes, fruit and papers and stop to chat'.(The Times 5 Jan 1915).

Thirty one of the internees and prisoners are buried in the local cemetery, many of whom died during the severe flu epidemic of 1918.

In Eastcote, the Grade II listed Barton Mead dates from the 17th century although the bays towards the east end were added in 1922.

I was surprised and delighted to see that the little Baptist chapel opened on the 17th October 1838 still has up to three services each Sunday.

The Boot Inn at Eastcote once had a large wooden boot that was displayed in the window. This boot was moved to Northampton Museum for safe keeping when the pub was closed.

The Eastcote Arms near the chapel is still open for business although there is no shop, post office or school.

PAULERSPURY

Three miles south east of Towcester
Population: 1801-859   2001 - 991

DOMESDAY BOOK
PIRIE

*The area was once famous for its orchards and this gave it its name pirie - pear tree. Although **Robert de Pavelli** was here in 1086 it was not until 1319 that the village became known as Paueleyespirye.*

This was once one of the *'out towns'* of Whittlewood Forest just off the main A5 London to Towcester road. Being alongside the old Roman Watling Street it is not surprising to learn of Roman coins, pottery, bones and a large quantity of dressed limestone being discovered in the area.
The village covers a wide area and has at least three segments - Pury End, Tews End and my favourite area Plumpton End.

Boudicca, Queen of the Iceni (Celts) is famed for leading tens of thousands of Britons in an uprising against Roman troops in 62AD.
A number of historians think her last battle was fought near Paulerspury at a site called Cuttle Mill and that she was buried in a field between Paulerspury and Whittlebury known as 'Deadquenny Moor' (Dead Queen Moor).

The church of **ST JAMES** the **GREAT** which dates back to the 12th century stands in a beautiful elevated position between two parts of the parish, Church End and Pury End.
I was particularly interested in visiting because of its connections with **William Carey** (Missionary and Charter Member of the Baptist Missionary Society) who was born in the village on the 17th August 1761 and who spent forty years of his life in India as a missionary where he died in 1834.

There is a memorial to him in the church porch near his father's tombstone.

The Perpendicular style tower contains a sanctus and six bells and the tower stairs are in the form of a very large buttress.
Among the many items of interest are the lovely round Norman font and the very ornate three seat sedilia and double piscina.

The window which caught my eye is in the south wall of the chancel in memory of the **Rev. Newbolt** who restored the chancel during 1854-5 at his own expense, he also built the village school. The window features the feeding of the five thousand and although there are not that many people depicted there are many more faces than I can ever recall seeing in any other window.

Monuments include the twelve foot long 17th century tomb in black and white marble of **Sir Arthur Throckmorton** (brother in law to **Sir Walter Raleigh**) and **Lady Throckmorton** and the well preserved 14th century oaken effigies believed to be **Sir Laurence de Pavelli** (d. 1349) and his wife. The wooden effigies had been covered in lime wash and have only fairly recently been cleaned. At one time churchgoers stuck candles on to the effigies which also meant that they had a good layer of candle wax.

Both the **Throckmorton** and the **Pavelli** families at one time held the manor which at the time of the Domesday Book was held by **William Peverel** (natural son of **William the Conqueror**).
There were at that time thirty two households, a priest and a mill rendering twenty six shillings and eight pence per annum.
It was quite a large and valuable settlement.

A local benefactor was responsible for the provision of the kitchen and toilet facilities at the west end of the north aisle.

The village has a number of interesting buildings including the **Henry Royce** Museum where the Grafton Hunt stables stood between 1892-2005 before being moved to Eydon.

The Old Village School - Paulerspury

A most unusual building is the wildly Gothic Victorian Primary School of 1860 with a little *Disney* like spirelet. The school was modernised and extended in the 1960's and given a sundial in 2008.

On the night of 25/26 September 1940 a bomb fell on the village damaging the Primitive Methodist chapel, The Bricklayers Arms and a number of houses.
Of the three chapels only the Independent chapel built in 1826 (now United Reform) with its own graveyard is still used for religious worship.

There is still a public house and restaurant - The Barley Mow and almost opposite the three hundred year old Vine House Hotel and restaurant. The village hall has an adjoining playing field but there is no longer a shop or post office.
The village sign is unusual as it comprises a post supporting an imitation tree bearing gold pears and topped with a golden crown.

Included in the parish although on the opposite side of the busy A5 and near to Towcester racecourse is the tiny hamlet of Heathencote.

HEATHENCOTE

Although not mentioned in the Domesday Book a manor is known to have existed here in about 1200 and a chapel maintained by St James Abbey of Northampton in the early 13th century.

In the 17th century it is recorded that there were about twenty houses but such has been the decline that little more remains than a farm and a few other buildings.

WILLIAM CAREY 1761-1834

William Carey was born in Pury End, Paulerspury on the 17th August 1761.
The house has long since been demolished but his memory is perpetuated in Carey Row on the site.

William's parents *Edmund* and *Elizabeth* were relatively poor. *Edmund* was a weaver before becoming schoolmaster at the Charity school in the village which *William* attended until the age of 12.
Originally he loved nature and wanted to become a gardener but had to give up this ambition owing to an allergy. As a result he found employment as an apprentice shoemaker in Piddington.
Here he met and married *Dorothy Plackett* in Piddington Church on the 10th June, 1781.

William's friendship with a fellow apprentice called *John Warr* led him to leave the established church and attend an Independent Meeting House in Hackleton.
In 1783 at the age of twenty two he was baptised in the River Nene in Northampton near Castle Station.

John Newton and *William Cowper* of Olney were great influences on his early Christian life and it was in the Baptist church in Olney where *William* was commissioned to be a minister. In 1785 *Carey* went on to become schoolmaster and Pastor at Moulton where he continued to make shoes to supplement his small income.
At the same time he started to study languages.
In May of 1782 in Nottingham he preached possibly his most memorable sermon:-
'Expect Great Things from God
Attempt Great Things for God'

Within a few months, following meetings at *Widow Wallis's* House in Kettering (now a Home for the Elderly) he became instrumental in the formation of the **Baptist Missionary Society** and volunteered to be its first missionary.

He left England with his wife and three sons for India in June 1793 and was never to return.
Life there was not easy for the family but he was able to undertake missionary work, translate the Bible into forty languages, set up the first printing press in India and establish a Bible College in Serampore.
He died in 1834 at the age of 73 years.

PIDDINGTON

Five miles south east of Northampton
Population: 1801-382
2001 – 1568 (inc. Horton and Hackleton)

DOMESDAY BOOK
PIDENTONE
*Situated on the edge of Salcey Forest it is thought that
the name derives from* **Pyda**'s *'ingtun' - homestead.*

At the time of the Domesday Book the manor was listed as being held by **Countess Judith** but others, it seems, had claims to it including
Bishop Geoffrey of Coutances and **Winemar** of Hanslope. There were ten households and a priest.

Today Piddington on the edge of Salcey Forest is a quiet backwater at the end of a 'no through road' just south of the B526 near Hackleton.
Although the village has a number of modern houses there are still some older and more attractive properties near the church.

It is not unusual for a church to change its name - some change according to the fashion of the day or to the preference of the Lord of the Manor.
At Piddington they have had three changes from **St Mary** to **St Thomas á Becket** and today **ST JOHN** the **BAPTIST**.

The church has an unusual west tower which dates back to the 13th century built in three stages and the spire with tall broaches carries on with a big collar like a parapet. The body of church was mostly rebuilt in 1877/8 by **E. F. Law**.

The village still has a public house - The Spread Eagle - but no shop, post office or school.

There was once a railway station named Piddington on the Northampton to Bedford Line but it was located in the middle of nowhere and much nearer to both Horton and Hackleton.
The line finally closed to passengers in 1951.

The Ministry of Defence had a store in Piddington with its own branch line which remained open until the 1980's.

Tiberius Claudius Severus

PIDDINGTON
ROMAN VILLA MUSEUM

The village has a long history going back to before Roman times.
On the outskirts of the village is the site of a late Iron Age settlement and an overlying large Roman Villa.

Excavations have been taking place over very many years and finds have included a Roman gladiator clasp knife made of copper alloy and iron - thought to be the only one of its kind in the whole of the Roman world.

Many artefacts are now on display in a museum set up in the former Wesleyan chapel thanks to the Heritage Lottery Fund and other grant giving bodies and individuals.

Exhibits also include a life size model of a second century villa owner - '**Tiberius Claudius Severus**.'

The museum is open on Sunday afternoons during the summer and autumn from 2 - 4 p.m.

PILTON

Three miles south of Oundle
Population: 1801-90 2001 - 55

DOMESDAY BOOK
PILCHETONE
The name implies that this was once
Pileca's 'tun' - farmstead.

Roger held the two and a half hide manor of the Abbot of the Abbey of Peterborough in 1086 when there were ten households.

This is a very tiny isolated settlement with a handful of houses separated by a meadow from the beautifully kept 13th century church of **ST MARY** and **ALL SAINTS** and the magnificent 16th century Manor House.
Together they make an absolutely wonderful scene which has hardly changed in centuries.
It is such a quiet and peaceful setting.

Just before the first gates into the meadow on the approach to the church is an unusual three storey stone building with a pyramid roof at one end.
It is known as Bede House or the Old Watch House and is thought to have been built around 1515.

A local tale concerning the *Treshams* of Pilton and those of Lyveden is that they are thought to have held secret meetings here and used the chimney like structure at the top to keep watch for approaching soldiers.

Entrance to the church is via a lovely Norman doorway with a tell tale chevron design carved into its surface.

The west tower has shafted bell openings, a spire with low broaches and two tiers of lucarnes.
The chancel was rebuilt in 1864 and the rest of the church restored in the next decade.

In 1630 *Erasmus Dryden* married *Mary Pickering* here, they were the parents of the Poet Laureate *John Dryden*.

The very attractive Manor House is thought to date from the 1560's and was once the home of the *Treshams* of Newton. The church porch has the trefoil emblem of the family carved in stone.

Nearby are the former fishponds and the quarries which provided stone in the 16th century for building Lyveden New Bield.

I was informed that at one time there were a number of small cottages in a lovely meadow but they were demolished on the orders of the *Lilford* family to clear the view from their family home across the Nene Valley and leave the sheep to safely graze.

The village was also once known as a tile making centre but today little appears to happen - there being no through traffic, no public house or shop and no school.

The Bede House.
Pilton

PIPEWELL

Three miles south west of Corby

DOMESDAY BOOK
PIPEWELLE
*The name is thought to derive from the Old English words 'pipe' and 'wella' meaning a spring with a conduit or pipe although another suggestion is that this was **Pippa**'s well, named after a local leader.*

Village Sign : Pipewell

Some reports suggest that Pipewell is one of the earliest deserted medieval villages in the County.
It has not completely disappeared but today is barely a hamlet lining a short stretch of a fairly minor road just west of Corby.
In 2000 there were just seventy two inhabitants in this quiet backwater but I doubt whether the very small church of **ST MARY** would hold even that number of parishioners.
In the Domesday Book Pipewell had nine households and was divided between three manors.
One of the earliest windmills in Britain is said to have been recorded here in the 12th century.
Prior to that date it was water that drove the mills.

The present church is the smallest in the diocese and was used as a private house on the **Hambrough** Estate until in 1880.
Mrs Hambrough decided that the village needed a church and set about raising £600 by public conscription for its conversion.
The work was completed by 1882.
The Grade II listed **Pipewell Hall** dates from 1675 and was built in limestone with a fish scale tiled roof although alterations were made in the 19th century. In 1922 it became associated with the famous **Lloyds** banking family, nowadays it houses weddings in a Lakeside setting.

A village sign was erected in 2006 opposite the church to mark the millennium.
It features a monk drawing water from a well with the current church in the background.
A millennium seat representing the continuous ring of time has been erected nearby.

PIPEWELL ABBEY

In its heyday Pipewell must have been very busy when the Cistercian Abbey east of the village founded in 1142 by **William Batevileyn** for thirteen monks was in use.
The Abbey had its own infirmary, brew house, bakery, gardens and fishponds
It was the scene in 1189 of **Richard I's** *'Great Council'* which was attended by most of the English nobility and Bishops to raise **Longchamp** and three others to the Bishopric.

The Abbey received its income from a number of local Rectories. I have read conflicting reports regarding its size and importance.
One said that *'at one time Pipewell was the most valuable in the County and the 3rd biggest Abbey in Britain'* - the other report said that
'it never grew to any considerable size or importance.'

Whatever the truth it fell on hard times and was dissolved in 1538 and demolished under the orders of **Henry VIII** after which its masonry and possessions found their way to other villages including the medieval screen at Brigstock and the stalls at Great Oakley.
All that now remains of the Abbey are a few humps in the fields and evidence of fish ponds. The site is on private land but can be viewed from the road.

Simon of Patteshull (d.1217) friend of **King John** and present at the signing of the Magna Carta was buried in the cemetery of the Abbey.

ITSFORD

Four miles north of Northampton
Population: 1801-339   2001 - 636

DOMESDAY BOOK
PIDESFORD/PITESFORD
A village existed here in Saxon times, the name deriving from Peoht's ford.

Pitsford had two small manors at the time of the Domesday Book. The smaller manor held by the *Count of Mortain* had a mill rendering two shillings per annum and little else, whereas the manor held by *Walter the Fleming* had twenty seven households but a less valuable mill rendering just twelve pence per annum.

The history of Pitsford is thought to go back even earlier. *Sir Henry Dryden* of Canons Ashby carried out excavations in Brampton Lane in 1882 and discovered fourteen urns containing ashes of which two at least were thought to be Saxon also bones and pieces of glass and 'brass.'

The present village stands at the western edge of Pitsford reservoir just east of the A508 and dates largely from the 17th century as the original settlement northwest of the church was completely destroyed by fire on the 18th August 1619.

Pitsford Hall was built in 1764 for *Lt. Col. James Money* but was later altered and extended.
It was then acquired by *Captain Drummond*, Master of the Pytchley Hunt.
During his ownership there were many royal visits and some older villagers can remember seeing the young *Princesses Elizabeth* and *Margaret* being walked around the village with a royal nanny.
The small conservatory at the front of the house was built so that *Queen Mary* could watch her young granddaughters taking riding lessons.

After the Second World War it was used as a Convent school by the Polish Order of the Holy Family of Nazareth.
Northampton Grammar school took over in 1989 and established Pitsford Hall Weather Station on the top floor.

Today it is known as Pitsford School - one of the country's leading independent schools for pupils aged 3-18. A bus service is provided to transport pupils from outlying areas.

In a delightful spot on the northern edge of the village with views over the valley stands the lovely rich ironstone church of **ALL SAINTS.**
The chief attraction is the Norman tympanum over the south door with a stone possibly representing *St George* and the Dragon and the *Archangel Michael.* This is protected from the elements by the south porch.
The church which was reconstructed in 1867 has a buttressed 13th century west tower with a one handed clock.

The village hall is an attractive early 20th century mock Tudor building. The Griffin Arms public house and restaurant always seems to be popular but there is no longer a shop or post office.

In an area once famous for an estimated three hundred local springs it is not surprising to find a reservoir on the edge of the village.

Sedgebrook Hall dating from 1861 is located one mile south west of the village and has a facade with a central pediment and a grand porch with Ionic columns. It is one of twenty three Landmark Hotels and Training Centres owned by Hayley Hotels and Conference venues - a popular venue for weddings, conferences and corporate events.

PITSFORD RESERVOIR

This is the third largest in the UK and supplies much of the water for nearby Northampton. It is about three miles long and when full holds about 4,000 million gallons of water.
Work began on the project in 1952 and it was opened by the late *Queen Mother* on Thursday 25 October 1956.
The western end is open to the public and is an ideal venue for walking, cycling, fishing, sailing and bird watching. The eastern end is a Nature Reserve and is restricted to licence holders
There is a seven and a half mile cycle/walk way around the reservoir accessible from various points.
The area was designated a Site of Special Scientific Interest in 1970.

PLUMPTON

Five miles west of Towcester
Population: 1801-56
2001 – inc with Weston and Weedon Lois

DOMESDAY BOOK
PLUNTUNE
*The derivation seems obvious - this was the
place of the plum farm.*

Plumpton is a small hamlet on a minor road
between Blakesley and Weston but was once
larger and much more important.

Today it is better known locally for 'Plumpton
Cutting' where the narrow road cuts through very
high hedges on the twisting road just outside of
the village although large vehicles and coaches are
doing their very best to widen the roadway.

In 1831 there were fourteen houses and seventy
five residents whereas today it is little more than a
church, farm and Manor House. Nearby is the
even smaller community of Oakley Bank which
was once part of Plumpton village.

The Domesday Book recorded two manors here
Leofnoth held the one hide manor of
Walter the Fleming in Towcester Hundred when
there were eight households and *Hugh* held of
Walter another manor in Gravesend Hundred with
thirteen households.

There has been a church here since 1229 when
Prior Nicholas of Weedon Pinkney (now Lois
Weedon) appointed *Simon of Northampton* as
minister. The present small church of
ST JOHN the **BAPTIST** is mostly a rebuild of
1822, but with the tower, arch, chancel, font and
box pews from the old church.
After it was declared redundant in 1973 a group of
local people bought the church in 1997 and
formed a Charitable Trust.

The attractive ironstone Manor House dates from
the 17th century and has two storeys with a gabled
porch and fine rusticated gate piers.
Plumpton was a civil parish until 1935 when it
was amalgamated with Weston and Weedon Lois.

POLEBROOK

Two miles south east of Oundle
Population: 1801-241   2001 - 453

DOMESDAY BOOK
POCHEBROC
*The name is thought to derive from the
Old English 'pohha broc' meaning
'the place with a pouch shaped feature by a brook'.*

Peterborough Abbey held the main manor here in
1086 when it had nineteen households whereas the
other manor had eight households and a priest.

On the 'Square' in the centre of the village is a
cluster of particularly attractive stone cottages,
some with a thatched roof including The Old
Dukes Head which was formerly a public house.
Many other houses have roofs of Collyweston
slate.

The grandest house is undoubtedly the Jacobean
Polebrook Hall with its two slightly projecting
gabled wings and imposing 18th century wrought
iron gates.

Although the village no longer has a post office or
stores it retains its Primary school and public
house - The Kings Arms.

13c North Porch - All Saints Church - Polebrook.

Dominating the village is the church of **ALL SAINTS** which is mainly Early English in style with remains of some Norman work.
Access is via the lovely Norman porch.
It is an interesting but rather oddly shaped church dating back to 1175-1250.
The tower at the south west end is topped by a gabled spire with medium high broaches and protruding lucarnes.

Piscinas for washing hands and sacred items are common in churches but I wonder if Health and Safety got involved at Polebrook where there is a highly decorated double piscina.

The church gets many American visitors as there was an USAF airbase nearby during the Second World War and the church has an American Memorial chapel with a Roll of Honour listing men who lost their lives flying out of Polebrook.

The new graveyard nearby has a number of headstones in memory of members of the circus fraternity who had winter quarters on the edge of the village.

The parish now includes the deserted villages of Armston and Kingsthorpe.

ARMSTON

DOMESDAY BOOK
MERMESTON
*The old Saxon name implies that this was once **Eorms** farmstead*

This is one of a number of lost settlements in the Oundle area.
In 1086 Armston and Kingsthorpe had between them a total of eighteen households and were held by five Knights from Peterborough Abbey.
In 1301 records show that there were twenty eight people wealthy enough to pay tax.
The manor of Armston and Kingsthorpe was held by Thorney Abbey in 1517 and was sold to **Sir Edward Montagu** of Barnwell in 1547.

There was once a Chantry and a Hospital here but following plagues and the enclosures around 1683 very little remains today but two farms and a few cottages although it is still marked on Ordnance Survey maps.

Polebrook Airfield

The airfield was built in early 1941 as a bomber base on land owned by **Lord Rothschild**.
Polebrook Airfield was the first to be completed in the Second World War out of a number planned for Northamptonshire and Huntingdonshire.

It was originally laid down for the RAF but became home to the 351st Heavy Bombardment Group of the 8th US Air Force. Between May 1943 and April 1945, one hundred and seventy five B17 Flying Fortresses were lost flying out of the base (see Lutton).

A triangular memorial has been erected on the site of the former airfield at the end of what was the main runway.

Clark Gable, the famous film star is said to have served on the base as an air gunner and whilst there had a private room for entertaining at the Old Three Cocks public house. Quite naturally his presence in the area attracted great media interest.

The airfield became inactive in October 1948 but eleven years later was brought back into use as a base for a Thor Missile Squadron of Bomber Command.
The land is once again back in the hands of the **Rothschild** Estate.

KINGSTHORPE

DOMESDAY BOOK
CHINGESTORP

Not to be confused with the large suburb to the north of Northampton town centre.
This settlement lay to the south east of Polebrook and in 1517 belonged to Thorney Abbey together with Armston.

After the Dissolution the joint manor was acquired by **Sir Edward Montagu** of Boughton who did what many land owners did - evicted the tenants and enclosed the land for sheep and by 1720 nothing remained.

The name is perpetuated in Kingsthorpe Lodge.

POTTERSPURY

Five miles south east of Towcester
Population: 1801-698   2001 - 391

DOMESDAY BOOK
PERIE/PIRIE

*The village was originally called 'pyrige' meaning
'the place where pear trees grow' but following
the introduction of pottery in the 12th century the name
was changed to Potters Perry.*

The village lies just off the main A5 (the old Roman Watling Street) between Towcester and Old Stratford and not surprisingly several ancient items of pottery have recently been excavated.

The three manors at Potterspury were, in the days of **Edward the Confessor,** held by **Earl Tosti, Bondi** and **Bisceop**. After 1066 they were divided between **Henry de Ferrers** and **William Peverel**.

The Domesday Book records a total of seventy seven households and a priest. In addition there were two mills, one rendering eighteen shillings and four pence per annum and the other twenty one shillings and four pence per annum.

Assuming an average of four and a half persons per household the population would have been around three hundred and fifty.

It would have been a sizable and quite valuable community and not too different to the population at the present time although in the past each property would have housed many more residents than today.

The millennium sign is simple in design and features the church, a pear tree and some pots which at one time were made locally.

There has been quite a lot of new building and more is on the way but some older thatched stone built properties remain which to my mind are usually far more attractive.

In the High Street is Grafton Terrace or Duchess Row, a row of eight houses erected in 1840, which was once a lace making factory.

Many women and girls some as young as five, worked in the lace making industry and most of the men were in agriculture until the arrival of the railway and the establishment of workshops in nearby Wolverton.

Still in use in the village is the large two storeyed brick built Congregational, now United Reformed, chapel founded in 1690 but rebuilt in 1780.

The **Wood** Memorial Hall next door was up for sale on my recent visit.

The present church of **ST NICHOLAS** dates back to the 13th and 14th centuries on the site of a previous church. Its tower with six bells was built in the 14th century and indications are that a spire was to be added but this never materialised.

It is a surprise when entering from the south porch to find six steps leading down to the nave.

The church has some box pews possibly for the Lords of the Manor and his staff.

Considerable alterations were carried out in 1848; the architect being **Richard Hussey** of Birmingham. A further major re-ordering was carried out in 1991.

Old pews have been replaced by modern comfortable seating and the church now has the benefit of kitchen and toilet facilities albeit in an unusual location just off the chancel.

The alterations exposed a piscina and a medieval three seat sedilia in the chancel which had been filled with rubble and plastered over by the Victorians.

I was particularly interested in the stained glass windows although they are relatively modern.

The *'Craftsman'* window in the west end of the south aisle commemorates the Ruby wedding of a **Mr & Mrs Holloway** in 1997 and features craftsmen (in modern guise) who would have built such a church.

Also in the south aisle is the millennium window featuring a modern nativity.

Sower Window - Potterspury Church.

Among those in the north aisle one lovely window depicts *'The Sower'* and is in memory of devoted Sunday school teachers.

Even the clerestory windows are worth looking at - they appear to be all identical but see if you can spot the subtle difference.

Of the original five or six public houses some are now private residences but The Reindeer now houses an antique shop by that name. The Old Talbot public house and restaurant still operates on the A5 and in the High Street is The Cock.

The village still has a village hall, shop and post office. The Primary school is dedicated to *John Hellins,* Vicar of Potterspury 1790-1827 who persuaded the 4th Duke of Grafton to donate land and money to provide a school.

To the west of the village was the famous 'Queen's Oak' - said to have been the place where *Elizabeth Woodville* of Grafton Regis first met *King Edward IV* whom she married in 1464. Their children included the ill fated Princes in the Tower.

The tree situated in fields behind Potterspury Lodge suffered during the drought in the early 1990's and finally died during a blaze in August 1997. It had not produced acorns for many years and attempts to root cuttings have all failed.

Across the busy A5 road which runs through the parish is the settlement of Wakefield.

WAKEFIELD

DOMESDAY BOOK
WACAFELD

This small settlement had just four households when it was held by *Count Alan* under the King in 1086.

It appears to have been his only manor in Northamptonshire.

Later it became part of the *Duke of Grafton's* Estate and in 1745 the Duke commissioned *William Kent* to build the Grade II * listed Wakefield Lodge on the site of a former Hunting Lodge in Whittlebury Forest.

The grounds were landscaped by *Capability Brown* who for the first time used water in the landscape.

Much Roman building material including dressed limestone, brick, roof and floor tiles and pottery have been dredged from the artificial lake in front of Wakefield Lodge.

Following the death of the 7th *Duke* in 1918 the whole Estate was broken up and sold.

Today Wakefield is best known for Wakefield Country Courtyard just off the A5. In addition to a farm shop, café, florist and craft workshop there are always some unusual hens running around.

In the fruit season it is very popular with the 'pick your own' fraternity.

PRESTON CAPES

Five miles south of Daventry
Population: 1801-380   2001 - 188

DOMESDAY BOOK
PRESTETONE

*Originally known as Prestetone as in the Domesday Book - the Priests Farm, however another settlement grew up a little to the south east and to avoid confusion the names Magna and Parva were added, later to be changed to Preston Capes (after **Hugo de Capes**) who held the Estate and Little Preston in the 13th century.*

In the Domesday Book mention is made of three manors one of which *'was waste'* and another had a priest. Although held by different tenants they were all part of the very large landholding of the **Count of Mortain.**

Preston Capes is situated around three ancient track ways including the Portway or Market Road and has a history dating back to Roman times.

On the site of a Roman encampment and a short distance to the east of the church is the ringwork of an 11th century castle which probably had a bailey. The site is now occupied in part by the Manor House.
In 1090 **Hugh de Leycester** founded a Cluniac Priory nearby but within quite a short time it moved to Daventry

The village which is mainly a Conservation area retains its old world charm and to a large extent has resisted change.

On the edge of the community with the Northamptonshire countryside coming up to its boundary is the church of **ST PETER.**
It dates from the 13th century but was drastically restored in 1853 when the chancel roof was raised making it higher than the nave.
The relatively large west tower with its prominent square blue clock houses five bells.
The two aisles in the church are most noticeable in that the north aisle is built of light coloured limestone whereas in the south aisle dark ironstone is used.
The 15th century font has been built into one of the pillars.

Preston Capes

What first struck me as I entered the church were the reddish brown walls in the chancel which I thought had been tastefully redecorated.

All the windows are either coloured or filled with stained glass. Of particular note is the impressive engraved glass East window installed in 1974 in memory of **George St John Ravenshead** who died in 1972 aged only ten.
His face appears as that of **St George**.
The window was given by his relatives and friends including **Lord St John** of Fawsley.

The churchyard with its lovely wrought iron gateway contains the base of a local Preaching Cross which was used for worship before the church was built.

Nearby is the old school which was built in 1845, enlarged in 1871 and was closed in 1965 but the bell is still in situ.

The school house dates from about 1690 but most unusual are the Archway Cottages built in the 18th century as four red brick cottages, (now two) for workers on the Fawsley Estate. They have a connecting archway with battlements which when viewed from Fawsley Park must look like a castle.

The village was part of the Fawsley Estate until 1932 when most properties were put up for sale.

The Knightley Way between Greens Norton and Badby passes through the village.

In 2000 a sundial which gives the population of the village at that time (195) together with its longitude and latitude was placed above the main door of the village hall.

The parish now includes the shrunken settlement of Little Preston.

LITTLE PRESTON

Just a few properties now comprise Little Preston which stands on the road from Maidford and never appears to have been very large.

A Manor House is specifically mentioned in a report of 1235 when *William de Montacute* had a chapel adjoining his house which is thought to have been moated.

The actual site of the old chapel is unknown but thought to be in the area of the present North Farm.

PRESTON DEANERY

Four miles south east of Northampton
Population: 1801-70   2001 – N/A

DOMESDAY BOOK
PRESTONE
Preston simply means 'priests farm' and 'deanery' from its having given its name to the Deanery of Preston.

This small hamlet near Hackleton consists of just the church, the Hall and a few Victorian cottages and never appears to have been much larger.

In the Domesday Book there were just six households and only ten people paid the Hearth Tax in 1674.

The church of **ST PETER** and **ST PAUL** dates mainly from 1200 although a small part is early Norman.
The west tower has many blocked up windows and a central pilaster with buttresses on each face.
It fell into disuse after the Reformation and was partly demolished, the remainder being used as a dog kennel and the tower as a pigeon loft.
It must have deteriorated into a sorry state but restoration has since been carried out.

The church which is very small with a single nave and square ended chancel was declared redundant in 1972 and is now in the care of the Churches Conservation Trust although it is still used occasionally.

Owing to the dwindling population the parish was abolished in 1935 and incorporated into the parish of Hackleton.
Preston Deanery Hall is a relatively modern building having been mostly rebuilt after a fire in 1872.

Pytchley

DOMESDAY BOOK
PICTESLEI/PIHTESLEA/PITESLEA

From its early spelling – 'Picts lei', or 'Phites leait' it appears that this was a settlement of the Picts, a tribe which occupied the northern part of Britain - possibly a group of them settled in the area on one of their forages.

On the many occasions I have motored through Pytchley I have always considered it to be almost lacking in buildings of beauty, history, or architectural interest except of course for the church.

In doing research for this book I ventured off the main street to the area called 'Top End' to find an oasis of beauty and tranquillity with some lovely old stone and thatched cottages.

Pytchley has been known for its hunting packs since before the Norman Conquest.

A huntsman, *Alwine* is mentioned in the Domesday Book when there were a total of thirty two households, four manors and a mill rendering eight shillings per annum.

The Lords of the Manor owed service to the King and maintained hunting dogs.

The church of **ALL SAINTS** dates from Norman times and evidence can be seen in the first two bays of the north arcade.

This is a large building reflecting the great number of people once living at Pytchley Hall and at other large mansions and farms in the area.

The embattled west tower with five bells is built of local sandstone and was heavily banded in 1840 with iron clamps to provide additional strength.

When the floor collapsed in the nave in 1843 it was discovered that an ancient cemetery lay under most of the church.

In 1973 the box pews were removed when the timber floor became unsafe owing to beetle infestation.

Items that caught my eye were the octagonal Jacobean pulpit, the round font (thought to be Norman) which was found in the churchyard in 1838 and the elaborate painted tympanum dated 1661 which was relocated to a position above the tower arch when the chancel screen was destroyed.

It features the royal Coat of Arms flanked by the badge of the *Prince of Wales* and an emblem of roses and thistles and is thought to be one of only two of its kind in the country.

Today funds are being raised to provide a toilet block and other facilities on the ground floor of the tower.

There is no longer a shop or post office but the village does have a village hall, a Primary school, a farm shop and a public house - The Overstone Arms.

The old chapel now houses an investment company and on the Isham side of the village is a yard with many coaches belonging to R.B. Travel (Taurus Holidays) who have been trading for over forty years.

Pytchley Manor House is dated 1633 and 1665 and has good chimneys, gables and mullioned windows.

Pytchley Hall

*A sad loss to the village was the demolition of **Pytchley Hall** said to have been a grand Elizabethan Manor which was ornate and richly gabled. It was built for **Sir Euseby Isham** in 1596.*

*When **Earl Spencer** took over Pytchley Hall in 1752 he started a hunting club with a pack of hounds from Althorp that was to become the famous Pytchley Hunt.*
The kennels were moved to Brixworth in 1966 where they still remain.
The Hall was demolished in 1824 when the Estate was sold due to the gambling debts of its then owner,
***George Payne** who was Master of the Pytchley Hunt. I read that he was so convinced of his bad luck that he gambled on any horse but his own although he won both the Cesarewitch and the 1000 Guineas in his time.*

Following the loss of the Hall in 1824 many local women turned their hand to lace making until machine lace from Nottingham ruined their livelihood.
*The Estate was bought by **Mr Lewis Loyd** whose son **Samuel** acquired Overstone Park and became **Baron Overstone** in 1854.*
Parts of the Hall were distributed far and wide - the gateway to Overstone Park, the porch to Glendon Hall, fragments to Isham and panelling to Cottesbrooke.

A small square gatehouse with a pyramid roof survives east of the church but very little else, in fact it is thought that the road to Isham goes straight over the site of the former Hall.

Pytchley Hall (from old Print).

QUINTON

Five miles south east of Northampton
Population: 1801-92   2001 - 194

DOMESDAY BOOK
QUINTONE

*The name is thought to have derived from **Cwena** – a common Saxon female name*
and 'tun' - farmstead - i.e. a woman in high standing in Saxon times.

The settlement may be small but it has a long history. Recent excavations have revealed the site of an Iron Age settlement south of the village where over one hundred worked flints were discovered together with pits, ditches and depressions and also a Roman site nearby where coins, jewellery and pottery were unearthed.

Countess Judith acquired the manor following the Norman Conquest. The Domesday Book records nine households.

This is a very quiet backwater although now not far distant from Northampton's southern sprawl towards the M1 which is only about half a mile away as the crow flies, although the journey by car to Junction 15 means a two and a half mile detour.

There is no longer a shop or school and apart from a few attractive properties there is little else of note other than the 13th century church of **ST JOHN** the **BAPTIST** which originally ended with the nave until the embattled tower was raised in the 15th century.

Most of the rest of the building was remodelled in 1801.The church is unusual in that it has rounded corners of the porch and chancel.

Buried inside is ***James Dallies Kellie -MacCallum*** (1845-1932) the oldest and longest serving Chief Constable ever in Northamptonshire, he served for fifty years.
The churchyard is well kept and framed with lime trees.

Church of St John the Baptist: Quinton

RADSTONE

DOMESDAY BOOK
RODESTONE
There appears to be some disagreement as to how we get this name as there are so many possible explanations including 'farm in a clearing'

The original settlement lay about a mile to the east of the present village which today is just off the busy A43 Towcester to Brackley Road.
Radstone has dwindled in size over the years and now consists of the church, farm buildings and a few properties.

Nowadays it is hard to believe that there were once two villages here - Upper Radstone near the church and the now deserted Lower Radstone.

In 1086 the Domesday Book lists one two hide manor with twenty one households - possibly up to seventy five people.

In his survey in 1720 **Bridges** recorded that there were nineteen houses and approximately one hundred inhabitants - the majority thought to have been in Upper Radstone.

The old school of 1869 still stands but no longer in use as such.

The delightful little church of **ST LAWRENCE** is situated in a field alongside some farm buildings and is approached by foot along a narrow grassy track.

It was given the **John Betjeman** Award in the year 2000 for exemplary repairs to churches and chapels still in use.
The west tower has a Norman base and a saddleback roof. Inside there is an unmoulded round arch towards the nave, a font, thought to be Norman, a blocked west window and blocked former bell openings, possibly early 13th century.

In the past when parishioners had to stand throughout a service, provision was made for the elderly and infirm to sit down on a stone seat along the wall - ' *the weak shall go to the wall* ' - a good example of such provision can be seen here.

The church is certainly popular with the bat fraternity claiming to have the largest colony of Natterer bats in the County plus a number of Pipestrelles, one of which obviously enjoying music took up residence behind the hymn board.

There has never been a station although the Grand Central Railway line once ran straight through the parish which includes the deserted settlement of Lower Radstone.

LOWER RADSTONE

This small settlement lay about one mile east of the existing village and sometimes went by the name Nether Radstone.

It was certainly included in the one manor mentioned in the Domesday Book and always seems to have been taxed with Radstone.

In 1260 a report stated that there was only a very small amount of cultivated land here.

I have not been able to discover any reason for the desertion of the community.

# RAUNDS

Four miles south of Thrapston
Population: 1801 – 890   2001 - 8275

DOMESDAY BOOK
RANDE
*Once this was a small settlement called 'rande',
meaning edge or boundary, indicating that the village
has always been close to the County boundary.*

At the time of the Domesday Book one of the two manors was held by the **Bishop of Coutances** with thirty households and two mills, one of which rendered thirty four shillings and eight pence and one hundred eels per annum.
The other manor was part of the royal manor of Higham Ferrers and had twenty households.

Raunds grew rapidly in the 19th century with the boot and shoe trade and the brick making industry and consequently has a lot of Victorian and 20th century housing. As is to be expected for its size the town has a good range of shops, public houses, public buildings and schools.

There are a few older and interesting buildings and a small 'village' centre but otherwise I do not find the place very inspiring.

The best feature of the town is undoubtedly the church of **ST PETER** which is considered by many to be one of the finest churches in the County. It is built of oolithic limestone known locally as *'Rance Rag'* or Raunds marble.

Archaeological digs have found items which support the view that the present church stands on the site of an ancient settlement with a Saxon church and burial ground.

The church has a Norman nave and an ornate Early English style west tower of fine proportions with a broached spire which soars to a height of one hundred and eighty six feet (58 metres), the third tallest in the County.
It was rebuilt in 1826 by **Charles Squirhill** after being struck by lightning.

According to my research the church has been hit by lightning twice more - in 1841 and 1895 - how unfortunate is that! Hopefully they have now installed a good lightning conductor.

On entering via the south door the visitor is confronted with the 15th century wall paintings on the north wall of the nave which were uncovered during restoration work by **Sir George Gilbert Scott** in 1874. Over the chancel arch is the red background colour of the 'Doom' with white spaces indicating where once the crucifix and the two figures at the foot of the Cross (the **Virgin Mary** and **St John**) were located.

Another unusual and possibly unique feature is the 24 hour clock above the tower arch. The stained glass in the East window is by **Kempe** dated 1907.

The churchyard cross is thought to be a memorial to commemorate victory at the Battle of Agincourt in the 15th century.

Whilst in the churchyard my attention was drawn to a marble obelisk on which I read that it is a memorial to **David Ramsay M.B.** who died on January 6, 1902 aged 35, and provided by the parishioners to commemorate his:-

'generous and sympathetic manner in which he, for 13 years, skilfully discharged the duties of his calling and as a memento of their regret at his untimely death caused by alleviating the suffering of others'.

I have since discovered that he contracted blood poisoning whilst carrying out an operation

Raunds Station on the Kettering/Huntingdon line closed to passengers in 1959 and the line was subsequently lifted.

The gateway to a former tannery on the north side of the road from Stanwick has a stone and brick entrance arch carrying the name 'Wellington Works' and surmounted by one of its famous boots.

RAUNDS MARCH

The shoemakers here were always independent and rioted at the time of the Enclosure Act (1794).

For over two hundred years the town was fondly known as the home of the British Army Boot but in 1905 when the Boer War ended work was scarce and wages were reduced.
One hundred and fifteen men decided to march to London (a forerunner of the famous Jarrow March) to try to get a better deal from the War Office.

They walked for five days (I hope they wore some of their better boots) but on arrival in London the War Minister refused to see them.

The leader of the march, *James Gribble* an ex soldier made the marchers frustration known from the Strangers Gallery in the House of Commons and eventually a small delegation were able to present their petition when presumably, like the *Grand Old Duke of York*, they marched back home again.

Their efforts were eventually rewarded with fair pay for fair work.

A plaque commemorating this march was placed on the wall alongside the Council Offices in Raunds on the occasion of its Centenary in 2005.

Council Gates - Raunds

The parish now includes a number of lost settlements.

MALLOWS COTTON
(WEST COTTON/MILL COTTON)

I was surprised to see the site of Mallows Cotton (or Middle Cotes) to the west of Raunds actually marked on a one inch Ordnance Survey map in 2004.
The map indicated that the village lay near what was once Ringstead and Addington Station on the line of the Northampton to Peterborough railway which was closed in the 1960's.

The three small settlements each known as Cotton seem to have been very close and I have placed them together in Raunds parish although they spread out into neighbouring Ringstead parish.

At one time Mallows Cotton seems to have gone by the name Middle Cotes and there is record of a chapel there dedicated to the Holy Trinity in 1292.
A settlement existed here at the time of the Domesday Book and may have survived until about the 16th century when the land passed to the *Green* family.

Jane Austen who was known for using high quality paper for her correspondence is said to have used paper made by *John Hall* at Mill Cotton in 1814.

Excavations in the area revealed a substantial late Anglo Saxon building adjacent to a mill of 9/10th century which is thought to be the forerunner of a Manor House built on the same site in the 12th century.

The history of Mill Cotton - sometimes referred to as Mill/Parva or Little Cotton in documents can be traced back to early 12th century.
Bridges notes that it was largely abandoned by the early 18th century and by 1840 nothing but the mill, Mill House and a farm remained.

Little can be seen today because of railway construction, gravel digging and modern ploughing but by what used to be Ringstead station it is not hard to imagine people living there.

RAVENSTHORPE

Seven miles north west of Northampton
Population: 1801-466   2001 - 656

DOMESDAY BOOK
RAVENESTORP

*It appears that the name has nothing to do with ravens
but rather comes from **Hrafn**'s 'torp',
Hrafn being a personal name.*

The three manors at the time of the Domesday Book had a total of sixteen households and were divided between the **Count of Mortain**, **William Peverel** and **Gilbert 'the cook.'**

This is an attractive village with a number of listed buildings set amongst farming countryside between Long Buckby and Guilsborough in the north west of the County. To the north east it overlooks a shallow valley which was flooded in 1896 to provide a reservoir (the oldest in Northamptonshire) to supply water to Northampton. Today it is a popular area for sailing, fishing and other leisure activities.

The oldest building is the brown ironstone church of **ST DENYS** (who was executed at Montmartre in Paris) which dates mainly from the 13th and 14th centuries. The only other church in the County with the same dedication is at Cold Ashby.
The tower with a ring of five bells was partly rebuilt in 1810 and the chancel in 1866.
The Jacobean pulpit is dated 23 April 1619.

Of particular interest is a very large old chest of uncertain origin said to weigh about three quarters of a ton. It is unusual in that unlike most parish chests which had three locks and three keys this one has six locks and six keys.
The parish chest was first introduced into churches in 1240 by the then **Bishop of Lincoln** to hold church treasures.
Thereafter it held parish records.

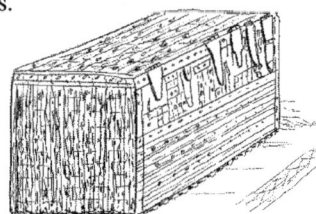

Great Chest : St Denys Ravensthorpe

The village was always basically agricultural and had no wealthy inhabitants or patrons so consequently there is a notable absence of monuments in the church although there is some armour reputedly used at the Battle of Naseby.

Sadly the local school was closed in 1962 and the Baptist chapel in 1972 - both have since been demolished. There is however still a public house - The Chequers - a shop and post office in a building dated 1610 and a village hall refurbished in 2011 at a cost of £87,000
In addition there is a plant nursery, a garage, a Pocket Park and even a Travel Company which organises School Study and Sports Trips and a Grade II listed K6 telephone kiosk.

Ravensthorpe always appears to be such a quiet respectable village that it came as a real surprise when a cannabis factory was discovered in one of the properties in January 2012.

The parish includes the shrunken village of Coton

COTON

DOMESDAY BOOK
COTA

Cota, as in the Domesday Book simply means cottage or 'cote'. Unlike many villages there is no addition to the 'cote' as in Holcot, Foscott, Muscott, etc. although for a short period in the Middle Ages it was known as Cotene Juxta Gildeburg - cottage next to Guilsborough.

In the Domesday Book Coton is recorded as an independent manor with nine households. By the time of the Hearth Tax in the 17th century, eight households were recorded and some fifty years later **Bridges** when writing his history of Northamptonshire noted that there were seventeen houses, much the same as today.

Little remains of the original settlement although it is still marked on Ordnance Survey maps about one mile south of Guilsborough.

The main property is **Coton Manor** which dates from 1662 and has gables and mullioned windows. The ten acre gardens with lakes, waterfall and wildfowl were created in 1920 by former family members and today they are a popular tourist attraction particularly in the spring when the snowdrops, helibores and bluebells are in full flower.

RINGSTEAD

Two miles south of Thrapston
Population: 1801-454   2001 - 1428

*The village does not appear in the Domesday Book
as it then belonged to the manor of Raunds and was first
documented in 1124.
It would have been a 'circular place' in Saxon times
according to its Saxon name of 'hring-stede'.*

Ringstead is located between Thrapston and Raunds just off the A45 (Raunds bypass) in the east of the County.

The large Baptist chapel tucked away behind some houses proudly displays the date 1887 marked out in coloured brickwork on the front of the building. This is still in use as a shared Baptist - Methodist chapel. The village hall was once the Temperance Hall established in 1861 to provide for the:-

*'Temperance, Intelligence and Happiness
of the people'.*

Opposite, the Ringstead Institute of 1908 now houses a play group.

At one time Ringstead workers were heavily involved in boot and shoe manufacture both in factories or small outbuildings although this has now ceased.

One factory the Ringstead Britannia Co-op Society built in 1895 is now office accommodation under the name 'Britannia House.'

The village has a number of 17th and 18th century stone buildings but was largely rebuilt in brick.
It is now quite a large community and still supports two public houses, a supermarket, post office, Primary school and even a fish and chip shop.

There is a considerable commercial presence in the village in the form of Dodson and Horrell's County Store with its large warehouses opposite The New Inn.

The church of **ST MARY** is basically a 13th century church consisting of a chancel with north chantry and a clerestoried nave which is separated from the only aisle, the north aisle, by a beautiful arcade.

The west tower is surmounted by a broach spire which houses the bell chamber thus resulting in the lower set of gabled lucarnes being unusually large. Inside the items which caught my attention were the beautiful tracery in the chancel windows, the unusual double aumbry and the stone base which at one time supported a decorated stone screen to separate the chantry from the chancel.

Ringstead was the birthplace of *Alf Roberts*, father of *Margaret Thatcher* (Prime Minister between 1979 and 1990) the only woman to date to have held the post.

There is still a Station Road leading out of Ringstead which eventually brings you to the site of the Ringstead and Addington station on the Northampton to Peterborough line. This closed in the 1960's and the station buildings have all been demolished but the original stone sleepers used in the early days of the line now provide excellent stepping stones for walkers who wish to avoid the boggy area during the winter months.

The parish includes part of the area of land in which were three small settlements known as Cotton (see Raunds page 347).

 ## KINEWELL LAKE NATURE RESERVE

A favourite spot of mine is the old gravel workings of Kinewell Lake just outside the village which have local Nature Reserve status.
Gravel extraction ceased in 1979.
Named after a spring that is now submerged, it is somewhat unusual in that the lake is connected to the River Nene allowing fish to migrate between the two.

The lovely lakeside walk can be extended to Willy Watt Mill and to include two other lovely villages, namely Woodford and Denford. The whole area is excellent for walking, picnics, bird watching, etc.
When in the area recently there appeared to be development work and building going on in the area of Willy Watt Marina.

ROADE

Six miles south of Northampton
Population: 1801-845   2001 - 2254

DOMESDAY BOOK
RODE

The name has not changed much over the centuries - the Saxon name was 'rod' meaning 'cleared land' or 'open woodland.' The area must have been covered with trees - Salcey Forest is still only a few miles distant.

There is evidence of a likely Roman settlement here as there have been many finds of coins, pottery and bronze pins.

When the Normans invaded in 1066 the manor was held by **Swein**. Following the Conquest it was tenanted by **Dodin** of **Gunfrid de Chocques**. There was land for only one plough and only two households are recorded.

However there is another entry relating to a four hide manor which **Sigar de Chocques** held of the King which may relate to Roade or Gayton.

The village stands astride what is now the busy A508 Northampton to Milton Keynes road.

By 1676 the population had risen to three hundred and in recent years it has expanded quite dramatically and now totals well over two thousand.

Naturally there is much modern building but quite a number of properties are of such an age that they have listed building status including the Baptist chapel built in 1736/7 and Hyde Farm (originally of the 14th century) and its medieval dovecote.

The hub of the village appears to be the area around the Green where there is a Methodist church which is still open, The Cock Hotel and number of retail outlets and a restaurant.

One of the biggest employers used to be Pianoforte Supplies which was founded in 1923.

It was heavily engaged in armament work during the Second World War and was substantially extended.

Its owner **Sir Cyril Cripps** provided some excellent sports facilities in the area.

At its peak the firm employed about seventeen hundred people many of whom came in from Northampton and the surrounding villages by bus.

Sadly from the point of view of its employees Pianoforte Supplies closed in 1980 however some buildings are still used for producing parts for Vauxhall cars.

Roade once had a busy Railway Station on the main west coast line and is the junction for trains on the Northampton loop. The station closed in 1964 but the line is still heavily used.

Just north of the station site is Roade cutting which opened in 1838 and was deepened and widened in 1875 to take the extra tracks for the Northampton Loop.

The present iron girders were installed after a landslip in 1891.

Whilst work was going on with the building of the railway cutting and station it is reported that up to a thousand navvies lived and worked in the area.

In my opinion Roade, being on the West Coast main line is an ideal spot for a station re-opening as was done recently at Corby.

At Roade commuters from the area including the sprawling southern suburbs of Northampton could gain access to main line trains to London and further afield whereas a Park & Ride scheme could quickly take shoppers to and from Northampton.

Near the Station was a public house originally named after the Chief Engineer of the railway **Robert Stephenson**.

This was renamed The George but like so many public houses at the beginning of the 21st century it was closed and has now been demolished.

The church of **ST MARY** dates from the 12th century, with the lower part of the tower, chancel, nave and the splendid south doorway dating from Norman times.

The lime tree avenue as you approach the main entrance makes it extremely difficult in summer months to view the church properly when trying to take a photograph.

A bell chamber was erected about 1450 to house four bells but this has now been increased to six.
During the 1800's various alterations took place including the provision of the north aisle.
The layout is quite unusual with the nave separated from the chancel by the central tower with an east and west arch giving very little room for the bell ringers.

The chief medieval monument is the plain unlettered altar tomb said to be that of
Richard Wake (of Courteenhall) and his two wives.

Once inside the church it is obvious that money bequeathed by local benefactor
Sir Cyril Cripps has been invested in new furnishings and lighting, a lovely modern church hall with full facilities and even a wrought iron spiral staircase giving access to the tower.
The East window dedicated to the memory of him and his wife is particularly impressive.

On leaving the church look to the top of the tower to see an enormous cockerel on the weathervane.
I am told that the cockerel was stolen when work was being done on the tower but it was found some distance away together with a £5 note to pay for its return.

On driving through Roade there are two things to look out for - one is the speed camera near the garage which in the past has caught many unwary drivers although it is now said to have been switched off and the other is the large Comprehensive school erected in 1956 and recently renamed the *Elizabeth Woodville* school which signals that you are leaving the village on the way south.

The Primary school in a different part of the village dates back to 1876.
Included in the parish is the shrunken medieval settlement of Hyde.

HYDE

This settlement once lay immediately east of Hyde Farm. The name is not recorded in documents until 1200 so I presume that if it existed in 1086 it was included in the record for Roade.

As much of the area has now been built on there is little evidence of the existence of this one time settlement.

Roade Methodist Church

-351-

ROCKINGHAM

Two miles north of Corby
Population: 1801-213   2001 - 115

DOMESDAY BOOK
ROCHINGEHAM

The name derives from **Hroca** *- ' inga' - 'tun'
the homestead of the people of* **Hroca**.

Rockingham Village

This is one of Northamptonshire's most attractive villages. It is dominated by the Castle which occupies a superb position on a hill overlooking the vast Welland Valley. The Castle dates back to the years immediately following the Norman Conquest and with it the village grew in importance and in 1272 the grant of a market was obtained.

The original Market Cross thought to have been situated near the Castle is said to have been destroyed during the Civil War but what was left was found in the mid 19th century and re-erected in the centre of the village. The present upper section of the Cross was rebuilt in 1894.

The village lies at the foot of quite a steep hill and has some delightful thatched stone houses and cottages dating from the 17th and 18th centuries.

The earliest domestic building is thought to be The Sondes Arms dated 1663 named after the family who owned the Estate in the Middle Ages.
On one side of this very popular public house and restaurant is the village shop and tea room and on the other side is the old school built by **Richard Watson** about 1845 but closed in the mid 20th century. It is now the village hall and is crying out for restoration.

One of my favourite County views is looking back up the hill towards the Castle.
It is a lovely view of a truly English village.
Take away the cars and you can imagine how peaceful it would have been in the past.

Between the Castle and the village stands the church of **ST LEONARD.**
Although its origins date back to the 13th century it was largely destroyed in the Civil War and was rebuilt in the 19th century.
The church is very low and of irregular construction consisting of a nave, chancel and memorial chapel to the *Watson* family with many memorials and monuments including *Lewis,*
1st Baron Rockingham.
On my recent visit I noticed that a considerable amount of plaster had been stripped from the south wall to allow the stonework to dry out before restoration work is undertaken.
The small square bell tower with octagonal pyramid roof was installed in 1845 - the design being taken from a church in Oxfordshire.

Rockingham had a station on the Rugby to Stamford cross country line following the Welland Valley for much of its route.
The station was actually in the village of Caldecott to the north and right on the Leicestershire border. The line closed in 1966 but the station buildings are still in commercial use.

Rockingham Speedway - a major national motor event centre is located about three miles east of the village. From the outside it is a hideous monstrosity and a real blot on the landscape.
I'm not surprised that they did not want it close to this most attractive village whose name it carries.

Watson

Rockingham Castle

Rockingham Castle, a Grade I listed building was once a royal fortress with commanding magnificent views over the Welland Valley and well protected by the lie of the land to north and west. There are traces of Roman occupation in the surrounding area where bones, pottery, tiles, coins and even a key were found.

*The Domesday Book states that the manor of Rockingham 'was waste' when **King William** ordered a Castle to be built on the site of an earlier fortification. This was in the form of a motte and double bailey.*
*His son **William II** was responsible for the first stone building on the site.*
It became an important seat of Government and the Great Council of the Realm was held here in 1096.
*Many medieval Kings visited Rockingham Castle including **King John** who frequently came to hunt in Rockingham Forest. On his last visit he is said to have left his treasure chest in the Great Hall giving rise to the legend that his treasures are buried at Rockingham and not lost in the Wash.*
Henry III strengthened the Castle with the addition of the iconic twin D - tower gatehouse.

*By the late 15th century the Castle had fallen into disrepair. **Edward Watson** acquired it from the Crown and obtained a lease in 1553 from **Henry VIII** to convert it into a fine private dwelling.*
***Sir Lewis Watson** bought the freehold from **James I** and became a Knight, Baronet and Baron.*
*He was a devout royalist but delayed his decision to fight for **King Charles I** and as a result the Castle was captured by Roundheads on 19th March 1643 and it remained in their control for the rest of the Civil War.*
***King Charles** was displeased with **Sir Lewis'** lack of support and locked him up in Belvoir Castle although he eventually regained control by which time the Castle was severely damaged, the curtain walls razed and the great keep destroyed. He lost a lot of his wealth and never fully recovered from the trauma.*

*Rockingham was in its heyday as a Victorian mansion filled with **Richard** and **Levinia Watson's** family, friends and servants. **Charles Dickens** was a frequent guest and it is reputed that David Copperfield and Bleak House were largely written whilst in residence there.*
*The Castle has passed through many hands including daughters, younger sons and nephews to the present **Saunders** family who have added the name **Watson** to preserve their heritage.*
The Castle and twelve acres of formal and wild grounds which are now in private hands are open to visitors during the summer months and host garden parties, equestrian events, conferences and concerts.
An impressive sight in the gardens is the four hundred year old Elephant Hedge.

Rockingham and its Castle was used by the BBC in the early 1980's for scenes of the English Civil War in its drama 'By the Sword Divided' and as the setting for the Bollywood film 'Kyan! Ho Gaya Na Dya'

In May 2013 the Castle will hold the Brigstock International Horse Trials for the first time following the sale of the host property Fermyn Woods Hall near Brigstock.

ROTHERSTHORPE

Four miles south west of Northampton
Population: 1801-197   2001 - 500

DOMESDAY BOOK
TORP
Simply known as 'torp' - village or secondary settlement, the name was expanded in about 1242
*to include the personal name of **Rethaer**.*

The two and a half hide manor was held by **Gunfrid de Chocques** in 1086 when there were twenty six households and a mill rendering thirty two pence per annum.

The main part of the village lies just off the Banbury Lane and the Midshires Way which runs through the County for a distance of forty six miles goes through the parish.
The village consists of two main streets, North Street and Church Street running parallel to Banbury Lane - an old Drovers' route.

How much longer it remains a village is unknown as it is gradually being approached by the expanding housing and industrial development of Northampton towards the M1 motorway which is less than half a mile to the north.
Many a motorist will have rested at Rothersthorpe (now Northampton) Services on the M1.

Similarly many will have journeyed along the Grand Union Canal by boat or on foot but few people seem to venture into the village itself.
At the moment it is lovely and quiet with some attractive properties together with a day nursery, a Primary school, a farm shop, a village hall and a public house - The Chequers.

The Baptist church which was rebuilt in 1892 stands close by the church but was closed for religious services many years ago.

Castle Farm has an interesting yard featuring old stables, red telephone boxes and old enamel advertising signs.

By the 17th century Manor House stables there is a large round sandstone dovecote approximately twenty feet diameter with a leaded roof topped by a little octagonal wooden cupula and over nine hundred nesting places.

For those who enjoy the countryside a lovely walk leads you through this historic village with its thatched cottages and along the banks of the Grand Union Canal with its multitude of flora and fauna, some rare plants, dragonflies and waterfowl and of course its narrow boats.

A focal point in the centre of the village is the church of **ST PETER** and **ST PAUL** with its distinctive saddleback roof, dating mainly from the 13th and 14th centuries, although the church has a Norman font.
It is thought that an even earlier church may have existed on or near the site with the discovery of the base of a 7th century Preaching Cross.
Of great rarity is an Early English style head of a wheeled cross which was discovered discarded in a barn in 1869.

The Old Dovecote
Rothersthorpe

The plain pulpit has one panel dated 1579.
The centre of the churchyard has been cleared of tombstones and with a well positioned wooden bench makes a peaceful place to sit and rest.

Although I like the black and white old Rectory alongside the church it looks a little out of place in its present setting.

As a teenager I spent many happy hours train spotting from the embankment near the signal box on Banbury Lane.

The line was always very busy and the level crossing was continually opening and closing.
The sight of the splendid long distance expresses will always remain with me.
Those days are sadly gone.

The line is still in use although steam trains have disappeared and the level crossing has been replaced by a rather expensive curving road bridge with traffic lights so as to allow the high speed trains to travel at higher speeds between London Euston and the north west.

THE BERRY RINGWORK

At the heart of the village between Church Street and North Street is an open area containing the Berry Ringwork.

Its origin appears to be somewhat obscure but this unusual defensive earthwork is thought to date from pre-medieval times but was used much later.

Ringworks are medieval fortifications built and occupied from the late Anglo Saxon period to the later 12th century.

As at Rothersthorpe they were small defended areas that contained buildings which were partly or entirely surrounded by a substantial ditch and bank usually topped with timber palisades.

In 918AD a Saxon army led by *Edward the Elder* defeated Danish forces who were occupying Northampton.
Two silver coins produced during the reign of *King Edmund the Elder* were found recently in the area by a metal detectorist.
Although an ancient site it is open at all times to members of the public.

ROTHWELL

Three miles north west of Kettering
Population: 1801-1409   2001 - 7108

DOMESDAY BOOK
RODEWELLE
*The name is thought to have derived from the Saxon
'rothu' (or rod) meaning clearing.
i.e. clearing near the well although some would have
you believe that it was 'the place of the red well.'*

The Domesday Book records Rothwell itself as having sixty four households, representing a population of over two hundred people and two mills rendering nine shillings and four pence per annum.

The large royal manor of Rothwell together with its appendages was worth £30 in 1066 but had risen to £50 by 1086 - a very valuable asset.

In 1156 the spelling was 'Rowel' and it is still known as such by local people even today.

During ironstone quarrying in the area evidence was found of an Anglo Saxon cemetery with at least eight Saxon urns, beads, brooches and rings and other bronze items.

It might seem unlikely today but in the early Middle Ages Rothwell had a town wall in which there were several gates.
It was a place of some importance and took precedence over nearby Kettering until the coming of the railway.

Like so many Northamptonshire towns and villages, Rothwell saw much growth in population with the arrival of the boot and shoe industry.
Many worked in factories but a large number of people were employed as outworkers in workshops and even garden sheds.

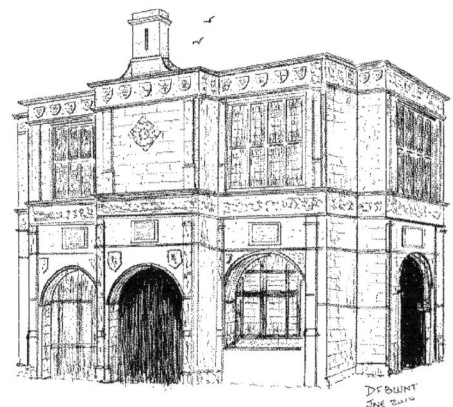
Market House. Rothwell

Some 19th century workshops still exist although footwear manufacture in the area virtually disappeared in the mid 20th century owing to the influx of cheaper goods from overseas.

Rothwell has more historic or architecturally attractive buildings than both Desborough to the north west or Kettering to the south east.
The most interesting and historic is the church of the **HOLY TRINITY.** This is a cruciform Norman church built of ironstone and once known as St Saviour's. It is the longest parish church in the County measuring 173 feet (53 metres) although it was once even larger.

Not only is this a big church it probably also had a large staff as it has a four seat sedilia and a triple piscina with three drain holes which is possibly unique in England. Inside are 14th century choir stalls and two groups of misericords.

The present tower is sturdy and rather short. Originally it had a spire but this was removed after being struck by lightning in 1660.

The Lady Chapel has a window in memory of *Catherine Maunsell* wife of *Captain Thomas Maunsell of* Thorpe Malsor and Rothwell Grange who died in 1931. The chancel contains a window dated 1912 in memory of *Jasper Booth* of Glendon and of more recent installation is the *Jessie Cleaver* window in *St Helens* chapel which was dedicated on 22nd October 2007.

The *Rothwell Imp* (likened to that at Lincoln Cathedral) is carved in stone on the south side of the chancel.

I love the sound of church bells but I am not sure how the surrounding inhabitants feel when all ten bells are being rung.

The church has good acoustics and as a result arranges many concerts.

I am sure that the visitors also appreciate the newly provided kitchen and toilet facilities.

The rib vaulted Bone Crypt or Charnel House is claimed to be one of only two in the country, the only other one I have discovered is at St Brides in Fleet Street, London. The crypt is said to contain approximately fifteen hundred skulls and thigh bones and is usually open for visitors on a Sunday afternoon in summer.

Research has revealed them to be mainly medieval in date - probably the remains of townspeople who died of natural causes but others like to tell you that they are of soldiers killed at the Battle of Naseby.

The local football team has quite aptly adopted the nickname *'The Bones'*

What is today known as the Rothwell House Hotel was built in the late 18th century of red brick as the Vicarage.
The 18th century Manor House with an elegant facade and columns has a particularly handsome doorway and is situated just to the west of the church opposite a park with medieval fish ponds.

A distinctive feature of the expansive Market Square is the Grade I listed Market House designed by *William Grumbold* for the somewhat eccentric *Sir Thomas Tresham* of Rushton Hall around 1578 but left unfinished for over three hundred years until it was finally roofed in 1895.

The building of Weldon stone is unique with ninety six heraldic shields and coats of arms of local landowning families depicted on the exterior walls.
In recent years the building has had various uses including a jail, council offices and a library.

Jesus Hospital south east of the church was founded by *Owen Ragsdale* a fellow of Magdalen College Oxford and a teacher in Rothwell in 1585, his tomb is in the church. The foundation for twenty four old men has at its entrance a lovely old gateway with *'Jesus Hospital'* carved in stonework above the arch. It was entirely reconstructed internally in 1962 following which the Governors admitted married couples.

On Desborough Road is the **Priory House** dated 1660 and possibly built on part of the site of an old nunnery which was founded in 1247 by *Richard Clare, Earl of Gloucester*.
The centre of the town is a Conservation area but always seems quite busy with traffic competing with people visiting the local shops, public houses, restaurants and library.

The United Reformed church off Meeting Lane was built in 1735 but Rothwell is said to be the birthplace of Midland non-conformity dating back to 1656 when a covenant was signed by its members.

ROTHWELL CHARTER FAIR

Rothwell had a market as early as 1154 and fifty years later *King John* granted a Charter for an Annual Fair to take place the week after Trinity Sunday, the Sunday after Whit Sunday.
It is the oldest Charter Fair in Northamptonshire.

King James I granted a second Charter in 1614 to *William Cockayne*, Lord of the Manor.

The annual Rowell Fair begins at 6 a.m. on Trinity Monday when the Bailiff for the Lord of the Manor seated on horseback outside the church reads the Charter.
Accompanied by his bodyguards of halberdiers and the Rowell Fair Brass Band he repeats it outside each of the town's public houses.
In return the ceremonial party receives a glass of traditional Rowell Fair rum and milk.
I have often seen the Fair but needless to say have not witnessed the opening ceremony.

Originally it was a four day Horse Fair but is now a pleasure fair which attracts thousands of visitors. The rides and sideshows are set up on both sides of the High Street and on the Market Square leaving the traffic to weave its way through as best it can.

In 2004 there were great celebrations on the occasion of the 800th Anniversary although this took place in June rather than May in the week following Trinity Sunday.

RUSHDEN

Four miles east of Wellingborough
Population: 1801-818   2001 - 25849

DOMESDAY BOOK
RISDENE

Etymologists suggest that the name comes from 'ryscen' or 'rysc' - rushy or rush and 'denu' - valley.

At the time of the Domesday Book Rushden was part of the Manor of Higham Ferrers.
There were nineteen sokemen and a mill rendering ten shillings per annum.

The Normans built a Hunting Lodge here which was developed into **Rushden Hall** by *John of Gaunt*. By the 15th century the settlement had become a small town.

At the junction of the old A6 and A45 roads there was a Toll Gate (now known as the Toll Bar) to collect fees from road users.
This point marks the boundary between the factory town of Rushden and its much more attractive neighbour the ancient Borough of Higham Ferrers.

Lace making flourished in the Middle Ages but with the coming of the boot and shoe industry and the building of shoe factories rapid expansion took place.

A major fire in 1771 destroyed most of Rushden which was then almost totally rebuilt.
Very few old buildings remain.

The population grew from 818 in 1801 to over 12,000 at the turn of the 20th century.
The town now has most of the facilities and resources to be expected to cater for quite a sizeable population.
In the High Street there is a mix of small shops with some superstores in close proximity.

In addition there are a number of chapels, public houses, restaurants, health centre, library, doctors' surgeries, etc.

Rushden was linked to the main railway line at Wellingborough by means of a Branch Line from Higham Ferrers.
Regular passenger services were withdrawn in 1959 and the last goods service in 1969.

The town retains its railway station but is no longer linked to the National Rail Network although since 1984 has been the base for the Rushden Historical Transport Society.
They regularly hold Open Days, special attractions and even run trains on a small section of restored track towards Higham Ferrers.

The station abounds with a wide assortment of rolling stock, old motor vehicles, platform equipment and furniture and enamelled advertisements.

Old Railway Station
Rushden

Strainer Arch
St Mary's Church: Rushden

Dominating the skyline is the crocketed 172 ft (53 metres) tall spire of **ST MARY'S** church which has been built essentially in Perpendicular style.

A particular feature is the ornate strainer arch which was installed in the nave to strengthen the side walls.
Similar features can be found at Finedon and Easton Maudit (Northamptonshire), Canterbury and most famously at Wells Cathedral.

Other features of note are the superb monuments to members of the *Pemberton* family of Rushden Hall in the *Pemberton* Chapel, the 15th century roof supported by angels, the fairly rare 14th century oak pulpit and the fine three seat sedilia.

The 15th century stained glass is said to be among the best in the County.

I got the impression that it is quite a lively church with plenty going on. It was certainly very busy and noisy on my visit when there was a gathering of youngsters from the 'Scarecrow Holiday Club' together with their nine enormous scarecrows.

Rushden Hall in nearby Rushden Park has a Jacobean east front, a two storeyed embattled porch and square bay windows.

Rushden was the birthplace of the novelist *H. E. Bates* - some of whose stories including *'Love for Lydia'* and *'The Darling Buds of May'* have recently been made into TV dramas.

During the Second World War a German aircraft dropped a stick of bombs over the town.
The Queen Victoria Hotel and some other buildings were hit. Unfortunately a teacher and several children were killed when one of the bombs hit Alfred Street Junior school.

The local football team, known as Rushden and Diamonds was the brainchild of *Max Griggs* of Dr Marten boots fame and was formed in April 1992 by the amalgamation of Rushden Town with Irthlingborough Diamonds Football Clubs.

A good modern stadium was built alongside on the main A6 road just outside Irthlingborough.
The team had a brief spell in the Football League when it was financially supported by *Max Griggs* but after relegation and a short spell in the Blue Square Conference League the Club was disbanded in 2011 and the ground taken over by Kettering Town Football Club.
This Club had a very short stay at the stadium before they themselves ran into financial difficulties.

Triangular Lodge - Rushton

RUSHTON

Three miles north west of Kettering
Population: 1801-434   2001 - 451

DOMESDAY BOOK
RISETONE/RISTONE/RICSDONE
The name appears to derive from 'rysc' meaning rush and 'tun' - farmstead - a dwelling in a marshy area or where rushes were grown.

Rushton has many 17th century buildings built of locally found oolite ironstone - more recently quarried locally for the nearby Corby Steel Works.

In the Domesday Book there were two villages here, Rushton All Hallows and Rushton St Peter.
In total there were fifty households and two mills rendering a combined total of forty four pence per annum.
In 1780 the two villages became one and by 1799 the Estate church of **ST PETER** located near the Hall was demolished.

Some of the stone was used to repair the remaining church of **ALL SAINTS** in the centre of the village which has an embattled west tower and a Norman west wall of the nave which is now completely hidden by massive organ pipes.
The church was restored about 1860 by *E. F. Law.*

The tomb of *Sir Thomas Tresham* MP who died in 1559 was transferred from the former church. His effigy wearing a long black mantle with the white flory cross over his heart, the traditional dress of a Knight Hospitaller is possibly unique and is thought to be the only one of its kind in England.

Another effigy in Purbeck marble features a 13th century cross legged Knight, traditionally *William de Goldringham,* the owner of an Estate in Rushton.

Just behind the church is probably the most picturesque cricket field in the County.
It is how I imagine village cricket should be played on a lovely sunny afternoon.

Rushton Hall, a Grade I listed building of Weldon stone is very large and impressive.
It was commenced by *Sir William Tresham* who bought the Estate in 1438 and the family lived there for nearly 200 years.
During that time they enclosed much of the parish resulting in a decline of population in the area.

The Estate was sold on about 1615 to *Sir William Cockayne,* Lord Mayor of London. He set about enlarging and embellishing the property.

A subsequent owner of the Hall for which she paid £165,000 was *Miss Clara Thornhill* after whom the local public house/restaurant is named.
On her marriage to *William Capel Clarke* in 1856 both took the name *Clarke-Thornhill.*

A former public house, 'The Three Cocks' ended up in the grounds of **Rushton Hall** when the course of the Rothwell to Pipewell road was altered and is now an outbuilding.

For about forty five years before it was sold in 2003 the Hall operated as a school for the RNIB. It is now a luxury hotel, spa and conference centre.

Rumour has it that an underground tunnel ran from the Hall to the Triangular Lodge and that a great treasure was buried there.

Whilst a search was being made to find this tunnel in 1979 a Priests Hole was discovered. These were a feature of many great houses of those who illegally held to the Catholic faith during the reign of *Queen Elizabeth I* as did the *Treshams.*

It is said that *Charles Dickens* conceived the idea of Havisham Hall for his novel *'Great Expectations'* on one of his frequent visits.

The Grade I listed Triangular Lodge, with alternating bands of light and darker ironstone was built for *Sir Thomas Tresham* between 1593-1595 as a rabbit warrener's lodge but in fact reflects his passion for the Roman Catholic faith. This bizarre Lodge is set in the north west corner of the Estate and has three storeys each with three windows on each of three sides.
In fact everything is in multiples of three - all hinting at the Holy Trinity.
Externally the building is quite amazing but in my view the inside is fairly plain.

There is still a Primary school but no longer a shop or post office and the Methodist chapel having closed is now used as the village hall.
Trains thunder through the village on the main line between St Pancras and the north but they no longer call at the little station although the old Grade II listed station buildings and platform still remain and are partly in residential use.

Included in the parish is the shrunken village of Glendon (see page 187) and the lost village of Barford.

BARFORD

DOMESDAY BOOK
BEREFORD(E)
The derivation is generally accepted as being a common term for a ford through which corn may be carried.

In 1086 according to the Domesday Book, Barford was held by the King and had a mill rendering thirty two pence per annum and seven households.

By 1327 there were fourteen tenants but almost the whole village was destroyed and the land converted to pasture by *George Boyville* in the early 16th century.

It is said that the church or chapel served by a monk from nearby Pipewell Abbey stood near the Ise Brook but by 1625 it is reported as having been levelled. Some people claim that a hooded monk still haunts the area.

Skeletons are said to have been found there before 1720 and *Bridges* in his history compiled about the same time reported that the marks of houses were still visible.

Today Barford Bridge over the River Ise to the east of Rushton is about the only indication of the former settlement.
The parish of Barford was abolished in April 1935 and became part of Rushton parish.

Tresham family

*The **Treshams** were a Gloucestershire family but their history in Northamptonshire goes back to **William Tresham** who married **Isabella Vaux** of Harrowden and in 1438 bought the Rushton Estate.*
*He acquired much of his wealth by virtue of his posts as Attorney General to **Henry V** and Speaker of the House of Commons.*
He was a staunch Lancastrian and was murdered near Moulton in 1450 (see Sywell).
*The Estate passed through various hands including **Sir Thomas** who died in 1559 and whose monument is in the church.*

*The most famous, some say the most eccentric, Tresham was another **Thomas** (1534-1605) who was Knighted in 1575 at the Queens Progress at Kenilworth.*
*Although brought up as a Protestant he turned to the Catholic faith. During his lifetime he was responsible for a number of unusual buildings including the Triangular Lodge at Rushton, the Market House at Rothwell and the New Bield at Lyveden - all expressions of his Catholic faith. **Sir Thomas** was a man of very strong religious convictions and spent fifteen years in prison or under house arrest for his religious beliefs and for harbouring Jesuit priests.*

*His eldest son, **Francis** who was described as a 'wild and unstayed man' was foolish enough to get involved in the Gunpowder Plot and died in the Tower of London in 1605 shortly after his father.*
*Although the family held considerable land they never recovered and deep in debt (owing about £1,700,000 at todays prices much of it as a result of fines) the Estate was sold about 1615. The line became extinct on the death of **Sir William** in 1634.*

SCALDWELL

Seven miles north of Northampton
Population: 1801-276   2001 - 271

DOMESDAY BOOK
SCADEWELL/SCALDESWELLE
SCALDEWELLE
*The name comes from the Saxon words,
'sceald' - shallow and 'wielle' - spring.*

In researching for this book I discovered that Scaldwell is one of the few villages in the County with no earthwork remains indicating that no movement or shrinkage has taken place.

There has in the past been ironstone mining in the parish during which were found 260 pennies and halfpennies from the reign of *William I.*

Up until the 1950's there were still ironstone quarries in the area.

At the time of the Domesday Book there were three manors with thirty three households.

One manor was given by *King William* to the Abbey of St Edmundsbury *'for the soul of Queen Matilda'*.

The village which lies just east of the busy A508 between Market Harborough and Northampton is a very attractive little place with stone cottages grouped around a lovely village Green with a pond which was the original source of water for the village pump which fed a series of horse troughs.

Numerous springs in the area now all flow into Pitsford reservoir.

From the Green the sight of the lovely 12th century church of **ST PETER** and **ST PAUL** standing on a slight hill makes a charming spectacle. There is a chancel with a north aisle and chapel, nave, south aisle, south porch and unbuttressed Norman west tower and a beautiful pinnacle sanctuary bell tower.

Extensive restorations in 1863 caused some dissension in the village with the removal of the old family pews. In the churchyard are the remains of a Preaching Cross.

The former Rectory dates from 1716 and originally had a five bay flat front but a porch was added later.

SHUTLANGER

Two miles north east of Towcester
Population: 1801-257   2001 - 270

*The village is not referred to in the Domesday Book and the earliest reference I can find is in 1162 when it was a daughter settlement for Stoke Bruerne and known as Shitelhanger from 'scytel' - shuttle or bolt and 'hangra' - wood on a steep slope.
The Victorians changed the name out of modesty.*

Shutlanger is a small limestone village with little of note except the monastery opposite the chapel. According to my findings this never was a monastery in the accepted term but simply a grand house and now exists as a Grade I listed private residence with a large vaulted porch.

Was this the building referred to by *Bridges* in the 18th century as *'a chapel converted into a farmhouse.'*

In 1884 an Infant school was established, designed by local architect *Matthew Holding* and a chancel dedicated to **ST ANNE** was added in 1886.

When the school closed in 1916 it became the village hall and the chapel continues to be used for occasional services.

There is no shop or post office although the remaining public house, The Plough Inn always seems to be advertising fish dinners when I travel through the village but there is little else to attract the visitor.

Although the Towcester to Olney railway line passed close by the northern edge of the village there never was a railway station.

One claim to fame is that it was for a time the home of *Derek Redmond* whose exploits on the track and in the Olympic Games earned him the title, the Shutlanger Flyer.

He is famously remembered for being helped across the finishing line by his father at the Barcelona Olympics in 1992 after suffering an injury.

SIBBERTOFT

Five miles south west of Market Harborough
Population: 1801-330 2001 - 343

DOMESDAY BOOK
SIBERTOD
The prefix is from Saxon origin - a personal name
Sigebeorht *followed by the Viking 'toft' - homestead.*

After the Norman Conquest the Estate (along with many others) was granted to the *Count of Mortain* when there were seventeen households and a priest. In 1299 *Lord Brabazon* granted the right to hold a Saturday market but this does not appear to have been successful.

Sibbertoft on the Northamptonshire/Leicestershire border lies at a height of 600 feet above sea level and once had a reputation for being a
'wild and lawless place'.
It appears to have consisted of two separate parts with an area called Westhorpe to the west of the main village. The River Welland rises in the cellar of the old Rectory and emerges north of the village reaching the North Sea at the Wash.
The bell ringers of Sibbertoft had the honour of starting a twelve hour cascade of church bells which rang down the length of the Welland valley to celebrate the Diamond Jubilee of
Queen Elizabeth II on Monday 4 June 2012.
A total of 35 towers over four counties took turns to ring at a pre-appointed time.

The peace of the area was disturbed in 1645 when the Battle of Naseby was fought close by.
King Charles' standard was raised at Moot Hill to the east and survivors fled north through the village after the Battle but there is little physical evidence to be seen today.
However in the Northampton museum is a stash of coins known as the *'Sibbertoft Hoard'* believed to have been buried by a soldier and trampled into the ground when the Royalist baggage train was pillaged after the Battle.
The total of the hoard was £2.3s.6d, about 65 days pay for a foot soldier at the time.

In the 19th century *Lady Villiers* who was a stickler for propriety was the Lady of the Manor and had acquired much land in the area including Sulby. Tenants of hers (and many villagers were) could not hang clothes out on a Sunday. All had to go to church and line up and curtsey or doff their hats to her after the service. Those that did not comply are said to have been evicted.

The church dedicated to **ST HELEN** dates from the 13th century but there is now little evidence following heavy restoration around 1862/3.
The Premonstratensian (White Canons) Abbey at nearby Sulby was very influential. Although not a wealthy Order they were in charge of the church and appointed the Vicars and as a result had a direct bearing on the village and its inhabitants.
A blue plaque on the wall of the Rectory states that *Rev. Miles Joseph Berkeley* MA FRS 'Mycologist' lived there between 1868-1889.
He is buried in the churchyard.
I was also interested in the tombs of *Elizabeth* and *Frederick Williams* lying side by side surrounded by a broken iron rail.

Nearby, the old school and school house are both now in private ownership. The buildings are quite attractive with some lovely two coloured brickwork incorporating the date they were built - 1814 - the second '1' being in the form of a cross reminding us that it was a church school.
The village still has a public house and restaurant, the three hundred year old Red Lion, a village hall and a recreation ground but no shop and both the Methodist and Baptist chapels have closed.
The Baptist chapel has recently been converted to a private residence. What caught my eye was a metal black and white plaque near the entrance gate with the inscription *'Any person who omits to shut and fasten the gate is liable to a penalty not exceeding 40 shillings.* Closer examination revealed it to be an old LNER sign.

At Castle Yard half a mile north east of the village there is evidence of a motte and bailey with the motte on the uphill side. No finds have been made. Little is known of its history but it is thought to date from the late 11th to the mid 12th century.
The Reading Room in Berkeley Street was provided in 1911 by *Miss Elizabeth Mansell* of Sulby Hall in memory of two brothers one a Major and the other a Colonel who were killed in the Boer War. Restoration was carried out in 2007.

SILVERSTONE

Three miles south of Towcester
Population: 1801-586   2001 - 1989

DOMESDAY BOOK
SELVESTONE/SILVESTONE
The name derives from ***Sigewulf*** *- a personal Saxon*
name and' tun' - i.e. ***Sigewulf's*** *farmstead.*
It is not thought that there was any silver found locally.

Three small manors are recorded in the Domesday Book one of which may have referred to Luffield.

The name Silverstone is known worldwide because it has been hosting Formula I Grand Prix Car Races since 1948.
The original track with its straw bales and wire fences is a far cry from the ultra modern, high tec and very expensive circuit of today.

The road between Towcester and Brackley was completely rebuilt and partially re-routed early in the 21st century partly to meet the needs of very heavy traffic on major event days.
Nowadays the centre of the village is much quieter but still has shops, a post office, Primary school, a public house - The White Horse, and a Recreation Association with playing fields.
There is even a mushroom farm although I recently witnessed the demolition of The Royal Oak public house which once stood on the old main road.
At one time Silverstone lay deep in the heart of ancient Whittlewood Forest, remnants of which still exist and inhabitants made their living by charcoal burning and other woodcrafts.
There was in the 12th century a Royal Hunting Lodge for *King John* although that has now gone, but the earthworks of the fish ponds can still be seen to the west of that part of the village known as **'Little London'** - so called because it was believed Londoners fleeing at the time of the Black Death settled here.

As I approached the village centre I was somewhat disappointed with my first view of the church.
It was not what I expected in such a large community, no tower and no spire.
There has been a place of worship here since around 1200 when a small wooden Chapel of Ease attached to the Royal Hunting Lodge came under the supervision of Whittlebury church. The Chapel was replaced with a small church in 1780.

Sir Robert Loder of Whittlebury Lodge when walking in the area decided that a more substantial church was required. As a result the church of **ST MICHAEL** with a small shingled turret instead of a west tower was built in 1884 using local materials and labour. The nave and aisles are under one roof. Inside I found it to be much more interesting with an octagonal carved font, attractive modern tapestries and stained glass from the demolished church of *St Edmund* in Northampton.
In 2011 Silverstone won the award as the winner of the best large village competition in Northamptonshire and runner up the following year.

Included in the parish is the lost settlement of Luffield.

LUFFIELD PRIORY

In the extreme south of the parish and partly in Buckinghamshire was the Benedictine Priory of Luffield founded by *Henry Bossu*, *Earl of Leicester* in the reign of *Henry I* (1100-1135).

This was once a thriving community but it is thought to have been wiped out when everyone perished at the time of the plague in the 14th century and the Abbey fell into ruin.
The last traces of the Abbey were obliterated when a Second World War airfield, home of the 17th Operational Training Unit was built over the site (now the home of the famous Silverstone Racing Circuit.

Anyone interested in Motor Racing will have heard the name Luffield in the context of the Formula I racetrack. Nothing now remains of the Abbey but it is remembered in the name of a farm on the site and by Abbey Curve on the racing circuit.

SLAPTON

Three miles south west of Towcester
Population: 1801-135 2001 - 91

DOMESDAY BOOK
SLAPTONE

*The name Slaptone comes from the words
'slaep' - slippery slope and 'tun' -farmstead
i.e. a settlement on a slippery slope.*

The Domesday Book records Slapton as having a single manor held by *Joscelin* of *Earl Hugh* with ten households.

The population appears to have declined from the 15th century possibly as a result of enclosure of part of the manor as sixty people over the age of fourteen paid the Poll Tax in 1377. Further shrinkage has occurred in the past 200 years.

This is now a very small village nestling in picturesque surroundings on minor roads south west of Towcester with no school, shop, or public house.

It does however still have a small Methodist chapel founded in 1814 and still in regular use.

The very small Anglican church which is dedicated to **ST BOTOLPH** was built over a relatively short period of time from the early to the mid 13th century and is relatively unspoilt.

The church with its west tower occupies a lovely peaceful spot on a grassy knoll above the River Tove with sheep grazing beside it.

It is famous mainly for its wall paintings dating from the 14th and 15th centuries.

They were re-discovered a century ago under a layer of lime wash painted at the time of the Civil War and restored in 1971 and attract visitors from far and wide.

One painting depicts *St Christopher* the Patron Saint of travellers and another *St Loi,* Patron Saint of farriers shoeing a horse. In their heyday they must have been a blaze of colour.

Until recently the two lanes off the main street continued to encircle the church, churchyard and Manor House.

SLIPTON

Three miles west of Thrapston
Population: 1801-128

DOMESDAY BOOK
SLIPTONE

Some experts think that the name derives as for Slapton whereas others believe the origin to be from the Saxon 'slip tun' - farm on a muddy surface.

Peterborough Abbey held this and many other manors nearby in 1086.

In this one street village there are a number of properties of architectural or historic interest
The popular public house/restaurant called The *Samuel Pepys* was recently refurbished with restaurant seating for sixty people but the village is not large enough to support a school, shop or post office.

The church of **ST JOHN** the **BAPTIST** is situated on its own in the fields to the east of the village and dates mainly from the 13th century.
In the churchyard is the War Memorial Cross fitted to the socket stone of an ancient churchyard cross.
From the church there is a pleasant walk through the fields to the village of Lowick which takes you alongside Drayton House and gives excellent views of this outstanding building.

In 1885 a detached part of Twywell called Curtley was added to Slipton enlarging the parish from 768 to 825 acres.

Ironstone quarrying has taken place in the area since 1877 and at one time the Islip Iron Co. who had mines in the area built tramways to connect these mines to the main railway lines.

The most famous of Slipton's sons is *Peter Wright* who was born in 1603.
He was a Catholic Priest who was hung, drawn and quartered for his faith on 19th May 1651 making him Northamptonshire's most recent religious martyr. *Pope Pius XI* beatified him on the 15th December 1929.

SOUTHWICK

Two and a half miles north of Oundle
Population: 1801-104 2001 - 180

*I could not find the settlement referred to in the Domesday Book
but in 1130 it was called Sudwic pronounced Suth-ick today.
This was the 'south farm' in relation to Apethorpe,*

Excavations have revealed a number of prehistoric and Roman settlements particularly to the west of the parish.
Evidence found in 1996 revealed that there was a thriving iron smelting industry here in the
10th century. As the village is not mentioned in the Domesday Book it must be assumed that it was included in a nearby manor.

In the north west of the parish is a chalybeate spring and its importance was recognised in the 17th century when bathing facilities were provided.

Today this is a small quiet one street village in the Nene Valley close to Rockingham Forest with no school or shop although there are some excellent walks in the area.

Adjacent to the Hall is the simple little church of **ST MARY** the **VIRGIN** which dates back to about 1230.
John Knyvett financed the 14th century west tower with its recessed spire.

The land on which the church stands is thought to have been used by the Romans to extract local ironstone and as a result heavy buttressing was required to strengthen the tower.

Of particular interest is the *Holditch* organ of 1840 which was originally in the Hall and the fine monument to *George Lynn* (1758) is thought to have been the last work of *Louis Roubiliac* (a friend and famous sculptor).

Like so many other local churches it was modernised in the Victorian era.

Southwick Wood is a fifty six acre Nature Reserve managed by the Wildlife Trust of Bedfordshire, Cambridgeshire and Northamptonshire. Unfortunately many trees were lost to Dutch Elm disease in the 1960's

The local public house now called
The Shuckburgh Arms is believed to date from the 16th century. It was brought into the Estate by the owner *George Capron* in 1840 and was renamed after his cousin, the *Rev. John Shuckburgh* who died unmarried and left him the residue of his Estate.

In the parish is the deserted village of Perio.

PERIO

Perio Mill about two miles east of Southwick appears to indicate the site of this lost settlement which like Southwick is not mentioned in the Domesday Book.

In medieval times it is thought that Perio may have been the mother settlement with a small Hospital dedicated to *St John* and *St Martin*. In 1329 it became a Chantry or free Chapel of Cotterstock College and retained this role until the 16th century.

There were once two mills here, one of which was thought to be the first in the County to make paper in the 1600's but in 1721 like so many such structures it was burnt down.
Alongside the present Perio Mill is the *John Bradshaw* gun shop.

Capron

Southwick Hall
and the Knyvett, Lynn and Capron families

*The first mention of a **Knyvett** in Southwick was in 1194 when they rented land from Peterborough Abbey.*

*The Grade I listed Hall was first built about 1300 by the family, possibly by **Richard** a prominent wool merchant and the Keeper of the Forest of Clive (or Cliffe) - part of the vast Rockingham Forest.*
The earliest parts are the two towers, one at the front of the house and the other in the courtyard at the rear.

*His son **John** was an MP and Lord Chancellor under **Edward III** and only the second layman in 300 years to hold this high office. He died in 1381. Another famous member of the family was High Sheriff of Northampton and was taken prisoner during the Hundred Years War. It is thought that the enormous ransom demanded was the reason why the family sold the Hall in 1441 although they had inherited another seat in Norfolk.*

*The Estate passed to **John Lynn** who had married into the family. His descendant **George Lynn** rebuilt and added to the Hall in the 16th century. He and his descendants lived here until 1840 when it was sold to a distant relative **George Capron** (a solicitor) who already held the manor in Stoke Doyle.*
*The **Caprons** rebuilt and enlarged the East Wing in 1870 and in 1909 an impressive entrance into the Hall was made through the undercroft or crypt.*
*One of the **Lynn** family, **George,** is credited with having twenty two children.*
*Another of **John Lynn's** descendants was banner bearer at the funeral of **Mary, Queen of Scots** and there is a legend that her burial certificate is walled up in the house.*

The Hall has been considerably altered over the years and contains architecture of every period from the 14th to the 19th century and illustrates the development of the English Manor House.
It is constructed mainly of local limestone with Collyweston slate tiles.

*The present owner **Christopher Capron** was head of BBC TV's current affairs programmes before setting up his own TV production company.*
*There was great secrecy when the BBC interviewed **Solzhenitsyn** at the Hall after he left Russia.*

The house and grounds are open to the public at certain times during the summer months.

SPRATTON

Six miles north west of Northampton
Population: 1801-776   2001 - 1099

DOMESDAY BOOK
SPRETONE/SPROTONE
*The Domesday spelling derives from
'spreot' - pole and' tun' - farm.
Literally the farmstead made from poles.*

In 1086 the four manors had a combined population of thirty nine households and two mills, one rendering six shillings and one sixty four pence per annum.

The village is a mix of relatively old and quite a lot of modern properties and is situated along the east side of the A5199 Northampton/Welford road. Most traffic passes by on the main road and fortunately misses the main part of the village where there is a shop, post office, hairdresser and a well patronised butcher's shop which has been run by the *Sauls* family since 1926.

The present public house, The Kings Head, is currently up for sale and two former public houses, The Chequers and The Fir Tree have been converted into residential use.

Until fairly recently the Manor House in Holdenby Road was a Country House Hotel offering accommodation, meals and facilities for weddings and functions. The signpost directing motorists to the Hotel is, at the time of writing, still in situ on the main road although since October 2011 it has been a fifteen bed mental health care facility run by St Matthews Healthcare of Northampton.

In 2012 plans were announced to increase the size of the former Country Manor six times to provide accommodation for an additional eighty four residential care beds much to the disquiet of the local population.

At one time Spratton was known for its lace making but nowadays most people have to seek work further afield.

ST ANDREWS was founded in 1120 and contains the remains of an early Norman church including the ornate embattled west tower and a doorway with an attractive zigzag moulding.
The spire rising from the tower dates from the 14th century.

Its real treasure is a memorial protected by iron railings to the Lord of the Manor, *John Swinford* (1371). The SS Collar is said to be the earliest example of its kind on record.
One wall bears a plaque to *Amphillis Twigden*, great, great, grandmother of *Lawrence Washington* who was born in nearby Little Creaton and was baptised in the church on the 2nd February 1602.

In the churchyard is an old Preaching Cross dating from the 14th century and also two table top tombs dated 1500 on which there is a Conservation Order.

The railway line between Northampton and Market Harborough was opened in February 1859 and a Station was provided for Spratton at the level crossing on the Brixworth road in 1864.
There were four stopping trains each way.
The Station closed in May 1949 and the line closed in August 1981. The trackway has been designated the Brampton Valley Way' and is frequented by cyclists and walkers.

The Grange of 1848 is built of brick and is gabled and barge boarded. In the early 20th century it was the home of the *Moorhouse* family who engaged *Emily Davison* as a live in Governess.
She was a staunch suffragette but met her end when on the 4th June 1913 she stepped in front of *King George V's* horse during the Epsom Derby and died four days later from her injuries.

Spratton Hall

The Georgian Manor House built in 1760 as a home for the **Clark** family is the largest property in the village. The three storey building has a slate roof and was built with limestone from Kingsthorpe.

The Hall was once the County seat of **Lord Erskine** of Restormel Castle in Cornwall.
The 5th Baron died here on the 8th December 1913 at the age of 72. He was admitted to Lincolns Inn in 1873 and practiced as a barrister and was a former Deputy Lieutenant of Northamptonshire.

After passing through various hands the Hall lay unoccupied between 1949-50 when it was opened as a boys' day and boarding school by **Mr K C Hunter**. It became co-educational in 1977 and a day only school in 1987. Today it has 400 pupils aged between 4 and 13.
Notable alumni include **Michael Ellis** the current MP for Northampton North.

Probably the best known former resident is **Charles Thomas Studd** who was born in 1860.
He was an excellent cricketer and played for England in the 1882 match won by Australia which was the origin of the Ashes. His fame lives on in the inscription preserved on the ashes urn to this day:-

> 'When Ivo goes back with the urn, the urn;
> Studds, Steel, Read and Tylecote return return
> The welkin will ring loud
> The great crowd will feel proud
> Seeing Barlow and Bates with the urn, the urn
> And the rest coming home with the urn!'

He became a Christian during the **Moody/Sankey** crusade in England.
As a British Protestant Christian Missionary to China he was part of the Cambridge Seven and later was responsible for setting up the Heart of Africa Mission which became the Worldwide Evangelisation Crusade (now WEC International). **Charles** died at Ibambi in the Belgian Congo in 1931.

STANFORD ON AVON

Six miles north east of Rugby
Population: 1801-45/NA

Cave

Cave Deus videt

DOMESDAY BOOK
STANFORD

The origin of the name is Stanford - stony ford. The name of the river on which it stands, the Avon was not added until the 16th century.

It is thought that both Stanford on Avon and Downtown were included together in the Domesday Book as one manor with twenty one households and a priest was given by **William the Conqueror** to one of his supporters, **Guy de Raimbeaucourt.**
William wished to build a grand Abbey at Selby in Yorkshire and called upon his supporters for assistance. In response the manor in Stanford became the property of Selby Abbey in 1069

The Abbot there appointed his nephew **Alan de Aslaghby** to be Vicar of Stanford and in 1307 he rebuilt the nave, aisles and tower of the church of **ST NICHOLAS** in grandest style.
In a religious survey in 1851 the Vicar reports that *'the church is manifestly too large for the present population'*.
It is certainly large for the present small village and with the absence of pews appears to be even larger.
From outside it almost looks as if it is falling into disrepair but when you enter you realise that windows have been blocked up simply to accommodate the many monuments.

Pippestrelle bats have decided that the church is a desirable residence and there is ample evidence of their presence. Efforts are being made to overcome the problem without contravening the law on bat preservation.

The church is well worth a visit if only to see the many *Cave* family memorials, including that of *Sir Ambrose Cave* (1568), MP, Chancellor of the Duchy of Lancaster and Knight of St John.
There is also some magnificent stained glass of the 14th to 16th centuries and a fine collection of Armorial Hatchments of the *Cave* family.

Standing on the Northamptonshire, Leicestershire border about five miles north east of Rugby, Stanford is a very small but attractive village with delightful thatched cottages and a wide expanse of grass between the main road and the church.

The original village was much larger and lay slightly north of the present one.
Depopulation seems to have started in the late 17th century and was completed by **Lord Braye's** great, great grandmother in the early 19th century when a row of roadside cottages were demolished and the occupants moved to Swinford.

It is unusual to find parish boundary markers on each road into the village.
The ones on the Yelvertoft road, erected about 1840 are of particular note.

The parish includes the deserted medieval settlement of Downtown.

DOWNTOWN

This long since disappeared settlement was at the time of the Domesday Book taxed with Stanford on Avon.
Its location is thought to be at the foot of Downtown Hill on which stood **Lord Braye's Folly.**

Excavations have revealed pottery indicative of occupation during the 12th to 14th centuries.
Many old records indicate that there was once a Chapel of Ease to Stanford church and also a water mill.
The site which has been destroyed by modern ploughing appears to have been cleared for sheep farming either by Selby Abbey who held the manor until the time of the Dissolution or by the *Cave* family who bought it in 1540.
The site is now cut in two by the Grand Union Canal.

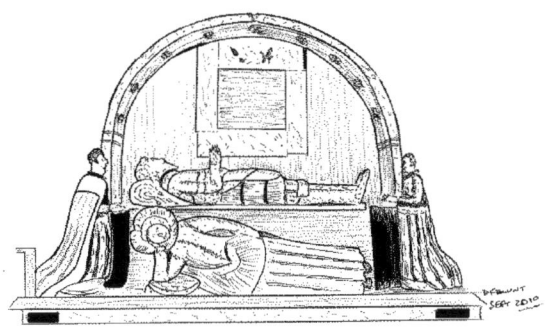

Tomb of Henry Knollys (d 1583) + his wife Margaret Cave (d 1600)
St Nicholas Church ~ Stanford on Avon

The Cave family of Stanford Hall

*Although the **Cave** family have lived locally since 1430 the present house dates from 1690 when **Sir Roger Cave**,
MP for Coventry commissioned **William Smith** the Elder, of Warwick to build a replacement on slightly higher ground.*

*The Hall, a dignified **William** and **Mary** house set in attractive parkland actually stands in Leicestershire although the
village is firmly within the boundaries of Northamptonshire. Unfortunately neither **Sir Roger** nor the architect lived to
see the house completed. In 1737 the 5th Baronet added the fine stable block and courtyard.*
*The **Cave** Barony was created in 1641 for **Thomas Cave**, a royalist who fought in the Civil War.*
*Later Baronets served in Parliament until the 7th **Baronet, Sir Thomas** died childless at an early age in 1792. The Estate
was then inherited by the 6th Baronet's only daughter, **Sarah Otway -Cave**, who became 3rd **Baroness Braye** in 1839.
Unfortunately she had an unhappy marriage and travelled widely as a means of escape although she must have spent
some time with her husband as they had five children. When **Sarah** died in 1862 without surviving male issue the Estate
was divided equally between her four surviving daughters but this led to general neglect.
Fortunately the Hall was restored in 1880 by her grandson **Alfred** - the 5th **Lord Braye**.*

*I like the story said to relate to **Adrian** the 6th **Lord Braye**. Not wishing to tear up floor boards to install electric lighting
he tied electric flex to the neck of a ferret which was then 'encouraged' to scamper under the floor boards between two
holes in search of a smelly piece of rabbit which was being used as bait. Job done!
In the Second World War the Hall was taken over by a Convent School. When they left the roof was in a very poor
condition but the building was saved when the Historic Buildings Council became involved and once again it is now the
home of the **Cave** family. It has lovely grounds, a rose garden, a small **Percy Pilcher** Museum and a highly successful
craft centre and tea room. The Hall is open on certain days in the summer and various events take place in the grounds.*

Percy Sinclair Pilcher (1867-1899)

Percy was born on January 16th 1867 and went on to become the first and most successful aviation pioneer.
At the time little was known about flight but one man, **Otto Lilienthal**, a German, was pioneering the art of gliding
and became known as the 'Glider King.' **Percy** and **Otto** became great friends and exchanged ideas.
In 1895 **Percy** began work on his first man-carrying glider and made considerable progress with his ideas, so much so
that in 1898 he turned his mind to powered flight which would give him longer in the air. The **Hon Adrian Verney**
(later 6th **Lord Braye**) offered workshop facilities and a place to fly but money was required to finance the venture.
A demonstration was arranged for 30 September 1899 and invitations were sent out to groups and individuals who, it
was hoped, would put money into the venture.
During the first attempt the towline snapped and on the third try the 50ft Hawk collapsed sending **Percy** crashing to the
ground. He died on Monday 2nd October 1899 at Stanford Hall and was the first man to lose his life flying in England.
The small **Percy Pilcher** museum in the stable block has a replica of the Hawk Flying machine.
In a field in the north east of the parish is a small classical column in memory of the pioneer aviator.

STANION

Three miles east of Corby
Population: 1801-248 2001 - 873

DOMESDAY BOOK
STANERE

*From 'stan' - stone and 'aern' - building,
the name suggests that this was the place
that began as some sort of stone house.
The village has a long history of stone quarrying.*

In 1969 during construction of a subway, evidence was found of a Roman road between Leicester and Godmanchester which passed through the parish. Not surprisingly a considerable amount of Roman coins, pottery, brick and tiles have been found locally.

This appears to be one of a minority of manors which were held by the same man before and after the Norman Conquest. *Edwin* held the manor freely before 1066 and after that date held it of the *Bishop of Coutances.*

The manor had just three households and a mill rendering thirty two pence per annum.

In medieval times the village was surrounded by trees in Rockingham Forest but today Stanion sits at the junction of the A43 from Kettering and the A6116 from Thrapston and has many picturesque cottages and houses. It has grown in size recently with much new housing and even more is planned.

The church of **ST PETER** has a commanding Perpendicular style west tower, with set back buttresses topped by a slender broach spire with two tiers of lucarnes. The dominant style of the church is late 13th century.

The original broach spire was at one time dismantled, lengthened and placed on a newer Perpendicular style tower giving it its lofty appearance. It is one of the tallest broach spires in the County.

When I visited the church I was interested to see the '**Dun Cows Rib**' about which I have read. This is about six feet long and legend has it that it is the curved rib of a gigantic cow that once supplied milk to the whole village. It's a nice story but I believe it to be part of a framework used by workmen when building the arches in the nave.

There is plenty more to see including the three decked pulpit, which were common in churches two hundred years ago, with a two decked reader's desk and a clerk's desk at the lower level, partnered by yet another two decker on the opposite side of the chapel.
The box pews in the aisles are placed sideways and tiered as in an auditorium.
In addition there are a number of medieval wall paintings including a kneeling stag and unicorn worshipping the place where a sculptured image once stood.

A notable feature is fifty one heads of men and women in the corbel table forming a frieze around the exterior of the church (could these depict some of the villagers at the time they were carved?).

The Methodist chapel was erected in 1907 and is still in use and a new Primary school caters for the needs of the younger children.

Still in use are two public houses, The Lord Nelson with a date stone of 1605 but actually of much more recent construction and the insignificant but grandly named *Cardigan Arms* after the *Earls of Cardigan* of nearby Deene Park who owned much of the land in the area.

STANWICK

Three miles north east of Rushden
Population: 1801-332   2001 - 1924

DOMESDAY BOOK
STANWIGE

From 'stan wigga' (10th century) and 'stanwige' (Domesday Book) it would appear that this was a place where there was a farmstead in a stony area or that the farmstead was built of stone.

The Abbey of Peterborough held the manor in 1086 when there were thirteen households and a mill rendering twenty shillings per annum.
By 1284 there appears to have been two manors.

The village once stood on the main road between Higham Ferrers and Raunds but life is now more peaceful with the opening of the dual carriageway bypass in 1987 on the busy A45.
During work on the bypass evidence was found of a Roman villa site including mosaics, bones and building foundations.

In the centre of the village and bounded by three roads stands the church of **ST LAWRENCE** built about 1225.
What is particularly impressive is the octagonal tower topped with a spire which rises to a height of one hundred and fifty three feet (48 metres).
It is certainly a magnificent piece of church architecture.
Entry is via the south porch which has a room above. Inside is a 16th century pulpit donated by the son of the Rector, *Sir John Dolben* a Royalist, who fought and was wounded at the Battle of Marston Moor and helped to defend the City of York. He eventually became Bishop of York where he is buried.
Of particular appeal are the richly carved 14th century font and the small flower shaped window high up in the west wall of the tower which is best viewed from the chancel.

Opposite the church is the shop - 'The Hub at Stanwick' and this in itself is worth a visit if only for the welcome and a warming cup of hot chocolate on a very cold day.

The Duke of Wellington : Stanwick

This friendly shop cum post office is obviously well stocked and well supported and for a number of years has won the title 'Best Village Shop cum Post Office' in the region in a competition organised by the Countryside Alliance.

In the 18th century the leather and boot industry grew. It is said that boots were made here for the famous *'Iron Duke'* and that this gives rise to the local pub being called The Duke of Wellington. Sadly like so many others the shoe factory closed in the 1970's but the public house is still in use.
The population has grown quite dramatically particularly in the past century and it is now the largest village in East Northants with a Primary school, day nursery, village hall and social club.

The Georgian **Stanwick Hall** which stands a quarter of a mile south west of the village was built by *William Smith* of Warwick in the early 18th century but was badly damaged in a fire in 1931. At the end of the 20th century the Hall was in danger of being demolished but it was purchased with a view to complete restoration and refurbishment and was the subject of a BBC Restoration programme in July 2012.

STANWICK LAKES

Quarrying in the area ceased in 2004 resulting in a very pleasant area of lake filled countryside which has been developed into the very popular tourist attraction of Stanwick Lakes just off the bypass.
Here there are six hundred and fifty acres of countryside with over seven miles of footpaths and cycle tracks around wide open spaces and tranquil lakes.
A new Visitor Centre with exhibition, shop and restaurant was opened in 2009.

STAVERTON

Two miles south west of Daventry
Population: 1801-437   2001 - 468

DOMESDAY BOOK
STAVERTONE
*The name has been associated with
'staefer' -staff and' tun' - farmstead, possibly it was
surrounded by staffs or poles for defensive purposes.*

Staverton stands on the watershed from which flows the Nene, Leam, Avon and the Cherwell and is alongside the main Daventry to Southam road, the A425.

On this road you can see the old Toll House with its decorative barge boards and a Venetian window at which tolls were paid by travellers to provide funds to improve the quality of the roads.

Before the early part of the 18th century the original village was located behind the church.

As you approach the church of **ST MARY** you will notice on your left a number of bricked up windows in the churchyard wall.
This is all that remains of a farmhouse which was gutted in a fire in 1720 which destroyed many haystacks, stables, grain stores and twenty two houses.
The total loss was thought to be about £3,000.
As a result of this fire the village received a bequest from *Elizabeth Darby* for a fire engine which was kept in the village
until recently and is now housed in Daventry museum.

The little barn with an
over large chimney
in the churchyard
 - the Sextons Barn –
used to provide
the church heating
via pipes which are
still visible in
places in the church.

The lower parts of the bell openings in the west tower have been bricked in, so I am told, to avoid annoying the villagers with the noise.
It was interesting to learn that a local school, as part of their music lessons, now sends some of its older scholars to practice ringing the bells. Staverton claims to have one of the best ring of bells in Northamptonshire.

There are some lovely stained glass windows with a weird assortment of window shapes and sizes and a Green Man high up in a side chapel on one of the old looking roof beams.
Inside is a grand monument to *Thos Wylmer* whose image appears on a brass plate together with his wife, six sons and four daughters.

A feature that interested me was the Restoration Appeal tapestry of 1988 on which are embroidered the signatures of the parishioners.

The old Vicarage dates from the 18th century and still stands but has been replaced by a new Vicarage for the current incumbents who went out of their way to welcome and help me during my recent visit.

The public house - The Countryman on the main road was once known as The New Inn.
Other public houses included The Windmill in Windmill Lane and The Crown opposite the Green both of which have now closed.

Primary school children are still educated in the village but there is no longer a shop or post office although there is a stove and fuel shop as you leave the village en route to Newnham.

The Jurassic Way between the Thames and the Humber runs through the village and a sign on the Green indicates that it is twenty two miles to Banbury and sixty six miles to Stamford.

Nearby is an old horse mounting block reminiscent of the time when life passed rather more slowly.

The Countryman : Staverton

STEANE

Population: 1801-15   2001 – inc in Farthinghoe

DOMESDAY BOOK
STANE
There can be no doubt that the name derives from the Old English 'stan' or stone - a stony place.

Crewe

At the time of the Domesday Book there were eighteen households and a mill rendering two shillings per annum.
This was a thriving and quite large village in the Middle Ages but was virtually wiped out as a result of the Black Death and enclosures and now only the Manor, chapel, farm and a few cottages remain.

A total of fifty one people paid the Poll Tax in 1377 but by 1428 there were only four houses.
The Manor here and at nearby Hinton was held by the *Lovell* family but was forfeit to the Crown in 1485. Later it was sold to ***Thomas Barker*** whose son farmed 1,000 sheep in 1547.

The Park and Estate was then acquired by ***Sir Thomas Crewe*** who was Speaker of the House of Commons for two Parliaments (1623-25).
One was known as the *'Happy Parliament'* and the other as the *'Useless Parliament.'*
His son ***John*** (1598-1679) was also a M.P.
He supported the Parliamentary cause during the Civil War but contrived to be one of the group to invite ***Charles II*** to return and as a result was created ***Baron Crewe*** of Steane in 1661.
He was succeeded in the peerage by
Sir Thomas who died without male issue when the title went to his brother the
Rev. Nathaniel who was Bishop of Durham and one of the longest serving Bishops of the Church of England.

The Barony became extinct on the death of ***Nathaniel*** in 1721.

Sir Thomas built the charming chapel of
ST PETER in 1620 in memory of his wife possibly re-using medieval materials .
It stands in a quite remote location but nevertheless is a grand building in a beautiful parkland setting.
The chapel is very imposing from the outside but I was not impressed by the interior which appeared neglected and dirty although there are splendid memorials to members of the ***Crewe*** family.

The original **Steane Park House** was the home of the *Crewe* family until the early 18th century when it was mostly demolished. The offices were made into a farmhouse which was converted into a Hunting Lodge in the mid 19th century.
The present house is gabled with mullioned windows and has some statues of dogs on the front lawn. Since 1990 the owners have restored the gardens in an attempt to capture its original glory.
A new feature is the '***Monet*** Bridge' built by craftsmen from Suffolk.

Prior to April 1935 Steane was a parish in its own right but is now included in Farthinghoe parish.

St Peters Chapel. Steane.

STOKE ALBANY

Four miles east of Market Harborough
Population: 1801-377   2001 - 330

DOMESDAY BOOK
STOCHE

Stoke may have been derived from the Saxon word for monastery or tree.
*The suffix derives from **William d'Aubigny** the Lord of the Manor in the 13th century*
who rebuilt the village on a grid pattern.

Of the two manors at the time of the Domesday Book one was part of the royal manor of Corby and the other, which had a mill rendering twelve pence per annum, was held by **Robert de Tosny.**

It is always real pleasure to visit Stoke Albany which in my opinion has some of the best features of a Northamptonshire village.
Around the tranquil village Green is set the Old Hall, parts of which date back to the 12th century, a former school, a medieval church, chestnut trees in the churchyard and a War Memorial.

It is a quintessentially English village scene which has hardly altered over a hundred years except for the trees on the Green which were planted to mark the Coronation of our present Queen.
I imagine it to be an even more impressive sight when all the wild flowers are out.

The position of this small nucleus of buildings at the north end of the present village leads me to think that there was a much older settlement at this spot.

The redundant village school was built in 1871 on part of the land belonging to the Old Hall and is now the village hall.

Fortunately the busy A427 Market Harborough to Corby road no longer goes through the village leaving it a much more peaceful place.

Like many places Stoke Albany has a mix of quite beautiful old buildings but at the same time many are fairly modern and rather mundane.

The White Horse public house is quite attractive apart from the fact that it had a most unsightly corrugated tin roof which I cannot help noticing whenever I am in the neighbourhood.

The house at no 2 Middle Lane displays a plaque indicating the award of the Best Conservation Area Improvement Design awarded by Kettering Borough Council in 1992.

Opposite is the lovely old Manor House which is oblong in shape with the left half pre-Reformation and the right half dated 1682 when it was enlarged.

The village was obviously well equipped with water in the past and at least two wells can still be seen in the main street.

The Old School : Stoke Albany.

The church is one of only sixty four English churches dedicated to **ST BOTOLPH**, a 7th century monk and Patron Saint of travellers. It dates mostly from the 1300's although the west tower with grotesque gargoyles at each corner was embattled during the 15th century.

At the entrance is a notice:-' *men are desired to scrape their shoes and women to take off their pattens*' (pattens were wooden soles for raising shoes above the mud).

Also in the porch is a great curiosity - a memorial tablet with its inscription: -

> *'Here lyeth ye body of Francis Parker who gave to ye pore of this parish ten shillings a yeare to be paid of Lamas day every yeare For ever, upon this grave stone, February ye 4th 1683'.*

On the stone seat beneath are holes in which the coins were placed.

Just inside the main door are the remains of the original font which was discovered under a tangle of weeds in the Manor House garden in 1954.

The church has a particularly wide south aisle which is taller than the nave but a very narrow north aisle and the chancel has a barrel like timbered ceiling.
A rather unusual feature is the three seat sedilia alongside the piscina with each seat set at a different level.

A brass plaque commemorates the crash nearby of a Boeing Fortress I AN534 from the 90th squadron RAF Polebrook on the 28 July 1941 with the loss of seven lives.

The Old Manor House : Stoke Albany

It is recorded that on one occasion having delivered a sermon the Rector decided that he had not been speaking long enough so simply turned the hour glass (like an egg timer) upside down and started again.

I also read a story about a lady who in the same church in 1885 put her umbrella up during a service as rain was pouring through the roof which looked perfectly sound when I visited.

On the outside of the building is a stone corbel of recent origin of a head wearing spectacles.

Buried in the churchyard with a memorial plaque in the church is *Thomas,* first *Lord Denman* (1779-1854) Attorney General, Lord Chief Justice, anti slavery campaigner and friend of *Charles Dickens*.

The Wesleyan chapel of 1833 appropriately enough in Chapel Lane is now a private residence

A Clapper Bridge (one of only three in the County) sits on the boundary with Wilbarston.

STOKE BRUERNE

Seven miles south of Northampton
Population: 1801-352   2001 - 395

DOMESDAY BOOK
STOCHE/STOCHES
There are at least three Stoke villages in the County (see Albany, Doyle)
the name could be a corruption of 'stoc' - religious place or more likely 'stocc' - trunk
as the village was located on the northern edge of Whittlewood Forest. The suffix 'Bruerne' to distinguish it from
*numerous other 'Stokes' derives from **William Briwerre** who held the manor during the reign of **King John**.*

Swein held the manor of the King at the time of the Domesday Book. The population was recorded as twenty one households plus a priest.
In addition there was a mill rendering thirteen shillings and four pence per annum.

Stoke Bruerne became Crown property when the *de Longeville* family surrendered it by forced exchange to *Henry VIII*. *Charles I* granted the park and manor to *Sir Francis Crane* director and founder of the Mortlake Tapestry works.
It was *Sir Francis* who was responsible for the two Stoke Park Pavilions to the west of the village.
In the 18th, 19th and 20th centuries much of the property was owned by the *Duke of Grafton* but has since been sold.

This very pretty village just off the main A508 between Northampton and Old Stratford had a railway station about half a mile north on the Towcester - Olney line - long since disappeared.
The station building itself was not in use for long but the house still remains and is in private hands.

The old brick pits which date from about 1792 have been converted into a wildlife reserve.

Standing on a hill overlooking the canal is the church of **ST MARY** which has a tower with a Norman base. The upper part dates from the late 14th century but was restored in 1900 and again in 1964. The clerestory with its circular windows was added in 1594.

The rood screen dates from the 15th century but was much restored during the 19th century with the result that little remains of the original structure.

Grand Union Canal : Stoke Bruerne

I was intrigued by the puzzling inscription on the wall to the west side of the churchyard. It reads:-

A 1893D
ParsoNGavE
WardeNDrovE
ClerKMadE
SquirEPaiD
God Save the Queen
To Our Own God.

Could it indicate those who had a hand in church restoration?

Local children still have the advantage of a Primary school in the village.

The reason why thousands visit the village each year is the Grand Union Canal which reached Stoke Bruerne in 1800.

Between 1800 and 1805 while workmen were constructing the one and three quarter mile tunnel to Blisworth all commercial traffic was taken off the canal and transported overland by a horse drawn plate railway to Blisworth.

Prior to the introduction of steam tugs, boats were *'legged'* through the tunnel by men lying on their backs and working their way through with their feet on the walls.
The tunnel is completely straight and is wide enough for boats to pass each other.

On a summer weekend or Bank Holiday when the village is packed with visitors a real bottle neck is the narrow humped backed canal bridge with two arches and robust curving brick and stone walls.
It was strengthened in 1972 but I wonder just how long it will be the authorities decide that it is no longer suitable for today's heavy traffic.

The bridge probably dates from 1835-40 when the canal was widened and double set of locks constructed. To the south is a flight of seven locks at the bottom of which is a pump to return water to the top in times of drought.

Apart from the canal itself another popular attraction is the National Waterways Museum which was converted in 1963 from a 19th century corn mill.
The museum tells the story of over two hundred years of canal life and children can dress up in traditional canal costume.
There is also a museum shop and waterside café.

The former Wesleyan chapel of 1879 has, since 1975, had a variety of uses including a farm museum, a tea shop and the Topiary Gift Shop.

Other attractions include Rookery Open farm on the edge of the village where children (and adults) can get close to the animals.

Stoke Bruerne is a great place to visit with a good choice of drinking and eating places including The Navigation Inn and the canal side Boat Inn built in the early 19th century.
There are some delightful walks in the area but for many people it is all the activities and sights of the picturesque canal that is the real attraction.

Unfortunately the village is a victim of its own success particularly during Bank Holidays and weekends so it is best to visit if you can on a sunny day in mid week in term time - you can then fully appreciate the village at its best.

STOKE PARK PAVILIONS

Stoke Park House was built by *Sir Francis Crane* between the years 1629-1635.
Crane brought the design of the house from Italy and had assistance from *Inigo Jones* to build it.
It was the earliest house in England on the plan of a Palladio Villa.

The house was flanked by two matching Pavilions linked to it by colonnades or screen walls.

Unfortunately the grand house burned down in 1886 and its replacement on a slightly different site was largely demolished in the late 1940's following its use by the Army in the Second World War.

What remains are the colonnades and the East and West Pavilions, one of which has been converted into a private residence.
The Pavilions are faced with cream oolite and dark brown ironstone and now stand either side of an ornamental pond.
They lie on private land at the end of a 'no through road' between Shutlanger and Stoke Bruerne but the West Pavilion and the gardens are open briefly during August for a small fee.

St Rumbolds Church Stoke Doyle

STOKE DOYLE

Two miles south west of Oundle
Population: 1801-115   2001 - 59

DOMESDAY BOOK
STOCHE

As in the case of Stoke Albany and Stoke Bruerne there are two possible explanations of the word stoke, in this case it was a reference to the fact that the settlement lived in a densely wooded area.

The village church has the unusual dedication to **ST RUMBOLD** (or *Rumbald*) who was born near Kings Sutton.
This is thought to be one of only two churches still dedicated to **ST RUMBOLD** in the country - the only other one I have discovered with this dedication and still in use is at Pentridge in Dorset.

The church is set in a lovely open situation which is slightly detached from the village and was built between 1722 -5 a rare date in Northamptonshire church history. The west tower has a balustrade with obelisk pinnacles at each corner.
Consisting of the simple ashlar nave cum sanctuary it is quite unusual both inside and outside and is very light with about 3,500 panes of clear glass in the Georgian windows.
I was very interested in the drawing of Northamptonshire fonts which is displayed in the church and in the two white angels above the East window. I was under the impression that the angels were in marble but am reliably informed that they are, in fact, wooden.

The church also contains a splendid memorial to **Sir Edward Ward** (1638-1714), Attorney General who passed the death sentence on **Captain Kidd** the notorious pirate.

An unusual tombstone is that of a recumbent figure of a priest which lies near the East window. This was once inside the old church but is now outside the perimeter of the newer, smaller church.

Another feature from the former church is a hanging monument with columns to **Mrs Frances Palmer** (d.1628). Her husband is portrayed kneeling in front of her together with two surviving children and four skulls of children who died in infancy.
The churchyard contains a good selection of native trees and shrubs and is managed carefully to maintain a rich variety of wild flowers. Also near the church door is the base of an old cross.

Stoke Doyle is now a very small village of about sixty people but contains thirteen buildings of special architectural or historic interest and has special landscape area status.

The manor was formerly within a royal forest and goes back to the time of the Domesday Book when it was held by Peterborough Abbey.
Edward D'Oilly in 1638 obtained licence to disafforest his land which contained 1,200 acres within Rockingham Forest.

Manor Farm House replaced the old Manor which was demolished in 1870 when the 18th century gates were moved to East Haddon Hall
A square stone dovecote with hipped roof and lantern survives from the old buildings.

A little distance from the church is the 17th century Rectory much altered over the years.
For decades the Rectory and the Manor have been associated with the **Capron** family and the public house, formerly The Swan was renamed
The Shuckburgh Arms in their honour.

Nearby is a lovely row of fourteen stone cottages.
At one time there were two stone quarries in the parish but today there is no longer a school, shop or post office although the village does possess a rare VR Post Box.

Stowe

NINE CHURCHES

(CHURCH STOWE WITH UPPER STOWE)

Five miles south east of Daventry
Population: 1801-311 2001 - 248

DOMESDAY BOOK
STOWE

*Was this a holy place as the ancient name
would imply, deriving from 'stow' meaning place,
holy place, hermitage, even church?
The accepted explanation is that the Lord of the Manor
had right of presentation to nine local churches.*

Gilbert de Gent held the manor here in 1086 when there were twenty seven households and a mill rendering sixty four pence per annum.

The hamlets of Church Stowe, prior to 1717 known as Great Stowe, with Upper Stowe once called Butter Stowe or Little Stowe together with various houses in between make up the parish of Stowe Nine Churches.

It is claimed that Stowe which is over five hundred feet above sea level in an otherwise fairly flat countryside gets its name because on a clear day nine churches can be seen (I tried but failed). On the other hand there is an old legend that it was only on the ninth time of trying to build the church that the workmen completed the task.
I have also read of a number of other explanations for the unusual name.

The small but beautiful church was re-dedicated to **ST MICHAEL** in 1560, prior to that it went by the names of *St Ninian*, then *St Peter* and *St Paul*. The oldest part is the rare Saxon west tower with medieval top which has been strengthened with the addition of iron straps.

The rest of the church is mostly late Perpendicular in style. Unfortunately the fabric looks as if it needs some money spending on maintenance.

It is claimed that a total of seven early carved stones are preserved within the church more than any other parish in the County.

The church is well worth a visit if only to see the splendid and particularly exquisite memorial to *Lady Elizabeth Carey* south of the altar.
She died in 1630 but the work was carried out by the Kings Master Mason, *Nicholas Stone*, ten years before her death.
It is said to be one of his best works.
Nearby is another splendid monument in Purbeck marble to *Gerald de L'Isle* of Stowe Manor who died in 1360.
Yet another great memorial is that to **Dr Thomas Turner**, President of Corpus Christi College at Oxford who died in 1714.

When visiting Church Stowe in 2010 landscaping was taking place on the hillside alongside the church to provide two ponds, giving the owners of Wyndham House (formerly the Rectory) opposite, a superb view over the valley towards the hills beyond. During the Second World War the house and grounds were used as a training school for Army Padres.
Alongside the 16th century Manor Farmhouse is a dovecote of the 17th and 18th centuries.

The Manor was once the home of **John Neville, 3rd Baron Latimer**, the second husband of **Catherine Parr** who inherited the Estate on his death in 1543. It is said that **Henry VIII** came here when courting **Catherine** who eventually became his 6th and last wife.
The Manor passed to the **Earl of Danby** who altered the house for his mother, **Lady Elizabeth Carey** whose marble tomb is in the church.

The church of **ST JAMES** in Upper Stowe opposite the popular visitor centre of Stowe Dairy Farm dates from 1855. It has a nave and chancel with steeply pitched roofs, a bellcote at the west end and a timber porch.
Next to the church is the Grade II listed Cavalier Cottage which was built in 1653 at the beginning of **Cromwell's** Protectorate.

The birth of Radar can be traced back to a field in the parish when on the 26th February 1935 **Robert Watson Watt** and **Arnold Wilkins** showed for the first time in Britain that aircraft could be detected by bouncing radio waves off them.
A commemorative plaque can be seen on the Litchborough road near the A5.

STRIXTON

Four miles south of Wellingborough
Population: 1801-57   2001 - NA

*Strixton is not mentioned in the Domesday Book
and is thought to have been included
under either Bozeat or Wollaston.
A man named **Stric** held land in each village and the
name simply means that this was his 'tun' - farmstead.*

The population of Strixton at the time of the Domesday Book is not known but thirty seven people over the age of fourteen paid the Poll Tax here in 1377.

It is thought that the population declined in the early 17th century when **Robert Parkhurst** of London had licence to enclose two hundred and sixty acres of land and convert it to pasture.

The Manor House, demolished in the late 18th century, once stood immediately south east of the church. Today this is a very small farming community just off the busy A509 Olney to Wellingborough road. Much of the village is owned by the Queen.

The church dedicated to **ST RUMWALD** is 13th century but according to **Pevsner** was almost entirely rebuilt along the lines of the previous church in the 19th century reusing the old stone. Kelly's Directory of 1910 refers to it as a *'curious'* church.

One unusual feature is that it has both a bell cote at the west end and a saddleback roof combined.

The windows in the church are mostly pairs of lancets and the west doorway has an unusual and attractive circular window of six lights above it.

Attempts to change the name to *St John the Baptist* in the 19th century failed to materialise.

SUDBOROUGH

Three miles north west of Thrapston
Population: 1801-241   2001 - 189

DOMESDAY BOOK
SUTBURG
'Suth burh' was the south fort in relation to Brigstock.

The Abbey of St Peter of Westminster held two manors in the County at the time of the Domesday Book, one here and the other at nearby Deene.
There were twenty three households, a priest and two smiths paying thirty two shillings per annum.
A mill is recorded as rendering six shillings per annum.
The manor stayed in the ownership of the Abbey until the Dissolution of the Monasteries by **Henry VIII** after which it passed through various local families including **de Vere** and **de Tichmershe**.

The village nestles in a wooded hollow off the busy A6116 Thrapston to Corby road and retains its old world charm with attractive thatched cottages. It is set in the heart of Rockingham Forest and is still in a lovely wooded area.

Added to the charm is Harpers Brook which flows through the village and many of the houses have lovely wooden bridges in their gardens spanning the gently flowing stream.
The village is well worthy of a detour.

On my recent visit to the church of **ALL SAINTS** in the main street the tower was heavily scaffolded and many of the surrounding windows were boarded up as restoration work was taking place.

The church itself was open but it was not empty.
It had become a prison for a considerable number of Red Admiral butterflies. I was able to gather up many of these, free them from their cobwebs and release them into the great outdoors.
Sadly some were beyond help or were too high up to reach.

Vane Arms. Sudborough

Although an earlier church is thought to have existed the present church dates from the 13th century and has a west tower with a blocked circular window on the west side and four thin pinnacles.

The south aisle is virtually devoid of pews although *'for the weak'* there is a stone seat running the length of the south wall.

In the chancel is an effigy of **Sir Robert de Vere**, a Crusader who fell in battle against the Saracens in 1249. He was the standard bearer to the son of the **Earl of Salisbury** who led the Crusade.

The church has a brass to **William West** 1390 with his wife and children which was engraved by his son, another **William** who went on to become a renowned London engraver.

I could not help noticing that three of the four gate piers in the church wall carried inscriptions.
One commemorates the Coronation of **King Edward VII**, another two thousand years since the birth of **Christ** and the other gives distances to London (eighty seven and a half miles) Peterborough (twenty one miles) and Northampton (twenty one miles) and the height above sea level one hundred and forty two feet.

Unfortunately it does not state in which direction the three places are located - compass required!

The Toll House at the east corner of the village street is circular with a conical roof and date stone of 1660.

Surrounding the old Georgian Rectory are some gardens which are part of the National Gardens Scheme and are open to the public regularly between March and September for charity.

The old school built opposite the Rectory in 1841 by the **Duke of Buccleuch** has now closed and there is no longer a shop or post office but there is a modern village hall - the **Francis Giffen** Memorial Hall with a quiet village garden, a seat and a sand pit to the rear.

The delightful little public house was built in the 18th century but has changed its name from The Cleveland Arms to The Vane Arms, owners of both Barnard Castle and land in Sudborough and Brigstock.

Sulgrave

Five miles north of Brackley
Population: 1801-414   2001 - 410

DOMESDAY BOOK
SULGRAVE

The present village is unusual as it has the same spelling today as that appearing in the Domesday Book. The derivation is from 'sulh' - channel or passage and 'graef' - pit or trench. The village being sited on a low spur in a deep broad cut valley.

This is a compact and attractive village located in a sparsely populated area of pleasant countryside of south Northamptonshire close to the B4525 Northampton to Banbury road.

The village is best known for its connection with *George Washington* who became the first President of the United States of America in April 1789.
His ancestors include *Lawrence Washington* who married *Amee (Amy) Pargiter* of nearby Greatworth who was five times great grandfather of *George*.

In addition to **Sulgrave Manor** the home of the *Washingtons*, other buildings of interest include the ivy clad Star Inn which is said to be over three hundred years old, the Rectory Farm Complex, the 18th century Vicarage and the 'Thatched House' in Manor Road which used to be The Thatched House Hotel.

The church has the unusual dedication to **ST JAMES** the **LESS** and was built between 1327-1377 during the reign of *Edward III* although the base of the tower including the west door is of Saxon origin.
Entrance is via the south porch which is thought to have been built for *Lawrence Washington* in memory of his wife *Amee* who died in 1564. *Lawrence*, his wife and son *Robert* are buried in front of the Washington pew.

The four panes of glass above the pew date from the time of *Elizabeth I* (1558-1603) and show the Coat of Arms of the *Washington* family.
It is thought likely that these Arms inspired the use of the stars and stripes in the American flag.

Of more recent date are two tapestry panels depicting forty eight scenes of village life which was completed in 1992.

I was particularly interested in three items one being the very large iron clad oak chest which *Lawrence Washington* purchased in 1539 and is said to have been used by the Culworth Gang to hold their loot when a member of the gang, *William Abbott*, was church warden. He is alleged to have carried firearms during church services.

The two other items are the rare small door in the south wall of the chancel used prior to the Reformation to sound the bell to announce the elevation of the Host at Mass and the delightful little stained glass *Jesus* window at the back of the church in memory of five children of one family who died over five hundred years ago from scarlet fever.

The grassy mound alongside the church was excavated in 1960 and 1976 and revealed a remarkable timber hall of the early 11th century beneath a Norman ring work.
The site appears to have been abandoned about one hundred and fifty years later.

Other unusual features around the village are a derelict tower mill, the stocks and the double whipping post which was reconstructed using some original timbers and ironwork and placed on the Green.

There is no longer a school or chapel and the former Sulgrave Stores in the centre of the village is abandoned and falling into decay but almost opposite is the present shop and post office which was opened some time ago as a result of the initiative and co-operation of local people.

SULGRAVE MANOR

The manor of Sulgrave was held by *Ghilo* in 1086 and tenanted by *Hugh*, *Landric* and *Otbert*. It had twenty seven households.

Subsequently it was owned by the Priory of St Andrew in Northampton but went to the Crown at the Dissolution and was sold to *Lawrence Washington* for £342 14s.10d in 1539.

The present fine Tudor House was built between 1540 and 1560 as the family home to ancestors of *George Washington*, 1st President of the USA and remained in family hands until it was sold in 1656.

There is a well founded tradition that in 1554 *Princess Elizabeth* took refuge at Sulgrave Manor when her life was under threat during the reign of her sister *Mary*.

After the *Washington* family emigrated to the USA the Manor was held by *John Hodges* and his descendants until 1840. It then changed hands a number of times and became run down and neglected but its future changed in 1914 when plans were put in place to purchase the House to celebrate the centenary of the Treaty of Ghent which officially ended the war between the UK and the USA.

These plans were delayed because of the onset of the First World War but it was eventually bought by public subscription. The Manor House was refurbished and opened to the public and held in trust for the peoples of both countries. It is now a very popular tourist destination with the largest collection of *George Washington* memorabilia in the UK and regularly hosts visitors from overseas.

The Stars and Stripes fly proudly alongside the Union Flag at the entrance.

SUTTON BASSETT

Three miles north east of Market Harborough
Population: 1801-189 2001- 88

DOMESDAY BOOK
SUTONE

*The original name obviously derives from 'suth tun' - south farm, probably because of its position
in relation to Weston by Welland.
Later in the 12th century it came into the ownership of **Richard Bassett**,
Chief Justice of England and it is from him that the suffix derives.*

At the time of the Domesday Book the manor was held by ***Robert de Bucy*** when there were eight households.
The present Manor House dates back to the 17th century.

Sutton Bassett which is only separated from Leicestershire by the River Welland is an insignificant tiny ironstone village of just eighty eight residents in the 2001 survey.

However it is probably better known than some larger places as it stands on the fairly busy B664 Market Harborough to Uppingham road and is only a short distance from Market Harborough.

There is no school or shop but surprisingly it still has its public house - The Queens Head which is said to have been purchased by a railway worker for £260 in 1884.

The Wesleyan chapel built about 1800 is now a private house and when travelling through the village recently I noticed that the whole of the roof was being replaced with modern solar panels.

Originally Sutton Bassett was a hamlet in the parish of Weston (by Welland) and its little church of **ST MARY** was a Chapel of Ease being an extra church without a graveyard.

It is well worth visiting for its Norman characteristics although it was rebuilt in 1856.
The simple little church comprises a small nave and an even smaller chancel and has an attractive double bellcote.

A new bell was presented to the church by its parishioners to celebrate the second millennium.

I was interested particularly in the Norman doorway into the nave and to see from a notice in the church that there were just seven people on the parochial register. I wonder how much longer such a small community can sustain its own church.

St Mary's Church : Sutton Bassett

SYRESHAM

Six miles south west of Towcester
Population: 1801-587   2001 - 805

DOMESDAY BOOK
SIGREHAM/SIGRESHAM
*The name is thought to have derived from a corruption
of **Sigehere**'s 'ham' - farmstead.*

In the Domesday Book Syresham is recorded as having three manors - one of which is thought to be the small settlement of Crowfield in the west of the parish.

Syresham is quite large and in part an attractive village with a wide main street and lies just north of the busy A43 Northampton to Brackley Road.

I was not surprised to learn that Syresham has won the 'Village of the Year' award in the past and in 2012 came second in the medium village category.

The church of **ST JAMES** has been heavily restored many times. It has Norman evidence in the font, south doorway, north window and dogtooth chancel arch of about 1200. The west tower dates from the 13th century but the short recessed shingled spire was added in about 1870.

The entrance is in an unusual position at the west end of the south aisle - maybe there was not sufficient room for it to be located on the traditional south side. In both the north and south aisles are some remnants of wall paintings.

Behind the altar are depicted *Jesus*, *St Johan* and *St Jacobus* in what appears to be a tricorn hat.

It is hard to imagine that the village once had as many as seventeen small shops including three butchers, five cobblers and two blacksmiths.
How times have changed!

The parish still supports a small shop cum post office, two public houses - The Kings Head and The Green Man on the main Towcester to Brackley road, a Wesleyan chapel dated 1846, a sports and social club and village hall and a Primary school opposite which is a house with unusual black quoins and window surrounds.

There is a very well planned and tidy play area for the village children to use.

John Kurde a shoemaker of Syresham is said to be Northamptonshire's sole Protestant Martyr.
He was sentenced to death at All Saints, Northampton in August 1557 for denying the Popish transubstantiation and was burned at the stake. His memorial in the Wesleyan chapel proudly records that he *'died for the truth'*.

As you leave the village in the direction of Silverstone there stands a tall Wellingtonia spruce. It was planted in 1897 for the Jubilee of **Queen Victoria** and is known as the 'Jubilee Tree' with a commemorative plaque placed there on the occasion of its centenary in 1997.

The parish incorporates the nearby hamlets of Pimlico and Crowfield.

CROWFIELD

Just a mile west of Syresham at the end of a 'no through road' lies the present hamlet of Crowfield.

There are just a few houses amongst which is the lovely little Bloomfield Memorial Hall.

The original settlement appears to have been sited to the south west of the existing hamlet.

It is thought to have been one of the manors of Syresham as I can find no reference to it by name until 1287.

I have no further information about the reason for the relocation of the site which was visible in air photographs in 1947 but the area since has been levelled and returned to permanent grassland.

PIMLICO

Two farms and a few other buildings now comprise the settlement of Pimlico which is to be found marked on Ordnance Survey maps south west of Syresham.
Like Crowfield Pimlico is also situated at the end of a 'no through road'.

I cannot imagine that it gets many visitors except on the occasional summer Sunday afternoon. *John and Jenni* ***Roberts*** of Pimlico House have a narrow gauge railway - grandly named *'The Pimlico Light Railway'* in their garden and open it for charity. Children and adults queue up to ride behind one of the tiny engines on a large figure of eight 5" gauge rail about a quarter of a mile in length. Teas and cakes on the lawn make for a great afternoon out.   It is well worth a visit.

SYWELL

Six miles north east of Northampton
Population: 1801-199   2001 - 811

DOMESDAY BOOK
SNEWELLE
The name would appear to be derived from 'seofon wiellen' meaning seven springs.

The four hide manor held by the *Count of Mortain* in 1086 probably included neighbouring Overstone which does not get a mention in the Domesday Book. There were twenty six households.

The village is located at minor cross roads about four and a half miles from Wellingborough and has some attractive stone properties many of which were rebuilt on the orders of the good *Lady Overstone* between 1860-4.
She was also responsible for the rebuilding of the old village school which is now the Grade II listed village hall and the enlargement of the Rectory both of which are gabled.

A row of cottages which stood in front of the church were demolished leaving an attractive area which became the village Green retaining its old world charm with stone built cottages, the village sign, the Celtic Cross which commemorates the 60th Anniversary of *Queen Victoria* and the old school.
The Primary school children now have a new school some distance away.

I was fortunate to visit the church when it was open due to the church clock being serviced although the key is available locally.

The church of **ST PETER** and **ST PAUL** with a short but formidable embattled and pinnacled tower is built of Northamptonshire ironstone and dates from about the 13th century but was restored between 1862-1870 when the chancel, which houses a medieval piscina, was rebuilt.

There are many monuments to the *Pell* family who succeeded the *Wilmers* as Lords of the Manor.

The East window with the date 1580 repeated a number of times caught my eye - it is quite unusual and seems a little out of place in the church. It has a heraldic design and was most probably originally used elsewhere as it was not installed until about 1839 by *Thomas Willement* who was an expert in medieval glass and who was at one time under the patronage of *Pugin*.

Another window which is quite memorable is the peace window depicting *Joshua* walking around the walls of Jericho.
It commemorates those who died during the First World War.

At the entrance to the churchyard is the wooden 'Wardens Gate.' It was erected in memory of *Major Peter* and *Cynthia Bletsoe Brown* whose family served as church wardens for one hundred and nine consecutive years between 1880-1989 - a remarkable achievement.

During the Second World War many young men, including those of the Free French Air Force learned to fly often on a five week intensive course at Sywell airfield which was also a centre for the repair of Wellington bombers.

Parts were transported on 'Queen Mary' lorries, put together again and flown out to resume their work.

The noise of light aircraft frequently breaks the silence in this otherwise tranquil location. Alongside the airfield is the Sywell Aviation Museum which began life in 1998.

On show in authentic wartime Nissen Huts is a variety of memorabilia mainly related to the Second World War.

In 2012 the Museum acquired the air frame of a Hawker Hunter which is undergoing restoration work.

Visitors are welcome at weekends and Bank Holidays in the summer and Air Shows are a popular tourist attraction.

The general store has closed but there is a baker and a cafe and two public houses -The Horseshoe on the edge of the village and The Aviator Hotel on the airfield.

Sywell Hall is an early 17th century house with a wide front, gables and mullioned windows.

It is thought that an earlier building on this site was for a time the home of the *Tresham* family of **Guy Fawkes** notoriety.

In 1451 *Sir William Tresham*, Lord of the Manor and Attorney General to *Henry V* was assassinated whilst returning home on the old road from Moulton to Sywell as a result of infighting between rival factions that led to the War of the Roses.

A fire in a hayrick at the Hall in 1809 during the tenure of *Mr Pell* resulted in considerable damage and the loss of four houses.

The Sywell Airgun Sports Club which was founded in 1983 provides a safe environment for air-gun and pistol shooting in the County.

SYWELL COUNTRY PARK

Just to the south of the village is Sywell Country Park.

The area has numerous springs and these provided the water to the 20th century reservoir nearby which is the central focus of the one hundred and forty three acre (fifty hectares) Country Park.

The County Council bought the reservoir from Anglian Water in 1983 and the park opened to the public two years later.

Apart from a car park, Visitors Centre, small tea room and toilets there is an Arboretum with several species of pine trees and a three mile waterside walk.

The shallow arms of the water consist of reed beds and marshland making this a good natural conservation area.

The sheep wash near the entrance to the Park was used by farmers until 1934.

TANSOR

Two miles north east of Oundle
Population: 1801-167   2001 - 185

DOMESDAY BOOK
TANESOVRE

This ancient village with a settlement since pre Roman times stands on the banks of the River Nene and this probably resulted in its name coming from ''tan - branch or fork and 'ofer' - shore or bank i.e. a branching river bank.

Alongside the old Roman road between Irchester and Water Newton which ran through the parish evidence has been found of a fairly sizeable Roman settlement. After the Norman Conquest the six hide manor with nineteen households and a mill rendering ten shillings per annum was held by the King.

The 19th century saw the advent of the railway with the line running through Tansor from Peterborough to Northampton although the village did not have its own station. The line closed in 1964 and the track way makes for pleasant walks to Fotheringhay and Nassington in one direction and to Oundle in the other.

The church of **ST MARY** which stands by the River Nene with Oundle School boathouse alongside has an intricate history with various parts attributed to different eras from about the 11th century.
It has a squat Norman west tower which houses three bells and has a long nave, the main part of which is Norman but a short chancel with an unusual wooden chancel arch. The incline from the nave up to the chancel is most noticeable.
In the church are seven carved misericords from Fotheringhay which are well worth seeing.
Look for the emblem - the falcon and the fetterlock - of the House of York

The font is of the early 14th century with large ball flowers although one is rough hewn and unfinished.

Almost hidden behind a high wall and dating back to the 16th century is the Manor House which was originally associated with the ***Westmorland*** family of Apethorpe. Surprisingly it does not get a mention by ***Pevsner*** in his book on *'Buildings in Northamptonshire'.*

About five hundred feet north east of the village is the Grade II listed shell of a medieval tower mill.

There are a number of fine houses of the 18th century some with date stones but today there is no school, shop or public house and much of the village now stands on a 'no through road' following the reconstruction of the busy A605 between Oundle and Peterborough.

As with most other villages some of the important properties in the past have been found a change of use.
The two former public houses The White Horse and The Black Horse are now private residences. The former school (closed in 1970) now houses Tansor Playgroup and The Lindens a former Rectory is now a Residential Home.
The shop and post office have now gone but there is an Art Studio.

Just to the south and now in the parish was a small settlement called Elmington adjacent to which was another settlement of the same name but now in the parish of Ashton.

ELMINGTON BY TANSOR

DOMESDAY BOOK
ELMINTONE

This deserted settlement is thought to have been sited south of Tansor alongside the present A605 road.

At the time of the Domesday Book the manor belonged to the Abbey of *St Guthlac* at Crowland and was usually taxed with Oundle. The land was enclosed between 1490 - 1513 when tenants were evicted and houses demolished and there is now little evidence that the settlement existed.

THENFORD

Four miles east of Banbury
Population: 1801-155   2001 - 74

DOMESDAY BOOK
TANEFORD/TEWORDE
*Thegn's ford- a thane being a lesser nobleman
in medieval times.*

The ford was over a tributary of the River Cherwell. The tiny village with no shop, post office or public house is delightfully situated on minor roads just off the A422 between Brackley and Banbury.

The Domesday Book records two small manors, one held by *Robert d'Oilly* and the other by *Mainou*.

Standing in splendid isolation is the church of **ST MARY** with an early Perpendicular style west tower with tall transomed bell openings and battlements.

There is a Norman font and a rounded arch over the south doorway. The rest externally mostly dates from about 1300.

The church has a lovely old stained glass window showing *St Peter* walking on the waves, an ancient Poor Box by the south door and also a recumbent effigy of *Fulk Woodhull* who died in 1613. He was an ancestor of *Michael Woodhull* a well known collector of books who rebuilt the present **Thenford House** to the east of the village between 1761-5.

This Grade I listed building is currently owned by the *Rt Hon Lord Heseltine,* a former Conservative MP.

It has strange twin hipped roofs with a cupula or belvedere between them.

There are attractive gardens and an arboretum on the four hundred acre Estate.

In the north east corner of the village is a Roman site where discoveries include foundations, hypocaust and a tessellated pavement together with coins dating from between the 1st and 4th centuries.

THORNBY

Ten miles north west of Northampton
Population: 1801-184   2001 - 162

DOMESDAY BOOK
TORNEBERIE
The spelling of the name has changed many times over the years but there is strong support for the idea that this was the settlement around a thorn tree or hedge.

The manor was held by *William Peverel* in 1086 but the Domesday Book does not reveal any specific details about population.

Thornby is an uninspiring village on the main A5199 road between Northampton and Welford which is the location of the traditional country public house - The Red Lion. There is no shop or post office and the Primary school built in 1862 has now closed and is used as the village hall.

The church of **ST HELEN** has a Norman font and an embattled and unbuttressed west tower dating from the 14th century although the north aisle and chancel were rebuilt in 1870.

The beautiful **Thornby Hall** with its stone Tudor style and gables and lake dates from the 17th century with later additions.

It lies in a secluded location off the single track road to Naseby. I have read that it houses a residential therapeutic community and special school for teenagers but you would not know it from signage or level of activity.

It is said that *Cromwell* slept here the night before the Battle of Naseby just three miles away.

The parish includes the lost settlements of Great and Little Chilcote.

CHILCOTE - GREAT AND LITTLE
DOMESDAY BOOK
CILDECOTE
The name implies 'young people's cottages' and probably refers to a secondary settlement.

The site of these deserted villages is thought to lie in the long narrow south west projection of the parish and to have been secondary settlements of Thornby.

In the Domesday Book it is described as a small manor with only two households. By the 13th century the land belonged to Pipewell Abbey. I have not yet been able to establish when and why they disappeared.

Thorpe Achurch

Three miles north east of Thrapston
Population 1801-208   2001 - 151

Thorpe Achurch is not mentioned by name in the Domesday Book.
The current name is a combination of Achurch and Thorpe Waterville, both once part of the Lilford Estate.

Evidence of a fairly large settlement possibly going back to the Iron Age has been found in the area of the old Roman road between Irchester and Water Newton which ran through the parish on the line of the modern A605 road.

The present village consists mainly of almost identical Estate cottages of 1830-40.
The oak canopy to the well in the village bears the inscription

> *In memory of*
> ***Thomas Alberton Powys***
> *MDCCCLXXXII*

At the end of a 'no through road' and somewhat isolated from the houses stands the church of **ST JOHN** the **BAPTIST** which was built in 1218 possibly on the site of an earlier church but with an interior mostly dating from the 19th century.
It has a late 13th century west tower and a spire with broaches.
Although the church is in quite an isolated position I can find no evidence to suggest that there has been any large movement of population in the immediate area.

This is the mother church of all that remains of the parishes of Achurch, Thorpe Waterville, Lilford and Wigsthorpe.

Approach to the churchyard is through an attractive lych gate erected shortly after the death of *Thomas, 4th Baron Lilford* in 1896.
He rests in the churchyard under his memorial East window.

Burials in the church include *Sir Thomas Powys* (1649-1719) Attorney General, MP, Prosecutor of the Seven Bishops, his tomb having been moved from the demolished church at Lilford.

Below the churchyard to the south west are some re-erected remains of the church of **ST PETER** at Lilford which was demolished in 1778.

The Rectory with its mullioned windows is a mix of architecture of the 17th and 19th centuries.

Robert Browne reputed to be one of the very first Dissenters was Rector here from 1591 to 1633.
He founded Independent congregations of those who had broken away from the established church - later known as Brownists.
He died in Northampton gaol after being imprisoned for non payment of tax and is buried in St Giles churchyard in Northampton.
His son *Edward* was one of the Founders of Maryland USA.

Alfred Leete who designed the famous World War One poster featuring *Lord Kitchener 'Your Country Needs You'* was born in the village in 1882. His sketches and cartoons regularly appeared in Punch Magazine until his death in 1933.

Another famous resident was *William Peake* who was Lord Mayor of London in 1686.

The Lych Gate : Thorpe Achurch

The parish includes the small settlement of Thorpe Waterville together with the lost hamlet of Achurch.

ACHURCH

DOMESDAY BOOK
ASECHIRCE
It would appear that the name refers to a Scandinavian name of Ase a man's name or Asa a woman's name and implies that this would have been an owned church.

This is just one of many lost settlements in Northamptonshire.
It had a Charter in 980 but diminished in size as a result of plague and enclosures when it became part of the Lilford Estate.
Azelin and two Englishmen held the six and a half hide manor of the Abbot of Peterborough Abbey in 1086. There were twenty four households but surprisingly no mention of a mill.
A famous descendant of the village was
John Quincey Adams, sixth President of the United States of America, who was related to local residents *Edmund* and *Judith Quincey* who emigrated to America in the 1630's.

The fairly isolated location of the existing church in Thorpe Achurch may indicate the site of the original settlement.

THORPE WATERVILLE

The name simply derives from 'torp' - secondary or outlying village and the name of the owners of the Estate in medieval times.

The tiny hamlet of Thorpe Waterville with some beautifully restored thatched cottages lies just off the A605 Thrapston to Oundle road.

Just opposite The Fox Inn once stood Thorpe station on the Northampton to Peterborough line which opened in 1845 and closed in 1964.
The station house is now a private residence.
There was a level crossing over the road at this point – one of the many of the line.

In the 12th century a fortified Manor House was founded by the *Waterville* family.
Licence to crenellate was given to *Walter de Langton*, the *Bishop of Lichfield* in 1301 and it was thereafter referred to as a castle.
All that remains are a farmhouse and the big thatched castle barn with a face formed out of two circular windows on one gable end and an unusual octagonal chimney.
It is thought to be a private chapel associated with the castle and until Victorian times was used for worship.

THORPE MALSOR

DOMESDAY BOOK
ALIDETORP

*Some experts have interpreted the name to mean 'an old secondary establishment' whereas others believe it to be a reference to land owned by **Aethelgyth** who was a Saxon lady.*

Edwin held the manor prior to the Norman Conquest after which it was held by **Fulcher** of the **Count of Mortain** and had twenty households. The name of the village was changed from just Thorpe in the 13th century when the **Malesoures** held the manor but lived most of the time at Milton Malsor near Northampton.

In this tiny village accessed by minor roads you will find the ironstone church of **ST LEONARD** standing proudly overlooking the main street. The original church consisted of a nave, a tower and a spire but it was enlarged in the 14th century and restored in the 19th century.

The massive **Casson** organ has recently been restored and has been used for the first of many concerts and music festivals that are being planned.
Look out for the unusual pulpit, the angels holding up the roof and the carved pelican bench ends.
Above the south porch is a delightful little private chapel provided by the **Maunsell** family.

The village, though small and without a shop, post office or public house is a delightful place to visit. Just to the north west is the almost one mile long Thorpe Malsor reservoir.
Rookery Cottage provides a delightful location for a care home for the elderly.

John Rand, a scholarly Rector was responsible for the provision of the well in the main street.
It was placed there in 1589 and has been twice restored. The unusual inscription in Greek is from **St John's** Gospel, chapter four verse twenty four referring to **Sychar** at **Jacob's** Well.

Thorpe Malsor Hall and the Maunsell family

John Maunsell acquired the Jacobean Manor in 1622 and its frontage has not changed much over the years apart from the installation of sash windows in the 18th century.
One family member was **Robert** who served as a midshipman under **Nelson** and became Captain of HMS Rodney prior to his appointment as Commissioner of Greenwich Hospital.
The best known family member is another **Robert** who took part in the siege of Cadiz in 1596 under the **Earl of Essex** and was Knighted for his gallantry.
In 1600 he was created Vice Admiral of the Narrow Seas and just three years later became Treasurer of the Navy. However his interest turned more to the creation of wealth by diverting his attention to the manufacture of glass rather than naval affairs. Together with a beneficial marriage into the wealthy **Cockayne** family at Rushton Hall he was able to develop the Estate.
At least two family members have been High Sheriff of the County - **Thomas** in 1821 & **Cecil John** in 1928.

The unbroken run of male **Maunsell** heirs to the Estate came to an end with the sudden death of **Major Cecil John Cockayne Maunsell** in 1948 and the female line carried on the succession.

The Old Well. Thorpe Malsor

THORPE MANDEVILLE

DOMESDAY BOOK
TORP
*Its original name means an outlying farmstead
possibly linked to Sulgrave.
According to documents dated 1252 the family who
owned the Manor was called **Amundevill** thus giving
the village name its suffix.*

Manor House : Thorpe Mandeville

As you approach the village from Culworth you pass Lower Thorpe with just a farm and three or four houses.

It has been in the news recently as a proposed new high speed rail link between London and Birmingham is threatening its very existence.

Thorpe Mandeville which was granted a weekly market in 1281 is itself a very small place but it has a fine church, one or two lovely old properties and The Three Conies Public House, a popular eating and drinking place which has a sun dial on its wall with the dates 1622 and 1847.

In former times it was the meeting place of the Bicester Hounds and before 1850 was the place for the Magistrates to hold their meetings.

Records indicate that there was a church here in 1163 possibly relating to Saxon times although no priest is recorded in the Domesday Book when the manor was held by *Ingelrann* of *Giles*, the brother of *Ansculf*.

The present church dedicated to **ST JOHN** the **BAPTIST** is mainly of the Decorated period and has a small stone figure, thought to represent *John the Baptist*, on the east side of the short west tower which has a pretty recessed saddleback roof. The tower has a plain parapet with four crocketed pinnacles and a gargoyle at each corner.

There is only one aisle which has fairly indistinct evidence of wall paintings.

Inside is a splendid monument to *Thomas Kirton* (1601) and his wife (1597) who are kneeling either side of a table with their twelve children and another monument to *Rev. Henry William Pullen*, a Rector who was Chaplain of the Arctic Expedition 1875-1876.

Many of the faces in the stained glass windows have now lost their colour.

The churchyard has a magnificent yew tree which according to a certificate in the church is in excess of a thousand years old. Its girth is said to be in excess of six metres but I haven't checked this.

The old Manor House which stood alongside the churchyard is said to have been garrisoned by *Oliver Cromwell* in the Civil War.

At the time the Manor was owned by the *Kirtons* who were related to *Cromwell* by marriage.

In the 13th century this was the site of Thorp Feast usually taking place on the Sunday following the 6th July.

Opposite the church is the current Manor House built by *Cromwell's* niece with a fine early 18th century front of five bays and an excessively large open segmental pediment.

The Old Rectory (now known as the Court) is over four hundred years old and was used as the Rectory until 1923.

A religious survey from 1851 records that there was no chapel of any kind in the village which was an unusual situation at the time.

The Primary school has now closed and the building is used as a village hall.

THRAPSTON

Nine miles east of Kettering
Population   1801 – 675   2001 - 4855

DOMESDAY BOOK
TRAPESTONE

There are various spellings of the name in old documents - the 'tun' obviously refers to a farmstead. Was the prefix a local name? Suggestions being Trapsta or Thraepst.

An old Roman road between Irchester and Water Newton is thought to have passed through Thrapston and although a possible Roman shrine or settlement was discovered to the east of the town little else of note has been recorded.

At the time of the Domesday Book there were two manors, one held by **Odelin** of the **Bishop of Coutances** and the other by **Ogier** - his only land holding in the County. The latter manor had a mill rendering twenty shillings per annum.

Thrapston is a low lying market town on the banks of the River Nene at the junction of the A45 and A605. It was first granted a weekly market by **King John** in 1205.

In medieval times it was an important river crossing with the narrow medieval bridge providing easy access to Islip and the villages beyond.

The present bridge over the River Nene which was built about 1663 is known locally as Nine Arches Bridge although only seven arches remain.

It has, of course, been repaired many times most importantly just after 1795 when five arches were destroyed in a great 'sea flood.'

A chapel dedicated to **St Thomas** the Martyr is thought to have existed near the Bridge.

At one time tolls were charged but soldiers and persons going to church were given free passage.

Over fifty houses were destroyed by fire in 1718 resulting in much of the town being rebuilt in red brick.

The church of **ST JAMES** has a Decorative style west tower with battlements, a recessed spire and a Decorative chancel. The church is thought to be sited near where an ancient castle once stood but of which there is no evidence.

The round headed priest's doorway dates from the 13th century.

The chancel with its double piscina and three seat sedilia also dates from this period although the seats now appear to be too close to the ground for comfort because the floor of the chancel was raised a foot in 1843 to make it level with the new nave. At this time the aisles were rebuilt and galleries added with their box pews.

In 1958 the church received some pews which had previously been installed in the Chelveston USAF base chapel.

Also of interest to American visitors is the Washington Memorial on the west wall of the nave. It is a stone tablet with three stars and two stripes - the forerunner of the American Flag - in memory of **Sir John Washington**, great, great, great uncle of *George Washington* who is thought to have lived locally at Montagu House in Chancery Lane which is now owned by a firm of solicitors.

He is thought to have been buried in the churchyard area.

Nine Arches Bridge : Thrapston

Set back from the street in Huntingdon Road is the red brick Baptist chapel dating from 1787 with alterations made in 1884/5,

The Methodist chapel was built in 1885 and is still in regular use.

In the Oundle Road Municipal Cemetery is the grave of *Henry Thurston* (1904-1988) well known in the eastern counties for his travelling circuses.

Thrapston grew rapidly in the 19th century with the growth of the leather and shoe industry and the coming of the railway when the town had two stations. One in Bridge Street which opened in 1845 served the London and North Western Line and one in Midland Road (1865) the Midland Line.
Both Lines are now closed and the Railway Stations both demolished.

A reminder of the railway era is a very impressive former viaduct over the River Nene which carried the Kettering to Huntingdon Line from 1920 to closure. It makes a very picturesque sight with the river traffic moving slowly beneath.

The former Corn Exchange in the High Street was built about 1850 and was originally known as The George Hotel.
It is a two storey building with a heavy doorway of Tuscan columns, above which is a hand drawn plough and carved sheaf of corn.

Opposite is the delightful Old Victorian tea shop with an ornate cast iron front where you can be sure of getting a warm welcome and lovely tea and cakes.

The Workhouse for sixty five inmates was erected in 1836 but was more recently occupied as Council Offices.

Washington Coat of Arms
Church of St James: Thrapston

The location in the Nene Valley has given rise to much extraction of sand and gravel.
The resulting areas have now been flooded and provide delightful areas for walking, fishing, boating, etc.

Thrapston was offered a bypass in the 1930's but this was turned down by the Chamber of Commerce who feared loss of trade.

By the 1960's traffic through the town was so heavy that the County Council had no alternative but to widen the road and as a result Thrapston lost much of its heritage not least being two three hundred year old coaching hotels and an even older inn.

In December 1990 a bypass was built but by then it was too late for some buildings and traders.
There is now very little of real interest either historically or architecturally.

At times the centre of Thrapston gets busy with a number of retail shops, a supermarket, public houses, a health centre, a library and schools.
The former Magistrates Court is now a restaurant.

THURNING

Five miles south east of Oundle
2001 - 93

DOMESDAY BOOK
TORNINGE
*The name seems to imply that this was once a place
overgrown with thorn bushes.*

The earliest reference to Thurning appears to be a Charter by **Burgred** (King of Mercia 852-74).

At the time of the Domesday Book there was a very small manor in this County under the Abbey of Peterborough and another in the County of Huntingdon.
Both areas of land were united in 1888 and the whole parish is now within Northamptonshire.

In 1263 **Berenger le Moyne** obtained a Charter for a weekly market on a Wednesday at his manor and a three day fair at Christmas but these do not appear to have been very successful as the village has never been recognised as a market town and it is certainly very far from that today.

Like its neighbour Luddington, this village lies on minor roads off the beaten track alongside the Cambridgeshire border.

The church of **ST JAMES** which has a Norman chancel arch was much altered by *'restoration'* in 1880 when it received its small spired bell turret.

What struck me on approaching the church was the very thin Disney like tower with a short broach spire.
It looks to be Victorian but I am informed that the tower appears in pictures which predate the Victorian period and was probably added in the 15th century.

The plain oak pulpit, lectern and desk are said to have come from All Saints Church in Barnwell which was partly demolished in 1825.

Church of St James the Great : Thurning

Opposite the church is the village hall which I assumed had once been the school but I was reliably informed that although it had been built as a school about 1900 it has never been used as such.

There is no shop, post office or public house but naturally rather a lot of horses around the Cromwell Equestrian Centre.

The house known as The Convent located in the north of the village is one of only a few timber framed houses in the district but I cannot find any evidence of a convent in the village.

Alongside the reed thatched Rectory is a 17th century tithe barn.

TIFFIELD

Seven miles south west of Northampton
Population: 1801-126   2001 - 370

DOMESDAY BOOK
TIFELDE

The old name appears to give rise to some uncertainty as to its origin. It is thought to mean a common pasture or open land at or near the meeting place.

The two manors, one in Warden Hundred and the other in Guilsborough Hundred were both lands of the **Count of Mortain** in 1086 but neither appears to have been very large.
Fortunately the village lies just off the extremely busy A43 road between Northampton and Towcester so most traffic passes it by.

To my mind the most attractive part is opposite the Primary school where there is a small green, a stream with a small wooden bridge and an attractive looking farmhouse.
The village no longer has a shop and has only one public house - The George.

In 1250 work began on the stone church of **ST JOHN** the **BAPTIST** to replace a wooden church on the same site. The work was carried out under the direction of the Master of the Hospital of St John in Northampton who owned a large proportion of the land. The earliest parts are the nave and the north aisle and there is a Norman font with lovely leaf carvings.
By the time of **Edward II** (1307-1327) the Master of the Hospital had been declared Lord of the Manor of Tiffield and Rector of the church.

The body of the church was renewed between 1859-73.

I was very surprised to see three quite large and dirty garden machines being stored in the aisles.

Two graves caught my attention in the churchyard, one in memory of **Thomas Fossett** of circus fame who had winter quarters in the village and the other to **Samuel Kenworthy** aged sixteen who died on 21 January 1880.

The tombstone was erected to his memory by his school friends at Tiffield Reformatory in 1881.
This Reformatory - known originally as the Northampton Societies Reformatory School for Boys was opened near the junction with the main road in January 1856. It was then used for a number of years as an Approved School.

In May 2008 HRH the **Duchess of Gloucester** officially opened the building as the home for the Gateway School with places for fifty pupils with behavioural, emotional and social difficulties.
The school had moved from its previous base in Raeburn Road, Northampton following a Government grant of £6.4 million.

For a period of just two years 1869 -1871 Tiffield had a simple wooden platform on the Towcester to Blisworth line but this was not popular with locomotive crews as the location meant making a difficult standing start on an uphill gradient.
The line has long since gone but I remember it from my cycling days as the embankments were teeming with rabbits and cowslips in the spring.
Today part of the old line has been converted to a Pocket Park.

TITCHMARSH

Two miles east of Thrapston
Population: 1801-569   2001 - 543

DOMESDAY BOOK
TICEMERSE/TIRCEMESSE
*Originally this was **Ticcea**'s mersc - marsh or swamp,
the village stands on a hill overlooking
the Nene meadows.*

Numerous Roman settlements have been found in the parish particularly at the junction of two Roman roads - one of which ran from Irchester to Water Newton and the other from Leicester to Godmanchester.
The manor was once held by *Azelin* of the Abbot of Peterborough Abbey. There were eighteen households.

The village occupies a high ridge overlooking the Nene Valley and the main Northampton to Peterborough road (A605).
On the far side of this busy road is Titchmarsh local nature reserve.

The outstanding feature of the village is the imposing Perpendicular style tower of the church of **ST MARY** said to be the best of its kind outside of Somerset which catches the eye and draws visitors to the village from every direction.
In my opinion it is certainly the best in Northamptonshire.
The church is unusual in that it has a ha-ha to the west and south sides of the churchyard.

The tower with sixteen ornate pinnacles rising to a height of about 100 feet (30 metres) is built of Weldon stone and houses a ring of eight bells.
The original porch was single storey but a second storey was added in 1583 and housed the *Pickering* family pew complete with fireplace.

Theophilus Pickering was Rector of the church and a relative of *John Dryden* the 17th century poet who spent his boyhood in the village.

Samuel Pepys attended the wedding here of his friend *John Creed* to *Lady Elizabeth Pickering* and there are fine memorials in the church to both families and also the *Dryden* family.
John Dryden's parents are buried in the church.

Pews were recently replaced with modern seating and money is currently being raised for the provision of a kitchen and cloakroom.

The Castle is thought to have been little more than a moated site on the south of the High Street.
Here stood one of the Manor Houses which passed to the *Lovell* family in the mid 13th century.
In 1304 *John Lovell* obtained licence to crennalate his house but by 1363 it was described as *'ruinous'*.
Its date of demolition is unknown and although the site was excavated in 1887 there is little evidence of its existence today.

The village is well worth visiting not only for the church as it has many very attractive stone and thatched properties of the 17th and 18th century including the *Pickering* Almshouses built in 1756.

The old chapel is currently up for sale or rent but the village still has a Primary school, The Wheatsheaf public house and restaurant and a community shop which is housed in the old Engine Shed where the fire engine was kept until the 1930's.

TITCHMARSH
NATURE RESERVE

The 150 acre Nature Reserve bounded by the River Nene and Harpers Brook to the west of Titchmarsh is owned and administered by the Northamptonshire Wildlife Trust. It opened in 1987 around gravel pits alongside the River Nene.
A variety of habitats and water levels together with seven islands of different sizes attracts wildfowl and wading birds while the grassland provides safe grazing for sheep. The heronry lake is the old duck decoy and is home to one of the largest breeding populations of grey herons in the County.
A walk around the area is always an enjoyable experience.

TOWCESTER

Eight miles south of Northampton
Population: 1801-2030   2001 - 8856

DOMESDAY BOOK
TOVECESTRE

The Roman name came from words meaning damp fortress but the Saxons called the place Tofeceaster from the local river - the Tove and Ceaster (Roman camp) recalling its Roman past.

Towcester with its Roman connections is thought to be the oldest town in Northamptonshire.
It lies on the banks of the River Tove on the line of an ancient British road later to become the Roman Watling Street which linked London with Wroxeter (the modern A5 road).

Just north of the junction of Park Street with the Watling Street was another Roman road to Alchester - it was obviously a very busy place.
It was here that the Romans set up a fortified station with the name Lactodorum which extended five hundred and fifty yards either side of the road.

The fortifications fell into disrepair in the 4th century.
Excavations in 1954 revealed a late 2nd century rampart overlaying a number of earlier houses.

The Romans were followed by the Saxons and in 873AD by the Danes who split the kingdom into two. Watling Street retained its importance and became the boundary between *King Alfred* and Danelaw.

Towcester was still a very important place after the Norman Conquest. The manor was held by the King and the mill rendered thirteen shillings and four pence per annum but I have no idea why in the Domesday Book *'the smiths' used to pay one hundred shillings - now pay nothing'*.

The Town Hall - Towcester

Recently the local council have restored the site thought to be the location of a late 11th century motte and bailey near the centre of the town as a tourist attraction. The spiral walkway to the top has events associated with the history of the town inscribed in the pavement.

The water meadows nearby have also been criss crossed with walkways which, in my opinion, adds greatly to the appearance and enjoyment of the area.

Towcester is still dominated by the main A5 road which runs right through the middle of the shopping area causing considerable traffic jams at times.

The population has increased dramatically since the Second World War and large modern housing estates have been built to the south west of the old town.

In recent years a bypass has been constructed on the A43 to the west, unfortunately this just means that traffic arrives more quickly at the bottleneck which is the roundabout at the junction of the A43 and A5.
There has been talk about a bypass for the A5 (the major problem) but to date no time table has been set.

.... TOWCESTER

The town has a number of supermarkets, a wide variety of retail shops, the Sponne Shopping Centre, public houses and restaurants, a library, health centre and schools for children of all ages.

Because of its location on the old A5 road there were at one time about twenty coaching inns to cater for the carriers and mail coaches and some inns still have courtyard entrances.

Establishments like The Talbot, one of the town's oldest Inns and The Saracens Head which was built early in the 18th century and is virtually unchanged, would have been well known to regular travellers.

When The Saracens Head was known as The Pomfret Arms it was graphically described in Pickwick Papers by **Charles Dickens.**

Saracens Head

The Pickwick Restaurant and The Brave Old Oak of the 15th and 16th centuries retain the original timber framing in the rooms and bar.

The opening of the London to Birmingham Railway in September 1838 which passed through Blisworth just a few miles to the north brought the coaching trade to an abrupt end.

Towcester was finally linked to the rail network by 1866 with the first of several routes but by 1952 all passenger traffic had ceased and goods traffic ended in February 1964 leading to the closure of the station and demolition of the site.

Central to the town is the church of **ST LAWRENCE** with its spacious churchyard. It is thought to have been built on the site of an earlier Roman Basilica as remains have been found of Roman flooring and tiles from a hypocaust.
The present church built mainly in the 13th and 14th centuries in rich gold ironstone has a Perpendicular style west tower and a tall nave arch but the body of the church externally is much restored.

A rare treasure is the *'Treacle Bible' of* 1549 with the text of Jeremiah 8.22 being printed as *'is there no traycle (treacle) in Gilead'*. In those days 'treacle' translated into cure-all as well as being a black sticky syrup but in modern translations the words 'balm' or 'medicine' are used.

William Sponne, Rector of **St Lawrence** church (1422-1448) was a great benefactor to the town. He started a fund to build a Grammar school and funded the building of the Chantry House about 1447. His tomb in the church bears two effigies - the one underneath being a realistic cadaver (skeleton).
Another Rector who went on to make a name for himself was **Benedetto Caetani** who became **Pope Boniface VIII** but it is doubtful whether he actually visited Towcester. In any event he proved to be quite an unpopular Pope.

The church, like the town suffered during the Civil War when it was the only Royalist stronghold in the County and was fortified by 14,000 troops of **Prince Rupert.**

The Congregational chapel (now United Reformed church) dated 1845 is still in use but the rebuilt Baptist chapel which is dated 1877 with a Baroque type pediment was sold at the beginning of the 21st century and the Baptist community now hold their meetings at the **Nicholas Hawksmoor** Primary school.

The Town Hall and Corn Exchange dated 1865 which occupy a prominent position on the Market Place is Italianate in design with a central tower.
As far back as 1220 there is a record of a market in the town.

A small Workhouse for forty people existed in the town in 1725 but was replaced by a new Workhouse in Brackley Road in 1836.

This was built of oolite stone from the hamlet of Foscote in the late classical style for up to two hundred and eight inmates at a cost of £3,000.

It was one of the first buildings of the architect **Sir George Gilbert Scott** who designed and built many other Workhouses.
He later went on to design the Albert Memorial and the St Pancras Station complex in London.

The 'new' Workhouse closed in 1931 and has been converted into a private residential estate called **Gilbert Scott** Court (I'm glad they decided to keep the name in memory of the architect).

Included in the present parish are the medieval settlements of Caldecote, Handley and Wood Burcote.

CALDECOTE

DOMESDAY BOOK
CALDECOTE

At the time of the Domesday Book this settlement was possibly included under the royal manor of Towcester.

It lies just east of the main A5 road and consists of little else but a few houses, a 17th century farmhouse which was built on the site of a 13th century monastery and a tiny Methodist chapel dedicated to **St Augustine** which is now used as an outlying church for **St Lawrence's** at Towcester.

Earthworks suggest that the hamlet once extended further north.

HANDLEY

The settlement is not mentioned
in the Domesday Book but was in 1220 part
of the Towcester Hundred when it was called
'hanle – egh' meaning a light clearing.

Handley or what was usually known as Handley Free Hay appears to have been located in the area around what is now Park Farm Handley.
The area being part of Whittlewood Forest was well wooded and the Park Keeper was ordered to provide the Sheriff of Northampton with three oaks for finishing the kitchen of the royal house at Silverstone

The land was sold by **Charles I** to **Sir Simon Beret** of Beachampton in 1605 for £6,000 and has long since been deforested and converted to pasture and tillage.

I did discover that **Dr George Pinckard** was born here and was baptised in Towcester in 1768.
He became a physician, army doctor and writer and was for a time Deputy Inspector of Hospitals.
In 1824 he set up what was to become the Clerical Medical Insurance Company.
What started as a small Company with just fifty two life insurance policies in its first year has now grown to a company with over 1.7 million policy holders and 4,000 staff

The quarry from which the tower and aisles of Towcester church were rebuilt by the bounty of **Edward IV** is not now worked but was known as The Delfe.

WOOD BURCOTE

This was formerly an independent settlement thought to have been included in the large royal manor of Towcester. **Bridges** in his 'History of Northamptonshire' about 1720 noted that there were twenty five families there. It now consists of a single street with a scattering of houses.

In 1219 it was mentioned as having a mill owned by **Aveline**, widow of **Geoffrey Fitzpeter** and **Joseph de Towcestre**.

TWYWELL

Three miles west of Thrapston
Population: 1801-230   2001 - 187

DOMESDAY BOOK
TEOWELLE/TUIWELLA

*The explanation for the name appears obvious
'twi' - two and 'wielle' -spring. In other words, the
settlement grew up on a 'double spring'*

In the Domesday Book the larger of the two manors was held by the Abbey of Thorney and had two mills rendering seven shillings and four pence per annum.

This is a delightful little village with some lovely old properties but sadly now lacking a school, shop or post office but still possessing a local public house and popular eating place - the *Egon Ronay* recommended 'The Old Friar' - a late 17th century thatched building.

I was surprised to see however that there is still the long established *Coales* butchers shop in the village with its own registered abattoir next door- very unusual in this day and age.

The small church of **ST NICHOLAS** is
Grade I* listed and is well worth a visit.
I gained access because the clock winder happened to turn up for his weekly routine.

There is evidence of Roman, Saxon and Norman architecture including a Norman font with a Jacobean cover.
On the south doorway are a remarkable eight scratch dials.
The tower has battlements and tiny pinnacles but the spire has gone having collapsed in 1699.

I found the church fascinating for a number of reasons. In the chancel is a most unusual Easter sepulchre with two aumbry doors and a stone book rest above. Also set in the wall near the altar are three small stones from Calvary which were sent to the *Rev. H. Waller*, by a friend of his, *General Gordon* of Khartoum.

The Rector also had links with *David Livingstone*, the great Scottish missionary and explorer and although he did not visit the church there are reminders of him in a glass cabinet including a piece of the tree bark in which his body was wrapped to convey him through the jungle and a pair of pliers used to release slaves from their shackles.

The beautifully carved oak choir stalls with animals and a procession of people including shackled slaves are dedicated to the *Rev. Waller*.

In 1876 a school was built for one hundred and twenty children (where did they all come from?)
It is recorded that *General Gordon* visited many times with the *Rev. Waller* and I can imagine the scholars looking forward to these visits with keen expectation. When it closed in 1979 the scholars went elsewhere and the building is now Macqueen House the Headquarters of the Northamptonshire Guide Association.

Twywell had a railway station on the line between Kettering and Huntingdon until its closure in 1951 although the line was partly used for ironstone traffic until 1978. The station was in the middle of nowhere and the only evidence nowadays is an occasional glimpse of the track bed.

The Manor House, west of the church is dated 1591 but has since been altered including the provision of a pantiled square dovecote in the 17th century. There is another dovecote attached to the 19th century Manor farmhouse.
I liked the Toll House of 1663 with its rounded front at the east end of the village. This building together with that at the rear which used to be the village Poorhouse is now a private residence

Twywell Hills and Dales Nature Reserve is a superb one hundred and thirty acre site in an area of two ironstone quarries which were abandoned in the 1940's & 1950's.
I enjoyed a lovely peaceful walk there but the locals tell me that whereas once it was a closely guarded secret and known to few people outside the village nowadays it gets very busy with visitors from further afield particularly at weekend and Bank Holidays.

UPTON

DOMESDAY BOOK
OPTONE
This was probably an Upper Farm being a little further up the River Nene from Northampton.

Upton, overlooking the Nene Valley just south of the busy A45 Northampton to Daventry road was, until recently nothing more than a church, Upton Hall and a mill which at the time of the Domesday Book rendered twelve shillings and eight pence per annum.

Like Mawsley it was listed as a deserted village but there has been massive development to the west of Northampton in recent years and as a result the increase in population in the area has given rise to shops, a doctors' surgery, a school, a community centre and a pub/restaurant.

The small Norman church of **ST MICHAEL** has been little used recently but may still have an important part to play in the lives of the new inhabitants but for the time being it is being preserved by the Churches Conservation Trust. Norman evidence is seen in the windows in the nave and chancel, the north and south doorways and the priest's doorway. A tower was built into the nave in the 14th century.

Upton Hall, a Grade I listed building has some 14th century parts but dates mainly from the 17th century.

The main portion is seven bays wide with a central pedimented Tuscan doorway. It was once the home of the *Knightley* family of Fawsley but was turned into a school in 1946. Today it is known as Quinton House School operated by Cognita Schools Ltd and provides co-education for children aged between two and eighteen years.

Upton Mill which ceased to grind corn about 1900 is in a beautiful setting on the banks of the River Nene. Unfortunately its isolation and peace has been shattered with the expansion of new properties on the western side of Northampton.

In 1841 *Daniel Spokes* was the miller with his wife and twelve children, many of whom became millers elsewhere in the County.

St Crispin Hospital or the County Mental Hospital just across the road from the church dates back to 1876.

I can see its big clock tower some one hundred and ninety feet high from my home in Kingsthorpe some five miles away.

It is no longer in use as a Hospital and the whole area is currently undergoing extensive re-development.

St Michaels Church Upton

WADENHOE

Three miles north of Thrapston
Population: 1801-237   2001 - 124

DOMESDAY BOOK
WADENHO
*The name appears to have come from the
Old English word 'waden' meaning a ford over a river
and 'hoh' which denotes a hill.*

This describes Wadenhoe perfectly situated as it is on the bank of the River Nene with its ancient church standing isolated on top of the hillside.

In my opinion this is a superb little picture book village and is well worth a visit.
The majority of the buildings have listed status.

The church occupies a superb location overlooking the nearby River Nene and it would appear that the community was once situated around the church if the surrounding earth works are anything to go by.

This is one of several in the country to have a double dedication.
ST MICHAEL and **ALL ANGELS** is thought to be the older of the two, a more recent one being to *St Giles.*
The church has a late Norman west tower with bell openings to the east and a small round headed window and a later saddleback roof and has a ring of six bells said to be the most musical in the County.

Inside is a memorial tablet to *Thomas Hunt* and his wife *Caroline Isham* who were shot by bandits whilst on honeymoon in Italy on 3rd December 1824. They are buried in a joint grave in Naples and their picture which was painted to commemorate their wedding can be seen in the Peterborough Museum and Art Gallery.

Cottages at Wadenhoe

Three of the four banditti were captured and guillotined but the innkeeper who informed them that he had wealthy guests in residence escaped justice and carried on his business for several more years.

When I attempted to visit the church in 2010 the building was swathed with plastic sheeting and scaffolding.

Work was being carried out so that fifty year old asbestos on the aisle and nave roofs could be removed and replaced with stainless steel.
The church is once again fully open.

Just outside the church is an interesting commemorative millennium sundial in slate.

Burgraed held freely two hides and half a virgate of land here at the time of *Edward the Confessor* but after the Norman Conquest this was granted to the *Bishop of Coutances.*
After the forfeiture of the Bishops lands under *William Rufus* the manor was granted to *King David* of Scotland and was included in his fee in the first half of the 12th century.
Another manor of one and a half virgates was held by the Abbey of Peterborough.

In the following years the land passed through the hands of the *de Vere* and *Lacy* families.

For a time *John Bridges* the Northamptonshire historian held the Manor although it seems doubtful that he ever lived there.

Eventually it came into the possession of *Sir Edward Ward* in the early part of the 18th century.
His daughter, *Jane*, married *Thomas Hunt* of Shropshire and thereby resulted the family name of *Ward-Hunt*.
It is their descendants who were murdered in Italy.

Wadenhoe House which dates from 1657 was extensively re-modelled by *George Ward Hunt* in the 19th century.

He also set up a Postal Telegraph Office in the village so that he could keep in touch with Government affairs in his capacity as Chancellor of the Exchequer and first Lord of the Admiralty in *Disraeli's* cabinet in 1868.

George is famous for forgetting his Budget Box on his one and only Budget Day.
Since then Chancellors have posed outside Downing Street with the red box prior to departure to the House of Commons.

In 1966 the House was converted into a residential training centre.
Today it is a popular place for high status weddings.
It is claimed that Wadenhoe was the first village to have street lighting by gas installed in 1869

Facing Manor House farm is a round dovecote which dates from the 17th century and is an excellent example of how a dovecote worked.
It contains a central wooden potence providing access to around six hundred and fifty lathe and plaster nesting boxes and is largely original, apart from the roof and glover (or lantern entrance), which were rebuilt in 1952.
Today it is a County Heritage Site and is open to visitors.

One of my favourite County locations is Wadenhoe Mill which stands on the site of a mill mentioned in the Domesday Book, in fact two mills were recorded in the Survey. One rendered twelve pence and the other thirteen shillings and four pence and sixty five eels per annum. The present building is 18th century with later additions but ceased production in 1972 when it was converted to residential use.

Sundial: Wadenhoe

This is a lovely peaceful spot to watch the wild fowl as the Nene meanders on its way to the sea.

The Kings Head public house in Church Street is of 17th century origin and nearby is the former school built in 1839 for sixty two children by *Miss Mary Caroline Hunt* and now known as Caroline Cottage.

At the bottom of Church Street is the village hall and a car park which I have used a number of times while enjoying walks in the area including one to nearby Aldwincle and another to Thorpe Achurch.

A Trust has been established to preserve the lovely old buildings and it is a real delight to gaze at the old mill by the river, the church standing isolated on the crest of a hill or simply stroll along the quiet streets.

WAKERLEY

Seven miles south west of Stamford
Population: 1801-194   2001 - 71

DOMESDAY BOOK
WACHERLEI
The village overlooks the Welland Valley and would have provided a good look out, this probably gives rise to its name – 'wacor' - watchful and 'leah' - clearing.

Evidence has been found locally of Iron Age, Roman and Saxon settlements in the area.
In 1971 excavations revealed what was in Saxon times a complete cemetery.
A large number of skeletons were found together with a vast quantity of grave goods such as spears, beads, pottery and brooches.
In the Domesday Book the manor was held by *Eudo Fitzherbert* and had twenty four households, a priest and a mill rendering five shillings per annum.

This sleepy little linear village alongside the River Welland on the boundary with Rutland was almost certainly much larger and nearer to the church than it is nowadays.

The church of **ST JOHN** the **BAPTIST**, which was declared redundant in 1972, stands outside the village on a slight hill. It has an excellent Norman chancel arch with a superb zigzag pattern and rests on beautifully carved capitals.
The magnificent embattled west tower is topped by a 15th century tall recessed crocketed spire.

In the early 17th century the Manor belonged to *Sir Edwin Griffin* of Dingley but in 1618 was sold to *Sir Richard Cecil* of Collyweston, 2nd son of the first *Earl of Exeter*, for £8500.
His monument is in the church.

The Manor House which occupied the site between the church and the river is thought to have been demolished in the early 18th century.

To the north of the village where the road crosses the River Welland marking the County boundary there is a fine five arch 14th century bridge which was repaired in 1793 and has markings indicating a *'Flood July 1868'* on the parapet.
Nearby stands the old station building on the Seaton to Wansford line which occupies a predominant location owing to the demolition of the railway bridge and removal of the embankment.

The early 19th century Exeter Arms, the former Red Lion, now extended and modernised, is named after the **Marquis of Exeter**, the **Cecils**, who lived at the Manor House prior to Burghley House.

Nearby are four unusual circular structures about thirty three feet in diameter with concrete bases and upper parts of red brick on two of them.
These were built by prisoners of war during the First World War but were never finished.
It is thought that they were to be used for refining iron ore from nearby quarries.

A reminder of the Second World War is an enamel sign indicating the house of the Air Raid Warden.
Although there is no shop in the village they do have the Barrowden and Wakerley Community Shop across the River Welland in Barrowden which opened in November 2009.

WAKERLEY WOOD

Just south of the village is Wakerley Great Wood which is one of the largest remnants of the ancient Rockingham Forest.
Since 1927 it has been a working forest but for the benefit of visitors contains a large picnic area, car parking, toilets and a number of forest trails.
Deer have always been a feature of Rockingham Forest and can still be seen in this wooded area.

In 1604 this area is recorded as having supplied twenty four deer for Christmas celebrations at Whitehall - the largest contribution of any forest and twice as many as were sent by the New Forest.

WALGRAVE

Seven miles north east of Northampton
Population: 1801-424   2001 - 822

DOMESDAY BOOK
WALDGRAVE/WOLDEGRAVE
WOLDGRAVE
*Walgrave adjoins Old and the first element
of the name is identical.
The second element 'grave' - is old English indicating
that this was once a grove belonging to Old.*

Boot Maker

At the time of the Domesday Book in 1086 the three manors had fifty one households so it was quite well populated.

The village stands just off the main A43 about midway between Kettering and Northampton.
One gets the impression that it was once a much busier place than it is today.

In its heyday the village was heavily engaged in footwear manufacture including boots for the British Army. *Cromwell's* boots are said to have been made there.

At the time of the expansion of the Boot and Shoe industry a terraced row of houses was built with workshops to the rear. These are located at Northall but were once known as Spionkop cottages after the battle of that name in the Boer War when many men from the northern towns lost their lives.

One of the larger Boot and Shoe factories '*Walkers*' was turned into apartments in 2003.
It is constructed of red brick and has white brick banding and linings to the arched windows on the upper storey.

The church of **ST PETER** stands proud of the main street and dates mostly from the 14th century.
It has a late 13th century west tower surmounted by a lofty spire with small broaches.
It is recorded that in 1633 when the chancel was embattled and the buttresses raised stone was used from the demolished Braybrooke Castle.
The spire was partly rebuilt and the clerestory added in 1867- 68.

The chancel is wider than the nave but the whole church is noticeably lacking in picture windows.
In the church is a chained Bible of 1611 and a Book of Homilies of 1676.

One Vicar, **John Williams,** eventually went on to become Archbishop of York although, so it is reported, he adopted doubtful methods to attain this high office.

In a quiet back street you will find the old National School Building erected in 1828 before education became compulsory. It continued in use as a school until 1910 when the present premises were built in Kettering Road. The old school has now been converted for residential use.

Near the village hall car park are the earthworks of what was thought to be a 12th century moated Manor House.

The present Baptist chapel was erected in 1788 and has an exceptionally fine interior and a small burial ground attached.

Other important buildings are **Walgrave Hall** with good gate piers bearing the Coat of Arms of the *Langham* family and the ironstone Rectory east of the church which is dated 1687.

The village still has a post office but whereas it once had five public houses only one, The Royal Oak, is still in business.
Others were The Langham Arms, The Robin Hood, The Travellers Rest and The Five Bells.

WAPPENHAM

Four miles south west of Towcester
Population: 1801- 477   2001 - 266

DOMESDAY BOOK
WAPEHAM
*This is another village supposedly named after a local leader - this time its **Waeppa's** 'ham' - homestead.*

Situated between Towcester and Brackley the village stood at the crossroads of England with the Welsh Lane and Oxford Lane crossing at the top of the parish. Many of the houses are large and attractively built of local Helmdon stone or red brick.

At the time of the Norman Conquest the single manor held by **Gilo de Pinkney** had thirty seven households and a priest together with a mill rendering four shillings per annum. A chantry for six priests was founded here in 1330.

In the Middle Ages it was a forest village within Whittlewood and was subject to special laws and privileges with direct connections to the King.

ST MARY'S church has an unusually wide chancel rebuilt in 1833 although much of the church is 13th and 14th century with a Perpendicular style East window and a fine pinnacled west tower.
The blue faced one handed church clock is said to be over three hundred years old and reckoned to be a fine example of its type.

There is a blocked up hagioscope (small window) in the aisle which allowed the priest in the chantry to see what was happening in the chancel.
Round pillars support the arches on the north side and octagonal pillars on the south aisle.
There are two fonts - a round one which is looking very worn and appears to be Norman and an octagonal one by a pillar.

In the Astwell aisle is a decorative hanging designed and made by **Mrs Kerstin Kappler**.
It formed part of her coursework for City and Guilds Creative Embroidery. She gave it to the church in 1996.

The hanging is modern in style but designed around traditional church and religious motifs namely fleur-de-lis and Alpha and Omega.

The church has brasses commemorating the **Lovatt** family of **Astwell Manor**.

Wappenham once had probably the most notorious Parson in the history of the County.
Theophilus Hart who arrived in the village in 1642 had a history of bribery and corruption and also was a womaniser and came to a brutal end at the age of sixty five when he was bludgeoned to death with a meat axe by the local butcher **George Tarry** who caught him once again in bed with his wife.
I have not been able to discover what happened to the butcher or his wife.

The Methodist chapel which dates from 1860 and was built in a modest Georgian tradition is still used as a place of worship but there is no longer a school and the local shop/post office has recently been forced to close.

Old buildings of note are the Manor, west of the church, dated 1704 with mullioned windows, the Laurels dated about 1700 which has a doorway with a steep open pediment and the Rectory, an elegant red brick house, close to the church.
This was designed in 1832 by the renowned architect **Sir George Gilbert Scott** and is most notable because it was his first project. He also designed the village school, two houses, a granary and a cart house in the yard of Rectory Farm.

Another listed structure is the old red telephone box on the village Green which was designed by the grandson of **Sir George Gilbert Scott**.

The village no longer has a public house,
The Old Bull by the playground and The Chequers becoming private residences.

Wappenham had its own railway station from 1872 until 1951 on the Towcester to Banbury Line which saw considerable goods traffic from the local farming community but few passengers.

The station buildings have been demolished and a sewage treatment works built on the site.

WARKTON

Two miles north east of Kettering
Population: 1801-220   2001 - 144

DOMESDAY BOOK
WERCHINTONE
*A personal name **Weorc** provided the prefix
this was his 'tun' - farmstead.*

Following the Norman Conquest the manor and church passed into the hands of **Queen Matilda**, wife of the Conqueror who gave them to the Abbey of St Edmund at Bury.

At the time of the Domesday Book there were twenty seven households and a mill rendering twelve shillings per annum.

The Abbey held the manor and church until 1536 shortly after which time **Henry VIII** settled them on **Sir Edward Montagu** and his heirs.

This is a small but very attractive Conservation village just off the main Stamford road only a stone's throw north of Kettering.

Much of the village with its lovely old thatched cottages and the surrounding lands are owned by the Buccleuch Estate of Boughton House.

ST EDMUNDS is one of the *'must see'* churches in the County. The west tower with its four pinnacles dates from about 1430 and is a very superior example of the Perpendicular style.

Inside there are Norman arches on both sides of the nave although these appear to have been chamfered smooth at the time of major alterations in 1748. The real treasures of the church are the four large monuments to members of the **Montagu** and **Buccleuch** families of **Boughton House** including two by the world renowned French sculptor **Louis Francois Roubiliac.**

According to my information twenty two members of the **Montagu** family are interred in the family vault together with six children with name plates on each coffin.

Of considerably more recent date are the extensions at the west end to provide a meeting room, office and cloakroom.

The church is included in **Simon Jenkins** book *'England's Thousand Best Churches.'*

WARKWORTH

Two miles south east of Banbury
Population: 1801 - 260   2001 - NA

*The settlement does not get a mention in the Domesday Book and the first reference I can find is that in the 12th century it was called Wauercuurt.
The suffix indicates an enclosure or village.
The prefix may be that of a Saxon name or maybe comes from 'waeferce' meaning spider.*

The actual village which never seems to have been very large is now little more than a church and a few houses and is quite remote even though it is within earshot of the very busy M40 Birmingham to London Motorway.

The medieval Manor House is thought to have stood immediately to the south east of the now isolated church. It was rebuilt about 1595 and survived until 1806.

Extant illustrations indicate that this was a large building around a central courtyard.

The whole building was surrounded by a balustrade which is probably why it is sometimes referred to as a castle.

Almost nothing remains except a stone in a farm wall with the Coats of Arms of former Lords of the Manor.

My vivid recollection of Warkworth is trying to complete a pencil sketch **of ST MARY'S** church on a freezing cold, very gusty afternoon in March and giving up as my hand was too cold to hold a pencil.

The church was much restored and rebuilt in the 1800's including the tower, chancel and south arcade.

Most of the original work is Decorative in style.

In the church are a number of monuments to the **Lyons** and **Chetwoode** families including a splendid table top tomb of **Sir John Lyons.**

WARMINGTON

Three miles north east of Oundle
Population: 1801-450   2001 – 874

DOMESDAY BOOK
WARMINTONE/WERMINTONE

*The name derives from an Anglo Saxon leader **Wyrma**
and 'tun' – settlement
the settlement of **Wyrma**'s people.*

The first documentary evidence of existence in Warmington appears to come from a Charter of 660AD and it is therefore one of Northamptonshire's oldest known villages.

In Roman times an ancient road between Water Newton and Irchester ran through the west side of the village. Roman coins and pottery have been found locally.

At the time of the Domesday Book there were two manors with a combined total of forty households.

Prior to the building of the modern bypass the main road between Oundle and Peterborough ran right through the main street. It is now much more peaceful and has become popular as a dormitory village for Peterborough which is very appropriate as the Manor belonged to Peterborough Abbey possibly from its foundation.

The main street is dominated by the fine church of **ST MARY** the **VIRGIN** which was built on the site of an earlier church by masons from Peterborough Abbey between 1180-1280 and the Lord Bishop is still its Patron.

It is generally accepted as being one of the best churches in the country in the Early English tradition. Its size indicates that it was once of some importance.

Careful and tasteful restoration has taken place over the years, particularly between 1875-1876 when it was supervised by the famous architect **Sir George Gilbert Scott**.

The west tower is topped by an impressive broached spire with very prominent protruding lucarnes.

The church is well worth visiting as it contains a number of excellent features including the wooden roof in imitation of stone vaulting.

Down the centre is a line of bosses with nine carved faces of the Green Man (a pagan representation of the Spirit of Nature) said to be one of the finest collections of Green Men in England.

The pews at the rear of the nave are 14th century and are decorated with poppy heads.

Also worth seeing is the beautifully painted and gilded chancel screen and 15th century pulpit.

Warmington Mill was mentioned in the Domesday Book when it rendered forty shillings and 325 eels per annum but the present building is 19th century.

It was closed on the retirement of the miller **Matthew Hayes**.

The Grade II* listed Manor House dates from the Jacobean era and the Wesleyan chapel built in 1881 to replace a smaller building is now a private residence.

Taylors Green is an old street in the hamlet of Souththorpe which declined after the Black Death in 1349.

The public house on the A605, The Red Lion, is a former 17th century coaching inn and a former public house The Hautboy and Fiddle (a most unusual name) is now a thatched private house 'The Old Hautboy.'

The village still has a Primary school which was built in 1830 and subsequently expanded.

Apart from visitors to the church many walkers are attracted to the area because the Nene Way runs through the village and there is a delightful section en route to Fotheringhay.

The parish now includes the old village of Eaglethorpe and the now deserted settlement of Papley.

EAGLETHORPE

*I can find no mention of this settlement in the Domesday Book but in 1297 it had the name Ekelthorpgrene suggesting that this was the secondary settlement of one called **Ecgwulf**.*

This small hamlet adjacent to the River Nene near Warmington once belonged to Peterborough Abbey.

In the 16th century it was depopulated when nearby Elton Park was enlarged but today it has been resettled as a part of Warmington village.

Just off Eaglethorpe Green is a dovecote which is thought to date back to the 15th century.
The 797 nest boxes were unique as they were constructed from a wood and lathe frame and covered with mortar.
The current nest boxes are a 1980's reconstruction.
Dovecotes are thought to have been introduced by the Romans and were a valuable source of food. The birds entered by way of the lantern or glover at the top.

Eaglethorpe Hall half a mile north is a 17th century building and is said to have a 16th century door and frame from Fotheringhay Castle.

PAPLEY

The first reference I can find of this settlement is in a census of 1301 when there was a population of twelve persons.
The Manor was owned by the *de Papley* family who sold it to *William Brown* of Stamford in 1456.
The settlement in the south east corner of the parish always seems to have been small and little evidence now remains although Papley Farm Cottage offer bed and breakfast and self catering accommodation.

John Elmes of Lilford appeared before the Court of the Star Chamber in 1539 charged, among other things, with having closed up highways in Papley and converting land to pasture.
Witnesses testified that there had been ten houses but by 1539 only two were inhabited.
Findings of the court are not known.

Green Man.

GREEN MEN

Since time immemorial mankind has felt the need to survive and to believe in something or someone to aid such survival.
Early man sought to explain everything that went on around them which they attributed to deities and spirits. In order to curry favour these deities and spirits were worshipped in various forms and ceremonies.

The Romans brought their own religious cults with them but when Christianity arrived in England from Ireland in the 6th century extreme difficulty was experienced in trying to convert the pagan inhabitants to their God and their religious rites.
The answer was to erect churches on pagan sites and to incorporate the pagan rites and ceremonies into the Christian service.

One deity 'the Green Man' held a special place - the spirit of nature and regeneration which mirrored the Christian concept of the Resurrection - death and rebirth. The Green Man portraying the human face in various forms was accepted by the Christian church in order to win over the population,

Green men come in three main forms - a face composed of foliage, a face surrounded with foliage and a face with foliage sprouting from the eyes, ears, nose or mouth.

Many examples can still be found in very many churches throughout the land and Northamptonshire is very well blessed in this respect. They are usually carved of wood or stone and can be found in roof bosses, corbels, capitals, screens and fonts.

Not only to they appear in churches but also figure in stately homes, art work, stones and even pub signs.
Many of those in churches date from the 13th to 15th centuries and they are well worth seeking out.

WATFORD

Four miles north east of Daventry
Population: 1801-356   2001 - 224

DOMESDAY BOOK
WADFORD/WATFORD
The name means 'Wading Ford'or 'Hunters Ford'
depending upon which interpretation you accept.

Watford (Northants) was firmly placed on the Motorist Atlas of England with the opening of the first stretch of long distance motorway in the country - the M1 between London and Crick on the 2nd November 1959.
It was here on the side of the M1 outside the village that the first motorway service area was opened and Watford Gap was born.
In its early days it was a popular stopping off point for Pop Groups travelling to and from gigs.
The Service Station got its name because it is located at a minor gap between two slight hills which found favour with engineers providing roads, canals and railways as evidence by their close proximity in the area.

Historically this was the crossing point on the old east/west stagecoach route across England and it is said that there was once a Coaching Inn in the area called 'The Watford Gap.'

The name of Watford appeared in the Domesday Book (1086) when the manor was held by *Gilbert the cook*. There were twenty seven households and the mill was worth twelve pence per annum.
It passed through various hands including the *de Braye*, *de Burnaby* and the *Parles* family.

In my research I also came across a 'depopulated' village by the name of Cumberford but it appears that Cumberford manor was a quarter of **Watford Manor** which came about when the *Parles* gave land to a daughter of the family of that name.

The shop and the school have now closed and the public house which was once known as
The Henley Arms is now a private residence.
There is a village hall which is used by the Daventry Christadelphians in the absence of a chapel.

The church of **ST PETER** and **ST PAUL** dates from about 1300 and has a Perpendicular style west tower with a tall arch towards the nave.
The external brickwork is in a very poor state and a notice advises visitors not to stand too close.

The nave has almost identical north and south aisles and high clerestory windows, two fonts and a decorated piscina in the south aisle suggesting that there was once an altar here.
The fine 14th century five light Perpendicular style East window depicts *Christ* and Biblical scenes.

In the chancel are memorials to the *Clerk*, *Henley* and *Abby* families all of whom have at one time lived at **Watford Court**.
At the entrance to the churchyard are millennium gates designed by *C. Fiddes.*

The Grand Union Canal passes to the west of the village through the famous Watford Gap.
The canal rises approximately fifty two feet at this point and gives rise to the Watford flight which consists of two single locks, a staircase of four and another single lock.

It was opened in 1814 and there was talk of installing an inclined plane like that at Foxton (which is now abandoned) but the plans were not carried out.

The long distance footpath, the Jurassic Way passes through the village and about half a mile north goes under a fine, ornate cast iron bridge with refuges like church pulpits at the four corners.
(Now quite logically known as the Pulpit Bridge).

Pulpit Bridge Watford.

-414-

The parish now incorporates the deserted medieval village of Silsworth.

SILSWORTH

This always seems to have been simply a hamlet and does not appear to be mentioned in the Domesday Book.
The first record I can find of the settlement is in 1213 but little of that time is known.
It always seems to have been included with Watford.
In the 14th century the land was shared between freeholders and three monastic houses but by the early 15th century much of it seems to have been acquired by **William Catesby** of nearby Ashby St Ledgers.
The land was enclosed in the 16th century which resulted in depopulation and the loss of the settlement which is thought to have been located alongside the Watford to West Haddon road.

PULPIT BRIDGE

This ornate bridge (known officially as Bridge 69) is on the West Coast main railway line Northampton loop and was built by the London and North Western Railway Co in 1877.

The Lord of the Manor, **Anthony Henley** was not at all happy about the new railway crossing his land and him looking out from his home at Watford Court at some unsightly bridge.
It is said that he specified the design of the bridge which marks the spot where the railway crosses the famous north drive of the Estate.
According to some reports the villagers objected to the proposed bridge and its location as it was due to be built near the point where Rogation Services were held by the Lay Rector (**Lord Henley**) hence the unique 'Pulpit' features and ecclesiastical style windows. In October 2011 following a local campaign the bridge was given a Grade II listing - a rare honour for an operational railway bridge.

Watford Court and the Henley family

The north porch of Watford Court carried the date 1568 but the house contained much work of the 17th and 18th centuries. Anthony Henley (3rd Baron Henley) was the son of Robert Henley and succeeded his father in 1841 but as this was an Irish peerage it did not entitle him to a seat in the House of Lords. He was instead elected to the House of Commons as MP for Northampton in 1859-1874 and High Sheriff of the County in 1854.

He married twice, first to Julia daughter of the Very Reverend John Peel, Dean of Worcester and then Clara Campbell Lucy daughter of Joseph Jekyll in 1870.
Clara was the cousin of the yet unknown garden designer Gertrude. It has been suggested that the young Gertrude may have had a hand in the design of the Pulpit Bridge.

Lord Henley died unexpectedly in 1975 at the age of sixty two without taking steps to protect his Estate from death duties. As a result most of the Estate was sold off and the Hall left to rot. Vandals stole material from the property and eventually the Hall was demolished in 1975 having been a family home for over 400 years.

All that remains are some garden structures including gate piers and footings of a walled kitchen garden. Watford Park an 18th century medieval park and garden has been granted Scheduled Ancient Monument status by English Heritage as it had been found to be of 'national importance'.
The open parkland is regularly used by local people for leisure activities.

WEEDON BEC

Seven miles west of Northampton
Including Upper Weedon,
Road Weedon and Lower Weedon
Population: 1801-750 2001 –2485

DOMESDAY BOOK
WEDONE
The name Weedon is a corruption of
'weoh' - shrine or holy place and 'dun' - hill
i.e. a hill with a sacred place.

Weedon is a village steeped in history lying as it does close to the Roman Watling Street which crosses the River Nene near the church.
The village of today is in three sections.

The old village of Lower Weedon has thatched cottages, brick terraces and Northamptonshire stone walls. Upper Weedon has modern housing and the historic royal Military Depot and Road Weedon has the traffic on the A5 and A45.
The whole area comprises the parish of Weedon Bec - the Bec indicates the connection to the Manor and the Abbey of Bec in Normandy, one of the most significant monasteries in Western Europe.

The manor of Weedon was given to the Abbey of Bec some years after the Norman Conquest.
However **Henry V** did not like the foreign Priories or Abbeys ('aliens' he called them) drawing rents from English manors and took them over so transferring income to the Crown.
About 1472 the manor was granted to newly formed Eton College who remained Lords of the Manor until the 1920's.

The area grew in commercial importance when the Old Stratford to Dunchurch and the Northampton to Warwick Turnpike roads were routed through Road Weedon in the early part of the 18th century and what is now known as The Crossroads Hotel was a Tollhouse.
This importance was enhanced by the arrival of the Grand Union Canal and the railway in the 19th century.

The focal point of the area is Lower Weedon where there are a number of shops, a Primary school, day nursery, post office and public houses including The Plume of Feathers.

When the London to Birmingham Railway was opened in 1838 the station at Weedon was to the south of the Daventry road but it was relocated slightly to the north in 1888 to improve access to the Barracks from the canal.
For a time there was a branch line to Daventry and Leamington but this, together with the station closed in 1958 although trains still rush through Weedon on the main line to and from London.

There have been two tragic accidents on the railway in the vicinity of the village.
In August 1915 two trains collided at Stowe Hill resulting in sixty four casualties and ten fatalities.
More recently on 21st September 1951 there was another crash at almost the same point when the engine *Princess Arthur of Connaught* plunged down the embankment killing fourteen passengers and a member of staff.

Just two miles north of Road Weedon on the A5 in old farm buildings is a popular tourist attraction the 'Heart of the Shires' shopping village with craft shops, boutiques, art gallery, workshops, delicatessen, a restaurant and tea shop.
The Nene Way, a long distance footpath alongside the River Nene passes through Upper and Lower Weedon.

Sandwiched between the railway line and the canal is the church of **ST PETER** and **ST PAUL** which has a Norman west tower. With the establishment of the Barracks in the early 19th century the building was too small and in quite a poor state of repair so most of the body of the church was rebuilt in 1825 in the Georgian style.
It is therefore fairly modern by church standards.

One interesting feature is the children's altar which was dedicated by the ***Rev C. Aylen*** of Flore in 1947. The octagonal Chapter House in Cotswold stone was added in 1969 and contains a choir vestry, meeting rooms, kitchen and toilets.

To the south of the church is the probable site of **St Werburgh's** Priory as large stones have been retrieved in the area.

St Werburgh was, in the 7th century, Patron Saint of Chester, Abbess of Weedon and other Priories. During her time in Weedon she is said to have locked up, and reprimanded, a flock of geese that were plundering the villagers' crops and fruit. Feeling very sorry for themselves the geese left the area never to return.

One of the oldest buildings is the Old School endowed by **Nathaniel Billing** in 1712 and known as the Free School - it provided education for twenty poor children.

The Congregational chapel now the United Reformed church, dates from 1792 although its roots go back much further.

It is recorded that in 1767 **John Wesley** was refused permission to preach in the parish church so *'accepted the offer of the Presbyterian Meeting House'* in the village

The Wesleyan chapel dates back to 1811.

Weedon Barracks

WEEDON BARRACKS

A major feature in the village is the Barracks which date from 1803 and once consisted of twelve large powder magazines, two Barracks for two regiments of the line and three pavilions.

The site was chosen (it is said) because it was thought that Weedon in the heart of England would be a safe place for **King George III** and other members of the Royal family to take refuge in the event of the expected French invasion.

A royal suite of three yellow brick Pavilions was built in preparation for the Kings arrival.

For a long period of time the Barracks were referred to as The Cavalry Barracks and I have ancestors who were stationed there with the Horse Artillery. Between the two World Wars the Barracks became the Army School of Equitation and an extensive indoor riding school and further stables were constructed.

The Barracks were demolished in 1955 but some of the other buildings are in commercial use.

At one time it was hoped to transform the area into a leisure complex using the canal as a feature and I also read that it was hoped to open a National Fire and Rescue Service Museum.

It will be interesting to see exactly what happens

In a religious survey in May 1851 it is reported that as the Roman Catholic soldiers at Weedon had *'no place (of worship) neither in nor out of the Barracks they are driven to the painful and humiliating necessity of performing religious services in the club room of a public house.*

The room will not hold half (of those wishing to attend) so that the service is repeated every Sunday morning'.

The club room concerned was at The Oddfellows. Probably the only 'painful' experience was not being able to buy a drink during the services.

At that time there were 763 soldiers at the Barracks of which 59.4 per cent were from Ireland and most were Catholics. As a result a Roman Catholic Chapel served from Northampton was opened in the village in 1851.

WEEKLEY

Three miles north of Kettering
Population: 1801-253   2001 - 242

DOMESDAY BOOK
WICLEI

*Wiclei in 1085 appears to have derived from the Saxon words meaning 'a dwelling place near the bend of a river'
in this case the Ise Brook but there are some who claim it means Wych Elm Wood - take your pick.*

Before 1066 the manor was held by **Earl Aelfgar** but following the Norman Conquest it became part of the Kings manor.

The number of households was recorded as twenty two possibly relating to a population of about one hundred and twenty people.
The mill rendered sixty four pence per annum but no church or priest is recorded.

The manor was then transferred to St Edmundsbury Abbey and remained in their hands until the Dissolution.
In 1541 all the lands of the Abbey in the area were granted for life to **Sir Edward Montagu**.

A later **Sir Edward** was created **Lord Montagu of Boughton** in 1621. The title **Duke of Montagu** was created in 1756. **Lady Elizabeth Montagu**, heiress to the estate married **Henry, 3rd Duke of Buccleuch** in 1767 and the Manor has descended with the Dukedom to the present day.

It is a charming little Estate village with no street names, only house numbers which do not run consecutively - a new postman may find extreme difficulty here.

Of particular note are the thatched cottages which are not troubled by the busy A43 Kettering to Stamford road which skirts the west side of the village.

Not surprisingly it has been designated a Conservation area.

At the entrance to the village is the popular **Jessica's** Teashop offering tea and cakes - very welcome after one of the enjoyable walks in the area.
The thatched tea shop was once a post office and is probably one of the most photographed post offices in the Midlands.

Opposite is the large gabled old Vicarage which dates from 1873 and is now a Care Home for the Elderly.

The village contains a number of lovely thatched cottages, one of which 'Corner Thatch' was the former Reading Room and library.

The village children have benefitted from (but not necessarily enjoyed), educational provision going back to 1624 when **Nicholas Latham** of Barnwell established a school in Church Walk.

A plaque over the doorway of the old school carries the inscription:-

'a free schoole for Weekley and Werckton (Warkton) Founded by Nicholas Latham, Clerke, Parson of Barnewell Saint Andrew. To teach theire children to write and reade. Anno Domini 1624'

Opposite is the village hall built at the end of the 18th century by the **3rd Duke of Buccleuch.**

The church of **ST MARY** stands in a particularly attractive and peaceful area close by an entrance to Boughton Estate Park which is formally laid out and is open to walkers during the year.

It is mainly of the Perpendicular period except for the Norman south doorway thought to be part of an earlier church. The tower has battlements and a short recessed spire.

Restoration took place in 1873 by *Arthur Bloomfield*.

Of particular note are grand table tombs to *Sir Edward Montagu* (died 1557) of Boughton House, Lord Chief Justice and his son, another *Sir Edward*, (died 1602) although they are not on the grand scale of the family monuments in nearby Warkton.

Buried in the graveyard is *Dennis Copperwheat* (1914-1992) one of only two George Cross holders buried in Northamptonshire.

He was awarded the honour because of his heroic deeds during the siege of Malta in March 1942.

When looking for his grave which I discovered stands close to the outside wall at the east end of the church I could not help noticing the incredible number of granite and marble crosses in the churchyard.

I counted over seventy crosses but am sure there may be many more as I did not have sight of the whole area.

Opposite the War Memorial and next to the church is one of my favourite buildings the former Almshouses or *Montagu's* Hospital dated 1611.

It is a very attractive two storey building with widely spaced mullioned windows.

Many people regard it as one of the most beautiful smaller houses of the Stuart period in the country and it has one of the best and most interesting sun dials I have come across in the County.

The dial has a large red painted background incorporating the Montagu Coat of Arms and carries the date 1631.

Above the doorway is the inscription:-

'What Thoe Doest Do Yt in Fayth'

The building was provided for a Master and six brethren with two women for cleaning, washing, making beds, etc.

The men were provided with blue gowns in order to attend church.

Today the building is a fine private residence.

Scenes for the 2005 film *'Pride and Prejudice'* starring *Keira Knightley* were filmed in the village.

Old Post Office: Weekley

Weldon

Great and Little

Three miles east of Corby
Population 1801 – 855   2001-1644

DOMESDAY BOOK
WALEDONE/WALESDONE
WELEDENE/WELEDONE
*Both Great and Little Weldon are
mentioned in the Domesday Book
and although the name is spelt in a
number of ways they all derive from words
meaning 'spring by the hill'.*

St Mary the Virgin – Weldon

Weldon has a history that goes back at least to the Roman era and the remains of a villa of about 4AD were found in the chapel field on the north side of the A43 in 1738 and re-examined in 1955/6.

Evidence has also been found of an even earlier settlement of the 1st and 2nd centuries AD including burials, pottery and coins.

Following the Norman Conquest Little Weldon (or parva Weledone) was held by *Hugh d'Ivry* of the King and Great Weldon by *Robert de Bucy.* Between them they had twenty five households. When the village was surrounded by the great Forest of Rockingham it was known as
'Weldon in the Woods'.

Weldon was enclosed by trees and it is said that one lost soul saw the tower of the church of **ST MARY** and was able to find his way home. So grateful was he that he left money to pay for a lantern to be placed on top of the tower.

When the tower was rebuilt during the 18th century a handsome and glazed lantern and wooden cupola with a scrolling iron weathercock were added. The lantern, lit by candles, acted as a guide to other travellers who got lost.
It is still lit today but no longer with candles.

Although Weldon is seventy miles from the sea the lantern gives the impression of a lighthouse.

The west wall of the tower contains 16th century Flemish stained glass depicting the 'Adoration of the Magi' and the inscription below shows it to have been given by *Lord Nelson* to *Sir William Hamilton.*
In 1897 it was presented to the church by the Rector, the *Rev. William Finch Hatton* in whose possession it had been for years.
One of the modern windows commemorates missions flown and lives lost by American airmen of the USAAF 401's Bombardment group from their base at nearby Deenethorpe.
In 1976 a treble bell was placed in the tower in memory of comrades who did not return from their mission.

In the churchyard is the gravestone to *Dr John Clarke*, surgeon and village doctor who served at the Battle of Trafalgar.
He gave the stained glass East window of the sanctuary.

An interesting feature of Weldon is the old lock up once a common sight which stands beside the village Green - the only known survivor in Northamptonshire.

It is a circular structure dating from the 18th century and looks like a small dovecote with a ball finial on the roof and a heavily studded oak door.

In the past it was used as a place of detention for those committing crime - is there a case for bringing back such deterrents?

The lockup became obsolete following the County Police Act of 1839 which led to the provision of Police Stations with secure cells.

Today Weldon which stands on the eastern edge of the sprawling town of Corby is a busy place coping with modern day life but it retains many old and interesting properties including the Manor House at the east end of the church, the 17th century Old Rectory Lodge and the curious looking Haunt Hill House west of the church with date stones of 1636 and 1643.

This is thought to have been the work of the Master Mason at the nearby quarry, **Humphrey Frisby**, and bears the Arms of the Masons Company on the gable.

Many of the old houses and two inns, The George and The Woolpack are built of Weldon limestone which was widely used in the Middle Ages.

The quarries were threatened with closure but have recently had a new lease of life and are now one of the leading masonry companies in the Midlands.

One house in the village was particularly unlucky during both the First and Second World Wars.

In the First World War it was struck by a bomb from a Zeppelin and in the Second World War it was damaged by the wreckage of a crashing Dornier bomber.

The bodies of the five crew killed in the second accident were first buried in the local cemetery but in 1963 and with due ceremony the bodies were disinterred and buried in the German Military Cemetery in Cannock Chase.

The Congregational church is housed in the chapel of 1792. Prior to that date the congregation met in the house of **Edward Nutt** and then a small barn on the present site.

WELDON STONE QUARRIES

Limestone is thought to have been quarried in the area since at least Roman times - there were once many quarries locally and remains of some old shafts can still be found.

Church Walk was an important area for quarrying and dressing limestone and here you will find a raised causeway or trackway dated 1755 which was used to enable villagers to avoid a stretch of water at a time of flood.

Weldon stone was greatly prized and used for buildings such as old St Pauls in London, Kirby Hall, Rushton Hall, part of Rockingham Castle and Kings College Chapel in Cambridge

John Bridges the Northamptonshire historian described the stone in the 18th century as *'so hard a texture as to admit a polish almost equal to Italian marble'.*

Some people claim that Weldon stone was used in the rebuilding of the new St Pauls Cathedral in London.

WELFORD

Seven miles south west of Market Harborough
Population: 1801-931 2001-1112

DOMESDAY BOOK
WELLESFORD
The name 'wellesford' in the Domesday Book derives from 'wiele' - spring i.e. the ford by the spring.

In 1086 the four hide manor was held by *Alvred* of *Geoffrey de la Guerche*.
There were seventeen households and a priest.
It would appear that Welford on the Northamptonshire/Leicestershire border has, for centuries, been quite a busy place and one of considerable importance.
In 1223 by Royal Charter a weekly market was established here with an annual Fair each August.
Its Charter was later sold to West Haddon.

Then followed the stagecoach era when Welford was an important staging post between Leicester and Northampton and had seven inns and coaching houses along the line of the High Street, some of which still remain but have been put to other uses.

The most famous is the Grade II listed Talbot Inn in the High Street which was immortalised by *Charles Dickens* in Bleak House.
Today it is a private residence.

In 1777 the village was listed as one of the main centres of weaving in the County.

Welford which is mainly a brick built village still has a shop, post office, garage, village hall, Congregational chapel dated 1793 with a lovely cupula and a Primary school with attractive black and red diaper brickwork.

Canal Milepost – Welford

The main road still winds its way through the village where there are a few interesting old properties.

Just off the main street is the 13th century church of **ST MARY** which was once a Chapel of Ease for nearby Sulby Abbey and an underground tunnel is said to have joined the two.
The list of Vicars dates from 1223 under the Abbey and Convent of Sulby.

Even older than the present church is the *Welford Chalice* a 12th century piece of church plate in lead which was found in the churchyard in 1968 and is now in a recess in the north wall of the church.

The massive and highly decorated organ which stands near the tower arch spoils an otherwise attractive nave.
The 15th century table tomb in the north aisle looks interesting from the photographs but on my visit was being used for a very moving Nativity scene.
It is said to have been damaged by *Cromwell's* troops who used it for sharpening their swords.

Behind the altar is an alabaster reredos of 1888 and nearby is a piscina and sedilia which were only discovered during restoration work in 1953.

The medieval parish chest is a fine piece of woodwork and is said to have been used for the safe storage of valuables for those staying overnight in one of the coaching Inns.

The north chantry is a delightful little chapel restored in 1921 by *Major* and *Mrs Guy Paget* in memory of one hundred and one men of Welford and Sulby who fought in the First World War of whom twenty seven failed to return.

The west tower now houses a very bright blue faced clock dated 2011.

One memorial which took my notice was that for the *Rt. Hon.* the *Lord Boardman*, soldier, lawyer, politician, and banker who lived in the Manor and who died in 2003.
My wife worked as his personal assistant at the time he was seeking election to Parliament.

The village hall dated 1894 is obviously very well used with many different activities featured in the posters in the window.

I was interested to see that about 10.30 on a very cold January morning the Hall was filled with ladies practising their yoga exercises.

North of the church is the Manor House a grand building in a superb location.

By the entrance gate there is a square red brick coach house with pyramid roof.

The brick built former George Inn (renamed The Wharf around 1947), has an embattled porch which projects into the roadway and the adjoining wharf area was once a busy place for coal, coke, granite and salt.

The Welford Arm of the canal fell into disuse after the Second World War but was restored and re-opened in 1969.

In my opinion this is a much more interesting area than the village itself.

Alongside the Wharf is a delightful little Pocket Park and the starting point for many walks one of which took me on a lovely sunny March day over the fields to Welford and Sulby reservoirs and the site of the lost village of Sulby which is now included in the parish.

Walks a Plenty -- Welford

SULBY

DOMESDAY BOOK
SOLEBI
It is thought that the name derives from 'sulh' meaning furrow or trench and 'by 'for a village or settlement.

Sulby is located to the east of Weldon on the border with Leicestershire.

Thirteen households were recorded in the Domesday Book in 1086 together with two Manors, one of which was described as *'waste.'*

The village is recorded as having eighty nine tax payers in 1377 but was reduced to less than ten households by 1428.

By the early 16th century the site had been converted to pasture and 2,000 sheep were grazed.

Today there are probably more houses in the area than there have ever been.

Sulby Hall dating from 1792 was designed by *Sir John Soane (*an architect, whose best known work was the Bank of England) for *Rene Payne* a London banker but when he died in 1799 it was inherited by his son *George*.

When he was in London to discuss the building of Sulby Reservoir he had an affair with a Governess.

Her brother challenged him to a duel on Wimbledon Common at which *George* was killed.

The Hall continued in use until 1952 by which time it was in such a bad state that it was sold for £2,000 for demolition. Some of the buildings in the area are thought to contain materials from the old Abbey

SULBY ABBEY

A Premonstratension (White Canon) Abbey was founded in 1155 by *Wm de Wideville* who gave them to the church in Welford. The manor, thought to be the one described as *'waste'* in the Domesday Book, was sold to the Abbey sometime after 1215. A regular visitor was *Edward II*.

From records it would appear that there were at one time about thirteen canons in residence.

The Abbey which stood about one mile south of the village of Sulby was dissolved in 1538 and the land acquired by *Sir Christopher Hatton*.

Abbey Farm stands on the site of the old Abbey which is marked by humps and bumps.

WELLINGBOROUGH

Eight miles north east of Northampton
Population: 1801-3328   2001 - 72519

DOMESDAY BOOK
WALETONE/WEDLINGEBERIE
WENDLEBERIE/WENDLESBERIE
The name is thought to come from
Waendal *- a person's name followed by*
'inga burh' - a fortified place.

The original name is remembered in the Waendal Walk which draws participants from over a wide area.

This is one of Northamptonshire's largest and most important towns with a long history. A large number of Roman sites with finds of coins, pottery and tiles have been discovered locally.

The manor including two hundred acres of land was given to the Abbots of Croyland by *Edred*, King of Mercia in 948AD and they remained Lords of the Manor until the Dissolution.

Croyland Abbey in Wellingborough which was restored after a fire in 1281 and reconstructed in the Jacobean style in the early 17th century is now used as office accommodation.

Nearby is the grand Grade I listed Tithe Barn erected in about 1400 to replace an earlier barn.
It is the only survivor of the original buildings attached to the nearby medieval grange.
The local peasantry paid their tithes and rents (10%) at the Tithe Barn usually in kind to the Lord Abbots Reeve.

Following fire damage (scorch marks can still be seen on the roof beams) in 1972 the Tithe Barn was restored as a result of co-operation between Wellingborough Tithe Barn Preservation Society and the Borough Council of Wellingborough.
It is now used by the people of Wellingborough for functions, dances, craft fairs, etc.

I was told a story of a farmer making butter at one end while his brother made coffins and laid out corpses at the other.

In the centre of the town is the open air market, the history of which goes back to a charter of *King John* in 1201. Alongside is the church of **ALL HALLOWS** and its churchyard with its old trees.

Much of the building is late 13th or early 14th century but there is evidence of an earlier church in the Norman arch over the south door.
The west tower dates from between the years 1250-1300 and is comprised of bands of ironstone and grey stone and is topped by a spire which rises to a height of 165 feet (52 metres).

The most notable carvings are those on the set of six misericords dating from 1383 probably brought from the Abbey of Croyland.

The church is notable for its collection of modern stained glass not all of which is to my taste.
The rose window above the west door is thought to be the oldest although the glass was only installed in 1964.

Of the other Anglican Churches the most notable is **ST MARY'S** church in Knox Road. Work began in 1906 in what appears to be a typical 15th century Perpendicular style but this give no indication of what lies within - it is amazing.
The building designed by *Sir Ninian Comper* is in golden Finedon ironstone and Welsh stone and was funded by three local sisters, *Gertrude*, *Harriet* and *Henrietta Sharman*.

Of particular interest are the rood screen and sanctuary and the north chapel, a complete example of the architect's planned decoration of the whole church and the south chapel with its interesting stained glass.

The whole ceiling throughout was intended to be painted blue and gold but owing to lack of funds only major areas were painted.

Sir John Betjeman stated that:- *'it was, in his opinion, the finest modern parish church in England'* and many other scholars echo this claim.

Simon Jenkins in his book *'England's 1000 Best Churches'* rates *St Marys* as the best in the County and among the best one hundred in England.

Another church worthy of note is the oval shaped neo Byzantine Congregational (now URC) chapel in High Street sometimes known as the *'pork pie'* church.

Wellingborough does not appear to have been much affected during the Civil War period but one highlight was when **Thomas Jones** the elderly Vicar was taken to Northampton jail on the back of a *'ferocious Wellingborough bear'* (probably a performing bear) for continuing to use the Book of Common Prayer which was frowned upon at the time. He was released but immediately returned to Wellingborough to continue his work and was once more returned to jail where he died.
He is depicted in stained glass in All Hallows church.

Had the Civil War not taken place Wellingborough is likely to have become a spa town like Bath.
At one time there were about thirty five springs in the area some of which, including the Red Well were claimed to have fertility properties.

In 1628 **Charles I** visited Wellingborough with his wife **Henrietta Maria** to take the waters as after ten years of marriage he was still awaiting an heir. It must have worked because they went on to have four children.

There is quite a large pavement mosaic just off Sheep Street recalling the names of some of these wells including Hemmingwell, Whytwell, Redwell and Holywell.
This area with its shopping mall, public houses, banks and restaurants is usually fairly busy especially on market days as would be expected in quite a large town.

On 28th July 1738 a great number of properties were destroyed in a Great Fire marked by a plaque in Silver Street. Two hundred and five houses were destroyed and six hundred homeless people took shelter in the church.

Another small plaque on the edge of the Market Place records the fact that on the 3rd August 1942 during the Second World War eight local people were killed in a bombing raid.

The Hind Hotel : Wellingborough.

One of my favourite buildings is the Grade II* listed gable fronted 17th century Hind Hotel - the hind being the symbolic sign of the **Hattons** who were Lords of the Manor and who sponsored **Drake**'s voyage around the world between 1577- 80 in a ship named the 'Pelican'.
In honour of his sponsor, **Drake** renamed his ship the 'Golden Hind' on his return to England.

Cromwell and his officers are reputed to have stayed here prior to the Battle of Naseby - he seems to have put himself about quite a bit!

In 1820 when HRH the **Duke of Gloucester** visited the town his horses were changed at the Hind Hotel. On leaving, the driver set off too fast and the carriage overturned and the Duke had to be rescued from the carriage window.

The central timber porch which extends over the pavement was added in about 1900.

An impressive new Museum and Heritage Centre has recently opened in the old Swimming Baths. **Dulley** and **Woolston** were Brewers in the 19th century and used water from one of the many wells in the town to make stout and mineral waters. After brewing the waste water was channelled into a specially created bathing area open to the public. The museum even includes a section of the baths.
It is well worth a visit with free admission but for how long I wonder?

.... WELLINGBOROUGH

It is said that a Castle once existed in this area and although no evidence has been found some parts of the town are named Castle Road, Castle Mews and Castle Fields and even the new theatre in the area was given the name Castle Theatre when it was opened on 30th March 1995 by *Jeremy Irons*.
It has a 500 seat auditorium and stages a wide variety of shows and exhibitions.

In 1905 the site housed the Cattlemarket but was also used by various supermarket chains in the 1970's and the 1980's.

Wellingborough School in London Road was built between the years 1879-95 but with later additions to cope with the growing population and popularity of the school.

Park Hospital in Irthlingborough Road was the former Workhouse with later additions.
The original brick building with its cruciform wings is dated 1835.

There was a dramatic rise in population with the arrival of the railway and the mining of iron ore between 1861-1901.

At one stage there were two railway stations in the town. One was at a level crossing on the London Road and served the Northampton to Peterborough line which closed in 1964 since when all track and buildings have been demolished and is now the site of the A45 flyover.

The other station at the bottom of Midland Road was built in 1857 of dark red brick with round arched windows and barge boarded gables for the Midland Railway between London St Pancras and Nottingham/Sheffield.
I am pleased to see that the main core of the station buildings has not changed too much since they were built.
It was the centre for a large locomotive depot with two roundhouses dated 1868 and 1872.

On the 2nd September 1898 there was a serious accident at the station when a trolley ran off the platform in front of a Manchester Express.
The train crew and six passengers were killed and sixty five people were injured.

We often used to take our young children to see the animals in the small zoo located just off Sheep Street. We even went by train to the London Road station before that closed. The zoo was open between 1943 and 1970 after which rules were tightened for keeping animals in captivity.
It was sold under auction for £1,500.

At the time of the Domesday Book there were one hundred and fifty five water mills in the County many of which were along the banks of the River Nene. Now there are only two in operation, the other being at Bugbrooke.

The one in Wellingborough was built by
J. B. Whitworth in 1866 after a previous mill at Turvey burned down.
It is still in regular use although electricity replaced steam in the late 1950's.
Kitchen cupboards regularly hold products from the mill in the form of flour and dried fruit.
I also read that they produce millions of the little sugar sachets that are a common sight in public houses and cafes.

Wellingborough Station

WELTON

Three miles north of Daventry
Population: 1801-488   2001 - 634

DOMESDAY BOOK
WALETONE/WELETON/WELINTONE
Waletone in the Domesday Book suggests a clear derivation from 'wielle tun' – spring farmstead. The village lies on limestone hills where there are numerous springs.

Prior to the Norman Conquest both **Wulfmaer** and **Leofric** held land in the area. After the Conquest they were still there but now as tenants to Norman noblemen.

This is a charming residential hill top village on the western edge of the County close to the Warwickshire border.

The church of **ST MARTIN** with its west tower and dominant blue faced clock is situated up a steep winding hill in the centre of the village and is mainly a 15th century church with some good wall tablets to the **Clarke** family who lived in **Welton Place.**

The tub shaped font is thought to be Saxon and is said to have been dragged all the way from the East coast in one piece.

The nave is made up of four bays of tall decorated arches supported by octagonal piers. Although the nave and both aisles are quite tall there is no clerestory but the white ceiling and black beams give the impression of space and light.

A small brass recalls that in 1899 five sons of the village carved the splendid pulpit *'for the love of the Church'*. They were also responsible for the delightful little Alms Box with an open hand appealing for donations.

An electrical fault in January 1997 caused considerable damage to the roof and destroyed some of the pews.

In the churchyard is a sad memorial to six year old **John Hewitt** who ran away from neglectful parents on January 16, 1806 and was found dead in a field in the parish two days later having starved to death.

Welton Place once stood beside a lake around which were planted rare cedar trees, some of which still survive.
It was built in 1758 for **Joseph Clarke** who was at one time High Sheriff of the County.
The family had a great interest in horticulture and the popular border plant the *'Clarkia'* is accredited to them.
Later the property was rented by the **Garrard** family, the Crown Jewellers, and it is said that they were often visited by members of the Royal family.

The 'Big House' as it was called locally was converted into flats but was subsequently demolished in 1972.
Excavations of the site revealed many Roman artefacts, coins, pottery and human remains.

The London and Birmingham Railway arrived in the area in 1838 and Welton had a station but it was located a long way outside of the village.
The line continues to this day as the West Coast Main Line but the station, one of the earliest in the County, closed in 1958.

The first school was established here in 1820 close to the present one which dates back to 1910 and has been upgraded and extended to offer education of a high standard.

The only public house is The White Horse and there is no longer a shop or post office.

The village once had both a Baptist and a Methodist chapel.
In a religious survey of 1851 one of the ministers, **John Gregory** records - *'I have been Pastor over this chapel for twenty years and have not been recompensed for my well wishes.'*

WEST HADDON

Seven miles north east of Daventry
Population: 1801-806   2001 - 1439

DOMESDAY BOOK
ECDONE/EDDONE/EDONE
The name Haddon derives from the Saxon words 'haeth' - heathland and 'dun' - hill.
To distinguish this from its sister village the East and West were added in the 13th century.

At the time of the Domesday Book the main manor was held by the Abbey of Coventry and smaller manors by **William Peverel** and **Gunfrid de Chocques.**
A market and a fair to be held in the town was granted by **King Edward I** to the Prior and Convent of Daventry in 1292. The church was later given to the Cluniac Priory at Daventry by **Hugh Poer**, grandson of the founder.

The fields of West Haddon were the location of an enclosures riot in 1765. As a result of an advert in the local paper a crowd assembled on the pretext of playing in or watching a football game.
Instead they pulled down fences which were then burnt claiming that it was public land and not the sole right of the wealthy landowners.

This is quite a large village about midway between Northampton and Rugby and close to junction 18 of the M1 motorway and until the recent construction of a bypass had the busy main road (A428) winding through its centre.
In fact six roads converge on the village including an old Drove road and no doubt cattle would have rested here on their way south.

The mainly 14th century church of **ALL SAINTS** stands in an elevated position alongside the main street in the centre of the village.
Its embattled west tower once had a wooden spire which fell into decay and was removed in 1648.

Entrance is made via the south porch over which is a rare sundial having three faces. The porch protects the south door with its 14th century studs and ironwork.
Inside is a rare and magnificent square Norman font carved out of one piece of stone and depicting the Nativity, the Baptism of **Christ,** Palm Sunday and **Christ** in Glory.

The chancel contains a piscina and there is also one in the south aisle near which appears to have been an aumbrey of the early 15th century.

According to information displayed in the church there are plans to install a new toilet and a kitchen - seems to be a must for most churches nowadays.

Among the memorial tablets are those of
William Lovett who in 1846 built and endowed six Almshouses at the west end of the village and **John Heygate** who built and endowed the school. Both men were also generous benefactors of other institutions.
The **Lovett** Almshouses are now run by the **Lovett** charity and are only offered to older people who have lived in the village or in a nearby parish.

In addition to the church there is still a Primary school which was extended in 2002, two shops, a post office, antique dealer, hair salon, a village hall and playing fields and a Baptist chapel (1882) although the Methodist chapel built in 1810 has long gone.

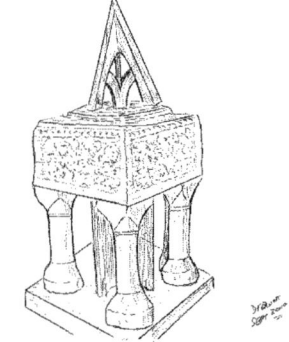

Norman Font : All Saints Church, West Haddon

The villagers seem to be well catered for although the village itself is not especially attractive.

One of the three public houses, The Pytchley Inn, was built as a private house but contrary to the general trend was converted into an inn which took its name from the local hunt.

The Sheaf Inn is an 18th century coaching inn whereas The Crown was the scene of a notorious murder trial. *Mrs Bates* murdered elderly *Mrs Gulliver* in Crick - the body being buried in West Haddon churchyard.

Mrs Bates took strychnine at the opening of the trial and died almost immediately.

An inquest was held at The Crown during the night for privacy and the two bodies were brought into the inn and removed again through a club room window.

Outside an antique shop stands an old milepost which originally read - Northampton eleven miles - London seventy seven miles but the wording was purposely obliterated in the Second World War to confuse the enemy.

Brownstones next to the church is a former Rectory dated 1676.

West Haddon Hall was built in 1827 and was used for military purposes in the Second World War. After the war the top storey was removed.

On my recent visit it was obvious from the posters on display that there is a lot of local opposition to a wind farm in the vicinity.

Almhouses: West Haddon

ALMSHOUSES

Although they represent an early form of housing for the poor and needy there are still many Almshouses to be seen in towns and villages throughout England where they first appeared in the 10th century.

The oldest known Almshouse still in existence is the Hospital of St Cross in Winchester which dates from about 1132.

Those to be seen around Northamptonshire are of more recent date.

Before the Reformation many Almshouses were associated with religious institutions and in many instances included a Chantry Chapel so that the residents could pray for the soul of the King and their Benefactor. These suffered badly at the time of the Dissolution of the Monasteries.

The Bede House in Higham Ferrers built about 1420 managed to avoid this fate.

In Northamptonshire many Almshouses were provided by local benefactors in the 17th, 18th and 19th centuries but they all had the same purpose of providing a good standard of accommodation, often at little or no cost to the poor and needy of the parish - many of whom were elderly. Sometimes they were provided by firms for their own workers. Many Almshouses were multiple small terraced houses either single storeyed or two storeyed as in the case of West Haddon. Sometimes they were congregated around a courtyard.

Over the years the accommodation has been upgraded which often meant reducing the number of individual properties to provide space for bathrooms in those remaining. The schemes are usually administered by a Charity or Trustees of the Bequest who decide on their tenants.

In addition to the Almshouses in West Haddon others are still in use in many places locally including Barnwell, Weekley, Higham Ferrers and Oundle.

Apart from the church and the Manor House they are often the oldest and most attractive buildings in the community.

WESTON & WEEDON LOIS

Four miles west of Towcester
Population: 1801-387   2001 – 330

DOMESDAY BOOK
WEDONE

From early times this area was known as 'weoh dun' (shrine hill) - it obviously had some religious purpose.
My Ordnance Survey map names this village as Weedon Lois but marks Lois Weedon House.
I cannot find any reference to Weston in the Domesday Book but the common name of Weston
simply means west farm so possibly the two settlements were combined at the time.

This is a community with so many names, Lois Weedon, Weedon Lois, Weston by Weedon, Weedon Pinkney, that it is difficult to establish where in an alphabetical list it should be placed and whether to separate them or bring them all together in one place.

The settlements of Weston, Lois Weedon and Middlethorpe nestle in the south west corner of the County in a delightful rural setting.

Weston itself is a delightful little village and has a good number of very attractive properties.

A particular favourite of mine is **Armada House** which dates from 1588 – the date the Armada was defeated.

Unfortunately the building suffered a disastrous fire in March 2011 and at the time of writing is just a shell covered with scaffolding and plastic sheeting. Hopefully it will be rebuilt in all its former glory.

Opposite is **Weston Hall** which was home to *Sir Sacheverell Sitwell* from 1927-1988.

He is buried together with his wife in the churchyard extension in Lois Weedon.

His sister, *Dame Edith*, a well known poet and authoress (1887-1964) is also buried there.

Her grave is marked by a tapering stone pillar on which is fixed a bronze plaque by *Henry Moore* depicting two delicate hands called *'Youth and Age'*.

The Hall is still owned by the *Sitwell* family and dates from the late 17th century although it has since been enlarged and modernised.

When travelling away from Weston towards Culworth look out for the llamas.

Although you cannot actually ride llamas, it is not uncommon here to see llamas trekking through the English countryside at a gentle pace.

The Crown public house is recorded as having existed in 1593 and has an old coach house indicating that Weston may have been on a minor coaching route.

Today it still provides meals, drinks and accommodation.

Weston possesses one of the oldest Baptist chapels in Northamptonshire.

The present building dates from 1791 although records of a chapel here go back to 1681.

Baptisms took place at an open air baptistry at Cathanger Farm in the parish of Woodend.

The chapel is now part of the Tove Valley Baptist Fellowship.

There is no shop and the school for younger children is in Lois Weedon whereas older children travel further afield.

A settlement existed in Lois Weedon well before the Domesday Book as Roman coins and pottery have been found locally.
In 1086 the manor of Lois Weedon was held by *Gilo de Pinkney* who held the adjoining manors of Sulgrave and Culworth.
He built a defensive fortification thought to be similar to those in his other two manors but all that remains is a small tree covered mound beside the village Green called Castle mound.

A small Priory dedicated to the Virgin Mary was established here early in the 12th century as a cell of the Benedictine Abbey of Lucien, Oise, France.

When the monks discovered a mineral spring to the south of the church they dedicated it to *St Lucien* of Normandy - it became known as *St Loy's* well. This attracted many pilgrims as did the relics of the saint thought to have been placed behind the altar underneath the East window.

At one time the monks used one part of the church and the parishioners the other and maybe this explains why there are two Easter sepulchres and two piscinas.
The monks are believed to have lived very well but had to work hard. The Priory is thought to have been sold in 1392 to the Cistercian Abbey of Biddlesden (just south of Syresham) but in 1440 the land was transferred to All Souls College in Oxford who are still major landlowners in the area.

It was a lovely sunny day the last time I visited the church of **ST MARY** in Lois Weedon but inside it was one of the coldest churches I can remember.
It is cruciform in shape with an Early English embattled central tower.
There is a stone pulpit dated 1849 with an unusual doorway approached up steps from the rear and wall paintings over the east arch in the south aisle.

On Sunday 2 July 1643 the parishioners witnessed a violent scene when twelve Parliamentary troopers rode from Northampton to arrest the Anglican priest - *William Losse* for his Royalist beliefs. *Losse* defied the troops, climbed on to the tower roof and removed the ladder but it is thought that he died from wounds sustained.
Of about seven thousand clergymen who stood up for their faith in the tenets of the Church of England only about six hundred survived at the time of the Reformation to resume their living.

The village is said to have witnessed the last person to be burnt at the stake in England - there is a tombstone to a woman who allegedly poisoned her husband but burning was normally for heresy not murder.

Although Lois Weedon does not have a shop or a public house it does have the Primary school for the area. This Victorian building dates back to 1848 but since then has been considerably enlarged and modified.

Armada House : Weston

WESTON BY WELLAND

Four miles north east of Market Harborough
Population: 1801-229   2001 - 141

DOMESDAY BOOK
WESTONE
This was the 'west tun' - farmstead connected to nearby Ashley.
It became Weston Bassett (after the holders of the Manor in the 13th century)
but is now known as Weston by Welland because of its location overlooking the Welland valley.

In 1086 the two manors were held by **Robert de Bucy** with ten households and by **Countess Judith** with five households.

The village lies on the quite busy B664 almost on the border with Leicestershire with fine views north over the Welland valley. There are some pretty ironstone houses but not much more of any note apart from the church and the old school.

The original church of **ST MARY** which stands alongside the main road was first built during the 13th century but was mostly rebuilt between 1863- 6 as a facsimile of its predecessor.
Part of the cost was met by the Rector the **Rev C. E. Danby** as was the enlargement of the churchyard. A plaque in memory of him and his wife **Susanna** has been placed in the chancel.

Above the altar is some lovely stained glass.
The west tower of ashlar has carved heads on the battlements and houses five bells.

I was interested in the large picture in the church with photographs of the residents of Weston by Welland in 1992.
What an invaluable record for future generations.

The old school standing close by the church is now in private ownership - the younger schoolchildren now have to travel to nearby Wilbarston.
These buildings are in the grand Victorian style and are topped by a magnificent group of five tall brick chimneys.
There is no shop or post office and in the absence of a village hall use is made of a section of the church.

The old public house, now known as The Wheel and Compass was built mainly of local stone in 1738. It was once a two storey building but a third storey was added to cater for the Irish labourers who laid the railway line about one mile from the village.

It is believed to be haunted by one of the workmen involved in a brawl over a card game.

Both the line between Rugby and Peterborough and the station which was shared with nearby Ashley have now closed but evidence of the line can still be seen.

Old School: Weston by Welland

WHILTON

Four miles north east of Daventry
Population: 1801-309   2001 - 296

DOMESDAY BOOK
WOLTONE

*The name probably derives from the Saxon words
'hweogol' - wheel and 'tun' - farmstead
describing a farmstead by a round hill.*

This was one of the many manors of the **Count of Mortain** in 1086. There were ten households plus a priest and the mill rendered forty pence per annum. Today the present mill and one hundred acres of land is the County's premier outdoor go karting facility.

The village has a history going back to Roman times with the site of a Roman settlement known as Bannaventa to the west.

This area is an amazing place because within the space of half a mile there is the old Roman road (Watling Street), the Grand Union Canal with a flight of six locks and a large marina, the West Coast main railway line between London and the north west and the 20th century motorway - M1.

Fortunately the village which lies on a minor road is not troubled by all the passing traffic.
It enjoys a relatively peaceful lifestyle with some lovely old properties. One of the most picturesque being a whitewashed thatched cottage but there are also some not so attractive modern buildings.

One of the smaller stone houses of 1689 is said to have floorboards made from the doors of the old prison in Northampton.

The church of **ST ANDREW** dates from the 12th and 13th centuries although much of the old church has been lost as a result of alterations in the 18th century and 'improvements' by the Victorians when the chancel which is higher than the nave was rebuilt. The only distinctive glass is found in the East window. Copper replaced lead covering the tower and nave in 1957/8.

Bat at Whilton Church

Several memorial tablets are dedicated to members of the **Rose** family who owned the Estate from the early 18th century. It was inherited by a nephew the **Rev. William Lucas Holden** who was Rector and who subsequently adopted the name **Rose** and paid for the installation of six bells in 1777. One peculiarity is the blue faced clock which has only four minutes marked to each five minute period - were the sermons cut short as a result? This church is one of a number in the County which have become home to a colony of bats and their evidence is everywhere.

Whilton is unusual in this area as it had a school housed in farm buildings as far back as 1768 thanks to the generosity of **Jonathan Emery**.
The former school house is now a private dwelling and the old school is the village hall and is used by a pre-school playgroup.
Today there is neither a school nor a shop.

BANNAVENTA

Emperor Antoninus in his 'Iter Brittanniarum' mentions a place called Bannaventa situated along the road twelve Roman miles from Lactodorum (Towcester). Weedon Bec and Daventry have been mentioned as two possible locations but the evidence discovered over the past three hundred years points to Bannaventa having been located on the site now occupied by Whilton Lodge which marks the junction of two Roman roads including Watling Street

It was a posting station for Roman travellers and would have operated in the same fashion as during the days of the stage coaches. The Roman settlement covering at least thirty acres indicates that this was a walled town.

It is said that **St Patrick** spent his early life here and in his Confession he said 'that he had been born in a settlement called 'Banavem Taburniae' and that when he was about sixteen was taken into captivity in Ireland where I was held as a slave'.
The Watling Street ran to North Wales the nearest port for travelling to and from Ireland.

WHISTON

Six miles east of Northampton
Population: 1801-56

DOMESDAY BOOK
WICENTONE/WICETONE
*This was once the farmstead - tun of the **Hwicce** tribe.*

The Domesday Book records that the three hide manor of Whiston and Denton had thirty four households and a mill rendering twenty shillings per annum.

Today it is a small but attractive village with no shop, post office, public house, chapel or school and occupies a hill position overlooking the Nene valley to the north.

The most attractive and impressive building is undoubtedly the fine church of **ST MARY** the tower of which can be seen from a wide area across the Nene Valley but no roads lead there.
A quite stiff climb up a footpath is necessary to gain access to the church so remember to obtain the key in the village before making the ascent. It is well worth the effort.

The body of the church is limestone whereas the splendid late Perpendicular style tower with fine tall pinnacles and gargoyles is of both ironstone and ashlar bands.
The masonry is of a very high quality and it is generally agreed that Royal stonemasons may have been involved.

The church is thought to have been completed in about twenty years around the year 1534 and funded entirely by **Anthony Catesby** who was a descendant of the **Catesby** family of Ashby St Ledgers and has not been altered since.

I can imagine that someone visiting after an absence of five hundred years would see little change apart from the memorials to members of the **Catesby** and **Boston** families.

The church is lit by candles and the electricity supply only seems sufficient for an electric kettle and a small organ so wrap up well if you are thinking of attending a service in the winter.

The original pump organ is still in situ.
Look out for the **Catesby** cat which appears in a roof boss and also on the two wooden staves either side of the pews.

I was very impressed and would include this church in my top ten for interest in Northamptonshire.

The Rectory near the church is Tudor and is dated 1852

The Moat House, a detached farm house on the west side of the village incorporates some parts of a former medieval building which is said to have accommodated **King John** on one of his visits to the County.

Catesby Cat - Whiston Church

WHITFIELD

Two miles north east of Brackley
Population: 1801-217   2001 - 215

DOMESDAY BOOK
WITEFELLE
The name is thought to derive from 'hwit' - white and ' feld' - open space or enclosed land.

The manor belonged to the royal manor of Kings Sutton in 1086 and had twelve households.

This small village stands on the Buckinghamshire border on a bend in the Great Ouse River in a quiet unspoilt backwater just off the busy A43 and gets very little through traffic.

The church of **ST JOHN** the **EVANGELIST** was rebuilt in 1870 in the Early English style with a broach spire after the previous spire was blown down in a gale on the 7th February 1869 totally wrecking the church fabric. The stained glass dated 1898-1914 is by *William Morris & Co*.

When I visited the church recently it was undergoing some restoration work.

Little else seems to happen here although I was interested to learn that in May 2009 Whitfield racecourse at Manor Farm became the new home of the Grafton Hunt Point to Point meeting.

The local public house is The Sun Inn but there is no longer a chapel, school, shop or post office although Illetts Farm does have some self catering apartments.

Church of St John the Evangelist: Whitfield

WHITTLEBURY

Three miles south of Towcester
Population: 1801-533   2001 - 586

*Although not mentioned in the Domesday Book it is thought that this was the place where **Witel**
a tribal leader, established his fortified place, the village being in the midst of woodland
now known as Whittlewood Forest which in the 13th century covered 20,000 acres.*

Whittlebury lies on the A413 Towcester to Buckingham road and has quite a lot of through traffic. The name is well known to many F1 Motor Racing fans as it stands close to one of the entrances to the famous Silverstone Grand Prix Circuit.
Unfortunately this means that you can often hear the drone of engines in the near distance even though there may be no racing going on.

King Athelstan is reported to have held court in the village in about 930AD but I cannot find the settlement recorded by name in the Domesday Book possibly because it was embedded in the Estate of Greens Norton.

The area is steeped in history and excavations have revealed that several Iron Age and Roman sites lay within that part of Whittlewood Forest which skirted the village.

In 1850 the site of a Roman Villa with at least twelve rooms was discovered in the north east corner of the parish near the Watling Street.
One of the mosaics found on the site was given by the *Duke of Grafton* to *Queen Victoria* and re-laid in a dairy at Windsor.

Media interest was aroused in 1983 when a local villager found a Roman skeleton in a shallow grave in his garden which is thought to have previously been a Christian burial site.
The skeleton was subsequently reburied in the churchyard.

During the latter part of the 18th century Dissenters' chapels began to spring up in towns and villages across the land.
One of the first Methodist groups in the area was established in Whittlebury when a farmhouse was licensed for preaching in 1763.

A chapel was built twenty years later and was enlarged in 1812. *John Wesley* the famous preacher obviously liked Whittlebury as he is said to have visited and preached on about twenty occasions.
On his first visit he recorded in his journal that he spoke *'to a truly loving and simple people....at the side of the new preaching house'*.
The chapel has now closed and is a private residence.

The village still has a Primary school and a public house/restaurant - The Fox & Hounds but no shop or post office.

Occupying an open aspect on the edge of the village with the churchyard entered through an attractive lych gate is the church of **ST MARY** which is thought to date from 1200 although the earliest mention of a chapel here was in 1236.

The church has a 13th century Early English style west tower although there is a Norman window high up in the tower which has a ring of five bells one of which is dated 1634.

On entering via the south porch look down at the blocks of slate placed edgewise - they are very unusual. I have not been able to establish when these were laid but the nave was repaved in 1815 and the whole church thoroughly restored by *J. P. St Aubyn* in 1877- 8 through the generosity of *Sir Robert Loder* whose grave is near the lych gate.

Before leaving the church admire the old 12th century patterned chest with ironwork and three double locks.

Whittlebury Lodge Hall was built about 1865 for the *Earl of Southampton* but was damaged by fire and rebuilt in 1871 in the Tudor style.
It is now a popular visitor attraction and is the venue for large scale and luxurious conferences, weddings and corporate functions. Accommodation is provided in two hundred and eleven double bedrooms many with panoramic views over the PGA Championship golf course.
The Hotel also offers private access to the Silverstone Race Circuit and is consequently booked well in advance of large Race Meetings.

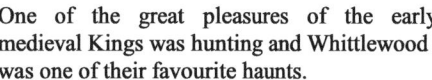

WHITTLEWOOD FOREST

One of the great pleasures of the early medieval Kings was hunting and Whittlewood was one of their favourite haunts.
During the late 12th and 13th century the royal forests of Rockingham, Salcey and Whittlewood extended in an unbroken band from the River Welland in the north east of the County to the Great Ouse in the south and encompassed almost half of the land area of Northamptonshire.

It was not all woodland but was subject to stringent Forest Law.
Punishment for those found trespassing, killing deer, clearing woodland, keeping hounds or even collecting wood was severe.

There was a common prison with a gaoler for the Forests of Salcey and Whittlewood at Hartwell Wyke.
The restrictions of Forest Law were relaxed at the end of the 13th century with the introduction of contracted disafforestation.

Research has revealed that within the forest there was a principal settlement in the parish and at least one other focus of occupation - i.e. a hamlet.

In the case of Whittlebury there were two such hamlets, Luffield (see page 364) and Nether End which is thought to have been sited about half a mile north west of the present village.
The forest also included a number of 'cotes' which usually referred to a simple barn for shelter i.e. Caldecote, Foscote, Astcote.

WICKEN

Six miles south east of Towcester
Population: 1801-367   2001 - 299

DOMESDAY BOOK
WICHA/WICHE
The Saxon word 'wicen' means specialised farms.

Wicken is tucked away at the southern edge of the County amid minor roads and yet quite close to the city of Milton Keynes.

Originally there were two villages here Wyke Dyve and Wyke Hamon divided by a small stream.

These were probably the two manors recorded in the Domesday Book. One was held by **Robert d'Oilly** and the other by **Baron Mano (Mainou)**.
The combined population was twenty four households.

Sir John Spencer of Wormleighton moved to Wicken in 1514 and built the original house in Wicken Park around 1571.
As he was owner of both Wyke Dyve and Wyke Hamon he set about the amalgamation of the two parishes in 1587.

The uniting of the two parishes is still celebrated annually on Ascension Day when after a service in the church the congregation repair to the Gospel Elm in Cross Tree Road to sing the *'Old 100th -* *'All people that on earth do dwell'* and then retire for cake (made to a special recipe) and a drink
(it used to be ale) in the village hall.

In 1938 the BBC Broadcast the service, I wonder if it was anything to do with the local pub -
The White Lion - donating seven gallons of beer to the festivities.

ST JAMES church in Wyke Hamon was only a short distance from the church in Wyke Dyke which was large enough for all the worshippers so it fell into disuse and was eventually demolished in 1617.

The house remained in the **Spencer** family for about two hundred years after which it was deserted and eventually demolished.

Charles Hosier who made his money in the City of London as a gold merchant bought the Estate in 1716 and set about building a new Manor House in Wicken Park.

In 1810 it passed to **Sir John Mordaunt** and eventually in 1945 the Estate was acquired by the Society of Merchant Venturers of Bristol.

The contents of the mansion were sold off and the house converted into a private school.

Today known as Akeley Wood School it provides a high standard of education to about nine hundred pupils in three locations with the junior school still in Wicken Park and the older children at two nearby sites in Buckinghamshire.

It is worth while taking time to visit the present church of **ST JOHN** the **EVANGELIST**, the body of which was, except for the tower which houses eight bells, rebuilt by *Thomas Prowse* in 1758 and finished after his death in 1767.

I wonder whether this is the reason why the nave roof and chancel roof look so different.
I could not believe that the superb vaulting in the chancel was papier mache rather than stone until I read it in the little church guide.
The nave has a pointed barrel vault of plaster but the presence of vaulting springs from the piers and corbels on the aisle walls suggest that the original intention was to have the whole roof vaulted.

Other notable features include the modern pews, medieval font (thought to have come from Wyke-Hamon church), the altar window telling the story of the Crucifixion and Resurrection, a magnificent brass across the floor in the chancel and the large number of memorials to local dignitaries.

It was unusual to see the names of Rectors going back to before 1263 inscribed in gold on two modern slate panels on the north wall.

The attractive lych gate gives entrance to the churchyard in which is the last resting place
Lord and Lady Penrhyn
(MP and race horse owner)
Just outside the porch is a poignant little medieval cross.

I can find no record of a non-conformist chapel in the village so can only assume that there were none (most unlikely) or that they travelled further for their meetings to avoid any confrontation.

The village contains a number of attractive thatched cottages, a sports club with new buildings and large playing fields, a village hall in the old school and a public house - The White Lion, but no longer a state school or shop.

Church Lychgate - Wicken

WILBARSTON

The Fox Inn. Wilbarston

Five miles east of Market Harborough
Population: 1801-755   2001 - 767

DOMESDAY BOOK
WILBERDESTONE/WILBERTESTONE
The original spelling would indicate that this was once
***Wilbeorth's** 'tun' - farmstead.*

In 1086 the larger of the two manors was held by **Robert de Tosny** and had twenty households whereas in the other manor held by the King there were five sokemen with three bordars.

This is a fairly large attractive village in a delightful part of north Northamptonshire overlooking the Welland Valley.
Originally it lay on the busy A427 midway between Corby and Market Harborough but thankfully the bypass removes all the through traffic.

The village is said to contain some of the oldest houses in the County.
In Barlows Lane is Barlow's cottage a lovely ironstone building carrying the date 1656.
Another house which caught my eye among many splendid old ironstone cottages is in Main Street with the date stone 1633 RAI.

The church of **ALL SAINTS** formerly All Hallows has been standing at the northern edge of the village for over eight hundred years and from its location there are splendid views across the meadows and the Welland Valley.

The well kept churchyard is subject to a Living Churchyard Project to encourage wildlife and a rich variety of wild flowers and plants.

As the church is cut into the hillside there is an unusual variation in levels including five steps down into the church and five steps up into the chancel. Most of the building is 13th century although Norman work includes the blocked priests arch in the south chancel and possibly part of the tower walls.

Much restoration took place in 1884 when the then Rector, the **Rev. W. Waudby** met most of the cost and commemorated his family in new glass for the East window. Restoration included new dark oak pews, pulpit, lectern and chancel screen.

The church must have looked quite spectacular when the nave, aisle and new chancel roof were painted. Time has unfortunately dulled their brightness somewhat.
Look out for the Victorian wooden lectern inscribed *'The gift of the poor of Wilbarston'* -
a shining example of class distinction within the church itself at that time.
On the 5th June 1982 lightning struck the broach spire resulting in the top fifteen feet being rebuilt. There is now a very substantial lightning conductor.

In the Second World War the village rejoiced in the safe return of all its service personnel – a list of which was placed on the internal north wall on Remembrance Day 2004.

The village still supports a shop and The Fox Inn with late 17th century origins.
The old school built in 1845 for ninety six children still stands alongside a modern school which now has to cater for children from other villages and not just Wilbarston.
Behind the school is the single surviving wall of a 17th or early 18th century rectangular dovecote with seven rows of open nesting holes set in a boundary wall – once an important source of food.

WILBY

Two miles south west of Wellingborough
Population: 1801-259   2001 - 621

DOMESDAY BOOK
WILEBI
*Was this once **Willa's** 'by' – village '- or does it derive
from the word 'welig' - willow tree?*

The village lies on the A4500 between Wellingborough and Northampton.

In spite of the fact that about half mile south is the relatively new Northampton to Wellingborough dual carriageway. I was amazed at the amount of traffic that still travels through the village.

In the Main Street are Wilby Working Mens Club and two public houses - The Horseshoe which was once a blacksmiths shop and The Crown.

There is no shop or post office but there is a large supermarket just beyond the parish boundary on the outskirts of Wellingborough.

Apart from the church, the old school and **Wilby Hall** which is a fine Georgian building the village has little that appeals to me.

The church of **ST MARY** has an unusual 16th century Decorative style west tower.
The square base with diagonal buttresses then turns octagonal with pinnacles which lead to the recessed spire connected by short flying buttresses.
Look out for the four large gargoyles on the tower.
I was so impressed with the tower that I expected something spectacular inside the church.
In this respect I was somewhat disappointed.

The approach to the south porch from Church Lane through a carefully tended churchyard is very pleasant although the tower clock was not working.

St Marys Church, Wilby

Countess Judith, niece of *William the Conqueror* who held the manor in 1086 when there were seven households, endowed the church.
In its present form it largely dates from about the reign of *King John* but apparently stands on the site of an older structure and the round stone font still in use most probably belonged to the original church.
There is some fine stained glass in the chancel which is divided from the nave by a wooden rood screen making it very dark.
The East window is interesting in that it is in memory of three Rectors, *William*, *Septimus* and *Robert Stockdale* who all served the church in the middle of the 19th century.

At the time of my most recent visit workmen were in the process of building toilets and kitchen facilities where once stood the north aisle which was demolished in 1839.
There are now only clerestory windows on the south side. I got the impression from the boards and certificates on the tower wall that they take bell ringing very seriously.

Next door to the church is the Primary school which was founded in 1854 and has since been extended.

Wilby Caravan Park was originally Wilby Lido an open air swimming pool much loved by the local people in the 1930's to 1950's, today it provides permanent accommodation in very well appointed caravans.

WINWICK

Eight miles north east of Daventry
Population: 1801-124   2001 - 85

DOMESDAY BOOK
WINEWIC/WINEWICHE

*The name has not changed much from its origins which means this was the place of **Wina**'s 'tun'*
possibly a specialist dairy farm.

This tiny village although only about one mile north of West Haddon is somewhat off the beaten track but is well worth seeking out.

Of the three manors the largest was held by the Abbey of Coventry. There were about twenty five households in total probably resulting in a population of about eight five - much the same as today.

It is a charming quiet little place with a superb display of wild flowers in the spring.

Bluebells

This is not surprising as two thousand daffodils were planted around the church to mark the millennium to add to the flowers already there.

The area has been designated a Special Landscape Area by Northamptonshire County Council and there was much local opposition to a wind farm in the area.
Unfortunately the Planning Inspectorate approved the application which will see the erection of six giant wind turbines each seven times higher than Winwick church.

The church of **ST MICHAEL** and **ALL ANGELS** stands on a grassy mound overlooking the peaceful countryside.

It is one of Northamptonshire's cruciform churches and dates back to the 13th century consisting of an embattled Perpendicular style west tower, nave, transepts, porch and chancel, the latter being replaced by the Victorians in 1853.

There is some superb bright and colourful stained glass in the west window of the tower. It was a millennium gift from friends and family of Winwick and partly funded by Daventry District Council and dedicated to the memory of *Lady Sarah Gibbs JP, MBE* who - *'brought joy and inspiration to everyone who knew her'*
It has already been described as being of national importance.

For some years during the 17th century there were more marriages in Winwick church than there were bachelors and spinsters in the parish.
It seems to have been the Gretna Green of Northamptonshire - I wonder why?

Near the church is the magnificent 16th century **Winwick Manor House** which together with the stables, old coach house and tithe barn have been converted to four separate residences.
It is claimed that men from *Cromwell's* cavalry slept in the tithe barn on the eve of the Battle of Naseby in 1645.

It is worth venturing off the road through the village to see the Crinkle-Crankle or
Crinkum-Crankum wall that was built near **Winwick Hall** to celebrate the millennium.
It is said to be the first wall of its type to be built in Northamptonshire and the first in England for one hundred and fifty years.

They were popular in Victorian times where they were built in areas of high prevailing winds because of the strength in the design.
According to the internet the Crinkle - Crankle wall is not the only unusual feature of Winwick Hall which has an aviary with peacocks and pheasants, South American ponies, several
ha ha's and in a cellar a twenty seat Art Deco private cinema.

One item which can be seen is a black and gold Victorian post box on an outside wall.

Sir Thomas Malory inherited the Estate in Winwick in 1434. He led the unremarkable life of a country gentleman, attending to his judicial and social responsibilities as Lord of the Manor until 1450 when, for unknown reasons, he turned to a life of crime. Apart from trying to murder the *Duke of Buckingham*, he stole livestock, extorted money with menaces, was accused of rape and attacked the monks in Coombe Abbey and stole their money and valuables. He was imprisoned on more than one occasion and used the time to write a book which was retitled Le Mort D'Arthur by the printer *William Caxton* in 1470.
It is said to have been the forerunner of poems, films and books about *King Arthur* and the Knights of the Round Table.
Winwick is a very quiet place indeed except when the village has its annual fete, with no shop,
post office, public house or village hall and with the closure of the school no public room of any kind.
It is hard to imagine such a notorious person as *Thomas* ever living there.

Gateway at Winwick

WOLLASTON

Three miles south of Wellingborough
Population: 1801-761   2001 - 3038

DOMESDAY BOOK
WILAVESTONE
*Initially **Wulflaf's** 'tun' - farmstead had become corrupted to Wilavastonhe by 1086.*

The village has quite a long history and I find the erection of descriptive wall plaques at points of interest useful and informative.

The local Heritage Society runs the excellent little Wollaston museum in the former Congregational chapel in the High Street.

The museum is free to enter and is open regularly during the summer. Part of the museum site includes Beacon Hill - a 34 foot high earth mound created about 1130 by *Robert de Newburgh* at a time when *King Stephen*, nephew of *Henry I* was at war with *Matilda*, *Henry's* daughter.

Later it was the site of Wollaston's first windmill.

The parish is notable for the discovery of many Iron Age and Roman settlements which have revealed hut circles, ditches, pottery, coins and tiles. Excavations in 1997 revealed evidence of occupation dating back to the 7th century when a grave of a high status Anglo Saxon warrior was discovered including a bowl with a highly patterned steel sword, a warrior helmet and a nose guard.

By the time of the Norman Conquest there were three manors, two of which were held by *Countess Judith* although one of them was claimed by *Winemar* of Hanslope.

There were a total of forty two households recorded and two mills rendering a total of eleven shillings and eight pence per annum.

The church of **ST MARY** which dates back to 1300 is an interesting building. Most of the church fell down in 1735 and was rebuilt over the next two years in the Georgian style.

Only the tower and north transept remain of the original structure.

When inside the church it feels more like a chapel although the balconies have been removed.

A lovely stained glass window was installed in the chancel in 1961 but otherwise there is plain glass throughout.

What did intrigue me was the random numbering of the pew ends. Apparently this was done during the Victorian restoration when the workmen did not bother to relocate the seats numerically or maybe they could not read or write.

Opposite the church is Keep House - *Mrs Keep* having provided the first school in the village between 1840 and 1873.

The village has grown dramatically in the past two hundred years from 761 in 1801 to over 3000.

Wollaston Museum

Boot and shoe manufacture was once an important feature but little of this now remains.

One company still in existence and priding itself as the UK's oldest surviving Works Co-operative is Northamptonshire Productive Society (Shoes) Ltd or NPS (Shoes) Ltd which was established in 1881.

Wollaston is the home of the iconic Dr Martens Boot which has become world famous. The first boot was produced in 1960 and is now worn by all ages across the globe.

The majority of houses and businesses date from the Victorian or 20th century era and are not particularly appealing but go down Hickmire near the church and you will find a small group of attractive ancient limestone cottages.

One of these, a 16th century house, is now called the Old Priory but was a medieval Rectory belonging to Delapre Abbey in Northampton.

On a recent visit I lunched at what I have always known as The Nags Head only to find that it had been rebranded The Wollaston Inn.
The building was first referred to in 1787 as *Mr Lucy's* hostelry.
In the late 1960's to early 1980's it had the reputation for staging shows by good rising young stars many of whom have gone on to top the international stage including *Rod Stewart*, *Led Zepellin* and *The Who.*
On the front of the inn is a clock marking the coronation of *Queen Elizabeth II* in 1953.
Other public houses include The Cuckoo in High Street and The Crispin Arms in Hinwick Road.
The Boot Inn in High Street was gutted by fire in April 2011 and has now been partly restored with a new thatched roof.
Plans have been put forward to convert the Grade II listed building into a private residence.

Wollaston Baptist chapel dates back to 1867 and appeared to be in fine condition and still in regular use until recently.
At the time of writing the area on which it stood is a building site. The chapel is being rebuilt with larger and improved facilities to meet current and future requirements - an unusual sight in an English village at a time when chapels are more likely to be closed for lack of support. I look forward to visiting when the work is completed.

Hickmire : Wollaston

In addition to the public houses, church and chapel there are a few retail shops, health services and a Primary school. The large fairly modern Secondary school on the Irchester road serves Wollaston and many of the surrounding villages and at the start and end of each school day the area is very busy with buses, taxis and private cars.

Wollaston Hall was built in 1738 and was bought for just £5,000 in 1940 when *Scott Bader* moved his chemicals company from London to Wollaston. In the 1950's the firm founded the *Scott Bader* Commonwealth gifting the whole company to its employees for all time

Now the company functions as a Co-operative with profits divided between investment in the company, bonuses for all employees and charitable donations. The company has grown into an international organisation but employs only about 250 people locally.

Jubilee Park near the church was provided through the generosity of *Scott Bader*, Northamptonshire County Council and Wellingborough Borough Council and was constructed to mark the Golden Jubilee of *Queen Elizabeth II* in 2002.

WOODEND

Five miles west of Towcester

The settlement is not mentioned in the Domesday Book but was once known as Little Blacolvesle and later Wood Blakesley. In Saxon times the settlement was surrounded by Whittlewood Forest, hence Woodend.

Until 1866 Woodend was part of Blakesley parish but since then it has become a parish in its own right although it has no church.

The old Baptist chapel built in 1813 is now a private house.

In the early days when those breaking away from the established church had to keep a low profile, baptisms took place in the open air and out of sight of the general public at Cathanger Farm in the south of the parish.
When I last visited it was very overgrown but you could still see evidence of the pool.

The two bakehouses (one of which was used for an old Hovis advert) and the former public house, The Royal Oak are now in private ownership.

After the First World War, Woodend was one of only two *'Thankful'* villages in the County where all the serving personnel returned safely - the other being East Carlton.

Only one soldier who was born in Woodend died but he had moved to Sutton Valence in Surrey before the war started.

Blakesley Hall . N. Towcester.
Demolished 1957.

During the Second World War two USAF Fortresses from Snetterton Heath in Norfolk collided over the village when they were flying to a turning point near Silverstone.
Eleven airmen lost their lives. After the main wreckage had been cleared the rescue workers had to search and clear over 150 fields.
It was not until 2011 that a memorial to those killed was erected just off the road to Plumpton.

The parish includes the lost village of Kirby.

KIRBY

I cannot find any specific reference to this settlement in the Domesday Book but it is thought that the land and the church which were granted to St John Hospitallers in 1194 may refer to Kirby.
This appears to have been a substantial village but in 1487 thirty eight people were evicted and the land enclosed.
The church has long since disappeared and all that remains is Kirby Grounds near to Hootens Farm on the minor road between Blakesley and Abthorpe which is marked on Ordnance Survey maps.

Blakesley Hall

*Blakesley Hall (within Woodend parish) was formerly a Hospital of the Knights of St John of Jerusalem who acquired land in the area in about 1194. Latterly it was the home of **Charles Bartholomew** (1875-1919). From all reports he did a lot of good for the area although he did have quite a reputation with the ladies! One of the many novel innovations he brought to the Hall was a 15 inch gauge railway laid down in 1903 linking the Hall to Blakesley station.*
*A miniature steam train, the Blacolvesley, was built by Bassett- Lowke of Northampton in 1909. In 1939/40 it was taken to Yorkshire. The engine is still owned by **Dr Bob Tebb** and is claimed to be the oldest workable internal combustion engine in the world.*
During the 1990's it worked on the Ravensglass railway in the Lake District.
It has been repainted in its original colours and is operated at Gala events.
The engine celebrated its 100th birthday in 2009 and is currently on static display at the Railway Museum in Cleethorpes.

During both World Wars the Hall was used as a Military Hospital and in 1947 the contents were sold during an eight day. The building fell into decay and was demolished in 1957 leaving only memories and two lodges on the road between Woodend and Blakesley.

WOODFORD

Six miles east of Kettering
Population: 1801-491   2001 - 1290

DOMESDAY BOOK
WODEFORD
*The name would appear obvious this was simply
a 'ford by a wood'*

The larger of the two manors recorded in the Domesday Book was held by **Robert** of the Abbey of Peterborough. It had thirty one households and a mill rendering two shillings per annum whereas the population in the smaller manor was just seven households with a priest.

This is quite a large village with much modern development and lies just south of the main A14 Kettering to Huntingdon road.

I particularly like the large green space with its Market Cross which lies at the heart of the village.

The ironstone mines and clothing factories which used to provide local employment have closed and most people have to travel outside the village for work although there is still a Primary school, convenience shop and post office, two public houses, The Dukes Arms which previously went by the name The Lords Arms and The Prince of Wales.
The Baptist chapel has been in continuous use since its erection in 1823. Prior to that date those not adhering to the Church of England doctrine would meet in private houses.

Situated to the east of the village is the church of **ST MARY** which has been referred to as the *'Cathedral of the Nene'* and is thought to have been started before 1250.
Its arcades are very long with the origins of a Norman church. The west tower with bands of ironstone and oolite below and ashlar above has pinnacles and a recessed broach spire.

During restoration work in 1867 a human heart wrapped in cloth was discovered and is now displayed in a glass case in one of the pillars.
It has been suggested that it was the heart of **Walter Traillys** a former Lord of the Manor who died in the Levant at the end of the last Crusade in 1290.

There are two oaken 14th century effigies - one of a cross legged Knight and the other of a lady.

Woodford House was originally a farm house and was bought in the early 19th century by **Charles Arbuthnot** who demolished the old buildings and rebuilt them a quarter of a mile south east of the original house.

The *Duke of Wellington* regularly visited his friends in Woodford and said that the area reminded him of the countryside around Waterloo in Belgium - the site of his most famous victory.
The Wellington Tower in his honour on the Finedon road is an unusual structure and has a large plaque bearing the words :-

> *Panorama*
> *Waterloo Victory June 18 AD 1815.*

Another unusual building is the black and white house dated 1890 on the corner of Eady's Row.

The Nene Way passes through the village which is a popular area for walkers.

There were once two mills on the River Nene in Woodford parish, only one of which - now known as Willy Watt Mill - survives.
It is a two storey mill of banded ironstone and limestone and has in the past served as a corn mill, a fulling mill, a paper mill and a bone mill.
In the summer months it is a very popular area for walkers, boaters, fishermen, etc.

WOODFORD HALSE

HINTON AND WEST FARNDON

Six miles south of Daventry
Population: 1801-629   2001 - 3456

DOMESDAY BOOK
WODEFORD

Here is another 'ford by the wood' but given the suffix to distinguish it from Woodford near Thrapston.
The Halse came from the Manor (near Brackley) to which the settlement belonged.

Among minor roads to the west of the County is a village which is noted on Ordnance Survey maps as Woodford Halse which I and many others, I suspect, used to call Woodford cum Membris.

In my teens my friends and I had many enjoyable cycle rides around the villages of Northamptonshire.
When we approached a new village we would often make a guess as to how the village got its name - this resulted in some very humorous but often incorrect explanations.

Woodford never caused any problems - it used to be heavily wooded and the infant River Cherwell which rises in nearby Charwelton divides Woodford from its neighbour Hinton, but where was Membris?
I had never heard of a village called Membris, it did not appear as a place on any map I saw and did not feature in the list of lost or deserted villages.

It was not until I started my research that I found that Woodford cum Membris simply means Woodford with members - i.e. Hinton and Farndon - now known as West Farndon to distinguish it from the Farndon near Market Harborough.
They became a single parish in the 12ᵗʰ century when Woodford was given preference because it is the only one of three places with a parish church not because it was the largest of the three - this being Hinton just across the infant Cherwell.

One of my first jobs on leaving school was to work in the post room at the Council's Education Department.
It was not unusual to send mail shots regularly to all the schools in the County many of which have now closed. One such school was Woodford cum Membris which is still in use.

In 1086 the two hide manor of Woodford Halse was tenanted by **Richard** of **Hugh de Grandmesnil** and had sixteen households and a mill rendering eight shillings per annum.
The Hinton manor was held of **Geoffrey de Mandeville** by **Wihtbert** and had fifteen households and a mill rendering two shillings per annum.
By 1329 the Lady of the Manor was **Matilda de Holland** who held the Manors at Woodford and Farndon (but not Hinton).

Woodford and Hinton increased dramatically in size when the Great Central Railway arrived.
This brought many new workers to the area and two terraces of artisan housing sprang up to accommodate them. The influx also resulted in extra shops and services.
Buildings, sidings, ninety one acres of marshalling yards, a loco department and the station and platforms wcrc built by 1899. Woodford became a very important railway junction. Sadly the line and buildings were axed by **Lord Beeching** and passenger services ceased in 1966 putting many people out of work.
Little now remains except some embankments, the two railway arches on Station Road and an industrial site on Great Central Way.

The former Hinton Gorse Hotel, an attractive black and white building on the corner of Hinton Road was built to cater for the railway traveller but was aimed at a higher class of customer with purpose built stabling so that the gentry could bring their horses with them on the train to join the many famous hunts in the region or simply leave them prior to making a rail journey further afield.

It is now the home of the Woodford Halse Social Club.

The only remaining public house is The Fleur de Lys.

Woodford Halse is more functional than pretty although there are a few attractive stone properties but I found it worthwhile just to walk around because of the history of the place.

I was interested to see the Moravian chapel behind which is a burial ground with identical flat numbered tablets marking individual burial positions. This system was used because Moravians believe that everyone is equal in the sight of God.

The history of Moravians in Woodford Halse goes back a very long way.

In 1787 *William Hunt*, a local farmer, who had been attending Moravian meetings in nearby villages, licensed his own house for meetings.

At first the community was supported from Bedford but was eventually recognised as a congregation in its own right in 1798 and started to build the chapel. By 1851 it had become the focus of the denomination in the County, this continued until quite recently.

The church has now closed and a planning application has been submitted for change of use to a residential dwelling.

The Methodist church of 1879 in Hinton and a small Roman Catholic church are still in regular use.

I was able to visit the parish church of **ST MARY** the **VIRGIN** in Woodford by getting the key from a workman on the roof who was busy replacing stolen lead.

The church has a long history going back to the 12th century and has a mixture of Early English, Perpendicular and Victorian architecture.

Ex Serviceman's Club - Woodford Halse

The north porch has recently been added which provides modern toilets and the all important kitchen for after service tea and coffee.

I was impressed with the Victorian stained glass windows depicting the life of the *Virgin Mary*. There is also a very large squint window so large I could have crawled through it - perhaps they weren't very good at squinting.

The Lady Chapel was dedicated by the Bishop of Peterborough on the 5th November 1978 to commemorate the centenary of restoration work. *Rev. Richard Walter* was Curate here for twenty six years before becoming Vicar in 1846. He died in 1851. Prior to ordination he was a naval officer and was injured at the Battle of Trafalgar.

The old school next door is now a village centre and a library.

Also on School Street is **Woodford Manor House**. It is a striking three bay 17th century property with additions in the 18th and 19th century. There is a beautiful central doorway under a segmented pediment.

Above the doorway is a sundial dated 1858 and a round ox eye window.

At West Farndon there is little but a few houses and farm buildings but I noted that the long distance footpath the Jurassic Way passes through the hamlet.

WOODNEWTON

Four miles north of Oundle
Population: 1801-268   2001 - 442

DOMESDAY BOOK
NIWETONE
*The village once stood in the middle of the forest
of Kings Cliffe and was given the prefix wood to
distinguish it from other Newtons
(new farms) in the area.*

Reginald held the manor of **Eustace** in 1086 when there were thirteen households and a mill rendering sixty four pence per annum.

This delightful village with its wide main street benefits by being somewhat off the beaten track.
It is a real delight to stroll around particularly when the roses and other flowers are in bloom but one building which looks completely out of place is the three storey Manor House.

The church of **ST MARY** stands in a superb position on a limestone crop just above the main street. It was originally a cruciform church with a central tower but when the tower was rebuilt with battlements and pinnacles in the 16th century it was placed at the west end.
In addition there is a clerestoried nave, chancel, south aisle and south porch. Comfortable seating has replaced the traditional pews.

Apart from the chancel there is plain glass throughout which makes for quite a light church which appears very well maintained.

One interesting item is a wooden swivel lectern for a chained Bible. There is also a plaque to US airmen whose plane crashed in the parish during the Second World War.

Thorough restoration of the church took place in the early 20th century by **H. L.C. Brassey** of Apethorpe Hall.
The churchyard has been designated an important site by the Wildlife Trust of Northamptonshire and has in the past won awards in Conservation Churchyard Competitions.

Buried on the north side of the church is **Nikolai Polakous** (1901-1974) famously known as Coco the clown with his enormous boots, baggy trousers and bright red hair. Nearby is the grave of his daughter **Helena Rowland.**
Nicholai lived in the village in a caravan between his extensive travels with the circus. His face is depicted on the new village hall.
Every other September a Clown Festival is held in the village to raise money for charity.

The early 18th century Woodnewton Mill now known as Conegar Farm was my starting point for a countryside walk to Apethorpe and Kings Cliffe. The present mill is one of my favourite viewpoints in the County.
One public house still remains in the village - the early 19th century White Swan Inn.
Schoolchildren now have to travel to school in Nassington as the former school buildings of 1876 were closed in the late 1980's.
The Methodist chapel built in 1840 has been a craft workshop where visitors have been welcomed since 1989.

Woodnewton Mill

WOOTTON

Three miles south of Northampton
Population: 1801-427   2001 - 15547

DOMESDAY BOOK
WITONE
The name comes from two words – 'wudu' and 'tun'
meaning farm by the wood.

The two manors were held by **Walter the Fleming** in 1086 and tenanted by **Winemar** and **Hugh**.
In total there were forty eight households meaning a total population of about one hundred and seventy five people.

The village with its adjoining Grange Park development is becoming increasingly popular with commuters and is rapidly being absorbed into the outer perimeter of Northampton as it stretches southwards towards Junction 15 of the M1 motorway.

At the heart of the old village is the church of **ST GEORGE** the **MARTYR** which has north and south doorways dating from about 1300.
The exterior was much renewed in about 1865 and further restored and rededicated in 1991 after a £93,000 restoration programme.
The church consists of a nave, north and south aisles, chancel and a Perpendicular style west tower with battlements and pinnacles.
Near the church is the local public house The Yeoman of England, the Primary school, Memorial Hall and the older stone built private residences which date from the late 17th and early 18th centuries.

The original **Wootton Hall** was demolished in 1911 and its red brick replacement is now the Headquarters of Northamptonshire Police.

From the mid 18th century many houses were built of brick from the brick works along Berry Lane.

On the B526 on the northern edge of the village stood Quebec Barracks later named Simpson Barracks, a base for the Northamptonshire Regiment and then the Pioneer Corps until its closure in April 1993. All that remains are two plaques at the entrance to the new housing estate with street names reflecting the military associations.

For a number of years coach loads of visitors were drawn to Turners Musical Merry Go Round where they could experience a ride on a large Carousel and listen to organ recitals and music of the 60s and 70's and enjoy Old Time Music Hall Shows. Today the only reminder is in street names such as Turners Court and Turners Gardens.
Opposite is the Northampton High School for Girls and nearby is a popular Garden Centre alongside which Waitrose have indicated their desire to build a supermarket.

Wootton's best known resident is probably **Caroline Chisholm** who was born in the village in 1808 and went on to become famous for her humanitarian welfare work with female immigrants in Australia. A new local school has been named in her honour and I have read of proposals to make her a saint.

The village made national headlines in April 2011 when four members of the **Ding** family were murdered in their own home.
The suspect disappeared for a long time in spite of numerous radio, press and TV appeals but was recently discovered in Morocco and extradition proceedings are in hand to have him returned to the UK for trial.

YARDLEY GOBION

Six miles south east of Towcester
Population: 1801-446 2001 - 1329

I can find no specific mention in the Domesday Book but in 1166 the village was known as Gerdeslai derived from 'hydra' - yards or poles and 'leah' - clearing i.e. an acre of woodland where poles were cut and made. The appendage **Gubbyn** *comes from* **Henry Gubbyn** *who held land in the area.*

The village lies in the south of the County just off the A508 Northampton to Old Stratford road.
There are a few thatched cottages and some other attractive properties mainly around the church but for the most part it is a village of new housing estates and has dramatically increased its size since the Second World War.

On a slight rise above the Green stands the church of **ST LEONARD** which has a pleasant aspect and well paved access but at the same time looks uninspiring. It was built in 1864 with financial assistance from the **Duke of Grafton** and consists of a nave and chancel with a bell cote at the east end of the nave.
What did surprise me was the clock over the porch which was added in 1889.

Inside the church is to my mind much more appealing with clever use of coloured brickwork over all the windows and arches.

Points of interest include the millennium needlework picture on the theme of the WI's anthem 'Jerusalem' and a curious 'Chinese Scroll' hanging on the organ which was given to the church by a member of the congregation **Jackie Pullinger** who worked amongst drug addicts and prostitutes in Hong Kong.

To the rear of the church has been added a small kitchen and toilet facilities.

The Coffee Pot Tavern : Yardley Gobion

The stained glass over the altar features:-

> *'Jesus*
> *the same, yesterday, today and forever'.*

The lectern, pulpit and priests stall were given by the villagers as a memorial to eight Canadian airmen who died when their bomber crashed on the outskirts of the village during the Second World War. Their names have been added to the memorial in the churchyard.
The aircraft avoided the houses and no civilians were killed (even the hens escaped death).

Near the church is an example of a millennium project. This time the replacement and restoration of the village pump, well head (surrounded by a white fence) and signpost.
It is a pity that nothing seems to have been done since then to maintain the feature.

The size of the village means that it still has its Primary school, a care home, shop and separate post office, The Coffee Pot Country Inn serving food and drink, village hall and playing field and Yardley chapel, a United Reformed church dated 1826.

Yardley Hastings

United Reform Chapel : Yardley Hastings

Seven miles south east of Towcester
Population: 1801-714   2001 - 792

DOMESDAY BOOK
GERDELAI

As in the case of Yardley Gobion the name probably means an acre of woodland where poles were cut and made. The name Hastings comes from **John de Hastings** *who, in the 13th century became Lord of the Manor on marriage to the* **Countess of Huntingdon.**

In 1086 the manor was held by **Countess Judith**.

The village was originally built by the Castle Ashby Estate of the **Marquess of Northampton**. Once it was just a small hamlet in Yardley Chase a medieval hunting park. Today it is quite sizeable with both old and new properties many of which overlook the stream flowing alongside the street.

The main Northampton to Bedford road skirts its southern end which appears to be the busiest area with a shop, post office, garage, fish bar, Indian takeaway and the thatched Red Lion public house.

At this point is the millennium sign with handily placed seats to sit and watch the world go by.
On the surrounding walls are brass plates listing the names of villagers street by street at the time, a remarkable record for the future.

Just to the east and on the main road is a Garden Centre with tea rooms.

The large and well preserved Congregational chapel (now the United Reformed church) was rebuilt in 1813 after a fire and has a big pediment which would not disgrace a Georgian mansion.

Close by is the Primary school with modern extensions, another public house, The Rose and Crown and the Memorial Village Hall.

The church of **ST ANDREW** has a short early 13th century west tower with twin bell openings under a round arch.
The connection between the tower and the nave is only a doorway with a slight chamfer.
A small part of the Norman nave wall still remains.

The church was much reconstructed between 1883-1888 by **George Sutherland**, the Clerk of Works at Castle Ashby Estate.

Around the large chancel arch are the words:-

*"Come let us worship and bow down
Let us Kneel before the Lord our Maker"*

Monuments include those to past Rectors and the local schoolmaster.

The Manor House which is situated immediately north of the church was built on the remains of a mansion which dated back to the early 14th century.
The old Rectory at the north end of the village was built in 1701 with a brick front of five bays.

In October 1940 there was considerable excitement when a German parachutist was discovered and captured by two local residents. When handed over to the Police he had £100 in English money and a false Identity Card.

Yarwell

Six miles north east of Oundle
Population: 1801-255   2001 - 316

*Although not mentioned in the Domesday Book it was known by the name Jarewelle
which is thought to have derived from 'gear' - fishing pool and 'wielle' – spring.'*

This small picturesque one street village stands by the River Nene where the river widens across the water meadows. A large number of Roman relics (particularly pottery) have been found in the area.

It is in the north east of the County close to the Cambridgeshire border and is about eight miles west of Peterborough.

The history of the village is dominated by agriculture although stone masonry played a significant part in the 1700's and 1800's utilising the natural limestone outcrops in the region.

On the main street is the quite small church of **ST MARY MAGDALENE** with its west tower and pyramid roof.
It was built in the 13th century when the building originally had north and south aisles but after a particularly heavy fall of snow and much rain in 1782, the walls and roof of the aisles became unsafe and were removed as the nave and chancel provided - *'more than enough room to contain the inhabitants'*.

As I entered the church recently I heard singing and not seeing anyone around assumed that as in some churches there was a CD playing somewhere in the background.
It was therefore a surprise, to me as well as to her, to suddenly come face to face with a lady who was busy under the tower arch arranging a floral display.

I then learned that the church once had a singing gallery at the west end of the nave - a great pity that it cannot be restored and brought back into use.

The church now serves both the Anglican and Methodist communities

Hidden away in the north chapel is a marble table tomb to **Sir Humphrey Bellamy** a London merchant who died in 1715.
It is said that as a boy he was making his way to London to make his fortune when he became destitute and ill and he was taken in by local people.

Sir Humphrey did eventually make his fortune and became an Alderman of London.

When he died he was brought back to Yarwell and in his will he left money to provide bread for the poor - was this the real **Dick Whittington?**

The village has a number of 16th, 17th, and 18th century properties built in local stone and these include Sundial Cottage, once the village bakery, with a lovely display of pink roses at its entrance in June.

Inside the building there are two early Victorian large baking ovens.

There is a modern village hall and the attractive looking Angel Inn of 17th century origin.

A former public house, the 16th century Fox was also a blacksmiths and is now known as Forge Cottage.

Younger children of the village now go to Nassington for schooling. The former school built in 1874 was closed in 1981 and there is no longer a village shop or post office.

For centuries Yarwell and Nassington disputed ownership of Sulehay wood (see Nassington) which lies between the two villages.

Old Sulehay Lodge is situated one and a quarter miles west northwest of Yarwell and has 17th century gables and mullioned windows.

There are many footpaths in the area and I enjoyed a very pleasant walk through Old Sulehay Forest (on the Wansford road) and on to Wansford and back along that stretch of the Nene Way which passes by Yarwell.

The Nene Valley preserved steam railway now operates to a newly constructed small Halt at Yarwell Junction at the end of a seven and a half mile running track from Peterborough.

This was the junction of the Northampton/ Peterborough and Rugby/ Peterborough lines both of which closed during the **Beeching** era.

From my research it appears that there never was a station at this point even when the lines were fully open.

From the Halt there is a pleasant little walk by way of Yarwell Mill back to the village.

A mill probably existed here at the time of the Domesday Book but as Yarwell is not mentioned it must have been included in one of the nearby manors.

The present three storey building is dated 1839 and was worked until after the end of the Second World War.

When last in the area it was quite busy with holidaymakers and campers on the twenty seven acre site.

In addition there is a five acre fishing lake.

The Angel Inn ~ Yarwell

YELVERTOFT

Six miles east of Rugby
Population: 1801-526   2001 –821

DOMESDAY BOOK
CELVRECOT/GELVRECOTE/GIVERTOST
Its name derivation obscured by the mists of antiquity is in two parts.
The personal name is Saxon in origin (consistent with many Saxon field names still found in the village)
*and was probably **Ceolfrith** possibly evolving later to **Gelver**.*
The name ending 'toft' denotes a small Danish settlement.

The manor belonged to *Roger de la Zouche* until 1296 and then to his son, *Alan* followed by other family members until it was forfeited to the Crown in 1399. The Manor House lay on the High Street between Swinnerton Lane and Elkington Road but it has long since disappeared.

Yelvertoft is a quiet little village situated in the wilds of Northamptonshire - the peace results from the absence of major roads.

It is not the most attractive village but the cottages which line the three quarters of a mile long main street between the village hall and the church have a charm of their own.

At the top of the hill is **ALL SAINTS** church and there has probably been a church on the site since Saxon times as a priest was mentioned in the Domesday Book.

An unusual feature is the addition of a second south aisle making three arcades in all with the magnificent south doorway of the earlier aisle rebuilt onto the outside of the third.
I like the lovely clock on the west tower.

The south window of the Lady Chapel was blown out during the Second World War but a little glass survived and can be seen in the nave windows.

It is said that the church was used as an armoury for *Cromwell's* troopers before the Battle of Naseby and that worn stonework on the sedilia indicates its use for sharpening weapons.

An outstanding feature is the monument which takes up almost the whole of the north side of the chancel to the *Rev. John Dycson* who was Rector between 1439 and 1445.

On the south wall is a memorial to the fourteen crewmen (12 Canadian and 2 British) of two World War Two aircraft from the RAF (a Halifax and a Lancaster) which collided over the edge of the village on the night of the 5th and 6th of December 1944. The Halifax had a full bomb load but fortunately they missed the village.

The churchyard is carefully managed to encourage wild life and flowers and has won a number of awards.

The Congregational, (now United Reformed) chapel here continues a long history of worship back as far as 1662 although the present chapel was not built until 1792 and a new frontage was added in 1832. It is well worth a visit.
Upstairs is a room with archives relating to local history.
Not only does the village have an Anglican church and a United Reformed chapel but also a Roman Catholic church.

Primary School: Yelvertoft

The Reading Room is the name now given to the former Charity school established in 1711 by a local man, **Richard Ashby**, for poor children.

The initial enrolment showed four boys and five girls *'clothed and taught.'*

In 1792 (the date on the sundial) it was enlarged to take twenty pupils and was used for the next one hundred years.

The building is now used as a meeting room for village societies.

The village pump has stood outside the Reading Room since about 1900 but was allowed to fall into disrepair after mains water arrived. Fortunately owing to local initiative the pump has been restored and was rededicated on May Day 2006 when the Yelvertoft Morris Men entertained the crowds. The pump even has a song dedicated to it.

The present school opened in 1876 and was enlarged and modernised in the latter half of the 20th century.

The village hall has an unusual history.

It started out as a Land Army Hostel but shortly after was turned into a prisoner of war camp.

Following this it was the home for displaced people from Czechoslovakia, Poland and Germany who were working on local farms.

The village acquired the building in 1952 and set about converting it to a village hall complete with caretakers flat.

Local residents also have the benefit of a shop, post office, Pocket Park, a public house –
The Knightley Arms, a butcher and even a stonemason.

The canal in this part of the County is quite lazy and meanders through the countryside covering a length of some five and a half miles to travel the straight line distance of about two and a half miles to West Haddon.

Yelvertoft marina is located near Flint Hill Farm and has facilities for a hundred and fifty boats.

TIMELINE - SIMPLIFIED

978-1016	**Ethelred II** – the 'Unready' married 1) Aelgifu of York 2) Emma of Normandy
1016	**Edmund** - 'Ironside' Son of Ethelred and Aelgifu married Ealdgyth. Agrees with King Canute of Denmark to rule England together Edmund was assassinated within the month.
1016 – 1035	**Canute** (Cnut) King of All England married Ethelred's widow Emma
1035-1036	**Alfred** son of Ethelred
1036-1040	**Harold I** (Harefoot) (illegitimate son of Canute)
1040-1042	**Harthacnut** –son of Canute
1042-1066	**Edward** - 'the Confessor' married Edith daughter of Godwin of Wessex No issue. Canonised in 1161.
1066	**Harold II** (Godwinson)
1066	**Edgar** 'the Atheling' proclaimed but not crowned
1066-1087	**William I** - 'the Conqueror'
1087-1100	**William II** -'Rufus Son of William the Conqueror
1100-1135	**Henry I** – 'Beauclerc' Son of William the Conqueror
1135-1154	**Stephen**- nephew of Henry I
1154-1189	**Henry II** - grandson of Henry I
1189-1199	**Richard I** – 'the Lionheart' 3rd son of Henry II
1199-1216	**John** - 5th son of Henry II
1216-1272	**Henry III** - son of John
1272-1307	**Edward I** - son of Henry III
1307-1327	**Edward II** - son of Edward I
1327-1377	**Edward III** - son of Edward II
1377-1399	**Richard II** - grandson of Edward III Son of the Black Prince
1399-1413	**Henry IV** - grandson of Edward III Son of John of Gaunt
1413-1422	**Henry V** - son of Henry IV
1422-1461 1470-1471	**Henry VI** – son of Henry IV born 1421 Regency until declared of age in 1437. Deposed and imprisoned in 1461 Restored briefly to the throne in 1470
1461-1470 1471-1483	**Edward IV** – youngest son of Edward III married Elizabeth Woodville – 10 children all declared illegitimate by Parliament
1483	**Edward V** son of Edward IV one of the Princes in the Tower
1483-1485	**Richard III** - uncle of Edward V born at Fotheringhay Castle
1485-1509	**Henry VII** grandson of Henry V
1509-1547	**Henry VIII** – son of Henry VII
1547-1553	**Edward VI** - son of Henry VIII
1553	**Lady Jane Grey** – the 'Nine Days Queen' Granddaughter of Mary the sister of Henry VIII Jane was executed in 1554 aged 16/17
1553-1558	**Mary** - daughter of Henry VIII and Catherine of Aragon
1558-1603	**Elizabeth I** – the 'Virgin Queen' daughter of Henry VIII and Anne Boleyn
1603-1625	**James I** - great great grandson of Henry VII
1625-1649	**Charles I** - second son of James I - executed
1649-1659	**The Commonwealth** – Cromwell
1660-1685	**Charles II** - eldest son of Charles I
1685-1688	**James II** - brother of Charles II
1688-1694 1694-1702	**William** of Orange –grandson of Charles I and **Mary** daughter of James II William ruled alone after Marys death
1702-1714	**Anne** - sister of Mary
1714-1727	**George I** - great grandson of James I
1727-1760	**George II** - son of George I
1760-1820	**George III** - grandson of George II
1820-1830	**George IV** - son of George III
1830-1837	**William IV** - brother of George IV
1837-1901	**Victoria** - niece of William IV
1901-1910	**Edward VII** - son of Victoria
1910-1936	**George V** – second son of Edward VII
1936	**Edward VIII** – abdicated
1936-1952	**George VI** – second son of George V
1952-	**Elizabeth II** - daughter of George VI

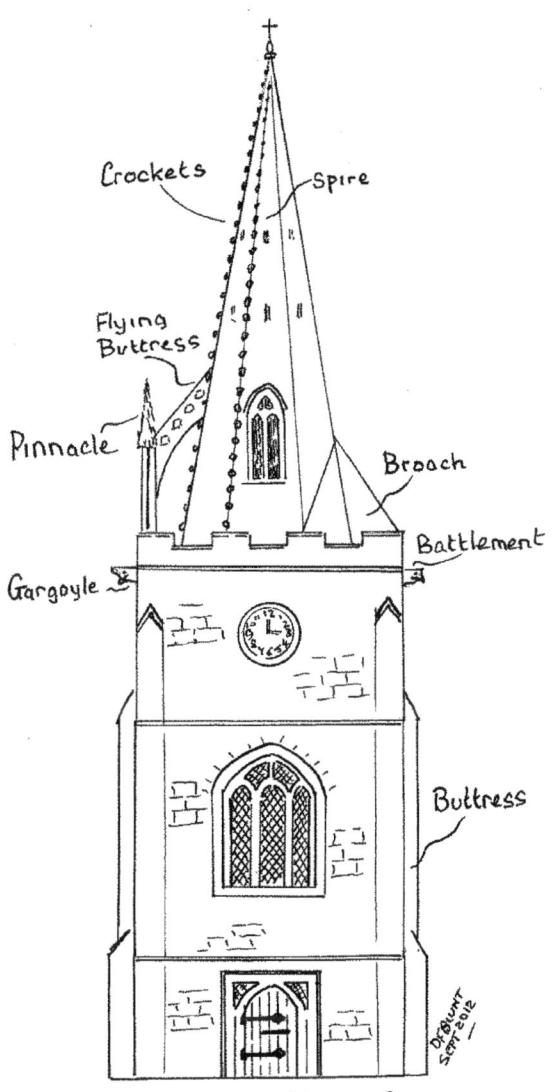

Features of a Church Spire

CHURCH DOORWAYS

NORMAN 1050-1200   EARLY ENGLISH 1150-1300   DECORATED 1250-1400   PERPENDICULAR 1350-1650

NORMAN — BILLET, CHEVRON
EARLY ENGLISH — DOG TOOTH, THREE LEAF FLOWER
NORMAN — BEAK HEAD, CABLE   MOTIFS
DECORATED — BALL FLOWER, TABLET FLOWER

ANGLO SAXON

Early Saxon Kings 978-1042
Edward the Confessor 1042-1066
Harold II 1066
Most buildings were made of wood ,few have survived. The stone built churches are more interesting for their decoration than their form.

NORMAN (ROMANESQUE)

William the Conqueror 1066-1087
William II 1087-1100
Henry I 1100-1135
Stephen 1135-1154
Henry II 11154-1189
Characteristic of the style are round arches,barrel vaults,walls decorated with interlacing arches and arcades,highly decorated doorways and an abundance of mouldings.

EARLY ENGLISH

Richard I 1189-1199
John 1199-1216
Henry III 1216-1272
Squat bulky structures give way to lighter taller buildings

DECORATED

Edward I 1272-1307
Edward II 1307-1327
Edward III 1327-1377
Early English innovations were improved resulting in larger windows, tracery work and a superabundance of decorative features covering surfaces,gables and arches.

PERPENDICULAR

Richard 11 1377-1399
Henry IV 1399-1413
Henry V 1413-1422
Henry VI 1422-1461
Edward IV 1461 – 1483
Edward V 1483
Richard III 1483-1485
A return to comparative simplicity. Buttresses were now deeper allowing even larger windows, tracery was at its most elegant the four centred arch appeared and fan vaulting reached perfection.

TUDOR

Henry VII 1485-1509
Henry VIII 1509-1547
Edward VI 1547-1553
The slow transition from Gothic to Renaissance. Large houses were built many of them in the new building material – brick.

CHURCH FONTS

SAXON AD 600-1100   NORMAN 1050-1200   EARLY ENGLISH 1150-1300   PERPENDICULAR 1350-1550

CHURCH WINDOWS

NORMAN 1050-1200   EARLY ENGLISH 1150-1300   DECORATED 1250-1400   PERPENDICULAR 1350-1550

ELIZABETHAN

Mary I 1553-1558
Elizabeth I 1558-1603
The growth of the new aristocracy and the wider distribution of wealth led to a vast increase in domestic building. The Renaissance brought a revival of classical features. In the larger houses – often a symmetrical E or H shape- galleries, grand staircases and carved chimneys appeared. Brick became fashionable.

JACOBEAN

James I (VI of Scotland) 1603-1625
The period of James reign was marked by profusely decorated open surfaces. The great houses showed even greater symmetry and Inigo Jones began to build in the Palladian style, derived from the work of the Italian architect Andrea Palladio.

STUART

Charles I 1625-1649
Commonwealth 1649-1660
Charles II 1660-1685
James II 1685-1688
The acceptance of classical architecture was incomplete until the time of Wren (1652-1723) Columns, cornices, and elegant proportions characterise this period.

QUEEN ANNE

William III and Mary II 1689-1702
Anne 1702-1714The age of the English baroque school which tempered pure baroque's florid ornamentation and over emphasis of detail with the classical

GEORGIAN AND REGENCY

George I 1714-1727
George II 1727-1760
George III 1760-1820
George IV 1820-1830
The Georgian era brought a return to the beauty of form and proportion. For the middle classes terraced houses were built. Towards the end of the period regency decoration emerged.

VICTORIAN

William IV 1830-1837
Victoria 1837-1901
The new rich class built to impress and architects designed in many styles particularly Gothic and Greek revival. Mass schemes of houses were erected for the working classes.

EDWARDIAN

Edward VII 1901-1910
The trend in architecture from 1911 to 1914 was largely a continuation of the Victorian style. The art nouveau movement influenced decoration.

GLOSSARY

ACRE – Unit of land equal to 4840 square yards

AISLE – A section of the church parallel to the choir or nave and divided from it by an arcade of columns or piers – literally – 'wing'.

ALMSHOUSES – see page 429

ANGLO SAXON CHARTER – Documents from the early medieval period in Britain which typically make a grant of land or records a privilege. The earliest surviving were drawn up in about 670AD. The oldest surviving charter granted land to the church but from the 8th century they were increasingly used to grant land to lay people.

APOLLO BELVEDERE (Pythian Apollo) - Celebrated marble sculpture rediscovered in central Italy in the late 15th century. The Greek god Apollo is depicted as having just shot a death dealing arrow. It is thought to date from the time of Hadrian and is a copy of a lost bronze original made by the Greek sculptor Leochares between 350 – 325 BC. Many copies were made as in Northamptonshire.

APSE – Semicircular or polygonal end of a chancel or nave.

ARCADE – A row of arches of columns or piers.

ASHLAR – Prepared or 'dressed' stone work in regular blocks.

AUGUSTINIAN – Order of Canons who followed a 'rule' based on the writings of St Augustine of Hippo drawn up in the 6th and 7th centuries.

AUMBREY – A recess in a wall which serves as a cupboard

BAILEY – The outer wall of a castle

BAILIWICK – A district over which a bailiff has authority.

BALUSTRADE – A row of posts that support part of a rail.

BASILICA – A large and important church given special ceremonial rules by the Pope.

BATTLEMENTS – A parapet with alternating high and low sections also called crenellations.

BELVEDERE – Architectural term for a structure designed to incorporate a view.

BENEFICE – Used to be a reward received in exchange for services rendered and as a retainer for future services. Now used by the Church of England to describe a parish or a group of parishes under a single stipendiary minister.

BLACK AUGUSTINIAN – Augustinian Canons were known as Black Canons because of the hooded black cloaks they wore over a black cassock. They were established at St Botolphs Priory in Colchester in about 1106 and were one of the first orders to set up religious houses in England and once possessed two hundred houses in England and Wales.

BLACK DEATH – see page 12

BODGING –A traditional wood turning craft using green(unseasoned) wood to make chair legs and other cylindrical parts of a chair.

BONE CRYPT – Building where corpses or bones were kept.

BORDAR – A villain who rendered menial service for his cottage. The cottar, the bordar and the labourer were bound to work on the land belonging to the Lord of the Manor.

BRASS –usually Roman coins – today we use the word bronze

BROACH SPIRE – A broach spire stands on a square base and is carried up to a tapering and octagonal spire by means of triangular faces.

BRONZE AGE – Refers to the period in British history from c2500 - c800 BC – marked by the introduction and use of copper and bronze for tools.

BUTTER CROSS – Located at market places where locally produced butter, milk and eggs were laid out and displayed on the stepped base of the cross.

BUTTRESSES – A mass of brickwork built against a wall to carry the thrust and provide strength.

CALVANISTIC BAPTIST – Also known as Reformed Baptists they go back to the 1630's. Notable early Pastors were John Bunyan, William Carey and Charles Spurgeon.

CANON – A member of the clergy on the staff of a cathedral.

CAPITAL – Top of a column.

CELL – Small room for a monk or nun.

CHANCEL – The holy area at the east end of the church, the usual location of the altar.

CHANTRY – A place (e.g. chapel) where prayers were to be said for the soul of the founder(s) who had left money for that purpose.

CHAPEL OF EASE – A consecrated building within a parish for those who could not get to the main church.

CHARNEL HOUSE – see Bone Crypt

CHARTER – Document granted by a ruler of government.

CHAPELRY – see Chapel of Ease.

CHAPLAIN – A member of the clergy attached to a chapel in a private house, institution or military unit.

CHRISTADELPHIANS – Greek for 'Brethren in Christ'. A Christian group developed in the UK and the USA. Founded by John Thomas their beliefs are based on the literal truth set out in the Bible.

CINERARY URN – Container for cremated ashes. Common in Anglo Saxon England

CIVIL WAR – See page 15

CISTERCIAN – Roman Catholic monastic order established in Citeaux in 1098 by St Robert de Champagne as a stricter form of the Benedictine.

CLERESTORY – Upper storey of the nave walls of the church lit by windows.

CLOISTER – A covered passage   around a quadrangle at the side of a church.

CLUNIAC – An order subordinate to the Abbey of Cluny in Burgundy. At the time of the Dissolution there were thirty five Cluniac houses in England including Daventry Priory, Delapre Abbey and St Andrews Abbey in Northamptonshire.

CLUNIAC PRIORY – In the Middle Ages from the 11th century a number of religious houses were established – those that were larger than cells were called Priories.

COACHING INN – Served coach travellers, stabled teams of horses and mail coaches and replaced tired teams with fresh ones. Traditionally seven miles apart – in some English towns there were as many as ten creating intense rivalry.

COLLEGE – Educational institution or a part of one.

COLLEGIATE CHURCH – Church attached to a college or college students.

COMMISSION TO THE SURVEY – Thomas Cromwell on behalf of Henry VIII undertook an inventory of the assets and income of the entire ecclesiastical estate of England and Wales and delegated his authority to handpicked Commissioners who were mostly secular clergy who were hostile to the power of the church and the monastic life in general.

COMMISSIONER FOR RECEIVING THE SURRENDER – see above – Selected men were authorised to receive 'the surrender of the monasteries' i.e. Sir Walter Mildmay of Apethorpe Hall.

COMMON PLEAS – The Court of Common Pleas (or Common Bench) was a common law court in the English legal system that covered 'common pleas' – actions between subject and subject which did not concern the King.

Created in the late 12th to early 13th century it served as one of the central English courts for about 600 years.

It was authorised by the Magna Carta to sit in a fixed location and sat in Westminster Hall for its entire existence.

CONEY – A rabbit

CONGREGATIONALISM – A Christian movement that arose in England in the late 16th and 17th centuries. Its theological position was between Presbyterians and the more radical Baptists and Quakers. Emphasis on the right of each properly organised congregation to determine its own affairs.

Robert Browne has been regarded as the founder of Congregationalism. Many were persecuted under Elizabeth I.

COPPICED – An area of woodland in which the trees and shrubs are periodically cut back to ground level.

CORBEL – Block of stone projecting from a wall usually to support a beam or some other stone feature.

CORBEL TABLE – Row of corbels often with carved heads on them set at intervals, sometimes carrying connecting arches but more often simply supporting a projecting wall, especially a battlement or parapet.

CORN EXCHANGE – Building where farmers and merchants traced cereal grains – common until the 19th century.

COTE – Cottage

CRENELLATION – See battlements

CRINKLE CRANKLE WALL – Also known as crinkum-crankum, serpentine, ribbon or wavy wall.   To economise on bricks it can be built one brick thick which if in a straight line without buttresses would fall. The wavy line provides stability. Normally facing south so they could be used for fruit growing – many in East Anglia.

CROCKET – A projecting stylised foliage knob of a stone.

CROMWELLIAN – Follower or admirer of Oliver Cromwell.

CRUCIFORM – Cross shaped church.

CRUSADER – Man joining military ventures between 1096 and 1291 especially to recover the Holy Land from Islam.

CRYPT – Literally 'secret place' originally used for martyrs, then saints relics under the high altar.

Now any underground room below a church.

CUPULA – Small, most often a dome like structure on top of a building.

CURATE – In England a clergyman assisting a parish priest.

DANELAW – Broadly speaking the area conquered by the Vikings in the 9th century. The boundary is roughly the line of the modern A5 between London and Chester.

DEFORESTATION – Removal of forest or stand of trees where the land is thereafter converted to non forest use.

DEMESNE – Land in 'Lordship' whose produce is devoted to the Lord rather than his tenants.

DIAPER PATTERN –A pattern of repeated squares of lozenges.

DISAFFOREST – See   deforestation

DISSENTERS – Christians who separated from the Church of England in the 16th, 17th and 18th century. They opposed state interference in religious matters and founded their own churches. The Act of Uniformity in 1662 required Anglican ordination for all clergy and many withdrew from the church it became known as non-conformists although originally this term referred to the refusal to use certain vestments and ceremonies.

DISSOLUTION OF THE MONASTERIES - see page 14

DOMINICAN – Catholic order of Friar preachers founded in 1215 by St Dominic. Also an order of contemplative nuns with black and white habits.

DOMESDAY BOOK – See page 10

DOOM PAINTING – Painting of the Last Judgement to remind medieval church goers of the afterlife by showing in graphic detail the dramatic difference between heaven and hell – often over the chancel arch so that it was constantly in view.

DROVERS ROAD – See page 59

EASTER SEPULCHRE – An arched recess generally in the north wall of the chancel in which from Good Friday to Easter Sunday were deposited the crucifix and sacred elements in commemoration of Christ's entombment and resurrection.

EMBATTLE – Having indentations like battlements.

EMPARKED – To be enclosed with a fence

ENCLOSURE – The process which ended traditional rights such as mowing meadows for hay or grazing livestock on common land formerly held in the open field system.

Once enclosed there uses of the land became restricted to one owner – no longer common land. Also used for the process that ended the ancient system of arable farming in open fields. Sometimes accompanied by force, resistance and bloodshed.

ERMINE STREET – Major Roman road that ran from London to Lincoln and York – the old North Road.

ESCHEAT – If a landholder dies without heirs the property reverts to the King.

EXCOMMUNICATION – In the Middle Ages acts of excommunication were sometimes accompanied by a ceremony where a bell was tolled (as for the dead), the Book of the Gospels was closed and a candle was snuffed out – hence the idiom 'to condemn with bell, book and candle'.

It meant the exclusion from public worship or the reception of sacraments but not exclusion from the rules of the church.

It was a formal ecclesiastical censure that deprived a person from the right to belong to a church.

FAIR CHARTER – Street or market fairs were established by Royal Charter – many date back to the Middle Ages and had their heyday in the 13th century. Originally most fairs started as street markets but since the 19th century the trading aspect has been superseded by entertainment and many now are the venue for funfairs run by travelling showmen.

FELLOWS – Most often used in an academic context – part of an elite group of learned people who are awarded fellowships to work together.

FETTERLOCK – A 'D' shaped fetter for tethering a horse's leg – now represented in heraldry.

FIEF – A piece of land held in return for military service.

FIELD OF THE CLOTH OF GOLD – Meeting in June 1520 between King Henry VIII and King Francis I of France arranged to increase the bond of friendship following the Anglo French Treaty of 1514. The 'friendship' was somewhat short lived.

FINIALS – Decorative knobs on top of a gable, post of other upright.

FLEMISH – Someone from the Flanders region of Belgium

FILIGREE BATTLEMENTS – Decorated battlements.

FLORY CROSS – A cross whose arms end in fleur de lys.

FLYING BUTTRESSES – A free standing arched buttress.

FORTIFIED MANOR – Manors were sometimes given a kind of defence – ditch, moat or palisade to protect them from being taken by an enemy or from damage from animals.

There were few fortified manors before the 12th century but in the 13th and 14th century it became fairly common for the King to grant licences to crenellate.

FOSSE WAY – Roman road linking Exeter to Lincoln

GARGOYLES – A grotesque water spout.

GILBERTINE – Order of Canons founded around 1130 by St Gilbert in Sempringham, Lincs where Gilbert was the parish priest. It was the only completely English religious order and came to an end at the time of the Dissolution.

GOTHIC – Style of architecture that flourished during the high and late medieval period. Originated in France – lasted to the 16th century characterised by pointed arches, ribbed vaults and flying buttresses.

GREEN MEN – See page 413

GROAT – Or fuppence – a long defunct English silver coin worth four pence.

HAPPY PARLIAMENT – The 4th and last Parliament in England in the reign of James I. It was referred to as 'Felix Parliamentum' in the Houses of Parliament by Edward Cope.

HAUTBOY – Archaic word for an oboe

HEARTH TAX – Known as hearth money, chimney tax or chimney money it was a tax imposed by Parliament in 1662 to raise money to support the royal household of Charles II. It was easier to count hearths because they did not move – unlike people. One shilling was to be paid for all fire hearths and stoves in all dwellings, edifices and lodgings payable at Michaelmas and Lady Day –
i.e. two shillings per hearth per year.

HECTARE – Unit of area – 10,000 square metres (2.471 acres)

HIDE – Unit of area originally sufficient to support one household but later became a unit used in assessing land for liability for land tax. On poor ground a hide was larger than on good ground – varied between 60-180 acres.

HONOUR (of Grafton) In medieval England an 'honour' could consist of a great Lordship comprising dozens or even hundreds of manors. Holders of honours (and the King to whom they reverted by escheat) often tried to administer the properties as a unit.

HOSPITAL – During the Middle Ages served different functions to modern institutions being almshouses for the poor, hostels for pilgrims or schools.

HOST (at Mass) – Sacramental bread

HUNDRED – Geographic division for administrative, military or judicial purposed under Common Law.

HYPOCAUST – An ancient Roman system of central under floor heating – literally – 'fire beneath'.

IMPARK/IMPARKED – See Empark

INCLOSURE – See Enclosure

IONIC – Forms one of three orders of classical architecture characterised by the use of colutes.

IRON AGE – Archaeological period generally occurring after the Bronze Age marking the use of iron.

IRON DUKE – Field Marshall Arthur Wellesley, 1st Duke of Wellington (1769-1852) soldier and statesman – famous for his defeat of Napoleon at the Battle of Waterloo in 1815.

IRONSTONE – Sedimentary rock containing a substantial proportion of an iron compound.

ITALIANATE – Style of architecture in the 19th century, first developed in Britain about 1802 by John Nash.

JESUIT – Member of the Society of Jesus, a Roman Catholic order of priests founded by St Ignatius Loyola.

KNACKERS YARD – A place where old or injured animals are slaughtered.

KNIGHTS HOSPITALLERS- Also known as the Knights of St John they were among the most famous of the western Christian military orders during the Middle Ages. They began in Jerusalem at a Hospital dedicated to John the Baptist founded around 1023 by Blessed Gerard to provide care for poor, sick and injured pilgrims to the Holy Land. After the western Christian conquest of Jerusalem in 1099 during the First crusade the organisation became religious and military and it was charged with the care and defence of the Holy Land.

LAMMAS DAY – Loaf Mass - 1st day of August – formerly observed as Harvest Festival.

LANCET WINDOW – A tall, narrow pointed early Gothic window.

LANTERN – A turret or tower on top of a roof or dome to let in light.

LEVELLERS - Political radicals in the mid 1600's associated with John Lilbourne, Richard Overton and William Walwyn. The term Levellers was coined by their enemies to imply that they favoured the abolition of popular rights and the equalisation of wealth – which they strenuously denied – unlike the 'Diggers' or 'True Levellers'. They promoted a programme which included religious tolerance, reform of the law, free trade and rights guaranteed under a written constitution and a government answerable to the people rather than the King or Parliament. Their beliefs appeared to be somewhat ahead of their time.

LISTED BUILDINGS –
Grade I – buildings of exceptional interest
Grade II* particularly important buildings of more than special interest
Grade II buildings of special interest warranting every effort to preserve them.

LONG PARLIAMENT – First called by Charles I on 3rd November 1640 six months after the dissolution of the Short Parliament and within weeks of the defeat of the English in the Bishops war against Scotland. The Long Parliament sat through the first and second Civil wars until December 1648 when it was purged by the New Model Army. The Purged Parliament (or the 'Rump' of the Long Parliament) was expelled by Cromwell in April 1653. The Long parliament was reinstated in 1660 after the fall of the Cromwellian Protectorate and was formally disbanded on 16th March 1660. The Parliament was formed to pass financial bills following the Bishops war. It received its name from the fact that through an Act of Parliament it could only be dissolved with the agreement of its members and those members did not agree until after the Civil War in 1660. In the chaos following the death of Cromwell in 1658 General George Monck allowed the members barred in 1648 to retake their seats so that they could pass legislation to allow the Restoration of the Monarchy and to dissolve the Long Parliament.

LOZENGES – A diamond shape

LUCARNES – Small opening to let in light usually a window in a roof or spire.

LYCH GATE – A roofed gateway to a churchyard originally from the old English 'body' referring to the former practice of using such gateways to shelter a coffin before burial.

MAGNA CARTA – Abuses by King John caused a revolt by rebel Barons who compelled him to execute this recognition of rights for both noblemen and ordinary Englishmen. It established the principal that no-one including the King or a lawmaker is above the law. It was granted by the King, under considerable duress at Runnymede on the 15th June 1215.

MANOR – The estate centre – varied in size.

MANORIAL PEW – Special area where the Lord of the Manor and his family sat.

MARKET CHARTER – Charter giving royal permission to hold a market.

MARKET CROSS – Structure used to mark a Market Square

MARLSTONE – Marl – rock or soil consisting of clay and lime.

MANOR – manor – in medieval times an area of land controlled by a Lord.

MARTIN MARPRELATE TRACTS - Most famous pamphlets of the English Renaissance. Printed 1588/89 on a secret press moved from one safe house to another. The seven tracts attack the Church of England especially its Bishops, hence: - Mar – Prelate - and advocated a Presbyterian system of church government.

MEDIEVAL – Relating to the Middle Ages.

MIDDLE AGES - Period of history between 5-15th century.

MINERAL SPRING – Naturally occurring spring producing water which contains minerals or other substances purported to have therapeutic qualities.

MISERICORD – Decorated shelf placed on the underside of a hinged seat in the choir stall to provide support against which to lean whilst standing.

MOOT HALL – Low ring shaped earthwork or mound where the elders of the hundred would meet to take decisions – some acquired permanent buildings. Many are relatively new sites.

MORAVIANS – Protestant denomination began in 1457 in Bohemia which places its emphasis on unity, personal piety, mission and music.

MORRIS MEN – English folk dancing to music – some say dating back to the 15th century.

MOTTE – A mound forming the site of a castle or camp.

MYXAMOTOSIS – Severe viral disease of rabbits which decimated the rabbit population in England 50 years ago.

NAVE – The main body of the church.

NEOLITHIC – The period 4000-2500BC

NINE MENS MORRIS – Strategy board game well known by the Romans – play peaked in England in medieval times.

OOLITHIC IRONSTONE – Limestone consisting of a mass of rounded grains.

OPUS SECTILE – Refers to an art technique in the ancient and medieval world where material was cut and laid into walls and floors to make a picture or pattern. Unlike mosaic, opus sectile pieces are much larger and can be shaped to define large parts of the design.

ORANGERY – Building in the grounds of fashionable residences from the 17th - 19th century given classical form. Similar to a greenhouse or conservatory mainly for growing citrus fruits.

ORIEL WINDOW – A bay window standing above ground level.

PACKHORSE BRIDGE – Bridge designed for horses loaded with panniers. Normally the width of one horse with masonry arches and low parapets so not to interfere with the horses load. Found on trade routes.

PALLADIAN – European style of architecture deriving from the designs of the Venetian architect Andrea Palladio (1508-1580)

PARLIAMENTARIAN – Supporter of the Parliamentary cause in the English Civil War

PASTOR – Ordained leader of a Christian congregation.

PEDIMENT – A low pitched triangular gable on the front of some buildings in the Grecian or Greek revival style of architecture.

PILASTER – A shallow pier attached to a wall. Slivers of columns fully adhered to the face of a building.

PILGRIMAGE OF GRACE – Popular rising in Yorkshire in 1536 in protest against Henry VIII breaking with the Roman Catholic church and the Dissolution of the Monasteries. Seen as a failure.

PINNACLE – A small turret at the upward termination of a buttress, wall or roof.

PISCINA – Shallow basin near the altar for washing hands and sacred objects.

POET LAUREATE – Poet officially appointed by Government and often expected to compose poems for State occasions and other governmental events. Dates back to Bernard Andre and Henry VII.

POLE – Five and a half yards

POLL TAX – A number have been levied over the years. There were three in the 1300's. The levy in 1381 was particularly unpopular as everyone over the age of 15 was required to pay one shilling – a considerable sum. This played a role in provoking the Peasants Revolt in 1381.

POLYGONAL – A plain figure with three or more straight sides and angles

POPPY HEADS – Head of a bench or pew end brought up to a carved figure or emblem originating from the French word 'puppis' meaning figurehead

POST MILL – Earliest type of European windmill. The whole body of the mill that houses the machinery was mounted on a single vertical pole around which it could be turned to bring the sails into the wind. Earliest in England was in the 12th century.

POTENCE – A rotating ladder in a dovecote allowing the collection of eggs or squabs and for maintenance.

PRE-REFORMATION – Before the 16th century schism within western Christianity initiated by Martin Luther, John Calvin and others which contributed to the creation of Protestantism.

PREMONSTRATENSION (White Canons) – Members of a Roman Catholic religious order founded at Premontre in Northern France in 1120 by St Norbert.

PRESBYTERY – Part of the church around the high altar to the east of the choir.

PRIEST – Person qualified to perform certain religious ceremonies in Catholic, Orthodox or Anglican churches.

PRIORY – Monastery or nunnery governed by a Prior or Prioress

PROVOST – Person in charge of certain university colleges or public schools.

PURITAN – Member of a group of English Protestants in the 16th and 17th century who sought to simplify forms of worship.

QUAKER – Religious Society of Friends began in England in the 17th century literally to 'tremble in the way of the Lord'

RABBIT WARRENER – One who owns or keeps a rabbit warren – gamekeeper.

RECESSED SPIRE – A spire which stands behind a balustrade or battlement.

RECTOR – An Anglican clergyman formerly entitled to the whole of the tithes in his parish as against a Vicar (deputy) who was only entitled to part.

RECUSANT – One who refused to attend Anglican services. The Recusancy Act began during the reign of Elizabeth I and was repealed in 1650. It imposed a number of punishments on those who did not participate in Anglican religious activity, including fines, property confiscation and imprisonment and in some cases,capital punishment.Catholics formed a large proportion together with Protestants and Dissenters.

REREDOS – Decorated panel above and sometimes around the altar.

REFORMATION – European Christian reform movement in the 16th century that established Protestantism as a constituent branch of contemporary Christianity, led by Martin Luther, John Calvin and other Protestants who objected (protested) to the doctrines, rituals and structure of the Catholic church.

REGENCY – refers primarily to buildings built during the period of the early 19th century when George IV was Prince Regent. Regency residences typically built in terraces or crescents with elegant wrought iron and bow windows.

ROOD – Cross or crucifix

ROOD LOFT – A display gallery above the rood screen

ROOD SCREEN – Also known as choir screen or chancel screen – an ornate structure of wood, stone or wrought iron originally surmounted by a rood loft carrying the Great Rood, a sculptural representation of the Crucifixion.

ROUNDHEAD – Supporter of Parliament during the Civil War – the name was a form of derision due to their short hair.

ROYALIST – Supporter of the Monarchy.

RUMP PARLIAMENT – Named after Colonel Pride it purged the Long parliament on the 6th December 1648 of those people who opposed the trial of Charles I for high treason. 'Rump' in this instance meaning 'remnant'.

SADDLEBACK ROOF – A roof with a ridge and two gables.

SANCTUS BELLCOTE – Bell rung to indicate the time for the celebration of the Mass.

SAXON – Style in vogue prior to 1066. Simple rounded topped openings and narrow windows but not very elaborate as the primary purpose was simply to shelter the altar.

SAXON GELD ROLL – Record of a tax based on ownership of land taxes were raised for Royal and Governmental expenses and for paying for wars

SEDILIA – usually in the south wall of the chancel – seats for priests during long services

SEVEN BISHOPS – Seven Church of England Bishops who were imprisoned and tried for seditious libel over their opposition to the Second Declaration of Indulgence issued by James I in 1688. They were found not guilty. The Declaration granted broad religious freedom in England by suspending penal laws enforcing conformity to the Church of England and allowing people to worship in their own homes or in a chapel. Anglican clergy felt it challenged their authority as many opposed the toleration of Catholics and other non-conformists.

SEXTON – Church officer responsible for the maintenance of buildings and/or the surrounding graveyard

SOKEMEN – Tenant between a free tenant and a villein – generally had personal freedom but had to perform most of the agricultural work of villeins

SPIRE – Tall tapering top of a church tower.

STAR CHAMBER – Court which sat at the royal Palace of Westminster until 1641 so called because of the painted stars on its ceiling.

STEEPLE – see Spire

STRAINER ARCH – Architectural feature used to reduce pressure on the side walls.

SQUINT – A hole cut into a wall or pier to allow the main altar to be views from where it otherwise could not be seen – hagioscope.

SQUIRE – Originally the shield or armour bearer of a knight. In the Middle Ages it became the term for the leader of an English village, often a JP or MP.

TEMPERANCE – Movement urging reduced or prohibited use of alcohol

TESSELATED PAVEMENT – (floor mosaic) Interior or exterior floor covering made of stone tesserae (Latin- dice) cubes in regular shapes to make a design

TESTER – A canopy

THIRD BRASS – Roman coins which were made of what we call bronze and were of different weight and shape

TITHE – Tenth part

TITHE BARN – Barn used for storing a tenth of a farms produce to be given to the church.

TOLL ROAD – (Turnpike) A privately or publicly built road for which the driver is required to pay a fee. Traditionally collected by hand. Originally dates from the 15th century when they were actually spiked barriers (pikes) designed to be placed across roads to prevent sudden attack by men on horseback.

TOURNEY – A tournament

TRANSEPT – Cross arms of a cruciform church normally running north to south.

TURNPIKE – Also known as a toll road - see page 89

TUSCAN – An order of classical architecture influenced by the Italian Sebastion Serlio who described the Tuscan order as 'the solidest and least ornate' The Tuscan Order was a primitive Italic architectural form predating Greek,Doric and Ionic.

TYMPANUM – the space between the lintel of a doorway and the arch above often sculptured

UNDERWOOD – below the trees of a forest

UNITED REFORMED CHURCH – Christian church in the UK resulting from the union of the Presbyterian church of England and the Congregational church in England and Wales in 1972. It is a Trinitarian church whose theological roots are Calvanistic. Each church within the URC is self governing.

USELESS PARLIAMENT – First Parliament of the reign of Charles I. It gained its name because it transacted no significant business making it 'useless' from the Kings point of view. It was dissolved on the 12th August 1625 'having offended the King'.

VIA DEVANA – Roman road from Colchester to Chester

VICAR – Priest in charge of a Church of England parish.

VILLEIN – In medieval England a poor man who had to work for the Lord of the Manor in return for a small piece of land on which to grow food for his family.

VIRGATE – Both a unit of assessment and a peasant landholding unit found in most counties except Kent and the Danelaw. Quarter of a hide – a notional thirty acres

WASTE In the Domesday Book describes settlements which the Norman army have passed through causing destruction.Also sometimes a term used for a manor not paying geld for some reason.

WATER MILL – A mill that uses a water wheel to drive a mechanical process such as flour or textile production.

WELSH ROAD – see page 59

WORKHOUSE – A place where those unable to support themselves were given accommodation and employment. The origins can be traced back to the Poor Law Act of 1388 which attempted to address the labour shortage following the Black Death in England by restricting the movement of labourers which led to the state becoming responsible for the support of the poor. Life was intended to be harsh to deter the able bodied poor. In the 19th century they increasingly became refuges for the elderly,infirm and sick.

WORSTED – A fine smooth yarn spun from long strands of coiled wool

YEOMAN – a man owning a house and a small area of farming land.

ZIG ZAG – A decorative feature often found in Norman arches.

ZIONIST BAPTIST – Theology that sees the return of Jews to the Holy Land as a fulfilment of scriptural prophecy. Israel must belong to the Jews as a pre-requisite for the return of Jesus to earth and that Armageddon will take place when Jesus returns.

LIST OF LOST SETTLEMENTS IN

NORTHAMPTONSHIRE

According to my research there are about a hundred villages in Northamptonshire that can be described as deserted or shrunken. In the vast majority of cases the desertion took place between 1350-1700. Causes include the Black Death, land grab by Monasteries and Abbeys, the introduction of sheep farming, or the wish of the local landowner to create a large park around his home.

ACHURCH – Thorpe Achurch
ALTHORP – Still a parish in its own right
APPLETREE – Aston Le Walls
ARMSTON – Polebrook
ASTWELL – Helmdon
ASTWICK – Evenley
BADSADDLE – Orlingbury
BARFORD – Rushton
BIGGIN – Benefield
BOUGHTON – Weekley
BRAUNSTONBURY – Braunston
BRAUNSTON CLEVES – Braunston
BRIME – Culworth
BROCKHALL – Still a parish in its own right
CALME – Clipston
CASWELL – Greens Norton
CANONS ASHBY – Still a parish in its own right
CHELVERSDECOTE – Possibly Newnham
CHURCH CHARWELTON – Charwelton
CHURCHFIELD – Benefield
COTES – Gretton
COTON – Ravensthorpe
COTON near Grendon – Grendon
COTTON MILL – Ringstead
COTTON MALLOWS – Raunds
CHILCOTE – Thornby
CHURCHFIELD - Benefield
DODDINGTON THORPE – Great Doddington
DOWNTOWN – Stanford on Avon
EAGLETHORPE   Warmington
EASTON NESTON   Still a parish in its own right
EDGCOTE – Still a parish in its own right
ELMINGTON in Ashton
ELMINGTON in Tansor
ELKINGTON – Still a parish in its own right
FALCUTT – Helmdon
FAWSLEY – Still a parish in its own right
FAXTON – Lamport
FIELD BURCOTE – Greens Norton
FOSCOTE – Abthorpe
FOXLEY – Blakesley
FURTHO – Old Stratford
GLASSTHORPE – Flore
GLENDON – Rushton
GREAT PURSTON – Farthinghoe
HALE – Apethorpe
HANDLEY – Towcester
HOLDENBY – Still a parish in its own right

HORTON – Hackleton
HOTHORPE – Marston Trussell
KELMARSH – Still a parish in its own right
KINGSTHORPE – Polebrook
KIRBY – Woodend
KIRBY – Gretton
KNUSTON – Irchester
LILFORD – Lilford cum Wigsthorpe
LITTLE CREATON – Creaton
LITTLE OXENDON – Great Oxendon
LOWER CATESBY – Catesby
MAWSLEY – Loddington
MURCOTT – Long Buckby
MUSCOTT – Norton
NETHER CATESBY – Catesby
NEWBOLD – Catesby
NEWBOTTLE – Still a parish in its own right
NEWBOTTLE – Harrington
NEWTON IN THE WILLOWS - Geddington
NOBOLD – Clipston
NOBOTTLE – Brington
PAPLEY – Warmington
PERIO – Southwick
PIPEWELL – Wilbarston
POTCOTE – Cold Higham
PRESTON DEANERY – Hackleton
ONLEY –Barby
OVERSTONE – Still a parish in its own right
RUSHTON ST PETER – Rushton
SEAWELL - Blakesley
SILSWORTH   Watford
SNORSCOMB – Everdon
STANFORD - Still a parish in its own right
STEANE – Farthinghoe
STRIXTON – Still a parish in its own right
STUCHBURY – Greatworth
SULBY – Welford
THORPE – Earls Barton
THORPE LUBENHAM – Marston Trussell
THRUPP –Norton
TRAFFORD – Chipping Warden
UPPER CATESBY – Catesby
UPTON – Still a parish in its own right
WALTON – Kings Sutton
WINWICK – Still a parish in its own right
WYTHEMAIL- Orlingbury

INDEX OF NAMES

-470-

ITEMS OF SPECIAL REFERENCE

INDEX OF PLACES